The PRINCIPLES of GARDENING

Hugh Johnson

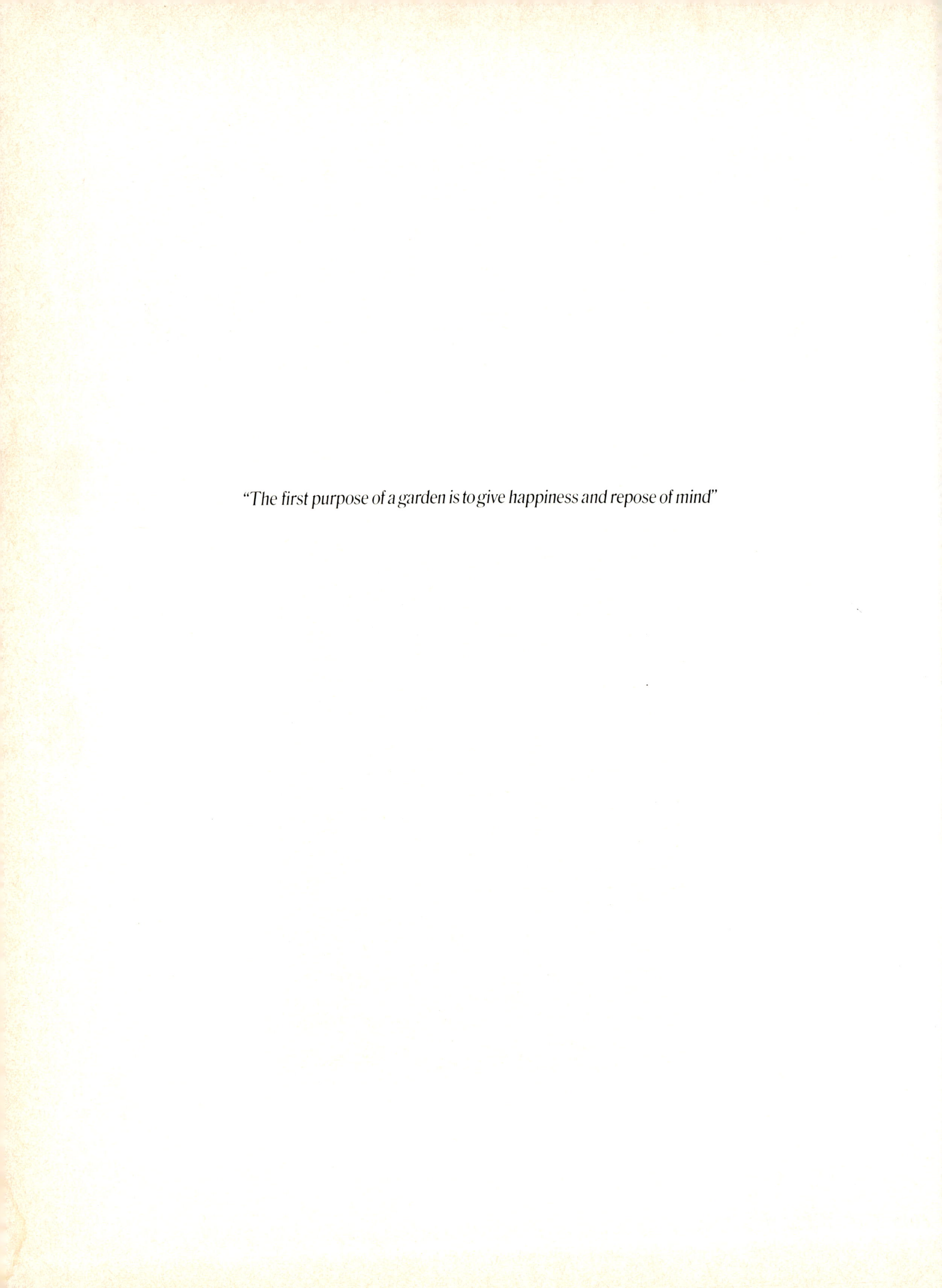

"The first purpose of a garden is to give happiness and repose of mind"

The PRINCIPLES of GARDENING

A guide to the art, history, science and practice of gardening

by Hugh Johnson

Simon and Schuster
New York

Editor	Michael Anthony Janulewicz
Art Editor	Leonard Lanivet Roberts
Assistant Editors	Jacky Baker Louise Callan Zuza Vrbova
Designer	Catherine Caufield
Assistant Designers	Valerie Hill Sean Keogh
Design Assistant	Alan Shorrock
Picture Researcher	Marilynn Zipes
Editorial Assistant	Margaret Little

Published by Simon and Schuster
A Division of Gulf & Western Corporation
Simon & Schuster Building
Rockefeller Center
1230 Avenue of the Americas
New York, New York 10020

Edited and designed by Mitchell Beazley
Publishers Limited, 14–15 Manette Street,
London W1V 5LB
Photosetting in Great Britain by
Servis Filmsetting Limited
Colour separations in Great Britain by
Gilchrist Brothers Limited
Printed and bound in Italy by
Arnoldo Mondadori, Editore, Verona
1 2 3 4 5 6 7 8 9 10

Library of Congress Cataloging in Publication Data

Johnson, Hugh.
The principles of gardening.
Includes index.
1. Gardening. I. Title
SB453.J64 635.9 79–14008
ISBN 0–671–24273–3

It would never occur to most gardeners to write a poem or paint a picture. Most gardens are the only artistic effort their owners ever make. Yet the one art that everyone chooses, or feels in some degree qualified to practise, is paradoxically the most complex art of all.

It is complex because it combines aesthetic judgements with science and craftsmanship in a kaleidoscope of variables. A poet is limited to the dictionary, a sculptor starts with a block of stone, but a gardener starts with a plot that is frozen one day and flooded the next, here in sun and there in shadow, teased by wind and tantalized by drought, plagued by insects, toyed with by birds, mined by moles. No two gardens are the same. No two days are the same in one garden. And yet on this flapping canvas an amateur without previous experience, holding the instruction book in one hand, tries to daub his vision of a better world—or if that is flying a bit high, at least to grow vegetables and feed his family.

Because gardening is so universal and has been going on for so long it has accumulated barns-full of folklore, libraries of literature, and a richness of reference that even fiction can scarcely equal. So many people have handled and delighted in so many plants, so many days have been spent in hard work, and perhaps not quite so many in tranquil contemplation, that to approach the subject for the first time is like being a raw recruit in a veteran army embroiled in an old campaign. What, whom, where are they talking about? Where can one start to pick up the thread?

I picked it up, and conceived the idea of writing this book, as I read one of the most perfect introductions to gardening that I know: Beverley Nichols's *Down the Garden Path*. In his Introduction he says, "I know that unless I write a gardening book now it will be too late to write it at all. For shortly I shall know too much. . . ."

I have started, therefore, as near as I can remember where I was about seven or eight years ago: at the beginning. I have tried to recapture the incomprehension of my first efforts with plants, and purposefully to go back over the ground trodden by so many generations that it no longer bears imprints. At the same time I have tried to comprehend the latest discoveries in the many sciences that have a bearing on gardening, to sum up the current state of knowledge and say what it means to the gardener of today.

From the feeling that there must be many like me, who wanted a vantage point from which they could survey the whole battlefield before deciding where they would stand the best chance of survival, I came to believe that there must be many veterans who would welcome a chance to stand back from their daily preoccupations and see what an outsider has to make of them. That is an author's job: to be an outsider with a passionate interest and concern. His aim is to weigh the options, clarify the objectives, balance the physical facts against the convention and tradition. Above all it is to identify the principles; to reach the nub of the matter. It is not easy to remain an outsider from such an enthralling subject for long.

As a relatively new gardener I have had to rely even more heavily than more experienced hands on others' written work, and have a profound debt of thanks to pay to the librarians who have helped me, particularly at the Lindley Library of the Royal Horticultural Society and the Cambridge University Library. I have also needed the encouragement and had to heed (or ignore) the warnings of many life-long gardeners, above all of Ken Beckett, who helped me so generously with *The International Book of Trees* and who once again has put his remarkable encyclopaedic brain, critical faculty and sense of humour to work on my behalf. I cannot thank him enough.

I have also consulted and been guided either over particular hurdles or in matters of philosophy by Ken Akers, Ted Allen, Mavis Batey, Miss B. K. A. Battersby, Richard Bisgrove, Chris Brickell, Roy Elliott, Valerie Finnis, Mike Janson, Christopher Lloyd, Tanya Midgley, Paul Miles, Fred McGourty, Elspeth Napier, Simon Relph, John Sales and Graham Stuart Thomas. In thanking them I hasten to dissociate them from anything hasty or untoward in what I have written. The same goes for my friends at Mitchell Beazley.

HUGH JOHNSON

The essence is control

Nature has her way in a once-great English garden. Was the garden in its heyday ever as beautiful as this?

What, if anything, do the infinity of different traditional and individual ideas of a garden have in common? They vary so much in purpose, in size, in style and content that not even flowers, or even plants at all, can be said to be essential. In the last analysis there is only one common factor between all gardens, and that is control of nature by man. Control, that is, for aesthetic reasons. A garden is not a farm.

The essence is control. Without constant watchful care a garden—any garden—rapidly returns to the state of the country round it. The more fertile and productive your garden is, the more precarious its position. Leave the lawn unmown, the beds unweeded for one summer and it will take a year, perhaps more, of hard work to restore it. Nor is it just a matter of unchecked growth. Even a minimal, super-simple garden, a Japanese courtyard of sand and rocks, has its pattern blurred by heavy rain, its emphasis altered by fallen leaves.

The rake, the hoe, the shears and the broom lie at the very heart of gardening.

Every natural community of plants has an inherent stability born of competition. Its inhabitants hold their ground in due relationship with each other by constant warfare. The only plants (and animals) present are those which have found an ecological niche for themselves; somewhere where their needs and characteristics dovetail with those of their neighbours. Each kind has slightly different requirements. Light, moisture and nutrients are available when it needs them. Woodland herbs and bulbs, for example, spring up and flower early in the year before the trees grow leaves and block out the light. Every wood, every meadow, every alp, every marsh has a distinct structure of taller and shorter plants. In fertile lowlands, which is where most gardeners garden, the natural state is a four-tier system with trees above shrubs above herbs above mosses and other humble earthbound things.

Not so a garden. Segregation is the tradition of gardeners—not into ecological but into horticultural niches. The plants that behave in such a way and like such a soil are grown together with as little competition as possible, protected from diseases, bugs, other plants and each other. When their protector goes on holiday their artificial world is immediately under threat. Instead of the stability of a hard-won Darwinian niche they occupy a pampered place which will be usurped by the quickest, most aggressive, coarsest plants—which are the ones we have come to know as weeds.

The most obvious form of plant thuggery is overwhelming neighbours with leaves to rob them of light. Light is essential for growth—although much more so for some plants than others; many are adapted to use low levels of light with great efficiency. Ultimately the plants that dominate are either the ones that can build tallest such as the trees, or those which can scramble and cling, making up for their lack of a structure by borrowing others'. Some trees are good neighbours, content with the light they need for themselves and not concerned with depriving others. Some, such as the beech, are dog-in-the-manger in the way they build a light-proof canopy so that their shallow roots can have the soil to themselves.

For as much competition goes on underground as over. Roots must constantly explore new soil for nutrients, at the same time withdrawing water not only from the soil they touch but by capillary action from a considerable area around. The more vigorous a plant the more questing its roots. Its hunt for food is at its height during its main growing season. If that coincides with its neighbour's its neighbour suffers. On the other hand it may co-exist happily with another plant which needs slightly different nutrients, or needs them at a different time of the year.

Shoving and elbowing for space is the kind of competition a gardener instinctively controls in the name of orderliness. But there are plants that use more overtly violent methods to compete: assaulting the growing tips of their neighbours with waving twigs as birches do, lacerating them like brambles, or strangling their host like the climbing honeysuckle, or even poisoning the soil as decaying grass roots can.

Competition is severest of all in the seedbed, where like jostles like. Unless the gardener thins the seedlings promptly, giving them elbow-room before they start competing, their growth is irreparably checked.

It is not only between one plant and another that the gardener must arbitrate. He is just as concerned with the internal competition between the different parts of one plant: the shoots, leaves, flowers, fruit. There is never enough food available to a plant to let all its potential buds open. If it grows madly it will flower little.

But most plants are grown in gardens for a particular contribution they have to make. The gardener desires the maximum number of flowers, or the maximum size and perfection in a few. Or he wants the most leaves, or the thickest stems, or the most distended and sugar-filled roots.

All the activities of cultivation—fertilizing, pruning, dividing, disbudding, grafting, even mowing—are examples of man directing plants in the way he wants them to perform; keeping them, in fact, under control.

Besides controlling plants, moreover, the gardener does what he can to keep pests at bay, to combat disease, to manage the soil and even to influence the wind and weather. Gardening in a greenhouse is the extreme example of man taking charge. There nothing is left to nature: light, temperature, soil and water are all his responsibility.

Different fashions of gardening call for different degrees of control. Traditionally the French see a garden as an artefact to be completed, then kept in order. The English, in contrast, see it as something ever-changing, emerging through time, calling for guidance rather than discipline.

On the whole, though, since control means work, and work is out of fashion, the more extreme forms of artificial gardening, whether it be the planting of floral clocks or maintaining the even more labour-intensive herbaceous border, have become backwaters of the art. Specialists will always be ready to sit up all night to have a perfect specimen ready to take a prize, but fashion, taking the hint from necessity, has moved towards a relatively relaxed style of gardening in which a little waywardness is considered a virtue. At the same time, with labour-saving as the vogue word, gardeners are looking for plants that take care of themselves to plant in combinations that have a degree of natural stability. The ideal modern garden, in some eyes at least, is one so close to nature (but of course with plenty of paved areas) that it becomes a mere view from the window, a framed picture with no job for the gardener at all.

In fact no such garden exists. For even under your daily surveillance the plants grow, almost always bigger and faster than you expected, or they die, or become tangled and ugly, or are eaten, or fall prey to a fatal fungus.

It is, or ought to be, the gardener's pleasure to be constantly adjusting, correcting, editing . . . editing is the best analogy; editors are forever adding commas, deleting paragraphs, changing phrases—the very stuff of gardening.

Most difficult of all to control, but most essential, is oneself. For a good garden is one with a plan, with variety but consistency, with a firm sense of purpose so that you know where to look and what you are supposed to enjoy. There is a perpetual temptation to anyone who loves plants to add another and another, bending his original intentions until they finally break; adding a colour that destroys a harmony, or a shape that jars, for the sake of growing something new.

The wind and the rain

Above One of the more dramatic stages of the hydrological cycle in its continuous round of evaporation, condensation, precipitation and flow. Clouds break over a Norwegian glacier and water transpired by plants, and evaporated from the sea, begins its downwards course.

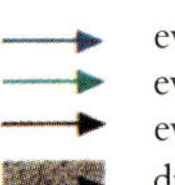

evaporation from sea
evaporation from plants
evaporation from soil
drainage into the ocean

Below Rain falling on the land drains directly to the sea, is transpired by plants, or evaporates directly from the soil. Of twenty-five inches of rain falling in central England eight inches drain away, five inches evaporate from bare ground and twelve inches are transpired by plants.

Rain never falls when we want it, but it falls in the end, and if it did not there would be no gardens, no plants—no life at all. Water is the life-blood of our planet. In living matter it not only circulates but forms the great bulk of the person or plant in question. Seventy per cent of your weight, and ninety per cent of your cabbage's, is water.

The hydrological cycle, to give the earth's circulation system its formal name, consists of evaporation, condensation, precipitation and flow. Precipitation and flow are powered by gravity; whether they are typhoons or Scotch mists, mountain torrents or field ditches or city sewers they are simply water sinking back to base level, the sea.

Water on its way down is visible, and frequently spectacular. It is easy to forget, if not hard to realize, that what comes down has to go up. Everything the clouds drop has been evaporated by the rays of the sun.

Plants play one of the leading roles in evaporation, second only to the sea itself. The process is dignified with the name transpiration, but it comes to the same thing: passively presenting water to the atmosphere to be soaked up and vaporized by the sun's energy.

The plant does it with its roots, drawing water from the ground and filling the open-pored vessels in its leaves with water for the sun to take away. It does it so efficiently that an open water surface like the sea is only marginally more efficient. Of all the rain that falls on a densely planted English garden two-thirds is promptly recirculated by the plants. Only one-third drains away into the ground. A big tree may draw three or four hundred gallons a day from the soil and release it into the atmosphere.

Why should it be in the plant's interest to transpire so much? First, because it has no other means of raising water and nutrients from the roots to the leaves. Second, because the whole growth process of photosynthesis depends on the pores being open to receive carbon dioxide from the air. And the pores are only open when all the cells of the plant are tight and distended with water.

Most plants have a way of throttling back when water runs short. Their pores half-close as the cells surrounding them become less distended. In drought they can close altogether, but as they do growth slows down and stops. It needs a water supply to complete the cycle, open the pores, and start the plant transpiring, and the water evaporating, again.

What then of condensation? What decides where and when the airborne moisture will form clouds, or the clouds break into raindrops? It is a question of pressure. The atmosphere is full of pockets and currents of warmer and colder air; usually warmer over the seas in winter and the land in summer, but affected and complicated by such factors as ocean currents, ice-sheets, deserts and lakes and mountain ranges.

Warm air is lighter than cold, just as warm water floats on colder water. Its atmospheric pressure is lower because its molecules are not packed together so tightly. In the spaces between them there is room for water vapour. For this reason warm air can also carry more moisture.

Cold air is dense and heavy on the mercury in the barometer, registering higher pressure but unable to hold much water in suspension. Where low pressure meets high pressure, therefore, it reacts as though it were meeting a mountain. The warm damp air is forced to ride up over the cold. But as it rises it cools—four degrees Fahrenheit for every 1,000 feet—until it can no longer hold its cargo of moisture. It condenses first into vapour as clouds, then as it cools further into bigger drops, which fall as rain.

Where the rainclouds go is determined on a global scale by the prevailing winds, which in turn are caused by the spin of the earth on its polar axis. At the equator hot air rises, and is

Left Morning dew in summer freshens the garden so much that it is hard to believe that it is a mere recycling of the moisture already present in the soil. There is unfortunately no net gain of water to plants however heavy the dew.

replaced by cooler air from north and south. But the equator, as it were the rim of the wheel, is moving fastest. The cooler air therefore lags behind the headlong equatorial spin and blows as a wind from north-east or south-east—the trade winds of the tropics; the steadiest and most reliable of all the winds.

Meanwhile the hot air of the equator, still spinning at equatorial speed, moves north and south, gradually cooling and falling. When it reaches the earth again it is still moving faster than the earth's surface. This is the prevailing wind of the temperate latitudes, blowing from the west, against the spin of the globe—the wind that for jets at 30,000 feet makes London an hour nearer to New York than New York is to London, and the wind that supplies the west coasts and western mountain slopes in its path with rain and to spare.

Between the trades and the westerlies, just north and south of the tropics, there is no steady airstream to carry water-laden air from the oceans over the land. These are the "horse latitudes", flat calm for sailors and arid for farmers. Most of the world's rainless deserts—the Sahara, Arabia, northern Mexico, central Australia, the Kalahari—lie in this windless region. The other great deserts, the Gobi and the western plateau of Nevada and Utah, are deprived of their share of the moisture in the westerlies by mountain ranges. It all falls on the Himalayas and the Sierras, leaving what is known as a "rain-shadow" to the east.

Such is the macrocosm; remote, perhaps, from a gardener's thoughts, however much it controls his behaviour. The same principles, however, apply to the microcosm. A house, too, has a rain-shadow. Warm air rises and cools as well in a back-yard as on a storm-bound coast.

THE WEATHER FORECAST

isobars
occluded front
cold front
warm front

A satellite photograph taken from 1,000 miles up shows the progress of warm and cold fronts (explained below) across northern Europe.

Cloud formations appear as white masses. Isobars join points of equal atmospheric pressure (at sea level) just as contour lines join points of equal altitude.

The "hills" delineated by isobars are anticyclones or high pressure areas in which the weather is usually settled and bright. The "valleys" are depressions or troughs of low pressure normally marked by wind and rain. The centre of a high is marked H, of a low, L. At present there is low pressure over the North Atlantic and eastern Europe and high over Greenland and northern France.

The closer together the isobars are, the stronger the winds, which generally blow almost parallel to the isobar lines, clockwise round anticyclones and anti-clockwise round depressions.

The boundary lines separating areas of different winds (and hence of different types of weather) are the "fronts". Whether warm, cold, or "occluded" (not greatly different from cold) fronts usually bring rain.

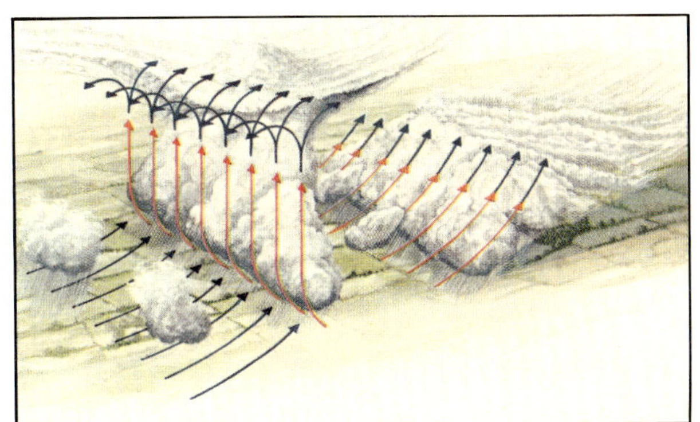

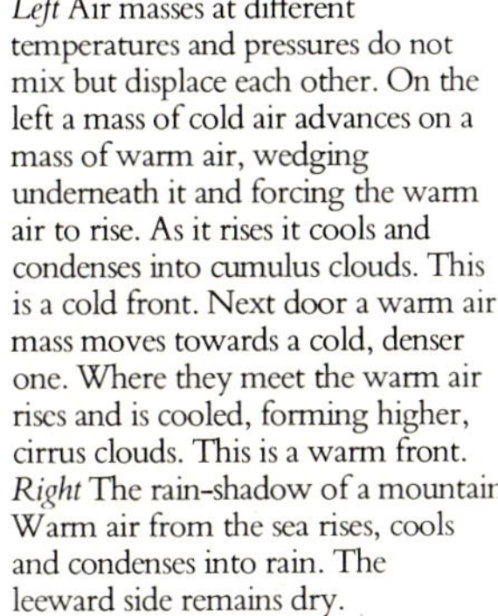

Left Air masses at different temperatures and pressures do not mix but displace each other. On the left a mass of cold air advances on a mass of warm air, wedging underneath it and forcing the warm air to rise. As it rises it cools and condenses into cumulus clouds. This is a cold front. Next door a warm air mass moves towards a cold, denser one. Where they meet the warm air rises and is cooled, forming higher, cirrus clouds. This is a warm front. *Right* The rain-shadow of a mountain. Warm air from the sea rises, cools and condenses into rain. The leeward side remains dry.

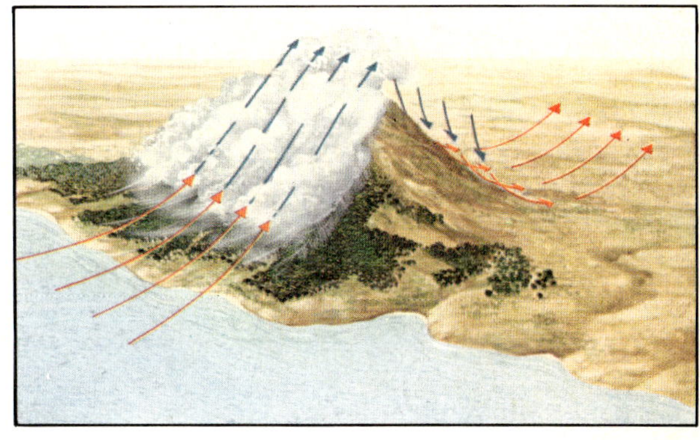

THE WORLD'S WEATHER

The principal influences on the world's weather are the prevailing winds, the oceans and their warm or cold currents and the land-masses and mountain ranges. In the temperate zones the prevailing winds are westerlies, which bring oceanic influence (high rainfall and moderate temperatures) to west coasts.

Land in the rain-shadow of mountains, or flat land on the coast with no mountains to cool the rain clouds, tends to be desert. Examples of the first are the Gobi and the second the Kalahari deserts. The combination of westerly winds and the warm Gulf Stream flowing north-west across the north Atlantic gives Britain a uniquely favourable position for growing the widest range of plants. Warm currents are represented by red arrows, cold currents by blue and wind directions by grey.

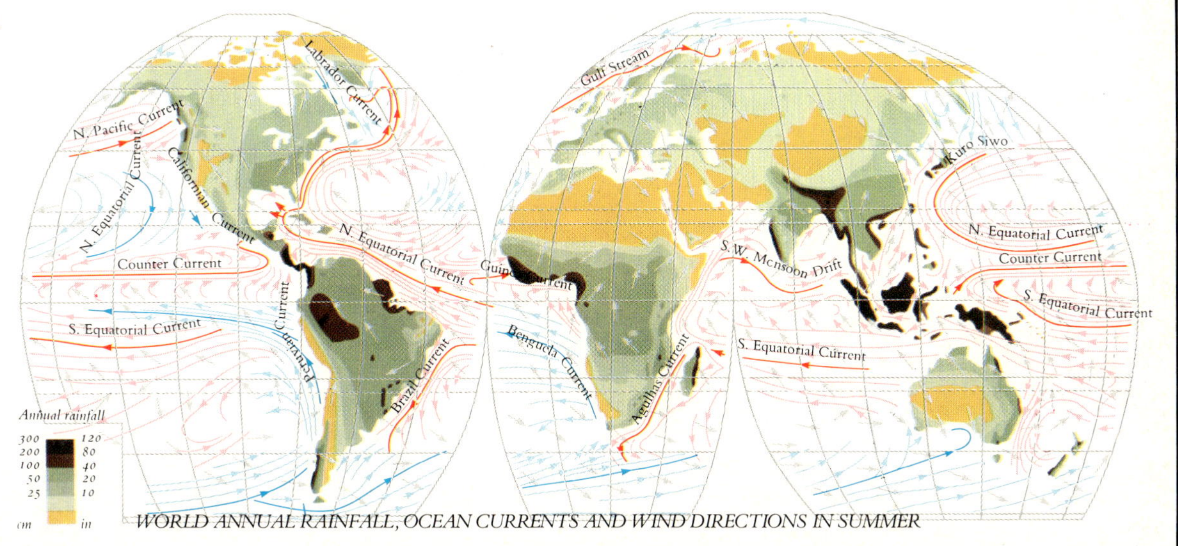

What is a hardy plant?

A crocus pushing up through snow is unaffected by the temperature of the air. Its cells are totally hardy: recurrent freezing and thawing do not affect them.

When a gardener says a plant is hardy he means it is adapted, or biologically programmed, to live in the particular climate he has in his garden. If it is killed or badly damaged, either by extreme cold in the dead of winter, by icy winds in spring, or by a sudden sharp frost destroying its unripe tissue in autumn or spring, it is called tender or half-hardy.

To many gardeners the most desirable plants are in the touch-and-go-zone, not because they are in any objective sense more beautiful than more rugged plants, but because each one is an illegitimate addition to his repertoire, holding all the charm of the forbidden and the chancy.

Plants in the tropics have nothing to fear from cold. The controlling factor in their lives is water supply; in an equatorial rain-forest they grow non-stop. If there were a drought they would rapidly flag and probably die. Plants that have to compete for light in deep jungle shade have big leaves with a high rate of transpiration and no equipment for reducing it.

At the other extreme the succulents are plants that have adapted to survive the almost permanent drought of near desert, with only the rarest cloud-bursts. They have reduced their leaves to the barest minimum and adapted their stems as reservoirs. The spines of a cactus are in fact its leaves and its swollen stem is a reservoir for holding water, with a thick or waxy skin that reduces evaporation to a minimum.

Plants that have evolved to inhabit the temperate zones have another problem to face: the seasons. Their survival depends on their being able to grow when it is warm and wet enough, and shut down operations when it is either too cold or too dry.

Shutting-down, or dormancy, can take many forms. For evergreens it is a mere pause; for deciduous trees and shrubs it means dropping their leaves. Both make new buds ready to grow when conditions improve. Herbaceous plants die down to ground level and shelter their buds in the ground; bulbs withdraw to their plump larders in the soil. Annuals disappear altogether, leaving only their seeds to come back to life when water and warmth give the signal.

In the warm-temperate regions (the Mediterranean, for example) the deciding factor is normally water supply. Summers are hot but so dry that growth is limited by lack of water. It is winter and spring rain that starts the bulbs sprouting, the seeds germinating, the herbs erupting from the ground and the trees putting on new leaves.

The most noticeable change in the landscape as you reach the zone of Mediterranean influence is that most of the woody plants are evergreen with thick, tough-skinned leaves. They can thus take instant advantage of growing conditions, but their leaves enable them to resist the summer-long drought. Plants of the extreme north (Canadian conifers for example) are evergreen for similar reasons: to have leaves ready to soak up the sun of a summer that comes and goes within ten weeks, but with thick leaves that resist excessive transpiration when the ground is frozen.

Between the warm-temperate and the downright cold lies the broad belt of well-marked seasons, and generally well-spaced rain, with temperature as its tyrant. Dormancy here is decided by cold. The overwhelming majority of plants are deciduous. Leaves in winter would do more harm than good, asking the roots in the cold ground for moisture they could not supply. Plants here wait for spring warmth, and grow new shoots often continuously all summer long. They ripen their seed gradually towards autumn (trees and shrubs ripen their new wood) and then shed their vulnerable soft leaves and harden their shoots before winter can harm them.

To temperate-zone plants timing is all. Their whole evolutionary adaptation to life with cold winters is based on their being safely dormant. If they put on new growth too

Above The west coast of Scotland, washed by the warm Gulf Stream, has a freak climate with little to fear from frost, despite being on the latitude of Labrador. Inverewe is the most famous of a number of coastal gardens where the enemies are gales and salt spray.

Right The famous fall colours of New England are caused by the concentration of sugar in the sap of the leaves as growth slows. Sunny days and cold nights destroy the chlorophyll and encourage the formation of other pigments that colour in the sugar-rich sap.

Left Grape-vines are among the plants often damaged by late frost that strikes after they have made new sappy growth in spring. This is one of the commonest forms of "tenderness" in what are otherwise "hardy" plants.

soon in spring late frosts will kill them. Wood which has not reached a safe state of ripeness and turned from green to brown before winter sets in will suffer the same fate.

Millenia of experience have perfected their timing. A plant in its native land is almost never caught out. The combination of day length and temperature is familiar and peremptory. The instinct of dormancy is so fixed that if you moved the plant to the tropics it would fail to open its buds: no winter means it must still be autumn.

As soon as it is moved to a foreign garden with different conditions its control mechanism receives the wrong data. In many cases the difference is marginal and unimportant, but in others the confusion is fatal. Many plants from harsh climates are tender in milder ones. On their home ground the first warm days are the certain sign of spring; so they start to grow. But in a Gulf Stream climate, warm spells happen in winter, to be followed by more frosts, often as late as May. New shoots, lured by false promise, are cut back in their prime. If this happens regularly the plant may die.

More mysterious altogether is the question of extreme cold. All temperate-zone plants are subjected to freezing from time to time. All will suffer if they are unprepared. But if they are prepared, and dormant, the degree of cold they can tolerate varies enormously. Ice crystals forming in the wood cells of an olive tree tear the delicate structures apart. But a sugar maple can be frozen into a solid block of ice and be unharmed.

The deciding factor, in these cases, is the concentration of sugar and proteins in the cell sap and also the permeability (the rate at which water can penetrate) of the central membrane enclosing the cytoplasm that contains the "works" or nerve centre of each cell.

Pure water freezes before water with sugar or salt dissolved in it. Therefore when a plant freezes, the least concentrated sap freezes first. In a hardy plant the pure water content rapidly migrates out through the walls of the cytoplasm and forms ice between the cells, leaving a highly concentrated solution of sap in the part that matters most. In a tender plant the water cannot do this and the dilute sap freezes in the plant, destroying the cytoplasm by breaking apart its surrounding membrane.

But even a hardy plant must have time to arrange matters. If you put a plant from the garden straight in a freezer there would be no time and it would die. Happily freezing in nature is normally a gradual process. Autumn weather constitutes a toughening-up programme for plants in itself. The common autumnal phenomenon of sunny days and cold nights is just the right regime. Transpiration (by day) is high while respiration (by night—see pages 40–1) is restricted by the low temperatures. Under these conditions (and no longer using up energy to put on new growth) the plant accumulates more and more carbohydrate in its tissue: the very concentration which will protect the heart of the cell when the real freeze comes.

What happens when it thaws is just as important: a very rapid thaw allows no time for the water to percolate back through the cell walls to where it belongs, and again the delicate membranes will be ruptured and the plant will die. Even otherwise hardy plants can be damaged by warm sunshine when they are frozen.

For this reason an east wall is a fatal place for plants that incline to tenderness. If the sun strikes them early after a frozen night the thaw will be too fast for them and their cell walls will break.

There are other kinds of tenderness besides susceptibility to cold. High alpine plants can sustain arctic temperatures but succumb to being wet in winter. Bog-plants might be described as drought-tender. Each plant, in other words, has a regime it will ultimately insist on.

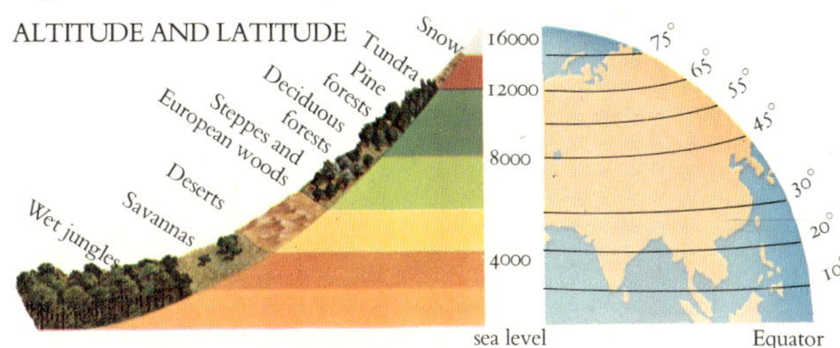

The direct correlation between altitude and latitude is expressed in this diagram *above* and in the picture *below* of Mt. Kilimanjaro. For every 250 feet of altitude the temperature drops 1°F. A mountain on the equator which reaches 16,000 feet contains on its slopes all the temperature zones from tropical to arctic, and therefore in theory could provide a habitat for plants from any latitude. The diagram shows the types of vegetation adapted to each altitude/latitude zone. Plant hunters looking for the hardiest forms collect seed from the highest possible stands.

Above Drought can kill as well as cold. When the loss of moisture from the plant by transpiration is greater than the intake by the roots from the soil the cells lose their "turgor", wilt and eventually die.

HARDY PLANT CELLS

The difference between a hardy and a tender plant cell is a question of whether or not, the cell contents are disrupted by ice crystals. A hardy plant cell prevents this by possessing a permeable cell membrane which allows water out of the cell in cold conditions. Thus the cell contents are more concentrated, lowering the freezing point by several degrees.

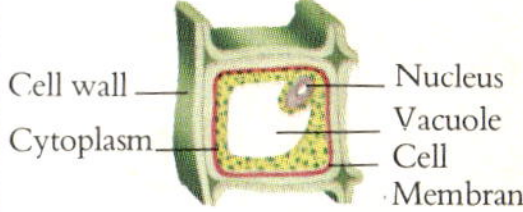

A plant cell in normal conditions with the cell membrane lying tightly against the cell wall.

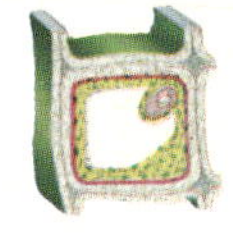

The diagram above shows a tender plant cell in conditions of frost. The membrane is relatively impermeable so there is no mechanism to prevent the cell contents from freezing up. As a result ice crystals form throughout the cell and rupture the cell membrane and the components of the cell. (above right)

The diagram above shows how a hardy plant cell (left) prevents itself from being killed by ice (right). In frosty conditions water moves out of the cell across the cell membrane. This increases the concentration of the cell contents and so lowers the freezing point. Ice forms outside the membrane, only distorting the cell.

Zones of plant hardiness

The number of days indicates the approximate length of the growing season, that is, when the temperature exceeds 43°F (6°C) (the temperature at which grass begins to grow).

The ultimate deciding factor in whether a plant will survive in a given spot (with adequate supplies of light, moisture and nutrients) is quite simply the lowest temperature it will have to endure. The mechanics of the destruction of susceptible plant cells by ice are shown on pages 12–13.

In the United States, where a huge land mass almost connected to the North Pole makes severe winters common over a great part of the country, this fact was long ago recognized and embodied in a famous system of plant hardiness zones. These were defined by the Arnold Arboretum of Harvard University, at Boston, Massachusetts, as zones of consistent annual average minimum temperature.

The map below is the one commonly accepted by the American horticultural industry. Opposite is one compiled on the same basis for Europe. The captions beside each give an account of the major climatic influences involved.

As an example of how the zone system works, a plant that is described as "hardy to zone 9" is one that will survive in temperature zone 9 (that is with an annual average minimum temperature of between 20°F/—6°C and 30°F/—1°C) or south of it, but only in exceptional circumstances in the next zone to the north, zone 8, where the temperature regularly drops to 10°F/—12°C. In other words it can safely be planted in gardens in Florida and along the Gulf coast or almost anywhere from Arizona up the west coast; or in Europe anywhere along the Mediterranean coast, in most of Spain and Portugal and in that narrow coastal strip of temperate winters all the way north to Scotland.

A map on this scale, of course, can only give the broadest picture. There are plenty of localities with exceptionally severe or mild climates. The biggest single factor in local conditions is altitude. For every 100-metre rise the temperature drops one degree Fahrenheit. While major mountain formations help to shape the hardiness zones on the maps the gardener must calculate for himself whether his own hill puts him at greater or less risk.

Other considerable local factors can be the presence of a large body of water, and shelter from the winter wind will be a matter of life or death in particularly exposed places.

Minimum winter temperatures, of course, have nothing to do with unseasonal frosts. A plant that has survived a severe freeze while it is dormant may yet be killed by having its new shoots destroyed in a spring frost.

On the right are examples of typical "indicator" plants for the ten hardiness zones. These give an example of the sort of garden vegetation you can expect to see. They were very kindly provided by Frederick McGourty Jr of the Brooklyn Botanic Garden, USA.

Zone 1
Below − 50°C.
100 days
Salix reticulata

Zone 5
− 10°C to − 5°C.
210 days
Cornus florida

Zone 8
10°C to 20°C.
270 days
Pittosporum tobira

Below The west coast of America is a law unto itself in horticulture as in everything else. In this richly gardenable country the same hardiness zone system does not work. The combined influences of the Pacific Ocean, the deserts, the Sierra Nevada and the coast ranges give peculiar pockets of totally different climatic conditions. Minimum temperature cannot be isolated as the overriding factor. A range of low hills can make the difference between desert and woodland. Under these circumstances the gardening staff of the admirable *Sunset Magazine* have charted the western states into no less than twenty four climate zones, based on combinations of latitude, altitude and susceptibility to the major influences of mild Pacific air and cold air from the interior in winter (in summer it is the other way round). The map (*below*) shows only the region round San Francisco Bay, where a break in the coastal hills allows Pacific air to penetrate inland.

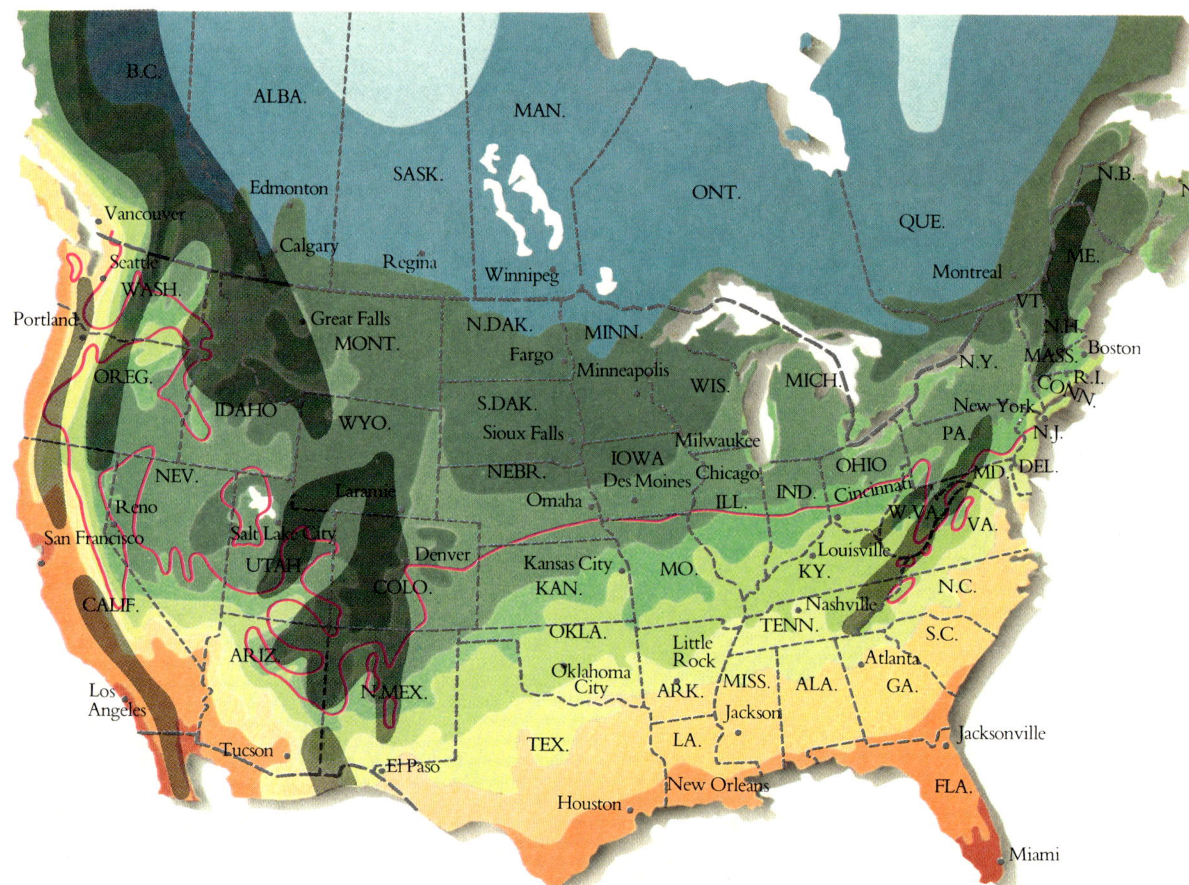

Zone 7
Zone 14
Zone 15
Zone 16
Zone 17

Above The minimum winter temperatures in the United States and Canada are dominated by the great land (and ice) mass to the north. You can picture the situation as intense cold radiating from somewhere in Manitoba. The main influences that distort this pattern of concentric bands and temper the severity of the climate are the mountain ranges of the east and west (the Rockies bring low temperatures farther south in the centre), the warm waters of the Gulf of Mexico and the generally moderating influence of the oceans—far more marked on the west coast than the east on account of the prevailing winds.

It is interesting to note that the Great Lakes are substantial enough bodies of water to have their own sphere of temperate influence, which is reflected in the vineyard industry of upper New York State, northern Ohio and even southern Ontario. Without the heat-storage of the lakes the vines would freeze to death.

The great influences on the winter climate of Europe are the cold land mass of Asia to the east, the warm air mass of the Sahara Desert to the south, and above all the remarkable effect of the Gulf Stream. The Atlantic Ocean is so effective in keeping winter temperatures up that, mountains apart, the hardiness zones of Britain and most of northern Europe run in bands from north to south rather than east to west. Even the northern tip of Scotland rarely suffers severe frost, lying in the path of the Gulf Stream, and its effects are still apparent on the west coast of Norway, which is at the latitude of southern Greenland but has minimum temperatures no lower than most of France.
Where the Atlantic and Saharan influences coincide in southern Spain, winter temperatures are as high as those in Florida, which is ten degrees of latitude and seven hundred miles farther south.

NORWAY
SWEDEN
FINLAND
Oslo
Helsinki
Stockholm
Edinburgh
UK
Dublin
DENMARK
Hamburg
NETH
London
Amsterdam
GERMANY
POLAND
USSR
Brussels
BELG
Frankfurt
Luxembourg
Prague
Paris
FRANCE
Munich
CZECHOSLOVAKIA
Vienna
Bern
SWITZ
AUSTRIA
Budapest
HUNGARY
RUMANIA
Bordeaux
Lyon
ITALY
Belgrade
PORTUGAL
Marseille
YUGOSLAVIA
Lisbon
Madrid
Barcelona
SPAIN
Rome
BULGARIA
ALBANIA
Gibraltar
GREECE
Athens

International boundaries

High ground

Your local climate

The grand movements of temperature, sunshine and rainfall are determined by oceans and landmasses, prevailing winds and pressure zones. They have their consequences in the distribution of plant-life that ultimately decides what we can grow in our gardens.

But the gardener's day-to-day worries are more local. A range of hills can have the same effect on conditions, though on a smaller scale, as a mountain range, and a lake can exert moderating influences similar to those of an ocean.

Several things can make remarkable differences to the local climate; the altitude, the flatness or slope of the ground, the type of soil, the nearness of the sea or a range of hills, and, perhaps most dramatically of all, buildings. The climate in a city can be so much warmer than in the surrounding country that it brings a different class of plants within range. An olive tree grows and occasionally bears fruit in London, six hundred miles north of its normal limits.

There is a rule of thumb about altitude which is, on its own, easy enough to remember and interpret. For every 250 feet above sea level the temperature drops one degree Fahrenheit. This is enough to shorten the growing season (defined as days with an average temperature above 43°F/6°C) by several days in hilly country.

More complex and usually more important to the gardener is the slope of the land, its aspect (to north or south) and whether he is at the top or bottom of a hill. It makes a great deal of difference whether the sun's rays strike the ground perpendicularly or at an acute angle—witness the difference between summer and winter, not to mention the equator and the pole. By having ground sloping towards the sun the angle is greatly increased and hence the effective radiation is greater. A south-facing slope is much warmer than a north-facing one, and will bring on growth noticeably earlier in spring.

Early growth, however, can be a snare and a delusion if the same south-facing slope is abruptly terminated by an answering north-facing one on the other side of the valley, or even by what looks like a snugly sheltering wall. For cold air behaves exactly like water. It flows downhill until it meets an obstacle; then spreads outwards and upwards, like water filling a pond. On a frosty night cold air flows off the upper slopes to mass at the bottom, and, according to how cold it is for how long, can make anything from a mere puddle to a whole valley-full of freezing air.

Any garden in a hollow is at risk from frost. The stillness of the sheltered air contributes to the risk as well. The exact mechanism that causes "radiation frost", the sort that occurs unseasonably on clear still nights, is surprisingly complex.

In the evening and the early part of the night the ground gives off its stored daytime heat to the cool night air. But there comes a moment when the ground cools to a temperature lower than the air immediately above it and starts taking heat back. The result is a thin layer of freezing air just above the soil surface. This air is denser and heavier than the air above it and therefore inclined to run downhill, like water, to the lowest available point.

The nature of the soil itself also affects its proneness to frost. Heavy soil heats and cools slowly like the solid block of a night-storage heater. But light sandy soil, or even a finely worked tilth over heavier soil, contains quantities of trapped air and acts as an insulation blanket between the atmosphere and the reservoir of heat in the ground. On cold nights the stored heat in the sub-soil is prevented from rising and frost soon forms at ground level. In the same way any vegetation has enough insulating effect to encourage radiation frost.

If a hollow is a frost trap, a hilltop usually suffers from the effects of wind. After sunlight and water supply, wind has more influence on growth than any other factor—not in the visible sense of bending and breaking shoots, but in making demands on the plant's plumbing that it cannot meet. Wind blowing over leaves is no different from wind blowing over washing: the stronger the wind the faster it dries. When the evaporation rate is more than the roots can keep up with, the plant's pores close and its whole life-process slows down.

Often, apparently sheltered corners of the garden are quite the reverse. Wind in an open field is damaging enough, but when it reaches solid obstacles like walls it is compressed into gusts and eddies at much higher speeds.

When it hits a house at right angles the effect can be devastating to plants at the foot of the wall. Perhaps half the body of air hitting the wall is forced up over the roof and round the sides, but the other half turns and blows directly downwards, crushing whatever is growing below.

Wind also, of course, affects where rain falls. The gardener's dream is of a steady, gentle, vertical shower on a still day, not falling hard enough to damage plants or compact the soil. In reality, he usually receives squalls of oblique rain on the prevailing wind. Westerly rain leaves a considerable area to the east of the house unwatered, and vice versa. On the other hand, the sunshine and wind on the south and west of walls dries out the soil there faster than anywhere else. It is not safe to assume that wall beds facing the prevailing wind can rely on rainfall.

Among all these imponderables at least one thing is certain: the course of the sun in the sky. It is easy to forget how much it varies from season to season. In winter it rises in the south-east and sets in the south-west, but in summer it rises and sets well to the north. A north wall that sees no sun all winter is well-lit, even baked, on hot summer evenings. This may make it suitable for an autumn-flowering plant, but too hot for something with delicate leaves that asks for perpetual shade.

THE PATH OF THE SUN

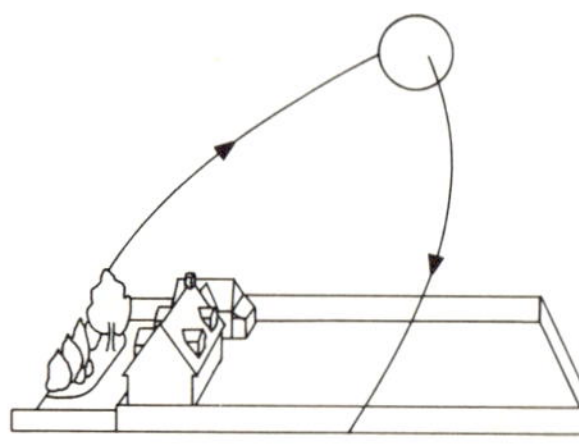

The sun in summer rises in the north-east and sets in the north-west, giving some light even to north-facing walls.

E N S W

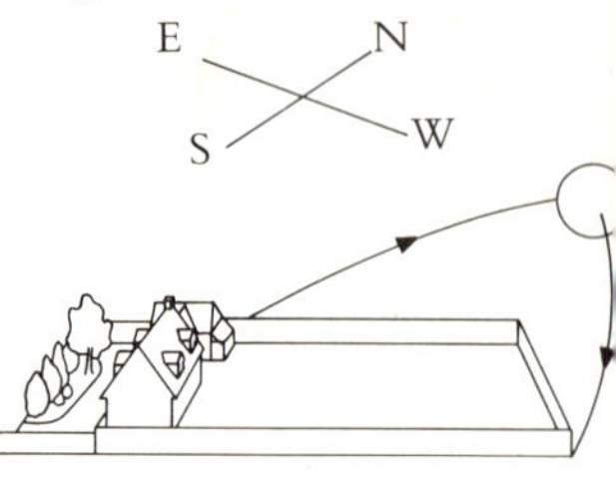

In winter the sun rises in the south-east and sets in the south-west; the north wall is in permanent shade.

Above The first fact to establish in any garden is its orientation and the angle of the sun at different times of year. On the latitude of central France (or Boston) its angle is 25 degrees from the horizontal on 1 January and 70 degrees on 1 June.

A small house and garden has a wide range of microclimates: spots where rain never reaches, which heat up quickly in sunshine, where winds funnel to create destructive draughts, where frosts form or water lies stagnant. The growth of the plants themselves creates more areas of shade, shelter or drought. The shadow of the house is usually a dominant factor: its north and east walls, being in shade most of the time, provide the equivalent of woodland light-conditions but without the shelter that woods afford. South and west walls enjoy most sunlight, but are also often windy. Some of the differing conditions in one small garden are described on the right.

The front entrance of this house faces north-east. In winter the sun never reaches it, but on the other hand illuminates the view in this direction. Birches and pines, hardy trees with interesting colour, are a good choice

The fan-trained tree facing almost due north, and in a passage-way with cold winds, is a morello cherry.

Right A south slope warms up in sunshine much faster than level ground. In winter an angle of 15 degrees to the horizontal facing south is enough to double the heat received from the sun, while the oblique rays falling on north slopes have hardly any effect at all.

Above Cloud-cover at night acts as an insulating blanket, keeping the heat received from the sun during the day close to the ground and so preventing frost forming. To some extent a canopy of trees, even when bare of leaves, has the same effect of preventing the (relatively) warm air from rising.

On a clear night there is nothing to prevent the earth radiating such warmth as it has back into the heavens. When the soil temperature falls below air temperature the soil cools the air still further. The layer of extra-cold air near the ground is a radiation frost, fatal to early flowers and new shoots.

Above Cold air collects at ground level and flows downhill like water to fill any hollow it can reach, just as if it were a pond. Such a frost pocket can easily be caused by interrupting air flow down a slope by building a wall or planting a solid hedge. Good "air drainage" is a vital consideration in any area subject to regular frost.

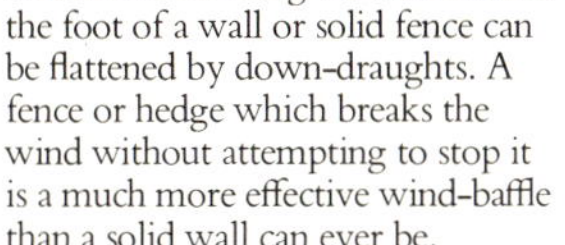

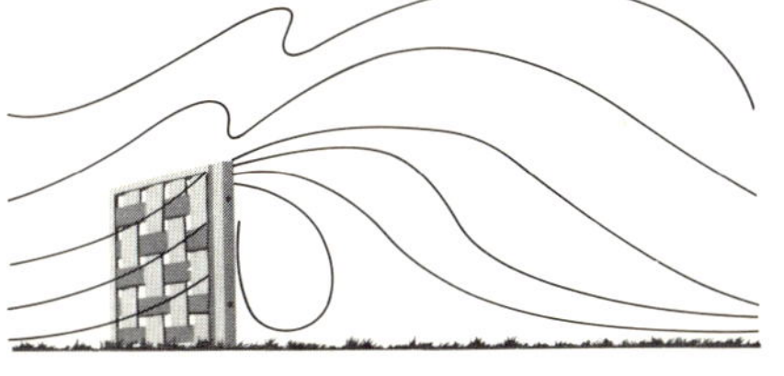

Right While walls have the advantage of storing heat they have the serious disadvantage of causing chaotic turbulence in strong winds. Plants at the foot of a wall or solid fence can be flattened by down-draughts. A fence or hedge which breaks the wind without attempting to stop it is a much more effective wind-baffle than a solid wall can ever be.

The south-west-facing terrace is a sun trap, which combined with the heat-retaining properties of walls and paving makes it ideal for Mediterranean plants. The sunniest and most sheltered spot is given up to a lean-to greenhouse. Plants in tubs on the terrace will need frequent watering, but those growing in the joints of the paving have the benefit of a cool root-run.

The nearer fence, facing just east of south, gives a good sunny border and an excellent situation for climbers. The clematis has its roots shaded by plants in the border and its top in sunlight: the perfect arrangement. The farther fence, with a north-west exposure, is shady in winter but well lit on summer afternoons. The pond is given a fully sunny position, as almost all water plants like sunlight. Cordon fruit trees provide a screen and shelter for the vegetable garden, again in full sun. Its north-facing fence is a good place for cold frames for propagation.

The plantsman's approach to a small garden like this without any variation of terrain would be to maximize the variety of plants that will thrive by matching the soil as far as possible with the microclimatic conditions. If cool and shady areas are to look the part their soil should be made as near as possible an imitation of woodland soil, free-draining but with a high organic content.

The sunniest spots will grow the plants of the Mediterranean and South Africa better if they are made as fast-draining as possible with rubble and gravel. A plastic sheet buried round the pond to impede drainage will allow bog-loving plants to grow. This approach sacrifices the unity of one soil type for the interest of diversity of plants. To compose a coherent picture this way is a considerable challenge.

Climate and the gardener

Gardeners don't give in easily. The challenge is to cheat the elements; to grow plants bigger and better than nature can manage unaided; to have more, earlier and more perfect fruit and flowers. Centuries of trial and error have produced an armoury of devices and techniques for protecting and encouraging plants against frost, heat, drought, wind and flood. Irrigation is climate control; so is drainage.

All the gardener's dodges arise from the same simple law: growth is ultimately controlled by the weakest link in the environmental chain. Whichever essential is in short supply governs the growth-rate, however much of the other ingredients may be available.

The environmental essentials are moisture, light, air and a high enough temperature. Different plants need different amounts of each, but normally there is one that presents the greatest problem for most plants in any given area. In southern California or North Africa the missing ingredient is moisture. In most temperate-zone gardens the controlling factor is low temperature. The chief fear is untimely frost.

There are stoical gardeners who believe in reducing the risks to a minimum: they plant doubtfully hardy plants in sharply drained, infertile soil where they will hardly grow at all. "Growing them hard" is the English public-school system applied to plants. Lusty shoots of exotic and susceptible growth are not allowed. Every inch has to be fought for. The theory is that by withholding nutrients and moisture, what growth there is will start late and stop early.

A less drastic precaution is choosing a cool and shady station for a precocious flowerer, such as a magnolia, hoping to delay its bud-break until warmer weather. Another is in the strategic timing of pruning, which encourages new growth. By leaving it late, new shoots are delayed. Another is planting late.

One insurance policy any wise gardener takes out is to choose fruit trees, for example, that flower at slightly different times. If frost or rain prevents the successful pollination of one kind, at least it will not affect them all.

Another approach is to use physical barriers between your plants and the elements. In Britain "the elements" means above all the wind. There are very few gardens where growth is not limited by the wind lowering air and ground temperatures. A recent research project in Germany showed that the one possible way of improving conditions in the country's best vineyards was to plant windbreaks of tall trees, and to align the vine rows so that the prevailing wind of summer blew at right angles to, and not along the length of, the lines.

The most effective windbreak allows some of the wind through, breaking its force rather than trying to stop it dead. Even a slight screen provided by a piece of fine-mesh netting supported on canes to windward of a plant can make the difference between life and death. Walls attempt the impossible, and only succeed in creating worse turbulence (see the previous page). The ideal windbreak is a hedge or shrubby screen with a fairly shaggy texture and a proportion of about two-thirds solid matter to one-third small holes. A beech hedge answers the description. Such a windbreak cuts the wind force to almost nothing for a distance of about twice the height of the fence in its immediate lee, and it still does some good at a distance of ten times the height. The windbreak should be at right angles to the prevailing wind. But not all gales, of course, come from the same quarter. Only a circular hedge can be effective against all winds.

Walls are used to grow fruit trees and tender climbers for a different reason: they absorb and store the heat of the sun, slowly giving it up again during the night. In the days of cheap fuel, whole walls up to twenty-five feet high were heated from behind by furnaces during the flowering season of the peaches.

Such lavish gestures of climate control are not for today. Very small gardens, indeed, can hardly spare space even for a hedge. Protection must often be on a plant-by-plant basis, even to the extent practised in the northern states of America of wrapping evergreens individually in sacking to keep off the desiccating winter winds. The Japanese do even better with their highly prized cycads, clothing them in hats and coats of plaited straw. The aerosol age offers a plastic spray to coat evergreen leaves and reduce transpiration. Damage from the weight of snow is another matter. Upright conifers are particularly susceptible. Some gardeners tie the branches up in autumn; others knock the snow off with a pole.

Above left A garden in northern New England battened down for the winter presents an extraordinary sight. The only hope of bringing evergreens through the long months of icy winds, often in deadly combination with bright sun, while the roots are locked in frozen ground, is to bundle them up in sacking. The plants are no warmer in their sleeping bags, but the protection prevents them having to transpire when there is no water available. Death would come from drought, not simply cold.

Above The light canopy of netting over a fruit cage is often a sufficient baffle for a slight frost, and serves the double purpose of lowering wind speed as well as keeping off the birds. Fine mesh, however, collects snow and can collapse under its weight.

Above Spring frost protection by sprinkling, coating shoots with a layer of ice, is increasingly popular.

Below right The roses at Sissinghurst Castle are made ready for winter by being tied tightly to poles and receiving a deep mulch of used hops from a local brewery.

Different mulches can have different effects on ground temperature. Dark-coloured ones absorb heat and encourage early growth—which may be a disadvantage. Transparent plastic is effective for warming the ground in spring and allows radiation at night, but black plastic prevents radiation and can cause low temperatures near the ground. A thick mulch on frozen ground can prevent frost heaving and consequent damage to roots.

Left One way of keeping rain from settling in the crowns of alpines and rotting them is to plant them on their sides, as here in a piece of porous tufa rock.

In very cold areas roses are buried for the winter, and Swedish friends tell me the only way they can keep rhododendrons alive is to turn the sprinklers on and coat them with a layer of ice for the winter. Spraying to form an ice layer is increasingly used against spring frost damage, too: a new shoot is safe at freezing point inside its ice capsule even when the temperature outside plunges many degrees below. Against less severe frosts it is surprising that only slight covering will make a difference: a canopy of bare branches, a wire-netting fruit cage; even a sheet of newspaper can save new growth.

So far we have talked only of defensive measures: baffles against wind and frost. But we can do better than that. By using glass we can push back the limits of the growing season. Glass, which nowadays includes transparent plastic, traps and intensifies the sun's rays. A note of caution is needed about polythene as a glass-substitute. It does not prevent the loss of heat by radiation. The so-called "greenhouse effect" (see pages 32–3) means that more heat comes into a glass structure than goes out. As long as the plant under glass has enough of the essentials of light, water and air, it can take advantage of the higher temperature to grow sooner and faster.

Glass is used for two basic purposes: either to bring a crop on ahead of its normal time in the open or to protect a permanent plant that would otherwise be killed by winter conditions. Winter conditions include damp as well as cold. Alpines, in particular, fall prey to rain when in their natural home they would be snug under frozen snow. A further use of glass is to provide an in-between stage for greenhouse-raised plants before they are submitted to the full range of natural conditions. Glass-covered frames are often used for "hardening-off" plants that have been pampered in propagation.

It need not only be the sun's heat that the glass encloses. The old-fashioned way of forcing early crops was to build a deep stack of fresh horse manure, cover it with soil and put a glass-lidded frame on top. The manure fermented, giving off enough heat to produce salads in mid-winter. The modern equivalent is to bury electric soil-warming cables in the soil under a frame. Compared with other forms of artificial heating, this is remarkably economical.

Above Glass "cloches" are used as portable miniature greenhouses. They warm up the soil for early crops.

Above Walls absorb heat from the sun by day and give it off slowly at night. This traditional system of climate control is valuable to such fruit as peaches in case of frost at flowering time; also in ripening.

Above Polythene tunnels have a "greenhouse effect" by day, but do not stop radiation heat-loss at night.

Above A bulb frame makes it possible to grow bulbs whose natural timing or whose tastes in weather cannot be met in the garden. Lights are put on when the bulb should be dried out for its period of dormancy.

The living soil

Left Peaty soils are the precise reverse of chalk soils: occurring in wet areas where lime and nitrogen are washed away. As a result vegetation fails to decompose and builds up an acid layer. The flora is limited to grasses and sedges, and such things as heather and other ericas.

Left Chalky soils, common in southern Britain and northern France, tend to be shallow and dry; humus is rapidly decomposed by the lime content. Their natural flora is among the richest.

Above The minute particles of heavy clay soil make it slow-draining but potentially extremely fertile. It warms up slowly in spring and retains heat well. Clay-soil flowers include hellebores, creeping bugle and *Narcissus pseudonarcissus*.

When a gardener is not complaining about the weather he is grumbling about his soil. It is not, however, quite such an arbitrary despot. Unlike the weather, soil can be improved. There are some soils that can even be perfected so that most plants will show every sign of satisfaction.

The perfect garden soil is a balanced mixture of five constituents: of solids perhaps two-thirds rock particles, of sizes ranging from small stones down to the tiniest specks of clay; one-third animal and vegetable matter, mainly dead and decayed but with a substantial population of living creatures; a considerable quantity of water and a remarkable amount of air. Unfortunately it is a rare occurrence for such a soil to form naturally. To understand why most soils have too much of one constituent and too little of another (at least from the gardener's point of view) we must go back to the ways in which soils are formed in the first instance—not just in prehistory but at this very minute.

When the surface of the earth is bare rock, as it all was originally and still is in such places as mountain-tops and sea cliffs, the weather is constantly chiselling away at the surface. Almost every mood of weather, except perhaps calm air and gentle sunshine, has its abrasive effect. Frost is one of the most powerful agencies for pulverizing rock. Extreme changes of temperature between day and night, causing rapid expansion and contraction, keep breaking pieces off. Heavy rain, strong winds, the pounding of waves and the grinding of glaciers all reduce rock, sometimes rapidly and sometimes imperceptibly slowly, to mineral fragments. This lifeless stony debris is the beginning of the creation of soil.

Soil is created when mineral detritus is colonized by living organisms. It is the interface between the solid rocky globe and the biosphere; the term for the mere film of life-supporting elements, oxygen above all, that envelopes us.

It is normal to distinguish between the top-soil, where the marriage of rocky matrix and biological life has gone furthest, and the sub-soil, where the influence of the biosphere is comparatively slight. Below the sub-soil lies the lifeless mother rock. The top-soil is rarely more than two or three feet deep—often far less.

So soil starts with geology. Its physical and chemical nature depend in the first place on the type of rock that was worn away. There comes a sharp difference, though, between soils that remain *in situ*, where they were weathered, and those that have been transported by water, as rain and rivers, by glaciers or by wind to end up far from their place of origin.

"Local" soils tend to be mixtures of particles of all sizes—a healthily heterogeneous mixture of everything from stones to silt. "Transported" soils tend to be sifted and sorted in the process of moving. The heavier particles are deposited first; the lightest last. If you follow the course of a river from mountain to sea the grading is obvious, from boulders in the upper reaches to finest silt in the delta or on the sea-bed. Transported soils therefore are inclined to be unbalanced: either all coarse particles or all fine ones, all sand or all clay. The main exception to this rule is the "boulder clay" often found where glaciers did the transporting. Its name tells its own story: clay in one spot and stones in another; here a stratum of sand and there a pocket of gravel.

Lichens will form even on unweathered rock, but other plants must wait until the accumulation of organic material

Below Sandy soils are "hungry", having an open structure that allows nutrients to be quickly washed away unless humus is constantly being added. They heat up quickly but cool down with equal speed. Sandy heaths have one of the most limited of natural floras, including birch, gorse and pine.

Glaucium flavum *Eryngium maritimum*

Right The effect of temperature and rainfall in deciding the nature of the soil is expressed as "Lang's Rain Factor". Generally speaking the higher the rainfall and the lower the temperature the greater the amount of organic matter in the soil, and vice versa. At any given average temperature the type of soil varies according to the rainfall. The diagram shows that in hot dry places the soil tends to be salty (mineral) dust; in cold wet places raw "undecomposed" humus.

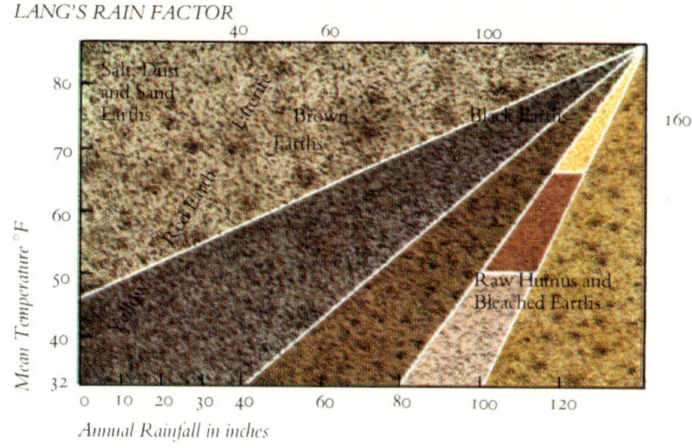

Above The relative proportions of different-sized mineral particles and organic matter in the four soil types illustrated on the left are shown by this simple experiment, which any gardener can carry out on his own soil. A trowelful of top-soil is shaken up in a big test-tube (or any straight-sided glass container) with water. As it settles the biggest mineral particles, stones, sink first, followed by the smaller particles in decreasing order of size to the smallest specks of clay, which either sink extremely slowly or even not at all, remaining in suspension. Organic matter settles as a dark layer on top of the mineral particles, or floats.

Above Earthworms are among the many inhabitants of the soil that are helpful to gardeners, improving its quality by passing it through their bodies and leaving tunnels that are exploited by roots and allow the entry of air. One species of earthworm, *Lumbricus terrestris* (illustrated above), pulls dead leaves down into the ground to eat them in private, a practice that adds valuable humus to the soil. In chalky clay, one of their favourite soils, earthworms may reach a population of 300 per square metre. Their net effect is entirely beneficial.

has started. In the rocky moraine below a glacier seeds may fall and have air and moisture enough to germinate. But the stones alone give no support or food for their roots and there is nothing porous to retain water. Then an animal may die, leaves and other plant debris may accumulate, bacteria and fungi can get to work, and the next seed that germinates can find a foothold in the scanty organic scrapheap. In turn it dies and adds to the organic layer. The mixture of stones, dead plants and animals, living ones, air and water has become soil. The same process continues with generation after generation of plants, each adding to the depth of soil, until big trees can find room for their roots. Steep mountainsides have been colonized or stabilized like this over millions of years of gradually increasing fertility.

The active agents in this process are the bacteria and fungi, and their lesser-known colleagues, whose feeding causes decay. Fertile soil has a colossal population of these micro-organisms: the bacteria in an acre of arable land, each one only visible under a microscope, may add up to a total weight of three thousand pounds. So fast do they multiply that under ideal conditions one bacterium can become two every twenty minutes. Others such as the actinomycetes, which are said to give the delicious fresh earthy smell to the soil, are just as abundant. Fungi are as active as bacteria in decomposing dead plant material. Without the activity of these creatures there would be no decay, and therefore no recycling of the carbon, the nitrogen and the other elements that plants need to grow.

The chief product of their industrious digestion, along with nitrogen and carbon dioxide, is the dark brown, crumbly, sweet-smelling decomposed vegetation known as humus—the chief component and sole object of the gardener's compost heap. Humus is constantly being made by the soil micro-organisms and as constantly being consumed. Its value to the gardener in improving the texture of no matter what soil is discussed on the following pages.

Even here, though, in this essential recycling process, climate plays a decisive part. In areas of heavy rainfall where nutrients (particularly nitrogen and calcium) are washed down—or "leached"—from the top-soil to lower layers few bacteria can survive. In the cold, wet, acid, lime-deprived forest of the north fungi are the chief agents of decay.

But where the land lies permanently waterlogged, as in peat bogs, not even fungi can live. Decay scarcely occurs at all; fertility is minimal and only a few specialized plants such as heather and cotton grass can grow at all.

The vital element that is missing from waterlogged soil is air. Oxygen is essential to all its inhabitants, including the roots of almost all plants. Its presence is the essential difference between the top-soil and the sub-soil. In top-soil, where all the action is and where most of the roots, even of the biggest trees, proliferate, the pores of air can occupy as much as half of the soil volume. Through them flows the soil-water. In them live the bacteria. The ideal soil of the gardener's dream not only all contains the elements in balanced and fertile proportion but the humus, the clay particles and the sand cohere into "crumbs" which remain separate, leaving ample air spaces between.

Exactly why some soils naturally remain "open" like this remains one of the many mysteries of nature. Which is not to say that you cannot achieve the same result by assiduous cultivation, conscientious drainage and applications of compost.

The soil as a reservoir

The soil provides three essentials to all plants: a firm foothold, food and water. If one of these three essentials could be called more important than the other two, it is water. Transpiration, as we have seen, is the motor of plant life. So the capacity of the soil to store water is a gardener's prime concern.

Soil holds water in two ways: in its organic content of humus and decaying vegetable matter which acts as a sponge, and in a thin film on each of its mineral particles. This film is strongly held together by surface tension.

The big variations between soils, therefore, come with the amount of organic matter involved and the surface area of the mineral particles. This is where sand and clay are poles apart. The comparatively few, relatively big, grains of sand have nothing like the total surface area of the millions of tiny particles of clay. So clay holds far more water than sand, and, since every little particle is equally reluctant to give up its individual film of water, grasps it much more tightly. As far as roots are concerned, then, sand has little water, but what it has is easily tapped. Clay has much more, but is miserly about letting it go.

When it rains, the open structure of sandy soil lets the water straight in. It percolates easily between the grains and travels down, drawn by gravity, until it reaches the permanently saturated level known as the water-table. As it goes it wets the humus in the soil and leaves a film on each grain. As each tiny cavity empties into the one below, air is drawn into it from above to take the place of the water. At the same time the flood of water passing through dissolves nitrogen and other foodstuffs and carries them with it—a process known as "leaching". A sandy soil, then, is an easy and airy place for roots to grow, but in rainy regions tends to be flushed clean of nutrients, so its fertility is low.

A heavy clay soil behaves quite differently. In the first place rain finds it hard to get in. The fine grains of the surface quickly coagulate to become watertight and the rain lies in puddles, only to evaporate again. What water does soak through moves slowly, its progress impeded by the tiny passages between the minute clay particles. Each particle claims its share. Until each layer is damp there is no surplus for gravity to pull lower. Nutrients are locked up in the same way as the water. Clay therefore is hard going for roots and tends to be airless, but holds its "goodness" well.

The gardener's ideal soil lies about half-way between the two extremes. A "good loam" is sandy enough to drain well, but has enough clay to hold essential reserves. Whichever way it tends, whether to lightness or heaviness, there is a ready way to improve it: to add more humus.

This is the chief value of peat, the compost heap, manure, straw or any organic matter. It may or may not have food value for plants, but it will certainly improve the texture of the soil. If it is sandy, it will clog the pores and slow down the exaggerated drainage. If it is clayey, it will open the pores and help the water (and the roots) through.

At the same time, the act of digging it in opens the soil to air and water. Undug, humus-starved soil is hard and heavy digging. The more humus the soil has, the easier the spade goes in and the lighter the load on the gardener's back. Both added humus and opening to the weather encourage the formation of soil "crumbs"; little conglomerations of particles which in turn give the soil a more airy, permeable structure.

But why this preoccupation with drainage? Surely, if water is so essential to plants the more they have the better? Would it not be best of all to have a high water-table that they could drink from as much as they wanted? It sounds a great waste of effort to water plants and at the same time to take elaborate precautions to drain the water away as quickly as possible.

The reasons are twofold. The first is that roots need air

Above Roots in a pot are in a more precarious situation than roots in the open ground, since they cannot grow away from stagnant, airless soil. Potting soil should therefore always drain quickly. Gardeners traditionally put a piece of broken pot over the drainage hole to keep it clear of soil.

Left The chief reason for digging is to open the soil to the air and allow the frost and the sun to break up clods into smaller crumbs, improving drainage and making it easier for roots to penetrate. A secondary reason is to mix in manure or compost, but this can be spread on the surface with as much effect.

Left Where soil lies wet and heavy there may be no alternative to laying drains. Here the tile drain-pipes are laid in a bed of rubble with a marked gradient as a foundation for a scree-bed for alpines which needs extra-thorough drainage.

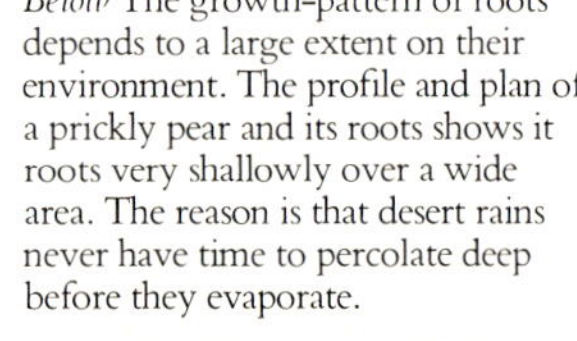

Below The growth-pattern of roots depends to a large extent on their environment. The profile and plan of a prickly pear and its roots shows it roots very shallowly over a wide area. The reason is that desert rains never have time to percolate deep before they evaporate.

Right A simple way to find out how much "rainfall" a sprinkler distributes, and whether it does so evenly or not, is to scatter a number of identical bowls within the area it covers and time how long it takes to put an inch of water in them.

Below The gardener's ideal is a long gentle shower of warm rain (preferably, of course, with fertilizer added). The same principle should apply to watering. A fine spray for a long period does least damage in compacting the surface and soaks in farthest. The golden rule is to water seldom and thoroughly.

almost as much as they need water. In saturated soil all the pore space, the gaps between the solid particles, is filled with water. Unless they are specially adapted to waterlogged conditions (as some bog plants are), roots kept for long under water will drown. Water passing down through the soil, on the other hand, renews the air in the cavities it vacates, leaving a healthy atmosphere with plenty of oxygen.

The second reason arises from the first. A high water-table restricts roots to soil near the surface, where the air is. Any sort of restriction is a disadvantage. They need as much room as possible to branch and re-branch in search of nutrients. But there is another problem with a root-zone limited to a few inches of the surface. It is inevitably unstable, helplessly subject to the changing weather. As it dries out in a drought, the uppermost roots die and lower ones take over, following the retreating water-table. But when rain returns and the water-table rises, the new roots will be too deep and be drowned. This is what happened to many beeches on shallow chalk soil in England in the wet winter after the drought of 1976.

The greater the depth of well-drained, well-aerated soil, therefore, the deeper plants can root and the safer they are in drought and flood. Investigation into the quality of vineyard land in Bordeaux has shown a direct relationship between the depth of drainage and the performance of the vines year after year. In the stony soil of the Médoc, vines will reach down thirty feet or more. At that level a passing shower means nothing; the plants grow in ideally constant conditions. To the gardener this means that occasional deep-digging, two spades deep, is a worthwhile operation—provided he puts plenty of compost or manure down in the lower layer.

For precisely the same reasons it is a fatal mistake to water plants little and often. If you merely sprinkle the surface, the roots will be forced to stay up where the water is, in the top few inches. Forget to sprinkle for a few days and there are no reserves of water below, nor any roots to tap them.

Traditional gardeners were for ever hoeing the surface of the soil between plants to keep a layer of broken "tilth" an inch or so deep. Although the main reason was to keep down weeds, they also thought that a dust-dry top inch of soil prevented surface evaporation.

Modern theory tends to decry the school of the hoe in favour of covering the surface with a mulch. This is in an attempt to return to the natural state of the forest floor with its fallen leaves, or the meadow with its accumulation of dead herbs and grasses. The mulch may be peat, leaf mould, compost, lawn-mowings, or even sawdust or pulverized tree bark. A two-inch layer spread over the warmed wet soil in spring has several beneficial effects. Preventing evaporation is the first, suppressing weeds is another (if they do seed in the mulch they are easily pulled up). Gradually adding to the soil-humus by the action of earthworms is a third.

In permanent plantings of trees and shrubs, mulching is undoubtedly beneficial. Heathers are happier for a mulch of peat and many alpines for a layer of gravel or stone chips. On the other hand, in parts of the garden where you are constantly planting and replanting, it is impractical to put down a layer you would constantly be disturbing.

Once the mulch has dried out, it works just as effectively preventing rain reaching the soil and preventing evaporation. It takes prolonged rain or irrigation to saturate the mulch before the soil can get even a drop. The great virtue of a gravel mulch is that this does not apply.

As a footnote on a recent discovery, it has been found by workers planting eucalyptus to reclaim the fringes of the Sahara that planting the trees two feet deeper in the sand than usual is beneficial, if the hole is filled with stones. Moisture condenses in the "mulch" at night and waters the tree.

SAND

NUMBER OF DAYS

Depth of wet soil in inches

Rain falling on a sandy soil sinks deep quickly. The graph shows that if one inch of water is added the top fourteen inches are dry in five days.

LOAM

NUMBER OF DAYS

Depth of wet soil in inches

In loamy soil with both sand and clay particles, drainage is more moderate. It takes ten days to dry out to the same depth.

CLAY

NUMBER OF DAYS

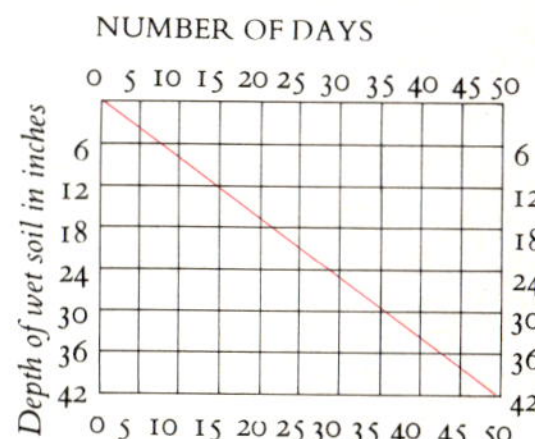

The tiny particles of clay soils slow down drainage and cause shallower rooting. To dry out a lawn to fourteen inches takes seventeen days.

Above Plants root deeper or shallower according to where the water is in the ground. The plant in this illustration is shown as its roots would be in heavy, moisture retentive soil and also how they would run deeper in light, fast-draining soil. Under normal conditions roots can adapt to fluctuations, but extreme drought, killing surface roots, followed by a very wet spell which raises the water-table and kills deep roots, can be a fatal formula. The inset shows how water percolates down through the air spaces in the soil, not reaching the lower ones until those above are full. The surface layer must be saturated before the reserves below begin to be topped up.

The chemistry of the soil

Below The bonfire is an essential part of garden hygiene. All waste plant material that is too woody to rot readily in the compost, or is full of weed seeds or tenacious roots, or is infected with fungus or virus disease, should be burnt as a regular routine. The fresh ashes of the bonfire are a source of potash.

Before the days of artificial fertilizers there was an ancient principle embodied in all farm lease agreements. The rules of good husbandry decreed that there were certain things the tenant might not take off the farm: the hay and the straw had to be fed to the animals and their manure put back on the land. If they were carted off and sold the land suffered. No one knew that essential potassium went with them. No one knew about potassium at all.

Early in the nineteenth century chemists were able to discover by analysing plants that they consisted of at least eight elements. They could account for the carbon, hydrogen and oxygen as coming from the water and carbon dioxide all around us. But that left nitrogen, phosphorus, potassium, calcium and magnesium, which must, they deduced, come from the soil. Manure, they discovered, also contains these elements. These, therefore, were what the old farming practice had unwittingly been recycling.

Manure, however, contains very little of the essentials in proportion to its bulk: only thirty pounds of all these elements together in a ton. It would be much more efficient to apply the elements direct.

Nitrogen was the first to be a practical proposition. It is easily available either in the form of sulphate of ammonia, a by-product of burning coal to produce gas, or nitrate of soda, which was discovered to exist in vast quantities underground in Chile. Either of these spread on the soil in spring had immediate and wonderful results in promoting lush green growth. Unfortunately they were also leached out of the soil by rain, so they needed to be applied little and often.

The next chemical to be found in a useable form was phosphorus. A young English squire, John Bennet Lawes of Rothamsted in Hertfordshire, became interested in why ground-up bones improved the fertility of some soils but not others. He dissolved some bones in sulphuric acid and found that the answer was simple: bone "meal" provided phosphorus (which is essential to good root growth) in acid soils that could dissolve it, but remained insoluble in alkaline soils. His invention of "superphosphate" made him a fortune and founded the artificial fertilizer industry. As luck would have it, he did not have to dig up the battlefields of Europe (as his enemies claimed) to find enough bones: he was able to use newly discovered natural deposits of calcium phosphate.

Nitrogen is all around us in the air. It should, the chemists thought, be reasonably easy to combine it with the hydrogen in the air to make ammonia. This in turn could easily be made into plant food by oxidation into its sulphate or nitrate. They found that a powerful charge of electricity could do the trick. In fact, lightning does it regularly; the rain in a thunderstorm is very dilute nitric acid. By World War I, German chemists had found a catalyst which made it a simple industrial process, to the great consternation of the British. Nitrates are a prerequisite for high explosives and Britain still had to import hers from Chile.

Potassium has long been applied to the soil in the form of fresh ashes from wood fires, which contain about ten per cent of potassium carbonate or "potash". Its value to plants lies chiefly in speeding the production of sugar in the leaves, and thus speeding the ripening process, the filling-out of beet and potatoes, the sweetening of fruit, the stiffening of grass stalks and the turning of new wood from green to brown.

The need for industrialized production of potassium fertilizers came later, as farmers abandoned their old recycling methods and turned to direct applications. Rock deposits known as kainit, which overlaid deposits of common salt in Germany and Austria, were found to be a mixture of potassium sulphate and magnesium sulphate.

Of the other major elements calcium was easily come by and indeed has been used for improving heavy clay soils at least since Roman times. Chalk or lime, or marl, which is limey clay, has the property of binding the clay particles together and making them more easily workable. (The word is flocculate, derived from the Latin for wool.) It is only very acid soils that normally lack enough calcium for most plant's chemical needs.

Magnesium, on the contrary, is often in short supply. Its function in plants is in the manufacture of chlorophyll, the essential green pigment. Where magnesium is lacking, leaves are parti-coloured, pale or sometimes flushed with purple. An excess of potassium and a shortage of nitrogen is often the indirect cause. A simple remedy is a dose of Epsom salts.

Since the early experimental days six more elements have been found to be essential to plants, but they are only needed in minute traces. These "trace" elements are iron, manganese, boron, copper, zinc and molybdenum. Lack of a trace element *could* be the problem with an ailing plant in your garden, but there are a hundred and one more likely problems to worry about first.

In practice, it is only the first three nutrient elements which need regular topping up, and that only where crops are being taken from the ground that are not returned to it.

The compost heap acts like the gardener's own cow, digesting his waste vegetable matter into a form the soil bacteria will enjoy. They have difficulties in soil that is too wet (and lacks oxygen), or too cold, or too acid. Decay is very slow in bogs or on the floor of rainy forest where acidity is high and nitrogen constantly being leached away.

A well-run compost heap (with lime and nitrogen added if necessary) can return to the soil the nutrients removed in growing most ornamental plants. The kitchen garden is another matter. There plants are being force-fed to maximum fatness and ripeness, then taken away bodily and not returned. They can certainly benefit from fertilizers—the choice of the

Above Such "natural" or organic fertilizers as ground-up hoof and horn or bones, dried blood, hair or seaweed have been used for centuries. The first man to patent the chemical manufacture of fertilizers was Sir John Bennet Lawes (1814–1900) of Rothamsted in Hertfordshire. His experiments showed that ground bones did little good on alkaline soil unless treated with acid because their calcium phosphate is insoluble in water. He processed first bones then mineral phosphates from Spain and elsewhere into "Superphosphate".

THE COMPOST HEAP

Compost is not only a way of returning to the soil what plants have taken out of it. Well-made compost improves the structure of all soils, lightening clay and giving substance to sand. The essentials of a compost heap are adequate air, moisture and nitrogen (food for the micro-organisms that do the work), and enough bulk of material to build up a high temperature to kill weed seeds.

The most practical method for a small garden is to build a double enclosure with air vents in the sides, and preferably ducts for air underneath (which can be made of bricks on edge, or a layer of small branches). Each box should be at least three feet square and high. Any animal or vegetable refuse can be put in. Ideally one whole box is filled at once, in six-inch layers of waste of different textures (e.g. grass-mowings alternating with stalky stuff) with a sprinkling of "activator", or nitrogenous fertilizer, in between. The heap is then thoroughly moistened and covered with a plastic cover or an old carpet.

It should take about a month in warm weather to heat up and cool down again. Another month or more of maturing, while the earthworms mix the compost up, is a good idea. Meanwhile waste can be accumulated in the second box for use the next time.

fertilizer depending on whether it is the leaves, the roots or the fruits of the plant that you intend to make a delicacy.

Compost or rotted manure are complete foods for the soil; they feed its structure as well as its chemistry. For those who have to do without them, there are alternatives—at a price: hop manure, spent mushroom compost, even wool waste ("shoddy") or minced-up refuse from the municipal dump.

Fertilizers, as opposed to composts, act more or less directly on the plant. "Balanced" garden fertilizers today are carefully designed mixtures of the essentials, with more of this element or that according to their purpose. The big three, N (nitrogen), P (phosphate) and K (potassium) are always included, and their proportions stated, always in the same order. Thus a tomato fertilizer might be N 6 : P 5 : K 9, heavy on the nitrogen and potash for growth and fruit, while a chrysanthemum fertilizer would have more phosphates for flowers.

"National Growmore", the classic formulation for Britain's wartime vegetable gardeners, is still widely used and has the all-purpose formula 7:7:7—that is seven parts in a hundred of each of N, P and K.

Gardeners without specialized knowledge do much better to stick to such brands rather than applying the particular fertilizers singly: they are powerful and quick-acting and can do more harm than good if they are overdone.

Some of the compound or balanced fertilizers are entirely mineral, inorganic or "artificial"; some (the more expensive) are natural or organic; some are a mixture. Of the traditional organic fertilizers, most are the dried and ground-up remains of some form of animal life, from fish meal to dried blood. Seaweed is a more recent addition with valuable properties. But still Squire Lawes' old bonemeal is one of the most popular and generally useful in gardens. It contains a little nitrogen and a good deal of phosphate which it releases slowly to the great benefit of newly planted roots. Too slowly, of course, for the Squire's liking.

Below Plants can only use nitrogen in the form of nitrates, which have only a short life in the soil. The picture below shows how different forms of fertilizer are converted to nitrates at different speeds through a continuous process of "digestion" by bacteria: from organic compounds to ammonia to nitrites to nitrates.

Left Legumes have nodules on their roots which contain bacteria that can short-cut the normal nitrogen cycle, "fixing" nitrogen directly from the air without having to convert it first into ammonia, then nitrites, then nitrates. For this reason peas and beans are given first place in the vegetable garden rotation.

Dead plants and animals contribute organic nitrogen compounds to the soil. Rain after lightening is very dilute nitric acid.

Manure, ammonium sulphate and ammonium nitrate all contribute ammonia. The nitrate provides usable nitrogen.

Ammonia decomposes to nitrites. Compost has already reached this stage.

Nitrites decompose to nitrates, which is the "nitrogen" plants need to grow.

Inorganic fertilizers (sodium and calcium nitrate) are a short-cut to this stage but their effect is short-lived.

pH VALUES

The acidity or alkalinity of soil determines to a large extent what can be grown in it. Acidity is measured in pH degrees. The rating is based on the concentration of hydrogen ions in solution: the higher the concentration the more acid the soil. A neutral solution has a hydrogen ion concentration of one in 10 million (i.e. 1:10,000,000, or 10^{-7} (ten to the power of minus seven). The figure seven is the pH. A lower pH is more acid, a higher more alkaline.

7.5 Many flowering shrubs do well, but not the heather group, azaleas, rhododendrons, lupins or most lilies. There is a reduced availability of phosphate, potassium manganese and iron.

7.0

6.5 Optimum for most plants. Maximum availability of mineral nutrients.

6.0 Phosphates fixed by soil; potassium, calcium, magnesium, and trace elements suffer loss by leaching. Bacteria affected more than fungi.

5.5 Nitrification reduced.

5.0 Many plants suffer from acidity; roots short, stubby often fanged. Phosphate largely unavailable.

4.5

4.0 Heaths and moorland plants; rhododendrons do well, many other flowering plants fail. Most mineral nutrients become much more soluble and liable to be washed out. Soluble aluminium appears in harmful quantities. Bacteria and soil animals affected.

Above Hydrangeas are tolerant of a wide range of soil acidity or alkalinity, but certain species have the peculiar quality of reacting like litmus paper, being red in alkaline soil and blue in acid. The reason is that the trace-element aluminium, which makes them blue, is not available to the roots in alkaline conditions. But similar inhibition of, for example, iron is what makes some plants impossible to grow in some soils.

MINERAL NUTRIENTS

POSITIVE EFFECTS	DEFICIENCY EFFECTS
Nitrogen (N) The rate and vigour of growth and colour of leaves. Protein building and photosynthesis.	Growth stunted; small yellow, or possibly bluish leaves. Thin weak stems.
Phosphorus (P) Root growth, ripening of seeds and fruit.	Stunted roots and growth. Small purple leaves and stems. Yield of fruit and seeds poor.
Potassium (Potash) (K) Close links with nitrogen. When nitrogen is increased, so must potash or a deficiency will appear. A fruit-forming fertilizer. Assists photosynthesis and the production of carbohydrate. Protects plants against diseases.	Fruits are poorly coloured, lacking in flavour. Leaves will appear scorched at edges, mottled, spotted or curled. Potatoes will cook badly turning black and soapy.
Calcium (Ca) Essential for sturdy young plant growth. One of the most important soil foods.	General lack of vigour, growing points die, growth stops. Without calcium, some species are unable to assimilate nitrogen.
Magnesium (Mg) Part of the chlorophyll molecule (which makes leaves green). It is necessary for the formation of animo acids and vitamins. Essential to germination of seed and synthesis of sugar.	Photosynthesis is effected and shows as yellowing of leaves, or purplish/brown patches between the veins. Leaves may fall prematurely.
Sulphur (S) Necessary for chlorophyll synthesis.	Similar to nitrogen deficiency—leaves become light green.
Iron (Fe) Helps in the formation of chlorophyll.	Chlorosis develops—yellow or very pale upper leaves, thin weak stem.
Copper (Cu) Plays a part in nitrogen metabolism.	Dieback of shoots, terminal leaves develop dead spots and brown areas. Branchless plants such as cabbage, become chlorotic and leaves fail to form.
Zinc (Zn) Legumes require zinc for seed formation. Formation of starch, chloroplast, auxin and internodal elongation.	Malformed leaves, "mottle leaf" of citrus, "white bud" of maize. Zinc deficiency leads to iron deficiency—both are thus similar in appearance.

Roots, the soil and the gardener

Above The orderly earthiness of the potting shed at the Royal Horticultural Society's gardens at Wisley. Potting is done at a central desk filled with the appropriate "compost". Plants are barrowed in (left). Shelves round the walls hold sterilized clay pots of a score of different sizes and shapes.

There is a crucial moment in the relationship of gardener and plant: the moment when he commits its roots to the soil. A gardener is constantly moving plants from one place to another when it is their nature, their very essence, to stay put. He pricks out seedlings from a seed tray when they have the merest thread of root, and he uproots well-grown trees with all he can manage of the ramifications of their roots to lug them to another station.

A large part of his success or failure depends on his care of the roots. However luxuriant the top, if its roots are mutilated it will wither away. If its roots are intact and well planted a flourishing top will follow.

The other vital factor is when he plants. His object must be to give the roots as long as possible to grow before the shoots start to make big demands on them.

Unlike the part of a plant above ground, which follows a precise plan of growth, roots are opportunists with no predisposition to one pattern. What is decisive is where they find the right combination of soil moisture, nutrients, and oxygen in a medium they can penetrate. Also unlike shoots, they grow all the year round if the soil is warm enough—above about 7°C/45°F.

A root bores through the soil by pushing a sort of warhead with an outer layer of expendable cells. The cells just behind the warhead are the ones that multiply to make it grow. As it bores the surface cells are left behind as lubricants to ease its passage.

But this is a soft and fragile instrument to contend with stones and solid clods. It will always take the easy path if there is one: an old worm-tunnel or the course of a former root that has died and rotted away. What it likes best is "open" soil, airy and uncompacted, yet rich in humus to conserve water and nutrients.

No one could express it better than the seventeenth-century writer who said, "Those that plant should make their ground fit [for rose trees] before they plant them, and not bury them in a hole like a dead dog. Let them have good and fresh lodgings suitable to their quality."

Most plants get their first taste of soil in the potting shed—probably of a nursery. There is no question of it being ordinary soil. The nurseryman talks about his "medium" or "compost" (not to be confused with the produce of the compost heap). Ordinary soil would be broken down by the constant watering a pot needs. Potting soil is designed to drain fast and keep its structure. The drainage, it cannot be said too often, is the most important thing of all. The conventional guarantee of free drainage is a crock over the hole at the bottom of the pot (see pages 22–3).

Any plant will grow happily in a pot until its roots have explored the whole volume of soil and extracted its nourishment. But then to keep it growing well and getting bigger, as opposed to becoming "pot-bound"—a condition only desirable for permanently potted flowering plants—it must be "potted on" into a bigger pot with more soil for its roots to exploit. Taking it out of its pot to see if its roots have filled it does it no harm. The way to do it is to tap the rim of the pot upside down on the edge of a table. If the roots are growing round and round it is time for a bigger pot.

More and more nurseries sell their plants in pots (or "containers" as they call them) so that the gardener gets them home

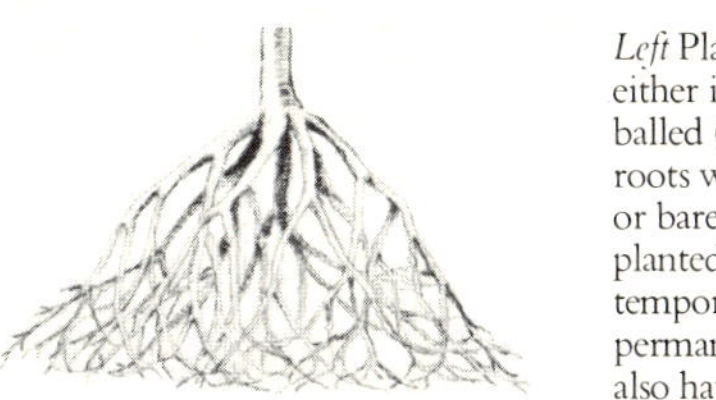

Left Plants are sold by nurseries either in pots (or other containers), balled (with a ball of soil round the roots wrapped in burlap or sacking) or bare rooted. Bare roots must be planted immediately, either temporarily ("heeled in") or permanently. Balled plants should also have their roots covered with earth, sand or compost while waiting to be planted, and be planted as soon as possible. Plants in containers can be kept and "grown on" if immediate planting is not convenient. They will need regular watering and feeding, and repotting into a bigger pot if they are not put in their permanent positions within six months.

Above The roots of a magnolia are thick, fleshy and brittle with relatively little branching, making it difficult to dig them up intact. Roots that are damaged should be cut off at the wound.

Below In contrast the roots of a *Hebe* (and those of rhododendrons) are fibrous and much-divided with a total length of hundreds of yards. Fibrous-rooted plants are more easily moved.

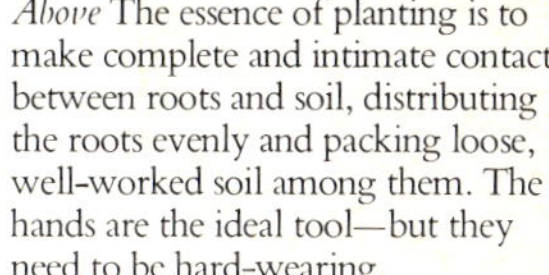

Above The essence of planting is to make complete and intimate contact between roots and soil, distributing the roots evenly and packing loose, well-worked soil among them. The hands are the ideal tool—but they need to be hard-wearing.

Above Bulbs also need careful planting. A lily bulb, best moved in summer just after flowering, while its new roots are growing, is given a bed of sand for good drainage in a very generous hole.

Above More summary planting for a daffodil with a tool that removes a core of soil. But still a handful of peat and sand in the bottom of the hole ensures close contact and good drainage.

with no disturbance to the roots. If the timing is right, and the roots have not outgrown the pot and started to spiral, this is the ideal arrangement. A containerized plant can be planted at any time (but preferably in damp weather) between spring and autumn. The essential is to prepare the ground over a much bigger area than the roots will immediately take up—say four times as big—making it as much like potting compost as possible: mixing the original soil with so much peat, sand and bonemeal that the roots will not know the difference. A thick layer of mulch over the soil (see page 23) will then keep weeds from taking advantage of the ideal conditions.

With bare-rooted plants the season is the first consideration. The ideal is for the plant to be dormant but for the soil to be warm enough for the roots to grow. In mild-winter areas this means autumn, as soon as the leaves fall. The roots will have most of the winter to expand ready for the big water-demands of spring.

Where the ground is either frozen or waterlogged in winter, though, the roots of a new plant may well be killed. It is better to delay planting until the ground warms up, even at the risk of having to water constantly in spring. Evergreens, which are never fully dormant, present the greatest problem. In mild areas September is probably the best time; the roots may get in four months' growth before the ground becomes really cold. In New England May is the month generally recommended.

Firm, careful, intimate planting is even more important when the roots are bare. Only by sifting fine soil down among the roots can you achieve the vital close contact. Bare roots can dry out almost instantly if they are exposed to sun or wind. Soak them well in water in advance, then keep them in a plastic bag until the actual moment of planting. Another trick is the old method of "puddling in": coating the roots with mud by dipping them in a very wet soil-and-water mix before planting them. Planting in mud, of course, would be fatal as the roots would get no air.

The only satisfactory way with plants that have become seriously pot-bound is to treat them as bare-root plants, gently breaking up the soil-ball and pruning off any intractable big roots that still insist on spiralling. If this means unbalancing the plant by leaving more top than root, then the top must be proportionately reduced too.

The same basic principles apply to transplanting. Dig up as much of the roots as possible and get them as quickly as possible into a spacious hole full of a moist but open and permeable soil. Roots that are badly injured should be cut off at the wound; they will not recover. For this reason such fleshy rooted plants as magnolias are almost impossible to transplant at more than a modest size. Thick fleshy roots are brittle, with relatively few branches. A large proportion of the root system is bound to be lost. Even fleshy rooted herbaceous plants such as peonies resent moving—whereas any plant with a dense mop of fibrous root can quite easily be unearthed intact. With all plants, stability in their new station is essential; if the wind can rock them, or if frosts lift them, their roots will never take hold. Trees and shrubs of any substance should always be given a solid stake for their first two years. Everything you plant needs the soil, open, porous and friable though it be, pressed down firmly and authoritatively round its roots and about its neck.

JOHN INNES COMPOST

The ideal potting compost was standardized to a set of formulae in the 1930s by the John Innes Institute. It was based on a priceless material known as fibrous loam, made by cutting turves from good pasture and stacking them with strawy manure till the grass rotted away, then sieving the result and sterilizing it with steam. Two parts of this with one of peat and one of "sharp" sand or grit is the perfect light "medium" for sowing seeds, combining the physical properties of water-retention and drainage in exactly the right proportions.

For potting up cuttings and seedlings the mixture is made heavier: seven parts loam to three of peat and two of sand. Fertilizers and chalk are added according to the kind and maturity of plant.

The cost of making ideal loam is so high today that soilless composts are more commonly used; i.e., just peat and sand (1:1 for seeds, 3:1 for potting) or (particularly in the USA) vermiculite or perlite, heat-treated minerals with remarkable powers of absorbing and retaining both water and air. Such composts have no natural nutrient value at all, unlike loam, so whatever the plant needs must be added.

Sunlight is energy

Above The sun is the ultimate source of all energy on earth. Green plants have the unique capacity to convert solar energy into food by the process of photosynthesis. But they differ widely in the amount of sunlight they need, or can tolerate. Lower woodland plants are proficient at converting the energy in low light levels.

There are two principal ways in which the sun's energy, its heat and light, are put to use to activate what would otherwise be a lifeless world—and plants are involved in both of them. The first, as we have seen, is the evaporation of water. Short-wave radiation, or heat, from the sun turns water to vapour. When it condenses and falls the solar energy that raised it is released to erode fields or drive turbines. The second is in the miraculous business of photosynthesis, in which plants feed on the sun's light.

It is a pity there is no pithy old Anglo-Saxon word for a process so central to life. The reconstituted Greek favoured by scientists makes everything sound equally unimportant and unintelligible. What sunlight does to plants is very important indeed, since all our lives depend on it. Directly for vegetarians, indirectly for the rest of us, plants and the sun together provide the world's entire diet. They also provide a large part of its oxygen.

Chlorophyll, the green pigment of plants, is the unique agent for this transaction. Its contribution is to convert the energy contained in light into the energy necessary for chemical change. The chemical change in question is the rearranging of the molecules of water and carbon dioxide to make oxygen and sugar. The sugar is stored energy—which is a way of defining food. Already we are in a tight conceptual corner. How does sugar store energy?

Energy is not the constituents of sugars but the force that holds them together. Carbon, hydrogen and oxygen are not sugar until their molecules are combined in the right pattern and proportion—$C_6H_{12}O_6$. But the force that combined them remains locked up until the process is reversed and the elements go their separate ways, or recombine in some other pattern. Then it is released to do other work—to make heat, for example, to build plant tissues or to move muscles.

Given the genius of chlorophyll, then, the three factors needed for photosynthesis are sunlight, water and carbon dioxide. Shortage of any of the three will slow the process down. Most plants grow better in sunlight than in shade.

On the other hand carbon dioxide is rarely in the air in such abundance that plants can take it for granted. Only three parts in a hundred of the normal atmosphere are this essential gas. Some plants can absorb it much more rapidly than others. The internal structure of the leaf is what makes the difference: some are made to take in and circulate gases quickly and easily—others have relatively sluggish diffusion.

The latter gain no benefit from floods of sunlight. Their rate of photosynthesis is governed by their intake of carbon dioxide. The shade for them is as good as the sun—better in fact, since they will not have to transpire so much. These are the shade-loving plants, adapted to life under the trees.

As far as the gardener is concerned the important thing is to give each plant the amount of sunlight or shade it needs. There are no general rules here—it is one of the many cases where a reference book is essential. But the point reference books cannot help with is the local intensity of sunlight. A plant that needs a degree of shade in the south of France would be happier in full sun in Scotland. Overmuch sun on plants not accustomed to it can create severe damage; scorching the leaves, and even the bark of trees.

Conversely a light-demanding plant obliged to live in the shade will distort itself in strange ways to get as much light as it can. The urge to reach the light is known as phototropism. It manifests itself in drawn-out, spindly stems leaning towards wherever the strongest light may be, with leaves often ingeniously rearranged to catch as much of it as possible. The control mechanism in the plant is simple. Cells on the lighter side stay as they are, transferring all their energy to cells on the shady side. These grow faster and bend the plant until the

Above Commercial chrysanthemum growers produce year-round flowering by manipulating the supply of light. The chrysanthemums are misled into "thinking" the nights are short and flowering is consequently delayed. Growers activate the pigment phytochrome, which controls flowering (see right), by using short periods of red light.

Below Fungi such as the mushrooms below, are devoid of chlorophyll, which means that they are dependent on other organisms, dead or alive, for their source of energy.

LIGHT AND PLANT PIGMENTS

The human eye and the pigments of plants are strangely unanimous about what part of the wide range of electromagnetic radiation constitutes usable (to us, visible) light. It lies between violet and red, or, as radiation is measured, between 390 and 780 thousand millionths of a metre (a unit known as a nanometre). When sunlight passes through a prism it is separated into the familiar coloured bands of the rainbow, each representing a different wavelength of light. The diagram right shows that plant pigments absorb and use all the visible spectrum except green, which is reflected. (Which is why the plants are green.) The different plant pigments, absorbing different wavelengths of light-energy, use them for different purposes. Some of these responses are shown below.

WAVE LENGTHS OF LIGHT IN NM.

390–500 CHLOROPHYLL 400–500 CAROTENOIDS 420 RIBOFLAVIN	PIGMENTS ABSORB LIGHT
500–600 NOT ABSORBED	
650–730 CHLOROPHYLL 660 PHYTOCHROME 730 PHYTOCHROME	PIGMENTS ABSORB LIGHT
730–810 NOT ABSORBED	

The pale blue pigment phytochrome, absorbing red light, is responsible for starting both seed germination and flowering.

Yellow-orange carotenoids, absorbing blue light, control such plant responses as leaf fall and the ripening of fruit.

Blue-violet riboflavin pigment, absorbing violet light, controls phototropism—the movement of the plant towards light.

Chlorophyll absorbs blue and red light. A plant without chlorophyll, such as the dodder above, cannot convert sunlight to energy.

illumination is equal all round. "Drawn" plants, making obvious efforts to reach the light, are common in crowded greenhouses and, indeed, in forests.

For plants not expressly designed for shade another effect of subdued light is to encourage leafage at the expense of flowers. If productivity in the sugar factory is low the tendency is to spend what stored energy there is on building more solar panels. It is when the balance swings the other way and the carbohydrate (or sugar) level is high that flower-buds are formed. Abundant sunshine one year can therefore have a noticeable effect on flower-production the next.

Plants are affected not only by the total amount of light received but by when it comes and for how long. We have gathered into our gardens plants from the low latitudes where days are nearly the same length all the year round (on the Equator all days and all nights last twelve hours) and plants from higher latitudes where a summer day, and a winter night, can be as long as twenty hours.

Since the growing season is the time of year when days are longer than nights, high-latitude plants need long periods of light (and are known as long-day plants). They may flower little, if at all, when grown far south of their natural homes. Plants from the hotter regions similarly need short days. The dahlia, which comes from Mexico, is an example of a short-day plant. It flowers after mid-summer, in the shortening days towards autumn. Long-day plants such as the delphinium tend to flower early and ripen their seed in the heat of the summer, "knowing" that a northern winter lies ahead.

PHOTOSYNTHESIS

$$6\,CO_2 + 6\,H_2O \xrightarrow{\text{SUNLIGHT}} C_6H_{12}O_6 + 6\,O_2$$

SUNLIGHT TRAPPED BY CHLOROPHYLL

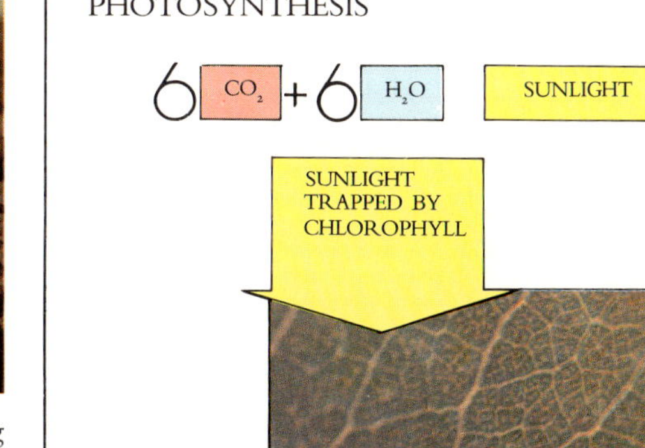

CARBON DIOXIDE (CO_2) TAKEN FROM THE ATMOSPHERE

WATER (H_2O) DRAWN UP FROM THE ROOTS

OXYGEN (O_2) EXPELLED AFTER PHOTOSYNTHESIS

SUGAR ($C_6H_{12}O_6$) STORED IN THE LEAF CELLS

The ingredients and the method for the basic process of capturing and storing the sun's energy are illustrated above. The whole process is known as photosynthesis. A section of a *Eucalyptus* leaf is shown absorbing the ingredients: the yellow arrow represents sunlight (absorbed by chlorophyll); the pink arrow carbon dioxide (entering through pores) and the blue arrow water (supplied by the roots).

The chemical equation above relates what happens to the molecules of each as photosynthesis takes place. In the presence of chlorophyll the excitement of the molecules by the sun's rays is transferred into chemical energy in the form of sugars (the purple arrow)—principally glucose. The oxygen released in the chemical reaction is diffused into the atmosphere (green arrow). The sugars are converted into starch for storage, then transformed into soluble sugars again for transport to the part of the plant where their latent energy is needed for growth or repair.

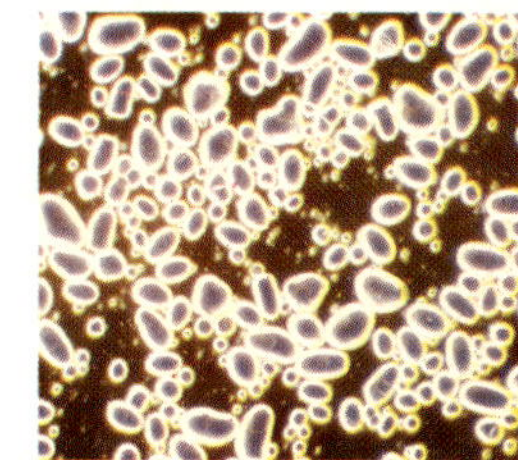

Above Starch grains (here magnified 50 times) are the solid form that energy takes for storage inside the plant.

Pests and diseases

The essence of gardening is control. But if control, or attempts at it, lead to neurosis, something has gone wrong. A garden which is a battleground against the less amiable and co-operative forces of nature can scarcely be a source of serenity. The gardener must be a philosopher, accepting that he and his have a place in the cycle of life which nothing, or very little, can ever alter.

Everything that grows is food for something else. Innumerable hosts of predators, both animal and vegetable, are constantly at work, not only on our precious plants but on each other. The best any gardener can do is to referee the performance with a bias in favour of his own side.

There are certain precautionary measures all gardeners can reasonably take. In a general way, a well-cultivated, well-fed garden is less prone to serious damage than a starved one. In plants as in animals, general health and vitality is the first line of defence against disease. The choice of plants can also help. Specialists are always more at risk, and so a wide range of kinds and species is an insurance policy. Some plants are inherently less prone to be eaten: rhododendrons, magnolias, weigelas and day-lilies come into this category. On the whole, the more highly bred a plant is, the more susceptible it will be to disease—another argument in favour of natural species as opposed to garden varieties. Certain modern cultivars, however, have been bred to be disease- and pest-resistant.

Occasional cataclysmic diseases alter the whole face of a country. Dutch elm disease is proving the point at the moment. Even more dramatic, in that it is destroying the most characteristic tree of a whole region, is the cypress disease which is devastating Tuscany. Both are caused by fungi. In such cases there is nothing to be done but to replant with a different tree.

Nor can anything be done about the unpredictable haunting menace, disastrous when it strikes, but by no means inevitable. Again, fungi are usually the culprits. In Britain honey fungus is the one that causes most spines to creep. Many old gardens, old woodlands and orchards in which trees have lived and died have it lurking somewhere in their soil, particularly if the soil sometimes lies wet. It lives on dead roots and attacks live ones —usually with fatal results. You get no warning. Suddenly your cherry tree, or peony, or rose, or even daffodil, wilts and is mortally sick. When it is dead you will usually find, just under the bark at soil level, tell-tale black "bootlaces"—the tentacles of the fiend. In the United States, Verticillium wilt holds a similar position of dishonour.

Coral spot fungus is another menace, though this at least you can see: tiny bright red pustules, at first on dead wood, but soon encroaching on to live. Fireblight is another—though this time a bacterium rather than a fungus—specializing in such members of the rose family as hawthorns and pears, hitting them with what looks like a blow-torch attack. Silver leaf disease is another fungus with a taste for the same victims.

None of these can be foreseen or guarded against, except by such commonsense general hygiene as burning rubbish, particularly dead twigs that harbour the coral spot, and protecting wounds and pruning cuts with a fungicidal paint or tar.

There is a more specific group of diseases, again mostly fungoid, that do the rounds of gardens where a particular plant grows. Hollyhock and snapdragon rusts are examples; black-spot on roses is another. The "wilt" that kills clematis back to ground level is a fourth. Most gardeners are prepared to fight with regular spraying for plants as important as roses, and to be patient and try again with clematis, but there are other things to take the place of snapdragons, and indeed of most plants that have ineradicable problems. The best advice here is to destroy them and plant something else.

The key question, of course, is to know if a sick plant is curable or not. If it merely looks ailing and unhappy, without any particular symptoms of blotched leaves or dying-back stems, it is worth looking for commonsense cultural reasons. Drought and water-logging are the first causes to eliminate. Look up the needs of the plant. Should it theoretically be happy where it is? Is it getting too much or too little sun? Is a more vigorous neighbour starving it? Is the soil suitable? If conditions seem to be right and the plant still reproaches you, your own temperament must decide whether to call in expert help or have done with it and make room for something new.

There are diseases—or perhaps conditions is a better word—that are so endemic in gardens that the only answer is to live with them. Powdery mildew is one. It is always ready to feed on plants when the temperature and humidity suit it. It weakens and disfigures the plants but seldom kills them, and can often retire for long periods. On balance it does not matter all that much. The less conspicuous downy mildew is a more serious complaint, crippling and occasionally killing the plant.

At least with fungus we can, if we want, go in to the attack. There are systemic fungicides such as Benomyl, which, when sprayed on the leaves, circulate in the sap and attack the fungus from inside. There is also the traditional sulphur dust and Bordeaux mixture to puff or spray from without.

Virus diseases spoil plants without remedy. They do not usually kill the plants, but make mottled or mosaic patterns on their leaves, cause them to grow in odd shapes and sometimes completely cripple them. Relatively little is known about these mini-microscopic organisms—which are also responsible for the "breaks" that give stripes to the tulip. The only course here is the bonfire.

As to the fauna of the garden that we regard as pests, there are said to be twenty-seven thousand species of insect alone that do damage, beside which you can line up the deer, rabbits, squirrels, slugs and birds.

In a small garden there is no need to tolerate the obviously damaging insects. Caterpillars that chew leaves are easily picked off (though you may be destroying a beautiful butterfly) and it is no great chore to take a puffer of nicotine or pyrethrum dust with you of an evening to discourage the aphids—the green- and black-fly. Aphids not only weaken plants by sucking their sap but also spread virus diseases.

In a bigger garden, unless you are prepared to spend considerable time stalking the little perishers, your best recourse is to encourage the birds to hold the ring for you. Mischievous they may be, and maddening when they strip your pyracantha of its brilliant harvest just as it starts to glow, but few birds are all bad. Provide plenty of evergreen shrubby cover, nest-boxes if necessary, food and water and the birds will repay you by eating up to four times their own weight in insects a day.

Birds will inevitably attack young greens, flower buds, seeds and fruit as well. It is just not possible to keep them bodily off each tempting plant in turn. But there are ruses to distract and discourage them. No bird likes running into an obstacle that it cannot see. A few threads of black cotton stretched between twigs can be as effective as complete netting in protecting, for example, primroses, which birds love to peck.

You cannot cotton a whole cherry tree to keep the bullfinches from stripping the buds, but try smearing some of the twigs near the buds with fruit-tree grease (intended for banding trunks to prevent insects using them as ladders) and the birds will soon learn to distrust such a slippery perch.

Your approach to predators is very much a personal matter. I do not shoot or poison anything except grey squirrels—and slugs, yes, I put down slug bait where I see they have been nibbling. But even with slugs there is a gentler (if less certain) alternative: a ring of sharp grit round the plant you want to protect. It hurts their feet.

Above The gardener has just as many allies as enemies among the fauna of his garden. The ladybird eating the greenfly is emblematic of the sort of natural balance a gardener should aim for as the ideal. Although reasonable control often means using poisons it is something to be avoided wherever possible.

Right Fungi are the principal parasites the gardener has to cope with. Of these the mildews are the commonest. The superficial powdery mildew, shown here, though disfiguring and weakening to the plant, is not too serious and can be sprayed. Deep-seated downy mildew, which feeds with long filaments probing into the heart of the plant, should be cut off and burnt.

VIRUS DISEASES

Virus diseases, often transmitted to plants by aphids and other insects that feed on sap, are a problem the gardener can do little about but burn the infected plants. Symptoms of virus disease are puckered and distorted leaves as in the strawberry plant (left), or light green or yellow areas, which when mottled are known as mosaics, or sometimes stunting and malformation of the whole plant.

Viruses are minute particles, too small to be seen through a light microscope, which depend on a host cell for existence and multiplication. As the host cell divides more viruses are created so that soon the whole plant is infected.

The current way to rid infected but desirable plants of virus disease is to make them grow very fast at a very high temperature, then remove the growth tips, or meristem, and propagate from that. With luck it will have outstripped the spread of the virus and be free of infection.

The greenhouse: total responsibility

Above No artificial heat is needed in a greenhouse or conservatory primarily intended to ripen grapes. The vine is planted outside the building and its trunk led through a hole at the foot of the wall. The geraniums and fuchsias in the foreground merely need to be kept dry and above freezing point when dormant in winter.

Left A conservatory used as a dining room at a comfortable temperature for people is warm enough for subtropical plants. There has to be a compromise on humidity: the ideal for the plants would be uncomfortable for most people.

While control in other parts of the garden is only relative, in a greenhouse it becomes total. The gardener takes responsibility for the plants' whole environment. Soil, water, temperature and light are taken, as far as possible, out of nature's hands and decreed by the gardener himself.

The object of the greenhouse is to increase the range of plants we can grow or to lengthen their useful seasons. It works partly by increasing the average temperature, but principally by keeping out extreme cold. As in the open, given adequate moisture and suitable soil, the ultimate factor that decides what will grow is the minimum temperature. A greenhouse, in other words, is a way of upgrading your local hardiness zone. Most people arrange conditions with a particular kind of plant in mind and heat their greenhouses to just above the minimum that the plant needs to survive.

The word greenhouse originated in the seventeenth century with the building used to protect what were then called "greens", and we now call evergreens. Keeping frost out was probably all they attempted. But when plant exploration started to bring in more and more desirable and exotic creatures from Central America and South Africa, higher temperatures were needed. Greenhouses became warmer and also lighter (the first had glass only on one side). By the nineteenth century they were hot, light and big enough for tropical palms. The greatest greenhouse ever built was designed by the Duke of Devonshire's gardener, Joseph Paxton, to house the Great Exhibition of 1855. It was given, and deserved, the name Crystal Palace.

While fuel and labour remained cheap there was no particular virtue in cooler greenhouses. Many plants were given much warmer conditions than they really needed—more for the comfort of their audience than themselves. There is little question of that today. Only a millionaire could keep a private tropical house—what used to be called a "stove". This needs to be kept above 65°F (18°C) for all but two winter months. Today each extra five degrees Fahrenheit doubles the cost of heating.

The warmest greenhouse climate commonly maintained in cold-winter regions is approximately subtropical, with a minimum temperature of 55°F (13°C). This is enough to keep many flowers in bloom in the winter, which was the role of the old-fashioned conservatory.

The general-purpose "cool" greenhouse, going down to 45°F (7°C), is much more common, and still allows the cultivation of such a range of plants that no one could feel deprived.

It is surprising what can be brought through the winter in a greenhouse heated only to 35°F (2°C)—just enough to stop it actually freezing. The most popular of all greenhouse plants, pelargoniums, fuchsias and chrysanthemums, will survive if they are kept dry enough to be dormant, though of course they will not flower in winter.

Without any heating at all, the function of a greenhouse changes: it becomes a device for keeping wind and rain, snow and ice away from the plants. But it still warms up in winter sunshine much more than the unprotected garden, which means an earlier spring for plants in its protection, and an earlier start for spring-sown seeds.

The alpine house is the most rewarding form of unheated greenhouse. It needs the maximum possible ventilation from the sides, day and night. Alpines are completely unaffected by cold: what they dislike is damp. The reward is to have the earliest bulbs in flower in January, undamaged by the weather, and to be able to enjoy them dry-shod.

Not that there is any need to make a final commitment to one regime. The same building will do for all purposes, given the heating capacity. The only structural distinction is that true alpine houses have continuous opening windows along

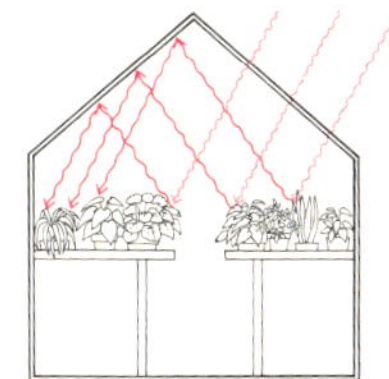

Left The so-called "greenhouse effect" ensures that heat from the sun is trapped inside the greenhouse. Sunlight enters as short-wave radiation which can pass through glass. Once reflected by the plants and soil it becomes long-wave radiation which cannot penetrate the glass to get out.

Left Growing conditions for orchids vary widely according to the species, but many demand minimum temperatures above 57°F (16°C) and an atmosphere at the same time both humid and "buoyant"—which means constant changes of air. The net result is that heating orchid houses is expensive.

the sides. But you can hardly overdo the ventilation in summer of any but a hot house.

The most practical plan in greenhouses longer than about twelve feet is to have a partition wall that will allow you to keep the two parts at different temperatures. The outer or door half could be used as an alpine house, stone cold in winter, while the inner half could be kept frost-free or warmer. The same arrangement lets you adjust the conditions in summer to suit two different kinds of plant; perhaps tomatoes in one side and begonias in the other.

It is the need for constant adjustment that makes a greenhouse so labour-intensive. Apart from temperature—which can be taken care of by a thermostat—the supplies of water, air and light are constantly critical. When the sun breaks through clouds, or a breeze gets up, the effects on the plants are exaggerated by their imprisonment behind glass. Excessive heat in summer is one of the main problems: anything over about 85°F (30°C) overloads the transpiration system of any but tropical plants. Full-time gardeners can afford to keep an eye on conditions and shamble back to the greenhouse to pull down a blind or open a ventilator. But absentee gardeners have no alternative but to rely on automation.

The most invaluable automatic aid is one that opens and shuts the ventilators in the roof according to the ambient temperature. It is simply a cylinder filled with a substance that expands and contracts as it gets hotter or colder, pushing (or not pushing) a piston upwards to open the skylight.

There are also devices for automatically raising and lowering slatted blinds over the roof glass according to the brightness of the light, but these are more complicated and expensive. Most gardeners compromise by painting the outside of the glass with a thin coat of special white paint in late spring and wiping it off in autumn. Roller blinds inside the glass are often used, but are much less effective than external ones.

The automation of watering has reached highly sophisticated levels in commercial glasshouses, but to a normal amateur with a mixed collection of plants there is no completely satisfactory substitute for going from pot to pot individually. Furthermore it is his opportunity to check the well-being of his plants—even to enjoy their beauty.

The simplest short-cut is "capillary" watering, that is standing the pots on a shallow tray of sand which can be kept wet automatically from a water tank with a ballcock standing at a slightly higher level. Alternatively, the sand can be watered daily by hand. Water is drawn up into the pots by capillary action (the pots in this case should not have crocks in the bottom for drainage, nor be taller than six inches). However, there are two principal snags in the system: all the pots stand on one level, making a tiered display difficult; and the roots soon find their way out of the pots and into the sand, tapping the unlimited water supply and making the plants grow embarrassingly fast.

Despite the snags, this system has the considerable advantage of raising the general atmospheric humidity. The air in most greenhouses is far too dry in hot weather, making the leaves transpire for all they are worth. Houses with concrete or tiled floors are particularly hard to keep humid enough, even if the floor is sprinkled with water twice daily. One way of maintaining a better atmosphere is to have beds or trays of damp sand under the benches (or "staging") as well as on them.

Perhaps the most important development for economy is the practice of heating the soil instead of the air. It makes it possible to use an unheated greenhouse (or indeed a frame) for propagation that needs heat. An electric cable, in effect a radiator, is simply buried a few inches under the soil or sand. By putting a plastic propagating cover over the soil you can have a greenhouse inside a greenhouse.

Above An alpine house in early spring with crocuses, irises, anemones and alpine primulas in bloom. An alpine house needs no heating of any kind, but maximum ventilation day and night. Flowering is only just earlier than outdoors, but the flowers can be enjoyed in perfect condition.

Left A warm greenhouse, heated to a minimum temperature of 55°F (13°C) allows such tropical and subtropical plants as *Dieffenbachia*, *Streptocarpus* 'Constant Nymph', the shrimp plant, fig plants and cordylines.

Below A cool greenhouse, with a minimum temperature of about 40°F (5°C), allows a wide general collection of plants, including the climbing blue plumbago, cactuses, kalanchoes. Tuberous begonias (see pages 122–3) are among its most brilliant summer-flowering plants.

Plants and the gardener

If in the end there is not very much we can do about the climate or the weather, and only a limited amount we can do about the soil in the garden (except to choose plants that suit it) at least the plants themselves are totally under our control.

The size, the shape, the health and the fruitfulness of what we grow need not be left to chance at all. Even before we began to understand the mechanisms of plants so many generations had watched them and experimented with them that a vast body of highly effective instructions had been built up. Our great grandfathers, who had scarcely heard of fertilizers and never heard of hormones, raised flowers and ripened fruit as fine as any today.

But today we have the advantage and fascination of knowing to a greater degree not just how, but why plants react to our attentions in the way they do. To understand their miraculous complexities is not just interesting in itself. It allows us to interpret the textbooks and judge for ourselves whether the conventional cultural methods make sense and why. It goes without saying that they usually do. On the other hand they are based on certain assumptions that may or may not apply—at least to you in your garden.

An obvious example is the routine instruction concerning how far apart to plant your vegetables. If a certain amount of light, water and nutrients are available the instructions can be used either to make few big plants or more smaller ones. Generally horticultural convention is to go for the big ones—in the teeth of gastronomic good sense that says plant them as close together as you like, and pick them before they notice.

Gardeners, particularly new gardeners, are usually ready to accept—indeed clamour to be told—the wisdom of the ancients on precisely how, and particularly when, to plant and sow and prune. The drawback to any such information, couched in exact terms, is that it can only ever be an average estimate over scores of soils and millions of microclimates. Reading and re-reading the textbooks is no substitute for a clear understanding of the principles, and a minute observation of the particulars. If you examine a plant closely, and use your common sense, the plant's health or debility, like the condition of the soil, is written all over it.

This section of the book is concerned with how plants work and can be controlled and multiplied, but also with the criteria by which we judge them, how they are classified and named, where they come from and how they have been improved.

A clear majority of the plants in most gardens are to some extent man-made, or at least man-influenced creations. As soon as man started to cultivate plants he instinctively selected the better ones; the better ones bred together and a whole separate race of "garden plants" began.

Were it not for the endless variety of new species which have been introduced from distant countries over the last four hundred years the process of selection and crossing among a limited range would presumably have gone so far that true species, or "wild plants", would be, by now, virtually extinct in gardens; as they are, for example, in most of China.

Happily we have still nowhere near mastered even the species that have been introduced to gardens from all over the world—let alone comprehended the contribution they may have to make in breeding even better plants. What is more there are still thousands more species and varieties to be collected, or in many cases re-collected because they have been lost in gardens for lack of knowledge of how to grow them. There is every reason, therefore, to hope for (and demand) better and more varied plants all the time.

Man interferes with plant. A rose-breeder on his dawn prowl looking for potentially good parents to cross is armed with genetic information new to the present generation.

How to look at a plant

Botanical illustration has reached perfection at various phases of its history. The discipline of exact observation has been coupled with astonishing steadiness of hand by a succession of distinct schools, starting (in Europe) with the German School of the early fifteenth century whose greatest master was Dürer.

The anemone above comes from what was perhaps the supreme period of flower-painting: early nineteenth-century France. Redouté is the most famous name of the school. This work by his contemporary Turpin shows that he had his rivals in exquisite portraiture. In a sense there was no progress, save in technology, between Dürer and Redouté.

It may seem pointless to the untrained amateur to follow such leaders, but the point is in the process, not the product. The act of drawing forces one to examine—and in examination lies the way to appreciation.

If control is the essence of gardening, the essence of plantsmanship is observation. As one who was habitually lazy in looking until he took up gardening I can speak with feeling on the pleasure of learning to observe.

It is too easy merely to recognize plants, mentally ticking them off as familiar or unfamiliar. Perhaps we look at the unfamiliar just enough to recognize it next time. But we do justice neither to the new nor the old. We seldom settle down quietly to study something—even things we find beautiful and satisfying. Even flowers.

Pick up an old Herbal and taste the freshness of clear observation in new-minted language. "The bulbous violet riseth out of the ground, with two small leaves flat and crested, of an overworne green colour, between the which riseth up a small and slender stalk of two hands high, at the top of which cometh forth of a skinny hood a small white floure of the bignesse of a violet, compact of six leaves, three bigger and three lesser, tipped at the points with light greene. . . ." Gerard had gazed long and lovingly at the snowdrop. He took nothing for granted.

I have found that a good way to get to know flowers is to pick them and keep them close to me for a few days in a vase. The vase on the kitchen table and the one on my desk always contain flowers (or other parts of plant) that I want to be better acquainted with. It is particularly good for watching the evolution from bud to flower. I do not think I would have noticed in the garden, for example, that the knapweed's elaborate black-fringed bud holds only a little embryo of its wide, starry thistle: it must grow and spread its ring of fine trumpets outside the bud. Or that the coneflower starts with a ring of insignificant greenish petals not worth the name that gradually lengthen and brighten until they surround the darkening cone with a corolla of yellow as brilliant as a buttercup. Or that the whole flamenco flower of the oriental poppy is folded like a parachute complete in the bud.

Perhaps the best of all ways of learning observation is to draw. Best not only because you have to look and look again (there are no hiding places for ignorance between pencil and paper) but also because drawing demands a more or less methodical approach: a general sizing up of the whole subject followed by more and more minute inspection of the details.

Without a measure of method you are immediately lost in the infinity of variables. Learning to look at plants means learning to analyse them, however informally.

It means first of all taking in the obvious points that distinguish, say, a shrub with permanent wood from a bulb with long, smooth leaves springing straight from the ground. Then the indication of a plant's nature and temperament in where it is growing: is it luxuriating in damp, leafy soil and shade—then surely it is a woodland plant—or happily cooking on a hot gravel bank? Or perhaps looking miserable and seemingly out of place in its garden station?

The nature and design of the flowers is the principal clue to a plant's relationship with others. In themselves the flowers may be the main attraction—or scarcely visible. At all events they deserve the closest appraisal of all.

The parts of a flower are set out on page 46. It is often not at all obvious at first which names to give to which parts. But a flower is a functional device, and a methodical examination, picturing how it works—what happens when it is pollinated; where the ovules are and how they will develop into seed—is fascinating, revealing, and plants that flower in the mind for ever. When you see its relations, moreover, you will probably recognize them as belonging to the same family.

Yet there are more basic points to consider. The pattern made by the buds, and hence the leaves and side shoots, is one of the most characteristic and consistent features, always falling into one of three categories, and usually the same for all the members of one plant family. Either the buds are opposite each other in pairs, or staggered (alternate) along the shoots, or they are in whorls of three or more. Out of this pattern and the relative size, strength and stiffness of the shoots or stems arises the plant's general stance or "habit". Two plants, for example, may reach the same height, but one of them does it on tiptoe, the other droopingly, with stems long enough to reach twice as high but without the rigidity to support them. The texture of the whole plant, and the way the light strikes it, also largely arise from the pattern of leaves and shoots.

In comparison, the actual shape and colour of the leaves, though always beautiful and interesting in themselves, are so variable that there is much less to be deduced from them. Deviations of leaf colour can apparently be almost at random. It seems to make little difference to some plants whether the basic green is suffused with red, or tinted blue, or variegated with yellow. Leaf shapes often have strong family resemblances. The maples are an obvious case. But if you were given a vine leaf, or the leaf of a Japanese anemone, to mention only two, you might think they were maple leaves. For that matter there is a maple with leaves just like a hornbeam. Chance seems to play a large part in leaf shapes.

Leaf texture has more messages than leaf shape. It is fairly easy to tell which leaves are evergreen, even in summer when all leaves are new. They have a harder feel, often a shiny wax-like upper surface and a more or less hairy, felty or scurfy underside. Among the many hundred rhododendrons the nature of the leaf surface is a main diagnostic feature. Both the hard waxiness and the soft hairiness are adaptations against water loss in whatever season, be it summer or winter.

Hairy leaves are also common among deciduous plants, but mainly in those from hot climates that face drought during their growing season. Most of the popular silver-leaved plants are examples. Not surprisingly, therefore, they want bright sun and sharp drainage in the garden too.

With closer observation and sharper focus less obvious points of detail become equally interesting. There are sometimes little tufts of leaf hairs just in the angles of the veins under the leaf. Some of the adjuncts to the basic stem-leaf-flower pattern can be as arresting as the protagonists: long, leafy calyces (the protective outer covering of the flower bud) or prominent prickly stipules (protective casing for the leaf bud) can give character to a plant. Even the shoot itself can be round or four angled, smooth or warty or furry, long jointed or short jointed, and almost any colour under the sun.

The need for order in this jungle of distracting detail is as clear as the difficulty of finding any. Botany, or more strictly speaking plant taxonomy, is the science of classifying the plant world. Gardeners usually steer clear of it as far as they are able. It is certainly not essential to them. They have their own ways of grouping plants by their garden uses. This book reviews garden plants horticulturally, not botanically.

Yet it must be said that botany illuminates our understanding of plants in such a way that keen gardeners eventually find themselves using its methods and terminology. It also dictates what plants are called.

Faced with an unknown, unlabelled plant there are three things you can do. You can take it to an expert. You can flick through the pages of a picture book until you find the plant that looks most like it—a highly unreliable method—or you can begin to botanize, just as you would begin to draw, methodically and analytically. If you can get as far as deciding on the genus: it is a tulip, say, or a cypress, botanists have devised an elimination game known as a key which practically makes the plant analyse itself. An example of a particularly graphic and well-expressed key is given on the right.

THE LANGUAGE OF BOTANY

The jargon of any profession can be provoking to anyone who feels excluded by it. A botanical description is so packed with trade terms of Greek and Latin derivation that most gardeners feel repulsed. Yet the jargon is an essential shorthand to prevent it becoming impossibly long-winded. Good botanists turn to it as little as possible, using everyday speech and imagery wherever they can. As George Bentham, in his introduction to the standard British flora universally known as "Bentham and Hooker", said: "The aptness of a botanical description, like the beauty of a work of imagination, will always vary with the style and genius of the author."

The only reason for a gardener to learn more than a few common botanical terms is to give him access to the more complete reference books, which he will need if he starts to specialize.

As an example of the genre, this is how *Hortus Third*, the authoritative American dictionary of cultivated plants, describes the common English primrose:

"To 6in.; lvs. oblanceolate to obovate, to 10in. long, tapering to petiole, wrinkled, irregularly toothed; fls yellow, purple or blue, $\frac{1}{2}$in. across, solitary, on pedicels to 6in. long, scape lacking. Spring. Europe."

Six inches, in other words, is the overall height; the leaves are up to ten inches long, tapering to the stalk (petiole) end. Oblanceolate and obovate are the extremes of a variable shape (see the key to leaf shapes on page 254). The pedicels are the flower stalks. They would normally be expected to grow from a central stem or "scape"—which the primrose apparently lacks.

To confirm Bentham's remark that botany is not an exact science it is interesting to see that Bentham and Hooker's account of the primrose disagrees. "If closely examined," they say, "the pedicels will, however, be seen really to spring from an umbel, of which the common stalk is so short as to be concealed by the base of the leaves."

Who are we to believe? Gerard's *Herbal* is no help. All he says is "the common whitish yellow field primrose needeth no description"

I am inclined to put my faith in Bentham and Hooker, if only because *Hortus Third* claims there is a blue primrose. But what clearer lesson could there be of the need to examine plants closely for yourself?

IDENTIFICATION BY KEY

Part of the key to Chamaecyparis and Cupressocyparis from Alan Mitchell's *Field Guide to the Trees of Britain and Northern Europe* demonstrates the analytical approach.

1.	Sprays very short, dense, bunched, upright; very slender; when crushed give warm gingery scent	thyoides, p.68
	Sprays long, open, flat, not bunched	2
2.	Leaves blunt and obtuse, bright green, marked bright white beneath.	obtusa, p. 63
	Leaves acutely pointed	3
3.	Leaves against strong light show translucent spots; points incurved; aroma of sour parsley	lawsoniana, p.60
	Leaves without translucent spots; points spreading	4
4.	Foliage fine, slender shoots; light or bright green	5
	Foliage thick, heavy, dark or medium green	6
5.	Foliage bright green, slightly upturned sprays, marked bright white beneath, aroma of acrid resin	pisifera, p.66
	Foliage pale, bronzed green; sprays arch down at tips; pale green beneath, aroma of seaweed	formosensis, p.68

The families of plants: a digression on names

Right The English bluebell exemplifies the disconcerting way well-known plants can change names repeatedly. As a widespread European native it has long had many local names. In the first wave of classification English hyacinth was translated into Latin, followed by a brief description. Linnaeus accepted the old idea that it was a hyacinth, but changed the specific name (see right). With advancing botanical knowledge the genus *Scilla*, bluebells included, was separated from hyacinth. Then it was noticed that *Scilla* keep their bulb from year to year while the bluebell renews it, so a new genus, *Endymion*, was created. Finally in 1934 the botanist Chouard rediscovered the name *Hyacinthoides*, coined in 1759 and since abandoned. By the law of priorities this was the correct name.

VERNACULAR NAMES

Vernacular names include bluebell, bell-flower, bummack, harebell, griggles, crowtoes, cuckoo's boots, culverkeys, jacinth, English hyacinth, Scille penchée, Sternhyacinth. . . .

EARLY HERBALS

Gerard, in 1597, called it *Hyacinthus anglicus* "for that it is thought to grow more plentifully in England than elsewhere".

A brief Latin description, "Hyacinthus corollis campanulatis 6-part. apice revolutis" followed and formed part of the scientific name before Linnaeus established the simple binominal system.

LINNAEUS 1753

Linnaeus (1753) classified it as *Hyacinthus non-scriptus* (which means "unmarked" or "not before described") in reference to Greek mythology.

Hyacinth was a youth loved by Apollo. When he was killed hyacinths arose from his blood inscribed with Apollo's cry of anguish, "Ai Ai". The bluebell has no such markings.

MC
SCIENTI

The short-lived post-Linnaean name *Agraphis* ("unmarked") *nutans* ("nodding") was succeeded by *Scilla nutans*, named by J.E. Smith in 1794.

The English bluebell is a nodding woodland flower of north-western Europe, almost invariably (in its pure form) blue.

It is a source of constant inconvenience and irritation to gardeners that they often do not know, and certainly cannot pronounce, the names of some of their favourite plants.

The problem is that most plants have no genuine vernacular common names. There is a safe area of old favourites and what are virtually man-made garden plants: varieties of rose or potato or dahlia or lettuce. But Latin is unavoidable to anyone who has ambitions beyond the most limited and humdrum range. And botanists are not generally given to letting considerations of simplicity or euphony stand between them and proliferating polysyllables. Worse still "they", the botanists, have been given power over us to change names, apparently at random. Some well-known plants have as many aliases as a Mafioso. To not-very-experienced gardeners names are a serious disincentive to branching out and getting more unusual and interesting plants.

The man who crystallized ideas about how natural objects could be concisely named and arranged in some sort of order of relationships was the great Swedish naturalist Linnaeus. Linnaeus made an immense collection of plants and other objects (his plants still exist at the Linnaean Society in London) and catalogued them with concise descriptions in what immediately became essential reference books.

His greatest single contribution to modern method was almost incidental to his work. He was the first naturalist (in his *Species Plantarum*, published in 1753) to apply a binominal or two-word name systematically to every object in his collection. Like other naturalists before him he gave a concise Latin description as the full name of each plant, but he prefaced each one of his twelve thousand specimens with the name of its genus and species; as it were its surname and given name.

All modern taxonomy revolves round this simple notion. Linnaeus certainly did not invent it. It is already there in such names as, for example, barn owl and brown owl, or for that matter armchair and dining chair. What was new was the discipline of finding a unique binominal for each plant and, as it were, registering it by attaching it to a particular specimen for reference. He added his signature to the description and published it, locked away the specimen, and that was that; the plant was officially, finally, universally named, once and for all.

But why are two words needed to identify a particular plant —and for that matter why are they enough? The answer to this lies in the concept of the species as the basic unit of identity.

When we speak of a species we mean a group of similar plants (or animals) that live together in nature, breed together, and produce offspring consistently like themselves. Genetic stability is proof of the integrity of the unit; it says that this is as far as evolution has travelled along this particular path.

When we speak of a genus we mean a group of such species, consistently different in detail, not normally interbreeding, but usually linked in a fairly obvious way. If we are shown a new rose we will know at once that it is a rose, although we have not seen that particular species before. These two broad categories have been recognized since ancient times.

A more searching scrutiny of the natural world has also suggested (in the first place to Aristotle) that there are broader groups and deeper relationships to be found. There is no lack of ways of classifying anything. You could make a list of plants with yellow flowers or heart-shaped leaves and have a system of a sort. But it would prove nothing because it would be limited to the characteristic you happened to choose. You could neither deduce nor predict anything from it. Aristotle guessed that there is a natural order of relationships where everything has a place. There was no clue, though, where to start looking for it.

By the late seventeenth century Pierre Magnol of Montpellier, the botanist whose name is remembered in the magnolia, had proposed the word "family" for a group of more than one genus with clear common factors not quite strong enough to unite them.

Linnaeus took a step further in looking for the "natural order". He classified plants by their sexual characteristics: numbers of stamens, ovaries, and so forth. His instinct was right, yet he admitted his system was artificial and would be superseded when the key came to light.

What natural links he did see he incorporated into a "fragment of a natural system". So far as it goes it still holds good. Taxonomists who followed him built on it until by the middle of the nineteenth century most of the genera of flowering plants had been assigned to families. The families were generally named after their best-known genus with the suffix "aceae". The family of the roses and their relations thus became the 'Rosaceae'. For old times' sake some of the earliest families to be recognized and named were left with the names they had first been given—examples are the Compositae, the Umbelliferae and the Cruciferae, whose family names describe the composite, umbrella-like and cross-shaped nature of their flowers.

Yet still the key, the link (if any) between genus and genus, between family and family, was unguessed at. It was left to Charles Darwin to supply it: plants are alike because they have common ancestors. Darwin wrote: "All true classification is genealogical. . . . Community of descent is the hidden bond which naturalists have unconsciously been seeking."

When the herbalists of the sixteenth and seventeenth centuries first tried organizing the plant kingdom into a comprehensible order they compared the plants around them with those described by the ancient Greeks and Romans; in particular Dioscorides' *De Materia Medica* of A.D. 60, the prime source of medical knowledge, and Pliny's *Natural History* of the same period, the sources of many legends and beliefs still current today. In many cases, including that of the bluebell, there was no classical description because the plant does not grow in Greece or Italy. John Gerard (above) (1545–1612) is the most famous of the English herbalists, though more on account of his style than his scholarship. He was an unblushing plagiarist.

In 1849 the botanist Clarke confirmed that the rival name *Endymion non-scriptus* (also first published in 1794) was correct.

In 1934 the botanist Chouard unearthed a 1759 description as *Hyacinthoides non-scripta*, correcting Linnaeus, antedating *Scilla* and *Endymion*.

The Spanish bluebell, *Hyacinthoides hispanica*, is an upright flower from south-west Europe, often purplish, pinkish or whitish.

Garden bluebells in blue, pink or white are nearly all hybrids of the English and Spanish species. There is no distinct botanical name for them.

Left The finale (so far) of the bluebell story could be described as a taxonomic cop-out. By applying the strict laws of priority they are now *Hyacinthoides non-scripta*. But even botanists sometimes have hearts. Everyone prefers the name *Endymion*, which was the name of the woodland lover of the huntress Diana. The R.H.S. Dictionary Supplement says "it is hoped that the better known generic name *Endymion* will be officially conserved". Rules are made to be broken, even in botany. If this diagram has not entirely clarified the history of the bluebell and its names it may have given a notion of the long struggle of the botanist and taxonomist over three hundred years to reach a final conclusion to where a plant belongs in the natural evolutionary order.

Right Each named plant has a type specimen, locked away dried in a herbarium. This is Linnaeus's own specimen of the plant he called *Linnaea borealis*—a woodland creeper.

The Swedish naturalist Linnaeus, or Carl von Linné (1707–78) revolutionized the science of naming and classifying natural objects by his sheer industry and application. No one before him had ever collected such a vast array of specimens—he had twelve thousand plants—and given them accurate descriptions and concise two-word names, embodying their relationships as far as he understood them. Such a work, published as *Species Plantarum* in 1753, immediately and inevitably became the standard reference book. Its system of keying names to dried specimens over the botanist's signature (plants named by Linnaeus are signed "L") is followed by taxonomists to this day.

NURSERY NAMES

The naming of plants by nurseries, as opposed to botanists, follows a rather different pattern. The example on the right shows the adventures in cultivation of two species of the genus *Pieris*, a spring-flowering ericaceous shrub, since they were introduced from the Far East early in this century. It illustrates the difference between a natural variety, which occurs in the wild and can be grown true to its parents from seed, and a cultivated variety or cultivar, usually the result of a chance mutation. This is selected as an outstanding seedling and propagated by cuttings, since its seeds will almost certainly produce seedlings like its parents, not itself.

Pieris formosa, a tall hardy shrub from the eastern Himalayas with white flowers and green young shoots.

Pieris japonica, a Japanese shrub with white flowers coming into growth in early spring; hence tender.

Pieris formosa var. (variety) *forrestii*, a local Chinese form of the above with slightly larger flowers.

Pieris 'Forest Flame', a hybrid between the two above made by chance at Sunningdale Nurseries. It has slightly less coloured young leaves than 'Wakehurst' and comes into growth earlier; hence is more tender.

Pieris japonica cv. 'Pygmaea', a selected dwarf form of the above from Japanese gardens.

Pieris japonica cv. 'Variegata', another dwarf cultivar with white-variegated leaves.

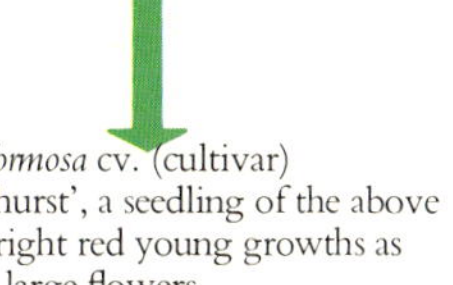

Pieris formosa cv. (cultivar) 'Wakehurst', a seedling of the above with bright red young growths as well as large flowers.

Meanwhile gardeners' interest in classification, far from wanting to chase relationships further and further back into history, lies in precisely the other direction.

For gardeners the species is normally the biggest unit of interest. What concerns them more are the minutiae of variations within species—whether they arise in the wild, in which case they are known as varieties, or in gardens. A gardener's variety—a double-flowered petunia in a bed of single ones, shall we say, or a purple-headed cauliflower—is not a "variety" but a "cultivated variety" (for which a botanical conference in Stockholm in 1950 adopted the repellent name of "cultivar").

To press home the point that a cultivar is a creature of a lower order of interest and importance than a naturally occurring variety, the International Rules of Nomenclature decree that cultivars must not be given names in Latin, but must have obviously modern "fancy" names.

Thus, for example, one of the best autumn-colouring maples from north central Asia, *Acer ginnala*, has a shrubby variety in Turkestan which is known as *Acer ginnala* var. (for "variety") *semenowii*. But a purple form of the Norway maple, selected by some misguided nurseryman in a row of green ones he was growing from seed, has to be called *Acer platanoides* 'Crimson King'. The former is a variety; the latter a cultivar.

The family is divided into genera, genera into species, species into (botanical) varieties and (horticultural) cultivars. The species is locked away in its herbarium with its name, description and the signature of Linnaeus, or whichever later botanist named it, attached. Why then are gardeners constantly being told that the name of a plant they have used all their lives is wrong and must be changed?

It can happen for one of two reasons. One is the application of the law of priority, which says that whoever published the name of a plant first with a correct Latin description was right. In many cases more than one botanist, perhaps in different countries, described plants within a few years of each other. Subsequent research unfortunately often discovers that we have been using a second or third name, which we are sternly told to change to the earlier model.

The other reason is simply that botanists, no doubt with the best motives, change their minds—usually about whether species should be "split" into different genera or "lumped" into the same. So long as botanists delve deeper and deeper into plant relationships gardeners will have to write new labels and unlearn old names.

How plants work

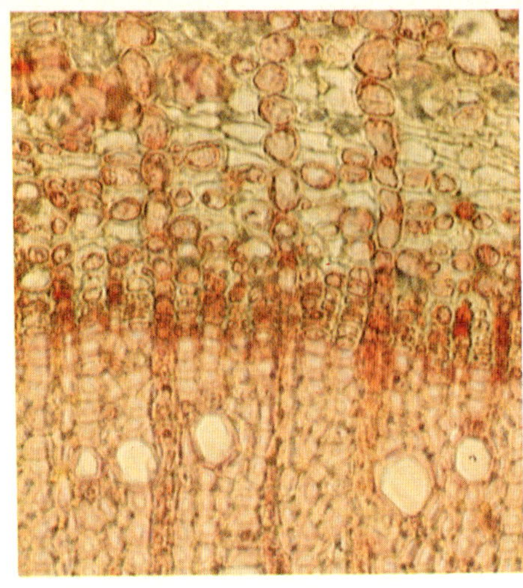

Above A section of an apple stem as seen through a light microscope and magnified approximately one hundred and fifty times. The phloem cells (top) are separated from the xylem cells (bottom) by the thin cambium layer.

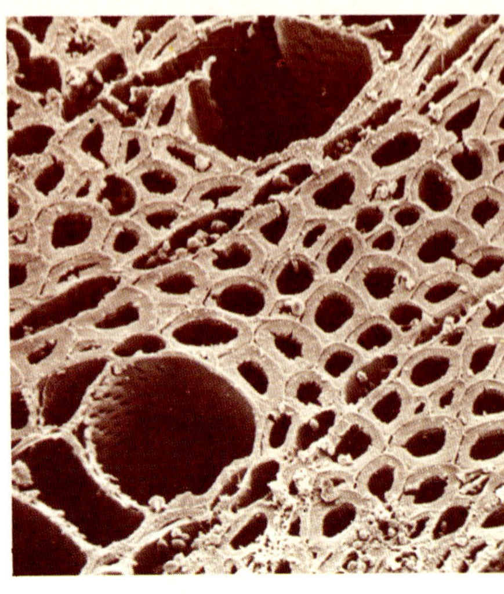

Above A section of wood from a birch tree, photographed through an electron microscope, magnified approximately two thousand two hundred times. The large "pipes" are lignified xylem vessels surrounded by supporting cells.

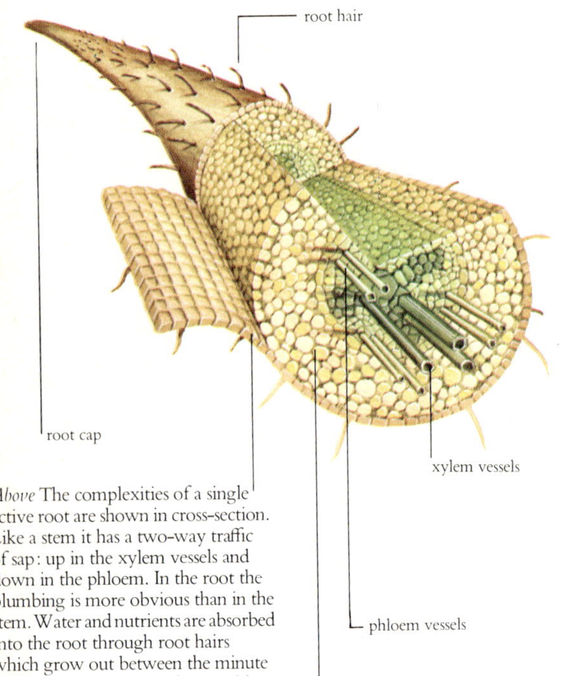

Above The complexities of a single active root are shown in cross-section. Like a stem it has a two-way traffic of sap: up in the xylem vessels and down in the phloem. In the root the plumbing is more obvious than in the stem. Water and nutrients are absorbed into the root through root hairs which grow out between the minute particles of soil. A cap of disposable cells protects the tip of the root.

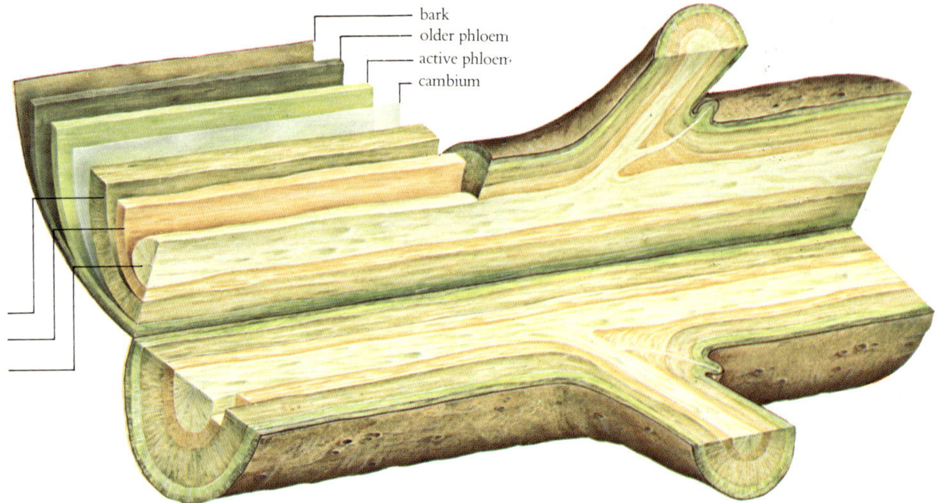

Right A section of a three-year-old twig shows the first year's growth, or pith, surrounded by the second annual growth ring, with the new xylem, the cells actively conducting water and nutrients upwards, being formed by the cambium layer. Outside the cambium the phloem is carrying the return flow from the leaves. The active phloem is protected by older phloem cells and bark.

When it comes to the way they function all plants, at least all green plants, are on common ground. Through the agency of chlorophyll in their leaves they combine water from the ground with carbon dioxide in the air. In doing so they trap and store some of the sun's energy. Using that energy they build more roots, stems and leaves to do the same job.

At a certain point in their career they channel some of this accumulated energy into making a different sort of organ—as well as more leaves they make flowers. The function of flowers is to produce seed, each of which is equipped with a small store of energy converted into food and a set of instructions as to how to become another plant.

In a nutshell, this is plant life. The precise design of the mechanism is decided by the lottery of genetics. Every time a flower is fertilized by pollen from another there is a new combination of genes which could lead to a better plant next time. The management of the routine, however, is entrusted to hormones—tiny particles of protein produced on genetic instructions to travel as chemical messengers through the plant, causing this part to grow or that to stop growing, this to produce a leaf bud, that a flower.

All the solid matter or tissue in a plant starts in the same way: as sugar produced by photosynthesis enriched by mineral salts from the soil. It becomes specialized as it is needed to build up one organ or another.

The sugar made in the leaves of a daffodil, for example, is transferred down to the headquarters of the plant, the bulb underground, and distributed through the diminutive central stem in its heart into thick fleshy storage organs, the leaves for the following year. Part of the sugar made in an oak leaf, to take a very different instance, may go through a chemical transformation into lignin, the solid matter that stiffens the cells of wood. Another part might go as starch into an acorn to be the energy supply for the next generation—or even into a pollen grain to be cast on the wind as the tree dutifully strives to reproduce its kind.

The principal organs of all plants are relatively few, and all the same. Apart from the flower (itself the most complicated structure) they are the leaves, the stem, the buds (which are future leaves or stems in embryo) and the roots, linked together by the vascular system, or plumbing.

The plumbing has two jobs to do: to move water and minerals up from the roots to the leaves, and then to redistribute what is left of this water after transpiration, along with the products of photosynthesis, to wherever the plants need nourishment.

There must therefore be two separate sap-flows in all plants: one up and one down. The mechanism for achieving this, with two kinds of veins separated by the cambium layer, is illustrated above.

Our understanding of the control mechanism of plants and the part played by such hormones as auxins, giberellins and kinins is only recent, and still by no means complete. The first growth-controlling hormone to be discovered was named auxin using the Greek word *auxe* for "increase"—the same root as in, for example, auxiliary.

It has been found that auxin is produced in the growing tips of plants and distributed from there via the sap back through the stems to the root. The concentration of auxin is always highest near the growth point, in the region where cells are dividing and active growth is going on.

Each part of the plant, it seems, has a different optimum auxin level; the level decreasing as it gets further from the growing tip. The main stem needs most; secondary or lateral

THE CAMBIUM LAYER

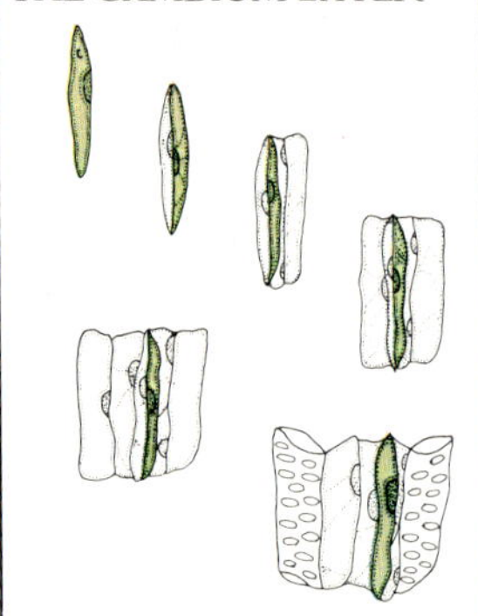

All the growth of a woody plant occurs in the cambium layer—a skin only one cell thick between the xylem, the inner wood, and the phloem, the tissue just inside the bark. The illustration above shows a single cambium cell in active growth. It is continuously producing new cells of three kinds at once: new xylem cells on its inner side; new phloem cells on its outer side; and new cambium cells to expand and keep up with the expansion of the twig, or trunk. It is these newly created cells on both sides of the cambium which are most active in the circulation of sap between leaves and roots.

Below A leaf cut open and with its layers of cells peeled back. The outer epidermis protects the two separate layers of active cells. The three ingredients for photosynthesis (sunlight, water and carbon dioxide) are brought together in these cells. The veins convey the water, and the carbon dioxide enters through the stomatal pores, chiefly on the underside of the leaf. At the same time the pores are needed to take in oxygen for the continuous process of respiration, which could be described as the burning of the fuel manufactured by photosynthesis.

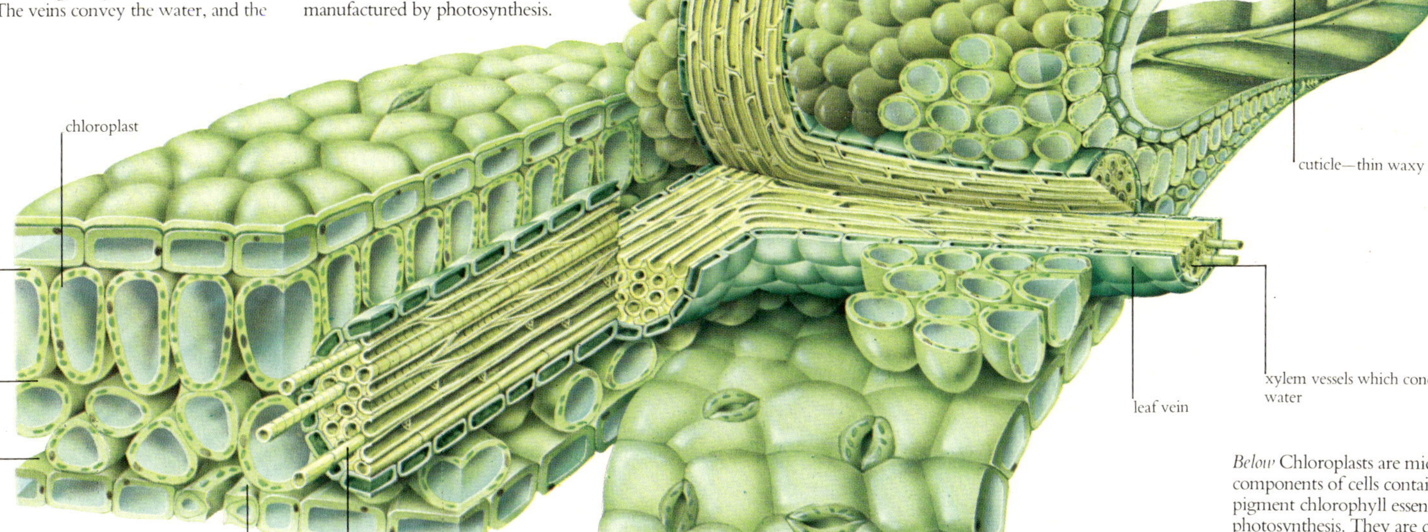

A PLANT CELL

cell wall

the cell membrane controls the substances entering and leaving the cell

vacuole—a space within the cytoplasm containing the cell sap or food

the nucleus is embedded in the cytoplasm. It controls the cell processes and cell division

chloroplast

the cytoplasm is a jelly-like transparent fluid containing cell organelles such as the chloroplasts

Below Chloroplasts are microscopic components of cells containing the pigment chlorophyll essential for photosynthesis. They are composed of a double membrane and contain stacks of "grana" joined by "frets". There are some half a million chloroplasts to each square millimetre of leaf surface.

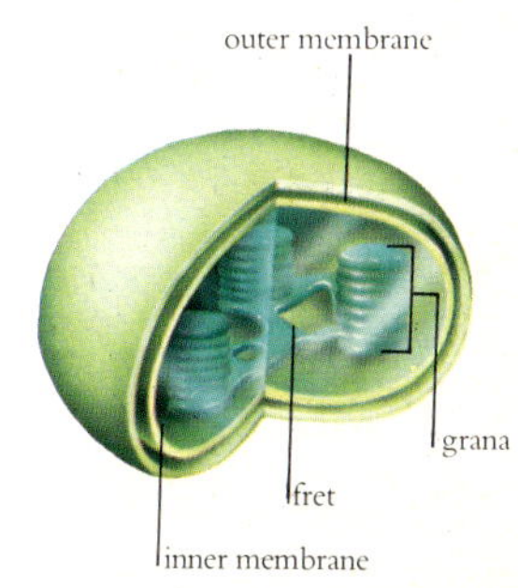

stems a good deal; the buds less and the roots least of all. A higher level has an inhibiting effect on growth.

If the normal balance is upset by removing the leader, the main growth point and source of auxin, the auxin level in the whole plant is lowered. The lateral stems find the new level to their liking and push on; at the same time the buds are favoured, and some of them will probably open.

This is the reason for the fact, known to gardeners since Adam, that pinching off the growing tips of, for example, a chrysanthemum, stimulates its branches to grow bushy.

In due course the newly-stimulated growth points themselves produce enough auxin to establish their dominance over the rest of the plant. In some plants, with naturally high auxin levels, this "apical dominance" is obvious. Christmas trees are spire-like for this reason: so much auxin is made by the leader that all the other branches are mere side-shoots in comparison.

It has been found that too much light destroys auxins. The control mechanism for phototropism (the bending of plants towards light described on pages 28–9) depends on there being more auxins on the shaded side of the growth point, causing the cells to grow faster on that side.

Gravity also affects the distribution of auxins. They sink to the bottom of whatever cell they find themselves in. In the case of roots gravity concentrates the auxins on the lower side, encouraging the upper side to grow, bending the top downwards. In the case of branches there is also more auxin on the lower side, but here it has a positive effect, promoting growth to bend the branch upwards.

Given the basic genetic programme that tells the cells to form the parts of, shall we say, an onion rather than an oak, all the decisions about the order of precedence are taken by hormones reacting to simple physical laws.

Above The movements of plant parts adjusting to external conditions is now attributed to hormone distribution. A bulb planted the wrong way up detects the pull of gravity and reacts accordingly.

Above Auxin is the plant hormone principally involved in opening flowers in response to temperature and light. Warmth makes the inner side of the petal grow faster. In crocuses cold reverses the process.

Left The tendrils of the passion flower (and many other climbers) respond to touch. When they contact a possible support the growth hormone moves to the outer side, speeding growth there so that the whole tendril curls like a spring.

Right Sundew plants, natives of boggy ground lacking nitrogen, trap insects for food by quick movements of their sensitive hairs—another example of the rapid redistribution of hormones in response to an external stimulus.

Controlling growth

Once having grasped how a plant works and what will be the next step in its routine, the gardener is in a position to anticipate and intercept its growth—to bend it to his will.

It is not too difficult for the specialist to know every mood and quirk of his sweet peas or his roses. To carry in your head the timings and inclinations of every plant in a considerable mixed collection is quite another matter. Here, as in so many aspects of gardening, only the gardener's temperament can decide whether he rushes neurotically from reference book to reference book or settles down to use his common sense. As Christopher Lloyd so wisely says in *The Well-Tempered Garden*, "the right time to do a job is when you have the time to do it properly."

There are not many plants we grow in gardens that are left entirely to their own devices. Naturalized bulbs and wild flowers are one common case, trees another—but more because they are out of reach than because pruning would not improve them. In most cases the gardener keeps sticking his oar in and taking away the plant's initiative. The essence, after all, is control—whether it is mowing lawns, force-feeding vegetables, trimming hedges, disbudding chrysanthemums or pruning fruit trees.

The natural plant has a balanced programme that allows so much growth for roots, so much for shoots, so much for flowers and fruit. It is not so much a question of harmonious government as equal competition between the parts.

The gardener's object, in each case, is to maximize the aspect of the plant that made him choose it. If it is the leaves he is interested in (as with lettuces) he will do his best to prevent it flowering. If (as with a fruit tree) flowers are the object he will discourage strong young leafy shoots and encourage the little spurs of old wood that bear flower buds. Experience shows that if a lettuce is grown fast, without check and with plenty of moisture, flowers will be slow in coming. It also shows that occasional hard pruning in winter encourages long leafy

Above Fruit trees trained *en arcure* are a show-piece of purposeful pruning. Stems bent over beyond the horizontal are apt to make an abnormal number of flower buds as a hormone-directed response. Arcure-training makes a pattern of this profitable fact.

Left In Japan the shaping of plants by pinching out growth tips is applied to many things from pines to chrysanthemums.

Below Topiary, here in one of its more extreme forms, is an annual stopping of growth tips to cause dense branching in one plane.

shoots on trees, whereas regular light pruning, especially in summer, provokes an apple tree into forming flower buds. So the lore and skills of gardening were moulded by generations of trial and error long before anyone understood the physical and chemical principles behind them.

We now know that the principles are the same whether we are dealing with a dahlia or a dogwood. They are summed up in the notion of apical dominance, which decrees the priority of buds from the apex, or main growth point, down to the roots. The role of auxins was discussed on the previous page. Pruning to control growth can be seen as telling the auxins where to concentrate their energies next. Strangely enough they rush to do man's bidding with extra energy. If pruning does nothing else it reinvigorates a plant.

The simplest example to take is a quick-growing herbaceous plant with a straightforward branching pattern: a chrysanthemum. If the grower's ambition is a flower of great size and splendour, he will pinch off the buds of side shoots that would produce flowers until he is left with a solitary flower bud. The plant will grow absurdly top-heavy, putting all its energies into one great football of petals on top.

Another grower with the same plant could have done exactly the opposite. He could have pinched out the centre bud, which would have made the side buds break. As each side shoot lengthened and formed buds, he could have pinched out the apical one again so that no one shoot could take over. The whole plant would have remained densely bushy, eventually to be smothered in hundreds of individually undistinguished flowers. The Japanese chrysanthemum garden pictured on the left is an extreme example—but not by Japanese standards: they apply precisely the same techniques to tall pine trees.

What complicates the pruning of shrubs, and makes it a stumbling block for so many gardeners, is the time scale. The essence is the same, but the structure of a shrub is made more complicated by its annual accretions of twigs. Unless you know whether it flowers on the new shoots it has just made, or the ones it made the previous year, there is a danger of cutting off the part that was about to bloom. The danger is avoided if you prune immediately after flowering. You can never go wrong because there will always be a year ahead in which to make new flowering growths, which is all any plant needs.

But there are drawbacks to pruning at odd times, particularly pruning spring-flowering shrubs in summer. For one thing it is hard to see the stems for the leaves; for another it usually means trampling on other plants; and above all you are too busy. It would be much tidier if we could do all our pruning in winter. Happily, with most shrubs we can limit ourselves to cutting out only stems that are clearly *passé*, much twigged and rough-barked, back to the point where vigorous young stems arise; whether from the base or part-way up the old stems. This method is foolproof.

One sort of summer pruning that we do regularly is dead-heading, or taking off spent flower heads. The object is not only tidiness. It prevents the plant using its energies in ripening seed, leaving it with more in its current account for the next lot of flower buds. Rhododendrons are dead-headed for the benefit of the next year's display, but with perpetual-flowering roses and many other shrubs (such as the buddleia pictured below), not to mention annuals and perennials, dead-heading is a good deed that has its immediate reward in the growth of a new flowering shoot within days.

"Pegging down" is another way of provoking more flowers in many plants, shrub roses in particular: if a stem is forcibly held horizontally it will often produce flower buds in protest all along its upper side. Another method, practised particularly with reluctant fruit trees, is bark ringing: taking off a narrow strip of bark to interfere with the sap flow and prevent the products of photosynthesis reaching the roots. Even a mere nick in the bark above a bud can increase its share of nutrients and galvanize it into action.

Left Dead-heading roses, or removing the stem that has flowered as far back as the next vigorous breaking bud, is a form of summer pruning. In removing the wood at the extremity it takes away a source of hormones which were having an inhibiting effect on the lower bud. This bud is now the new leader and responds by growing with sudden vigour (*below left*).

Right The pecking order of flower buds in the opposite-branching buddleia. The top flower spent, the two laterals below it open their flowers. Meanwhile the laterals behind those prepare their buds.

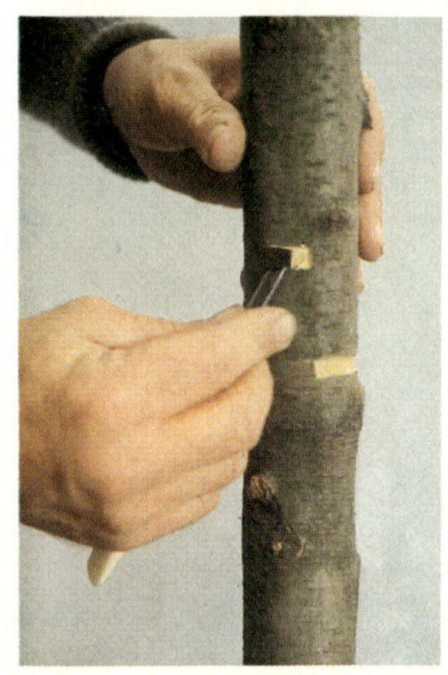

Right Flowering and fruit can be encouraged in trees that are tending to grow only leaves and stems by interfering with the downward flow of sugar-rich sap to the roots. The process, known as bark-ringing, involves removing with a knife or chisel either a whole ring of bark one-quarter of an inch wide or (as here) two half rings a half inch wide on opposite sides of the trunk, three inches apart. The increased concentration of carbohydrates in the top of the tree results in extra flowers. Root pruning is a more laborious way of achieving the same object.

Far right "Stopping" a geranium to make it more bushy is done simply by breaking off the growing tip.

Weeds

What is a weed? The classic definition is "a plant in the wrong place". But half the plants in half our gardens are condemned by this definition. There is more to it than that. Weeds are a race of super-plants, of unfair vigour and tenacity. Either by prolific and fertile seeding, or by delving deep with brittle roots that can regrow from the smallest scrap left in the ground, they hang on to their places in the garden when any well-bred plant would give up. It is their efficiency and aggressiveness that make them so unwelcome. If a weed were a meek little thing, reluctant to grow at all, we should call it a "difficult subject" and coddle it in a cold frame.

We can only spare garden space for plants of rampant vigour and productiveness if they have something special to offer: brilliant flowers; delicious leaves; perhaps an indifference to wind that makes them valuable as a screen. Weeds are the ones that not only volunteer too readily but are dull and dowdy even at their best.

The objections to such well-adjusted plants are two. They compete with, starve, overshadow or throttle the better things we are trying to grow. And they hide the desired effect, or at least blur its outlines. They spoil the focus of the picture.

Getting rid of weeds, therefore, has its immediate rewards to offer. To me it is the most basic of gardening activities: the essential editing, the blue-pencilling without which the garden as such would cease to exist.

I would go further and say that unless you hand-weed your garden you do not know what is in it. Down in the undergrowth with a hand-fork, sorting out the sheep from the goats, you are faced with the task of identifying every plant. I make it a rule not to pull up anything I cannot name. In fact, I name them as I go: a homely catechism of fat hen, shepherd's purse, groundsel, twitch (with a few expletives deleted), until suddenly there is a little plant which is none of these. Perhaps just a new-born seedling. One gets to know the seed-leaves of the local weeds: but this is different. Is it holly? A hellebore? Perhaps it is honesty or foxglove. Perhaps something I had never expected to set seed and germinate in my garden.

Then comes the decision. Do I leave it here to see what develops? Some of the happiest effects in every garden, even in the greatest and most meticulously planned, are created by plants in unexpected places. I might collect a batch of hellebore seedlings and marshal them into one spot, or pot them up and give them to friends—or just leave them where they are.

Whether weeding is a pain or a pleasure depends more than anything on the condition of your soil. To weed in baked, dry ground is utterly frustrating—in fact, virtually impossible: the fork won't go in, and the roots won't come out. On very wet ground it is just a muddy mess. Your hands and your tools become clogged, slippery and unusable.

The time to weed, therefore, is after, but not immediately after, a good downpour—the interval depending on how quickly your soil drains. Failing rain, weed after a long, steady soak with the sprinkler. Take a small "border" fork, a hand-fork, a bucket for the spoil, something to kneel on . . . and prepare for a gently pleasurable afternoon.

Paradoxically, the better a weed is growing, the easier it is to extract. Soil in really good heart—open, fertile, well-stocked with humus—yields up its weeds as readily as it nourishes your plants. Furthermore, a well-fed weed is in less of a hurry to flower, set seed, and multiply our troubles. A weed which has germinated in a soft bed of mulch comes up easiest of all: another sound argument for mulching.

The alternative to hand-weeding is to decide that, like Pilate, what I have planted, I have planted—and that anything else is by definition a weed. For the parts of the garden where you are growing crops, be it a row of beans or a bed of petunias, discrimination among odd seedlings is impracticable.

This is where the hoe comes in. All a hoe is, although there are scores of different designs, is a blade that you push or pull just below the surface of the soil to cut off the weeds at their roots. It is only good for one specific job: killing young weed seedlings. So you have to do it often. To hoe deep-rooting permanent weeds, whether with tap-roots like dock or running stolons like ground elder, is worse than futile: it encourages them to sprout and multiply. The only way is to fork them out.

With hoeing as with hand-weeding, the better the soil, the easier the job. The ground should be rather drier—though not baked hard, or the hoe will just skim the surface.

The chart on the right sets out briefly the three classes of weed killers, how they kill and where they might effectively be used. In large gardens they are essential. But in small gardens, they are best avoided. They are not only unnecessary and potentially dangerous, but they put a distance between the gardener and his plants. Weeding is not just about weeds: it is about getting to know your garden better.

Above and above right The aesthetic rewards of weeding are immediate. In the classic gardener's phrase, "you can see where you've been". Here the whole point of a planting in harmonious textures and colours is obscured through spring-time neglect. Grassy weeds in particular can establish themselves unnoticed and gradually blur the definition of the picture. For the gardener the act of concentrating on leaf shapes, to spot any rogue plant before it does any harm, is a good way of training the eyes to appreciate subtleties of form. The more you notice, the more you enjoy. Weeding the bed above was done in the morning (after watering the evening before) using a long-handled border fork and being careful to move the feet as little as possible. Footmarks were then prodded over with the fork.

Above By kneeling to weed the gardener is deeply involved. *Right* Among crops, mulches are more practical. Black plastic prevents weeds, and looks tidy if not natural.

Above A weed with all the survival techniques: rosebay willow-herb not only produces tens of thousands of fluffy, far-sailing seeds but forms a permanent network of deep and brittle roots. It is a wild flower of woodlands: a weed in gardens.

Below A weed in one country: a crop in another. However pretty they are to us their promiscuity condemns them. But the French grow dandelions as a salad and for their roots, which make a tolerable coffee substitute.

WEEDKILLERS

Chemical weedkillers work in one or more of three different ways. "Contact" weedkillers kill only the green parts of the plant they touch, which is enough for short-lived weeds but ineffective for perennial, deep-rooted ones. "Translocated" weedkillers are absorbed into the plant's system by its leaves, reaching through the stem into the roots. Hormone weedkillers work in this way, stimulating the plant into growing so vigorously that it dies. "Soil-acting" weedkillers are taken into the plant from the soil by roots. With thorough study weedkillers can be made an important ally of the over-stretched gardener. But these powerful chemicals should never be casually used.

THE PRINCIPAL MODE OF ACTION FOR EACH CHEMICAL **c**= contact **t**= translocated **s**= soil-acting	ammonium sulphamate	sodium chlorate	2, 4, 5-T	dalapon	propachlor	paraquat + diquat	dichlobenil	simazine	mecoprop or dichlorprop	MCPA	2, 4-D	ioxynil or morfamquat
		s	**t**	**t**	**s**	**c**	**s**	**s**	**t**	**t**	**t**	**t**
Total Vegetation control	★	★				★						
Woody weeds	★		★								★	
Problem weeds (grasses)				★		★	★					
Problem weeds (broad-leaved)	★		★			★	★			★	★	
Flower beds and vegetable gardens					★	★						
Fruit bushes and trees				★		★	★	★				
Rose beds and shrubberies						★	★	★				
Paths, drives, patios		★		★		★	★	★		★	★	
Established lawns									★	★	★	
New lawns												★

Flowers

Right The bee foraging for nectar in the heart of a daisy flower is being covered with pollen from the anthers. When it visits the next flower some of that pollen may be left sticking to the stigmas.

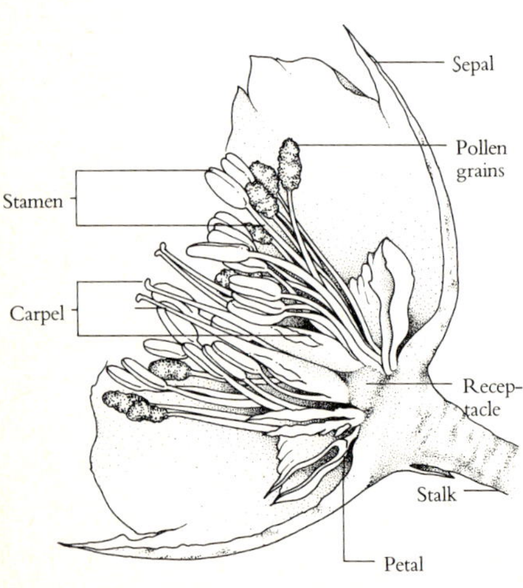

The parts of all flowers are borne either in whorls (concentric circles) or spirals. The hellebore above and left is an example of a "perfect" flower—that is one with both sexes—in the usual whorl arrangement. The outer whorl or calyx acts as the protecting bud before the flower opens. It consists of sepals, which in this case look to the layman like petals, being much bigger than the next whorl or corolla, which consists of the true petals. The petals of hellebores are small and tubular. The more usual arrangement is for the sepals to be small and green and the petals, large, coloured and often scented.

The next whorl is of male parts: the stamens, each consisting of a filament (the stalk) and an anther, which contains four pollen sacs. A hellebore has about sixty stamens. The innermost ring is of female parts or carpels. Each carpel has an ovary at its base, then a stem (the style) ending in a stigma. For fertilization to take place a pollen grain must be deposited on the stigma. Hellebores have thirty or forty carpels. Nectar is produced in nectaries, at the base of the ovaries.

We now accept without surprise the fact that flowers are the sexual organs of plants, responsible for the awkward task of mating with another individual of the same species, without the facility of strolling over and asking for a dance.

In the eighteenth century when Linnaeus proposed the idea it was considered both improbable and an affront to public decency, if not morals. It still remains a mystery how plants came to evolve a sexual system. For it seems clear that flowers are merely stems with leaves modified to perform their specialized, ambitious and complex functions.

It becomes more strange when you think that most plants can, and do, reproduce their kind vegetatively—that is by means other than seed. Making flowers is a considerable investment of the plant's resources in something which will give it, as an individual, no benefit. The two hundred thousand flowers on a cherry tree draw out something like twenty-five pounds of carbohydrates from the tree's reserves. Fattening up the cherries to tempt birds to take them will use even more.

Whatever primeval algae first dropped differentiated male and female spores started the exchange of genetic material and the chance of a more efficient plant. Somewhere in the aeons of evolution the basic vegetative parts of plants began to specialize and become male and female organs. The branch of the evolutionary tree that advanced farthest along this path inevitably evolved fastest (as its sexual system grew more efficient) and produced most variations on its theme.

Those variations are, today, our flowering plants, from primitive attempts like the conifers (botanists are loathe to admit that their sexual organs are truly flowers at all since the female seed is naked, without an ovary to contain it) to such relatively primitive flowers as the magnolia (which have all the parts together—the term is "perfect"—and thus are in theory in danger of fertilizing themselves) to sophisticated models such as the orchids.

One of the biggest steps along the way was the recruitment of insects as part of the team. The most primitive flowers are all wind pollinated. In order to have the slightest chance of landing a pollen grain on an appropriate female organ by means of wind alone vast clouds of pollen are needed. Pollen is largely protein and therefore expensive in terms of energy for the plant to produce. But attract a bee to the flower with a bright colour, a sweet smell and a little nectar, and a mere dab of pollen will be sure of finding its way straight to the mark.

To the gardener flowers can be either a means to an end or an end in themselves: the former when he wants fruit; the latter when it is simply display he is after.

There are many reasons why the fruit is not always forthcoming. It can of course just be a matter of bad weather or lack of bees. Gardeners deal largely with highly selected, often highly bred, cultivated varieties. In the course of their raising their sexual efficiency often suffers. A fruit-grower, for example, is faced with a baffling array of cultivars whose flowers may or may not be compatible with themselves or others. Unless he plants sorts that are compatible he will have barren trees. Nature plays similar tricks to guard against what amounts to floral incest. Sometimes the pollen ripens at the wrong moment for the ovule; sometimes it simply fails to fertilize it. Occasionally the fertilization takes place but the fruit, as though it knows it was conceived in sin, fails to mature and drops off. Yet there is no general rule about this: many plants regularly self-pollinate and thrive on it. Most garden weeds, indeed, seem to prove it is positively beneficial.

Where the flower is an end in itself, as in most of our garden flowers, its sexual efficiency is of no account, but if anything a drawback. Many flowers stay brilliant and pristine for days or even weeks on end, until they are visited by an insect, but once they are fertilized their colour fades, their petals fall. The plant's

Left The fig is a peculiar example of a close relationship between an insect and a particular plant. Its flowers are of separate sexes, both enclosed inside a little urn (later the fruit) with an orifice surrounded by the male flowers. Fig-wasps, which use figs as incubators for their eggs, are covered with pollen as they emerge.

Above Cymbidium orchids make certain that a visiting insect follows the right routine. The flower has a prominent lower lip which invites the insect to land. Its weight springs a trap which brings the lip smartly up, enclosing the visitor, which can only escape by crawling out backwards. In doing so it passes first the stigma, which it pollinates if it is carrying pollen; then the stamens, picking up pollen for another *Cymbidium*.

Above The aquatic eelgrass, *Valisneria spiralis*, has solved the problem of pollinating floating female flowers from submerged male flowers. When the pollen is ready the male flowers break off and float to the surface (the photograph above). After pollination the female flower stem twists in a spiral carrying the fruit to the bottom to ripen.

Above Conifers (here, the Scots pine) have separate male and female flowers, usually on the same tree with the males ones on the lower branches and the females higher up.

Above The female flower of the pine becomes the cone. It depends for fertilization on the wind blowing pollen from another tree, since its own pollen is unlikely to reach it.

Above The male catkins of a willow shed their pollen on the wind in early spring before insects emerge. Male plants with their golden pollen are much more ornamental than females.

energy is transferred from flowering into forming seed.

It is partly for this reason that the improvement of garden flowers so often takes the form of depriving them of fertility. A "double" flower is a flower whose sexual parts have been transformed by mutation into more petals. Both because it cannot be fertilized and because it has more petals it will last longer and be more ostentatious in display.

The gardener in any case wants to know what conditions encourage flowering. In general they are the ones that make strong growth of leaf and stem impossible. There is a chemical balance in every plant between its store of carbohydrates (sugar and starch) and the supply of nutrients for growth. While nitrogen, in particular, is plentiful, and there is plenty of water to carry it surging through the cells, it will go on making more leaves and shoots. When the supply of nutrients dwindles, often because of a shortage of moisture to dissolve them and make them available, the balance tips and the hormone messengers draw on the carbohydrates to make flowers. In woody plants the great years for flowers often follow dry and sunny years, when the plant was under stress. They are its effort to perpetuate itself: at least to leave seed on earth.

Above Maize has its male flowers at the top so that the pollen drops straight onto the female flowers, which develop to become the "cobs" Such self-fertilization is the exception. Maize is grown in blocks rather than rows to encourage it.

FERTILIZATION

When pollen grains land on a stigma (above, magnified approximately seventy times) their adventures are not over. The male cell still has to reach the ovule in the ovary. To do so it grows a root-like pollen tube. Nourished by secretions in the stigma and guided by chemicals in the style the tube grows down until it reaches the ovule. The male sex cell then swims along it to fertilize the female. The fertilization itself is in two parts: one of the embryo, the other of the endosperm; the food storage tissue which will be contained in the seed in the cotyledons.

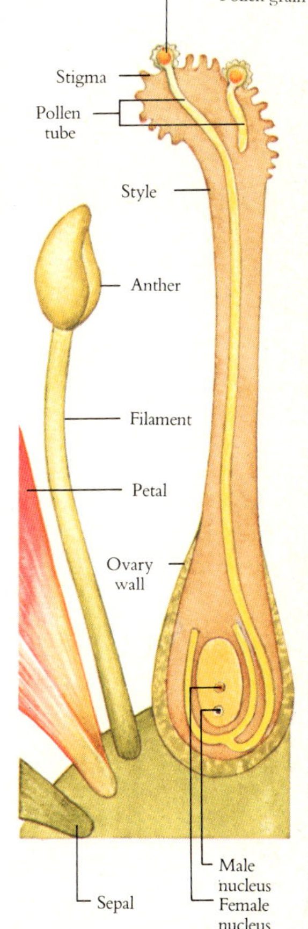

How plants are improved

Above Rose breeders out at dawn, before insects have started pollinating the newly-opening flowers, are looking for buds at just the right stage for hand-pollination.

Left A rose prepared for hand-pollination. Just before it opened the petals were cut off, then the stamens—if any of the anthers had opened to release pollen it would have to be rejected. The stigmas are then brushed with pollen from the proposed bridegroom and the flower protected from insects by a bag while the seeds ripen.

	C	c
C	CC	Cc
c	cC	cc

MENDELIAN INHERITANCE

If pollen from a climbing rose is dusted on the stigma of a non-climbing rose the plants that grow from the resulting seed will all almost certainly be climbers. The gene for climbing is therefore "dominant"; that for non-climbing "recessive". This first generation of a cross is known as F_1, meaning first filial. If the F_1 generation is self-pollinated the result will be as shown *left*, where the gene for climbing is represented as C and that for non-climbing as c. CC or Cc is a climber. Only the one-in-four chance cc is a bush. This experiment in Mendelian genetics was done by Jack Harkness when he self-pollinated the scarlet climber 'Danse du Feu'. Of 100 seedlings 75 were climbers; 25 bushes. If the recessive character is the desirable one to the breeder it can thus be isolated in the second generation and perpetuated in the third. Two cc bushes crossed cannot produce a climber.

For many hundreds of years men gradually improved the plants they grew by the common sense of planting the seed of the better specimens. They also discovered a very long time ago that you could graft a branch of a better tree on to a less good one. In China the selection of varieties for cultivation was in an advanced state a thousand years ago. The notion of improving on nature's productions is not new, but until the last century it could be no more than careful selection of what Nature chanced to provide.

The word hybrid came into use in the eighteenth century to describe such things as mongrel dogs that were obviously the result of crossing two varieties or forms of the same sort of creature. Darwin used it more scientifically in describing the false oxlip as a hybrid between a cowslip and a primrose. But it was not until the work of Gregor Mendel (1822–84) came to light and was seized on and examined at a conference called by the Royal Horticultural Society in 1899 that the science of genetics was born. The ways that characteristics are transmitted from one generation to another, getting mixed up in the process, have since become clear enough to guide breeders in a half-light growing more dawn-like all the time.

Improvements come to plants in many ways. Breeding is only one of them. Natural mutations account for great numbers of our better plants. A nurseryman or a keen gardener is always on the look out for seedlings of unusual character, or "bud sports", when for no discernible reason a plant puts out a branch or a flower different from the rest. If it looks worth having he will cherish it and propagate from it, thus starting a new "clone". But seedlings from his clone will very often go straight back to the ancestral norm: it will always have to be propagated by cuttings to keep its character.

The object of breeding is to combine the best points of different plants. Two varieties of one species can be "crossed"; two species of one genus can be "hybridized"; very occasionally two species of what are considered different genera can be persuaded to mate—though some botanists take this as prima facie evidence that the genera in question are really the same.

Some plants, of course, are much quicker to breed than others. With an annual there is a chance of an improvement every year: hence the great strides in vegetable breeding. Trees in contrast have never been consciously bred for improvement until very recently. It takes years to find out whether the work was worthwhile.

If the microscope were not there to tell us what goes on in the swopping over of sex cells what would we know? Simply that there are certain odds on particular characteristics of parents turning up in their children. The classic Mendelian experiments were made with peas. Mendel showed that when peas of different sizes and colours were crossed (that is bred together under controlled conditions, so that he knew which pollen fertilized which ovule) certain characteristics regularly reappeared in their offspring, suppressing their opposites. A tall pea crossed with a short one gave tall offspring; a red-flowered pea with a white one gave red offspring; a smooth pea with a wrinkled one gave smooth offspring. He coined the term "dominant" for characteristics that suppressed their alternatives, which he called "recessive".

By then letting the offspring fertilize themselves he discovered that a recessive character was not suppressed once and for all, but reappeared in the next generation in a simple mathematical relationship to the dominant character: 1 to 3.

To explain this he supposed that there must be "genetic factors" (we now call them genes) in the sex cells which have to be paired when mating takes place. When the pairing includes a dominant gene its character will take over. But there is a steady chance of the pairing of the recessive genes. When this happens the recessive character (e.g. a short or

Below The popular house plant *Primula malacoides* has been treated (right) with the drug colchicine which has the effect of increasing the number of chromosomes in its cells, or making it "polyploid". Each cell is therefore bigger. In this case the proportions of a naturally graceful plant are ruined

Bottom Hybrids are often more vigorous than either of their parents. In this case two species of *Eranthis* have been crossed to produce the lower flower, *Eranthis× tubergeniana*, with its much more showy petals. The reason is that in the swapping of genes weakening factors tend to be displaced by normal or healthy ones.

white pea) will take over. Pictured on the left is a recent experiment with a climbing rose that demonstrates precisely this.

The mechanism of the mixing of characteristics was discovered early this century. The panel on the right is an attempt to elucidate a subject which is far from simple. In its broadest terms, and leaving out the jargon, every living cell has in its nucleus at least some chromosomes—worm-like bodies that carry the genes. Sex cells (sperm and egg) are formed by dividing the genetic material in half so that when fertilization takes place the right amount of (i.e. at least two) chromosomes will be present, half from each parent.

Chance, or various agencies, frequently leads to variations in the mathematics. It is quite common for the first stage of cell division (the pairing off of the chromosomes) to take place but then for the cell to fail to divide: the result is a cell with double the normal number of chromosomes and hence double the size. The whole plant may therefore be bigger and may be considered an improvement (see the primula, above).

In practice, if a breeder is concentrating on various desirable characteristics in, let us say, a cabbage he is trying to improve, he will cross and recross the plant with its sister seedlings and "back-cross" it with its parents to try to concentrate the desirable qualities ineradicably in it. With certain annuals this process has gone so far that the chance of their "reverting" is minimal. But in some cases this is not easy, and by far the best results come with the seed of a fresh cross of two slightly different strains, both selected for similar characters. The term "first filial", or F_1, is used for this fresh cross. F_2 seed, from the second generation, is less vigorous and will contain a proportion of throwbacks to undesirable characters.

MEIOSIS

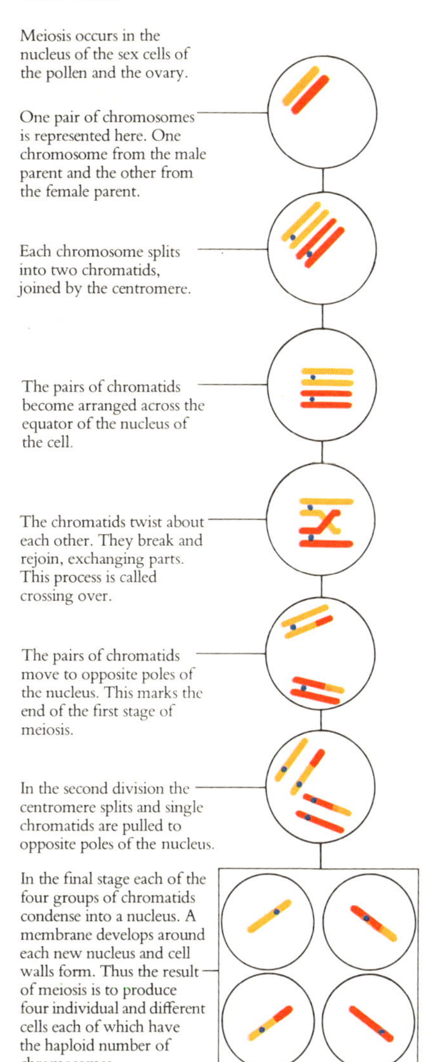

The chromosomes are the carriers of genetic instructions in the form of genes. During normal growth, when new cells are formed, the chromosomes simply divide to provide an identical set for the new cell—a process known as mitosis.

When sex (i.e. sperm or egg) cells are formed, the chromosomes divide in a different way. The number of chromosomes in the nucleus is halved and the genetic instructions are slightly altered. This process is known as meiosis. The full number of chromosomes is restored when the sex cells are united at fertilization. The diversity in life is due mainly to the combined effect of meiosis and fertilization on the chromosomes.

The number of chromosomes in a plant's sex cell is known as its haploid number. Double that (i.e. the normal number for any of its cells) is its diploid number. For various reasons many plants have more than twice their diploid numbers. If each cell contains four times the haploid number the plant is known as a tetraploid; if six, a hexaploid. Any plant with more than the diploid number is a polyploid. Sometimes chance produces an odd-numbered polyploid. Each of these factors will influence the breeding potential of a plant. As more is learned about them, more deliberate breeding becomes possible.

CROSSING OVER

On the pair of chromosomes represented here, one bears a gene A, which determines resistance to disease. It also bears gene B, which causes late maturity, in another position. On the other chromosome, in corresponding positions, are gene a, causing susceptibility to disease, and gene b, causing early maturity. If, during meiosis, crossing over occurs at the appropriate place, part of a chromatid bearing gene A becomes attached to the part of a chromatid that bears gene b. Thus genes A and b are on one chromatid, producing a plant which is resistant to disease and early maturing.

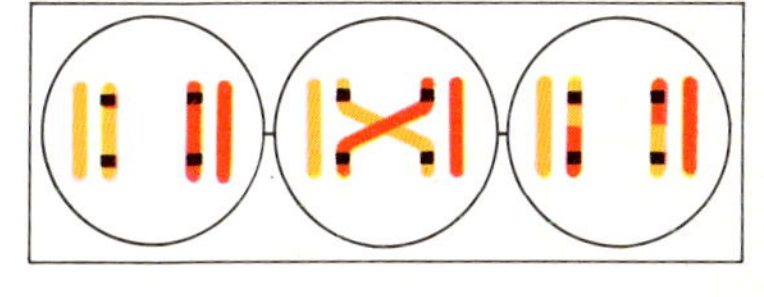

Above Genetic mutation is one of the principal sources of variety, and the main means of evolutionary improvement. Most variegated plants in gardens are genetic mutants of green plants. Often, as on this bush of *Eleagnus pungens* 'Maculata', a branch will undergo another mutation back to its plain green form. When this happens the wise gardener cuts it off, since it is usually more vigorous than the variegated branches and will eventually grow up and starve them out.

Above Mutation can also be induced artificially by radiation. The variegated African violet seedling below was experimentally subjected to radiation which rearranged the sequence of genes on its chromosomes. This may result in a favourable characteristic appearing in the plant which can be bred into new strains by normal methods of crossing or hybridizing. This method of changing the character of plants is becoming more popular with plant breeders.

Fruits and seeds

Below In an apple the ovary is "inferior"—i.e. below the base of the corolla, in a swelling in the flower-stem—"the receptacle". As the flower withers it is the swelling stem that becomes the apple. The tree lavishes nutrients on the 'fruit' to make it palatable to birds, and a possible reserve supply of food for the germinated seed.

Above The progress of a lily from flower to seed. *Lower left* The ovules are fully formed as the flower blooms. Next the stamens have shed pollen; the carpel withers; the ovules are fertilized and start to swell. *Top* The corolla has withered; the ovules are seeds, beginning to fill the ovary.

Right A beanflower is fertilized; the ovules are already tiny embryo beans in the ovary at the base of the carpel. The flower is shed and the ovary extends to become the pod, the beans gradually filling the space.

Flowering plants developed from their non-flowering ancestors because they found a way of communicating with each other and pooling the results of their most successful (though entirely haphazard) experiments in design.

The physical form this collaboration took was the seed. Far more than being just a fertilized ovule ready to start a new life, the seed is in itself an elaborate product of evolutionary improvement. For what could be more vulnerable than a minute plantlet with no resources of its own dropped under the shadow of its parent? Before it became an effective means of propagation the seed had to learn the trick of waiting until conditions were favourable before it started to grow, to develop its own food reserves, to be able to find out which direction was up, and to find a way of leaving home.

So although a seed is still undeniably a miniaturized plant it has a number of extra characteristics plants do not have. It can remain dormant, in some cases for many years. All seeds have a limited period of viability, ranging from a few days to upwards of a hundred years. The seed can sense when it is right to wake up and start growing. It has a built-in food bank to power its first stages of growth. And it has, in many cases if not all a means of transport, or at least a chance of hitching a lift.

Of all these adaptations dormancy was undoubtedly the most important; the one that gave flowering plants a unique advantage over their ancestors. Every time you turn the earth and find you have brought new weed seeds to the surface you can see what a powerful weapon it is.

Every seed has developed a form of dormancy suitable for the conditions it expects to encounter. The chemical computer in a seed coat can calculate whether it is buried at the right depth for germination by taking readings of the fluctuations of temperature, light, moisture, the presence of oxygen and other gases and nitrates in the soil. Perhaps most wonderful of all, this computer can compromise. Seed-coats are sensitive to temperature, moisture, light, oxygen and other gases either separately, or in certain combinations, or in certain sequences, or even in both sequence and combination—rather like the lock of the most sophisticated possible safe.

All this sounds as though it will cause the gardener endless trouble getting conditions exactly right. In practice it does not. Most of the seed that gardeners buy for regular use (vegetables and annuals make up the vast majority) are either not difficult at all, or any necessary treatment to remove inhibition to germination has already been given by the seed merchant.

Certain classes of seed do present special challenges. Many trees are awkward, demanding either that they be sown very fresh (the oak, willow, Japanese maple, walnut are examples) or be subjected to dampness and low temperatures over a long period. The treatment for the latter, known as stratification, consists of mixing the seeds with wet peat or sand and leaving

Above In the prolific and vigorous shrub *Lycesteria formosa* from the Himalayas the flower-spikes continue to grow and flower as the seed ripens. Flower, ripe fruit and all stages between can be seen together.

Germination

A typical dicot seed such as an acorn consists of two seed leaves or cotyledons, which act as food stores, a plumule or first shoot and a radicle or first root, enclosed in a hard outer coat. Germination starts when the outer coat absorbs enough moisture for the cotyledons to swell and burst it open. First the radicle and then the plumule emerge, bending respectively downwards and upwards. In most dicots the seed leaves emerge on the plumule. In acorns they remain concealed, acting as the energy source until the first true leaves appear.

Three days

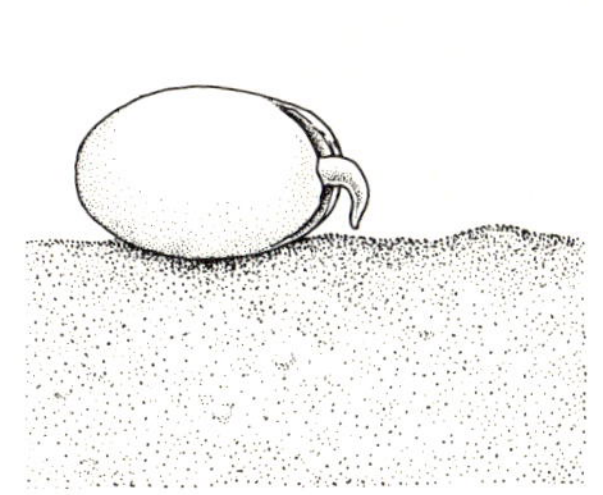

The swelling cotyledons force the acorn open and the radicle appears. Gravity attracts it downwards.

One to two weeks

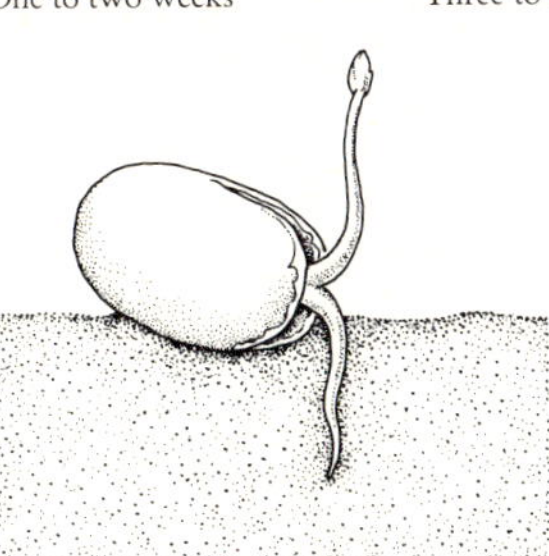

As the radicle begins to function as a root the plumule emerges, away from the pull of gravity.

Three to four weeks

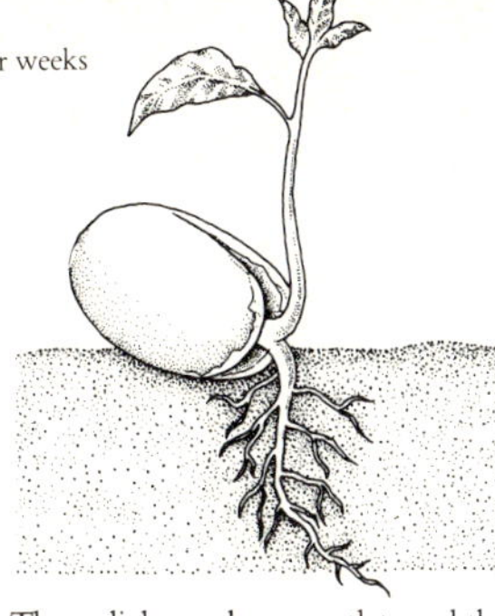

The radicle produces rootlets and the plumule leaves. The oak is now independent of its food store.

Left Depth and spacing of seed sowing depends on the size of the seed. Sweet corn can be handled as individuals and sown at regular spaces. The "drill" is drawn straight and only twice as deep as the seeds are thick.

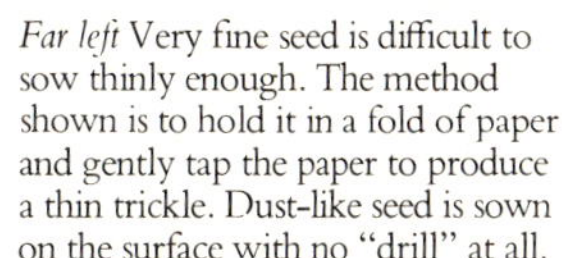

Far left Very fine seed is difficult to sow thinly enough. The method shown is to hold it in a fold of paper and gently tap the paper to produce a thin trickle. Dust-like seed is sown on the surface with no "drill" at all.

Below As soon as seedlings are large enough to handle they must be "pricked out" to a wide enough spacing to give them light and air and prevent their roots from competing with each other. They are lifted gently by one leaf and put in holes made with a pencil in fine soil. The younger they are when they are first moved the better. The second move will be with a ball of soil round their roots.

Dispersal

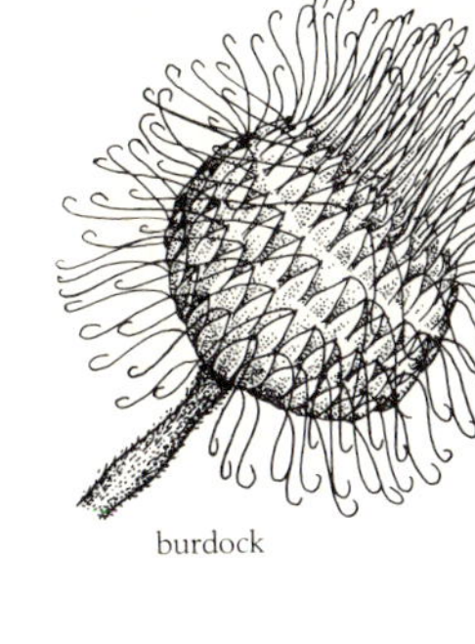

burdock

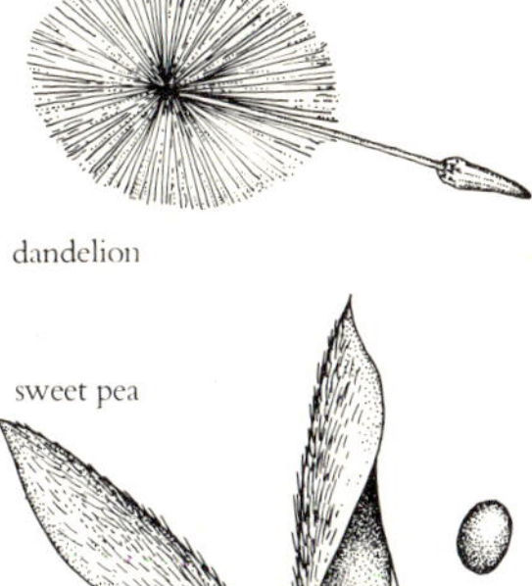

dandelion

sweet pea

poppy

Nearly all seeds have some sort of dispersal mechanism. Examples are (above) palatability to birds, (above right) hooks to catch on animals' coats, (right) the poppy's scattering device which disperses the tiny seeds through the circle of slits when the stem moves in the wind.
enough force to carry them yards.

Above Other seed dispersal mechanisms are (top) fluff to carry it on the wind and (above) the spring-action of the sweet pea plant, which ejects its fairly heavy seeds with enough force to carry them yards.

them exposed to the elements through a cold wet winter. Many of the rose family, many conifers, many maples, azaleas and magnolias need stratifying.

The seedlings of alpines would stand little chance if they germinated in the autumn. Alpine seed is programmed to undergo a cold winter and then germinate quickly next spring. Bulb seed often germinates quickly, but in many cases develops to flowering size only very slowly—which is why most bulbs are propagated by offsets rather than seed.

The majority of seed dries out as it ripens and is stored and sold dry. Before it can start to germinate it must absorb water. A number of seeds have impermeable coats that initially resist any soaking. Examples are some sorts of sweet peas and *Sophora microphylla*. In nature this resistance eventually breaks down, but in cultivation they must be chipped or scratched to allow water in. Rubbing them on sandpaper is one method (known as scarifying). Peas and many other plants, with what seems truly remarkable forethought, naturally produce a proportion of seeds much harder than the rest simply to stagger the timing of their imbibition (as the preliminary absorbing is called) and subsequent germination.

The process of germination is illustrated at the top of the page. It needs not only moisture but oxygen. A balance of these two factors determines how deeply a seed should be sown. A very rough and ready guide is its own diameter. The soil should be fine-textured and just moist ("a good tilth") to give close contact all round and yet allow air in. Dust-like seed should be scattered on the surface with at most only the faintest powdering of soil on top. A broad bean on the other hand can be planted one inch deep in winter, when the ground is wet, and two inches deep in summer, when the moisture level is lower (and oxygen has penetrated deeper into the ground). But too-deep sowing is the commonest cause of failure to germinate. All other things being equal, bigger seed is better for the simple reason that it has a bigger food supply.

The normal safe time to sow any seed in the open is in spring, as soon as the soil warms up and dries on the surface. Some will germinate at near freezing point, but most not until the temperature approaches 55°F (13°C). Some slow seed may not germinate till autumn, or until the following spring. If you are experimenting with seed whose habits you do not know, collected perhaps in the wild, it is a mistake to give up hope before two years are up.

The object of sowing seed in a greenhouse or frame is earlier germination, and hence a longer growing season, or earlier crops. In this case, as in any where the seed is sown closely in a restricted space, transplanting is inevitable. The golden rule is the sooner the better. As soon as the seedlings are big enough to take hold of give them a wider spacing. In this respect the fatter your fingers the less likely they are to be green.

Above The willow-herb has feathery hairs projecting from its seeds. These act as a parachute and as the seed sinks to the ground very slowly it is more likely to be carried away by air currents.

Shoots into roots

Below A mist propagation unit works on the principle of keeping cuttings in a condition as much like growing plants as possible. They are kept permanently moist with an intermittent spray while gentle heat is applied from below. Under these conditions even such difficult plants as rhododendrons usually root freely.

Right An impressive example of the propensity of plants to perpetuate themselves from their own tissue. A huge old chestnut is producing a forest of young trees by "layering" its long branches, which root when they touch the ground.

Above A famous old plant collector, "Cherry" Ingram, responsible for introducing most of the popular varieties of Japanese cherry to England, crouches under a rhododendron to inspect the branches he has pegged down. Layering is a method of propagation that eventually works even with plants that are impossible to root from cuttings. It may be necessary to wound the bark of the branch before pegging it down.

Above Layering is still possible even when no branch is low enough to peg to the ground. "Air-layering" is done by wounding a young branch and surrounding the cut place with damp moss or peat which is then tied securely above and below it in a wrapping of polythene. Eventually the branch will put out roots into the moss. When there are enough it is cut off and potted up as a new independent plant.

Plants are not like animals, which must mate or see their kind perish from the earth. As a fail-safe device for procreating, whether they succeed in fertilizing and scattering seed or not, they have evolved, in parallel with their flowers, a marvellous range of ways of renewing themselves from their own tissue.

Bulbs make offsets, strawberries send out runners, daisies form wider and wider clumps, brambles arch over and root their tips, irises multiply rhizomes, trees and shrubs layer their branches to surround the decrepit old parent trunk with vigorous offspring. Each is a natural method of increase which a gardener, adopting it for his own purposes, would call vegetative propagation.

Sometimes it is more convenient to make more plants this way than by sowing seed. Often it is easier or more certain. But in many cases it is essential, either because fertile seed is not available or is likely to produce a hybrid. Or most often because the plant the gardener wants to reproduce is a garden clone, a cultivated variety which must be kept away from the genetic melting pot if it is to keep its identity. Plants propagated vegetatively are as identical as if they were all part of one great plant—which in a sense they are.

If it is just a few plants the gardener wants, one of the natural or quasi-natural methods of propagation will often suit his purpose. But for larger numbers it is essential to make the most of the parent plant: to take cuttings; short lengths of stem, preferably in growth and with a few leaves on. Such is a plant's will to live that in most cases a cutting given a suitable rooting medium will become an independent plant.

A daunting number of variables surrounds the question of which piece of stem to cut and when. Some stems root best as cuttings if they are still green and sappy; others when half-ripe; others not until they are completely mature. Some root best if cut between joints; others at joints—others with a little "heel" of older wood torn or cut off with them. The younger and more vigorous the stem is (and also the parent plant) the sooner the cutting is likely to root. Flowering stems are less likely to root than non-flowering ones.

The essential condition for all soft or half-ripe cuttings is that they should be kept in a growing, functioning state during the period while they are rootless. Ideally they should have leaves, but not too many leaves, so that their normal process of photosynthesis continues without making excessive demands for moisture which there are no roots to supply.

Many cuttings will root in water, but roots made like this are brittle and difficult to transfer to soil. The usual rooting medium for soft cuttings is a 2:1 mixture of sharp sand and finely sifted peat, kept permanently moist.

One of the best ways of achieving the ideal conditions on a small scale is to put the cuttings round the edge of a clay flower pot within which is a smaller one filled with water. The space between the two, which need not be more than an inch, is filled with the mixture of sand and peat. Water percolates through at a rate that keeps the mixture both damp and airy. Another way is to cover a pot of cuttings with a polythene bag, prevented from touching them (and thus risking fungus problems) by hoops of stiff wire.

The difficulty is often to find a balance between damp and fresh air. In frames this is done by keeping the frames shut (and shaded if the sun is hot) all the time except for an hour or two in the morning, when they are opened for a change of air. Perhaps the nearest to the perfect rooting conditions yet achieved is in the mist propagator, where the cuttings are placed in an open bed in a greenhouse, with soil-warming cables to provide "bottom-heat", under fine spray jets which keep up an intermittent drizzle. It works both for quick-rooting soft cuttings and summer or autumn cuttings of such evergreens as rhododendrons and those conifers that are notoriously difficult.

The discovery of rooting hormones has made the process easier still. Every garden centre now sells little containers of hormone powder which, in very modest quantities (you just dip the base of your cutting in it before potting it up), can stimulate root formation within a mere week or two.

Hardwood cuttings are always a slower process, but in compensation are less demanding. Many woody plants can be rooted simply by half-burying a vigorous shoot in autumn in a shady corner in soil mixed with a good proportion of sand. By next autumn they will be rooted and ready to move.

Above Simple division is the usual way of propagating herbaceous plants. Sometimes they can be pulled into pieces by hand. Tough old clumps yield to the leverage of two forks back-to-back. A clump can be divided into as many pieces as there are growing points with roots attached. The moribund middle should be thrown away and the vigorous growth round the edges divided and replanted. Most border plants need dividing every three or four years.

Above Nearly all bulbs have a way of reproducing themselves vegetatively. Most naturally produce "offsets"—young bulbs beside the old—which can easily be used to increase a clump. A lily bulb is formed of scales (which are abbreviated food-storing leaves) that can be gently pulled apart and will form roots independently if they are planted in damp sand. Some lilies form little bulbs on their stems above ground level, which eventually fall off and begin a life of their own.

Above Carnations and pinks are propagated by a unique form of cutting known as "piping". A young stem is quite easily pulled out of its socket in the node just below it. This piece of stem will root easily in sandy compost. Many more strictly herbaceous plants (pinks are really evergreen sub-shrubs) are also easily propagated by cuttings of sappy young growth taken in spring. Dahlias and delphiniums are among the plants often propagated in this way.

Above Even the leaves of many plants can be persuaded to produce roots. The big leaf of the South African "Cape primrose", *Streptocarpus*, here, has simply been slit with a knife in several places along its mid-rib and pinned down on damp sand. Roots soon form at the cuts and new leaves arise from the roots. The smaller leaves of, for example, sedums or African violets are simply pulled off and planted upright in sand in the same way as the scales of the lily bulb.

MERISTEM CULTURE

The most recent development in plant propagation has been the discovery that the extreme growing tips of shoots that consist of a few actively-dividing cells, known as the meristem, are enough material to make a new plant. They are cut off with surgical precision and hygiene and made to root in an aseptic nutrient jelly based on agar (seaweed extract). The great advantage of this method is that virus diseases appear not to reach the meristem. Good but infected strains of plants can be "cleaned" of virus. Another advantage is that so little plant material is needed: where necessary (as with rare plants or new mutations) one plant could furnish hundreds of offspring if only a few cells are needed for each.

GRAFTING AND BUDDING

Grafting a cutting, known in this case as a "scion", from one plant on to the roots of another may be necessary for a number of reasons. The cutting may refuse to root; its roots may be sickly and weak or prone to a disease or pest (as European vine roots are to phylloxera); extra vigour may be wanted—which is why most roses are grown on briar roots; or the reverse—fruit trees are generally grafted on to dwarfing rootstocks, which limit the ultimate size of the tree. Also it saves time; the cutting is immediately given established roots. The roots and top must be of closely related plants to be compatible—of the same family, but not always necessarily of the same genus. Pear is always grafted on quince roots; peach on almond; Japanese cherries and ornamental crab apples on seedling stocks of wild cherry or crab; many weeping tree cultivars onto normal rootstocks of the same species.

There are many forms of graft, but one objective: to bring together the cambium layers (see pages 40–1) of scion and rootstock and keep them pressed tightly together until they unite. Below are several of the many ingenious forms of surgery found efficacious over the centuries. "Budding" (bottom) is the form of grafting now preferred for many commercial purposes, being most economical of precious scion-wood and generally quicker.

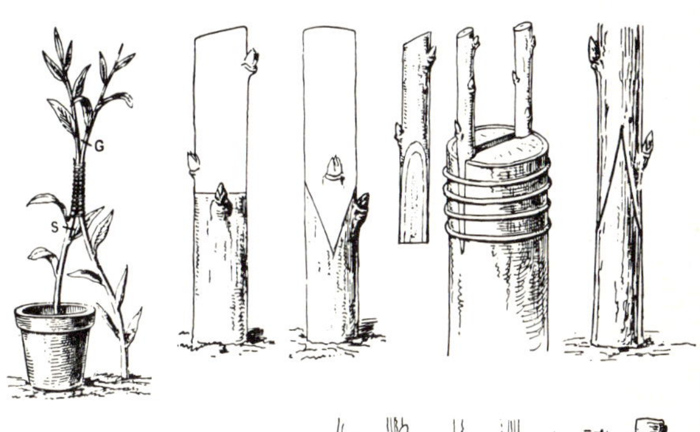

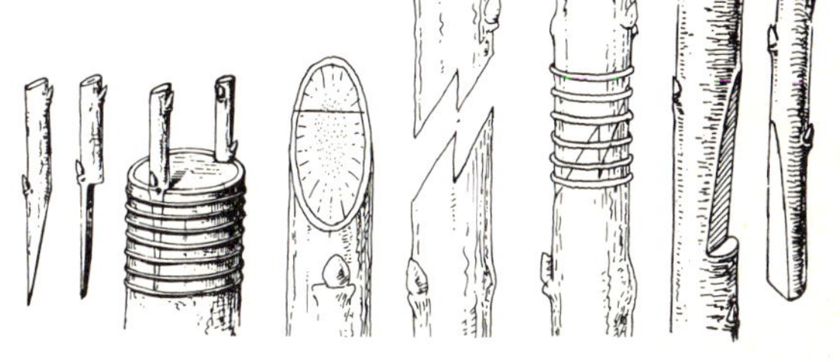

Above The various forms grafting can take are self-explanatory, given the principle that the cambium layers of scion and root must be kept in contact. The most convenient and/or efficacious for a given plant depends on whether the stock and scion have the same diameter, whether the graft is expected to "take" quickly, whether it is sheltered in a greenhouse or out in the open and subject to the wind. Centuries of experience have established which method suits which plant.

Above Budding is the method generally used for propagating large numbers of such plants as roses. A single bud of the desired variety is all that is needed. It is cut off with a sharp knife in spring, taking with it a little sliver of wood. The pith from this is removed and the bud with its surrounding bark alone is slipped into a little slit made in the bark of the rootstock. Once the bud has opened and made a new shoot the top of the rootstock is cut off immediately above it.

The nursery routine

It is hard to say what constitutes a "typical" nursery, since nearly all nurseries today specialize to some degree. Many sell all categories of plants in their garden centres but produce only one or two categories themselves, buying the rest in from trade suppliers. Others are intensely specialist, perhaps in rare alpines, which constitute as much a hobby as a business. Yet others are no more or less than factories, producing standard popular lines of bulbs or trees by the million.

On this page we analyse the routine of a fairly large nursery producing trees, shrubs and herbaceous plants, including groundcover plants, conifers and heathers. The representation is based on a combination of two famous British nurseries, Notcutts of Woodbridge, Suffolk, and Blooms of Bressingham, Norfolk.

Since (with the exception of intensively bred annuals and some vegetables) only species can be propagated true to type by seed, and most nursery plants are selected garden forms or cultivars, most nursery propagation is necessarily by cuttings, grafting or division.

The nursery's business is to rationalize the production of hundreds of diverse plants, each of which needs slightly different treatment, particularly in the matter of timing. There are for example at least twelve types of cuttings: greenwood, softwood, semi-hardwood, hardwood, basal, heeled, nodal, internodal, stem, leaf, leaf-bud and root. Experience shows that although almost any cuttings of some plants will take root, others must be taken from a certain part at a certain stage of development to stand any chance of success. Others will not root at all but must be grafted or budded on to appropriate and compatible roots.

Since most of this development depends entirely on the weather, industrial programming is not easy. Luckily the discovery that cuttings of many plants can be stored for up to two or three months, provided they are kept just above freezing point, has meant that they can be taken at precisely the right moment, even if a log-jam of work makes it impossible to process them straight away. Yet to a nurseryman, as to every gardener, the weather has the final say. If the ground is frozen or water-logged all orders can be held up for weeks on end: it may become impossible to send out plants at the right time for gardeners. Hence a greater reliance on growing more plants—even trees—in containers from start to finish.

There is a constant commercial pressure on every nursery to narrow its range of plants, simplify its routine and give itself the breathing space either to lower prices, take higher profits or take over less-efficient competitors and expand the business.

A depressing number have yielded to the temptation. The range of plants on general sale today is a mere fraction of what it was at, say, the beginning of this century. Many, if not most, garden centres today are predictable to the point of dreariness, with almost nothing to offer but the plants you see in every front garden.

But the contrary pressure also exists: to excel by producing new and better plants. Good nurseries are constantly working on the qualities of their favourite genera. Unfortunately the "new" tends to be confused with the "better". What is all too rare is the nursery that critically examines the vast range of old selections, chooses the best and reintroduces them to the country's gardens. Even where public trials are held, for example by the Royal Horticultural Society at Wisley, very few nurseries take advantage of the experience gained.

Keen gardeners know that very often the only way to obtain a highly desirable plant is to find another keen gardener who already has it. The keener the gardener, in fact, the more anxious he is to give away pieces of his best plants—not to do nurseries out of business but to ensure the survival of something excellent.

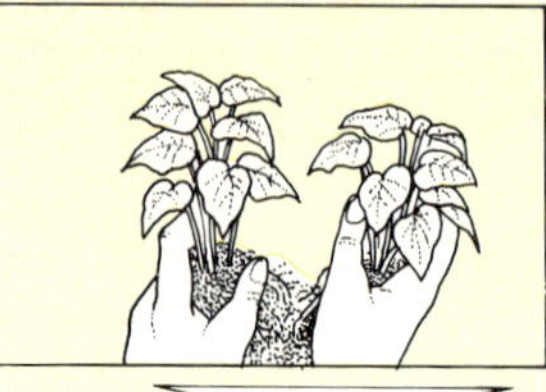

Herbaceous plants are propagated by either division (*above*), cuttings (*above right*) or seed (*above far right*).

Divisions are made in spring or autumn depending on the plant and are planted straight out in well-prepared and fertilized soil to grow to saleable size.

Above Herbaceous cuttings taken from mother plants in spring or early summer are rooted in sandy compost in cold frames. Rooting is usually completed in six to eight weeks.

Above Seeds of herbaceous plants are sown in seedbeds (or boxes if the seed is rare, very small or otherwise difficult). They are thinned or pricked out in the usual way.

Above Planting out into the field is done by a gang of four sitting on a low trailer behind a slow-moving tractor which straddles the prepared growing-on bed.

Above When large enough to handle, seedlings and rooted cuttings are potted-up in plastic pots on a rotary machine which dispenses compost with a slow-release fertilizer. This machine can pot 1200 plants an hour.

Above During the summer the beds are hoed and watered. Within six to eight months (usually by October) most herbaceous plants have reached saleable maturity and are lifted by a tractor equipped with an undercutting device. *Below* Plants are then individually forked by hand into a trailer.

Above The potted plants are stood out on raised gravel beds with an overhead watering and feeding system until ready in autumn for lifting and despatch (*below*).

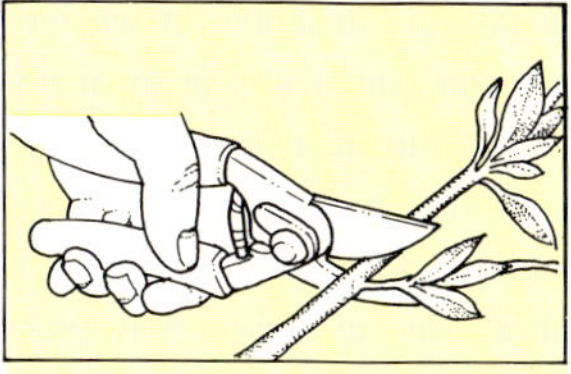

Left Shrubs are generally propagated by cuttings (though sometimes by seed, layering, grafting or budding). Cuttings are taken from young vigorous mother plants, kept for this purpose. At the appropriate moment in the ripening of their new wood they are cut, dusted with fungicide and dipped in rooting powder.

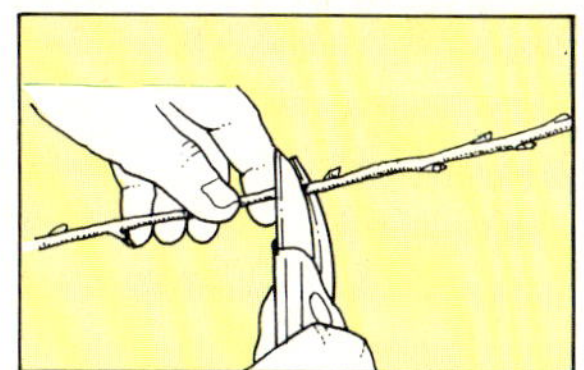

Above One economical method of rooting woody cuttings is to plant them in a sandy compost warmed by cables below and covered with polythene, with frames over to provide shade.

Above The surest way of rooting most difficult cuttings is in a "mist unit" (see pages 52–3). From the mist cuttings must be potted in small peat pots for weaning before mechanical potting-up.

Above After rooting under mist or polythene, potting-up and potting-on, the young plants are moved to an unheated tunnel house to be grown on. They are then gradually hardened off by admitting cooler air.

Above Trees rooted under mist, like shrubs, must be given a weaning period in a tunnel house before they can be planted out.

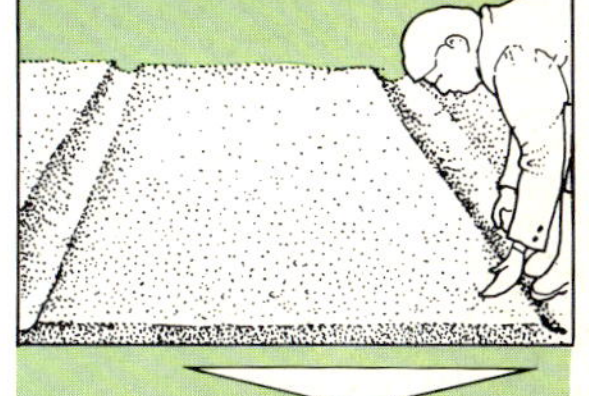

Trees are either bought in as young seedlings (*above*) or propagated by cuttings (*above left*), seed (*above right*) or grafting or budding (*below*). *Left* Cuttings are sometimes rooted under mist like shrubs. *Right* Seedbeds are thinned by hand. *Below* Seedling trees are planted out from a tractor-drawn rig.

Below Many tree cultivars can only be propagated by grafting or budding on to appropriate rootstocks. Budding is shown below. When the bud has "taken", its new shoot must be tied in to make it grow as a trunk rather than a branch. The top of the rootstock is soon pruned off and replaced by a cane. The young tree will then be trained and pruned for four more years.

Above Trees are "lined out" for growing to the various recognized selling sizes. A full standard takes up to seven years. During this time they are trained, pruned, sprayed, irrigated and fertilized regularly, while their roots are undercut at intervals to keep them dense for their eventual lifting (*left*).

Above The fully weaned young shrubs are stood out on sand beds where they are watered from below with dilute fertilizer by capillary action. Some shrubs are grown on for about a year; but others and conifers need longer. Being grown in containers they can be sold all year round.

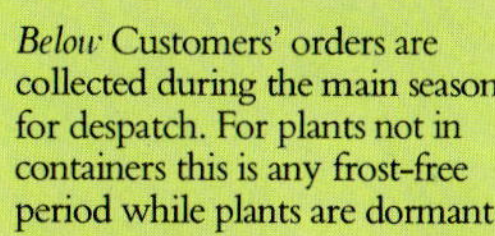

Below Customers' orders are collected during the main season for despatch. For plants not in containers this is any frost-free period while plants are dormant.

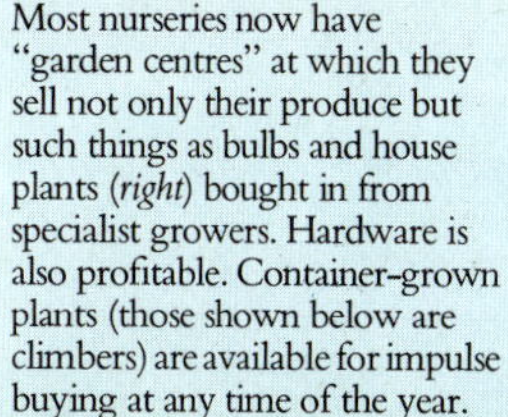

Most nurseries now have "garden centres" at which they sell not only their produce but such things as bulbs and house plants (*right*) bought in from specialist growers. Hardware is also profitable. Container-grown plants (those shown below are climbers) are available for impulse buying at any time of the year.

What makes a plant gardenworthy?

Above Perhaps the first criterion of all is that a plant should give pleasure. This spectacular three-foot saxifrage 'Tumbling Waters' is the pride and joy of its young owner.

Above right It has taken forty years for this perfect specimen of *Juniperus* 'Compressa' to reach the height of the saxifrage. Snail-like slowness can also be a virtue in plants.

Below In contrast the foxtail lilies (*Eremurus robustus*) earn their place in the garden by a short-lived early-summer display of vegetable fireworks that nothing else can equal.

There is an old Hollywood comic's gag: "New is easy. Funny is hard." There has never (or not for four hundred years).been a shortage of new plants to grow in gardens. But whether they have been better than the old ones is not always clear. It depends on what the gardener is looking for. There are so many aspects of quality in plants that it is worth pausing to consider what makes a good candidate for our limited space.

There is a rough and ready division, of course, between the beautiful and the useful. Any plant that can fairly claim to be both has a head start. But there are many other categories of plant character that have their garden uses. Critical gardeners keep a mental score-card of points for and against plants in order to decide whether they are suffered to remain, enthusiastically propagated, or are torn up and consigned to the bonfire.

Most fundamental—except perhaps to a masochistic kind of gardener most often found in an alpine house—is a good constitution; a plant's ability to thrive and wax fat. This does not mean the hooligan temperament of a weed, but the inclination, given an appropriate site, to grow steadily and strongly without sudden fits of the vapours. If shoots regularly die back, or a succession of pests and diseases make it their headquarters, or the plant sits in an apparent coma, it may of course be the gardener's fault. But once he has satisfied himself that he has given it a fair chance it must either thrive or be scrapped. I can think of otherwise unexceptional plants whose chief beauty lies in their rubicund appearance of enjoying life. It is a principal virtue of the tulips (and many other bulbs); the peony; some wild roses; planes; willows; many pines.

A more specialized form of the same virtue is to be able to thrive where little else can. Plants thus acquire local merit points which do not apply elsewhere. Few trees will stand a full salt-laden sea blast, for example. The sycamore, often regarded as little better than a weed, has won its battle honours as the first line of defence against salty south-westerlies—a lop-sided thing, perhaps, but tough enough to allow something better to grow in its lee.

Similarly there are plants adapted to what can scarcely be called soil; grasses that can bind shifting sand, heathers for dank peat, gorse for dry heathland or spindle for chalk.

In Arctic winters the ability to survive at all makes a plant gardenworthy, whereas in temperate places the sheer perversity of gardeners gives an extra half-point for glamour to plants that are liable to succumb when the occasional hard winter arrives.

Straightforward speed of growth is one of the most obvious qualities a gardener may be looking for. Hedge-plants are generally (but mistakenly) judged on how soon they will reach the required height. The word "vigour" means both speed and overall willingness to keep growing. But very slow growth is a character equally in demand. Small gardens need scaled-down plants. There is a premium on tiny shrubs and dwarf conifers that take a long time to reach saleable size.

If flowers are the first thing that come to mind as desirable in a garden, there are many ways of judging the quality of a flower. There are those who see true beauty only in the naturally evolved balance and proportions of wild flowers, whether from Sikkim or a local ditch. Others judge a flower on the breeder's success in packing in the maximum number of petals. Others count on the brilliance of its colour. Others put stress on its oddness. A blue rose would be a best-seller regardless of its intrinsic merit. A very few have the depth of knowledge to judge the merits of a flower in the context of its peers, its ancestors, its breeding history and its record in cultivation.

The shape, colour, texture, scent, leaves and habit of a flower are all matters for critical debate. But there are other aspects beside its looks. A plant may gain merit by flowering earlier or later than others and so extending the season for that

Below Bark of bright colours is one of the most valuable winter garden resources. Certain of the white willows and shrubby dogwoods are the most vivid providers, completely impervious to weather. For the clearest colours of yellow, red, purple or white the plants are cut hard back to a stump every spring.

Right Flowers have no need of a lofty pedigree to provide a perfect garden picture. Under the shade of a Japanese maple in this garden on the Welsh borders is a simple combination of bluebells and Welsh poppies—both wild flowers which some people would class as weeds in the garden.

genus or species—or the very same quality may tell against it by making it liable to damage by late or early frosts.

The length of its flowering season is critical too. Most of the saga of rose-breeding over the last 180 years has been concerned with making the term "perpetual" come true. Such autumn flowers as Michaelmas daisies and chrysanthemums have immensely long periods in bloom. If the poppy flowered at that time of year it could not compete.

Flowers which having flowered die well or leave beautiful seed heads are worth extra points: those that leave sorry brown rags lose merit. There is extra credit, too, for flowers that dry off on the stem still keeping their perfect form, or that can be picked and dried. Dried delphiniums keep their potent blue.

Scent is a quality not much discussed except in general terms, and little understood. There is a small category of plants grown as much for their scent as for their other qualities. Such herbs as lavender, rosemary and mint; summer jasmine and Dutch honeysuckle; philadelphus; balsam poplar are examples. With most plants, though—even with roses, which surely have a duty to be fragrant—we put too little stress on scent.

Flavour was once the chief criterion for fruit and vegetables. Now it is considered secondary to appearance, uniformity and regularity of cropping. The reason for this is because expensive research takes commercial factors into account first. But this is a powerful argument for the planting and study of old sorts by amateurs who want taste, not supermarket shelf-life.

This is only to touch on the inexhaustible list of the contributions plants can make to gardens. Thorny plants make good barriers. Some plants take kindly to clipping and grow dense and snug. Some make dramatic gestures and some take up quaint poses. Some cover the ground as close as a rug and save us having to weed. Some we love for their anthology of associations. Some we must have simply because they are rare.

Left A plant that attracts beautiful insects with its flowers or birds with its fruit has an additional asset. The herbaceous *Sedum spectabile* is often covered with red admiral butterflies in late summer.

Below The wise men of horticulture. A committee of the Royal Horticultural Society votes at one of the Society's London shows on whether an alpine deserves an award. The Society's awards are internationally accepted. For their details see under AGM, AM and FCC in the glossary.

The first garden plants

A list of the plants grown in European gardens in Shakespeare's time—one of the early Herbals in fact—is startlingly limited in its scope. Few of today's ornamental plants are there at all. The emphasis is on plants useful for food, flavour, medicine, cosmetics or perfumery.

The flowers that were grown compose a list of lovely nursery-rhyme naïveté: "Roses, red and damask, snapdragons, sweet williams, sops in wine [carnations], sweet briar, pinks, pansies, hollyhocks, cowslips, bachelor's buttons, wall-gillyflowers [wall-flowers], columbines, daffadowndillies, lilies, lily of the valley, primroses, marigolds, valerian, love-in-a-mist, lavender, peonies and poppies" are all that are mentioned by Thomas Tusser in his *Five Hundred Pointes of Good Husbandrie*, published in the 1570s.

Botanical curiosity, like all the studies awakened by the Renaissance, was concerned at first simply with interpreting the ancients. Theophrastus or Dioscorides recommended such and such a plant for dysentery or the ague. Which is it? Frequently none of the plants in cultivation matched the description.

Pierre Belon, a Breton physician, was one of the first to go plant hunting abroad when he spent three years, from 1546 to 1548, in the eastern Mediterranean looking for the plants—and not only plants of course but all the wonders—described by the classical writers. He was an observer rather than a collector.

A much more potent influence at that time was the diplomatic bag. Turkish gardening (in the Persian tradition, see pages 206–7) had long before reached a point of sophistication undreamed of in Europe. The Viennese ambassador to Constantinople in the mid-sixteenth century was the admirable Ghiselin de Busbecq, who sent home such Turkish specialities as tulips, hyacinths, anemones and the Crown Imperial, the first hint of the fabulous harvest of bulbs that has poured ever since, and continues to pour, from the eastern Mediterranean and beyond.

At various dates now forgotten (but often quoted as 1596, the year of publication of John Gerard's *Catalogus* in which many of them are first listed) a steady stream of plants from the nearer and more accessible Mediterranean was collected into gardens.

One of the first Englishmen to go out and look for them was the royal gardener John Tradescant the Elder, who visited Alicante and Algiers in 1621 and brought home plants cultivated by the Moors; notably an apricot and the Persian lilac.

It was another 50 years, though, before Sir George Wheler visited Greece and Turkey on a methodical plant hunt (he introduced St John's Wort, *Hypericum calycinum*) and not until 1700 that Joseph de Tournefort, with Claude Aubriet—remembered by the aubrieta—as his professional painter, set off on the first major expedition through Greece, round Turkey and as far as Persia. Tournefort's finds included the common *Rhododendron ponticum* and the yellow azalea *R. luteum* on the south shores of the Black Sea, and the oriental poppy in Syria.

With its characteristic summer drought the Mediterranean is essentially a region of spring-flowering, summer-dormant plants. Most bulbs are typical. And the herbaceous plants that flower through our northern summer are over and beginning to die down in the Mediterranean by June. Most of its trees and shrubs are evergreen for the same reason. Many of the plants of the sun-baked rocky garrigues are highly aromatic: our garden herbs.

The map shows some of the most popular garden plants native to the area and some of the plant hunters who have explored it—a process that is by no means over yet. Each year another botanist sets out in the spirit of Pierre Belon.

Names of a selection of the best-known garden plants are printed on the map in italics in the area(s) where the plant grows wild. The dates refer to when they were introduced into cultivation. Names of the principal botanist-collectors are printed over the areas of their expeditions, with the dates of their first visits when they are known.

Along all coasts of the Mediterranean Sea
Anemone coronaria 1596
Arbutus unedo
Centranthus ruber
Cistus salvifolius 1548
Clematis cirrhosa 1596
Clematis flammula 1590
Colutea arborescens 1568
Erica arborea 1658
Helichrysum italicum
Iris germanica 1573
Lavandula angustifolia (spica) 1568
Lilium candidum 1596
Muscari comosum 1596
Nerium oleander 1596
Nigella damascena 1570
Quercus ilex 1581
Rosmarinus officinalis 1548
Viburnum tinus 1596

AMSTERDAM
LONDON
RHINE
BONN
SEINE
PARIS
LOIRE
Maw 1869
Barr c.
Wheler 1675
RHONE
Paeonia officinalis
Tournefort 1700
Fraxinus ornus
EBRO
Tournefort 1700
Hyssopus officinale 1548
Narcissus spp
MADRID
BARCELONA
Rhododendron ponticum 1763
TAGUS
Masson 1783
Maw 1869
Matthiola incana
Barr *c.* 1880
Webb 1825
Tradescant 1611
LISBON
Linum narbonense 1759
Masson 1783
Barr *c.* 1880
Euphorbia characias
Maw 1869
Acanthus mollis 1548
Webb 1825
Boel 1607
Dianthus caryophyllus
ALGIERS
Alstroemer 1760
Iris unguicularis (I. stylosa)
Masson 1783
Hooker and Ball 1871
Cytisus battandieri 1922
Webb 1827
Cedrus atlantica 1845
Cosson 1852
Maw 1877
Balls 1936

Above Iris germanica has been cultivated in Europe since classical times. Linnaeus called it German because Strabo, a ninth-century German monk, recorded growing it.

Right The hardy cyclamen are natives of the Mediterranean shores. The more tender *Cyclamen persicum* is the parent of our modern house-plants.

Right Acanthus was one of the Mediterranean plants admired by the classical world. Its leaves were the inspiration for the capitals of Corinthian columns.

Right The oriental poppy, now universal in gardens, was brought home by Tournefort from Syria in 1702.

STOCKHOLM
LENINGRAD
NHAGEN
BERLIN
VISTULA
WARSAW
DNIEPER
LBE
PRAGUE
VIENNA
Maw 1869
BUDAPEST
Hyssopus officinale 1548
Crocus vernus
Pyracantha coccinea 1629
Sibthorp 1787
BELGRADE
BUCHAREST
DANUBE
clamen neapolitanum 1824
Crocus imperati
Hyssopus officinale 1548
Prunus cerasifera 1629
Arabis albida 1798
Wheler 1675
w 1869
Iris xiphium 1596
Phlomis fruticosa 1596
SOFIA
Ball 1911
Tournefort 1700
Wheler 1675
Sibthorp 1787
Wheler 1675
ROME
1546 *Campanula pyramidalis 1596*
Campanula pyramidalis 1596
Webb 1827
Chionodoxa sardensis
Salvia officinalis 1597
Lilium chalcedonicum 1596
Belon 1546
ISTANBUL
Gypsophila elegans 1828
Rhododendron ponticum 1763
R. luteum
Convolvulus cneorum 1640
Sibthorp 1787
Iris pallida 1596
Chionodoxa luciliae 1877
Sibthorp 1787
Philadelphus coronarius 1596
ANKARA
Narcissus jonquilla 1596
Maw 1869
Balls 1936
Maw 1869
Tulipa gesneriana c.1554
Balls 1932
ATHENS
Elwes 1874
Lathyrus odoratus 1700
Webb 1827
Belon 1546
Genista aetnensis
Tournefort 1700
Wheler 1675
Webb 1827
osson 1852
Sibthorp 1787
Belon 1546
Tournefort 1700
Webb 1827
Sibthorp 1787
Prunus amygdalus 1548
Hyacinthus orientalis 1596
Michaux 1782
Cyclamen persicum 1731
Iris histrio 1873
TIGRIS
Cedrus libani 1638
Belon 1546
Rauwolf 1573
Michaux 1782
BAGHDAD
EUPHRATES
Hibiscus syriacus 1596
JERUSALEM
Rauwolf 1573
Delile 1798
Belon 1546
CAIRO
NILE
Forsskòl 1761
Hasselquist 1749
Brunnera macrophylla 1830
Papaver orientale 1714
Polygonum baldschuanicum 1883
Nepeta mussinii
Fritillaria persica 1596
Parrotia persica 1841
Epimedium pinnatum 1849
Lychnis chalcedonica 15
TEHRAN

Above John Tradescant the Elder, gardener to King James I of England, was one of the first to travel abroad for new plants: to Russia in 1618 and the Iberian Peninsula in 1621.

Above Joseph Piton de Tournefort explored the Levant from Greece to Persia for Louis XIV from 1700 to 1702 on an elaborate and well-prepared botanic expedition.

Above Conrad Loddiges's nursery in London published its first catalogue in 1777. He spread newly found plants far and wide, and perhaps introduced *Rhododendron ponticum* to Britain.

Throughout the Balkans and Turkey

Anemone hortensis 1597
Aubrieta deltoidea 1710
Crocus chrysanthus
Crocus flavus c.1597
Genista lydia 1926
Helichrysum plicatum 1877
Prunus dulcis
Prunus laurocerasus 1629

Eastern coast of the Mediterranean Sea from Yugoslavia to Israel

Acanthus spinosus 1629
Borago officinalis
Cercis siliquastrum 1596
Chrysanthemum coronarium 1629
Cupressus sempervirens 1548
Euphorbia characias wulfenii
Gladiolus byzantinus 1629
Ruta graveolens 1562

Above Rhododendron ponticum was found by Tournefort in northern Turkey in 1701, but not grown in gardens until over sixty years later.

Above The common herbaceous peony of cottage gardens was introduced from the eastern Mediterranean, possibly from Crete, before 1548. Claude Aubriet, Tournefort's painter and companion, painted it. The double crimson form, which is now the cottage peony, appeared as a natural mutation in Antwerp shortly after.

Above Seventeenth-century Dutch painting expresses the wonder and pleasure of newly found flowers, including here tulips, hyacinths, poppies, peonies and narcissi, with *Rosa centifolia*, the "Painter's Rose", bottom right.

PLANT HUNTING CONTINUES

Professor Tom Hewer of Bristol is one of the number of botanists who still bring home unrecorded species from regular expeditions to the Middle East. Below he is seen lunching with his son and a guide in the Zagros mountains of Iran, where he went in search of rare alpines in 1973. Some of the more important recent introductions of the twentieth century are listed below.

European introductions since 1898

Anemone blanda 1898
Anthemis sancti-johannis 1928
Arum creticum 1928
Cistus palhinhaii 1944
Crocus goulimyi 1955
Genista lydia 1926
Geranium dalmaticum 1947
Geranium renardii 1935
Salvia haematodes 1938
Sempervivum giuseppii 1935
Sempervivum kosaninii 1925
Viola delphinantha 1933

Plants from the New World

Right Michaelmas daisies are typical of the North American meadow flowers, introduced since the seventeenth century, that have enriched our herbaceous borders.

Widespread north to south in eastern USA

Acer negundo 1725
Acer saccharinum 1688
Amelanchier laevis 1870
Aster novae-belgii 1710
Cornus florida 1731
Crataegus crus-gallii 1680
Dicentra eximia 1812
Helenium autumnale 1729
Kalmia latifolia 1726
Liatris spicata 1732
Lilium superbum 1727
Liquidambar styraciflua 1681
Liriodendron tulipifera 1663
Lobelia cardinalis 1626
Monarda didyma 1744
Oenothera tetragona 1820
Parthenocissus quinquefolia 1616
Pontederia cordata 1759
Quercus coccinea 1691
Robinia pseudacacia 1590
Tradescantia virginiana 1616

MISSOURI
Juniperus horizontalis 1836
CHICAGO
Rudbeckia hirta 1714
Michaux 1785
Kalm 1748
Bartram 1730
Betula papyrifera 1750
BOSTON
More 1722
Cornus canadensis 1774
NEW YORK
Aster novae-angliae 1710
Michaux 1785
Rhus typhina 1629
Kalm 1748
WASHINGTON
Catesby 1712
Tradescant Jr 1637
Phlox paniculata 1732
Banister *c.* 1680
Michaux 1785
Catalpa bignonioides 1726
Bartram 1730
Fraser 1785
Magnolia grandiflora 1734
Juglans nigra 1634
Lyon 1802
Yucca gloriosa 1550
Young *c.* 1764
Yucca recurvifolia 1794
MISSISSIPPI
RIO GRANDE
Catesby 1712
Bartram 1730
Michaux 1785
NEW ORLEANS
Coreopsis basalis drummondii 1825
Agave americana 1640
Begonia fuchsioides 1846
Choisya ternata 1825
Cobaea scandens 1787
Cosmos bipinnatus 1799
Cuphea ignea 1845
Dahlia spp 1789
Echeveria spp 1826
Euphorbia fulgens 1836
Euphorbia pulcherrima 1834
MEXICO
Fuchsia fulgens 1837
Ipomoea purpurea 1629
Lobelia fulgens 1809
Tagetes erecta 1596
Tagetes patula 1573
Zinnia elegans 1796

Mexico: Plant collectors

Hernandez 1570
Sessé and Mocino 1788
Humboldt and Bonpland 1798
Coulter 1824
Hartweg 1836
Linden 1838
Roezl 1868
Balls 1938

Left The tiny creeping herbaceous dogwood, *Cornus canadensis*, is one of the enchanting new flowers introduced from North American woods in 1774.

Right Dahlias are Mexican, long cultivated by the Aztecs before they were brought to Europe by the Spanish.

Above John Tradescant II (1608–62), the royal gardener, like his father, travelled three times to Virginia for "varieties of flowers and plants".

Above John Bartram (1699–1777), the first American-born botanist, collected plants for correspondents in England.

Above André Michaux settled in South Carolina to collect plants for the French government and made the first study of American oaks.

Joyfull Newes out of the newe founde Worlde was the English title of the first book on American plants, published in London in 1577, the year Sir Francis Drake left to sail round the world. It was a translation of the work of a Spaniard, Dr Monardes.

Spain's new South American empire was tropical and subtropical, with Florida as its northern extreme. Its economic plants, which included tobacco, potatoes, tomatoes, marrows and such flowers as marigolds and sunflowers, were the first American plants to reach Europe in the sixteenth century.

Samples of the flora of North America, hardier and therefore potentially of more interest for Europe, came later. It is John Tradescant the Younger who is generally credited as the first European gardener/botanist to go plant hunting in North America. He travelled to Virginia three times in 1637, 1642 and 1654. He kept no diary, but his catalogue published in 1656 shows that the famous Tradescant collection in London included such new American plants as Virginia creeper, tulip tree, red maple, swamp cypress, false acacia, and such future garden flowers as Michaelmas daisies and rudbeckias.

The equable climate of western Europe has no equivalent in eastern North America; its immense size and southerly latitudes (Boston equates to Rome, and Atlanta to somewhere in the Sahara) make both winter and summer capable of vicious extremes. Generally, the plants of eastern North America are happiest in the continental climate of central Europe. The Gulf Stream summers of Britain can be altogether too tepid for them, failing to ripen their new growth or their seeds, although a wide range of trees and shrubs from north-eastern North America is successfully cultivated. The number of its species, however, dwarfs that of Europe, almost rivalling that of China, the only other country to have escaped the attrition of the Ice Ages. Whereas European plants in retreat from the ice reached the Mediterranean and were extinguished on its shores, American and Chinese species retreated south in good order, and in due course advanced north again. The magnolias are an example of a family long extinct in Europe, first discovered in America and later in even greater variety in China.

Missionaries despatched to the colonies by the botanically minded Bishop of London, Henry Compton, kept up the flow of new plants in the latter part of the seventeenth century. North America's first home-grown botanist was John Bartram of Philadelphia, whose employment by a group of plant enthusiasts in England was extremely fruitful. His methodical explorations of Indian country from Florida to the Great Lakes brought more than two hundred new plants into cultivation. Bartram was followed by others, notably John Fraser and André Michaux.

Until the mid-eighteenth century, the rich hunting-ground of South America was kept under lock and key by its Spanish masters. Chile was destined to be the country of most significance for gardeners; its plants do splendidly in the Gulf Stream climate of North West Europe. The 4,000-mile Pacific slope of the Chilean Andes provides every possible climatic niche for a range of plants very unlike those of the rest of America: indeed, some species are related only to the flora of New Zealand, south-eastern Australia and Tasmania. But glimpses into Chile were rare until it gained independence in 1817. Most of the important plants were collected by professionals employed by the nursery firm of Veitch, particularly William Lobb in the 1840s. Harold Comber also made an important and successful visit in the 1920s.

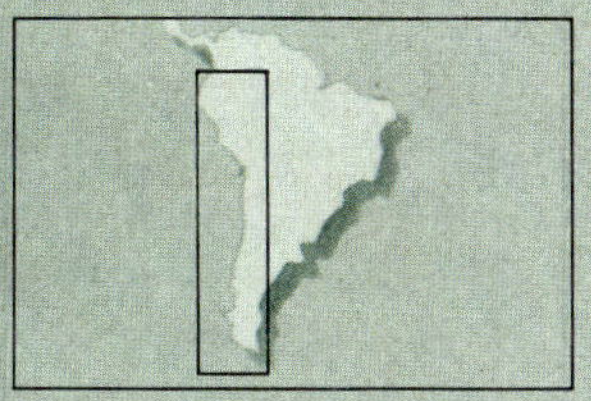

QUITO

de Jussieu 1735
Humboldt and Bonpland 1801
Cuming 1826
Hartweg 1840
Balls 1939

MARAÑÓN

Mathews 1830
Dombey, Ruiz and Pavon 1777
Frézier 1712

LIMA

PERU

Pearce 1859
Heliotropium peruvianum 1757
Tropaeolum majus 1686
Roezl 1869
Balls 1939
de Jussieu 1735
Cuming 1826

Frézier 1712

Hippeastrum spp 1830
Alstroemeria ligtu 1838
Alstroemeria aurantiaca 1831
Elliott 1927
Bridges 1840
Poeppig 1827

CHILE

Schizanthus pinnatus 1822
Buddleja globosa 1774
Eccremocarpus scaber 1824
Escallonia rubra 1827

SANTIAGO

Fuchsia magellanica 1823
Lippia citriodora 1784
Mimulus luteus 1826
Salpiglossis sinuata 1824
Comber 1925
Feuillée 1709
Berberis linearifolia 1925
Lobb 1840
Lapageria rosea 1847
Araucaria araucana 1795
Cuming 1826
Berberis darwinii 1849
Calceolaria integrifolia 1822
Embothrium coccineum 1846
Bridges 1840
Eucryphia glutinosa 1859
Geum chiloense 1826
Lobb 1840
Gunnera tinctoria 1840
Tropaeolum speciosum 1846
Abutilon vitifolium 1837

Darwin 1834

Elliott 1927

Above Alexander von Humboldt, who made a five-year journey (1799–1804) through South America was described by Darwin as "the greatest traveller who ever lived".

Above Harold Comber searched the Andes on the Chile-Argentine border for hardier forms of good plants. His successes include *Embothrium coccineum*, the flame tree.

Above Clarence Elliott with his natural history specimens on his way home from South America in 1928, drawn by John Nash. Elliott made two trips with Dr Balfour-Gourlay.

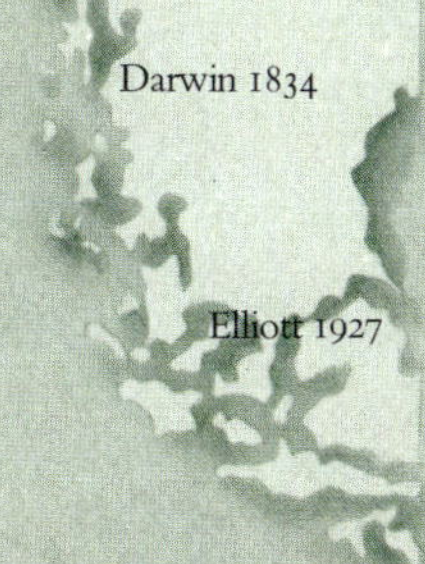

Above Fuchsia magellanica grows in the woods of southern Chile as a tall bush. In northern gardens frost often cuts it to the ground.

Above Embothriums were considered tender until Comber (*left*) found a hardier form.

Above The evergreen *Berberis darwinii* commemorates Darwin's voyage up the Chilean coast in 1834.

Above The lovely tree-mallow, *Abutilon vitifolium*, grows in the temperate rain forests of southern Chile.

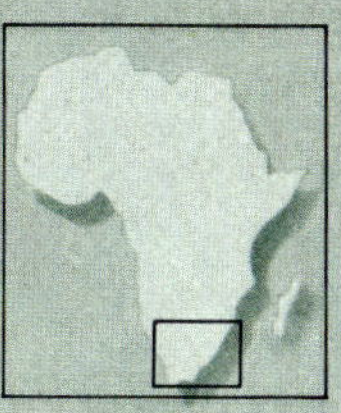

Left Francis Masson, sent to the Cape by Kew in 1772. His fortune in finding almost virgin territory had spectacular results, especially among heaths and pelargoniums.

Throughout South Africa
Agapanthus africanus 1629
Agapanthus orientalis
Aloe variegata
Amaryllis belladonna 1712
Aponogeton distachyus 1788
Asparagus densiflorus 1890
Asparagus setaceus 1876
Crassula falcata 1785
Crinum spp
Crocosmia spp 1846
Dierama spp
Dimorphotheca spp 1752
Erica gracilis 1774
Erica spp
Freesia spp 1816

PRETORIA
JOHANNESBURG
SWAZILAND

Zantedeschia aethiopica 1731
Strelitzia reginae c.1773
Plumbago capensis 1818
Pelargonium spp 1690

ORANGE

LESOTHO

DURBAN

Ornithogalum thyrsoides 1757
Nerine bowdenii 1889
Mesembryanthemum spp 1714
Lobelia erinus 1752
Kniphofia spp 1707

CAPE TOWN

Ixia spp 1757

PORT ELIZABETH

Galtonia candicans
Gazania spp 1755
Gladiolus spp 1756
Gerbera jamesonii 1887

Hermann 1672
Auge 1761
Thunberg 1772
Masson 1772
Boos and Scholl 1786
Niven 1798
Burchell 1810
Bowie 1816
Cooper 1859
Ingram 1927

Below Pelargoniums, endless species of *Erica* and varieties of bright daisies are among the characteristic Cape plants. For its size the Cape has contributed a high proportion of the most colourful garden flowers.

Erica gracilis

Pelargonium acetosum

Gazania pavonia

Florists that they are, the Dutch who made the Cape their land-fall on the way to the Indies in the seventeenth century must have been fascinated by its strange and brilliant flowers.

Cut off by equatorial Africa and the oceans from contact with other temperate lands, South Africa's plants have evolved in isolation. Although there are floristic links with distant western Australia and South America, the Cape has scores of plants that have no close relations elsewhere. Certainly the most famous is the pelargonium, popularly known as the geranium, but red-hot pokers, agapanthus, kaffir lilies, nerines, galtonias and freesias, crocosmias and dieramas and the startling daisies of gazanias, dimorphothecas, mesembryanthemums and arctotis are all unique to the Cape. The Cape is the world headquarters of the *Ericas*, the heaths: 470 out of 500 species are Cape natives. It is also famous for Proteas.

The coastal part of South Africa has a Mediterranean climate, with long seasonal droughts, and many of its plants retreat into bulbs for the summer. Others, such as pelargoniums, protect themselves with hairy leaves and aromatic oils.

The early Dutch, oddly enough, did little exploration or systematic exploitation of South Africa's plants. It was not until the botany boom of the eighteenth century, with Linnaeus conferring celebrity on plants and plant collectors alike, that the action really started. In 1772 Linnaeus's pupil Carl Peter Thunberg stayed at the Cape on his way to Japan. At the same time, Sir Joseph Banks at Kew sent out Francis Masson, who spend three years amassing more than five hundred new species. "The famous journey to the Levant made by Monsieur Tournefort . . . at enormous expense," wrote Banks, "did not produce so great an addition of plants to the Paris gardens as Mr Masson . . . has to those at Kew."

More plants from the New World

Above California poppy (*Eschscholzia californica*) was one of the many brilliant annuals introduced to gardens by David Douglas.

Above The evening primrose (*Oenothera missouriensis*) was found in 1811 by Nuttall and Bradbury while exploring the Missouri.

Above Many species of ceanothus, the blue-flowered evergreen that covers the coastal hills of California, are known collectively as California lilac.

Above David Douglas had the West almost to himself from 1825 to 1834. His introductions, especially conifers, changed the face of gardens.

Above Lewisia rediviva commemorates Captain Meriwether Lewis, who with William Clark made the first overland crossing to the West.

Above This scene greeted Douglas and the early botanists in the north-west: Douglas fir, redwood, red cedar and western hemlock.

The plains and mountain ranges west of the Mississippi are a barrier to plants as well as to people. When Captain George Vancouver sailed up the West Coast in 1792, and twelve years later Captain Meriwether Lewis and Lieutenant William Clark made the first continental crossing, they entered a whole new botanical realm.

Climatically western North America has more in common with Europe than the rest of North America: the north perpetually rainy, the central coast tempered by the famous fogs from the cold Pacific, the south so dry that it corresponds well enough to North Africa.

In the Ice Ages it was a sea-locked last resort where such species as the redwoods and the Monterey pine and cypress survived in isolated coastal groves. Behind the barrier of the Sierras the familiar plants of the rest of the continent have evolved their distinct West Coast forms: dogwoods, larches, rhododendrons, currants, lupins, penstemons, lilies, poppies, oaks . . . almost everything is different in the West.

Above all it is the world's great repository of conifers. David Douglas, sent from London by the Horticultural Society in 1825 to explore (and to become the most famous of all professional plant hunters) wrote home, "you will begin to think that I manufacture new pines at my pleasure". Such trees as the Douglas fir and Sitka spruce have revolutionized the forestry of the northern world as the hardy western cypresses have its gardens: the Lawson in its many forms is quasi-universal today.

Of uniquely western flowering plants the most influential have been the ceanothus, which covers the coastal hills with a blue mist in spring, perhaps the Oregon grape (*Mahonia aquifolium*), the garrya with its tassels, or the ground-covering *Gaultheria*. Certainly a whole host of annuals: California poppies, *Godetia, Clarkia, Nemophila, Phacelia, Limnanthes* . . . plants that can take instant advantage of rain at any time of year to begin their brief life-cycles.

Australia's plants began to be added to the catalogue in the closing years of the eighteenth century. It was no less a figure than Sir Joseph Banks himself, already at the age of twenty-five an eminent scientist, who sailed with Captain Cook in the *Endeavour* and in 1770 commemorated his excitement by christening his landfall Botany Bay.

The ancient island, so ancient that its very mountain ranges have been eroded away leaving a colossal plain, has developed a flora and fauna after its own fashion. Nowhere else do so few plant genera dominate the landscape. *Acacia* (or "wattles"), *Eucalyptus* and *Grevillea* make up a vast proportion of the total of trees and shrubs. *Eucalyptus* is unique on earth in its ecological diversity and dominance: the 500-odd species lord it over dry bush, rain-forest and snowy pass alike.

Australian flora has close links with South Africa, perhaps surprisingly considering the distance. The important *Protea* family, famous in South Africa for its spectacular flowers, has its headquarters in Australia with *Grevillea, Banksia, Hakea* and *Lomatia*. But few of these are familiar names to gardeners, and indeed Australian plants have generally been found difficult to cultivate in the temperate north.

The heroes of Australian botany were pioneers of the sort who are given to a John the Baptist regime. Most notable of a hardy company were Allan Cunningham, who scoured the bush for 15 years from 1817, and also visited New Zealand, and James Drummond, who explored south-western Australia for plants from the mid-1830s until his death, in 1863.

By then, flourishing botanical gardens, still some of the world's finest, had been established in each of the Australian colonies. More recently the hunt has been for hardier forms of the more desirable Australian plants in higher altitudes and in cooler Tasmania, to the south.

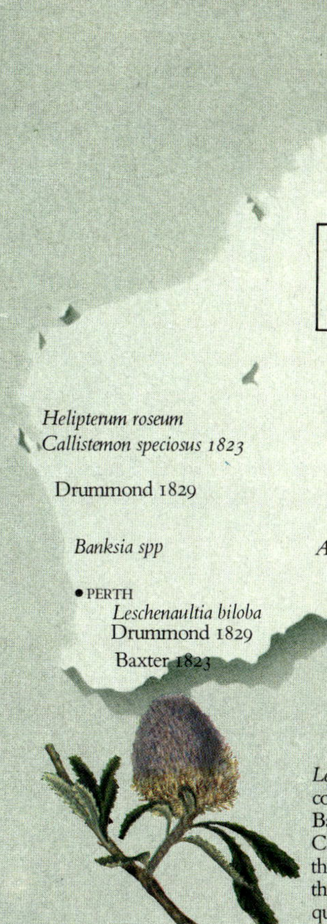

Left The banksias commemorate Sir Joseph Banks, who botanized with Captain Cook. Their family, the Proteas, have two-thirds of their number in Australia, one-quarter in South Africa and the rest in South America.

Left Wattles, or acacias, are almost as widespread as gum trees in Australia; particularly *Acacia armata*, the kangaroo thorn, which reached England in 1803.

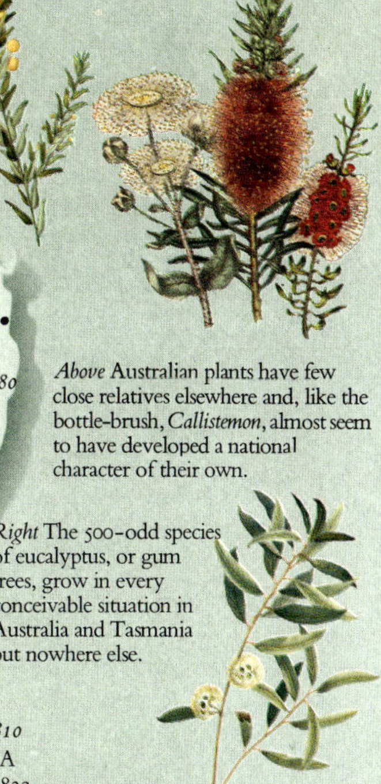

Above Australian plants have few close relatives elsewhere and, like the bottle-brush, *Callistemon*, almost seem to have developed a national character of their own.

Right The 500-odd species of eucalyptus, or gum trees, grow in every conceivable situation in Australia and Tasmania but nowhere else.

Above Alan Cunningham spent fifteen years from 1817 plant hunting in New South Wales. His brother Richard died on his first sortie in the bush in 1834.

Above James Drummond (1777–1863), pioneer of botanical exploration in Western Australia, spent nearly thirty years finding extraordinary plants.

PLANTS FROM NEW ZEALAND

New Zealand is even more of an enigma than Australia. A very high proportion of its plants are endemic, that is known nowhere else. What links it has are evidence of the land-bridge which must have joined Antarctica with New Zealand on one side and South America on the other. Before the Ice Ages such genera as *Nothofagus*, the southern beech, now found in Chile, Argentina and New Zealand, with a remnant population in Tasmania and south-east Australia, must have covered the Antarctic continent.

New Zealand's climate ranges from the subtropical in the north to the alpine and cool-temperate in the spectacular mountains and fiords of the south. It produces few garden plants of brilliant colouring, but a horde of quiet evergreens of subdued design which have made their mark in sophisticated modern gardening, in zones of no very hard or prolonged frost. *Hebe* and *Olearia* are the biggest groups, and *Senecio* perhaps the best known. Another is *Pittosporum*. Unfortunately the two splendid New Zealand conifers, *Agathis* and *Dacrydium*, like her tree ferns, are tender in most of Britain, but the very striking cordylines or cabbage trees and flax (*Phormium*) are first-class garden plants in zone 8. To alpine gardeners New Zealand is a treasury of plants of subtle beautv. including *Acaena*, *Celmisia*, *Parahebe* and *Raoulia*.

Below The many species of *Hebe*, almost all endemic to New Zealand, make excellent small garden evergreens. *H. colensoi* was discovered by William Colenso.

Left Olearias, or daisy bushes, are another New Zealand contribution to mild gardens. This is *O. macrodonta*.

Widespread in both islands

Acaena microphylla
Brachyglottis repanda 1890
Cassinia fulvida
Cordyline australis 1823
Corokia cotoneaster 1875
Griselinia littoralis 1872
Hebe elliptica 1776
Hymenanthera crassifolia 1875
Leptospermum scoparium 1772
Muehlenbeckia axillaris
Muehlenbeckia complexa 1842
Olearia macrodonta 1886
Parahebe catarractae
Phormium tenax 1789
Pimelea prostrata
Pittosporum tenuifolium 1789
Sophora microphylla 1772

Dieffenbach 1839
A. Cunningham 1826
R. Cunningham 1832
AUCKLAND
Bidwill 1839
NORTH ISLAND
Clianthus puniceus 1831
Hebe speciosa 1835
Senecio greyii
Olearia albida
Sophora tetraptera 1772
Colenso 1834
Dorrien-Smith 1909
WELLINGTON
Celmisia coriacea c.1880
Gentiana saxosa
Hebe salicifolia
Hoheria lyallii 1871
Olearia × haastii 1858
CHRISTCHURCH
Colenso 1834
SOUTH ISLAND
Carmichaelia enysii 1892
Clematis australis
Bidwill 1839
Cotula atrata
Sinclair 1841
Travers 1849
Hymenanthera alpina
Haast 1858
Wahlenbergia albomarginata 1881
DUNEDIN
Dorrien-Smith 1909

Above Missionary William Colenso, arriving in New Zealand in 1834, became an ardent collector remembered for many important introductions.

Above Captain A. Dorrien-Smith visited New Zealand in 1909 to collect plants for his famous sub-tropical garden at Tresco in the Scilly Isles.

Above New Zealand flax, *Phormium tenax*, has leaves like a giant iris which yield one of the finest fibres known.
Left Kowhai (*Sophora microphylla*) is one of the few plants native to both New Zealand and Chile. It must once have had pan-Antarctic distribution.

Asia: the jackpot

Before the Ice Ages the same plants were spread in a glorious mixture throughout the northern temperate world. It was the Ice Cap that edited them by degrees of hardiness, eliminating thousands of species from North America and even more from Europe. As the Ice Cap stayed much farther north over the Asian land mass than over the "western" side of the globe, China and Japan still have the descendants of almost the complete set, with local variations.

This vast treasure-house of plants remained unknown, apart from a few tantalizing glimpses, to Western gardeners until the last century. Chinese and Japanese gardeners had meanwhile been selecting and breeding the best garden plants for far longer than anyone in the West. At the same time intensive cultivation left no room for wild plants in the populous regions around the ports, so that what the first Western visitors to China and Japan saw was entirely a cultivated flora: their botanizing was done in nurseries.

In 1698 John Cuninghame, a surgeon with the East India Company, was first into China, where he bought plants and paintings of plants. The camellias he sent home were the first ever seen in Europe. Next, and more significant, were French missionaries, admitted on sufferance by the suspicious Chinese for their scientific skills. Father Pierre d'Incarville arrived in 1740 and stayed 15 years, sending back to London and Paris all the seed and information he could collect—enough, together with East India Company contacts, to start a craze for chinoiserie in all the decorative arts, including gardening.

Gardeners pestered the captains of merchant ships to bring home all they could for them from China: by this means the China roses reached the West. In 1804 William Kerr, an official plant collector from Kew, was sent out and the stream of plants increased. But China remained obstinately closed to foreign exploration of the interior until after the disgraceful episode of the Opium War in 1842, when she had no option but to let Europeans in. Thus in 1843 the exploration of inland China was begun by Robert Fortune.

Japan, not unwilling at first to talk to foreigners, had been quickly disillusioned by Western deceit and closed her doors to all but the Dutch, who were allowed a trading post at Nagasaki. Two doctors with the Dutch Company, Englebert Kaempfer in 1690 and Carl Thunberg in 1775, were until 1823 the only Western botanists to have seen her plants. As a result many Japanese plants bear their names.

From the 1840s the flow of new plants to Europe became a spate. The Himalayas turned out to be the centre of rhododendrons, providing hundreds of species from forests of unimagined richness and variety, thick with the primulas, poppies and lilies that were to revolutionize gardening. Inland China had more trees and shrubs to offer than any other corner of the globe. Japan had azaleas, maples, roses, magnolias, lilies and, of course, flowering cherries. At first this harvest was gathered in mainly by British and French collectors, later also by Americans.

One of the most famous collectors was E. H. "Chinese" Wilson, who worked in the early 1900s for Veitch's nursery in London and for the Arnold Arboretum of Boston, USA. Wilson alone introduced at least one thousand new plants to cultivation. At the same time other parts of western China (then a wild and dangerous country racked by civil war and infested with bandits) were being combed for plants by George Forrest, Reginald Farrer (who started the cult of the rock garden), Frank Kingdon-Ward, William Purdom, Frank Meyer and Joseph Rock.

Unfortunately, a large proportion of the great flood of Chinese plants has been lost to cultivation: there was simply too much at once. Nor was the ground completely covered. There remain regions of great promise on the borders of Tibet.

West China (chiefly Szechwan)

Berberis verruculosa 1903
Berberis wilsoniae 1903
Betula albo-sinensis 1901
Ceratostigma willmottianum 1908
Cotoneaster salicifolius 1908
Hamamelis mollis 1879
Hypericum patulum 1862
Jasminum polyanthum 1891
Lilium regale 1903
Kolkwitzia amabilis 1901
Rosa willmottiae 1904

Cornus alba sibirica 1741
Jasminum officinale 1548
Rheum rhabarbarum (rhaponticum) 1573

Bergenia cordifolia 1779
Bergenia crassifolia 1765
Rheum palmatum 1763

ULAN BATOR

David 1862

MONGOLIA

Farrer 1914

Paeonia lactiflora 1548

Clematis macropetala 1910
Buddleja alternifolia 1915

Jacquemont 1829

Throughout China

Juniperus chinensis 1804
Magnolia denudata 1789

KASHMIR

Amherst 1826

Wallich 1809

Kingdon-Ward 1914

Viburnum farreri
Rosa moyesii 1894
Euphorbia griffithii
Farrer 1914
Rock 1922
Potanin 1884
Gentiana farreri c.1915
Gentiana sino-ornata c.1910–
Incarvillea delavayi 1893
Delavay 1867
David 1862

HIMALAYA

Androsace sarmentosa 1876
Rhododendron spp
Betula utilis 1849

Fritillaria imperialis c.1590

TIBET

Betula jacquemontii 1880
Clematis montana 1831
Cotoneaster frigidus 1824
Cotoneaster microphylla 1824
Rhododendron spp

LHASA

Hooker 1847
Elwes 1870
Kingdon-Ward 1911
Cooper 1913

Cotoneaster conspicuus 1934
Forrest 1904
Rhododendron spp
Primula florindae 1926
Meconopsis betonicifolia 1924
Ludlow and Sherriff 1933

YA

SZECHWAN

CHUN

Farrer and Cox 1919
Wilson 1899
Kingdon-Ward 191

Magnolia campbellii 1868
Primula denticulata 1840
Aesculus indica 1851
Begonia rex 1858
SIKKIM
Cotoneaster simonsii 1865

NEPAL

Kingdon-Ward 1911

ASSAM
Hooker 1847
Leycesteria formosa 1824

MEKONG

Juniperus squamata c.1824

YUNNAN
Forrest 1904
Callistephus chinensis 173
Rock 1922

South-west China

Camellia reticulata 1820
Camellia saluenensis 1924
Clematis chrysocoma 1910
Pieris formosa 1858
Osmanthus delavayi 1890
Primula malacoides 1908
Rosa banksiae normalis 1796

The Himalayas, particularly at their Chinese end, are the world headquarters of the rhododendrons, with scores of species growing together. Some of the most important Himalayan species are:
Rhododendron arboreum (right)
R. augustinii 1918
R. calophytum 1903
R. discolor 1901
R. intricatum 1903
R. lutescens 1903
R. orbiculare 1903
R. sargentianum 1903
R. souliei 1903

Above Primulas abound in the Himalayas in the same conditions as rhododendrons: wet summers with sharp drainage.

Left The grandest of all hydrangeas was discovered in China by E. H. Wilson and named for C. S. Sargent.

Above The blue poppy, found by the French missionary J-M. Delavay in 1886, remained a legend until F. Kingdon-Ward brought home seed from Tibet in 1926.

Right Lady Amherst, wife of the Governor-General of India in the 1830s, introduced *Clematis montana* from Simla, north of Delhi.

Above The early-flowering *Kerria japonica* commemorates the first professional collector to live in China, William Kerr from Kew, from 1804 to 1812.

Maximowicz 1860
Meyer 1905

East China

Chaenomeles speciosa 1796
Forsythia suspensa fortunei 1833
Lilium tigrinum 1804
Rosa banksiae 1807

Weigela florida 1845

Astilbe chinensis 1892
Ailanthus altissima (glandulosa) c.1750
Potanin 1884
PEKING
d'Incarville 1740
NTSIN
Fortune 1843
David 1862
KOREA
ANG HO

Central China (chiefly Hupeh)

Acer griseum 1902
Actinidia chinensis 1900
Anemone hupehensis c.1844
Berberis candidula 1895
Chimonanthus praecox 1766
Cotoneaster dammeri 1900
Cotoneaster horizontalis 1879
Cotoneaster lactea 1913
Davidia involucrata 1905
Hydrangea sargentiana 1908
Macleaya microcarpa 1896
Primula obconica 1880
Trachycarpus fortunei 1844

Gardenia florida 1754
NANKING
Ginkgo biloba 1727
Jasminum nudiflorum c.1830
Fortune 1843
SHANGHAI
Mahonia japonica
Mahonia bealei c.1850
Buddleja davidii 1896
on 1899
ry 1881
Kerria japonica 1834
Lonicera nitida 1908
Cuninghame 1698
Fortune 1843
David 1862
Henry 1881
Trachycarpus fortunei 1844
James Main 1792
Kerr 1804
Fortune 1843

Above The first plant collector to see inland China was Robert Fortune, sent by the Horticultural Society in 1843. Later he took tea to India.

Above The Japanese anemone of autumn, *A. hupehensis*, was one of the treasures brought from China in 1844 by Robert Fortune, with *Forsythia*, winter jasmine and the snowball tree.

Above Sir Joseph Hooker holds court in Nepal in 1849. Collecting looks luxurious: the reality was strenuous.

Above The first Chinese plants known in the West were from gardens, including many forms of *Camellia japonica* (brought to Portugal at an unknown date before 1600).

Above The catalogue of Veitch's nurseries in 1907. E.H. Wilson had sent a flood of superlative new plants.

Above Charles Sprague Sargent, founder of the Arnold Arboretum, USA, travelled in northern Japan in 1892 to collect flowering cherries and crab apples

Above The botanic garden of St Petersburg under Carl Maximowicz was the great centre for the study of Japanese and Siberian plants in the 1860s.

Above Engelbert Kaempfer, after whom many Japanese plants are named, was the first European botanist there in 1690.

Left The most sumptuous of all irises, the water-loving *Iris kaempferi*, is an old Japanese garden plant, developed in Tokyo from the seventeenth century and before.

Right Chrysanthemums, which, like most plants introduced from Japan, have been cultivated there for centuries and developed into innumerable forms, were introduced to Japan from China in about AD 800.

SAKHALIN (USSR)

Prunus sargentii 1893

Sakhalin, Hokkaido, Honshu, Shikoku, Kyushu

Anemone hupehensis c.1844
Dicentra spectabilis 1816
Hydrangea petiolaris 1878
Magnolia liliflora 1790
Prunus serrulata 1822

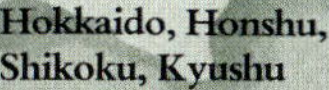

Above The hostas, or plantain lilies, are natives of Japan, where many garden forms, including exquisite variegated miniatures, are treasured.

Above Japanese garden maples were introduced to Europe about 1815 through the Dutch trading post in Nagasaki harbour.

Maries 1877
Sargent 1892
J.H. Veitch 1892
Prunus sargentii 1893
HOKKAIDO
Acer japonicum 1864
SAPPORO
Maximowicz 1860

Hokkaido, Honshu, Shikoku, Kyushu

Acer palmatum 1820 (not Kyushu)
Euonymus japonicus 1804
Euonymus fortunei 1860
Hamamelis japonica 1862
Hemerocallis fulva 1576
Hydrangea macrophylla 1790
Iris kaempferi 1857 (not Shikoku)
Parthenocissus tricuspidata 1862
Rhododendron kaempferi 1878
Spiraea japonica 1870

Left Sargent's cherry, native of northern Japan (see C. S. Sargent, above), is one of the earliest in flower and colours fiery red in early autumn.

HONSHU

Prunus sargentii 1893
Acer japonicum 1864
Hosta sieboldiana 1829
Kaempfer 1690
Thunberg 1775
Siebold 1823
J.G. Veitch 1860
TOKYO
Fortune 1860
Maximowicz 1860
Lilium auratum 1862
Magnolia stellata 1877
Malus floribunda 1862
Prunus incisa 1913
J.H. Veitch 1892
Sargent 1892
OSAKA
Lilium speciosum 1832
Wilson 1914
KITAKYUSHU
SHIKOKU
Lilium speciosum 1832
Lilium longiflorum 1862
Prunus mume 1878
Kaempfer 1690
Thunberg 1775
Maximowicz 1860
Oldham 1861
Ingram 1926
KYUSHU

Honshu, Shikoku, Kyushu

Acer rufinerve c.1859
Arundinaria japonica 1850
Aucuba japonica 1783
Berberis thunbergii 1883
Camellia japonica 1739
Chaenomeles japonica 1869
Cornus kousa 1875
Cryptomeria japonica 1842
Elaeagnus macrophylla 1879
Elaeagnus pungens 1830
Fatsia japonica 1838
Ligustrum ovalifolium 1842
Rosa wichuraiana 1891
Skimmia japonica 1838
Wisteria floribunda 1830

A garden place for every plant

Considering the vast differences between their origins it is remarkable how many plants have settled down to a quiet suburban life: North American with South African; Chinese with Chilean; plants whose natural habitats are as unalike as the dry veldt and a water-meadow are found growing side by side in gardens.

Today we can look up any plant we are ever likely to encounter and discover its potential size, its habit of growth, its taste in soil and temperature, and in most cases its conventional or habitual place, if any, in gardens. Yet as each new discovery was added to the catalogue, from the first Turkish tulips to the early eastern American trees to the latest alpines from New Zealand, it has been planted by tentative gardeners, not knowing whether they were handling a fragile gem or had a potential menace on their hands, in this soil and that and in various situations of sun and shade. Many plants never survived their first encounter with cultivation. The ones with the best chances were those accompanied by field notes from their discoverers, saying whether they were found clinging to cliffs or buried in forests, at what altitude, with what rainfall, in what depth of what kind of soil.

Until the latter half of the eighteenth century garden designers were extremely conservative about plants, using only those that had been known for centuries. To collect plants was another matter—certainly nothing to do with garden design. The English landskip school (pages 226–7) was particularly austere; curiously enough at the very moment when the passion for new discoveries and the pressure to find garden places for them was rising to a peak.

As we shall see, the austerity of the original designs was usually short-lived; they soon began to accumulate irresistible curiosities. Within the first thirty years of the nineteenth century the sifting of the great stream of novelties was well under way. As new plants came into cultivation they began to be assigned to their places in gardens that were becoming more and more like a microcosm of the natural world.

Field and meadow plants were accumulated in herbaceous borders; rockeries were built, at first for ferns and then for alpines; bog plants were packed off to pond gardens. The rose garden came into being to accommodate the many new kinds of rose. "American" gardens were filled with rhododendrons and azaleas, shrubberies with shrubs and arboreta with trees, while patterned bedding was devised as a way of displaying outdoors all the tender plants that could not pass the whole of their lives in the garden.

This section of the book is a review of these horticultural niches, which have now become the backbone of all gardeners' references to plants, supplemented in some cases by the forms they take—bulbs or tubers for example; or their natural habit, as in the case of climbers.

The modern tendency, however, is to abandon the segregation which the nineteenth century introduced and to treat plants on the basis of common needs, putting all the peat-loving plants together in a damp shady corner, or massing Mediterranean-climate plants in beds of gravel where they can sizzle to their hearts' content. This is certainly the most satisfactory way for gardeners whose concern is concentrating on the plants themselves. The alternative, which is perhaps the most ambitious of all ways of gardening, is picture-making in terms of design and texture and colour alone, drawing on the whole plant repertoire—an awe-inspiring undertaking, but the way in which the great English gardens of this century have been made.

The "wild" garden at Kastel Twickel in Holland is a supreme example of the assembly of plants from different countries and climates to form a coherent picture with a sort of dream-like naturalness.

Trees in gardens

Above Trees as a backdrop. The luxuriant drapery of a weeping willow transforms a pleasant but unremarkable garden into a stage set with dramatic potential. The obvious attractions of these obliging trees often prove too tempting; they spread too fast for small gardens.

Below Trees as a *corps de ballet*. A chequered planting of standard mophead false acacias (*Robinia pseudoacacia* 'Inermis') seen through stems of London planes at the Hotel Pompadour, Fontainbleau. The false perspective is heightened by the shaded foreground.

Trees are the most prominent and the most permanent plants in any landscape. Whatever else you may plant or build, trees determine the scale. Their roots, their shelter and their shade dictate the conditions that other plants have to suffer. Their textures and colours and tracery form the background to your compositions. Their domes and spires create the skyline.

For anyone fortunate to garden in old woodland there can be no compromise. The trees tell you what sort of garden you have. The only way to success is to recognize the character they impose and take advantage of it, stressing its cool beechiness or wild pininess, either by complement or contrast, in everything you plant.

But the more common situation is a jumble of trees of no particular persuasion, some inside the garden, some (just as important) next door or in the street. Some perhaps perfect for their place, others wildly unsuitable; greedy, messy or just plain ugly.

We tend to accept trees because they are there, and because they take so long (we think) to grow. Yet a tree should have a reason for being there as much as any other plant. Furthermore it should, and can, be the right tree. For the range is almost infinite—in size, shape, colour, texture of leaf, interest of form, speed of growth, time of flowering. If we consider only one of these aspects—usually it is either speed of growth or flowers that is given priority—there may well be a catch in store. The fastest trees nearly always have the greediest, farthest-ranging roots. The most lavish-flowering are frequently dull as ditch-water once their three-week performance is over.

The trick in choosing trees is first to consider what role they have to play, and secondly how many virtues and how few vices we can combine in the plant that is going to loom so large for so long on our horizon.

It applies to existing trees as well as new ones. There is no garden where an ugly and unnecessary tree must stay. Only take time to consider: is it always ugly, and always unnecessary? You must watch it carefully for four seasons before you can answer that. The common alder receives little praise in summer, but in winter its dense clutter of cones and catkins catching the low sun is a major pleasure. The common maple may be considered a bore in spring but ends the year with a lingering glow of gold.

It helps to consider the necessity or otherwise of trees if we enumerate the possible jobs they can do for the gardener. We can codify them as the seven S's of (if you must) silviculture.

Shelter is the first and perhaps the most essential for the sake of the rest of the garden. The power of the wind to reduce the efficiency and performance of plants (see page 17) is something the gardener must always bear in mind. In a small garden hedges or shrubs may be all there is room for in the way of shelter, but a big garden needs big trees to windward, even at the expense of a view. If the view is so wonderful that it draws all eyes out of the garden it may be better to dispense with the distraction of foreground planting altogether—and hence with the need for trees to shelter it.

In far more cases some kind of compromise is possible, with an oblique glimpse through sheltering trees. But it is a mistake to take off the lower branches of trees on the windy side so as to be able to see under them: the wind, baffled by their tops, will come through between the trunks faster than ever. If on the contrary the view is spoiled by an eyesore, near or far, a quick-growing tree is the only practicable way to blot it out. The rule to remember here is that the screen near the eye hides more than the screen near the object. A mere bush by the window or on the terrace will be as effective as an oak on the boundary—at least locally, and while your main screen grows.

Seclusion is perhaps the strongest psychological effect trees have to offer. A sense of privacy is not everyone's first thought in planning a garden. Americans seem to get on very well without it in those suburbs where all the houses are set in one big lawn. Yet privacy is a strong feeling in most European countries. To me it is essential not to be seen taking my pleasure among the flowers, or grunting over the potatoes.

Seclusion means more than just privacy. It means the indefinable sense of enclosure and security that a garden should give. Wide skies are stimulating and invoke adventurous feelings; the reverse of the garden spirit of timeless calm. It is an old axiom of gardening that the centre should be kept open—in order that the sides should be seen to be encircling.

The role of trees here is to limit the amount of sky you see by creating the third S, the skyline. It is the strongest line in the whole landscape, yet one which is generally ignored, and very rarely consciously composed. Its dominance is obvious, however, once you become aware of it. The best time to look at the skyline is as the light fades and details blur on a clear evening. The light sky is a definite shape above the dark masses of buildings and trees. Is it a pleasing, interesting shape or monotonous or unbalanced? If there is a pond in the picture the skyline has an added importance, appearing upside down as well. Look at it in the pond. Mirrors always show a fresh aspect of what they reflect.

Shade is a more practical reason for planting, or not planting, trees, according to whether your summers are torrid or temperate. In North America it is probably the single most important factor—witness the fact that the professional amenity tree association is called the Shade Tree Conference.

There are heavy shade trees such as sycamore and horse chestnut, and light-dappling ones such as birch, willow or eucalyptus. The choice of public planners is often a late-leafing tree such as the plane, *Robinia* or *Gleditsia*, whose shade develops late and lasts only for the hottest months.

An exact calculation of where and when the shade of a particular tree falls can be helpful. The diagrams on page 16 that map the movement of the sun in the sky show that, for example, a tree to the southwest gives most shade to a house during the hottest hours of summer.

The sense of scale in a garden is influenced by trees more than any other single factor. The pictures to left and right show just how much. On the left the contrast between tall foreground and miniature background trees gives a powerful perspective to the view: the miniatures seem a whole landscape away. To the right the mounting layers of crown on crown surmounted by the distant giant elm have the effect of telescoping distance and miniaturizing the house in the foreground. The Japanese are specialists in false perspective. By isolating a stunted pine on a rocky outcrop they manage to convey the idea of boundless space in a mere courtyard.

Consciously or not, deliberately or not, the trees give a garden its basic divisions of volume: its structure. Where they are all deciduous the structure can disintegrate at leaf-fall—the great argument for including a proportion of evergreens in the basic shape-giving planting.

All this is strategy: the use of trees for what they can contribute as the biggest plants in the garden. Most important of all, of course, is the value to the senses of the tree itself, as sculpture to be admired for its own sake.

Above Fastigiate trees such as these Lombardy poplars or Italian cypresses are, as Russell Page has said, like trumps at bridge. Here the reflection doubles their tremendous verticality.

Below The perspective effect of the picture opposite is reversed in this view at Saling Hall, Essex. The repetitive crowns of the apple tree in the foreground, then the walnut, the Scots pine and finally the towering elm telescope the distance.

The characters of garden trees

Below It is remarkable how many of our best small trees we owe to Japan. Sargent's cherry is an ideal tree for a small garden: one of the first cherries to flower, in clear pale pink, and reliable in turning to fiery colours in early autumn. It is always one of the first trees to change colour.

Trees must be functional: their share of garden space demands it. Their function also dictates whether you choose tall-growing forest trees or orchard-size flowering trees, dense smothering agglomerations of green (or evergreen) or airy balletic structures of much limb and little leaf.

I find it useful to categorize the characters of trees under half a dozen general headings. First I divide the deciduous from the evergreen. Then those whose main season of attraction is spring from those which do their thing in autumn—leaving in a special class of their own those which have two worthwhile performances (or indeed are lovely year in, year out).

In small gardens one annual performance is not enough. However many pink petals some of the cherries and ornamental crabs rain down in spring their leaden leaves for the rest of the year condemn them, unless, like *Prunus sargentii*, they produce an autumn blaze, or like *Malus* 'Golden Hornet' they hold heavy crops of glowing fruit far into winter.

The small or medium-sized trees that get on this exclusive list include most of the birches, whose elegant architecture and fascinating bark are as effective in winter as summer; several of the hawthorns, but particularly *Crataegus* × *lavallei*, which flowers as lavishly as an elder and holds its gleaming leaves as long as its glistening berries; the amelanchiers, for their delicate flowering as the new leaves open and their bonfire orange in October; the medlar, for wide white flowers and a strange medley of autumn colours; several *Sorbus* species, but specially *hupehensis*, pale grey all summer and yellow with white berries in fall; flowering dogwoods for all the qualities; the golden acacia, *Robinia pseudoacacia* 'Frisia', for sustained substitute sunshine; the weeping willow for every quality except moderation and some little willows for pretty leaves, brilliant bark, and furry catkins in the dead of winter; a number of maples for lovely leaves at all times and unparallelled fieriness before they fall; and magnolias, not just for their wonderful waxen flowers but for the air of aristocracy that never leaves them. It is a crime to stop: the pear tree should be on the list; the Italian alder, the quince, the sumach, the catalpa. . . .

There are situations where the one thing that counts is speed. Every tree has its characteristic growth curve, given reasonable conditions for growth. Some that start out like hares end as tortoises; others that dawdle for their first years suddenly startle their proprietors by putting on a yard a year.

Wherever eucalyptus will grow they are champions for instant and sustained speed. A cider gum grew twenty feet in two years in my garden. Again for mild climates the two conifer relics of the Monterey peninsula in California, the Monterey cypress and pine, are both alarmingly fast—a Monterey pine, in fact, once grew twenty feet in one year (its fifth) in New Zealand. The nearest equivalent evergreen for cold climates is the Leyland cypress, which should manage ten feet in three years. Among hardy deciduous trees it is poplars and willows that hold the records: seventy feet in fifteen years is fair for a black poplar, the same height in twelve years for a white willow. Other trees with remarkable growth rates, depending on local conditions, include the wingnut, *Pterocarya*, the silver maple, *Acer saccharum*, and the southern beech, *Nothofagus obliqua*.

It would be right, however, to label these trees (at least the big poplars and willows) For Emergency Use Only as far as most gardeners are concerned. There comes the moment when they dominate the whole scene and reach their roots into every corner of the garden. Dismantling them can be extremely expensive.

The rule should be to plant the fastest trees only when necessary, and always to plant the tree you really want in the long term at the same time. Although what I call the three-year rule (for three years not much happens) applies to most trees and many shrubs, even oaks, reputedly so laggard, make long enough shoots to give you immense satisfaction when the three years are up.

The categories continue, to help you in your choice, with the overall shapes of trees, distinguishing those that are cloud-like in maturity (the oak, the sycamore) from those that tower (the elm, the lime); those than fan out with several stems (Japanese maples, magnolias) from those that throw out a few important branches from a single stout trunk (old pines, for example, and cedars); those with regular whorls of branches (poplars, alders, most conifers) from those with many unimportant little branches that stay close to the stem (cypresses, and fastigiate trees such as the Lombardy poplar); weeping trees—there are many besides the willow—from rigid spires such as young spruces and firs.

Some are right for one garden job; some for another. Lightly engineered trees or those with dramatic silhouettes are right for the foreground, framing the view beyond. Solidly billowing ones end the view. Birches, Japanese maples, pines, cypresses and olives are the kinds of tree to plant near the eye; oaks, beeches and yews to keep for the bottom of the garden.

In every department of gardening there is a tug of war between variety and unity. With trees it is most obvious. Let us say you have room for six small trees in your garden. The temptation is to collect the six most startlingly different—one gold, one silver, one purple, one pointed, one with leaves like dinner plates, and one with dazzling autumn colour. I will not suppose you could not compose them to great effect, along with your roses, your rhododendrons, your herbs and your delphiniums. But it would be a restless, unfulfilled effect—a furniture showroom, not a furnished room. Plant it now with six similar, if not identical, trees: six fruit trees, for example, or any six with the same general colour and bearing. The suggestion of an orchard is immediately reassuring. The room is furnished to a purpose, not just to display its wares.

Left America's flowering dogwoods combine all the virtues of a long and lovely flowering season, fine autumn colour and usually a graceful stance. But their needs are fairly specific. The combination of acid soil and continental climate which brings out their best performance is not found in Western Europe.

Magnolias have the most individually splendid flowers of any trees. The showiest are those that flower before the leaves emerge, such as *Magnolia stellata*, *left*, and the pink or white *M. soulangeana*, *below*. They have an air of distinction at all times of year whether in bare structure or in leaf.

Left The Japanese flowering cherries provide the most exquisite tree-pictures of spring. The early-flowering and scented Yoshino cherry, *Prunus yedoensis* that makes graceful arching little trees, is a favourite in Japan. An evergreen background makes all the difference to the impact of such early flowers.

Above The Japanese maples are more particular than cherries about soil and site, thriving best in deep slightly acid leafy soil. But they combine first-class structure and texture better than any other trees, and the best forms, such as this 'Osakazuki', provide some of the most brilliant reds in autumn.

Right The birches declare their identity by the range of their bark colours. The finest is the rare Himalayan *Betula jacquemontii*, which has a creamy-white bloomy texture. Others are golden (*B. lutea*), coppery-pink (*B. albo-sinensis*), brown and crackling (*B. nigra*) or white like the silver birch shown here.

Evergreens: winter furnishing

Below The oldest and the newest of garden evergreens: the black-green of a yew tree demonstrates its value as a foil for spring blossom. On the left a young cider gum (*Eucalyptus gunnii*) is already a substantial tree. Several species of eucalyptus are proving hardy in southern and western Britain.

Above Evergreen interest is important at ground level, too. Leaves of cyclamen in January among rocks under the golden *Elaeagnus pungens*.

Above The masterly use of evergreens to provide a formal garden stage for the performance of the seasons. At the Johns Hopkins Hospital, Baltimore, sprawling old boxwood hedges emphasize the lake-like level of the lawn, while cypresses lead the eye into intriguing woods. Four urns and a pair of flowering dogwoods are superbly dramatized in their evergreen setting.

Left Evergreens as a natural maquis-like mass on a rock bank at Wakehurst Place, the Royal Botanic Gardens in Sussex. They include azaleas and tree heaths.

Below Small-leaved evergreens such as box invite the ancient art of topiary—at its best abstract but disciplined.

Left The loquat (*Eriobotrya japonica*) is perhaps the hardiest tree (to zone 7) that gives the tropical look of huge evergreen leaves. Other possibilities are *Magnolia grandiflora* and in suitable conditions some of the giant-leaved Himalayan rhododendrons.

Of all the things that far-northern gardeners might envy in a garden in a more balmy climate the most valuable are surely the broadleaved evergreen trees, shrubs and even the lowlier plants that look alive all winter.

In a bare winter garden the cheerful shine of a laurel leaf or the benevolent bulk of an old box bush are pleasures as great as any flowers. They stabilize the garden. They furnish its draughty spaces. They reassure us that spring will bring back the leafy enclosures.

In a Mediterranean climate this scarcely calls for comment. It is the normal regime of many plants to hang on to their leaves all winter, and let them go as the new ones come in spring. By being dressed all year they are theoretically in a position to grow whenever the ground has moisture enough. The risk they take is that a hard frost and a nasty wind will sere them instead. Very rarely is the damage more than temporary.

There are conifers with tough little needle-leaves that can take the same gamble in the far north. A covering of snow usually protects them from the worst of the winter. But broadleaved evergreens are much more vulnerable. Even those whose cells can withstand freezing and thawing are in trouble. Snow can help them (though it can also break their branches), but bare to the icy blast, their metabolism in a frigid trance, their leaves become dehydrated. They emerge into spring at best disfigured, at worst dead.

The Ice Ages put paid to whatever evergreens there may have been in Britain up to that time, leaving only (as native) the holly (which is odd, since English holly is not all that hardy), the ivy and juniper and yew.

The history of gardening in northern Europe, and the northern United States, since the seventeenth century has been a history of slowly bringing them back to their pre-Ice Age range—at first gingerly, protecting everything "green", as they were called, in greenhouses—then with more confidence; now with a fairly comprehensive knowledge of their tolerance for cold, which is far more than our ancestors believed possible.

The great advance in knowledge has been the realization that wind and sun are as much the enemies as very low temperatures. By providing shelter and shade the northern limits of many evergreens can be pushed back surprisingly far. A few years ago the notoriously windy city of Chicago could hardly boast a single evergreen beyond a few unhappy-looking rhododendrons—the northern species such as *Rhododendron catawbiense* and *R. maximum*, which have earned the often-used epithet of "iron-clad". Now after trials at the Morton Arboretum the list of evergreens for zone 5 is growing.

The battle-proven kinds include *Euonymus fortunei*, a low shrub with the useful capacity to climb walls, particularly north walls; English ivy; American holly (which unfortunately lacks the lustre of English holly); Oregon grape, *Mahonia aquifolium*, which does have a good gleaming leaf; *Pieris* (both *P. japonica* and *P. floribunda*, with their respectively drooping and erect creamy flowers in spring); drooping *Leucothoe*, which has something of the stance of a short bamboo; the little-leaf boxwood (very slow and low); even, apparently, a form of the evergreen magnolia of the South. Probably the best all-round garden plant on the list is mountain laurel, *Kalmia latifolia*. If *Kalmia* came from the Canary Islands we would heat greenhouses for it.

Life is easier for any evergreen if snow falls early and deep, but those mentioned above have managed without it, given soil to their liking (which is on the whole light and acid), good drainage, shelter on the side of the prevailing winter wind, and preferably the shade of pines overhead. These are the considerations that should govern their placing in a cold garden.

Even among this limited range there is room for some interesting combinations; of dull leaves with shiny leaves; of upright forms with spreading forms. True while they are covered with snow it makes little difference whether they have leaves or not, but as soon as it melts they furnish a background to the first flowers of the year.

In milder climates the list of evergreens in general use is a pusillanimous nibble at the range of possibilities. The bigger rhododendrons are the mainstay of many winter landscapes, but none are at their best in winter. They seem to fill their space with patient gloom.

Leaving flowers aside and concentrating on what leaves can contribute to the garden in winter, the many variegated hollies and several forms of elaeagnus have glints of gold and silver. Nothing in the garden shines brighter in winter than *Elaeagnus pungens* 'Maculata'—unless it be the monarch of the female hollies, 'Golden King' (*sic*), which combines scarlet fruit with dashing yellow-edged leaves.

Both the cherry laurel and the Portugal laurel have polished leaves (the first bigger and brighter green). Aucubas lost their good name when their yellow-spotted leaves were flaunted in every Edwardian front garden—but there must be some exciting way of using this most singular plant. Skimmias are excellent for dense and interesting dark shapes, growing eventually as high as a man, garnished, for the fortunate at least, with red marbles. Pyracantha and some of the cotoneasters are rose-relations profuse in their fruiting as well as useful for their winter green. There are evergreen viburnums and berberis, arbutus and escallonia, cistus and brooms—in fact it seems as many evergreen as there are deciduous shrubs.

To these we must now add an increasing range of Australasian evergreens, which are turning out to be tougher than anyone expected. Experiments with eucalyptus show that at least half a dozen forms from colder corners of Australia can be trusted in zone 8. To have big, fast-growing, broadleaved evergreen trees is a revolution: holm oak, virtually the sole candidate before, is maddeningly leisurely.

Above Of several evergreens that win their laurels in spring *Pieris* is the loveliest: its new shoots, bright red in such selected forms as 'Forest Flame', appear with its white lily-of-the-valley flowers. The Japanese use photinias for similar effects, clipping them over to ensure an even flush of coppery leaves.

Above The varieties of English, American and Japanese hollies are innumerable, but it is English holly that produces almost every combination of gold, silver and green, spreading or weeping.

Right The New Zealand hebes are a varied race with all the qualities of good evergreens, but like most New Zealand plants are accustomed to mild winters. *Hebe rakaiensis*, one of the hardiest, is not unlike box, compact and always a cheerful green, with the addition of short spikes of white flowers in summer.

Far right The golden oval-leaved privet (known as California privet in the USA; it comes from Japan) is evergreen in mild winters but loses its leaves in severe cold—a useful mode of self-defence. Gentle use of the shears in summer gives it a solid sculptural quality.

Conifers

As the great forest trees of the northern world, holding all the records as far and away the tallest and oldest vegetables alive (367 feet and 4,900 years respectively), conifers may not seem cut out for gardens. But they have certain advantages over the equivalent full-scale broadleaves. Neither their branches nor their roots spread so far in maturity. Their leaf-fall is of no consequence, but can be left where it lies as an instant mulch, and most of them come into their own in winter.

They are the only big evergreens for very cold gardens. But in any garden they are some of the strongest creators of atmosphere, conveying a sense of changeless calm, gently scenting the air with resin. Few offer any real beauty, but all offer character, and each has its moment of glory, either in its bright bold new shoots, its surprisingly scarlet flowers, or its richly detailed cones.

As far as gardeners are concerned the big conifers in their early life can be easily classed as either spires or columns. The cypresses, false cypresses, thuyas, incense cedars and all trees with frond-like foliage fall broadly into the column category. Most of the rest, with a few exceptions, start life in Christmas-tree style, developing their strongly characteristic shapes only after thirty years or more.

The spruces and the silver firs go on as unrepentant Christmas trees all their days. Their most gardenworthy members are the Colorado blue spruce for its icy colour, Brewer's weeping spruce for its mourning veil of near-black and the Korean fir for its heavy crop of purple cones while it is still below eye-level.

Pines are much harder to choose. In habit the pines billow out, forgetting their upright youth and striking fierce poses as they grow older. They vary vastly from the droopy long-leaved white pines to some of those from California with huge bristling brushes of stiff needles, from the intricate curly green-and-blue needlework of the Japanese *Pinus parviflora* 'Glauca' to the heavy bottle-green foliage of the Monterey pine. Finally, common though it is, it is hard to beat the combination of steely blue needles, salmon-orange bark and the wild highland poise of the Scots pine.

Cedars, and their leaf-losing cousins the larches, grow beamy with age. It takes a hundred years for the cedar of Lebanon to form its famous plateaux in the sky, but the blue Atlantic cedar, the most popular of all conifers by all accounts, starts demanding elbow-room much sooner and will eventually overwhelm a small garden. The deodar, its more relaxed-looking brother from the Himalayas, is potentially no less of a cuckoo in the nest.

A larch is perhaps too humdrum a choice, but there is one deciduous conifer I cannot overpraise—the swamp cypress. It does not demand a swamp, but in any decent soil will form a narrow tower of fine fresh green all summer, turning in autumn to a dark squirrel brown for weeks on end. The recently discovered Metasequoia grows faster and is similar in many ways, but in colour, texture and floppy habit it is not so good.

The more conventional evergreen relations of these two are the Japanese *Cryptomeria* and the California redwoods, none of them garden trees in the usual sense. However, the *Cryptomeria* has a form, 'Elegantissima', with soft curly foliage which turns a unique reddy-purple in winter; a strange tree which, when it reaches a certain height, falls over and lives recumbent.

The attraction of the cypresses is principally as background material of rich texture and many colours. But they also have the merit of simple form, making them perfect exclamation marks when they are placed apart. For a rapid and reliable screen of rather dull matt green the Leyland cypress (× *Cupressocyparis*, a hybrid between *Cupressus* the true cypress and *Chamaecyparis* the false one) has no rival. The biggest Leylands have grown to 100 feet in 50 years and kept a perfect flame shape, green from the ground up. Fifty years hence, when all the millions recently planted are full-grown, Britain will be unrecognizable.

Happily for gardeners the false cypresses have produced more "sports" than any other trees. These wayward seedlings are our main source of coloured evergreens. There is a roster of a hundred or more of varying colour, size, texture and form—all well worth serious study. The blue-greys are at their best in summer; in winter they can look merely drab and cold. The Lawson cypresses 'Columnaris Glauca' and 'Triomf van Boskoop' (the latter much bigger and broader) are two of the best blues. The brightest yellows, much more telling in winter and fairly radiant in summer, are the Lawsons 'Aurea Smithii', 'Lanei' and 'Stewartii'. *Cupressus macrocarpa* 'Donard's Gold' is even better, but can be damaged by cold winters.

Above The quintessence of pine. A superbly trained Japanese black pine in a Kyoto monastery. It is hard to know whether the pine is imitating the eaves or the eaves the pine.

Left Juniper and yew are two conifers that have what appear to be berries instead of cones. The fine foliage of the bushy *Juniperus communis* is full of subtle shadings of colour. It was one of Gertrude Jekyll's favourite trees. Yews and junipers are unusual among conifers; each tree is either male or female.

Left The silver firs (*Abies*) have some of the prettiest cones, usually grey-purple (this species is *A. koreana*), plump and always upright. They fall to pieces on the tree. Spruce cones hang down and fall off in one piece.

Above The narrowest of spires and one of the most effective of the spruces is the Serbian spruce (*Picea omorika*). It grows on dry limestone in Serbia. A hardy, handsome and adaptable tree.

Left This unique forest of garden forms of the false cypress is at the British National Pinetum at Bedgebury, Kent. They create an unreal, dream-like atmosphere in their sheltered valley beside a murmuring stream.

DWARF CONIFERS

Conifers are particularly prone to what nurserymen call "sporting"—producing freak growth, either as ugly ducklings in the seed bed or as witches' brooms—outbreaks of congested or deformed growth on the branches of normal trees.
If these sports can be persuaded to grow and can be propagated they provide a whole new range of miniature plants in shapes, textures and colours never seen before.

True dwarf conifers are some of the slowest-growing plants and can live happily in a pot for twenty years—but there is no clear dividing line, and many advertised as "dwarf" are no such thing.

It takes restraint to use pygmy plants effectively in the garden. They must be segregated into a world of their own. They have become part of a whole new gardening idiom in conjunction with beds of low heathers (see pages 148–9). Rock as a background is also suitably neutral in scale: they are gaining ground in many rockeries (often at the expense of more interesting but more temperamental plants).

The identities of dwarf conifers is a study in itself. Many were christened by their captors in a form of pseudo-Latin even worse than the botanical variety—though today the code permits only vernacular names.

It is impossible to choose from such a gallimaufry, but the most popular dwarfs include miniature bush spruces, ground-hugging junipers, congested weeping hemlocks, tiny globular thuyas, shrunk cedars, deformed *Cryptomeria* and, above all, endless variations on the already endlessly various false cypresses. *Chamaecyparis* is the big name among dwarfs. The plants in the picture are front left *Thuja plicata* 'Rogersii'; centre left *Thuja orientalis* 'Semperaurea'; top left *Juniperus chinensis* 'Armstrongii'; centre right *Thuja orientalis* 'Minima'.

Hedges

Above Williamsburg, Virginia, is famous for its hedges, particularly of the American favourite, boxwood or box. They fill every role from tall barriers to playful patterns, giving the sense of order and control which the seventeenth century demanded from gardens.

Right The yew hedges at Crathes Castle, near Aberdeen, Scotland, are 300 years old. With age yew creates a unique architecture of its own, at the same time impressive and slightly comical. Its soft shapes and sombre yet subtle colouring make it the perfect foil for other plants; the ideal background for bright flowers in a border.

In the twin roles of dividers of space and protectors of gardens, walls have traditionally been the functional choice, hedges the ornamental one. Walls encircled the outer boundaries of great estates, and supported the fruit trees in the kitchen garden. But in the pleasure grounds, as a setting for fine trees and flowers and sculpture, the ideal for centuries has been close-clipped evergreens—box, yew, holly, holm oak or cypress. Today the price of walls makes hedges the almost inevitable choice.

We have seen the virtue of hedges as shelter from the wind; how effective they are in speeding the growth of the plants they protect (pages 16–17). We will turn later (pages 172–3) to the merits of dividing the garden space to give variety of scene, making the whole seem bigger than the sum of its parts.

Here we are concerned with hedges as plants—the principles of choosing, establishing and maintaining them. Or not plants, perhaps, so much as crops. It is a good starting point to look on a hedge as a permanent crop; a row of identical plants planted at unnaturally close spacing to give the effect of one long narrow plant. Like crops, hedges make special demands on the soil.

A good hedge starts with a good trench. It is well worth digging a full spade's depth and a yard wide, and putting a generous layer of compost or manure in the bottom, to give the roots easy luxurious feeding while the top is building up a solid structure. At least, as a minimum, loosen the soil with a fork over the same area and spread fertilizer before you plant. Not only do the little plants need it to grow fast and keep you happy, but it makes weeding the new hedge infinitely easier if the soil is well cultivated—and weeding is vital in the first years before the roots have colonized the ground and the branches thickened to shade it.

Below The Château de Beloeil near Brussels, home of the Princes de Ligne since the fourteenth century, has six miles of 20-foot hornbeam hedge: a total surface of eleven acres to cut and trim. They turn what is otherwise a flat landscape into one of Europe's most romantic and theatrical gardens.

Right The hedges of the Generalife gardens at Granada are of Mediterranean cypress. A taut line guides the shears along the top edge and a second line indicates the slope for the side.
Below right Well-fed roses make splendid informal hedges for country gardens. This particular rose is *Rosa alba* 'Celeste'.

For the same reason—ease of weeding—do not be tempted to plant a double or "staggered" row of plants, however thick you want the hedge to be. It is far easier to weed a single line, and the final result will be just as impressive.

The new hedge will certainly need watering in its first few summers. But water in winter can be fatal. When young yew hedges die off in patches, which they often do, the reason is often that the roots are drowning. There does not have to be puddles on the surface to drown them. Good drainage below is essential. If the soil is very heavy or the site low-lying it may be necessary to cut drains leading away from the hedge to a ditch or sump (see pages 22–3).

The more often you trim the sides of a young hedge, within reason, the better. The idea is to encourage it to sprout and sprout again until it forms a dense thicket of twigs. The top should be left to grow straight up until it reaches the height you want, then trimmed as often as the sides.

The best hedge plants are those most apt to sprout again where they are cut—one of the reasons why yew is unbeatable: cut an old yew tree back to a bare pole and it will be green-fuzzed all over in the following year. When it comes to the rejuvenation of a dilapidated old hedge this is a vital consideration. Grubbing out a hedge and replanting it is a major operation. Much better to cut it right down to the ground, feed it liberally, and trim the sprouts from the stumps into a new hedge. But certain conifers, notably the cypresses, have no equipment for sprouting from old wood. When a cypress hedge gets bare there is nothing you can do but replant.

The trouble with fast-growing hedges is that they need cutting so often. The ideal, no doubt, would be a hedge that grew like cress up to a preordained height, then only a demure few inches a year. It is a decision the hedge planter must make: whether the quick screen or the eventual saving of effort is more important to him. Among the classic hedge plants, yew, box and holly are relatively slow to start—though yew should grow a foot a year—while beech, hornbeam and other deciduous trees gain height quickly but take longer to thicken into a screen. Once grown, one cut in August is all these need. Leyland is the best behaved of the cypresses—not only in being extremely hardy but in shooting up three feet a year so long as you let it, then slowing down obligingly once you start cutting it. But a fairly light trim is all it will take: once it has got away you cannot make drastic reductions. The fastest (and cheapest) hedges are privet and *Lonicera nitida*, the tiny-leaved bush honeysuckle (but without flowers). But both need trimming aggravatingly often.

I have spoken of hedges only as barriers—not as objects of beauty in themselves. While there is beauty in the subtly varying colours of yew and box, or the russet of beech in winter, and satisfaction and amusement in the shapes that can be cut in any solid hedge, there is another class of hedge which is really a way of displaying a favourite plant. Shrub roses, for example, can make a head-high screen. Musk-roses such as 'Felicia' or rugosas such as 'Blanc Double de Coubert' work well. Both can be trimmed lightly with shears in summer. A large part of the pleasure, for me, is in the scent: I find the spotty effect of big flowers in a hedge rather irritating.

For low hedges beside paths some of the herbs are ideal. Lavender, rosemary, lavender cotton (*Santolina chamaecyparissus*) and southernwood (*Artemisia abrotanum*) are all well tried—if not as well tried as that ageless component of grand gardens (and friend of slugs) the dwarf box.

Above Many botanical gardens have demonstration plots where hedges can be compared. This is at Edinburgh.

Below Hedges should taper towards the top to allow plenty of light to reach the sides. This device measures the exact angle of "batter" against a plumb line.

Shrubs: the backbone

Right Japanese maples need no flowers to qualify as first-rate garden shrubs. *Below* Hibiscus bushes clipped into domes and trained as little trees are the whole architecture of the formal parterre at Chenonceaux on the Loire. As in the Japanese garden (*left*) their flowering in late summer is a bonus, not their *raison d'être*.

Above Azaleas are used almost as sculpture in a modern garden in Japan. The inherent interest of their natural tiered habit is enough. The flowers are enjoyed as an incident, but the design of the garden is complete without them.

Right The variegated leaves of a dogwood (*Cornus alternifolia*) hold the light and give depth to the recesses between the branches.

Below Most powerfully purple of shrubs, the smoke bush *Cotinus coggyria* 'Royal Purple' absorbs almost all light.

The essence of a tree is that it puts its strength into a single trunk to reach as high as it can towards the light. The trunk thickens as the tree builds a larger head. There are many shrubs that grow in just the same way, the only real difference being their size. Rhododendrons and azaleas, cotoneasters, cistus and osmanthus are examples of steady builders. But another large class of shrubs is more distinctly "shrubby". In contrast to a tree they put up a set of equal stems to carry their leaves and support their flowers. Up to a point the stems thicken, but then they tire and just tick over. The plant's energy goes into putting out new shoots to replace them. The essence of these shrubs is replacement and rejuvenation. A healthy shrub has a canopy which is part old, part new; the new part performing most of the useful work and being the more attractive.

In garden convention the term flowering shrub is used to distinguish those (mostly deciduous) grown chiefly for their flowers from those (mostly evergreen) that are traditionally used as upholstery. A gathering of shrubs constitutes a shrubbery. A shudder goes with the very word. It conjures up a sooty no-man's-land in nineteenth-century villa gardens, the last of which has not even yet been cleared away. Lazy gardeners would throw the lawn-mowings there and small boys learn to smoke.

Its purpose was to fill space once and for all with a substantial mass of vegetation, whether for shelter, to separate one part of the garden from another, to hide something one would rather forget or simply to cover the ground. Each shrub no doubt was bought in response to an enthusiastic catalogue description, usually laying stress on its profusion of flowers. As it took its place in the shrubbery, however, its charm deserted it. It grew lank and spindly and scarcely flowered at all. This, at least, is the account we find in reforming gardening books.

What went wrong? There is nothing inherently wrong with the idea of massing bushes. Nature often does it. The first mistake was lack of control. The notion of permanence, of having "done" that part of the garden, was fatal. The second

Below Shrubs integrated with border plants to make a pattern of light and shade in interesting shapes against a wall. A ceanothus cascades over *Helichrysum rosmarinifolius*, a native of Tasmania like a tree heath with daisy flowers. In the foreground are day-lilies, an herbaceous Jerusalem sage and a geranium.

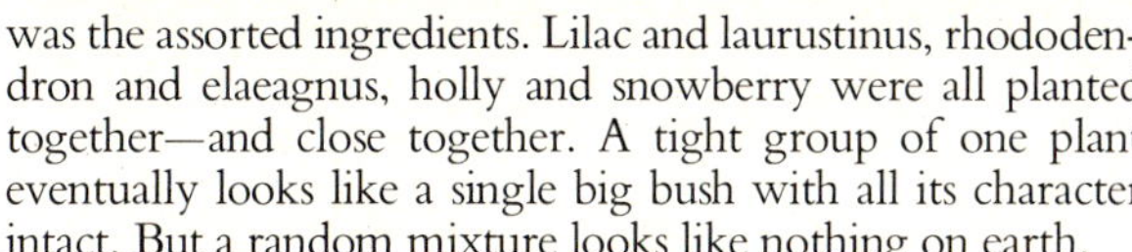

was the assorted ingredients. Lilac and laurustinus, rhododendron and elaeagnus, holly and snowberry were all planted together—and close together. A tight group of one plant eventually looks like a single big bush with all its character intact. But a random mixture looks like nothing on earth.

The function of shrubs is as valid—indeed essential—today as ever it was. The winds still whistle, the washing still needs hiding from the parlour window, and, though there may be much less ground to cover, there is far more ugliness to hide.

But the fashion of using them has changed—to treating them as individuals with a precise contribution to make to the garden, not just in flower but if possible all year round. With little space to spare there is no room for passengers. Lilac, for example, and philadelphus, however lovely in flower and sweet in smell, have to admit to being just a mound of nondescript leaves all summer—and in winter, just a clutter of nondescript twigs.

The shrubs that pay for their space all year long are those with a singularity of deportment, or a texture or colour of leaf that is always interesting. It does not have to be loud, but it must have character.

The sort of character they can contribute is a pronounced and deliberate dome, a violent uprearing of stiff stems, a tiered wedding-cake look or a softly weeping habit. In terms of texture it could be strikingly intricate and fine like parsley or coarsely detailed like fig-leaves, matt like sea-buckthorn or glittering like a camellia, or smooth and solid like an aloe. The leaves could be aluminium or brass, verdigris or burgundy.

It would be catastrophic to collect all these eccentrics and make them socialize. There must be a theme running through the garden that embraces the shrubs along with the trees, the herbs, and indeed the landscape. Acid-soil gardens have the widest choice of shrubs and at the same time a built-in ecological theme, which is why they are so often harmonious. But the theme could equally be a colour range, or a repetition of shapes. One of the most reliable contributions shrubs can make to the garden is their combination of highly coloured fruit and leaves in autumn.

The ultimate aim must be to integrate the shrubs completely with the other plants, treating them as equal partners with herbaceous plants and bulbs, composing scenes in which all the forms of plant life shelter and complement one another.

One class of shrubs can usefully be segregated from the rest for special mention—the almost instant ones that grow to full size in a mere two or three years or even, sometimes, in one year. With this extreme vigour usually goes great profusion of flowers and often a ready willingness to root from cuttings. *Ribes sanguineum*, many philadelphus, cistus, *Lavatera olbia*, *Abutilon vitifolium*, some buddleias, some ceanothus and almost all willows come into this category.

These are the best plants of all for giving a look of maturity to a new garden. They can be interspersed with slower-growing permanent shrubs and trees as temporary gap-fillers—though it is worth remembering that their roots are greedy.

Pruning shrubs is very much a matter of personal philosophy. Gardening books often give the impression that it is an essential operation. They come near to threatening that the poor thing's life will be in danger without regular surgery.

The purpose of pruning is fully discussed on pages 42–3, but it is right to add here that wherever space allows almost all shrubs do best with only the judicious removal of old wood from the base when it loses its vigour. A little snip here and a little snip there may be the gardener's idea of a perfect afternoon, but the shrub in most cases would rather be left alone. If the real reason for pruning is that the shrub is too big for the space allotted to it then it is much better to admit it, dig it up and plant a smaller one.

The next six pages follow the flowering and fruiting seasons with some of the shrubs that give the best value for space. Convention today segregates the two great groups of roses and rhododendrons from the ruck of shrubs—though they are no less. This book follows that convention.

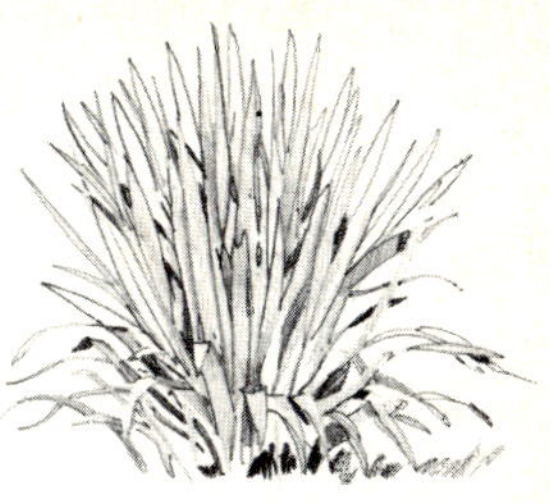

Above Size and shape, and the colour and texture of the leaves, are (or should logically be) more important in the choice of a shrub than its flowers. New Zealand flax (top), *Spiraea veitchii* (middle) and *Fatsia japonica* (above) are examples of stiff, relaxed and emphatic shrubs, each of which will create a wholly different atmosphere.

Below Dwarf and slow-growing conifers must be included with the shrubs that are grown for their shape and texture alone—but not planted with them. They mix badly. Their foliage is easily shaded out and killed by neighbours. Grouped together they form a little world on their own.

The early shrubs

Left The flowering currant, *Ribes sanguineum*—introduced from the West by David Douglas in 1826—is one of the earliest and hardiest red-flowered shrubs. A dozen forms have been named, ranging from white to crimson. It is often seen flowering in snow, and forces well when cut and taken indoors.

One gardening writer coined the phrase "overcoat plants" for anything that flowered in winter, and would have none of them. To most of us, though, the few courageous flowers that choose winter for their annual display are doubly welcome. We love them first for their own, usually short-lived, beauty, but even more as tangible evidence that roots are busy in the ground, sap is moving and cells are forming.

Once you become an overcoat gardener you begin to notice and enjoy not only the few frost-proof flowers but also the subtle swellings of buds, whose promise is almost as great a pleasure as the eventual flower and leaf will be. And shrubs, by the nature of things, with their buds where we can reach and see them, are more prone to this kind of enjoyment than most trees or virtually any herbaceous plants.

We in England hardly know the total clamp-down that grips land-locked countries in winter. There is always something stirring. Mild spells in December and January often tempt premature flowers from shrubs that should wait for the true spring. Happily the return of frost, though it may destroy the flowers, will do no other harm. It is hopeful young shoots that are vulnerable.

It is surprising that any shrubs are naturally programmed to flower at what seems the worst moment. But the approach of the shortest day is the signal for some of the mahonias to spread their sweet-scented sprays of yellow flowers. The witch-hazel uncurls its strange spiders of yellow and orange. Mezereon, the mauve winter daphne, is a poignant little plant with its tiny scented flowers on bare, stiff twigs. Even camellias, whose flowers are easily spoiled by frost, start with the sasanquas in November and keep up a sequence of one or other member of the family in flower all winter.

There is leisure in winter to enjoy flowers that we would pass by if summer was their season. Many of the earliest flowers are catkins, designed for wind pollination. They have no reason to invest in gaudy pigments for advertising, yet even in monochrome their progress from tight bud to full extension is enthralling to watch. Best of all are some of the shrubby willows that first spangle themselves with silver; then the male catkins miraculously develop a sheath of sparkling gold as the pollen grains emerge.

When all is bleak and bare we are ready to accept the brown catkins of hazel and the grey-green ones of *Garrya elliptica* as worthwhile colours. The flowers of wintersweet (*Chimonanthus*) and the strange stiff tassels of *Stachyurus* are in the same minor key that seems to fit the season.

The enjoyment of winter plants depends entirely on their setting. Scattered in the open on a prairie of frosted grass, with nothing but bare twigs as background, they can seem a poor reward for venturing forth. But given a sheltered corner with the solidity of a hedge, a wall, or best of all the deep green of pines behind them, their flowers can seem like jewels.

The Cambridge University Botanic Garden has a small enclosure devoted entirely to winter pleasures. There is a collection of winter-flowering viburnums, pink and white, of great beauty. This garden also demonstrates that flowers are by no means the only rewards of shrubs in winter. The brilliant red and yellow barks of Siberian dogwoods and white willows, the startling white hoops of a bramble, *Rubus biflorus*, the spiralling twigs of the contorted hazel, even the dangerous armament of the bizarre *Colletia armata*, a plant composed entirely of thorns, make a picture full of colour and interest. The floor is largely winter-flowering heather, sheltering winter bulbs. The trees are birches with gleaming trunks and the wonderful cherry *Prunus subhirtella* 'Autumnalis', which flowers repeatedly in every spell of mild weather between November and April.

Come spring, however, the authorities shut the gate. There

Above and left Camellias are by far the most sumptuous of winter flowers. For long after they were first imported from China it was assumed that such ostentatious evergreens must be tender and they were kept under glass. The plants are in fact hardy at least to zone 8, but frost damages the flowers. The protection of the greenhouse is therefore still a good idea in frost areas.

There are at least two thousand varieties of *Camellia japonica*, the common camellia (*above*), besides numerous other species, of which the most important are the large-flowered but more tender western Chinese *C. reticulata* and the Japanese *C. sasanqua*. *C. saluenensis*, a close relation of *C. reticulata*, was crossed with *C. japonica* by J.C. Williams in Cornwall in the 1920s to produce *C.× williamsii*, combining hardiness with exquisite flowers that last over a long season. 'Donation' (*left*) is the most famous and reliable of a score of such crosses.

Right The mahonias include some of the hardiest of evergreens with the noblest of leaves and provide some of the very few mid-winter flowering shrubs. The hybrid *Mahonia× media* is a reliable rather gaunt shrub growing to eight feet, and is sweet-scented as most winter flowers are.

Right Daphnes are intensely sweet-scented shrubs that start their season very early with the purplish or white Mezereon. It is followed by the voluptuous evergreen *Daphne odora*, then many species in spring, including *D. cneorum* 'Garland Flower' and its hybrid (here) *D.× burkwoodii*, flowering in May.

is nothing here for summer enjoyment. This is the catch with a garden well-laced with winter pleasures, or with a warm corner given up to them. The ideal is to concentrate your earliest flowers and any plants you love in winter in one sheltered place, near the house, where you will not have far to walk, and perhaps can see from the windows, and is sunlit at noon, not before. Dawn sunshine on frozen buds can be a great destroyer.

Once spring arrives subtlety goes out of the window. The stalwarts of the first great flowering season do not mince their colours. Forsythia is a brave burst of yellow—unfortunately in most forms the most lurid imaginable. The flowering currant shouts back in hard pink. The flowering quince adds scarlet to the riot. *Berberis darwinii* plunges in with vivid orange. In rhododendron country fierce fights break out. Overhead the cherries and crabs spread a canopy of bronze and blue-pink. Underneath, the bulbs see no more reason to show restraint than the multicoloured pansies and polyanthas of the spring "bedding".

This is the season that garden centres sell hardest. The gardener's sap is rising too and he is ready to spend. Cheerfulness is easy in the garden at this time of year: an individual and memorable effect much harder.

One answer lies in knitting together the individual splashes of colour with plenty of leaves. A bold green matrix gives the picture cohesion. Most of the leaves must be evergreen if they are to be in place in time for the early flowers. Luckily conifers are at their best in spring, starting their pale new growth in thrilling contrast to the old, dark needles and flowering in their quiet way at the same time.

Such work as shrubs entail for the gardener—remarkably little once the shrubs are well planted and away—is largely concentrated into winter and spring. This is the time for an annual inspection to see whether any old stems are becoming decrepit and need cutting away to encourage new ones, to curb the excesses of shrubs that are bullying their neighbours, and to prune those that flowered in summer and autumn. Warm, damp weather any time between autumn and spring is also the time to cover their roots with a thick mulch of leaves—by far the best way to feed and protect them.

Above The flowering quinces, properly *Chaenomeles* but often called 'japonica', flower in early and mid-spring with weatherproof but scentless flowers in red, orange or white. This is *C.× superba* 'Knap Hill Scarlet'.

Above The pendent grey-green catkins of the North-west American *Garrya elliptica* lengthen as spring begins. The evergreen leaves are crinkly and decorative, but need protection against severe frost.

Above Witch-hazels are true mid-winter-flowering shrubs with completely frost-proof flowers. The Chinese witch-hazel, *Hamamelis mollis*, has been improved on with such cultivars as the wide-spreading 'Pallida', shown here, and hybrids such as the orange-flowered 'Jelena'. The hazel-like leaves colour beautifully in autumn.

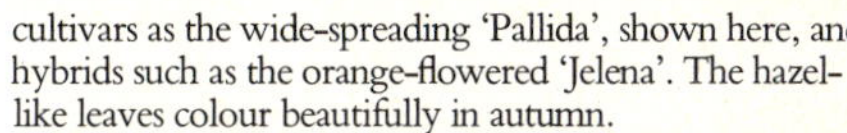

Above The shrubby willows come in such a range of leaf shapes and colours, with such variations in catkins, bark, size and habit, that they are well worth collecting. One of the best for smaller gardens is *Salix hastata* 'Wehrhahnii' with dense clusters of silvery male catkins in early spring which turn gold as the pollen appears.

Above The *Berberis* flowering season starts in mid-spring with the evergreen *B. darwinii* from Chile. One of its hybrids, *B.× stenophylla*, has a dozen forms, generally yellow to orange, gracefully arching but like all berberis armed with painful thorns.

Above The first sumptuous wide-open flowers with all the confidence of high summer are the moutans or "tree peonies" in an endless range of colours. This is the Japanese 'Shujakamon'. Their new growth is often caught by late frosts, and some protection is needed.

Shrubs: spring into summer

Below Such mid-summer shrubs as ceanothus and the mauve-flowered *Abutilon vitifolium* are given the backing of a wall in this garden at Abbot's Ripton in East Anglia. The subdued foreground of grey, with the sturdy evergreen mound of *Viburnum davidii*, sets off the lushness of the big shrubs.

Below Summer and autumn-flowering shrubs are freely mingled with border flowers and roses to give year-round substance to this double border. The shrubs include potentillas, *Cistus*, *Buddleia* 'Lochinch', Jerusalem sage and *Hebe salicifolia*. Upright "Irish" junipers march down each bed.

Above The common European lilac has given its blood to a wider range of variations than any other single shrub. Yet among all the colours and single and double flowers it remains stolid and uninspiring. There are many more graceful species from the East, but with less showy flowers.

The early-flowering shrubs have bulbs as their only rivals. There is little doing among the border plants, hellebores apart, until spring is well under way. But then suddenly the petal count is so high that there is no room in the garden for a fraction of the possible contenders. Mere wildling species tend to be elbowed aside by selected varieties with bigger or longer-lasting flowers.

The tree peonies are perhaps the first flowers that have the feeling of the fully open spring: broad, fragile petals in extravagant numbers. As we saw on the previous page they unfortunately tend to flower before it is safe to be so sumptuous.

Hard on their heels comes the common lilac in its many forms, single- and double-flowered, varying from heavy hanging trusses of white ('Vestale' is as white as a shirt in a commercial) to wine-red ('Souvenir de Louis Spaeth') via creams, purples, pinks and even lilac. "As with other plants which become the victim of the specialists," says the catalogue of Hillier's Nurseries severely, "far too many forms have been selected and named." Gardeners in the far north are none the less grateful to Miss Preston, who developed some super-hardy hybrids for Canadian conditions in the 1920s. 'Hiawatha', purply red, is the most memorably named of them.

I have already hinted that lilac is a dull, space-consuming plant when its flowers are over. And yet there is no other smell quite so magically spring-like—and the flowers are very fine.

All at once brooms, spireas, viburnums and ceanothus are on duty. The last is called wild lilac in California, despite its little leaves and tight soft blue flowering heads. Ceanothus is on the very fast but not very hardy list. The evergreen spring-flowering ones (*Ceanothus veitchianus* is the commonest) are less hardy than the deciduous summer-to-autumn-flowering group which is led by the first-class 'Gloire de Versailles'. There are pale pink ones too—but not worth growing.

There is no season without its viburnums, and scarcely a viburnum without merit. Their name does not exactly quicken the heartbeat, perhaps because their flowers are white or pale pink, or perhaps because they are cousins of the vulgar elder, rather than having the blue blood of the ericas or roses.

Viburnum farreri (alias *fragrans*; but several of them are wonderfully fragrant) flowers all winter. So does the evergreen *V. tinus*. In early spring the beautiful deciduous *V. juddii* and the evergreen *V.* × *burkwoodii* start up; then the guelder rose, *V. opulus* (the variety 'Sterile' is best known as the snowball tree), then *V. tomentosum*, which has a form in such bold horizontal brush-strokes of white that nobody can resist it. Other viburnums are grown for their splendid leaves (*V. rhytidophyllum*, the "leatherleaf" and *V. davidii*, low-growing favourite of architects for adding dignity to facile buildings) and yet others (*V. betulifolium*, and *V. opulus* again) for their red berries and yellow and red leaves in autumn.

Left The evergreen "sun roses" or cistus are unflagging flower-bearers in June and July, but each flower only lasts a day. Most, like the gum cistus, *C. ladanifer*, shown here, are white with dark markings. The hybrid *C.* × *cyprius* is similar but hardier and more vigorous. 'Silver Pink' is a fine and hardy pink.

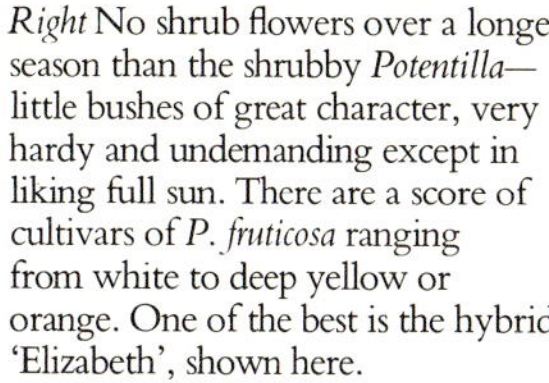

Right No shrub flowers over a longer season than the shrubby *Potentilla*—little bushes of great character, very hardy and undemanding except in liking full sun. There are a score of cultivars of *P. fruticosa* ranging from white to deep yellow or orange. One of the best is the hybrid 'Elizabeth', shown here.

Above *Olearia cheesemanii* from New Zealand leads into the summer with its profusion of little white aster-flowers covering its very pretty evergreen leaves.

Above All *Philadelphus* (mock-orange) are white or cream; most have a wonderful fragrance. 'L'Innocence', shown here, is one of the most elegant.

Above The American elderberry, *Sambucus canadensis*, with its splendid leaves and vast flowers and heads of fruit is a hardy shrub for big, even wild, gardens.

Above The Chinese dogwood, *Cornus kousa chinensis*, holds its star-flowers on the upper sides of its graceful branches and turns rich crimson and bronze in autumn.

Above *Viburnum tomentosum* 'Mariesii' is boldly tiered like a wedding cake. This detail shows the flowers composed of sterile florets surrounding fertile ones.

Above The spireas, with their arching wands covered with tiny rose-like flowers, begin in May with the popular 'Bridal-wreath'. Different species flower all summer.

At this time of year spireas are "only" white, but generous with their flowers, and always graceful—Bridal-wreath (*S.* × *arguta*) particularly so. The brooms are principally yellow, in all shades from lemon to cream, but include varieties in brown and purple and orange, and mixtures of these. Three genera, *Cytisus, Genista* and *Spartium*, are lumped together as brooms, and indeed you could sweep the floor with any of them. They all consist of thin, evergreen twigs-cum-leaves, which bear their bright pea-flowers. The tallest (to fifteen feet) is the Mount Etna broom, flowering in midsummer. One of the lowest and most shapely is *Genista lydia*, a two-foot hummock of piercing yellow in spring. The toughest (though not proof against a hard continental winter) is the Spanish broom of summer and autumn. The most beautiful is *Genista cinerea*: silky and languid—and of course rare.

Midsummer also sees the start of the longest-running show in the entire shrub garden: the tireless potentilla, cheerfully flecked from now to November with its little rose-like yellow, cream, red or white flowers. The air is languorous with philadelphus (or mock-orange, or syringa). The dainty styrax —known in America with characteristic bathos as snowbell— lines its long branches with drooping flowers. A battery of escallonias, deutzias, weigelas, kolkwitzias, daphnes, rubus and one proud choisya are in action. But then so are the roses. A shrub has to pass rigorous tests to win a place in high season.

Above The earliest-flowering, most graceful, and one of the biggest-growing *Buddleia* is the June-flowering *B. alternifolia*, which has been described as like a lilac-flowered weeping willow. It can be trained as a small tree or allowed to spread uncontrolled into an impressive arching mound.

Shrubs for late summer and autumn

Above The season of the fullest colour. Autumn brings such rich harmonies that precise planning for them is scarcely necessary. Acid soil gives the widest variety.

Left Viburnums are back in autumn after their summer pause with the evergreen *V. tinus*, alias *laurustinus*—a shrub rather out of fashion.

Below Their flowers show quite clearly that the oleanders are bush periwinkles. They need the warmth of their native Mediterranean, where they flower in many colours.

Above *Hypericum* 'Hidcote', named after the Cotswold garden, flowers throughout summer and autumn.

The second commonest complaint among gardeners, though admittedly following a long way behind the weather, is that there are certain inevitable seasonal "gaps" when nothing is in flower. To hear some gardeners talk you would think that winter arrived in August.

It is possible to achieve a very dull garden by concentrating on the shrubs of spring and early summer. Most of them pass into a coma after flowering, though many come out of it again with fruit and falling leaves of lovely colours.

But it is not difficult to interweave with your spring-flowering shrubs others that spend the early year forming flower buds to open in the summer holidays. Most things that flower later also flower longer. There is as wide a choice of shrubs as ever, with, curiously enough, a wider range of richer colours. While the earlier season, roses and rhododendrons apart, seems to have been dominated by yellow and white flowers, the later season has a wider and warmer spectrum, leading, it seems with a sort of vegetable logic, to the time of year when green is the exception rather than the rule.

For sheer volume of colour, in gardens or in the wild, autumn stands alone. In summer a yard of rich scarlet in a border delights us. In autumn we can have it by the furlong. Whole trees are the colour of our most vivid flowers. With the turning leaves come the ripening berries. Even the quality of the light, with the sun lower in the sky, intensifies the chromatic climax of the year.

The chief shrubby components of this feast, before the leaves take over from the flowers, are the hydrangeas, the hypericums, the fuchsias, the hebes and hibiscus, the buddleias, the potentillas (still going strong) and in the south the oleanders.

Right A mere sample of the harvest. Some of the best berrying shrubs are (left to right) berberis (this is *B. wilsoniae*) for red berries; mahonia for blue; *Viburnum opulus* for red; pyracantha for orange. Others are spindles, blueberries, gaultherias, pernettyas, hollies, cotoneasters, elders, sea-buckthorn and roses.

Above The lacecap of *Hydrangea villosa* consists of a central cluster of fertile florets surrounded by sterile "ray florets".

Below Three lacecap hydrangeas in the sort of tree shelter they enjoy. The tallest (left) is *H. sargentiana*, then *H. villosa*, then *H.* 'Bluewave'.

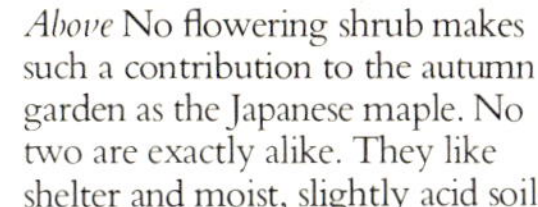

Above No flowering shrub makes such a contribution to the autumn garden as the Japanese maple. No two are exactly alike. They like shelter and moist, slightly acid soil.

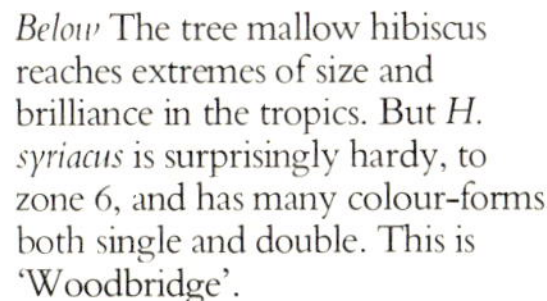

Right The hebes reach the peak of their long flowering season in late summer. One of the most attractive is *H.* × *andersonii* 'Variegata', here with 'Jackson's Blue' rue.

Below The tree mallow hibiscus reaches extremes of size and brilliance in the tropics. But *H. syriacus* is surprisingly hardy, to zone 6, and has many colour-forms, both single and double. This is 'Woodbridge'.

There is no shortage here. Remember there are ceanothus still to flower, and I have not touched on the rarer plants: the plumy buckeyes, the tender clethras of ineffable sweetness, the stately eucryphias and hoherias, Japanese bush-clover with its rosy purple panicles, bright blue ceratostigma or violet-blue caryopteris, nor invaded the world of sub-shrubs, where lavender and its associates are going full tilt.

The hydrangeas are the most various and potentially the best garden material of all the summer shrubs; taking over where the viburnums left off—even (though they are apparently not related) to having the same trick of producing two kinds of flowers: one set for marketing and the other for production.

The typical florist's hydrangea that first comes to mind is marketing material only: a mop-head of sterile florets. I find it helpful to think of these by their old-fashioned name, *hortensia*, which has just the right ring of horticultural pretence about it. Hortensias look well in pots, or in combination with architecture. They are at home at the foot of a shady wall, perhaps the entrance yard of the house, if given enough moisture. For either doing a solo in mid-lawn, or blending with other plants in the light shade of trees (which is what they prefer) there are many other hydrangeas, all better.

The lacecaps have both sorts of flowers. Of these 'Bluewave' is justly the most famous. They also include the smaller *Hydrangea serrata*, which carries to perfection the hydrangea's particular virtue of dying gracefully. In its best form, 'Grayswood', the sterile florets, instead of fading, darken from pink to intense mahogany-crimson. There are lacecaps of all sizes (see the photograph above).

Below Another tree mallow, not so splendid as hibiscus and less hardy, but easy, fast-growing and endlessly in flower: *Lavatera olbia* 'Rosea'.

The third flower form is the panicle, or branched flower cluster, best known in *H. paniculata grandiflora* and *H. quercifolia*, which has splendid leaves like an American red oak, even to their autumn colour. Both of these have white flowers.

The coloured hydrangeas are litmus paper for the chemistry of the soil. Where it is acid they are blue; where alkaline, pink. In alkaline soil their supply of aluminium is cut off. Since their blue is altogether a more striking colour, gardeners often achieve it even in the wrong soil by adding aluminium sulphate.

Hypericums offer nothing like the same variety. Their virtue is a guaranteed supply of big buttercups on small bushes for months on end. The best known, St John's Wort, appears on the groundcover pages. The best is 'Hidcote', a five-foot bush which flowers so freely for so long that one begins to tire of its relentless cheerfulness.

Yet in a small garden it is the plants that flower and flower again that must take priority. In this hardy varieties of fuchsias can hardly be beaten. The tender varieties are discussed on pages 122–3. If anything can beat them it is some of the hebes, above all the extraordinary 'Midsummer Beauty', often in flower in southern England at Christmas.

Buddleias come and go all too quickly, leaving dull brown dead-heads to regret them by. Without their scent and the butterflies it brings they would hardly hold the place they do in gardens. Hibiscus times its single flowering well: after we have expected to see new faces appearing. It is also far hardier than its Mediterranean look suggests.

Not so, alas, the oleander. This is really Monte Carlo material; but so loaded with agreeable associations that anyone with a conservatory should begin to collect the set.

Roses: a family tree

The ancestry of roses may seem a laborious way of approaching a delectable subject. But if one is to make any sense out of the bewildering variety of flowers grouped under that name today the only place to start is with the wild roses whose sap, in a cocktail of inextricable complexity, runs in their veins.

Until recently no one knew, or had even really tried to guess at, the early matings that produced the rich old pink and purple roses of European gardens up to the last century. From the Persians and Greeks, via the Romans, certain strains of cultivated rose had gone on, scarcely changing. There were no roses that flowered more than once, either in early or late summer, only two yellow or orange middle eastern species (the Australian Brier and the Sulphur Rose), and no huge climbers. The "tea" scent was unknown.

But a mingling of the genes of a dog rose, two distinct strains of climbing musk roses and the deep pink *Rosa gallica* with perfumed petals (which goes back to at least 1200 BC) had produced a range of Damasks, Gallicas and Albas in all the shades of clear pink or bluey pink between white and purple. They had heavenly scents—the Damasks in particular inheriting from the musk roses, whose scent is in their stamens, the trick of sending their fragrance far downwind. Their flower shapes developed over the centuries from single to densely double with charming flat faces of puckered petals. The Gallicas were mainly low bushes, but musk-rose vigour made the Damasks tall, even rambling, plants. While the Gallicas were thorny with rather dark, dull, roundish leaves the dog rose in the family was a smooth, pale-foliaged plant, which gave the Albas their greyish leaves and a mere sprinkling of thorns.

The high point of breeding with this relatively limited range of genetic possibilities was reached by the Dutch in the seventeenth century, when repeated crossings of Albas and Autumn Damasks gave them the rose of a hundred petals, otherwise known as the Cabbage, the Provence, or the *Rose des Peintres*. Its heavy head makes it better in a vase (or indeed in a painting) than on a bush. But no flower could be more sumptuous.

The end of the eighteenth century is the turning point in rose history. In the 1780s and 1790s merchant ships came home with the roses the Chinese grew in gardens—themselves the results of centuries of selection. Chinese roses derived from two wild species: the "giant" rose, a huge climber with big silky yellow flowers and the wonderful "tea" scent, and *Rosa chinensis*, a pink or red once-flowering climber that grows in the Ichang Gorge of the Yangtse River. At some unknown date this had "sported" to produce a dwarf bush with the priceless attribute of flowering on and on, ceaselessly pushing out new shoots, with every shoot forming flower buds.

Four of these new introductions to Europe have been dubbed "the four stud chinas". All the ramifications of rose breeding since 1792 can be traced back to one form of *Rosa chinensis* and three hybrids of the Chinese and the giant rose.

The man who coined the phrase, and worked out the story, was the great Cambridge geneticist Dr C. C. Hurst. His work, in partnership with his wife Rona, using chromosome counts to reveal forgotten relationships, is the basis of the family tree opposite. It shows how the old roses rapidly interbred with the new wherever they were introduced to produce new classes with new characteristics, which again interbred in a more and more deliberate and commercial process leading to today's Hybrid Teas and Floribundas. The only hitch was that the longed-for gene for perpetual flowering was a recessive one (see pages 48–9). Two generations of each cross had to pass before this quality could be handed down.

The process is far from stopping at the bottom of this page. This is where modern rose breeding begins. On the following pages are some of the new developments of rose breeding as more wild species are brought into the genetic pool.

ROSA CORYMBIFERA. A single dog rose from the Near East, flowering throughout June.

A RAMBLING MUSK ROSE, From the Near East, with rich far-carrying scent. Probably the white ROSA PHOENICIA from Asia Minor.

ROSA GALLICA. The red Apothecary's Rose, a low suckering bush cultivated for more than 3,000 years. June-flowering, with many scented petals. Gallica cultivars vary from deep pink to light crimson to purple.

THE SUMMER DAMASKS. An ancient group, double, red, pink or white, with a strong scent. "Damask" refers to Damascus; the crusaders are said to have brought them home. The striped 'York and Lancaster' rose, shown left, is an example.

ROSA × ALBA. The White Rose of York, a bush with pale leaves and great vigour from the dog rose, sweet scent and white or delicate pink colouring from its musk and Gallica grandparents. Flowering from June to July only. 'Celeste' is still a famous example.

THE CABBAGE OR PROVENCE ROSE, ROSA × CENTIFOLIA, shown right. This is the densely double heavily scented result of intensive Dutch breeding in the 17th century. Once-flowering and heavy-headed but uniquely sumptuous.

R. GALLICA

THE BOURBON ROSE

HYBRID CHINAS. Many crosses, starting with Brown's 'Superb Blush' and 'Bengale Descemet' of 1815. Also crosses of ROSA GALLICA and Hume's Blush. Lovely flowers but once-flowering; Gallica character dominating recessive recurrent China character.

MOSS ROSES. Sports of the Cabbage and Damask roses with strange glands giving a luxurious mossy effect to stems and buds. There are many cultivars.

ROSA FOETIDA (below). A bright yellow (sometimes scarlet and yellow) rose from Persia, cultivated for centuries as the Austrian briar. This rose is almost sterile.

HYBRID PERPETUALS. Seedlings of Hybrid Chinas crossed with Portlands and Bourbons, thus with enough China genes to be perpetual-flowering or at least twice-flowering. 'Princess Helène' (1837) was the first. Excellent hardy large-flowered roses—the principal class from 1840 to 1890.

A cross raised with great trouble by the French breeder Pernet-Ducher in 1888. Not remarkable in itself but bringing ROSA FOETIDA genes into breeding.

The rose family tree is so ancient and intricate that it can never be known in full. This family tree is a necessarily simplified attempt at charting a story spread over many centuries. It shows (upper left) the roses of old European gardens—and before them of the classical world—and the revolutionary effect on them of oriental blood (upper right).

At most stages of the story crosses between species were repeated many times. The roses illustrated are simply examples typical of their groups. The later groups number many hundreds of cultivars.

A MUSK ROSE. Probably ROSA MOSCHATA from the Mediterranean. White, late summer flowering, richly scented, single or double.

ROSA CHINENSIS. In the wild a single once-flowering climber, but through selection in Chinese gardens a recurrent-flowering bush, often double-flowered, and in many colours between red and pink, but not yellow. The young leaves and thorns are red.

ROSA GIGANTEA. The original tea-scented rose—a wild climber from the Sikkim–Yunnan highlands with big silky, limp, pale-yellow flowers in summer only. Tender in Britain.

ROSA × ODORATA. A range of old Chinese garden roses of many colours, both climbers and bushes, mostly once-flowering, but with some valuable recurrent forms. 'Hume's Blush' is shown above.

THE AUTUMN DAMASKS. Probably grown by the Greeks and Romans. Pink or white, well scented and twice-flowering, showing musk-rose influence.

'SLATER'S CRIMSON CHINA'. A small semi-double perpetual-flowering bush rose, a selected form of ROSA CHINENSIS introduced to England by the East India Company in 1792.

'PARSONS'S PINK CHINA'. A pale-pink, semi-double, perpetual-flowering bush from Chinese gardens, possibly the same as the "Monthly Rose" sent to Sweden and England in the 1750s.

HUME'S BLUSH TEA-SCENTED CHINA. A small, pale-pink, perpetual-flowering Chinese garden bush rose sent to England by the East India Company in 1809.

PARKS' YELLOW TEA-SCENTED CHINA. A small shrub with big double yellow flowers, recurrent, sent from China to the Royal Horticultural Society, London, in 1824. Now lost.

MILLER'S WHITE MUSK. A garden form of ROSA MOSCHATA, musk scented and late-flowering.

'CHAMPNEY'S PINK CLUSTER', 1802. Champney was a nurseryman in S. Carolina. His rose was once-flowering, but a seedling from it raised by Philippe Noisette and distributed in Paris in 1814 was recurrent like its China grandparent, cluster-flowering, with the musk scent. This was ROSA × NOISETTIANA, shown right.

R. GALLICA

R'S CRIMSON CHINA'

UNKNOWN

YELLOW NOISETTE/TEAS. The first European roses with yellow tints. Both bushes and climbers. Many crosses, starting with 'Lamarque' and 'Jaune Desprez' in 1830.

'PARSONS'S PINK'

THE PORTLAND ROSE. A bright red rose, slightly recurrent, perhaps found near Paestum in Italy by the Duchess of Portland. A chance seedling of 'Slater's Crimson China' and an unknown rose.

THE BOURBON ROSE. A chance cross in 1817 on the Isle of Réunion (then called Bourbon). Vigorous, prickly, with tight-packed shell-like petals, fragrant and a fine pink, repeat-flowering. 'Zéphirine Drouhin', shown above, is an example.

HUME'S BLUSH

ROSA MULTIFLORA. A creamy-white summer-flowering Japanese climber, introduced to France in 1860. Its flowers are in dense clusters.

A DWARF SPORT OF 'PARSONS'S PINK CHINA' (ROSA × ODORATA) in 1805.

PINK BOURBON TEAS. The first was 'Adam', raised at Reims in 1833. They are beautiful, fragrant and perpetual, but not very hardy.

Crossed in Guillot's nursery, Lyons, to produce in the second generation (1872) the first POLYPOMS, 'Paquerette' and 'Mignonette': dwarf continuous-cluster-flowering bushes. 'Cécile Brunner' is shown right.

Many TEA ROSES were bred between 1840 and 1890. Dr Hurst called these "the most exquisite roses ever produced". But few were hardy enough for the garden. 'Gloire de Dijon' (1853) is perhaps the best of this kind today.

'ORLÉANS ROSE'

PINK HYBRID TEAS. 'La France' (1867), shown left, was the first rose to combine the delicacy, shape, scent and eagerness to flower of the Teas with the hardiness and strong growth of the Hybrid Perpetual.

'SOLEIL D'OR' 1898. The first Pernetiana rose, shown left. It brought deep yellow colouring into the mainstream of rose breeding—but also liability to suffer from blackspot.

HYBRID TEAS

POULSENS. Hybrid Tea 'Red Star' and polypom 'Orleans Rose', crossed by Poulsen in Denmark in 1924. These Poulsens' roses, crossed with Hybrid Teas, are the parents of modern Floribundas. 'Korona', shown left, is a popular cultivar.

Many yellow, orange and parti-coloured HYBRID TEAS.

Shrub roses

The early European roses reached the peak of their fortunes in the famous collection of the Empress Joséphine at La Malmaison, recorded in the world's most popular flower paintings by Redouté in the years 1817 to 1824.

From the 1830s on the "China" characters of repeat-flowering, of silkier flowers and subtler scent were so highly prized that the old favourites seemed to have been consigned to history. In due course, the same fate overtook each new step towards an ideal combination of brilliance, hardiness and constancy in bloom. The emphasis grew more and more on flowers and less and less on plants. Some of the Victorian masterpieces needed a groom and a footman in constant attendance to show at their sumptuous best. By the time the Hybrid Teas took over as the supreme roses in the 1900s, rose routine was established as something quite separate from the rest of gardening. The virtues of the rose as a self-sufficient shrub were almost forgotten.

Luckily the old breeds still had a few admirers who kept them going, mostly in France and North America. Their reinstatement began in the Jekyll-inspired return to older, homelier and subtler ways with flowers and continued with such sensitive gardeners as Victoria Sackville-West and Constance Spry. Then, in the 1950s, Graham Thomas, in his book *The Old Shrub Roses*, made the case for them and catalogued all he could find. He pointed out that if they are shorter in flowering season than modern cultivars, they last as long as most other one-season shrubs—and the hold the rose has over the heart is even stronger in these more tender, muddled and feminine flowers than their well-organized, often strident, descendants.

Meanwhile new wild species had arrived in the wave of

Above The old shrub roses can be massed for glorious effect at midsummer, giving the garden an atmosphere and fragrance that nothing else can.

Right A single shrub rose as a commanding feature in grass. This is the modern shrub 'Frühlingsgold', a cross between a Hybrid Tea and the most widely spread of all wild roses, variously known as the Burnet or Scots brier, in this case an Asiatic form *Rosa spinosissima altaica*.

Below right The Scots brier is a little suckering plant with great delicacy of flower, leaf and fragrance and sometimes rich autumn colour.

Above One of the oldest of all garden roses, *R. gallica officinalis*, the red rose of Lancaster. Gallicas have rough foliage and spread freely by sending up suckers. Their scent is rich and powerful.

Above Several of the ancient Albas are still common in gardens: 'Great Maiden's Blush' and 'Céleste' are among them. They are upright thorny shrubs with grey-green leaves and flowers of exquisite soft pink. This is 'Queen of Denmark', a nineteenth-century Alba with the most perfectly formed flowers of any and darker leaves than most.

Left An unspectacular ancestor of modern roses. 'Old Blush' or the "monthly" rose (so-called for its habit of flowering constantly from summer to Christmas). It may be the same plant as 'Parsons's Pink China'. If so it is the only one of the original "stud chinas" still common in cultivation, though neither vigorous nor very hardy.

Left Rose-hips can be highly ornamental in the garden from late summer onwards. Two of the best species for fruit are *far left Rosa rugosa* from East Asia, with hips as big as small tomatoes, and *R. moyesii* from China, with bottle-shaped hips of sealing-wax red, often in very large numbers.

Asiatic introductions to widen the whole concept of the rose and its possibilities, and to re-awaken interest in the lovely, simple, single flower. The Japanese *Rosa multiflora*, which brought profuse cluster-flowering, appears in the family tree on the previous page. Another eastern Asian species, *R. rugosa*, brought recurrent-flowering combined with extreme hardiness and splendid foliage. Yet another, *R. wichuraiana*, was to revolutionize the breeding of rambling roses (see pages 92–3). The butter-yellow *R. hugonis* and the cherry-red *R. moyesii* arrived from China in the 1900s.

Breeders began to turn back to wild roses nearer to home whose genetic potential had never been investigated. Lord Penzance, for example, used the sweet brier in the 1890s in combination with various Hybrid Teas to produce the Penzance briers. Wilhelm Kordes in Germany, one of the greatest of all rose-breeders, crossed a Scots brier with Hybrid Teas to make the great 'Frühlingsgold' and 'Frühlingsmorgen'.

Thus another category of rose, the "modern shrub", came into being; strong and healthy, good-looking as garden plants, without the special needs of the florists' roses. Far from detracting from the name of the old roses it enhanced it, for more gardeners began to think of roses as an integral part of the whole garden picture.

What sort of picture then do the shrub roses, old and new, paint in the garden? Despite the grandeur of their Rothschild drawing-room names—'Assemblage des Beautés' and 'Gloire des Rosomanes'—the general effect of the old pre-China roses, and even of such Bourbons and Hybrid Perpetuals as have proved themselves over a century and more, is rustic and cottagey. This has more to do with the bushes themselves than with the flowers, which can be picked and arranged in high-drawing-room style. But the big, rather coarse-leaved shrubs, drooping under the weight of their blooms, can hardly be made to look formal as modern bedding roses can.

Above The Hybrid Perpetuals were the reigning class of roses from the middle to almost the end of the nineteenth century. 'Mrs John Laing' is one of the best.

Above 'Nevada', one of the finest of modern shrub roses, is a cross between *R. moyesii* and a Hybrid Tea. It makes a big bush smothered with creamy flowers at midsummer and another lesser batch in autumn.

Shrub roses are not only better mixers in the garden, taking part in the general border scene, but they need to be mixed, so that other plants can make up for their lack of later flowers and hide their leaves—a strong point of the Albas but of few others. It is impossible to go wrong among their harmonious colours of crimson, purple, violet, mauve and white. All lie safely on the blue side of the spectrum (see pages 198–9). Their problem is only a tendency to heaviness *en masse*. They need very definite punctuation, both in colour and form. White, grey and blue are the best colours to "lift" them; hot modern rose colours are wrong. The simple verticals of irises, delphiniums, foxgloves and tall campanulas provide contrast.

As for pruning, they need only the same attention as any long-lived shrub: the occasional removal of the oldest worn-out stems from the base. To keep them tidily within bounds the strong new shoots can be shortened by a third.

The same pruning precepts apply to most roses being grown as shrubs, multifarious as their habits are—varying from the low-growing Burnet or Scots brier, spreading by means of fiercely armed suckers, to the huge round bush that 'Nevada', for example, eventually makes, or the gauntly upright *Rosa moyesii*. Nothing will make a neat bush of this.

Among the less familiar species, those from western China for example, and modern shrubs, all the rules are broken. The colour-barrier is down, with bright red and yellow appearing. Autumn flowers are available, beautiful ferny leaves make features of shrubs not in flower and rose-hips are important autumn ornaments.

Above 'Blanc Double de Coubert' is perhaps the best-known form of the East Asian *R. rugosa*. An easy, hardy and strong-growing bush.

Above left The moss roses have stems and buds covered with strange, sticky, fragrant glands. They were nineteenth-century innovations. 'William Lobb' or 'Old Velvet' here grows up to eight feet.

Left New Chinese species early this century gave us roses with particularly delicate foliage, including the popular 'Canary Bird'.

Right Many roses tend to hang on to leaves in winter. One of the few with fine autumn colour is the American *Rosa virginiana*, a single, pink, late-summer rose with abundant red hips.

Bedding roses

The difference between roses as fully fledged shrubs and roses as well-drilled flower machines is emphasized by borrowing the term "bedding". Bedding to a gardener means massed display over a long season: the job of summer annuals, in fact. The Hybrid Teas were developed to provide exactly this, in as many and as dazzling colours as possible. Their productivity is extraordinary: the "China" urge to go on making new growth, with every shoot ending in a single flower, is developed to the limit.

But they also had another goal; to win prizes for perfect blooms. Prize flowers need long stalks, and have heavy heads; qualities scarcely compatible with giving a good show in the garden. Hybrid Teas thus became schizophrenic plants that need patient nursing and guidance all their lives to perform either of their possible roles well. Moreover, as they have become further and further inbred in the search for new colours and shapes, they have grown more susceptible to disease.

Those who grow and love them have forgiven them all their faults and are ready to feed, spray and prune them, even to put up with their appearance in winter—like a sinister device for impeding infantry—for the sake of their flowers. And certainly among man-made flowers there is nothing more elegantly sensuous than a modern rose bud. As cut flowers, at the just-about-to-open stage, they are supremely graceful and may never be surpassed. The full-blown flower is not nearly so good: there seems strangely little pattern among the many petals that made the sculptural bud.

For bedding purposes—that is to keep consistent colour going in a flower bed as evenly and as long as possible—they have already been superseded by the Floribundas. Our rose family tree showed how cluster-flowering was interbred with Hybrid Teas (from *Rosa multiflora*, via Polypoms and then the Poulsen roses) to create a new class, combining profuse sprays of flowers with the Hybrid Tea colours and the Hybrid Tea urge to flower and flower again.

Floribundas not only give a more even spread of colour than Hybrid Teas; on the whole they need less cossetting—advantages that are now being bred into Hybrid Teas by combining the two races. Already there are big-flowered Floribundas (known in America as Grandifloras) and Hybrid Teas with significantly more flowers.

Apart from the elusive blue, which is thought to be genetically impossible, modern roses cover the colour spectrum. Bright yellow tea roses arrived with the twentieth century. About 1930 a genetic mutation produced a new pigment in roses which added a new degree of brilliance: a harsh fluorescence which has been widely used for intensifying reds and oranges. Its ultimate use at present is in 'Super Star', which you almost feel you could pick to use as a torch.

As to scent—which many hold to be the soul of the rose; the

Above left Bedding with Hybrid Tea roses in a great country-house garden at Rockingham Castle, Northamptonshire. They furnish colour, fragrance and atmosphere all summer long as no other plants can.

Top An alternative to formality: Floribundas used in a German garden as small shrubs in a sea of lavender, which softens their angular shapes while emphasizing the quality of their flowers.

Above Full-frontal formality with Hybrid Tea roses in Queen Mary's Rose Gardens, Regent's Park, London. The roses in each bed are all of one kind, here 'Wendy Cousins' with standards of the same kind to add height behind. Standards are simply bushes grafted on the top of bare stems of a vigorous rootstock rose, usually *Rosa rugosa*.

Above left and *above* The flowers of a Floribunda 'Scarlet Queen Elizabeth' and a Hybrid Tea 'Precious Platinum' compared. Floribunda clusters give a more even effect, especially at a distance, but nothing can compare with the individual bloom of the Hybrid Tea for form and texture.

Left The Hybrid Musks flower in clusters like Floribundas but on substantial, healthy shrubs. 'Felicia', here, is one of the best all-round garden roses.

Right Miniature roses, suitable for pots but difficult or impossible to place in the garden, are derived from a dwarf China rose, which gave them a long flowering season. 'Royal Salute' is a new cultivar.

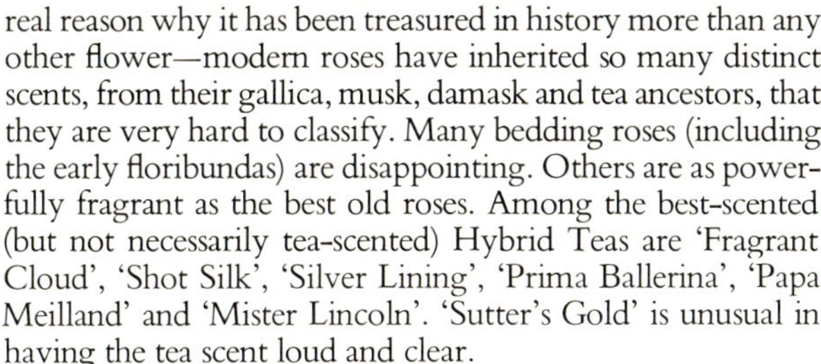

real reason why it has been treasured in history more than any other flower—modern roses have inherited so many distinct scents, from their gallica, musk, damask and tea ancestors, that they are very hard to classify. Many bedding roses (including the early floribundas) are disappointing. Others are as powerfully fragrant as the best old roses. Among the best-scented (but not necessarily tea-scented) Hybrid Teas are 'Fragrant Cloud', 'Shot Silk', 'Silver Lining', 'Prima Ballerina', 'Papa Meilland' and 'Mister Lincoln'. 'Sutter's Gold' is unusual in having the tea scent loud and clear.

Scent was bred into the Floribundas from the 1950s onwards ('Tonnerre' being perhaps the first). The yellow 'Arthur Bell' (1965) and pale pink 'Michelle' (1970) are two with particularly powerful fragrance.

This is where a third group of modern roses, the Hybrid Musks, suggest themselves as the answer. They are not bedding roses in the strict sense, but shrubs of such profuse and constant flower that they can serve the same purpose, at least where there is room for a bush six feet wide. They start flowering late in the season, when the first flush of roses is over, keep going fairly steadily and have a triumphant autumnal show of flowers—all richly scented. 'Buff Beauty', 'Felicia', 'Penelope' and 'Vanity' are among them.

What happens to bedding roses if they are not given the full bedding treatment, pruned hard back and force-fed to flower to their utmost? It depends on the variety in question. Those that are particularly prone to black-spot, rust or mildew, the three chief enemies, may well succumb. On the other hand, mildew pounces on just that sappy young growth that pruning and feeding provoke. "Grown hard", with little feeding, particularly of nitrogen, they will be more resistant. There is no law that says that Hybrid Teas must be hacked almost to the ground every winter. Some of them, for example the lovely soft-toned 'Peace', will make tall shrubs and flower well.

Floribundas can more easily be treated as shrubs—though no doubt at the expense of some of their flowers. In their case, one method is only to dead-head them (cut off their flowered stems down to the next opening bud), which amounts to a light pruning after flowering, and otherwise only to cut away whole stems from the base when they are past their prime.

Disease and insects apart, the principal penance for growing roses is the sucker problem. Almost all commercially grown roses are budded on to a vigorous rootstock of either the dog-rose or the eastern Asian *R. rugosa* or *multiflora*. Sooner or later, usually in reaction to a jab from a probing fork, the rootstock will send up suckers. Unless they are promptly removed, all the vigour of the plant will go into them. But cutting them off is worse than useless: they must be torn off below ground where they leave the root.

THE MOST POPULAR

Britain's Royal National Rose Society keeps an annual register of the most popular kinds of Hybrid Tea and Floribunda roses. Below are the lists for 1978 of the most-grown roses which have been in cultivation for at least ten years, during which time they have had to prove their merit.

Hybrid Teas

'Grandpa Dickson'
'Peace'
'Pink Favourite'
'Wendy Cousins' (Most fragrant)
'Ernest H. Morse'
'Piccadilly'

Floribundas

'Iceberg'
'Evelyn Fison'
'Queen Elizabeth'
'City of Leeds'
'Elizabeth of Glamis'
'Southampton'

Climbing and rambling roses

Below left The wild musk roses are some of the world's most powerful climbers (or strictly speaking ramblers). This single plant of 'Kiftsgate' is over thirty feet wide, completely enveloping a shed in July with flowers and fragrance. Other similar roses are 'La Mortola', *Rosa longicuspis*, and 'Wedding Day'.

Below Still powerful but more amenable is the wichuriana rambler 'Albéric Barbier', whose pliant stems can be made to follow the contours of a wall, a tree or (as here) a rope. Creamy flowers are perfectly set off by dark green glossy leaves. Regular pruning is unnecessary, and indeed scarcely possible.

Far left 'Gloire de Dijon', one of the first and best climbers for colour, scent and perpetual-flowering.

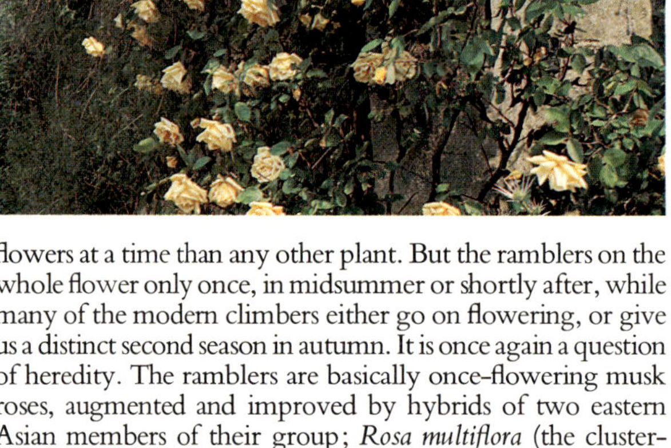

Left Climbing 'Lady Hillingdon' has a unique rich tea scent and warm colour with gracefully drooping flower-stems.

Above 'Albertine' bridges the gap between climber, rambler and shrub Coppery buds open to rose-pink petals with a heavenly scent.

Above 'Mermaid' is one of a kind: a cross between a tea rose and the MacCartney rose, a tender Chinese species. It is slightly tender but in warm areas it makes a huge almost evergreen climber, flowering all summer even in the shade. Its prominent stamens give it a distinctive wild rose look.

The urge to impose order on a thoroughly heterogeneous lot has led gardeners to classify their longest-stemmed roses, which in nature are given to pouring down cliffs or mounting into trees, as climbers or ramblers according to their conventional garden uses. No rose climbs in the sense that a vine does by deliberately taking a grip on the next hand-hold in the direction of the light. The rose method is to put up canes, sometimes of amazing length—as much as thirty feet at a time—in hope that support will be forthcoming. Its thorns help it to hang on: the big climbing musk roses have particularly vicious curved thorns behind their leaves.

But a rose of almost every stature can be found somewhere, in a steady progression from a short shrub to a size to challenge forest trees. Along with differences of size come other important variations: stiffness of stem and a tendency to send up new stems. All three greatly affect garden performance.

To gardeners, climbers are those which tend to produce stiff stems in relatively small numbers (not "breaking" very often from the base), but capable of reaching, let us say, the eaves of a house. Ramblers usually have more pliable and whippy shoots in larger numbers, tending not to grow so long because new ones are regularly coming from ground level to take over.

Just as important as their manner of growing is their manner of flowering. By virtue of sheer size, the tall roses give us more flowers at a time than any other plant. But the ramblers on the whole flower only once, in midsummer or shortly after, while many of the modern climbers either go on flowering, or give us a distinct second season in autumn. It is once again a question of heredity. The ramblers are basically once-flowering musk roses, augmented and improved by hybrids of two eastern Asian members of their group; *Rosa multiflora* (the cluster-flowering rose which lies behind our Floribundas) or *R. luciae wichuraiana*, a sweet-scented, late-flowering evergreen rose given not to climbing but running along the ground.

The musk roses (multiflora and the shrubby American Prairie rose excepted) are only white or cream, but include the most gigantic members of the genus: roses such as *R. brunonii* and *R. filipes*, whose best-known form, 'Kiftsgate', will occupy a space forty feet high and wide. Their flowers hang down in trusses of extreme grace; hundreds of strong-scented, five-petalled, yellow-stemmed flowers at a time.

R. multiflora contributed a purple pigment to a small band of roses via its offspring 'Crimson Rambler'. *R. wichuraiana* has been so important as a parent that a whole class of roses is often referred to by its name. The famous 'Albéric Barbier' might be taken as the type of these: lax and flowing, growing to twenty feet, dark green glossy leaved, with a sweet-sharp scent like fine German wine; and apt to produce more creamy

Below and *below right* The climbing Hybrid Teas can create a richer effect on a wall than any other climber. 'Souvenir de Claudius Denoyel' is a superb example, flowering early and again later with generous fragrance. It is important to tie the stiff stems of Hybrid Teas to the wall as near to the horizontal as possible.

Right The superlative white Floribunda 'Iceberg' has produced a climbing sport, here perfectly trained.

Below 'Madame Gregoire Staechelin' is a gloriously sensuous Hybrid Tea, profuse even in shade, but only once-flowering and with a tendency to flower at roof level, with bare stems.

Above Pillar roses are a vague class of short-growing climbers or ramblers, not overtopping about nine feet. 'Phyllis Bide' is an excellent but little-known example, often still in flower at Christmas.

Left The grand manner of displaying ramblers in Regent's Park, London. The graceful curves of ropes between pillars emphasize the elegance of the roses, which are from left to right 'Silver Moon', 'City of York' and 'New Dawn'.

Below 'New Dawn', raised in the United States in 1930, is near to perfection as a rambler or climber. It is as good used formally (left) as lighting up an old yew tree with its falling sprays. It is healthy, fragrant, and flowers for months on end.

flowers, though not effusively, after its early-summer climax.

A totally different blood-line produced the climbers. The musk rose is still there as a distant ancestor, but the major influence is Chinese. The family tree on pages 86–7 shows the complicated series of crosses that produced first the Noisettes (the first recurrent-flowering climbers) then the climbing teas, then added old-rose blood—via the Hybrid Perpetuals and Bourbons—to produce Hybrid Teas, and explains why at each stage the genetic potential to produce a climber is present. 'Zéphirine Drouhin', for example, is a Bourbon climber which is still often grown.

Some of the noisette and tea climbers were as good as any made since, in gentle tones of buff and apricot and cream. 'Gloire de Dijon' and 'Climbing Lady Hillingdon', 'Mme. Alfred Carrière' and 'Alister Stella Gray' are among them. Some missed the gene for recurrence but were so beautiful and so different from their fellows that they have survived anyway. 'Paul's Lemon Pillar' and 'Mme. Gregoire Staechelin' are among these.

The Hybrid Teas, though bred as a race of recurrent-flowering bushes, also have the family tendency to "sport" into climbers. There are Hybrid Tea climbing sports in most colours. Among pinks, for example, 'Climbing Ophelia'; among flame colours, 'Climbing Mrs Sam McGredy';

Above 'Golden Showers' is one of the most perpetual-flowering roses.

Below 'Parkdirektor Riggers' is a new *kordesii* climber with a similar length of season.

among crimsons, 'Climbing Ena Harkness' (and the darkest of all red velvet roses, 'Guinée'); among yellows, 'Casino'. Whites are rare. All can be assumed to be recurrent to some degree—some of them as perpetual-flowering as their sister bushes. For anyone who likes Hybrid Tea flowers but dislikes their bushes, these climbers are the ideal way of growing them.

To this very broad structural and genetic division must be added the filling-in that breeders have inevitably done, though much less in climbers and ramblers than in bushes.

It is generally recognized that the fault with the climbers, Hybrid Teas in particular, is their stiffness. The loveliest thing is the cascade. Enlightened gardeners now want every possible colour in manageable disease-resistant plants that are as recurrent as climbers and as graceful as ramblers.

'Albertine', an early cross between *R. wichuraiana* and a Hybrid Tea, is a wonderful example of the potential. It is not exactly graceful, or recurrent, but it remains a universal favourite. Floribundas can also "sport" into climbers. 'Climbing Iceberg' and 'Climbing Korona' are examples. Another promising development is the new fertile species *R. kordesii*, produced in Germany by a stroke of genetical good fortune, which combines the hardiness and healthiness of *R. rugosa* with the qualities of *R. wichuraiana*. The old distinctions between climbers, ramblers and shrubs is becoming blurred.

Rhodoland: species and series

Below The Himalayas are the heart of Rhodoland. Plant-collecting parties like this, crossing a clearing in *Rhododendron arboreum* forest in east Nepal, have been scouring the mountains for new, better and hardier species since the 1820s. Almost all hybrids have some Himalayan blood.

A future historian looking back at the gardens of the last hundred years might well christen the period the Erica Dynasty. The Ericaceae is the one plant family that has imposed a whole fashion of gardening. In fact it has imposed two. The modern heather garden is the latest manifestation of their compelling, uncompromising character. But their greatest and most enduring innovation was the rhododendron woodland—a style that became the rage a hundred years ago and continues to this day.

Like all good dynasties the ericas have a strong family look about them—particularly in the shape of their flowers and their imperious manners. They are not good mixers. They grow best and look best in the company of their own kind. Their kind includes strawberry-trees, mountain-laurel, *Pieris*, *Enkianthus*, sorrel trees, gaultheria, blueberries and bilberries, cassiope and clethra . . . an astonishing diversity of woody plants of every size. Most remarkable of all is the genus *Rhododendron*, which alone has over eight hundred species. There is nothing else we grow in gardens that can compare in richness and range, from creeping alpines to towering trees. All (or nearly all) rhododendrons are flamboyant in flower and at least neat, but often spectacular, in leaf.

Other plants that have diversified so widely have adapted to almost every soil and climate. The ericas, the rhododendrons particularly, have gone the other way and specialized. Somewhere in the history of their evolution (from a branch of the tea family that includes the camellias) they struck up a profitable relationship with mycorrhizae or soil-dwelling fungi, which enabled them to exploit very acid soil that is unfertile for most plants. Most of their development has taken place in the cool and rainy mountains of the world, where acid soil follows on the endless leaching of nutrients by the rain; ideal country, with its wet summers and deep snow in winter, for the big evergreen leaves which most of them have. They exist on all the continents except Africa and South America, but proliferate in species upon species, as no other plant proliferates anywhere, in the monsoon belt of the eastern Himalayas. The dripping forests and deep gorges between Yunnan and Sikkim, to the north of Burma, where the Irrawaddy, Mekong, Brahmaputra, Salween and countless other rivers rise, was christened by one explorer, quite simply, Rhodoland.

I have borrowed his word for the title of this chapter because a word is needed to express the whole world of the rhododendron; its fascination, its cultivation, the fanatics who follow it, the garden style they have built round it, and the botanical wrangles it provokes.

For a tidy taxonomic mind rhododendrons are one of the great challenges. They demand a system, to group the species into bigger units that have something more in common than just being rhododendrons. Classifying them has provided a life's work for several scholars, notably at the Royal Botanic Garden in Edinburgh. To this day there is no agreement and the major reference books adopt different systems. The one described here, which seems to lead the layman some way at least into the maze, is the one set out in four hundred admirably lucid pages of the eighth (1976) edition of Bean's *Trees and Shrubs Hardy in the British Isles*.

It divides the whole genus into three principal sections: the lepidote, the elepidote, and the azaleas, which gardeners consider a separate issue (see pages 98–9).

Lepidote means scaly. The scaly rhododendrons are the largest group, with some 500 species, and also the widest ranging, with half its members in the tropics of Malaysia and Indonesia (the "Malesians"), but including also the tough little alpines and the epiphytic kinds that live on trees in warm rain-forests. Although the botanical character of scaliness (chiefly under the leaves) is not obvious, that and the way the leaves are

rolled in the bud, bottom side out, does seem to link all these species to a common ancestry.

Elepidote means "not scaly". In practice the leaves of this group are very often hairy underneath instead, and always rolled top side out in the bud. But more important, the great majority of gardenworthy rhododendrons fall into this group. They are on the whole bigger plants than the lepidotes, but more limited in their range, not venturing into high mountains or low latitudes.

Within these groups the species are mustered on the basis of their apparent affinity into smaller groups or "series", each named after its best-known member. There are twenty-three lepidote series, but only sixteen elepidote, so we are beginning to reach a comprehensible number. On these pages are set out a dozen of the best-known series, covering most of the species that concern the gardener.

It is not so difficult to grow rhododendrons as it is to choose them, or to site them satisfactorily in the garden. Their needs are simply stated: they must have acid soil, and they prefer damp air. They would rather that the soil was deep, decomposed leaf litter, but they can grow on a mere few inches if necessary as long as it never dries out, or is ever flooded. Being surface rooting they are some of the easiest plants to move, even when fully grown. But they do not like starvation: they need a regular diet of more and more leaves in the form of a mulch over their roots. If the leaves are supplemented with mature manure so much the better.

The grand manner of rhododendron gardening is to plant them in thinned woodland, where tall oaks, larches and firs filter the sunlight into dappled shade. It was devised by the grandees of the last century in imitation of the Himalayan forests, to provide shelter from wind, frost and excessive sun for plants whose massive features, both flowers and leaves, can easily be blemished by the elements. The myth emerged that they like deep shade, which is far from true. Most will tolerate it, but flower little and become thin and leggy looking for the light. Where they need shade and coolness is at the roots. Once they have equipped themselves with low branches or grown together in a solid phalanx, so that the soil is in permanent shade, their heads can only benefit from sunshine, within reason. Long dry spells are the enemy. Without their ration of mists and rain their noble leaves hang like the ears of a whipped spaniel. They react in the same way to winter cold. Dry, frosty weather is cruel to them; icy winds worse. For all these reasons the best climate, aside from monsoon-lashed mountains, is in the mild, damp, west of Europe and north-west of North America and New Zealand. The more splendid kinds find the east altogether too bracing.

The hardiest kinds, however, are well signposted after more than a century of experience and breeding. Precise codes of relative hardiness have been developed for each country.

Twelve of the thirty-nine series (groups of species) of rhododendro are represented on the right. Although lepidote, or scaly, species are more numerous in nature they are far outnumbered in gardens by the elepidote (unscaly) species. The lepidotes are largely either alpine o tropical. Flower-shapes often vary enormously even within one series, from trumpet- to funnel- to bell-shaped, or something in-between. The position of the flower is slight more characteristic.

Lepidotes are apt to flower not only from the terminal (end) bud c each shoot but also from several le axils below it, whereas elepidotes are more inclined to flower from t shoot-tip only. There are also differences in the numbers of chromosomes which makes crossin between the two groups less easy than within them.

The series represented here as a sample of the most important are:

s. Arboreum: mostly trees or big shrubs with long leathery leaves, hairy below, and many flowers in dense "truss" in the white-red-purple colour range.

s. Campanulatum, a wide-spread and heterogeneous Himalayan gro recognized by blunt-edged elliptic leaves, usually hairy below, and more or less bell-shaped flowers ranging in colour from yellow or white to deep red.

s. Falconeri is usually grouped together with **s. Grande**. The two are predominantly stout plants wit hairy shoots and hefty leaves. Thei flowers are generally bell-shaped ir terminal trusses in a wide range of colours. They can be spectacular in wet mild-temperate gardens.

s. Fortunei has several sub-series (including **Griffithianum** and **Calophytum**) but all are large bushes, have blunt-ended leaves an flower at the shoot-tip with funnel to bell-shaped flowers in the pink-white range.

s. Griersonianum is another one-species series of the greatest value f its beauty and as a parent of hybric Its uniqueness lies in the form of it bud, and its scarlet and crimson trumpet-flowers felty at the base.

s. Neriiflorum is another broad grouping based on the loose formation of the flower-heads, the flowers being unspotted and their ovaries densely hairy, but most of the species are small and their flowers red or near-red.

s. Ponticum has two representativ opposite. It circles the globe north the Himalayas. Their leaves are generally smooth and their rather long-stalked funnel- to bell-flower form candelabra shapes.

s. Thomsonii is another broad an mixed collection of small to medium east Himalayan species w thin leathery leaves and loose terminal trusses of flowers, often be shaped (as in the well-known dwa *R. williamsianum*).

s. Cinnabarinum are tall shrubs with small leaves, densely scaly below, usually tubular, rather flesh flowers, from purple to orange, an with three times the normal chromosome number.

s. Lapponicum are dwarfs with tiny, scaly aromatic leaves and sho funnel-flowers in many colours. Again with extra chromosomes.

s. Triflorum has three sub-series, lightly-branched, thin-leaved, sometimes deciduous, with speckle funnel-flowers, in a huge range of colours from yellow to near-blue.

Left R. auriculatum from west China is named for the earlike lobes of its leaves. Its importance is its very late flowering, after mid-summer, which is useful to breeders. A famous hybrid is 'Polar Bear'.

Below R. impeditum represents the Lapponicum series of alpines, forming dense bushes in dry upland areas. The related *R. fastigiatum* and the deep purple *R. russatum* make good rock-garden plants.

Above The (lepidote) Himalayan *R. cinnabarinum* is a parent of 'Lady Chamberlain' and other famous hybrids. Its series includes the apricot *R. concatanens*.

Above R. haematodes, R. sanguineum and others in the Neriiflorum series are chiefly small or dwarf shrubs from west China. *R. forrestii* is a good hardy rock-garden plant.

Left The beautiful dense-growing *R. yakushimanum* from southern Japan is the aristocrat of the Ponticum series, which includes the common European *R. ponticum* and hardy American species. Now much used for breeding.

Left R. decorum is a Fortunei, together with the tender Himalayan *R. griffithianum*, parent of the famous 'Pink Pearl', and the Chinese *R. calophytum*, a splendid hardy tree.

Above R. griersonianum was one of Forrest's best discoveries with its exquisite flowers. The most used of all rhododendrons for breeding.

Above R. campanulatum has given its name to a heterogenous dozen of Himalayan species. In Victorian times it was considered outstanding.

Right R. arboreum was the tree-species whose introduction from the Himalayas in the 1820s first showed gardeners the brilliance of the genus. Its natural range is so wide that variations proliferate. The best is blood-red.

Above R. maximum, the "rosebay", was the first American rhododendron to reach Europe (1736) and was bred into the "hardy hybrids". These *R. catawbiense* are the American Ponticums.

Above left R. augustinii is highly prized for its blue flowers, improved by selection. Its series, Triflorum, are mainly thin shrubs, including the bluish-white *R. yunnanense*.

Right R. fictolacteum represents the very similar Falconeri and Grande series—all tall Himalayans including some, with the grandest of all leaves, such as *R. sinogrande*. *R. fictolacteum* is one of the hardiest.

Left R. campylocarpum was Hooker's favourite Nepalese rhododendron; one of the best yellow-flowered species, which tend to lack vigour. Its series, Thomsonii, includes *R. thomsonii* with blood-red bells and the popular little *R. williamsianum*.

Rhodoland: hybrids

The first rhododendrons to be grown in European gardens were the pink-flowering rosebay, *R. maximum*, introduced from eastern North America in 1736, and the mauve Pontic, which came from Asia Minor in the 1770s. A third, *R. caucasicum*, brought in yellowish flowers in 1803. And a fourth, *R. catawbiense*, came from America in 1809. They were all thoroughly hardy, good-looking evergreens, but on the strength of these alone the rhododendron would never have taken off. Their flowers are at best pleasant, at worst dowdy.

The real launching of Rhodoland took place in the 1820s, when the first of many Himalayan species, sent home as seed from Kashmir, flowered in England. This was a different matter: a tall plant (christened by its botanical godfather *R. arboreum*, the tree rhododendron) with magnificent blood-red flowers. No other known shrub could compare with it.

There was unfortunately a snag. The flowers came in March or April, when they were almost bound to be destroyed by frost—and indeed the whole plant needed protection. It was not by any means a satisfactory garden plant. But it was the cue for nurserymen to embark on a breeding programme that for a century went on at fever pitch, crossing the old hardy sorts with the new Himalayan ones in efforts to combine hardiness with bright, beautiful and, above all, late flowers. Unless the flowers could be delayed until the end of May there was at least an even chance that frost would damage them. It takes little frost to spoil so sumptuous a flower.

The fruits of these labours are known as the hardy hybrids. The nurserymen, above all the Waterer family at Knapp Hill in Surrey and Bagshot in Berkshire, and the firms of Standish and Noble at Ascot and Sunningdale (all on the sandy heaths south of London which are still ideal nursery and horse-racing country) worked in high rivalry and deep secrecy, crossing and recrossing species with hybrids and hybrids with more hybrids. Many of the plants they produced are still among the best of their kind. 'Lady Eleanor Cathcart' (*R. maximum* × *R. arboreum*) and the early-flowering white *R. nobleanum* (*R. caucasicum* × *R. arboreum*) are examples of well-known plants that were the first generation of breeding.

Of later, more complex crosses of the same blood, a score are still in cultivation. Strangely enough, though by now breeding was in full spate in France, Holland and Belgium as well, nearly all were English raised. Apparently English nurserymen were shortening the generation gap from seedling to flower to as little as four years by grafting seedlings on to mature roots. By 1870 they had crosses already seven or eight generations removed from the tender *R. arboreum*, but still carrying its desirable traits.

In 1850 Joseph Hooker returned from his famous expedition to the Himalayas with forty-three more rhododendrons of great quality but questionable hardiness. The pick of them was *R. griffithianum*. The nurserymen looked hungrily at this lovely flower when it first opened in captivity in 1858. They crossed it with hardy species and hardy hybrids, but its tenderness remained in all its progeny until 1897, when Waterers of Bagshot put on show what still remains one of the most famous and beautiful hardy hybrids—'Pink Pearl'.

Dutch nurserymen were quick to follow up with their own hybrids, the firm of Endtz using 'Pink Pearl' as a parent to produce the well-known 'Souvenir de Dr S Endtz', Koster & Sons using other *griffithianum* hybrids to make such famous hardy plants as 'Betty Wormald', and van Nes & Sons taking over the *griffithianum* breeding programme of the Berlin Porcelain factory (including the beautiful but tender 'Queen Wilhelmina') to produce in due course the splendid scarlet 'Britannia'. Evidently they had their eyes on the lucrative British market.

Meanwhile rich amateur breeders were at work on the increasing number of Himalayan introductions, motivated simply by their curiosity and the restless search for new forms of beauty. Cornwall, possessing a mild, damp climate, became a centre of cultivation of delicate species. Names such as 'Tremough' and 'Penjerrick' began to appear on beautiful but generally tender crosses. The term "species hybrid" is often used to distinguish these later, often amateur, productions from the old hardy hybrids of the nursery trade.

To the flow of new kinds from Nepal and Sikkim was added a stream, later to become a spate, from China. The first was *R. fortunei*, discovered by Robert Fortune in 1855 and in due course a famous parent of hybrids. In 1900 Sir Edmund Loder of Leonardslee in Sussex crossed *R. fortunei* with the comely *griffithianum* to produce perhaps the most famous "grex", or group of hybrids from two species, ever made—*R.* × *loderi*. This grex (the word literally means flock) has gone on to sire many other hybrids. *R. fortunei* too has been repeatedly used as a parent, particularly in the series of crosses made in this century by Lionel de Rothschild at Exbury in Hampshire.

Three great amateur names dominate twentieth-century rhododendron breeding: de Rothschild, J. C. Williams of Caerhays in Cornwall, and Lord Aberconway at Bodnant in North Wales.

The 1900s had seen a virtual invasion of western China by plant collectors. If "Chinese" Wilson stands at the head of the list for the variety and sheer number of his discoveries, the greatest gatherer of rhododendrons was George Forrest. By the end of the First World War many of their new species were beginning to flower in gardens. J. C. Williams in Cornwall was a subscriber and received seed from both Wilson and Forrest, and was the first to make hybrids of their introductions. Among many fruitful marriages those of Forrest's wonderful red trumpet-flowered *R. griersonianum* from Yunnan are probably the most numerous and important. Wilson's (lepidote) *R. augustinii* was another notable addition, bringing the nearest thing to blue into the range of rhododendron colours in such crosses as Williams's 'Blue Tit'.

Above Country-house rhodoland provides the greatest of all shrub spectacles in spring. High walls of 'Pink Pearl', the most famous of all the hardy hybrids, line the drive of a Norfolk mansion.

Above George Forrest was the greatest of all collectors of rhododendrons in the wild. Between 1904 and his death in the field in 1932 Forrest introduced more than three hundred new rhododendron species. He worked with incredible industry and efficiency, employing native collectors, chiefly in Yunnan Province in China and on the borders of parts of Tibet and Burma. Most of his introductions came from rainier and warmer regions than Wilson's. Many of them are tender, but have had enormous influence as hybrid parents.

Right The beauty and variety of rhododendron leaves is a study in itself, particularly as the pale young leaves emerge in contrast to the dark old ones in spring. From left to right here are *R. macabeanum, R. sinogrande, R. yakushimanum* and *R. fictolacteum*.

Above 'Britannia', raised in Holland in the 1920s from a complicated parentage including *R. griffithianum*, is still considered one of the best hardy scarlet rhododendron hybrids. It grows to about ten feet.

Above R. loderi, a cross made in 1901 between *R. fortunei* and *R. griffithianum*, is generally considered to be the finest hybrid rhododendron; a small tree with richly-scented flowers. 'King George' (above) is a very good form.

Above 'Lady Rosebery' and 'Lady Chamberlain' are two similar groups of crosses made at Exbury with basically the same parentage as 'Bodnant Yellow' (bottom left). A pink form of one parent gave the crimson 'Lady Rosebery'.

Left The royal gardens at Windsor have tried to improve on perfection by crossing the pink *R. Loderi* 'Venus' with the Rothschild cross 'Hawk Crest', the best yellow hybrid. The new cross is as yet unnamed.

Exbury is famous for a vast range of hybrids, both of rhododendrons and azaleas. 'Lady Chamberlain', 'Lady Rosebery', 'Jalisco' and 'Hawk Crest' are among the best known —each being a grex with several members of differing colour and quality. Bodnant also produced many well-known crosses between the wars; many of them red flowered and of a useful medium size, such as 'F. C. Puddle' and 'Bodnant Yellow'. Slocock's nursery at Woking, Surrey, is another famous breeder. Dietrich Hobbie in West Germany is another, specializing in small and very hardy plants suitable for modern German gardens. The best known are 'Elizabeth Hobbie', 'Baden-Baden' and 'Oldenburg'. In the United States the best-known producers of rhododendrons tough enough for north-eastern winters include David G. Leach, Orlando S. Pride and Gustav A. L. Mehlquist.

In the case of rose-breeders it is often said that novelty is all; that there are no real advances to be made along the lines they are following. Species which might have much to offer are not given a chance. In Rhodoland it is different. There are exciting new developments happening all the time. At the moment perhaps the most important concern the Japanese *R. yakushimanum*. Breeders have their eyes on the unique combination of hardy good temper and aristocratic good looks of this incomparable species. Though it is hard to imagine what would constitute an improvement on a plant already so richly endowed.

The aesthetics of placing rhododendrons in gardens are less simple than they appear. Small modern gardens cannot imitate the forests of Nepal. The little alpine kinds are at home in rock or peat gardens. But the bigger rhododendrons have so much presence that they seem to want to banish all except their own kind from the garden. Roses look wrong with them. The usual cheerful border flowers and annuals look tawdry and out of place. Other shrubs look trivial. Only a select band of flowers, such things as lilies, trilliums, the Asiatic primulas and the Himalayan blue poppy that tolerate the acid soil, feel right in Rhodoland.

Above 'Bodnant Yellow' is one of the most famous hybrids made at that great North Wales garden in the 1930s. Its principal parents were the orange-yellow *R. cinnabarinum*, crossed with the late-flowering *R. maddenii*.

Above Hybridization also includes improving on a species by crossing two particularly good, slightly differing forms. *R. augustinii* 'Electra', is an example, made by Lionel de Rothschild at Exbury in the 1930s.

Rhodoland: azaleas

Below The evergreen Japanese Kurume azaleas flower in May in a wide range of colours from scarlet to cream. They are in their element here in the light shade of thin oak woodland on the famous Battleston Hill, at the Royal Horticultural Society's Wisley garden.

Linnaeus believed that azaleas and rhododendrons were two different things—based on the fact that (most) azaleas have five stamens, while rhododendrons have ten. As far as botanists are concerned his grave error was corrected in 1870 by Carl Maximowicz of St Petersburg. As far as gardeners are concerned, Linnaeus was right.

Rhododendrons are almost always evergreen: azaleas drop their leaves, or most of them, in winter. The "evergreen" azaleas shed the few leaves they keep all winter in spring. Azaleas tend to be small, or at least thin branched, and their flower formation, too, is distinct: never in a raceme or spike like many rhododendrons. Above all they are known for smothering themselves in so many flowers that leaves are invisible. They make solid mounds of colour in a wider colour range than anything else except roses. Great beauty is possible with carefully chosen azaleas: loud jangles if they are planted indiscriminately.

Their tastes in soil are the same as rhododendrons': damp leaf-mould is their favourite food. Whereas most of the bigger rhododendrons are happiest in modified or tree-filtered sunlight, most azaleas are creatures of open scrubland where the sun reaches them all day. A baking does them no harm.

For practical purposes there are two main groups of azaleas, the deciduous and the evergreen—or nearly so—roughly conforming to a botanical division into two "sub-genera". It is too much to hope that we should be allowed to call them "series", just when we were getting used to the word.

Each of the two groups is now a tangle of hybrids so numerous that they are referred to by historical names. Ghent, Knap Hill, Kurume, Exbury are the places where the crosses were originally made. Mollis, the name of the other main deciduous batch, is one of those fossilized blunders that pepper the pages of gardening literature. *Azalea mollis* was at the time the name of the Japanese parent of the group. The same plant is now called *Rhododendron japonicum*. To make matters worse the old *Azalea sinensis*, the Chinese parent, is now called *Rhododendron molle*. Hence, you may well suppose, the retreat into hybrids with names that stick, even if they are in Japanese.

The family trees opposite are the only clear way of telling this complex story and explaining how divers qualities of hardiness, habit, size and brightness of flower and time of flowering have been combined over the last hundred years into such reliable garden plants.

In general the colours of the deciduous azaleas are better in the hotter part of the spectrum, the flame colours; while the evergreens, where they are hardy (generally not below zone 8), have pinks, mauves, lilacs and blue-purples to offer.

But flowers are not all. The deciduous azaleas often form distinct tiers as they grow older, making bushes with much character. In autumn few things in the garden turn more glorious or more various colours. Among the evergreens are plants that mound up prettily or spread massively. The Japanese habitually shear them all over to encourage dense bushiness. The Western method is to pinch out the growing tips.

I must not give the impression that it is only hybrid azaleas that are worth growing. Few if any of the hybrids have the range of qualities of the common yellow European wildling *R. luteum*, the great-grandfather of them all. For flower, for leaf colour, for stature and for an intoxicating sweetness of breath it is still superlative.

One azalea seems to have been unofficially christened Royal for its combination of qualities. The rosy pink *R. schlippenbachii* is exquisite, from its early unfolding of purply red leaves to its sumptuous autumn colour. It lacks scent, but otherwise its only fault is that springtime eagerness that dogs gardeners in Britain. April warmth woos it from the bud, only for May frost to cry "got you" and bite its head off.

Below 'Harvest Moon' (front) and 'Hugh Wormald' are two of the modern Knap Hill deciduous hybrids. Most grow to about five feet, with bronze young leaves, sweet scent and autumn colour.

Right Rhododendron luteum, formerly called *Azalea mollis*, photographed in its own country on the south shores of the Black Sea. It is as fine a plant as any of its hybrids, with glorious fragrance and autumn colour.

Below The deciduous azaleas give an autumn display of colour almost as bright as their flowering. The azaleas that William Robinson planted at Gravetye, Sussex, are still healthy sixty years on.

Right 'Palestrina' is one of the loveliest white evergreen azaleas, a hybrid of *R.* × *malvaticum* and *R. kaempferi*. When it flowers in May its new leaves are the most brilliantly fresh green.

Above Of all the Kurume azaleas the strident pink 'Hinomayo' is the most popular. Unlike most of its kind it is almost deciduous, though very hardy.

DECIDUOUS AZALEAS

R. luteum (*Azalea pontica*). Caucasian, European. To 10ft. Flowers May, bright yellow, very fragrant. Lovely autumn colour. Well worth growing.

R. calendulaceum (flame azalea). Allegheny Mts, USA. To 10ft. The May to June flowers are small but brilliant red-orange-yellow. Brings scarlet tones into hybrids.

R. periclymenoides. Widespread in eastern United States. To 9ft. The May flowers are in the red-pink-purple range, with a longer "tube" than the flame azalea.

R. viscosum (swamp azalea). Carolina to Cape Cod. Flowers June and July—sticky, white or pinkish, long tubed, very fragrant. To 7ft.

Other eastern American deciduous species: there are fifteen in all.

The story of the deciduous azalea hybrids, which include most of those grown in gardens, is told in this chart. The Ghents are the equivalent of the early hybrid rhododendrons in which European and American blood was first mingled. Bigger, brighter and more showy flowers became possible with the introduction of Japanese and Chinese blood (*R. japonicum* and *R. molle*). The richest genetic mixture (the left-hand line of the chart) has resulted in the finest combinations of qualities, culminating in the Exbury hybrids.

Ghent hybrids. Originated in Belgium in 1820s. Upright; some to 10ft. Relatively small flowers with the new leaves in late May. Sometimes "hose-in-hose" or double-flowered (e.g. the yellow 'Narcissiflora'). Good autumn colour and very hardy. 'Rustica Flore Pleno' is a related double-flowered strain.

R. molle (*A. sinensis*). From eastern China. To 6ft. Has fine big yellow flowers in April and May but lacks vigour in cultivation.

R. japonicum (*A. mollis*). Japanese. To 5ft. Flowers in May before the leaves appear. A wide range of colours, mostly red and orange. Scentless.

Knap Hill hybrids. First made by Waterer's nursery, Knap Hill, Surrey, in the 1850s but only came to prominence in the 1920s. To 5ft. Young leaves often bronze. Fairly fragrant flowers in May stand up well, sometimes with a darker "flare". Very hardy. Good autumn colour.

Mollis hybrids. Originated in Belgium in 1860s; developed by Koster in Holland in 1890s. 4 to 5ft. Flowers, in early May before the leaves, are sometimes spoiled by frost. Very hardy, likes full sun; brilliant flaming hot colours, but no scent.

R. occidentale. The one azalea of the western United States. To 8ft. Lovely white flowers, yellow blotched, in June and July when leaves are fully out. Fragrant.

Above Azalea breeding for bigger and more sumptuous flowers has reached its climax in the Knap Hill-Exbury hybrids with such plants as 'Silver Slipper' shown here.

The Exbury strain. Developed since 1920 at Exbury, Hampshire, by Lionel de Rothschild, by repeated crossings and ruthless elimination. Heights vary from 5 to 10ft. Very hardy. Big flowers with strong bright colours, often with darker markings. So inbred that seedlings are all good, but many of the best have been named and won awards, e.g. 'Basilisk', 'Strawberry Ice', 'Silver Slipper', 'Sun Chariot' and 'George Reynolds' (the yellow original of the strain).

Occidentale hybrids. Originated in Holland (Koster, 1895). To 7ft. Late May to early June flowering, fragrant with fine, delicate pastel colours, not to be mixed with Mollis hybrids.

EVERGREEN AZALEAS

R. mucronatum. A group of Japanese garden azaleas. To 4ft, spreading. White flowers at the end of May. Hardy but also good indoors.

R. indicum. S. Japan. 3 to 6ft. Bright red June flowers, slightly hardier than *R. simsii*, but not so good indoors.

R. simsii. S. China. 3 to 8ft. May flowering, red with darker markings. Tender.

R. kaempferi. Kyushu Island, Japan. To 10ft. Shades of red in mid-May. Fairly hardy.

Various other local species on Kyushu.

R. kiusianum Kyushu Island, Japan. To 10ft hardy, flowering May to early June. Mauve or white.

Various other species and hybrids.

"Indian" azaleas. Modern Belgian sorts are largely derived from *R. simsii*.

The hardy deciduous Korean *R. poukhanense*.

A wide range of other hybrids.

R. 'Obtusum' is one such cross: low and dense with small glowing-red flowers.

Kurume azaleas. Old hybrids between species on Mt Kirishima in Kyushu, S. Japan. E. H. Wilson chose a famous fifty out of 250 garden kinds in 1918. Many small flowers in late April to May. Not all hardy.

Gable hybrids. Pennsylvania, USA. Some of the hardiest evergreen azaleas, e.g. 'Rosebud', 'Stewartstonian'

Glenn Dale hybrids and many other species and hybrids. Maryland, USA. Bred in the 1930s for big flowers and bright colours to be hardy in the middle Atlantic states, e.g. 'Martha Hitchcock'.

Exbury evergreens. Very high quality. Moderately hardy, e.g. 'Pippa', 'Leo'.

R. 'Malvaticum'. Very hardy, mauve, not now grown.

Evergreen azaleas divide broadly into those intended for indoor use as pot-plants and those fit for garden life. The term "Indian" is often used for the many indoor cultivars that are principally bred in Belgium. Japan has a centuries-old tradition of breeding and selecting hardier garden forms that has been continued in Holland and the United States. Many points of parentage remain obscure, but the basic blood lines emerge fairly clearly.

Vuyk hybrids. Dutch. Small, hardy and reliable. Include the superb white 'Palestrina' and 'Vuyk's Scarlet'.

Koster's hybrids. Dutch. May flowering in a wide range from orange to red-purple. Leaves colour in Autumn, e.g. 'Anny'.

Climbing plants

Right Climbers attach themselves to the plants they use as hosts by an ingenious variety of methods. But if they are to be asked to climb up walls only those with ariel roots or "holdfasts" (sucker pads) are self-supporting. The rest need a trellis or system of wires, designed to support a considerable weight.

The great advantage of climbing plants is that they add the vertical dimension of the garden to the space you can cover with leaves and flowers. The smaller the garden the more important this is. A little urban backyard has more wall than floor. Climbers take very little ground space, yet can clothe any wall with beauty, or at least with soothing greenery.

Not that it is a climber's nature to grow on walls. A climber is a plant that decided (in an evolutionary way) to concentrate on length rather than strength, to throw all its energies into gaining height rather than becoming a responsible self-supporting citizen of the woods.

The majority of climbers are woodland creatures that rely on bushes and trees to support them as they grow upwards to the sun. They are light-demanding plants. That is why they climb. But their roots are accustomed to the cool, shaded soil beneath the trees. A wall provides no all-round shelter, but brusque draughts; no deep damp humus at its foot, but rubble and dust. On south-facing walls the whole plant is grilled all summer long.

Climbers have varied and ingenious ways of hanging on. Plants such as ivy and Virginia creeper use the adhesive method: ivy has aerial roots, the creeper small sucker pads. Tree trunks are their natural home: walls are not so different.

Then there is a class of climbers that hardly deserves the term at all. They simply put out long lax shoots directly upwards and hope to find something to support them. Climbing roses are the commonest example. You might count their curved thorns as crampons, but unless they encounter a branch overhead they will eventually flop to the ground. Another shoot will rise, fail, fall on top of the first, until the rose is a huge tangled mound.

The most ingenious kind of climber uses something that seems remarkably like muscular reaction to grab hold of a twig or branch on the way up. The grape vine is a good example. It is a tendril-climbing plant. The tendrils are like long leaf stalks without leaves, which can weave about like the limbs of an octopus until they touch something that feels promising as a hand-hold. Then the cells on one side of the tip grow with amazing speed while those on the other side stay as they were, and the tip quickly forms a curl. Many clematis use the same muscular-seeming reaction, but having no specialized tendrils, curl the long stalks of their leaves round any likely support.

The commonest of all climbing techniques is the serpentine spiral or twining motion adopted by honeysuckle, bindweed, wisteria, summer jasmine and a score of other well-known plants. Again it is faster growth of one side of the stem than the other that causes the curling motion. Some twine clockwise, some anticlockwise. Whether like bathwater they change their minds at the equator I have not discovered.

In each category of climbers there are both permanent woody plants and herbaceous ones that start again each year. The woody ones can eventually strangle their hosts. Once honeysuckle has wound its wiry loops round a twig it is only a matter of time before the twig, trying to grow thicker, throttles itself. I have seen wisteria in the forests of Japan with a main trunk twelve feet in girth. The tree it originally climbed had long since died and decayed and the monster was held up by half an acre of tentacles proliferating in the forest canopy above. It was a salutary reminder that the size of a climber must be matched to the size of its host plant if the poor climbing-frame is to survive.

This Japanese forest contained wild wisteria and tall paulownia trees, in bloom simultaneously with flowers of the same pale lilac tint—not an arrangement any economically minded gardener would allow. The sensible thing is to grow an early-flowering climber over a late-flowering bush or tree, or *vice versa*, giving a double performance. I do it with the light-weight *Clematis macropetala* over a browny red form of the smoke bush, *Cotinus coggyria*. First comes the clematis with its violet-blue flowers, just as the young brown leaves of the bush appear. Then, when the bush produces its purply puffs of "smoke" in summer, the clematis has silky, silvery seed heads.

Alternatively, a climber that flowers at the same time as its host, but in a different colour, can be a remarkable sight. The white *Clematis montana* over a scarlet hawthorn works perfectly. Or there is the contrast of leaf colour to play with. One day I hope to see the white wisteria I have planted under the outskirts of a copper beech hanging its snowy tassels all over the tree's purple dome.

Climbers on walls need support suitable to their mode of gripping, which could of course be an established tall shrub or tree, a ceanothus or a magnolia perhaps, planted against the wall. But this takes time. To do the job quickly, for climbers without directly adhesive habits, there is nothing for it but to provide a system of wires or trellis. The essential here is that it stands out well away from the wall—four inches is not too much—and that its supporting nails or screws are strong enough to hold what could eventually be a very heavy weight. There is of course no need to limit yourself to one climber per pitch. A strong one can easily support a lighter one on its back. A rose can take a clematis, or a wisteria a passion flower.

Whether on walls or under trees climbers need generous planting, with due regard for the normal poverty of the soil in such places. It is a good plan never to plant closer than eighteen inches from the foot of a wall, and then to dig deeper and make a richer soil mixture than for other plants. My technique for planting under trees and among shrubs is to excavate well, then to bury a large cardboard box (the dozen-bottle size), fill it with compost and plant in that. By the time the box has rotted away, the climber's roots are ready to compete.

Above The aim of climbers is to reach up through the woodland canopy to the light. Virginia creeper climbs equally fast on house or tree, turning scarlet in autumn. Boston ivy, in reality Japanese, is often mistaken for it, but has variable, eventually coarser, leaves.

Below Artificial (and unfortunately intrusive) support for a large-flowered clematis. The clematis would grow as well and look far better supported by a wall shrub. Or the trellis could be hidden by another climber, flowering at a different season, or evergreen.

Left Clematis montana allowed to run amok over an old fruit tree: the most natural and rewarding way to grow a vigorous climber, though eventually the tangled unprunable mass will destroy the tree unless it is cut right down and made to start again from scratch. The next step is to build a pergola.

Above The grape vine has been used from time immemorial to form leafy shade over garden walks, an adaption of its natural habit of building a canopy in the tree-tops. If fruit is not the object the purple-leafed vine gives a rich effect. For vigorous growth and autumn colour the huge-leaved *Vitis coignetiae* is best.

Left The honeysuckle is another climber, and eventually strangler, of trees. It luxuriates in shady corners and dislikes hot walls. None is more fragrant or lovely than the early and late Dutch forms of the European woodbine. Their fruits are glistening red berries.

Two ways of using ivy. *Above* it is clipped into impeccable architectural pilasters. *Below* it runs riot and almost buries the Hotel Lechat in Honfleur, Normandy. Scarlet geraniums in the window-boxes give life to what might otherwise appear to be an abandoned building.

Climbers for four seasons

A south-facing wall is the gardener's equivalent of prime time on television. A tantalizing choice must be made between the plants that demand the wall's shelter and warmth to grow at all and those that show their gratitude by producing twice as many flower buds from their well-ripened wood. On the whole climbers are likely to come into the second category. Remembering their native woods, they will grow satisfactorily (in appropriate hardiness zones) with any aspect. The south-facing wall should therefore be saved for plants that will repay VIP treatment with outstanding quantity and quality of flowers.

The two real florists' climbers are roses and clematis. If you are looking for the longest, brightest, finest show of flowers, and you can provide for them, you need look no further. Climbing roses are discussed on pages 92–3, and clematis, all too briefly, at the foot of this page.

Once you become climber minded, not just walls but every potential support in the garden—every tree, every shrub—become volunteers to be climbed on. There are flowering climbers for every moment of the unfrozen year, and ivy in endless variety to close the winter gap.

From time to time violent debate breaks out as to whether ivy is harmful to trees and buildings. The best authorities agree it does no harm to tree trunks or walls, despite its vigour. Trouble begins if it reaches out along branches and steals light in the canopy of a tree, which is very rare, and of course when it reaches, and starts to grow among, roof tiles.

At least a hundred cultivars of ivy have been given names. They vary in leaf shape and colour, often variegated yellow or white, very much in vigour and to some extent in hardiness. All, however, do the same strange thing when they are about to flower: they cease to be climbers and become shrubs, sending out stiff branches from the top of tree or wall. Cuttings taken from these will root and grow—but only as bushes.

Common green ivy, especially the big-leaved variety known as Irish (the one commonly sold as groundcover in the USA), is too powerful to be allowed among garden shrubs and trees of value. But many smaller cultivars are ideal. 'Goldheart' has small almost triangular leaves with radiantly cheerful yellow centres. 'Glacier' describes itself. Then there are curly-leaved, arrow-leaved, parsley-leaved. . . .

The flowering season for climbers starts (and finishes) with clematis (see below). Winter jasmine—a climber by convention only, in truth a spineless shrub—seizes the first mild spell to spangle its wall with yellow. But the great event in the climbing calendar is the eruption of the wisteria as spring turns to summer. Other climbers have flowers that could belong to a shrub, or be at home in a border. But wisteria has flowers that only a tree, and a big one at that, could possibly bear. The most manificent racemes—a word surely worth learning to describe such a cascade of flowers—are found on a form of the Japanese wisteria, *Wisteria floribunda macrobotrys*. The record length is said to be six feet; three is common. The Chinese wisteria (*W. sinensis*) has shorter racemes but generally more of them, rather earlier. Both are honey scented and enormously vigorous once they have started, creating a total tangle unless the gardener takes command. Pruning by shortening the long whippy growths is well worth while, ideally in summer and again (more savagely) in winter.

With full summer, the honeysuckles are starting: 'Early Dutch' first, then a dozen kinds, scented or unscented. Elegant and unusual though they are, I would not give space to a scentless honeysuckle. An evergreen one, *Lonicera japonica halliana*, has great virtue as a fast-growing sweet-scented screen, though its flowers are small. I have mixed it in a wild scramble on a north-facing wall with the powerful climbing hydrangea.

Most climbers flower together in summer: the climbing potato, *Solanum crispum*, and the far more beautiful but more tender *S. jasminoides*, which can flower on far into autumn; the summer jasmine, which makes little show, but on an upwind fence exhales a whole Arabian Night of perfume; the passion flower, intricate and bizarre; the Russian vine, of all plants called mile-a-minute the one that most deserves it, yet with a lovely froth of cream to cover a worn-out tree; in Mediterranean climates, bougainvillea; on warm walls farther north, towards autumn, the orange-trumpeted campsis; in cool woods, the flame-flower, *Tropaeolum speciosum*.

Then there are the annual climbers that rush up a trellis or a wall or inside an airy bush, to flower all summer long. Sweet peas, morning glory, *Cobaea scandens* and *Eccremocarpus scaber* are instant ways to add the climbing dimension to the garden.

Above A bridge is ideal support for a wisteria; the water adding the beauty of reflection. On a house wall they need strict management to flower well and stay within bounds.

THE CLEMATIS YEAR

Clematis armandii

Clematis macropetala

Clematis montana

Clematis 'Nelly Moser'

The clematis year starts in mid-winter with a lacy leaved evergreen, *C. balearica*. Its scented flowers like little creamy hellebores hang down from high on sheltered walls and trees. The Chinese *C. armandii*, white or pink with thick, hard, evergreen leaves, comes in early spring. Full spring brings *C. alpina* and *C. macropetala*, blue-purple lanterns on lightweight scramblers.

Clematis montana from the Himalayas flowers in late spring in rampant sheets of white or strong mauve-pink (*C. montana rubens*). Then early or late in summer—in some cases both—come the large-flowered cultivars, single or double, from white and pale pink to blue and royal purple. 'Lasurstern' is one of the best blues, 'Marie Boisselot' a splendid white (best in shade), 'Ville de Lyon' a clear red, and ×*Jackmanii* the most prolific purple. Blue is perhaps the most valuable of all, since no roses are this colour. Varieties with a darker bar on each sepal, which need rich feeding, are typified by 'Nelly Moser'.

Another group with abundant small white, red or purple flowers, *C. viticella*, has a long summer season. Then late summer brings the "lemon-peel" clematis, *C. orientalis*, with silky seed heads, and the heavenly scented *C. flammula*, with a mist of tiny white flowers.

Clematis tangutica

Above The flame-flower, *Tropaeolum*, is a herbaceous (non-woody) climber of prodigious energy in cool woodland soil. Yew is a perfect background for its trails of scarlet.

Right A small town garden uses climbers on a pergola to hide the boundary line. Ivy for winter is mixed with the Japanese vine, *Vitis coignetiae*, for summer and autumn.

Above The Brazilian bougainvillea is the best known of subtropical climbers. It is a spiny evergreen with no natural means of climbing, easily adaptable as a pot-plant for frost-free greenhouses. The striking colour is in the three papery bracts round the flower, itself a nonentity. With food and warmth it will flower for almost all the year.

Above Sweet peas are in that category of flowers that enthusiasts will go to any lengths to perfect. They can be casually grown as a very effective annual climber with a long season (lengthened by steadily picking bunches for the house). Or they can be meticulously trained up strings or canes and disbudded until they form a few flawless blooms for the show bench. But all need plenty of food at the roots and plenty of water in full sunshine. Some modern cultivars with bigger flowers lack the sweet scent which is more than half the point of growing them. Grandifloras (which have small flowers) are the sweetest of all.

The herbaceous border and its flowers

Above The heyday of the herbaceous border: George Elgood's painting of a border at Blyborough from Gertrude Jekyll's *Some English Gardens*, published in 1900 when the massing of hardy perennial plants in wide borders of their own was all the rage. Yew hedges provided the perfect background.

The French term *plantes vivaces* sounds at once more lively and nearer the truth than the awkward technical term herbaceous perennials by which we designate our finest and favourite flowers.

Herbaceous signifies merely that they have no wood: they are all soft material that dies back to the ground every year. Perennial distinguishes them from annuals and biennials with a limited life-span: perennials go on and on, growing bigger and bigger at each yearly appearance.

These are in fact the cream of the world's wild flowers, marshalled from meadows, prairies, woodland glades, the bush and the veldt.

By combining the permanence and certainty of shrubs with the brilliance of annuals they make themselves indispensable. They were probably the first flowers ever grown in gardens, and have always dominated the garden scene from early summer until late autumn.

The idea of segregating them into their own separate quarters is a late arrival. In the more extravagant Victorian gardens the flower beds were filled from the hothouses with spectacular displays of tender "bedding". Hardy perennial plants were forgotten, or relegated to borders round the kitchen garden and used simply for cutting for the house. The reforming William Robinson was among those who detested garish seasonal "carpet bedding" and advocated the use of permanent plants instead, replacing the formal "beds" scattered on the lawns with long deep "borders" along the sides of the garden, leaving the centre open. To this day the terms have kept the meaning he gave them: a "bedding plant" is temporary; a "border plant" permanent.

The fully fledged herbaceous border, a massive bed filled entirely with hardy perennials, was a *tour de force* of the last decade of the nineteenth century and the first generation of the twentieth. The artist who perfected it was Gertrude Jekyll. She carried the careful grading of heights and colours to its extreme. In her borders there was never a bare or flowerless patch, never an untoward hue. Graham Thomas remembers her own garden. "To see in reality those wonderful borders of graded colour was like an entry into a new world, or walking through a static rainbow."

It was too good to last. The static rainbow needed not only a consummate artist to design it but endless painstaking craftsmanship to keep it going. To hold all those perfectly graded plants in place a comprehensive system of corsetry was required. To urge them to maximum performance they must be constantly lifted, divided, replanted, fed.

But worst of all, out of season there was nothing to see but bare earth. A few of the plants have evergreen leaves; a few beautiful seed heads that last until winter gales destroy them. But a purely herbaceous border is a purely summer treat.

Above The planting plan for Miss Jekyll's main flower border, showing her carefully varied clumping and grouping to maintain months of perfectly harmonious colour and form. From her enormously influential book *Colour Schemes for the Flower Garden*.

Left Border flowers in their natural setting. A meadow in northern Greece in spring.

Right An alternative approach: border plants (in this case *Rodgersia podophylla*) massed on their own make a garden incident as telling as any shrub, and very much faster.

Above The price to pay for a summer spectacle: underpinning for a herbaceous border in the Royal Botanic Gardens, Edinburgh.

Thus the wheel has turned full circle, back to the old system of mixed planting, with border plants taking their place beside and among and under shrubs and trees and annuals, with bulbs between them to flower early in the year while they are just stirring. Not only is there less work to do and a far longer season of flowers, but in a mixed planting each plant can be given the conditions it prefers.

Where border plants will always score over shrubs is in their generosity of flowering from the first year of planting, their rapidity of increase and the fact that most of them are eminently portable: if you do not like them where they are, or you are moving house, or want to give a friend a piece, it is a minute's work to fork out a plant and move it or divide it.

They need good nourishment like any other plant, but no pruning; just the removal of their dead stems when they become unsightly. The more vigorous of them do, however, become congested in time as they constantly make new shoots from their outer edges. The middle is starved and dies. It is time to dig up the whole plant, divide it and replant the pieces.

Mixed planting solves most of the old border problems. It can even help with supporting tall plants by sheltering them and giving them something to lean against. There remain splendid flowers such as delphiniums, which will always need discreet help from thin stakes or canes to stand up proud. Breeders have produced short-stemmed versions of most of the popular border plants, including delphiniums, to save the trouble of staking. But is a short delphinium what you are looking for? Isn't that soaring spire the whole point?

Almost all the common border plants have been selected and "improved" and selected again by nurserymen looking for ever brighter and longer-lasting flowers. The improvements in most cases are real as far as they go, but by concentrating on the flowers the breeder neglects the whole plant. Inbreeding often weakens it, making it more prone to disease. Bigger flowers unbalance it, making it top-heavy. Gardeners are now tending to look more and more at the whole plant. It must take scrutiny from all round. Are its leaves pretty when it is out of flower? Does it stand gracefully? In many cases the answer is no. What started as a wild flower has become part of a paintbox, and lost its integrity.

In the survey of border flowers that follows, the emphasis is on species: the true unaltered flowers. The flowering season is divided into three parts, which obviously overlap but which help us to visualize the garden at different stages of the summer. The first pair of pages of each of the three is concerned with the general character of the garden at that time of year and the commonest—almost the essential—plants that dominate it. The second is an assortment of less common plants, almost all true species or close to them, arranged according to their preferences of soil and sun.

Below An alternative overall method of support for border plants: wide-mesh netting stretched horizontally between posts driven in at the corners of the planting.

The early border

Below The thrilling harmony of this spring scene is achieved with what seem simply the natural colours of a northern woodland glade: the plants are pale blue forget-me-nots, the Corsican hellebore 'Boughton Beauty', a spurge, the annual and the perennial forms of honesty, lungwort and periwinkle.

It is still too early in the year for the ground to be hidden with leaves and flowers. The essence of spring and the first days of summer is not massed colour but brilliant touches against a background of brown earth and the radiant green of young leaves. Chlorophyll green is the dominant colour of the season; so piercing that for the month or so that it is in its full burgeoning no scarlet or magenta can be brighter.

All other colours are seen as complements or contrasts to the eye-filling green. Flowers that pick it up and intensify it still further, such as the lime-green and golden-green spurges, are wonderfully effective. As contrast to the green, anything works from bright mauve (the biennial honesty is a prolific provider of this colour) to baby blue. There are still bulbs to add their notes of yellow and red, blue and white. More shrubs are flowering now than at any other season.

Coherent colour schemes are almost impossible at this time of year: it is better to concentrate on particularly happy pairings and groupings—which will occur by chance anyway—taking account of foliage as much as flowers. Young day-lily leaves, for example, sword-like in form and of a most telling yellow-green, are a useful ingredient. Hostas are grown as much for the excitement of seeing their salad-fresh leaves sprout from the ground, unfurling as they go, as for their summer flowers.

There is one family that cannot be overdone: the hellebores. Alone among border plants they stand up to the winter and announce the spring with incredibly long-lasting flowers of incomparable texture and quality, quiet coloured but forming with their deeply sculpted evergreen leaves some of the most satisfying plants you can grow.

HELLEBORES

Above Hellebores, the Christmas and Lenten roses, are the infallible sign of a keen, even a highbrow, gardener. They are a confusing race, but it scarcely matters as all are worth growing for their excellent, in most cases, evergreen leaves and winter or early spring flowers. They like shade, even a north-facing wall, and appreciate shelter. Under deciduous shrubs is an ideal place to grow them, although one species, the Corsican hellebore, builds itself up almost into a low shrub. They like fairly damp soil and have no objection to lime. The four best-known kinds are the Christmas rose, *H. niger*, with broad leaves and white or faintly pink flowers rising from ground level, often open by Christmas; the stinking hellebore, *H. foetidus*, with a striking combination of narrow, black-green leaves and pale green flowers with purple margins in late winter; the Corsican hellebore, *H. lividus*, the biggest of the four, with stiff, toothed, white-marbled green leaves and pale green flowers that last for months; and the Lenten rose, *H.× hybridus*, with less-important leaves and flowers in any colour from white to maroon, often beautifully speckled within.

Above The hostas have a unique place in the garden for the simple beauty of their leaves. Later in summer or autumn come lily-like, usually fairly modest, flowers. There is a vast and bewildering range of names to choose from; Japanese gardeners have been selecting them for size and colour for centuries. Above (in its emergent state) is *Hosta sieboldiana*, whose blue-grey leaves often grow to a foot wide and turn a vivid buff in autumn. The variegated forms are almost as various as hollies, yellow or creamy-white with green either in the centre or as a rim round the leaves, which in *H. crispula* and *H. undulata* have elegantly wavy margins. Among the best are *H. fortunei* 'Albopicta' (yellow leaves with green rims), 'Thomas Hogg' (green leaves with cream rims) and *H. plantaginea grandiflora* for both leaves and sweet-smelling flowers.

Left Wood anemones are almost as valuable early in the year as Japanese anemones are in late summer. They light up woodland, or any shady spot, with their delicate white, pink, or lavender-blue faces. The florists' bright red and blue creations cannot compare with them for the real freshness of spring flowers.

Left Aquilegias, the columbines, are up early with their graceful greyish ferny leaves. They hybridize eagerly: the wild *A. vulgaris* will dominate and muddy the clear colours of the better kinds. The two names, meaning "eagle" and "dove", refer to the flower's bird-like shape.

Above Oriental poppies are briefly splendid in early summer, in colours from pure poppy red to pink, and a dramatic white with jet-black markings. They like dry soil and sun. Their pale, hairy, deep-cleft leaves are excellent up to flowering time, then rapidly degenerate and need hiding. A sprawling, top-heavy plant; in a tidy garden it needs support. Like many poppies these can be prolific self-seeders.

Above Garden lupins have been bred from the blue wildflower of the American West into a whole spectrum of colours, popularized by Russell's nursery at York. Russell lupins can be bought as seed (mixed colours) or plants of a named variety. Unless dead-headed they seed themselves prolifically, usually in unclear pink. Dead-headed they will often flower again. Their pale fingery leaf-clumps are welcome in spring.

Above The peonies are the earliest border plants to produce such sumptuous flowers in such resounding colours. The old double red form from the Mediterranean (above) is a cottage-garden tradition, though scores of varieties in all colours except blue, and shapes ranging from simple to outrageously frilly, have been bred. They are based mainly on forms developed in Chinese gardens from *Peonia lactiflora*. They are all slow moving and apparently immortal, encouraged by feeding but reliable even under neglect given deep soil and sunshine. Their season is short, but their leaves are good-looking, red when they open and often red again in autumn. One species of great beauty is *P. mlokosewitschii*, with single yellow flowers among flushed grey-green leaves. The equally gorgeous "tree" peonies appear at the same time.

PRIMULAS

Primula auricula

The 500 species of the primrose genus embrace alpines, meadow-flowers and bog-plants, all spring flowers of almost childish charm—the very opposite of the sophisticated silk-and-satin irises below. A tendency to "mealiness", or a coating of leaves, stems and buds with "farina", adds to their crisp, laundered look. All like leafy soil with humus, though some like it drained; some not. Many, despite the air of mystique that surrounds the genus, are very easy to grow. All are perennials—though a few are very short-lived. Most grow rapidly from seed. Auriculas, from the European Alps, have been highly bred into exquisite show-flowers in endless colour combinations. They have thick evergreen leaves and flower early in spring. Some need alpine-house treatment; all like good drainage. The alpine aristocrat *P. marginata* belongs in the same "section". They propagate simply by offsets from the base or by division. The common English primrose begins to flower in winter. Garden forms of the primrose crossed with cowslips are called polyanthus—in colours relentlessly called "jewel-like". They need dividing regularly or growing as biennials (pages 118–9). The Himalayas are the real family home. Himalayan kinds include the winter-flowering *P. malacoides*, *P. obconica* and the hybrid *P.* × *kewensis*, lovely graceful flowers which need a frost-free greenhouse and are usually grown as annuals. The "drumstick" primula, *P. denticulata*, comes from Kashmir. It needs wet ground and prefers cold winters. From Sikkim comes *P. florindae*, the tallest and latest to flower; an easy hardy perennial for moist or wet ground. Most rarefied looking, but not at all difficult in damp soil, are the "candelabra" section, including the crimson *P. pulverulenta* ('Bartley Strain' is a pink version), the orange *P. aurantiaca*, magenta *P. beesiana* and *P. japonica* in various colours. Colours of seedlings soon become muddled with crossing if several species are grown together.

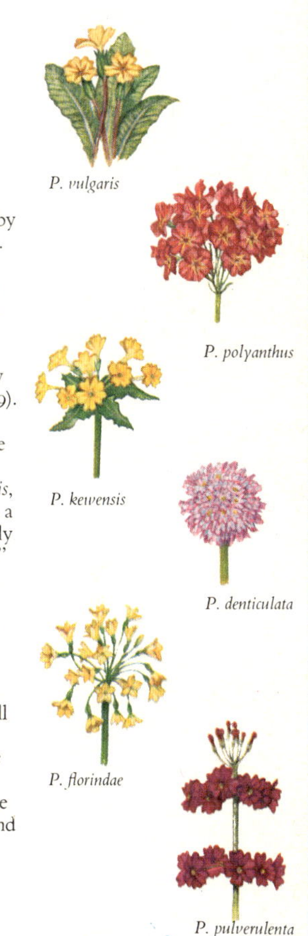

IRISES

Bearded iris

Early summer brings the climax of the long season of the irises. Few genera are so consistent in their style of flowers over so many species (there are 300) yet so diverse in their way of life. Roots vary from rhizomes to bulbs or tubers, and habitats from dust to mud. The flower of the bearded, or German, iris, *above*, epitomizes the design: three petals upright (the "standards") and three drooping (the "falls"). The "beard", appearing in this group only, is a soft, hairy patch on the upper surface of each fall. Bearded irises like well drained soil in full sun. Endless cultivars have been produced in all colours except red, and many combinations, in a range of sizes from April-flowering dwarfs to four-footers that flower in June. The unbearded Pacific Coast hybrids are of medium size, in subtle colours, and enjoy the same conditions. Slightly damper soil suits cultivars of *I. sibirica*, with much smaller flowers and grassy leaves. Close-to the veining of the falls is exquisite; these are elegant and easy plants. Similar soil suits the bulbous irises of early summer: the Dutch, Spanish and English kinds, which flower in that order. These have slender leaves and stems and fair-sized "flags". Any soil and any degree of shade satisfies the evergreen *I. foetidissima*, or Gladdon, which is grown not for its flowers but its brilliant autumn berries. The miniature winter-flowering bulbs *I. histrioides* and *I. reticulata* need sharp drainage; alpine conditions. The tuberous *I. bucharica* of spring simply needs a snug spot. Mid-winter iris, *I. unguicularis* (alias *stylosa*), likes it very dry. The flowers emerge from deep in dull foliage but their delicate mauve colour and sweet scent are ravishing indoors. Really damp soil, and even shallow water, suits the yellow flag, *I. pseudacorus*, and the Japanese *Iris kaempferi*, with the most regal flowers of the genus.

More early flowers

Below Meconopsis grandis The most perennial **Blue poppy** of the Himalayas. Not easy to grow. It hates lime, likes good drainage in winter and a wet summer, with shade and shelter all the time, but worth it for its electric-blue flowers.

Right Trillium grandiflorum **Wake robin** Easiest of the lovely family of wood lilies, likes cool, moist shade, forms an 18-inch clump with glistening white three-petalled flowers. A superb double-flowered form is very rare.

Right Veronica gentianoides Earliest of the spiked **speedwells**, with delicate spires of palest blue. *V. spicata* and *V. incana* are similar, later; *V. incana* has silvery leaves. *V. teucrium* in midsummer is the strongest blue.

Left Omphalodes verna **Navelwort** A little woodland version of the forget-me-not, creeping with running roots. *O. cappadocica* is slightly larger, to ten inches. Both make good groundcover.

Above Polygonatum × hybridum **Solomon's seal** A most obliging plant for the patient, slowly spreading its graceful wands of white bells by creeping roots. Will take deep shade but not hot drought.

Left Saxifraga umbrosa **London pride** A humble workhorse that demands nothing but always looks neat and, in spring, forms clouds of delicate pinky-red flowers. Evergreen.

Right Doronicum plantagineum **Leopard's bane** The earliest of the border daisies; sunny yellow to go with late tulips and honesty. Easy in almost any soil but best partly shaded and not too dry. *D.* 'Miss Mason' is another favourite: slightly shorter and stouter.

Left Dicentra spectabilis **Bleeding heart, Dutchman's breeches** and many other names. A clump of ferny leaves with a delicate air and arching stems dangling bizarre red and white lockets.

Left Epimedium × youngianum More useful than spectacular, with sharply serrated, almost evergreen leaves turning orange-red in autumn. Flights of little pink flowers.

Left Pulmonaria angustifolia **Lungwort** Variable pink to blue flowers. Early and easy though its mid-green leaves are dull for the rest of the year. Some species have white-spotted leaves.

Below Convallaria majalis **Lily of the valley** Worth growing for its magical fragrance, but not always easy to start. Best to plant a whole clump, soil and all, if possible.

Left Brunnera macrophylla Forget-me-not flowers above mounds of impressive heart-shaped leaves. Not fussy; sometimes seeds itself. A white-variegated version is very fine but rare.

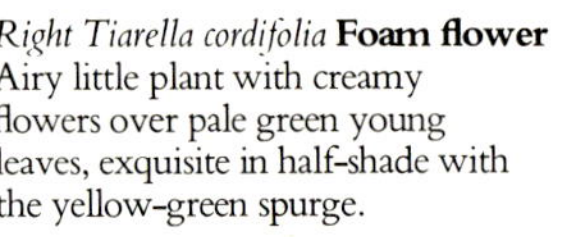

Right Tiarella cordifolia **Foam flower** Airy little plant with creamy flowers over pale green young leaves, exquisite in half-shade with the yellow-green spurge.

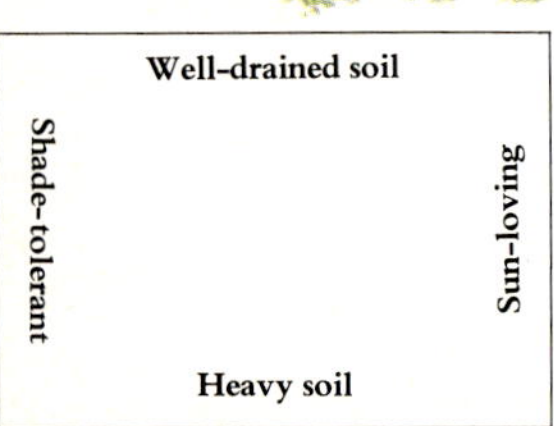

Well-drained soil
Shade-tolerant
Sun-loving
Heavy soil

Most of the early flowers on this page are creatures of the woods, accustomed to dappled sunlight (if to any sun at all) in summer, but shooting up in good time to flower in the spring sun before the roof of leaves closes over them. In the garden they are ideal for half-shady places; under late-leafing trees or shaded by a wall for half the day. The other side of the equation, however, is that they need plenty of humus in the soil, provided in nature by the leaves of the trees.

On the whole early flowers, flowering in the longest days of the year as midsummer approaches, tend to have a shorter season than those that flower in the shortening days of late summer. Partly it is a question of simple size: later-flowering plants have all summer to put on more bulk and make more flower buds.

Large areas occupied by these early plants may easily be flowerless, untidy or even empty altogether in high summer,

Right Adonis amurensis **Pheasant's eye** A Japanese buttercup, one of the earliest of all herbaceous plants (one form, Fukujukai, flowers in January). A double form has flowers that turn green. Its European counterpart, *A. vernalis*, flowers slightly later. Both disappear in summer.

Below Euphorbia characias wulfenii Impressive shrub-like **spurge** with grey-green bottle-brush stems, long-lasting bract-flowers with brown centres.

Above Geum 'Borisii' **Avens** An easy plant for early summer cheerfulness. Use carefully, well away from fragile shades of pink. *G. chiloense* 'Mrs Bradshaw' is twice the height, double, scarlet, and flowers all summer.

Below Euphorbia polychroma, alias *E. epithymoides*. One of many **spurges** whose cheerful yellow-green bracts serve the gardener as flowers. *E. griffithii* is similar but bright brick-red.

Above Pulsatilla vulgaris **Pasque flower** Silky haired anemones of great beauty rising from filigree tufts of grey leaves. A native of Europe, including Britain.

Below Heuchera sanguinea **Coral bells** A native of the SW States yet hardy in all of them. Evergreen, to two feet, with versions in pink, crimson and white. Needs deep planting. *Heucherella* is a *Heuchera* crossed with a *Tiarella*.

Below Cheiranthus allonii **Siberian wallflower** Tender in cold gardens; best used as a biennial, but grows shrubby on walls in warmer areas. With spikes of orange flowers.

Right Bergenia purpurescens 'Ballawley' A saxifrage with big leathery leaves, most valuable in winter, when they take on beetroot tints.

Above Centaurea montana **Knapweed** One of several perennial versions of the cornflower. None are such true blue, but the knapweeds are boldly Scottish in design and the white form a lovely thing.

Below Rheum alexandrae Ornamental rhubarb from China, its flowers hooded with yellowish bracts. Likes moisture. *R. palmatum* with red flowers is bigger and easier to grow.

Below Trollius europaeus **Globe flower** The noblest buttercup, needing heavy, damp soil. There are single and double forms in shades from pale lemon to moderately strong orange.

Above Symphytum × uplandicum **Comfrey** An ecologist's plant, astonishingly nourishing as green manure or compost, but also hairily handsome. The flowers dither between blue and purple.

unless later plants are interspersed with them. Dicentras and Virginia cowslips for example disappear by midsummer. No harm can come by planting a late flower, such as a Japanese anemone, hard alongside in the same plot. Lupins and oriental poppies need a sequel to cover their shabby leaves after flowering: Acanthus or *Artemisia lactiflora* would blot out any sign of them. Bulbs require the same approach. The notion of following bulbs with hostas has occurred to thousands of gardeners. Annuals can also be grown in the kitchen garden, brought out ready to flower and planted in the spaces between the early perennials.

There are other early plants whose leaves are worth as much as their flowers and do them credit all summer. Of the plants on this page, the evergreen bergenia, London pride, epimedium, heuchera, the deciduous Solomon's seal, lily of the valley and brunnera are all good-looking without flowers.

The selection of spring and early summer border flowers on these pages includes some of the lesser-known, neglected and more specialized plants. Far from being just for massed display, border plants provide flowers for every corner of the garden in conditions ranging from groundcover in obscure shady corners to front-line positions in full sun.

The plants are positioned on the page according to their preferences (or tolerances) for more or less sun, and for more or less free-draining soil. The extreme left of the page represents shade, the extreme right a sunny and open position. The top of the page is fast-draining (though not necessarily dry; see for example *Meconopsis*) and the bottom has heavier, more water-holding soil.

In practice it is the middle of the page that should be most crowded: the majority of border plants will do well enough in "average" conditions.

The mid-season border

Right A border in full cry in mid-summer, its components flowering shoulder to shoulder with apparently little room for later plants.

Below Delphinium 'Loch Maree'. White, pink and even red forms are now available.

Although it is arbitrary to divide the continuous succession of flowering into groups, there is no question that the mid-summer season represented here (or strictly, in Britain, the season starting at the end of June) is the climax of the year for border flowers.

While the true spring flowers are over, many families that had a few outriders in spring now arrive in force; genera such as the hardy geraniums and day-lilies, and above all the daisy family. Even the latest-flowering plants have filled their allotted spaces, at least with leaves if not yet with flowers. There is no natural break between now and the waning year.

A really ambitious traditional border, based on the premise that everything in it should be flowering at once, would inevitably be based on this period. Every colour is available in almost every shape; which makes the task of choice and organization not easier but very much more difficult. There are all the annuals to consider; and such late bulbs as some of the alliums. At the same time the roses have reached their first peak, adding to the opportunities for rich but controlled, or riotously muddled, combinations. On pages 198–9 there are examples of what can be achieved in fine-tuned colour harmony at this time of year.

There is a danger of overdoing the daisy motif from now onwards. There are so many of them (see the panel below, and the Michaelmas daisies, cornflowers, chrysanthemums and dahlias in the third border period) that they need to be consciously kept away from each other by alternating them with different flower forms.

Delphiniums are inescapably the stars of the show; nothing else either early or late challenges their true-blue steeples for everything we desire in garden decoration. Campanulas are their rivals, but they never quite achieve the same brilliance. These pages touch on the basic ingredients: overleaf are some interesting alternatives.

HARDY GERANIUMS

The hardy geraniums or cranesbills cannot be fitted tidily into a single season. The bloody cranesbill *below* is out in May, while *Geranium wallichianum* 'Buxton's Blue' ends the summer. They are underrated because their individual flowers are modest by border standards, but few flowers have longer seasons, and they have the virtue of hearty leaf-clumps of great character that make bushy ground-cover without fuss. Several also give good autumn colour. The brightest summer cranesbills are the early *G.× magnificum, right*, and the mid-season *G. psilostemon*, four feet tall with magenta flowers.

SALVIAS

There are a score of handsome herbaceous salvias, related to the shrubby kitchen sage. All are hairy, aromatic plants with spikes of hooded dead-nettle flowers. The best known is *Salvia superba*, with sheaves of violet-purple three-foot spikes. The most beautiful is the sapphire-blue *S. patens*, which needs winter protection in cold areas. Bigger species include bright silver *S. argentea* and the pale lavender *S. haematodes*. The scarlet bedding salvia is *S. splendens*, a half-hardy perennial grown as an annual.

THE DAISY CHAIN

The daisy family, the Compositae, is the largest of all families of flowering plants, with more than 13,000 species in up to 900 genera. Most of this vast array are herbaceous plants. Inevitably the garden risks being overwhelmed with these cheerful and easy flowers; particularly the border in mid- to late summer when many of them bloom at once. The family includes plenty of less obvious daisies: thistles, for example, and such varied border flowers as yarrow and golden rod. Hundreds of them are annuals or biennials. The eight genera shown here are probably the best-known border daisies beside chrysanths, Michaelmas daisies and dahlias, which are shown on pages 114–5. They are illustrated in approximate order of flowering. *Anthemis tinctoria*, the ox-eye chamomile, is a good border plant from June to August, its leaves fresh and finely cut, its flowers ranging from pale to deep yellow. It will flop without support. The slightly earlier silver-leafed, white-flowered *A. cupaniana* is another good plant, forming a dense carpet. *Erigeron* (Fleabanes) have been bred in all colours from pink to purple, with single or double flowers. The effect is like early Michelmas daisies flowering June to August. *Coreopsis* (Tickseed) has some of the prettiest leaves, and at only two feet needs no support. 'Goldfink' is only one foot high (June–September). *Gaillardia* (Blanket flowers) are the most brazenly painted, in circles of red, yellow and brown. At three feet they need support for their long season from June to October. *Heliopsis* are brassy and loud in July and August; four feet and need props. *Helianthus* (the annual sunflower is one) are tall, spreading, greedy, but bright from July to September. *Inula* include some huge plants, but the best is the two-to-three-foot *I. hookeri* with greeny yellow narrow petals. August to September. *Helenium* (Sneezeweed) is last to go —August to October—with suitably autumnal colours including velvety brown. The taller kinds need support.

Above Day-lilies are among the most highly bred of all border plants. The scent and charm of such species as the early *Hemerocallis flava* has been traded for splendour in such productions as 'Black Prince'.

Below Border phlox has a uniquely sweet far-carrying smell. Soft pinks and plain white suit it best, particularly in evening light, but there are crimsons and purples too. Staking is rarely necessary.

THE CAMPANULAS

It is easy to recognize the bell-flowers, but hard to remember which is which of six tall species and six short. *Campanula lactiflora, left*: 'Pritchard's Variety', is among the best of the tall ones, growing to four or five feet, along with *C. latifolia, C. pyramidalis* and *C. persicifolia*. *C. carpatica, below,* shows the value of the small ones—this grows to one foot. They all share a clean-cut freshness in their simple flowers, and always hover on the grey and purple side of blue. But their colours, their shapes and their timing fit them perfectly to accompany old roses, and they need little special care, beyond well-drained soil. Caution: they include a few, such as *C. rapunculoides*, which are pretty, but ineradicable weeds.

DIANTHUS: PINKS, CARNATIONS AND THEIR KIND

With the big genus of *Dianthus* we hover between perennials and annuals and biennials. There is no clear-cut line, but none of them can be called permanent. Frequent propagation is necessary—but happily easy; from cuttings with some, seed with others. There are countless named cultivars, breaking down into eight or nine essential kinds. They are rock rather than meadow plants by nature; all like dryish limy soil and full sun. Most have more or less narrow grey or greyish leaves; the perennial pinks mounding up into low ever-grey shrublets.

Illustrated *above* are: Old-fashioned, Garden or Cottage pinks; one foot, summer-flowering only. The most perennial kind, lasting for up to five years. Single, or double-flowered, classified by colour-pattern into Selfs, Bicolours, Laced and Fancies.

Modern or Allwoodii pinks; (the above crossed with perpetual carnations), summer and autumn flowers. Faster-growing, but shorter lived.

Indian pinks; grown as annuals, often dwarf, single or double, colours usually mixed.

Sweet William; flowers in midsummer, often with concentric rings of different colours. Best grown as a biennial.

'Loveliness'; the best pink for shade or damp soil. Wide colour range, long flowering. Use as a biennial.

Border carnations; descended from the Elizabethan Clove Gilliflower, clove scent, two feet, needs support. Double flowers in midsummer, perennial but short lived.

More mid-season flowers

Left *Alchemilla mollis* **Lady's Mantle** Easy and highly fashionable, with charming soft leaves that hold dew-drops like pearls. Bright lime-green flowers flop and need cutting off, or seedlings will follow. Good groundcover and a perfect foil for any bright colour or grey.

Right *Eremurus robustus* **Foxtail Lily** Stateliest of all border flowers, rising to nine feet from fleshy radiating roots. The clump of bent strap leaves needs hiding. Well-drained soil; plant like asparagus, carefully, on a sand mound.

Above *Eryngium × oliveranum* **Sea Holly** A good hybrid among many good species, all contributing spiky architecture to the border. The hard metallic flowers dry perfectly for winter use. Good in very dry soil. The white form of *E. giganteum* is 'Miss Willmott's Ghost'.

Above *Lychnis coronaria* **Dusty Miller, Rose Campion** Almost too easy and more vivid than smart. Seeds itself in any dry spot; seedlings are rosettes of pale grey flannel. *L. flos jovis* is easy, pink-flowered and half the size.

Above *Nepeta × faasenii* **Catmint** Easy, long-flowering, weed-smothering; for dry, sunny places. Traditional groundcover for rose beds. Cats revel in it: a few thorny twigs discourage them. Cut it back in midsummer for more flowers.

Above *Aruncus dioicus (sylvester)* **Goat's Beard** Worth growing for its clumps of fern leaves, and noble in flower with its creamy plumes. Not fussy but likes moisture. Adds form and structure to beds of droopy shrub roses.

Above *Astrantia major* **Masterwort** Long-lasting flowers of most delicate construction and subtle green-pink, loved by sophisticated flower-arrangers. Shapely dark green leaves. Easy to grow in any well-drained soil.

Below *Monarda didyma* **Bee Balm** (or **Bergamot**) A rough minty plant with whorls of long-lasting hooded flowers. 'Cambridge Scarlet' is brightest of a range of pinks and reds. Likes moist soil. The leaves make "oswego tea".

Above *Astilbe* 'Bronze Elegance' A useful dwarf form of a popular plant for boggy ground, though any moist soil will do. Available in many colours, some lurid. The leaves and seed heads are worth leaving for winter.

Left *Viola cornuta* **Horned Violet** Representative of a lovely race that includes little sweet violets and the big biennial pansy. Makes a spreading clump in a dampish spot, not too sunny. Flowers repeatedly if watered.

Above *Thalictrum dipterocarpum* **Meadow Rue** Most dainty of tall plants, graceful and airy in flower and leaf, but needing shelter and deep moist soil mixed with peat. *T. aquilegifolium* is easier but less elegant.

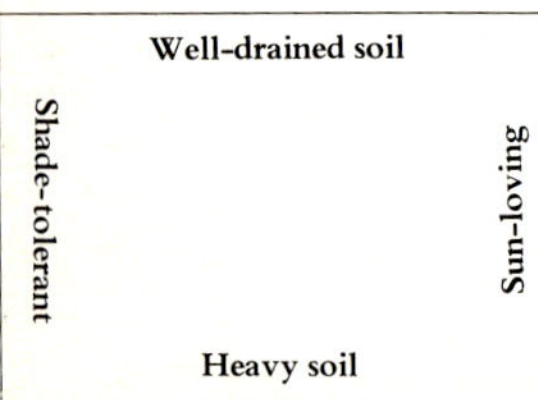

Whereas among spring flowers there was an almost even division between those that liked sun and those that preferred some shade, all the emphasis here is on sunshine. The sun-shade axis is therefore over on the left-hand side of these pages. Tastes in soil remain as various as ever.

Compared with the generally low, even ground-covering, spring flowers, the mid-summer field is tall (and may well need support). These are mainly meadow and prairie flowers—a good number of them from the prairies of North America.

For solo performances, as a garden feature in a corner or by a door, divorced from others of their kind, some of the most architecturally interesting, reliable and longest-lasting in flower are *Acanthus, Aruncus, Crambe* (which is capable of looking after itself in long grass) and *Macleaya*. *Eryngium, Astilbe* and *Achillea* have beautiful seed-heads to decorate the border later, or dry for winter decoration indoors.

Above Acanthus spinosus **Bear's Breeches** A classic Mediterranean plant, worth growing for its splendid fretted leaves alone. Magnificent flower spikes of white and dusky purple. It spreads, even in total drought.

Above Crambe cordifolia The king of the cabbage family. Colossal dark leaves and explosions of tiny white sweet-smelling flowers like gypsophila. Splendid in grass.

Above Alstroemeria ligtu hybrids **Peruvian Lily** Slow to start (needing deep planting) but eventually far-spreading (and rather floppy). Flowers in azalea-like mixtures of pink and orange on lily-like stems. Sun and dry but fertile soil.

Right Linum narbonense **Perennial Flax** Wispy little grey-leaved plants, not long-lived or very hardy but smothered all summer in satiny funnel flowers of a strong sky-blue. Take cuttings in autumn to be sure of next year's supply. Or sow seeds in spring.

Above Verbascum vernale (and others) **Mullein** Grey-flannel leaves and stem; flowers mostly yellow, but white, pink, purple and brown forms are available. Yellow *V. bombyciferum* is most spectacular, to ten feet, but only biennial.

Below Scabiosa caucasica **Scabious** Wide-eyed innocent flowers of well-washed blue; otherwise a dull plant. Young plants flower all summer, so divide the clumps every other spring. Chalky soil and sun is best.

Below Anchusa azurea 'Loddon Royalist'. A good strong blue on a rough boragey plant; earlier than most on this page but usually short-lived. Propagate by root cuttings.

Above Penstemon ovatus (and others) **Beard-tongue** Rather tender evergreen, dull of leaf but endlessly in flower in reasonably moist soil. *P. ovatus* is truly blue, *P. barbatus* red; other species and hybrids many colours.

Left Achillea 'Moonshine' (and others) **Yarrow or Milfoil** Ferny leaved and evergreen with flat heads of tiny flowers in white, cream or yellow that last months and dry well.

Left Oenothera 'Yellow River' an excellent perennial **Evening Primrose** with a long mid-summer season of silky golden flowers. Full sun and moisture for best results.

Above Althaea (Alcea) rosea **Hollyhock** Soaring favourite of unique value, single or double, in a wide range of warm colours. But short-lived and often unhealthy; best grown from seed to flower the next year. Sometimes self-seeds.

Above Sidalcea malviflora **Checkerbloom, Greek Mallow** Good-looking, pale, fingery leaf-clumps; flowers like small silky hollyhocks—the pale pink form is prettiest. Fast and easy like most mallows, but needs some support.

Right Macleaya microcarpa **Plume Poppy** Most unpoppy-like member of that family, with the best leaves of any border flower; chalk-white below with orange sap in branching veins. Invades other plants, but splendid alone, seen full length.

The late border

Somewhere about the middle of August the mood of the garden imperceptibly changes. The sun is lower in the sky; the morning wakes with dew on spiders' webs; trees and shrubs are a heavy green with few flowers; the first leaves fall.

The shift, one might suppose, would be into a minor key as the year wanes. But the richest and most splendid passage of tone and harmony is still to come. The tints of turning leaves add to the colours of flowers. As flowers fade, curious intricacies of seed-containers and bright gems of fruit appear. Strong full-grown plants, uncorsetted, billow and lean at improbable angles and in voluptuous curves.

There are still pinks and blues as clear as in the spring among the flowers, but the mood of the season is best expressed in rich and subtle tones of violet and crimson, cream and bronze. Chrysanthemums and Michaelmas daisies are vital ingredients: a garden cannot be said to be truly autumnal without them.

Japanese anemones, above all the stately white form, are essential. The succulent sedums, especially 'Autumn Joy', with its slow transition from sea-green to mahogany, provide an anchoring dome-like mass.

For sword-leaves and upright or arching flowers with the smoothness of bulbs, montbretias and red-hot pokers follow the departing agapanthus. South African plants and bulbs have their big season in late summer. Galtonias, the white cape hyacinths, are followed by the sugar-pink nerines and the pink or scarlet Kaffir lilies.

Conscientious picking-off of dead flower heads keeps the season going for most border plants as well as for roses and annuals. Dahlias in particular seems to have endless reserves of flowers that only frost can stop.

Above Agapanthus, the blue lilies of South Africa, are often grown in tubs and stored indoors in winter, although they are hardy in zone 8. They range from white to dark blue. In the foreground, love-in-a-mist; behind, red *Fuchsia magellanica.*

Below The sweet dishevelment of the autumn border, with the warm tones of dahlia and chrysanthemum in the low-angled sunlight.

MICHAELMAS DAISIES

The Michaelmas daisies are a surprisingly complicated bunch, mainly natives of North America. *Aster novae-angliae* (from New England) tends to be tall and pink. *A. novi-belgii* (the "true" Michaelmas daisy) is shorter, to four feet, and has been bred in every colour from white to crimson and purple. These all make vigorously spreading clumps that tend to go bald in the middle. Every two or three years the best parts from the perimeter should be replanted. Half a dozen less showy species from America are also worth growing, including the airy white *A. tradescantii* and *A. divaricatus*, and the violet *A. spectabilis*. The pictures show *top A. sedifolius* (*acris*), a wild European species; *middle A. novi-belgii* 'Patricia Ballard', and *bottom* the Euro-Asian hybrid *A.×frikartii* 'Mönch', flowering from late summer until frost.

RED HOT POKERS

The red hot pokers, or torch lilies, including such cool and elegant numbers as 'Maid of Orleans', *right*, are South African and only reasonably hardy, but worth warm corners and well-drained soil for their value as exclamation marks in the brimming late-summer garden. The "original" red hot poker is *Kniphofia uvaria*, tall and orange-red. Now most are hybrids, available in heights from two to five feet and colours from cream to flame. The hotter shades are beautiful with the lavender and mauve Michaelmas daisies. One lesser known but very hardy species, *Kniphofia caulescens*, has an almost aloe-like rosette and flowers in subtle green, pink and plum. *Below* is *K. galpinii.*

Above A jumble of South African iris-relations are called montbretias. The stooping red *Crocosmia*× *masonorum* is good. *Curtonus paniculata* is a bigger orange one.

Below Rudbeckias, the coneflowers, are some of the most characterful American daisies. 'Goldsturm', here, reaches two feet. 'Herbstsonne', reaches seven.

CHRYSANTHEMUMS

Chrysanthemums are the most indispensable of the daisies. They appear in marvellous variety all summer long, coming to a climax in autumn with brown, red and yellow flowers that epitomize the season. The mop-headed late-summer ("early-flowering") kinds were originally developed in China and Japan, where they are still enormously popular. Like the dahlias, below, they have their own exhibition jargon. The Chinese favoured them "incurved"; the Japanese "reflexed". Breeding still continues unabated. For general garden use, having the same autumnal flavour, derivatives of the hardy Korean chrysanthemum with flowers in sprays are prettier and less trouble. The colour range only lacks anything approaching blue—which can be supplied by Michaelmas daisies. Chrysanthemums ask only for sun and well-drained soil. *Below* is a sampling of the range, covering most of the summer. Feverfew, often used as an edging to beds, is liable to become a weed. The grey-leaved marguerite, or Paris daisy, is shrubby by the Mediterranean but tender in frost. Cuttings taken each year are ready for bedding-out the next.

Feverfew, *C. parthenium*, flowers all summer. This is the gold 'Aureum'.

C. rubellum is a long-flowering late-summer perennial. Pink 'Clara Curtis' is best known.

The shrubby marguerite, never-ending in flower, is *C. frutescens* from the Canary Islands.

The summer Shasta Daisy, single or double, always white, is the Pyrenean *C. maximum*.

The Korean chrysanthemums are hardy and flower into autumn in many colours. This is 'Daphne'.

Heavy-headed exhibition chrysanths come in many forms. This is the reflexed 'Ryland's Bronze'.

DAHLIAS

The variety of dahlias, such as it is, is almost entirely man-made. They all come from two or three variable Mexican species (possibly already hybridized in Aztec gardens) imported to Europe early in the nineteenth century. From the beginning a never-ending succession of variations of colour, shape, size and petal arrangements were produced. The botanist soon shrugged his shoulders at what to him was a load of haberdashery. The classification in use today (illustrated right) has been developed by florists. Culturally they divide simply into bedding dahlias, small slightly variable plants raised from seed each year, and border dahlias, larger plants sold as tubers and by precise name.

Their propagation is easy, either by dividing the tubers with a piece of stem attached to each, or by short cuttings from the new growth in spring. The joy of the dahlia is the ease with which it makes a big plant laden with flowers in any colour except blue. All it asks is deep-dug soil with a high organic content to keep the roots moist. Competitive growers double-dig in autumn, lacing the bottom spit with mature manure. The disadvantage is that the sausage-like tubers will rot left in cold, wet ground. But it is easy to lift them and keep them in a dry, frost-proof place in winter. Staking is the other problem; such lush plants need firm support, which is hard to hide.

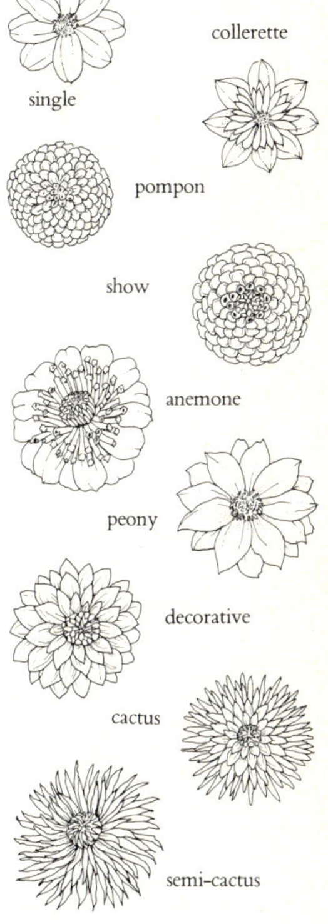

Above The range of shapes of dahlia flowers. *Left* Large border dahlias are traditionally grown in beds of their own, in full sun and with shelter from wind.

More late flowers

Left Limonium latifolium **Sea Lavender, Statice** A clump of broad dull evergreen leaves. Wide branching heads of hundreds of diminutive lavender flowers. Dried, they last all winter.

Left Aconitum carmichaelii **Monkshood Wolfsbane** Poisonous and somehow sinister-looking with its strange hood- or helmet-shaped flowers and good leaves. *A. napellus* is darker and earlier flowering.

Below Veronica virginica **Culver's Root** an invaluable plant for its determined geometry: stands up for orderliness in a muddle of flowers. Not fussy about soil.

Above Liriope muscari **Big Blue Lilyturf** Evergreen and grassy, popular as edging in the USA. Grape hyacinth-style spikes of violet flowers in autumn. Rather dull on its own; needs a contrasting companion. Nerines would be good.

Above Sedum 'Autumn Joy' The best border form of **Stonecrop**. The pale, fleshy, radiating leaves are good by midsummer. Flower-colour develops steadily from pink to rich red-brown.

Left Artemisia lactiflora **Mugwort** Surprisingly related to silvery sprawlers. This is green, upright, and bears loose spikes of small creamy flowers. Good bulky backing material. Needs moisture.

Above Gentiana asclepiadea **Willow Gentian** Leaning sheaves of stems with willowy leaves in pairs. The flowers of dusky blue ride the stem between the leaves. From meadows in the lush foothills of the Alps. Not bright but memorable.

Above Cimicifuga racemosa **Bugbane, Black Snake-root** One of several species of great grace. Distinguished leaves and narrow flower-spikes.

Above Saxifraga fortunei. So late-flowering that frost can often spoil it, but worth growing even for its leaves alone. Airy white flowers with a long bottom petal giving a comet-tail effect. For cool moist shade and shelter.

Above Crocosmia × masonorum **Montbretia** One of the best of a wide variety. Bright red flowers face upwards on arching stems. *Curtonus* (alias *Antholyza*) *paniculata* is like a somewhat taller, dark orange version of the same.

Left Lythrum salicaria **Purple Loosestrife** Reliable for strong bright colours between pink and purple for a long period. For vigour rather than refinement; could become a weed.

	Well-drained soil	
Shade-tolerant		Sun-loving
	Heavy soil	

There is still a distinct preference for full sunshine among the latest plants to flower. Only those on the extreme left of these pages are happy in more than dappled shade. Those at the top prefer their soil on the dry side: the bottom row like it heavy enough to hoard some moisture all summer.

Leaves and overall habit and structure become more and more important as the climax of flowering passes. The plants here are more than mere border-fodder, with pretty faces to hold up in serried ranks like a school photograph. Any of these plants will make a feature where it can be seen from the ground up, leaves and all.

With late-flowerers it is important, too, that the burgeoning clump looks interesting before it flowers. Most of these pass that test. It is some of the popular classics of the previous page (Michaelmas daisies, red hot pokers, rudbeckias for example) that need help from interesting neighbours, whether in flower

Below Solidago 'Goldenmosa' **Goldenrod** A refined and miniaturized form of the coarse, spreading goldenrods of North America—which also have their value as an emblem of autumn.

Above Verbena bonariensis **Vervain** A complete original. Lanky square-sectioned stems, opposite-branched, tipped with clusters of bright purple flowers for many weeks. Not very hardy.

Left Anemone × hybrida 'Honorine Jobert' **Japanese Anemone** The finest form of one of the indispensables—permanent, self-supporting long-lasting and exquisite.

Above Echinops nithenicus **Globe Thistle** A compelling combination of blue globes, white stems and dark green leaves. The best of an easy and tenacious genus.

Left Romneya coulteri **California Tree Poppy**. Slow to start but eventually enormous and ineradicable. Supremely beautiful grey leaves, white crêpe petals and golden stamens.

Above Schizostylis coccinea **Kaffir Lily, Crimson Flag** Smooth and bulbous-looking leaves with flowers rather like small crocuses, red or pink, in spikes. One of the last flowers to start; likes damp and warmth.

Above Hosta plantaginea 'Grandiflora'. **Plantain Lily** The last and best of hostas grown for their flowers. Tall, white and smelling like a lily, but the narrow lettuce-green leaves are lovely too. Likes sun and some moisture.

Above Polygonum amplexicaule **Knotweed** The aristocrat of a family with some dangerously weedy members. Even longer-lasting than the Japanese anemone.

Above Dierama pulcherrimum **Wand flower** The most graceful of all border flowers, but not for cold climates. Evergreen leaves, waving stems, dangling lilac or violet bells.

Right Lobelia cardinalis **Cardinal flower** A North American at home in hot summers, cold winters and rich retentive soil. Several hybrid forms offer different colours, but truly scarlet flowers like this are rare.

or not, in the building-up period before they start to bloom.

As the border-plant season ends there comes the question of what to cut down and clear away, and what to leave to outface the winter in its withered brown state. Soft, leafy plants make their own decision and collapse with the frosts. Others that have made almost woody stems stand with still-recognizable flowers or dried seed pods until gales or snow cut them down—sometimes until spring.

The tidy-minded often like to clear the ground of such vestiges, prick it over with a fork and stare virtuously at the flat bare earth all winter. But there is far more interest in a garden with an evergreen shrub here, a raised brown fist of flowering thistle or truncheon of polygonum there. Any plants that turn deep reddy-brown and crisp are worth keeping. Some Michaelmas daisies do. In winter sunshine it is remarkable what value warm patches of brown assume.

Annuals and biennials

I am unlikely in the short space of two pages to convert a confirmed once-for-all landscaper into an ardent annualist. We are talking of different garden disciplines: alternative notions of what gardening is all about. My best chance is simply to say turn the page. See what a feast you are missing.

Annuals are out of fashion. Like vegetables they mean work, which however pleasant and rewarding goes against the grain of the modern gardener. The phrase "labour-saving" has conditioned us to think we are saving the labour *for* something. But labour saved pays no dividends. While seed sown. . . .

For annuals are at the same time a crop and a celebration. They are the most eager of all plants to put their energies into display—which means in most cases brilliant flowers. They have only one season in which to grow, flower and set seed. Given good conditions they do it with an abandon that gives more colour for a longer period than any other plants.

The good conditions are a prerequisite, and meanness in providing them is probably the commonest reason why gardeners who have tried annuals have been disappointed and given them up. If they are to be worth stooping over they must be sturdy, hearty plants. And there is no second chance—no "giving them a good feed next winter". They must grow strong roots and a bushy top from the start. They want just the same treatment as vegetables—total indulgence. Their will to live and urge to reproduce is such that if you can get round to picking off the fading flowers before any seed is set, more and more flowers will follow.

But that is as much as, and really more than, you can say about annuals in general. They vary in their tastes less than most plants, but enough to need careful study.

Certain definitions are essential. The three terms hardy, half-hardy and biennial each trigger off a sequence of operations which are simple in themselves but confusing until you know which is which. Biennials of course are not annuals at all but two-year plants. But since they entail yearly sowing and transplanting they slot naturally into the sequence.

It must be remembered that these are gardeners', not God's, terms, based on the most successful management of the plant—which is why there are perennials which are conventionally treated as annuals for top performance, and "annuals" which will go on for years in hot, sheltered or particularly dry places. A giant sage which dies every winter in good soil in my garden has sown its seed high in a wall and shows every sign of becoming not just a perennial, but a shrub. A wallflower in a bed is usually grown as a biennial: in a wall it can live for years and years . . . but back to the rules.

Hardy annuals germinate at low temperatures and suffer spring frosts gladly. They are therefore sown, usually where they are to flower, as early in the year as the soil is fit for them; perhaps in March. "Fit" means loose and friable—neither frozen nor dusty nor muddy. A number of annuals could well be placed in a separate "very hardy" class. These do best of all if they are sown in autumn, as nature intended, to germinate and spend the winter as small plants. The spring and summer forget-me-nots, love-in-a-mist, poppies, the baby-blue nemophila and the gentian-blue phacelia are all the better for this early start—which in a sense reclassifies them as biennials.

Biennials are sown in summer in order to have half a growing year to establish themselves before winter. From the garden management point of view this normally means sowing them in the vegetable plot, where they can be thinned and pampered along with the salads, then moving them as substantial plants in autumn, winter or spring, according to the climate and the state of the soil, to what the text-books charmingly call their "flowering stations". Most biennials flower in spring. Foxgloves and Canterbury bells are about the last to perform—and by August the next generation of foxgloves has already started its little rosettes around its parents.

Half-hardy annuals behave like hardy annuals, with the all-important difference that they must be kept indoors until after the last frosts. They must be sown early to be ready to flower in summer. But they need a temperature in the 50s Fahrenheit (10°C plus) to make them germinate (some higher; some lower; *vide* the seed packet), and once they have germinated they have to be housed, in their growing bulk, in good light and reasonable warmth. Like all seedlings they must be thinned, pricked out, if necessary potted on and generally kept on the go: it is fatal to try to slow them down by letting them become crowded. Thus the space problem grows ever more acute as spring goes on. Cold frames will do to keep the last frosts off them, but by that time frame space for "hardening-off" is at a premium. For all these reasons most gardeners buy their half-hardy annuals ready-grown at planting-out time in boxes or flats from commercial nurseries—which greatly limits their choice and by no means guarantees that they will get the best varieties.

If you are ready to go to the trouble of raising half-hardy annuals, intensive study of seed catalogues is worth your while.

There is not the slightest reason to segregate annuals into a separate bedding department of the garden, as tradition would have us do. Where segregation comes naturally, as in window boxes and tubs, annuals are ideal. But they can also add their special vitality to every sort of planting: traditional border, shrub bed, modern mixture of the two, kitchen garden (in the French style, both for general *agrément* and for picking)—anywhere they can be offered a good start in well-prepared soil.

To make handsome plants of annuals, the thinnest sowing, the most conscientious thinning, appropriate pinching-out to make them branch, and where necessary support with brushwood or canes, are all essential. As to choice—turn the page.

Above Annual bedding of a kind now chiefly practised in public parks, and nowhere better than here in Melbourne, Australia. From front to back of the bed are alyssum, three kinds of pansies, poppies, stocks, marigolds. Notice the stand-pipes for watering.

Right Cornflowers, California poppies and convolvulus with nasturtiums, whose leaves are just visible, to follow them; a good example of grouping annuals with similar tastes and harmonious colours. All these will put up with dry conditions.

Left A good example of spring bedding, composed largely of biennial wallflowers and forget-me-nots, with polyanthus primulas also planted out as biennials. Across the lawn, under the flowering cherry, a herbaceous border is just waking.

Right The two stages in the life of a typical biennial; a foxglove. From seed sown in summer the plant has formed a substantial rosette of leaves by autumn. If necessary this can be transplanted in early spring. In spring it sends up its flowering stems. Foxgloves have tiny seeds in enormous quantities.

Below The joy of annuals is that the simplest means can be used to create the most brilliant effects. The sunk garden at Packwood House, Warwickshire (a property of the National Trust) is planted with such kindergarten plants as nasturtiums and marigolds. In the background sweet peas are trained up tripods.

Above Spring-flowering annuals can sometimes be hastened along with careful cultivation to flower in a greenhouse or conservatory in winter. *Salpiglossis sinuata* is a half-hardy annual, like an aristocratic three-foot petunia, which submits well to this treatment. If seeds are sown in July or August and the plants are kept at a minimum of 45°F (cool greenhouse temperature) with modest watering and plenty of light, they can be in flower by the end of January. Alternatively, April-sown seed will flower in August. *Calendula* and *Nemesia* are other suitable flowers that can be forced for decorating the greenhouse in winter like this.

Annuals: the choice

HALF HARDY ANNUALS

1 *Aster novae-angliae*
2 *Cleome spinosa*
3 *Cosmos bipinnatus*
4 *Schizanthus pinnatus*
5 *Echeveria gibbiflora*
6 *Zinnia elegans*
7 *Nicotiana affinis*
8 *Venidium fastuosum*
9 *Salvia splendens*
10 *Dimorphotheca ecklonis*
11 *Kochia scoparia*
12 *Salpiglossis sinuata*
13 *Heliotropium peruvianum*
14 *Tagetes erecta*
15 *Verbena hybrida*
16 *Ageratum houstonianum*
17 *Nemesia strumosa*
18 *Petunia hybrida*
19 *Antirrhinum majus*
20 *Phlox drummondii*
21 *Gazania splendens*
22 *Lobelia erinus*
23 *Portulaca grandiflora*
24 *Mesembryanthemum criniflor*

HARDY ANNUALS

1 *Lavatera trimestris*
2 *Lathyrus odoratus*
3 *Amaranthus caudatus*
4 *Delphinium ajacis*
5 *Helianthus annuus*
6 *Nigella damascena*
7 *Coreopsis drummondii*
8 *Impatiens glandulifera*
9 *Centaurea cyanus*
0 *Rudbeckia hirta*
11 *Papaver somniferum*
12 *Chrysanthemum carinatum*
13 *Clarkia elegans*
14 *Calendula officinalis*
15 *Salvia horminum*
16 *Gypsophila elegans*
17 *Reseda odorata*
18 *Tropaeolum majus*
19 *Eschscholzia californica*
20 *Godetia grandiflora*
21 *Linum grandiflorum*
22 *Iberis amara*
23 *Matthiola bicornis*
24 *Convolvulus tricolor*
25 *Phacelia campanularia*
26 *Limnanthes douglasii*
27 *Nemophila menzeisii*
28 *Alyssum maritimum*
29 *Bartonia aurea*

Bedding with tender plants

Above The art of carpet-bedding can still inspire much admiration when it is done with such geometrical precision as in this successful example in the public gardens at Lyon in France.

Below The subtropical style of tender bedding aims at the opposite effect: the gaudy lushness of a jungle garden. Several of the plants here are familiar, but it is the big-leaved ingredients that provide the jungle touch.

To discourse on the beauties of summer bedding today would be like proposing a polka at a disco. The seasonal setting-out of thousands of plants to form patterns and pictures is a garden fashion that has come and gone. It lingers on in resort towns in Britain, and perhaps more in France, where civic pride can also take some childish forms at times. But the panache has faded. Such examples as the masterpiece above are rare, and found in only the public parks of the richer towns.

When summer bedding was new it was the embodiment of the Industrial Revolution come to horticulture. It bespoke acres of glass, tons of coal, and squads of house-proud gardeners. It was almost forced on gardens, one feels, by the pressure in the greenhouse boilers. Here was all this exotic stuff: what were they going to do with it? At great Victorian mansions it was not unknown to change all the flowerbeds between weekends, with the household linen.

Much of the bedding was done with annuals raised from seed sown in heat in late winter, but another major source of bright, strong and exotic plants was the tender perennials imported from South Africa and Central and South America. The stock plants, kept in greenhouses, supplied thousands of cuttings or seeds to be grown on in pots and bedded out when the risk of frost had passed. Of all these plants by far the most successful and popular were the South African geraniums.

The Royal Horticultural Society Dictionary, whose chapter on bedding reads as though it was written in 1850 rather than 1950, sets out a choice of "three distinct styles of summer bedding": "Ordinary Summer Bedding", "Subtropical" and "Carpet Bedding".

By "Ordinary" is meant a still-familiar style consisting usually of a mixture of annuals and tender perennials. Geraniums, fuchsias, tuberous and other begonias and ageratums are mixed with red-leaved coleus and beet and the silver of

FUCHSIAS

Fuchsias have most of the advantages that make geraniums such popular bedding plants. They are fast-growing, colourful (at least at close quarters), have a very long flowering season that lasts well into autumn and are extremely easy to propagate by cuttings. Two geranium qualities they lack are drought resistance and infinite variety. Many feel they make up for them in the elegance of their dangling flowers and their sometimes startling colour combinations in the range purple-red-pink-white.

They are principally natives of Central and South America, where in the extreme south *F. magellanica* is the hardiest species. Most cultivated kinds are hybrids of this with *F. fulgens* from Mexico. *F. magellanica* (below) with its small red or pale pink ('Alba') flowers is hardy in Britain.

'Display'

'Winston Churchill'

'Snowcap'

BEGONIAS

There are three broad classes of begonias, all of which have similar uses to fuchsias and geraniums and are managed in greenhouses in much the same way. Like fuchsias they need plentiful food and water when in flower. Tuberous-rooted begonias are lush show flowers, the equivalent of Regal pelargoniums (see below). Most are cultivars of *B.* × *tuberhybrida* in brilliant colours and with exciting crystalline petals. Rhizomatous-rooted begonias are chiefly grown for their striking, usually ear-shaped leaves marked with various colours. Fibrous-rooted begonias include the bedding plant *B. semperflorens* with small red, pink or white waxy flowers.

GERANIUMS

Geraniums have had a unique role as *the* bedding plant since the Victorians discovered their qualities. They are highly coloured in endless variety, perfectly adapted to mass production and as near indestructible as can be. Strictly speaking they are all really pelargoniums. In popular use the name pelargonium is applied only to the showiest of them with the biggest flowers: The Regals. It is one of the rare cases in horticulture where democracy has successfully routed botany.

Their South African origin explains one of their great virtues—ability to survive drought. None of them can withstand freezing, but because their metabolism can slow down to almost total dormancy they are as easy to overwinter as if they had tubers like begonias or dahlias.

But an even greater virtue is that cuttings root with effortless ease any time from spring to early autumn. They need slightly different treatment from most other cuttings—but what it amounts to is simply less water at every stage, including airy rather than close conditions.

There are six simple categories to be aware of. Within these their variety is prodigious.

First are the zonal geraniums, so-called because their leaves have a darker central zone, sometimes distinct, sometimes faint. These are the common bedding kind, with red or pink, often veined or marbled flowers all summer. They may be single or double but are individually relatively small.

Coloured-leaf geraniums have been bred with emphasis on shades of gold or brown or "silver" in the leaf and have more modest flowers. They are used similarly for bedding.

Miniature geraniums are just that: no more than eight inches tall, very varied and good for windowsills.

Ivy-leaved geraniums have trailing stems with much smaller leaves, like miniature ivy. They are chiefly used for hanging baskets and window boxes. 'L'Elégante' (below) is the best.

Scented-leaved geraniums, though not showy in flower, are some of the most interesting to collect for their enormously varied leaves that range in shape from round to lacy, in texture from corduroy to velvet, and in scent encompass lemon, rose, pine, peppermint, apple and spices.

Regal, Fancy or Show pelargoniums have by far the most luscious flowers and are usually displayed in the protection of a greenhouse, where they come into flower earlier than the "geraniums".

Regal: 'Aztec'

Zonal: 'Mrs Henry Cox'

Coloured-leaf: 'Freak of Nature'

Scented-leaved: *P. graveolens*

Scented-leaved: *P. crispum* 'Variegatum'

Ivy-leaved: 'L'Elegante'

Senecio (Cineraria) maritima, with calceolarias and celosias, heliotropes and *Salvia splendens* and gaillardias, using blue lobelia and golden feverfew as the low edging, all laid out with elaborate geometry.

Subtropical bedding demands greater resources. Botanical gardens and the major parks departments are alone in using it today. It is largely a matter of moving out into the open plants that would normally live under glass all year and rather gingerly plunging them, pots and all, in the most sheltered bed for the hottest months. Big-leaved plants such as agaves, palms, bananas, cordylines, yuccas, ficus, grevilleas, *Eucalyptus globulus* and tree ferns get pride of place, along with such fast-growing annuals of tropical appearance as castor-oil plants and herbaceous solanums, and the tender perennial cannas.

Carpet bedding is defined as forming carpet-like patterns with dwarf coloured-foliage plants, which, the RHS Dictionary notes, need "constant attention with regard to pinching and keeping them within their allotted space". Alternanthera, calocephalus (leucophyta), sagina, tresire and echeverias are perhaps the arch-carpet-bedders. Where a taller plant is used to stand up among the dwarfs it is known as a "dot plant".

The significance of all this to most modern gardeners is fairly remote. Having moved on to the labour-saving philosophy of permanent ecologically-inspired planting there are few who would return to the painting-by-numbers approach.

On the other hand there is a place in an eclectic modern garden for every sort of plant. If you have a greenhouse it is irresistible to use it to propagate the most sultry-looking plants you can find . . . geraniums are only the beginning.

Above all the old bedding game applies to pots, urns, vases, tubs and every sort of container. A noble vase overflowing with plants that could not possibly be growing in the garden around is the richest eye-catcher of all.

Bulbs and other packages

Right The principle of the bulb is food storage in an underground organ. Such organs can be buds, swollen stems, leaves or roots.

Bulbs were surely invented by a Dutch industrial designer. The functional lines, the built-in packaging, the sheer convenience of a plant that can be handled so easily during such a long dormant period . . . they all point to a backroom genius in the garden-centre business.

The tidiness of the whole idea is immensely appealing. Out of this capsule, on a signal received from the atmospheric temperature and moisture, come the roots to drink, the leaves to feed, the stem and flower to mate. They build up a replacement module, make their attempt at reproducing their kind. Then they fall away, their jobs done, to be recycled in the soil. The refuelled, or rather rebuilt, bulb lies low, as safe as a plant can be, oblivious to lack of water, waiting for the right sequence of cold and wet to set it going again. Meanwhile it can be poured down chutes into boxes, displayed on counters, put up to auction: the perfect packaged flower.

These eminently satisfactory arrangements, however, evolved with another object in view. The bulb routine, in the case of the most familiar examples, is an efficient way of life in countries with brief rains, usually in spring, and long dry summers. The Mediterranean and the Near East and countries with Mediterranean climates such as South Africa are the homes of most bulbs. Our crocuses come typically from shallow soils in Greece and the islands; tulips from parched hills and plains in the steppes of central Asia; daffodils from Spain, Portugal and North Africa. True there are Pyrenean daffodils accustomed to wet summers—and lilies tend to break the rules by growing in damp but porous woodland soil—but with all the exceptions taken into account there is remarkable homogeneity in the broad group that the layman calls bulbs.

Nearly all, for a start, are monocots like the grasses, with long, smooth leaves with parallel veins. They tend to flower on "scapes" or stems that rise straight from the ground independent of the leaves—also smooth, with an inclination to be brittle and sappy. With one possible exception they never exceed about eight feet in height, nor grow woody, nor show a tendency to climb. Most of them belong to only three families, which in turn must have a common grandparent.

Of the three main families the Liliaceae has the widest range. It includes lilies, hyacinths, tulips, fritillaries, alliums (the onion tribe), scillas, grape-hyacinths, trilliums, colchicums and erythroniums, the "dog's tooth violets". The Amaryllidaceae, besides of course the amaryllis, includes narcissi, snowdrops, nerines and sternbergias. The Iridaceae, besides irises, contains crocuses, gladioli, montbretias and freezias.

Not all the members of these families have evolved as bulbs. Among irises the truly bulbous are in a minority. The notion of food-storage is there, however, in all these flowers in one form or another. And a bulb, though the word is convenient for the broad category, is strictly speaking only one particular design of storage organ. The others should be called by their proper names of corms, tubers, tuberous roots and rhizomes.

All share not only the storage habit but the habit of bypassing the sexual process and making new plants by some form of division; either by forming new buds which soon become independent bulbs, or building new corms on top of, or new tubers beside, the old. They are like herbaceous plants in this: they renew themselves centrifugally whether they have any luck sexually or not. Unlike herbaceous plants which stay in one piece, bulb "off-sets" detach themselves and live independently, making them ideal units for commerce.

As far as bulb catalogues go it is not the botany but the package that counts. They include flowers with the same convenient habit which are quite unrelated: notably cyclamen, which are a kind of primrose, and anemones and aconites which are cousins of the buttercup.

The next six pages survey the range of expensive temptations that bulb nurseries offer, with particular attention to the three genera that dominate the bulb world: narcissi, tulips and lilies.

There are many ways of using bulbs in the garden. The same flowers can give quite different effects used formally as bedding and casually as incidents. But whether they are dressed by the right, tucked away among shrubs, naturalized in grass or woodland, given a sun-baked cranny or rockery, or even treasured in pots and sheltered in frames, certain principles of cultivation apply.

All bulbs need good drainage. Even those that like perpetual drizzle must not lie in saturated soil while they are dormant. With few exceptions bulbs like to be planted as deep as they are tall. If they need to go deeper they pull themselves down by their roots. All bulbs demand to have their leaves left intact while they feed, flag and finally wither. If you cut them off during the period after flowering, next year's bulb is deprived of its rations. After flowering is the time to feed and water established clumps if you have any reason to think they need it.

In formal bedding-out schemes, particularly of tulips, this is the time they are lifted and moved to a quiet sunny corner to ripen off. Once the leaves have withered the bulbs are dried and stored, to be replanted in autumn.

Curiously enough the best time to shunt any bulbs round your garden is not during the commercial break while they are dry and dormant, but when they have just flowered and are in full leaf. Then you can clearly see and get hold of them without stabbing them with your fork, and you can remember which is which. The sooner they are moved the quicker they will become re-established.

Above Tulips with their symmetrical form and paint-box colour seem to demand formal treatment. Certainly the tall Dutch tulips, as opposed to the more reticent species, look best in substantial blocks of one colour at a time, as here at Duke University, Durham, North Carolina.

Right It is hard to be convincingly formal with daffodils, except perhaps the tallest and stiffest. The nodding stem flowers of the more natural kinds are best clustered and dotted in grass almost as long as their leaves. A close-mown lawn gives them too much emphasis.

THE BULB ROUTINE

The hyacinth has a true bulb, consisting of overlapping swollen leaf bases or scales on a basal plate surrounding the embryo flower, the whole thing wrapped in a coat of expended scales.

The flower is completely formed, surrounded by food in the swollen scales.

Roots from the basal plate absorb water; then leaves force the path for the flower.

Within three months the flower blooms, the leaves photosynthesize.

The flower-stem withers first; the leaves continue to restock the bulb with food.

Two months later the bulb has a new leaf and flower bud from the basal plate.

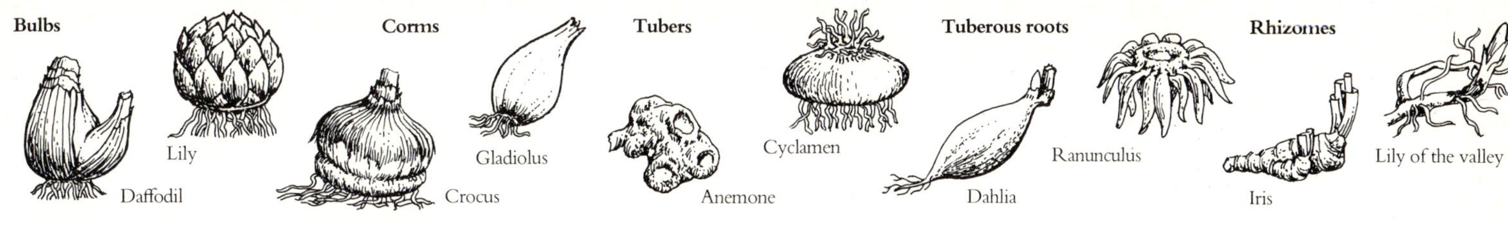

Left Tulips had long been cultivated by the Turks before the Ambassador from Vienna to Constantinople in 1560 first procured bulbs for the West. In Holland they caused a sensation: bulbs changed hands for fortunes.

Turkey lies on the western edge of tulipland. The epicentre is in the desolate wastes of Turkestan beyond the Caspian. Here, wrote the botanist Regel, "sport anemones, crocuses, irises, tulips, fritillarias and long-shafted eremuri." Winter is long and cold, spring wet and summer hot and dry. Only in the last eighty years has this treasure-house been explored—once more largely by the Dutch, with firms such as Van Tubergen taking the lead.

THE BULB TRADE

The international bulb industry has had its base in Holland for four hundred years. The volume of the bulb trade today is remarkable. In 1976 there were more than 5,000 hectares of tulips in Holland, 2,000 of gladiolus, 1,600 of daffodils, 880 of irises, 500 of crocus and many more of dahlias and the smaller or more specialized bulbs. Britain, the biggest export customer, bought a total of some 7,000 tonnes, although growing most of her own daffodils.

Regular auctions are held and visits to the bulb fields round Hillegom and elsewhere are important spring tourist attractions.

THE CORM ROUTINE

A crocus "bulb" is strictly speaking a "corm": a very short underground stem swollen with stored food and enclosed within overlapping fibrous leaf bases.

The flower is already formed, surrounded by the food supply in the swollen leaves.

The built-in food supply is used to produce roots and leaves.

By early spring leaves grow and the crocus blooms. Flowering uses all the "food".

New food supplies gathered by the leaves build a new corm on top of the old.

The new corm on top of the old one has contractile roots to pull it to the right depth.

Bulbs for spring

Right The European name of "Dog's-tooth violet" is less appropriate than the American 'trout lily' for the shade-loving erythroniums—plants with marbled leaves and flowers like small hanging lilies. All except the pink and white *Erythronium dens-canis* are from North America. This is *E. tuolumnense* from California.

Bulbs and the spring are almost synonymous in most gardeners' minds. No sooner has the snow gone, leaving grubby heaps in corners and the grass pale, blotched and ill-looking, than from the chilly soaking ground green dagger-points begin to poke. Within two days the snowdrop has freed its upright white antenna from the protecting leaves. For a few more days it lengthens its stalk. Then, at a moment I have never caught, its capsule opens and the bell nods down. If you must start spring somewhere it is surely here.

There is a texture to the flowers of spring bulbs which is easy to recognize but hard to describe. E. A. Bowles came very close when he described them as "crystalline": there is a sense of seeing through a transparent skin into faceted layers inside. The freshness and tenderness of the effect, and the clarity it gives to their colours, is unique to the season—except, says Bowles, for the sumptuous glittering petals of tuberous begonias in summer. I find the magic also in the thick petals of some camellias; this extra dimension of reflecting light both coloured and clear—like, indeed, a diamond.

The first bulbs to show themselves may not be the snowdrops but crocuses or the tiny irises, blue *histrioides* or yellow *danfordiae*, flowering no more than three inches above the soil. You might expect to find a certain disproportion in the size of the flowers. In practice the little bulbs which are all flower and no plant have the same kind of charming illogicality as the tiny alpines that wear flowers several sizes too big. But like the alpines they need to be either in the palm of your hand or in unusually large sheets on the ground to be really effective. A dozen or a score of crocuses in a bed thirty feet away is of little value. It is better either to plant extravagantly or to grow them in a pot, a frame or a raised bed by a path, where you will stop and take in the details.

The Dutch, of course, have an answer for this, breeding great fat strong-coloured crocuses almost like young tulips. But those who have only seen Dutch crocuses have missed the fairy delicacy of the genus—not to mention its variety, or the fact that it furnishes flowers all winter and well into spring and again in the autumn. An ice-bound winter delays the performance, but the earliest crocus species flower in a warm December to be followed by a succession up to March.

The Greek *Crocus laevigatus* and the Italian *C. imperati*, two of the earliest, are the kind that beg for close-up inspection: they blend so many subtle colours and patterns in their petals, their outsides veined or feathered with dusky mauve. *C. aureus*, a clear yellow, appears at the same time, and only a little later *C. chrysanthus* offers almost every colour from ivory to gold to deep lilac, all with flushes or feathers of deeper colours. In practice, for scenic effect, the important differences between these species are the overall colour and the time of flowering.

In reasonable conditions (which includes relative freedom from mice) these early crocuses will spread and spread. The mauve-to-purple *C. tomasinianus* ("Tommies" to their friends) are the most prolific of all. The finest living memorial to the extravagant Miss Willmott, whose Essex garden at the turn of the century kept a hundred men busy, is a whole roadside field of perhaps ten acres which has been colonized by her crocuses since she departed: an incredible sight in February.

What the crocuses do not provide is true blue: all their blues

Above The snowflakes are distinguished from the snowdrops by their six "petals" all being the same length. *Leucojum vernum* flowers in late winter. The "summer" snowflake, *L. aestivum*, is later and taller.

Below left and below Crocuses are flowers for the open lawn; bluebells for the wood. The earliest crocuses flower in mid-winter; large Dutch hybrids in spring; bluebells just as the woods break into leaf.

Right The winter aconites' clumps of deeply fringed leaves are some of the first herbaceous-looking arrivals of spring, along with the rich green shoots of the cuckoo-pint, or lords and ladies. The bright buttercup flowers of the aconites have conspicuous green ruffs, fringed like the leaves. They naturalize freely.

Right The "windflower" anemones vary from the white English woodland *Anemone nemorosa* to blue *A. blanda* of the Greek mountains to the "poppy" and "peacock" anemones and others grown in gaudy colours. The red flowers here are *A. coronaria*, the poppy anemone; the blue *A. blanda*.

are more or less washed with purple or lavender. The early daffodils cry out for a strong blue to set off their yellow—happy and gleaming as it is. Luckily one of the earliest and easiest little bulbs to naturalize is the Siberian Squill, *Scilla sibirica*. *S. sibirica* 'Spring Beauty' is the perfect brilliant blue to pull the daffodils up with a jerk: a plant only eight inches high with diminutive flowers, but with the impact of a gem lying in the grass.

There is a fairly strong blue among the variable anemones, too. But even the bluest, the Greek *Anemone blanda atrocoerulea* (literally "dark blue"), looks washy beside 'Spring Beauty'. (They flower at the same time). The grape hyacinth will provide a low background of a rather light blue for the later daffodil season, at the same time as their big brothers, the bedding hyacinths. But these last belong to a different school. Hyacinths and daffodils, even the grossest and stiffest of daffodils, were not meant for one another.

Perhaps the greatest joy of spring bulbs is that they are an extra dimension you can add to any part of the garden. Because they come and go before the garden fills up, they, with hellebores and early woodland flowers, are a scene in themselves which you can develop over the years. The only place not to put bulbs is in beds where you are constantly digging and planting. Plant them in places which will be undisturbed for years. By far the best value are the bulbs that naturalize. As clumps grow thick you can divide them after flowering, lifting them gently with a fork, holding them by their leaves and pulling them apart to separate them; then replanting them at wider spacing.

Above The Crown Imperial fritillary is the grandest of all spring bulbs. Mary Grierson's painting is of the orange form: there is also a lemon yellow.

Above The snake's head fritillary, *Fritillaria meleagris*, European sister of the Crown Imperial, settles down in damp spots more as a wild flower than a garden bulb.

Above Grape hyacinths, species of *Muscari*, are some of the easiest bulbs to naturalize. Their light blue spikes come just a little too late to be exciting, but a pool of them with daffodils is a pretty plan.

Left Snowdrops are among the few small spring bulbs that are best seen alone rather than carpeting the ground. A small clump with a stone vase to give scale and definition is a complete picture.

Bulbs: the great three

DAFFODILS

Narcissi, and daffodils, which are narcissi with trumpets as long as their "petals", are among the hardiest and easiest to grow of all bulbs. Starting with about sixty species, mainly from the Mediterranean, over eight thousand named varieties have been produced. They are officially classified into Divisions by the proportions of their flowers, and sub-divisions by colour combinations. For most gardeners this is academic. A dozen kinds is ample to furnish the garden from earliest spring to May with distinct forms. Temperature largely decides flowering time. The first flowers are out in January in warm areas, March in cold ones. Times of flowering given here for comparison apply to the south of England.

The hoop-petticoat daffodil, all trumpet and practically no petals, is a species with no "improved" forms but naturally variable. It naturalizes well in damp spots, flowering in late March and early April.

'Golden Harvest' is one of the commonest yellow daffodils, grown by the field-full for market in March. Technically it is Division 1, sub-division 1a. Sub-divisions 1b and 1c are for yellow-and-white and plain white.

'Edward Buxton' (*top*) is one of the best "large-cup" and 'Carlton' (*bottom*) is a good "small-cup" narcissus, flowering respectively in March and April, though there is no simple relationship between shape and timing.

Double daffodils, with the simple trumpet replaced by a scramble of "petaloids", have not been fashionable since the seventeenth century. 'Texas' (March-flowering) is one of few available.

Narcissi with the blood of the little Portuguese species *N. triandus*, have drooping flowers in clusters, their petals usually swept back. 'Thalia' (*above*) is one of the best.

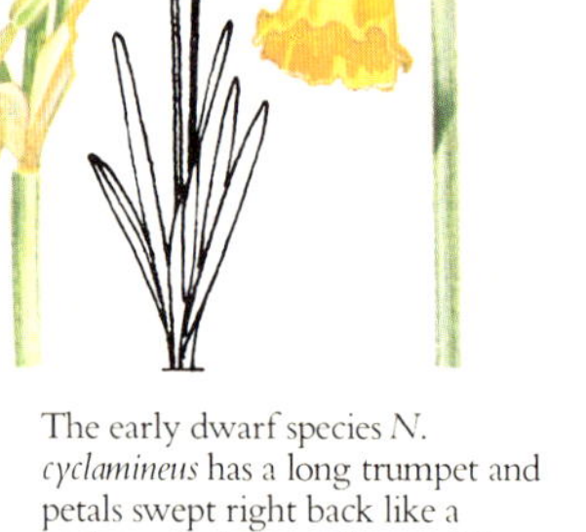

The early dwarf species *N. cyclamineus* has a long trumpet and petals swept right back like a cyclamen's. It naturalizes well in damp soil. 'February Gold' (*above*) is one of the best of its garden hybrids.

The jonquils with their long rush-like leaves have the strongest scent of all but flower rather late and need a warm corner. They are lovely in bowls indoors. 'Trevithian' is one of the best garden forms.

'Paper White', flowering in mid-winter and therefore usually grown indoors, is the only common form of *N. tazetta*, cluster flowered and sweet scented, the most widespread of all species, reaching east to Japan.

The Pheasant's eye or poet's narcissus, *N. poeticus*, flat faced with a red or red-rimmed cup, is one of the latest to flower. These crossed with tazettas are called "poetaz".

Three bulbs dominate the garden in turn from early spring to late summer. Even such familiar friends as crocuses and such seasonal spectacles as Crown Imperials must be classed as minor themes and embellishments beside them. The narcissi, tulips, and recently lilies have been bred in infinite variety.

Over the centuries other bulbs have come in for intensive breeding. Thousands of varieties of hyacinths, ranunculus and anemones have been raised with great excitement, only to be lost again. For none of these were garden flowers.

The tulips were the first of the big three to attract breeders because of the range of their colours, and because they are subject to viruses that make the colours "break" in bizarre patterns. Tulip fever, when fortunes were made and lost on single bulbs, raged in Holland from 1643 to 1647.

"Daffadowndillies" were popular in Elizabethan times, but the fact that yellow was their only colour moderated enthusiasm for breeding. Modern narcissi began in the last century.

Lilies were regarded as difficult and cussed plants (as most of them still are) right up to the last thirty years or so, when intensive hybridization, mainly in Oregon, has produced reasonably easy cultivars of the most spectacular of all bulbs.

Now all three are elaborately categorized for judging purposes by the size and shape of flower, or the historical backgrounds of the strain. The limitation of this system is that it treats most of the natural wild species as second-class citizens.

LILIES

Lilies demand a high price for their undoubted glamour. They are among the wayward plants that demand both plentiful moisture and rapid drainage. Unlike other bulbs they have no protective "tunic" and never entirely stop growing. The fleshy scales of their bulbs are therefore always vulnerable; above all to drying out if they are dug up and stored. They should always be kept moist. Never buy desiccated lily bulbs. Virus and botrytis are the other problems lily growers must face. They are not plants for casual disposal round the garden for summer colour. They ask for woodland soil and semi-shade. Lilies have been hybridized partly for bigger and brighter flowers but also to make them easier to grow. The selection here is of some of the best of the more elementary kinds.

The Madonna lily, *Lilium candidum*, has been in gardens for 3,000 years and is still unsurpassed for scent and simple beauty, flowering at mid-summer. It is almost alone in preferring dry limy soil and full sun on its shallow roots.

'Enchantment' is perhaps the most famous of all the hybrids from the Oregon Bulb Farms. It carries up to sixteen flowers, six inches across, on each stem in July and tolerates hot weather and most soils, or a pot.

TULIPS

The broadest division of tulips is between the garden varieties, the result of breeding begun in the sixteenth century, and the "botanical" or species tulips, which are more recent imports from the East, generally shorter-stemmed, often smaller and in some cases much earlier-flowering. The former are conventionally treated as bedding plants, planting them in late autumn and lifting them after flowering in spring. The latter are grown with more or less success as permanencies in sunny dry soil; the smallest in rock gardens. There are fifteen official classes of tulips, based partly on when they flower, partly on shape and partly on ancestry. Those illustrated here represent the six most distinct bedding categories and three of the species which are first-class garden plants, arranged in their approximate order of flowering.

One of the earliest and easiest of tulips is the charming little wildling *T. turkestanica*, which carries as many as seven star-like flowers on each slender nine-inch stem in February.

The water-lily tulip, *T. kaufmanniana*, is a variable species with wide leaves and narrow petals, flowering in March. It has produced excellent hybrids, many with the mottled leaves of the scarlet *T. greigii*.

'Red Emperor' is a selected form of the biggest-flowered species, *T. fosteriana* from Samarkand. It flowers in early April. Crossed with Darwins (*see below*) it has produced the earlier and finer Darwin hybrids.

Single early and double early are the first categories to flower, about mid-April (though they grow well in pots for forcing in February). Peach (*above*) is a typical double.

The "mid-season" (mid-to-late April) tulips are principally the Mendels and the slightly bulkier 'Triumphs'. 'Athleet' is very striking.

Lily-flowered tulips are distinguished by their pointed petals, curling over as they open, that make them the most elegant of their race. They flower in late April. One of the finest tulips is 'White Triumphator'.

Parrot tulips (above is 'Red Parrot') have their petals twisted and dishevelled and bordered with a jagged fringe. They are mostly sports of Darwins and like them flower late, in May.

The ultimate in stately formal tulips are the Darwins, up to thirty inches high, biding their time for good weather in May. Their flowers are square-bottomed and their petals blunt. Above is 'La Tulipe Noire'.

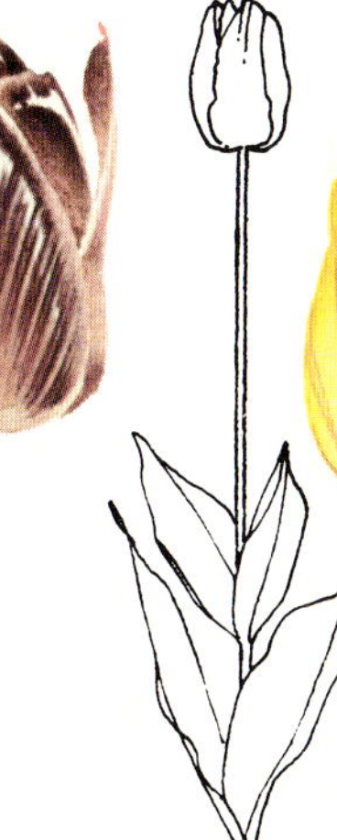

"Broken" tulips, made from "breeder" tulips by injecting them them with virus-infected sap, were the passion of early Dutch florists. 'Absalon' *above* is a Rembrandt, or broken Darwin.

'Marhan' is an improved version of the European martagon or Turk's cap lily, made by crossing it with a similar species from Korea, *L. hansonii*. It combines the scent of the Korean with the tolerance of the martagon—and hybrid vigour.

Lilium regale was one of E. H. Wilson's most valuable Chinese finds: deeply fragrant, easy to grow, increasing quickly by seed and offsets. Like many lilies it is top-heavy and profits from a supporting shrub.

The Bellingham hybrids are big West Coast Americans, of the reflexed Turk's cap persuasion and hot colours, demanding lime-free soil and semi-shade but responding with rude vigour, growing to seven feet or more and making big clumps.

'Green Emerald' is an example of the Oregon trumpet-flowered lilies, July- or August-flowering, for semi-shade. Their names are hypnotic: 'Black Magic', 'Black Dragon', 'Golden Clarion', 'Golden Splendour'. Olympic hybrids are similar.

The Oriental hybrids include the most artificial-looking of all lilies, with wide-open, banded and spotted, heavily scented flowers. They like full sun. 'Imperial Crimson' (*above*) flowers in late summer.

Bulbs for summer and autumn

Above Cyclamen naturalized in the conditions they enjoy: the edge of woodland on light soil. At several long-established Bordeaux châteaux (here at Langoa on the gravel dunes of the Médoc) they have formed dense carpets over many years, woken to life by August rain to flower at vintage time. *Cyclamen europaeum* is a native of southern France and northern Italy, yet curiously enough is not so hardy as the autumn species from southern Italy and Greece, *C. hederifolium* (*neapolitanum*).

Right One of the most elegant of the onions, the June-flowering *Allium siculum* (see also below).

Later bulbs forgo the psychological advantage of answering our anticipation of spring. They have to compete for our interest with many things that might be growing on the same spot.

Lilies, the aristocrats of summer bulbs, have nothing to fear. They can command attention in any company. Lilies apart, though, there is a general midsummer pause, as though few bulbs were willing to risk comparisons they might lose. The big gladioli parade themselves in their paint and powder. They leave me, I fear, completely unmoved. Otherwise only the onions, more politely known as the alliums, have the cheerful self-assurance to keep going.

There are characters among the onions that should be more widely known. The flower shape is an interesting one for a start: a star-burst of bells on stalks. In some species stiff stalks form a drumstick shape; in others they droop gently. The colours are never brilliant, but there are half a dozen species that earn their modest keep. Sun is all they ask.

The bulb world reawakens towards the end of summer with performances that cannot be ignored from South African bulbs, and also with the start of the long-running cyclamen and crocus, alike in having a season that pivots round the winter rather than the summer.

The true autumn crocuses are easily confused with other flowers of remarkably similar construction, until you get down to the details. Autumn crocuses look very like spring ones, though rather taller and less robust. They tend to be knocked flat by autumn gusts. Colchicums, which are usually called "autumn crocuses" as well, are lily rather than iris relations, showing it by having six stamens instead of three, and stressing their differentness by having not modest grassy leaves like real crocuses, but wide floppy ones that follow like retribution after the flower is past. Instead of the vertical streaking that marks the crocuses, their superficially similar goblets are often patterned more or less distinctly with a pink chequer-board or tesselated effect. In some rare and tricky species it is clearly drawn. In common ones, *Colchicum autumnale* and *C. speciosum* and their forms and hybrids, it can usually be faintly traced. Moreover they are pale pink, which no crocus is, whence their vulgar name of "naked ladies".

It is just as well that cyclamen are timed to go off at intervals: some such basic clue is needed in telling them apart. The dozen-odd species vary more in their tenderness or tractability than their looks. The whole plant is so captivating, from its clear-pink little long-eared flowers, like a spaniel in a wind-tunnel, to its deep green shield-, heart-, or kidney-shaped, often

Above Out of about 450 species of *Allium*, the onion genus, some twenty are worth growing for decoration. The red-purple *Allium pulchellum*, above, is an easy, even invasive plant, flowering in July and August, seeding freely as most alliums do. The colour-range extends from the pearly-white *A. neapolitanum* in spring to the little yellow wildflower of midsummer, *A. moly*, the bluebell-blue August *A. cyaneum*, and the joker of the race, *A. albopilosum* whose violet flower heads rise like balloons eighteen inches above the border in July.

Above Autumn sunshine dramatizes the nakedness of the leafless *Colchicum* in October. This form of *C. speciosum*, 'Conquest', is one of the last in flower and among the strongest in colour. There is also a rare pure white and a double pink. The broad leaves that follow the flower easily distinguish colchicums from the true autumn crocuses.

notched or scalloped leaves, that I will uncritically plant as many as I can lay my hands on of the kinds that are reputed hardy. They are Mediterranean flowers, sold in bunches in markets in Italy, Greece and the South of France. It is remarkable, therefore, that at least two are very much in evidence right through an average British winter. *Cyclamen neapolitanum*, which flowers in late summer, decorates the winter ground with its leaves alone. *C. coum* flowers in early spring, sometimes as early as December, combining flowers and foliage in a picture of grace that leaves me speechless. The bun-shaped brown tuber that produces this vision is almost comical. The Neapolitan cyclamen is so absurd as to root from the upper side of this moribund-looking lump, leading many gardeners to plant it upside down. (It can survive even this if planted shallowly enough.) But given a dry, rather shady place and a soft bed of old leaves, (even the needle-fall of a giant old cedar), ground too starved for even grass to grow, the tubers will grow to loaf-size, seedlings will spread, and a great tribe of marvellously varied plants will spring up. They would be worth collecting for their leaves alone: no two seem to be alike. The florist's cyclamen, an inflated version of the tender *C. persicum*, entirely lacks the sense of humour of its country cousin.

Most of the South African bulbs are tender or risky in zone 7. In zone 8 they ask for the sun-baked foot of a south wall where they will receive a Veldt-type baking. They then need a late-summer soaking to start them off.

The rule applies to the pink-trumpeted *Amaryllis belladonna*, which flowers without leaves, to *Crinum* × *powellii*, which sprays its pink or white lily-flowers allium-fashion in a long succession above a bushy leaf-clump, and to the nerines. Nerines are the ones to choose if hot spots are rare in your garden. *Nerine* × *bowdenii* is the hardiest, and worth making efforts for. Its flowers are like spun-sugar spiders with unique qualities of catching and holding the light. As cut flowers they have unusual stamina—up to a two-week life in water. If your treatment satisfies them, they will multiply to form dense clumps and last for ever. The only quality they lack is scent. Best tempered of the South African bulbs, unaccountably out of fashion today, is the Cape or summer hyacinth, *Galtonia candicans*, which asks no more than a fairly sheltered spot, not too dry, to raise its four-foot steeples of white or greeny-white bells. Tucked in among border flowers that are beginning to hint at autumn, their waxy whiteness is like a theme from the first half of the symphony gently repeated by the woodwind in the second.

Left The true amaryllis, *Amaryllis belladonna*, is a smaller and hardier plant than the huge trombone of a bulb grown under the name in pots—which is really a *Hippeastrum*. Amaryllis will grow in a warm wall-border in Britain. The leafless stem rises two feet and carries four pink trumpets, redolent of the Riviera.

Above There is a strong family resemblance to the amaryllis in the *Crinum*. *C.* × *powellii* is the only one generally grown in temperate gardens. Planted in well-fed ground and left to become congested over the years it makes a subtropical mass of leaves and pink and white flowers.

Above A bright satiny yellow crocus with six stamens early in autumn can only be *Sternbergia lutea* from the eastern Mediterranean. A narrow-leaved form, *S. lutea augustifolia*, is said to be readiest to flower, but does best after a very hot dry summer on a gravel bank.

Above The Kaffir Lily (*Schizostylis coccinea*) is yet another South African branch of the iris family, with the latest season of all, sometimes still in flower in November when frost knocks it down. The grassy leaves and flowers suggest a bulb; in fact it is a star-like rhizome.

Above The snowflakes are the snowdrops of the late spring and summer. They are Mediterranean and central European bulbs of the same family. Above is the eighteen-inch summer snowflake, *Leucojum aestivum*. *L. vernum*, of spring, is between this and the snowdrop in size.

Above The South African *Nerine* × *bowdenii* appreciates the protection of a wall in British gardens. The even lovelier *N. sarniensis*, known as the Guernsey lily (apparently because bulbs from a ship-wreck were found on a Guernsey beach) is best grown under glass for the summer baking its bulbs need. Pure white as well as lighter and darker forms can be had.

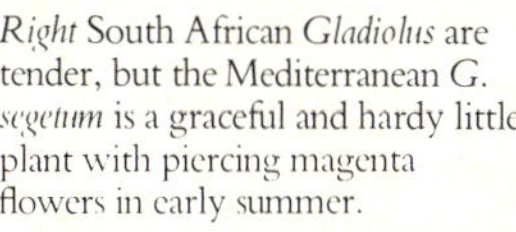

Above The Cape Hyacinth is one of the most reliable bulbs of the late summer, at home in a border with herbaceous plants where its long-stalked bells make a great impression.

Right South African *Gladiolus* are tender, but the Mediterranean *G. segetum* is a graceful and hardy little plant with piercing magenta flowers in early summer.

Alpines and rockeries

Right In their urgency to flower and set seed, some of the plants of the high alps generate enough warmth to melt the last of the snow. *Saxifraga burseriana*, one of the characteristic lime-loving plants of the Dolomites, is one of the loveliest of its race, with wide round-petalled flowers from a cushion of blue-grey leaves.

Above The shattered crags of the Dolomites of northwestern Italy are skirted with screes of broken limestone. The pink moss campion, *Silene acaulis*, flowers there as it rarely does in gardens, with yellow toadflax, *Linaria alpina*.

The notion of growing mountain plants in gardens goes back perhaps 150 years, to the time when the Alps were suddenly discovered to be beautiful as well as forbidding. Romantic gardeners of the early nineteenth century were more interested in the rocks and caverns than the flowers. They had climbed no higher than the lower cataracts, still overhung with larch and fir. Mosses and ferns were their idea of alpine plants. The gardeners enjoyed the gloom, and made more or less convincing imitations of it when they returned home.

Then tourists climbed higher. Above the tree-line they found another world, where low bushes of rhododendron and juniper and willow were exposed to bright sun and high winds, where the snow lay thick and late and revealed a host of hidden plants when it melted; all rushing into flower at once. The higher they climbed the shorter the plants became, hugging the ground closer and closer, all their parts foreshortened to avoid the gales and find what warmth and shelter there is in the ground.

All foreshortened, that is, except the flowers, which seemed to get bigger and brighter the higher they climbed. On the high alps little cushion-like plants were often totally hidden with a mantle of intensely coloured flowers.

The conditions that produce these brilliant midgets are simple enough to understand. Their whole growing season is packed into a scorching three-month summer. Winter means snow cover, under which roots can lengthen and buds form. Snow can lie for years in some deep glens, only melting in an exceptional drought. But as soon as the snow goes, everything needed for growth is there in abundance: moisture from the melting snow, warmth from the sun high in the cloudless sky, and light of an intensity we never see in the lowlands.

Flowers take priority because the season is so short. They must have time to ripen seed before winter comes again. At high altitudes annuals are almost unknown: there is no time for the necessary germination, growth, flowering and seeding in one year.

But why the short joints; the stunted growth? Because, it seems, the periods when cells can divide and tissues grow are

Below A small, fragrant mountain daphne, *D. striata*, thrives at 6,500 feet in the alps in what appears to be a pile of loose rocks without soil. It pushes long underground shoots for yards under boulders, eventually colonizing large areas.

Right Tufa rock; limy, light, porous, soft enough to carve but hard enough to weather, provides well-drained niches for rock plants: here yellow *Euryops acraeus*, white *Saxifraga cochlearis* and green *Helichrysum coralloides*.*

only those between bright day, when the plant is under too much stress of transpiration, and the alpine night, which is too cold: only, in other words, the brief twilight. Any vigorous upward growth, moreover, would soon be wrenched away in a storm. On a mountain, safety and such warmth as there is (out of the sun) are found lying flat on your stomach.

If the alpine climate is fairly uniform, given that there are slopes facing north, south, east and west and all points between, the terrain is not. There is first of all the basic rock: granite in the Alps, the Himalayas, the California Sierras, limestone in the Dolomites, the Pyrenees. There is every degree of slope, from soilless precipice and overhang to flat, stagnant marshland where sedges grow high among the peaks. Below cliffs there is scree: the deep accumulation of rock debris, a dry habitat in summer where plants must root yards down to reach the retreating water. Below glaciers there is moraine, where water runs below the rubble all summer long. There may even, in some gully, be a pocket of deep soil. Each will have its characteristic flora, in colonies which eventually become familiar to observant climbers and walkers with their eyes on the ground.

One of the happiest discoveries of modern gardening is that it is possible to reproduce a great range of different habitats within the confines of a tiny garden by imaginative use of stone, soil and water. The keen alpine gardener today is a creative ecologist, ready to build the precise crag or cranny a particular plant needs, taking account of shelter or exposure and the depth, texture and chemical make-up of the soil it comes from. The scree, the moraine and the mountain tarn are all in his repertoire. Alpines in fact present the perfect opportunity for an intelligent flower-lover and naturalist with a small garden to combine the pleasures of forming a collection with the satisfaction of experiment and research.

Unspecialized gardeners are not too particular about what they call an alpine, so long as it is low growing and looks more or less at home on a rock garden or in a dry-stone wall. Dwarf shrubs and bulbs quite unconnected with mountains are usually included. Over the page is a selection of some of the

Below A campanula has established itself upside-down on a ledge of crumbling shale above a stream. Such apparently completely soilless lodgings are exactly what many alpines like: the one proviso being a steady supply of water passing through the roots as it drains down the mountain.

Below A natural outcrop of rock has been used as a rock garden. Pockets of soil were first made on ledges and in crevices. Eventually seedlings appeared in apparently soilless places.

Left In common garden use there is no essential distinction between alpines and other small plants. Overemphasis on rock plants to cover banks is a common temptation, but can lead to dullness after the brilliance of the spring display.

most worthwhile and commonly-grown "rock" plants.

In a temperate lowland garden it is, above all, the weather that is wrong for growing true alpines. It is mild and damp when it should be dry and freezing; it should indeed be deep in snow. And when it should be sunny and hot it is more than likely to be drizzling. The soil is usually almost as bad: too rich, too slow draining, and full of organic matter (including slugs). Both factors keep the crown of the plant damp and its roots near the surface, when what it needs is a dry surface and every inducement to root as deep as possible—to find the equivalent of the mountain crevices.

A well-built rock garden goes as far as it can to combat these disadvantages. It is built with excellent drainage underneath: an immediate soak-away for any surplus water. Its component rocks tilt backwards into the slope to carry the rainwater deep into the ground, never letting it run down the surface. At least half, better three-quarters, of its rock is below ground, providing the long, cool root-run that alpines need. It stands out in the open, away from trees, where sun and wind can keep the surface dry, and its surface is mulched with rock chippings to help keep the crowns of the plants well-drained and protect them from rot, and to discourage slugs. A stony background also sets off the character of the little plants that are essentially individuals.

Yet for all these precautions rock gardens rarely serve to grow the plants from the highest alps that have the most demanding natures and in many cases the loveliest flowers. If they cannot have snow they must have some other covering. The answer, in practice, is an alpine house: an unheated greenhouse with double the usual amount of ventilation, or a frame, or a special raised bed with a cover, where the plants can be kept dry in winter, and if necessary given a good baking in high summer.

For convenience specimens of these temperamental highbrow plants are normally grown in pots or "pans" in alpine houses and frames, and so that they can be moved to the front line (or proudly carried to shows) when they are at their best, and hidden when they are not.

Above Photographing alpines in their habitat is the horticultural equivalent of big game hunting. Here the German photographer Wilhelm Schacht captures the yellow pulsatilla in the Alps. It is worth taking the correct equipment to a rendezvous that may never happen again. A tripod is vital, a macro-lens (100mm) is best for close-ups of small plants. It is also worth taking something to shelter the plant from the wind. Take several exposures and keep full notes for each photograph.

Above An alpine house is an unheated greenhouse with copious ventilation, where difficult alpines can be protected from winter damp, easy ones can flower to perfection, and the gardener can admire his early-spring treasures in comfort. The late Clarence Elliott, one of the pioneer alpine nurserymen, was photographed in his alpine house in January.

Above Rock gardens are not necessarily associated with alpine plants accustomed to snow and ice. At the famous gardens of Tresco Abbey in the Scilly Isles a rock bank is covered with such sub-tropical plants as aloes (with pink spikes), red mesembryanthemums, aeoniums (the grey rosettes) and white freesias, with Chilean pujas and an araucaria.

Common (or garden) alpines

Below left The two-and-a-half-acre rock garden at the Royal Botanic Garden, Edinburgh, has been called the greatest in the world, both for its construction (with every conceivable combination of aspect and drainage) and its plant collection. Note that conifers planted as dwarfs can look very different after fifty years.

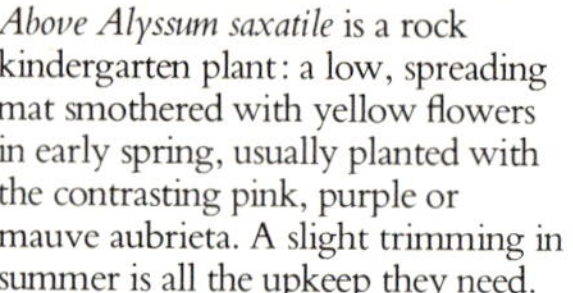

Above Alyssum saxatile is a rock kindergarten plant: a low, spreading mat smothered with yellow flowers in early spring, usually planted with the contrasting pink, purple or mauve aubrieta. A slight trimming in summer is all the upkeep they need.

Above The baby of the rose family: the two-inch creeping acaena from New Zealand. There are several species, all with pretty greyish leaves and contrasting burrs. They creep freely in gravel and between stones. This is *Acaena novae-zelandiae.*

Above Alpine pinks are common in the mountain ranges of Europe and make easy rock garden plants, often seeding themselves and sometimes hybridizing. They flower in early summer.

Below The prostrate willows slowly form intricate gnarled mats. This is *Salix reticulata*, named for the netted pattern of its leaf veins, lovely in early spring when golden catkins crowd its branches.

"Rock-plant" is a non-exclusive category for anything, herbaceous, shrubby or bulbous, that stays in scale and does not seem to betray the personality of a rock garden. This rather nebulous definition takes into account speed of growth and permanence as well as simple size. Annuals seldom look good in a rock garden. Soft, sprawling nasturtium is a good example of the wrong sort of plant, whereas (over a big rock) the equally sprawling *Clematis alpina* is exactly right. If we said that the plant should be hardy, and be fine in all its parts, we would be approaching a definition, although the rule would not apply to the subtropical rock garden at Tresco on page 133.

One reason for the harmony that reigns in a good rock garden is that with few exceptions its plants are natural species and their selected forms. Florists' inflated flowers are almost absent and hybrids are scarce, with such notable exceptions as the saxifrages. The flowers of mountain plants are already out of proportion by normal standards, but they have their own internal logic.

The aesthetic difficulty in having part of the garden on a smaller scale than the rest is that a natural-looking transition is very hard to achieve. A rock garden needs either to be big enough to be a whole view in itself, or so frankly miniature that it detaches itself as a convincing set-piece from the rest of the garden. Old stone troughs and sinks used as miniature rock gardens do this perfectly.

There is no such difficulty with wide-spreading mat plants. They will mantle a bank or a low wall in bright colour without raising questions of alpine propriety. Yellow alyssum, purple or mauve aubrieta and white iberis are the universal favourites of the spring, often associated with tulips.

Saponaria, creeping phlox, creeping gypsophila, helianthemums, thymes and campanulas carry on through the summer. A low wall suits their sprawling habit perfectly. It also answers their need for speedy drainage. These are all easy to grow, and have become one of the happy clichés of gardening.

Form and foliage are as important in rock gardens as they are in any landscape. Plants of deliberate and striking design, and above all evergreens, are needed to punctuate the sprawlers, relieve the sheets of colour, and keep the rocks company in winter. Between them cushion plants and rosette plants, together with dwarf shrubs and dwarf conifers, provide plenty of scope. Some of the genera that have most to offer are dianthus, the pinks, both as grey tufts in winter and pink or white massifs in early summer; the primulas, with many alpine

Left The easiest and one of the prettiest of the harebells, *Campanula cochlearifolia*, white or pale or dark blue, flowers in late summer.

Right The Swiss rock soapwort, *Saponaria ocymoides*, flowering in early summer, spreads its pink seedlings around.

Below The intense deep blue of a gentian makes *Lithospermum diffusum*, a sprawling little shrub of the borage family, one of the most universally popular rock plants for acid soil. 'Heavenly Blue' is the brightest form with a liking for a well-drained bank and full sunshine.

Above The flowers of the perennial candytuft, *Iberis sempervirens*, are startlingly white in early summer against its yew-like evergreen leaves. A most valuable plant on rocks or walls or anywhere that a low evergreen mound is needed.

Below Gypsophila, the "baby's breath" of the summer border, has its alpine version in *Gypsophila repens*, no more than eight inches high, easy and effective to hang down dry walls. Normally it is white; this form is *G. repens* 'Rosea'

Above Of the many alpine primulas the European *P. marginata* is one of the prettiest and most reliable. It likes lime and good drainage, but contrarily dreads drought. The mauve 'Linda Pope' is one of the best forms.

Below *Dryas octopetala* is one of the loveliest European mountain plants. It has oak leaves and strawberry flowers, is evergreen, summer-flowering and followed by silky globes of seed heads.

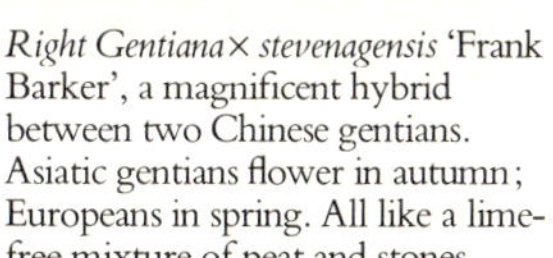

Right *Gentiana* × *stevenagensis* 'Frank Barker', a magnificent hybrid between two Chinese gentians. Asiatic gentians flower in autumn; Europeans in spring. All like a lime-free mixture of peat and stones.

or suitably miniature members, some easy and some very difficult; and the three great "rosette" tribes of saxifrage, sempervivum and sedum (for which see page 137).

To give more emphasis to cushions and rosettes, small as they are, it is helpful to have very low stretches of totally prostrate plants. In relatively damp and shady places the moss-like saginas and *Arenaria balearica* are ideal for this. In full gritty sun acaenas, the prostrate burr plants from New Zealand, creep briskly about. Some of the raoulias, also from New Zealand, are so low they are almost like lichen.

Dwarf conifers can be, and often are, overdone in rock gardens. Once the gardener starts there seems too much temptation to collect the whole set, and there are hundreds. Other dwarf shrubs include several that creep as low as infantry under fire: notably some willows of great character, the mountain dryas and such ground-hugging cotoneasters as *Cotoneaster dammeri* and *C. adpressa*, which seem indifferent to wet or dry, sun or shade. There is no end to the tiny shrubs that stand up, again including willows with sparkling catkins to go with early bulbs. Such small winter flowers as cyclamen, snowdrops, crocuses and irises rarely look better than cradled in a rocky cranny, where they set the scale of the self-sufficient scene.

Highbrow alpines

Above The low dome or cushion is a characteristic shape of high mountain plants. This specimen of *Diosphaera asperuloides* from Greece has been growing in a pot for twenty years to reach a height of three inches.

Left The lewisias, from the western United States, have some of the most sumptuous flowers of any alpines. The evergreen *L. tweedyi* needs rich but dry lime-free soil and shelter.

Above Great impetus was given to alpine growing in 1911 by the publication of *La Flore Alpine* by the Swiss botanist Correvon, with superb plates by Ph. Robert. This is his painting of *Pulsatilla vernalis*.

Below An aristocratic nasturtium: *Tropaeolum polyphyllum* from the Andes sends up its sprays from deep among rocks in summer, promptly disappearing after flowering.

The alpine and rock garden plant catalogue is immense. I am purposely only dipping into the extreme ends of it: everyman's alpines and those one might call highbrow, part of whose appeal, at least, is that they are very difficult to grow. Only a fanatic will waste time on a dull plant just because it seems intent on dying. The challenge is that if you can find the formula the results are sensational.

The miraculous beauty of some of these plants can only be seen either by climbing the right mountain at just the right moment, or by visiting a show where the crack alpine gardeners are competing. It is not just the plants that are worth seeing but the way they are presented, in hand-made pots that are almost heirlooms, the pot in proportion to the plant, the surface dressed with stones that set off, in colour and size and texture, the character of the "subject". Even the labels are considered part of the exquisite still life: the favourite being a narrow ribbon of dull lead with the name embossed, curling round the rim of the pot.

But they are hard to grow, and the reason may be obvious or it may be a mystery. There are alpines such as moss campion that grow perfectly well in gardens, but never flower as they do in the mountains. Nobody really knows why. One of the commonest hazards is rot in the damp of an un-alpine winter; a risk chiefly for plants whose leaf formation traps water in their crowns. Rosette plants such as lewisias and ramondas are examples. When they are grown outside they are commonly planted on edge in a crevice where rain cannot settle in them. Under glass, watered from below and with a deep mulch of stone chippings to keep their "collars" dry, they are safe.

Another problem is a decided taste in soil which the grower can only meet under the controlled conditions of a pot: and it may take him years to discover exactly what that taste is. It can range from peat and sand—with plenty of sand—for alpines from the woods, to almost pure ground-up tufa rock; a way of administering lime and drainage together in the maximum possible dose.

A further problem is the imperative that desert plants, bulbs in particular, have their period of total drought at the right time of year. Yet another is simply that some plants flower too early to be a practical proposition outdoors. Many bulbs are grown in pots simply to be better enjoyed, tranquil and unmuddied. Early-flowering saxifrages are another example of impetuosity. Some of the most desirable androsaces, which might be described as something between a saxifrage and a primula, come into the same bracket.

Pots are essential for moving alpines about and taking them to shows, but they add greatly to the labour of growing them. If there is a key to success with alpines it is drainage: indeed water supply both coming and going. In nature their roots occupy large volumes of stony ground with water flowing through it. It is the flow that matters: the water is always fresh and full of oxygen. The way to achieve the same effect in a pot is to mix plenty of sharp little stones with the soil—be it peaty or limy—and to make the pot fit the roots as tightly as possible. The roots should occupy all the soil all the time to prevent it stagnating. It follows that if the plant is to grow it must be repotted into a slightly bigger pot at least once a year. Keeping the pots plunged up to their rims in damp sand or peat is essential for even temperature and humidity. It all adds up to a considerable operation.

An easier way to provide the right conditions is to build up deep beds in your alpine house or frame and fill them with suitably stony soil—acid in one bed, alkaline in another, according to what you are going to grow. Alpines planted directly into this will root as they do in nature, often avoiding the trap of stagnant soil and constantly pushing on to fresh feeding-grounds.

Above The finest and the most difficult of the alpine phloxes, *Phlox nana*, from New Mexico, needs light lime-free soil and the protection of an alpine house, but flowers for weeks on end when satisfied.

Above right *Primula allionii*, from the Alpes Maritimes, is a low cushion made up of tight rosettes, susceptible to winter wet and needing gritty soil in an alpine house. It is among the first primulas to flower, producing large flowers in the early spring.

Right The rare Cretan *Anchusa caespitosa* has the reputation of being exceptionally difficult to grow. The picture shows the generous layer of stone chippings used as a mulch in the pot to keep the collar of the plant as dry as possible.

SAXIFRAGES, SEDUMS AND SEMPERVIVUMS

The difficulty with this trinity of rosette plants is not so much growing them as knowing which is which. **Saxifrages** (rockfoils) are alpine aristocrats, their rosettes forming beautiful spiral patterns. The 300 species are divided into fifteen sections, with hundreds of hybrids. The best-known sections include kabschias, which flower very early, need gritty soil and shade from hot sun. About eighty are in cultivation, mostly under glass. The silvery *S. grisebachii* with velvety red flowers is one of the best. "Mossy" saxifrages have whitish (sometimes red) flowers in April or May, like shade and moisture and make spreading green mats. "Silvery" or "Encrusted" refers to the crisp leaves of another section with white or cream flowers in arching sprays. *S. aizoon* is the best known; 'Tumbling Waters' (see page 56) the most beautiful. A very different section, diptera, includes *S. fortunei* (pages 116–7) and *S. stolonifera*, or mother of thousands. Another includes London pride.

Sedums (stonecrops) have even more species but few hybrids. Their leaves are fleshy, tending to turn red in drought or old age. Flowers are mostly white, pink or yellow. They love sun. One series, telephium, includes such border plants as *S. spectabile* (pages 116–7), another the tiny wall-pepper, *S. acre*. Rock garden kinds include 'Cappa Blanca' and the red-flowered 'Schorbusser Blut'.

Sempervivums (houseleeks) are a tribe of only twenty-five species but many hybrids from southern Europe, related to sedums, hardy, thick-leaved. At their coarse extreme, *S. tectorum*, which grows on roofs, they are like sedums. At their most delicate, *S. arachnoideum*, festooned with spiders' webs, they approach the saxifrages.

The peat garden

Above Peat is the accumulated vegetation of boggy ground which never entirely decays because of the acidity of the water. The structure of the dead plants (largely sphagnum moss) remains, providing a perfect root-run.

Below In these peat beds, built with railway ties against a north wall pink *Phlox subulata*, scarlet musk, celmisias, the grey-leaved daisies from New Zealand, orchids and lilies are among the plants that luxuriate.

Surely the human race can be divided into the moist and the airy: into those who love cool, damp air and the scenery and plants that go with it, and those who must have wide open spaces and uninterrupted sunlight; into those who dream of the highlands of Scotland and those whose hearts are in the isles of Greece? Scotland itself would not be such a cradle of gardeners and botanists if the swirl of mist and the patter of rain did not excite deep horticultural emotions.

The manner of gardening that epitomizes the joy of the rainy heath and the dripping copse was one of the latest to come into being. It was the invention of Scottish gardeners in the 1950s, rapidly brought to perfection at the Royal Botanic Garden, Edinburgh; its lore and learning set down in a book by Alfred Evans, head of that department of the garden, in 1974. The book is *The Peat Garden and its Plants.*

The word peat always brings a faraway look into a keen plantsman's eyes. No doubt racehorse trainers feel the same about oats and rally drivers about octanes. Peat looks, feels and is the stuff that plant roots like best to burrow in. Not that it has great food value: it has very little. Its virtue lies in its texture and its ability to absorb and retain vast volumes of moisture.

The peat garden was conceived as a way of cultivating and cossetting small plants that need damp acid soil and the moist atmosphere immediately above it. Such plants are found almost everywhere in the world's rainy highlands; in the Himalayas, Japan, the Rockies, Scotland, the Alps. Many of them are alpines in the strict sense, but not rock plants: their only interest in a rock would be to hide in its shade. The peat garden is therefore complementary to the rock garden. The same sort of devoted plantsmen revel in both. But from the practical point of view it has marked advantages. It is far quicker, cheaper and easier to build. And the range of plants that can be satisfied by slightly modifying its conditions (adding, for example, more stones for drainage, or lime) is enormously wide. It can be adapted to give almost any plant short of a confirmed rock-dweller the time of its life.

A peat garden is a bed of acid soil richly and deeply laced with peat, in a proportion of about half and half, sloping preferably to the north, well-supplied with rain or other soft water but also adequately drained, with rubble below if necessary. The softness of the water is crucial; water from a chalk spring would be useless.

To vary the slope and provide degrees of shade and drainage outcrops are usually arranged, often as low walls, ideally built of solid blocks of peat. In Europe such blocks are cut from peat beds, brick size, both for fuel and for gardening. Logs of wood are sometimes used, but they are a poor substitute: the advantage of peat blocks is that plants will root and seed in them, covering them with a mantle of vegetation and at the same time binding the structure together.

A north-facing slope, or the north side of a wall, can thus be

Left Some of the species of *Meconopsis*, including the blue poppy, are worth a place for the beauty of their leaves alone. Best is *M. regia*, which forms broad leaves over two or three years, then flowers with creamy poppies, sets seed and dies.

converted from a problem corner to one where a wide range of plants is in seventh heaven, the only proviso being that weeds with running roots like it too.

For this original sort of peat garden, the rules are simple. Do not attempt one in areas of very alkaline soil or water supply, or very low rainfall. It will be a great deal of trouble and probably only a moderate success. Take infinite pains to exterminate perennial weeds before you start. Build with damp materials. Once dry all peat is extremely hard to re-wet. For the same reason bury the greater part of each block to prevent it from ever drying out. Build walls with a backward tilt into the slope, nailing the blocks together with thick wire if necessary, and firm down the peat-soil mixture at every stage as you go, especially between the blocks. Welcome the shade of trees but do not build directly under big ones: their drip and their fallen leaves can both be a problem. If the bed is too big to reach across, install small stepping stones; your full weight when working would compact the soil too much.

It was only a short step from the idea of the quasi-naturalistic peat garden, laid out on the ground, to the idea of a frankly artificial peat shelf: a raised bed made of two parallel walls with the space between filled with the same sort of peat-soil (or indeed any other) mixture. To the plant collector, more interested in the intensive care and enjoyment of large numbers of (usually tiny) individuals than in scenic effect, this is perhaps the very best way of enjoying the greatest number of plants in the smallest space.

The plant families that provide most candidates for this special treatment are the ericas, the primulas and the lily family. Among ericas the dwarf rhododendrons are the obvious first choice; there are hundreds of them. Then there are such creepers as arctostaphyllos, the "bear grape", gaultherias (which include the pretty "partridge berry" and the over-vigorous *Gaultheria shallon*), and vacciniums (including cranberry, bilberry and blueberry). There are some lovely little shrubs; cassiopes with reptilian scales; elegantly tiered enkianthus, shedding its leaves in scarlet and gold; kalmiopsis, the baby brother of the calico bush; leucothoe, faintly resembling a bamboo; pernettyas, which keep their purple or white berries all winter . . . it is a long list. The heath and heather part of the erica family would love it here, too, but would soon take over at the expense of more precious things.

The primula list is almost as long. This is the ideal place for such rare and otherwise difficult species as *Primula vialii*, with a sharp spike of violet flowers, or *P. whitei* with a gentle nest of icy-blue ones.

Most lilies love peat beds. So do their relations the trilliums, fritillarias, erythroniums, and above all, from the plantsman's point of view, the rare high-Himalayan nomocharis. Gentians luxuriate in peat. So does the Himalayan blue poppy and its relations. The list, in fact, is far too long to investigate here.

Left Rhododendron 'Carmen' is among the many dwarf ericaceous plants ideally suited to peat beds.

Right All the meconopsis, including the Himalayan blue poppy and, here, its close relation *Meconopsis grandis*, love damp, peaty conditions and look particularly beautiful with raindrops weighing down their delicate flowers.

Above Part of the peat beds at the Royal Botanic Garden, Edinburgh: the original example of this style of gardening for enthusiasts, now richly mature and full of beauty from spring to autumn.

Below A young peat garden, showing how peat walls can be made to blend in with rock-work to provide a wide range of growing conditions, from a boggy ooze to a well-drained plateau.

Plants for the waterside

Left The musks are species of *Mimulus*, bright summer-flowering water-lovers with one fast-moving weed (the yellow *M. guttatus*); but otherwise well-behaved. The two-foot *M. cardinalis* is the best red species. Several hybrids, including 'Whitecroft Scarlet', are smaller and flower for many weeks.

I might almost have used the same introductory distinction to this chapter as to the last on peat. There are those to whom big-leaved plants growing strongly in wet ground are rank weeds in a ditch; others who feel that this is where the plant world reaches its most luxuriant and fulfilled. It is certainly where temperate gardens come nearest to the tropical jungle.

Plants that live in water or at the water's brink, in permanently wet ground, must be physiologically adapted to airless soil. Where the soil is always saturated there is no drainage; hence no air being drawn down into the pores of the soil; hence very little and seldom enough oxygen for the roots. The roots need a peculiar structure or chemistry to acquire oxygen. Swamp cypresses put up woody knees above the water as they grow old, apparently simply in order to breathe. Other plants have long air ducts from the surface into the mud-delving roots. True bog-plants, in other words, form a distinct class separate from the much more numerous ones that need the air in a "moist, well-drained soil".

The easy and obvious way of using wet-ground plants is in conjunction with a pool or stream. Where there is abundant water, above all flowing water, the gardener can take his pick of all such plants; making a true bog here, a damp bed of open, porous soil there. Many bog plants will happily grow in shallow water and most artificial ponds are built with shelves to accommodate them in the exact depth of water they seem to prefer. On the other hand the surface of the water itself is the prime aesthetic attraction of a pond. It is a pity to mask it with too many plants—certainly plants that do not need to be in water. To keep a patch of ground really wet it is a simple matter to excavate a shallow basin, line its bottom and sides, (not quite to the top) with plastic sheeting, refill it with fertile soil and then let the hose or the overflow from a pond run in.

Remember, though, that you cannot hoe in mud, and forking is extremely unpleasant and difficult. Under these circumstances some weeds, once installed, are there for good. The ground elder in my bog garden is a particularly fine example.

It is worth going to great pains to begin without weeds; more to the point be well advised on what is and is not a weed in wet ground. A number of plants sold as suitable for water-gardens are uncontrollable: the yellow musk, *Mimulus guttatus*, for example; certain rushes and reeds. . . .

The best way to achieve a moist, well-drained bed depends on the water-table: if it is very high it may be necessary to raise the level of the soil; if the drainage is good it may be necessary to bury a plastic sheet, but this time to cut drainage holes in it and fill it with grittier soil; even with some half-bricks in the bottom. Where water is in short supply the out-and-out bog garden is easy enough, but the moist bed, needing a constant flow, may not be possible.

The great advantage water-plants have over all others is that moisture stress is unknown to them; the sun cannot ask them for more water than they can supply. They are always free to transpire to their hearts' content. Hence their tendency to make lush growth and often to have big, sometimes prodigious, leaves. Waterside plants in fact have the tendency to produce nothing but leaves without plenty of sunlight.

By far the biggest leaf of any plant we can grow in Britain belongs to the Brazilian *Gunnera manicata*, like a rhubarb with a ten-foot wingspan, which luxuriates in boggy ground. Among other plants whose impressive foliage is the main reason for growing them are two members of the rhubarb family (the gunnera only looks like rhubarb), *Rheum alexandrae* (page 109) and *Rheum palmatum* 'Rubrum', whose unfurling in episcopal tones in spring is one of the events of my boggy calendar.

The rodgersias are a clan of several species with big leaves of strong character; the best known of them suggesting a horse chestnut. *Peltiphyllum peltatum* (*right*) has a more delicate but still almost tropical effect. Hostas grow to great size and substance in rich, damp ground. Even better is the *Lysichitum*, or skunk cabbage, which follows its foot-high buttercup-yellow or white spathes of early spring with simple great paddle-leaves of enormous size.

Long thin leaves are even more numerous among water-plants than long wide ones. There are all the rushes and reeds, for a start. The great reed mace (commonly known as bull-rush) is scarcely a plant for gardens, but its three-foot cousin *Typha stenophylla* is almost essential to a boggy scene. Sedges, galingale and several tall grasses (see pages 144–5) have emphatic character to contribute—bamboo even more so; making the best of all backgrounds and windbreaks for a bog-garden. As leaves for leaves' sake, two of the finest ferns, the royal and the shuttlecock-shaped ostrich fern (*Matteuccia*), need boggy ground to be seen at their best.

Perhaps the most important single genus of wet-ground flowers is the primulas (see page 107), from *Primula denticulata* in early spring to *P. florindae* in summer, with a long succession of graceful candelabras in endlessly changing colours between. Next must come the water-irises—but only in June and July. *Iris kaempferi* is the most impressive, with its wide, flat flowers. *I. laevigata*, on the other hand, is hardier and has a lovely form with vividly white-variegated leaves, which look superb rising from shallow water, and greatly lengthen its ornamental season.

For the spring the yellow kingcups are essential. In early summer trollius, the globe-flowers, take up a similar theme. Later in the summer come the musks, brilliant in yellow, scarlet and orange; and the astilbes in colours from mahogany to candy-floss. Day-lilies love the brink of a pond.

Once we are out of the mire and into the drainage area, we can simply start adding border flowers. There is no hard and fast dividing line, any more than there is between plants that like bog and those that will stand knee-deep in water.

Above A bog garden scene relying mainly on leaves of character for its atmosphere. They include day-lilies (left foreground), ostrich fern (*Matteuccia*) (second rank, left) and the giant *Gunnera manicata*—its flower is the brown prickly excrescence. Candelabra primulas and lilies ring the far side of the pond, which is partly covered by the dreadful duckweed, *Lemna minor*. In the centre and right foreground are hostas, *Iris laevigatus*, and leaves of *Echinops ruthenicus*, the globe thistle (in a dry spot) and the giant hogweed, *Heracleum mantegazzianum*.

Left A perfect waterside combination where stepping stones cross a brook. *Salix lanata*, the woolly willow, with the yellow-variegated leaves of *Iris pseudacorus* 'Variegata'.

Above Looking down to a stream in a woodland garden with plants that enjoy the moisture but reasonable drainage of the bank. From the left: foxgloves, the blue parasols of *Campanula persicifolia*, *Kirengeshoma palmata*, which produces showers of soft yellow bells in autumn. In the right foreground is masterwort, *Astrantia major*, and below in the ditch ferns and bamboos.

Left Double kingcups and the earliest bog primulas, *Primula denticulata*, flower together in a pondside bed.

Above *Peltiphyllum peltatum*, or umbrella plant, is an eccentric and valuable member of the saxifrage family. It puts up tall stems topped with pink flowers from bare ground, then follows them with foot-wide leaves on individual stalks as much as three feet long in marshy ground.

Above *Lysichitum americanum*, American skunk cabbage, emerges from the mud in early spring. Its bright yellow spathes are followed by leaves that eventually grow huge. *L. camtschatcense* is more refined.

Above *Iris kaempferi* has been developed in many forms, emphasizing its wide, flat flowers. Many colours are available. It will grow in shallow water, but prefers a moist soil.

Plants for the water

Right Of the smaller water-lilies suitable for domestic pools up to two feet deep, *Nymphaea laydeckeri* 'Fulgens' is one of the most popular. Smaller still, needing only six inches of water, is *Nymphaea pygmaea* with tiny white and gold flowers, or its cultivar 'Helvola' with yellow flowers.

There is a mystery and calm about water-lilies which reaches everybody. That such marvellously modelled flowers should emerge from the bosom of the lake is always a source of wonder. Far out among the water-weeds the crowding of rich green plates, each with a triangular notch, tells you where to look, then one morning in midsummer a perfect chalice of white, or yellow, or throbbing red suddenly lies open on the surface. More and more follow, in incredible numbers. The leaves rise up, jostling and shoving as though the hidden plants were erupting. It is rather as though the most splendid and prolific of peonies was anchored to the bottom and could only produce its leaves and flowers in one plane.

The marvel of it all is that water-lilies are exceedingly easy to grow. If they look at their most romantic far out across the mere, they are a most intimate joy nestling among their perfect gleaming leaves in a wooden tub by the garden door. There is no need to have a lake or even pond to grow them; there are water-lilies for every depth of water.

India and the Middle East are the richest source of species, though there are water-lilies native to almost every country. They include the sacred lotus of Egypt (*Nymphaea lotus*) and perhaps the most beautiful of all water-plants, the lotus of the Far East, *Nelumbo nucifera*, in whose flower Buddha sits. This lotus raises its pale sea-green leaves and fragrant white flowers, pink tinged, high above the water. Alas it cannot be counted among the hardy kinds.

Most of the coloured water-lilies we grow today are hybrids arising from the work of the great French breeder of the last century M. Marliac, who crossed some of the more richly coloured but less hardy species with the hardy European *Nymphaea alba* and others. Of common kinds it usually can be said the warmer the water the better they will thrive.

To plant water-lilies in a natural pond is a simple matter. In late spring take a piece of an established plant, complete with roots and at least one shoot, and tie it up in a sack with a load of good soil—old manure and chopped turf for preference—the shoot emerging. Weigh the sack down with stones and drop it into water of the appropriate depth. By the time the sack has rotted the roots will have taken hold of the bed. In a concrete or plastic pond or a tub the plant will have to grow in a plastic or wire container, full of compost and lined with turves, and weighed down with stones.

Of the scores of full-size cultivars available the classics are the red 'James Brydon' and 'Escarboucle', the yellow 'Sunrise' and the magnificent gold-centred white 'Gladstoniana'. These are for water from two to even six feet deep and would completely fill a small pool. M. Marliac's 'Layerdeckeri' strain are more suitable for small pools, but are all in shades of pink, purple and crimson. Another Marliac hybrid, 'Chromatella', provides a first-class yellow of moderate size.

Nothing rivals the display of the water-lilies, but there are plenty of other fascinating or quietly charming plants for open water—all of them good for the healthy balance of the pond. The page opposite displays a selection, some of which need to root on the bottom, while others float free and take all their sustenance from the water. Several (not shown) live most of their lives completely submerged, but are none the less valuable for the oxygen they produce. Water moss (*Fontinalis antipyretica*), water starwort (*Callitriche platycarpa, verna* and other species) and hornwort (*Caratophyllum demersum*) are three with very pretty foliage which are easy to keep in control—the first consideration when choosing water plants.

Above Full-scale water-lilies in a pool at Bodnant, North Wales, against the background of a famous blue Atlantic cedar. The way the lilies form rafts with open water between is ideal. They should never cover the whole surface.

Below The water hyacinth, *Eichornia crassipes*, is a Mexican cattle-fodder plant which will either live afloat or take root. It needs warm shallow water and full sun to flower in cultivation and can be killed by frost.

Above The plant we commonly call bullrush is properly reed mace, *Typha latifolia*. It is tempting to plant it for its brown velvet flowers (here dispersing their seed) but it is a voracious colonizer, stopping only at deep water.

Left Water soldier (*Stratiotes aloides*) is a curious spiky rosette with a habit of resting on the bottom, then floating to the surface to flower.

Right Swans are particularly fond of the roots of the green pondweed, *Potamogeton natans*, endlessly confused with water hawthorn.

Right The water violet or featherfoil, *Hottonia palustris*, should really be called water primrose, since it belongs to that family and flowers like a miniature candelabra primula in early summer. It floats free; just throw rooted pieces in the pond.

Above Water hawthorn or Cape pondweed, *Aponogeton distachyos*, is in flower almost all year, and sweetly scented, too. It roots in the bottom of water up to two feet deep.

Above The Indian lotus needs warm water and protection from frost, but can be grown in a tub and overwintered indoors, or put out in a pool in early summer.

Above Golden club, *Orontium aquaticum*, is one of the most striking hardy plants for water up to eighteen inches deep, with handsome wax-covered leaves. It flowers in spring.

Above The water buttercup (or celandine), *Ranunculus aquaticus*, covers the surface of ponds and streams in spring. Like many easy water plants it is apt to become a weed.

Above Common marestail is another vigorous water plant which will become overwhelming without discipline. Confined to a box of soil it makes an ideal mid-pond feature.

Left The florists' arum lily is a South African plant that seems to reverse the usual rules, being hardier in six to twelve inches of water than in a drier place.

Grasses and bamboos

Right Grasses that deserve a prominent position, with leaf colour that ranges from nearly blue to golden-yellow and a variety of different flower spikes. The grasses shown are, from left to right, *Stipa gigantea*, *Miscanthus sinensis*, *Molinia caerulea*, *Phalaris arundinaceae* and *Helictotrichon sempervirens*.

Ornamental grasses are an unappreciated by-way of gardening, considering the impact they can make as a contrast to more conventional garden plants. Hardly anyone can name the lovely things that wave their feathery flowers in a summer meadow. Nobody would consider moving them wholesale into the garden—to most people the waving meadow effect is the very antithesis of gardening. It is easy to forget that an isolated clump of what is by nature a plant to be seen *en masse* can be immensely striking.

The simplicity of the drawing, the reiterated line of the narrow leaves rising parallel, then bending, criss-crossing and swaying, can make impact enough in a scene of broad leaves, fingery leaves and general jumble. But most garden grasses have been selected for eye-catching colours as well, many for very graceful and beautiful plumy flowers, and some for magnificence of stature.

There are grasses that grow ten feet in a season, then die off leaving a great straw-coloured fountain to the mercy of the winter weather. And of course there are dwarfs that stop at a couple of inches. There are grasses that will grow in liquid mud, though most prefer sunny steppe-like soil. There are also grasses such as couch that are a major menace, sending brittle running roots with uncanny speed to invade their neighbours—roots that snap at the first sign of an avenging gardener, every little white scrap ready to explode into an incredible yardage.

The first principle of gardening with grasses is to avoid any that spread by runners underground. They include, alas, the very decorative white-striped gardeners' garters (one of the few that has a well-known common name).

The other aggressive way grasses can break their allotted bounds is by seeding. Several of the prettiest are annuals—the delicate pearl grass, *Briza maxima*, with hanging heads like a cross between an oat and a Chinese lantern is one; Bowles's golden grass, slight, stooping and wonderfully yellow, is another. Bowles's seedlings, being bright yellow, are easy to identify, but most grass seedlings, annual or perennial, are more or less interchangeable to the lay eye—so it is better to treat them all as enemies unless you know them to be friends.

Grasses look best as individuals or small clumps, used as a punctuation mark in a stretch of other plants. The place for a full stop is at the end of a sentence—say the corner of a bed or where a path turns out of sight. But grasses are equally good as the less emphatic commas and semi-colons of the garden; to form a gentle interruption in a stretch of low planting, or to provide neutral colouring and soft texture in contrast to plants of strong colour or hard etching.

The bigger grasses can stand on their own as singular features rising from a lawn, or even from the gravel of a drive. Such blatantly artificial isolation, where you can see the whole plant from top to toe, shows off their extreme elegance perfectly. Pampas grass grown like this is a cliché, but the ten-foot *Miscanthus sacchariflorus*, given plenty of moisture, would be a splendid landmark.

The association of tall grasses and water is always successful. The waterside, of course, has its own range of grass-like plants—the rushes, reeds and sedges. Pictorially they all work well by contrasting their vertical or drooping lines with the smooth horizontal of the pond. The sedges (including the graceful *Carex pendula* and the brilliant golden *Carex morrowii* 'Variegata') and the *Cyperus* (umbrella sedges or galingale, like the Egyptian papyrus) are the only ones normally planted.

Bamboos are grasses that aspire to be trees by forming permanent woody stems. Some of them actually achieve their ambition, reaching sixty or seventy feet, but these alas are of the tropics. The tallest bamboos of moderate hardiness (zone 8) reach no more than twenty-five feet, and that with such thin stems that they need the shelter of thick woodland. The common hardy (to zone 7) bamboos do well to reach twelve feet, but form such dense evergreen clumps and screens that nothing can match them. They provide the atmosphere of the jungle, complete with sound-effects.

Many of them have the failing of running roots. Rather than exclude them for that reason, it is worth forming concrete barriers that they cannot pass; eighteen inches is as deep as they need to go. Or simply mow around them. A mower will destroy new shoots coming up out of bounds.

Unfortunately bamboos are a botanist's paradise. The faintest difference of stem colouring provides an excuse for a new name. Perhaps as a result few nurseries grow them. Metake (*Arundinaria japonica*), which is unfortunately a spreader, is the only truly common one, although the similar *A. nitida* can be trusted to stay in a clump. The shorter broad-leafed *Sasa palmata* makes an admirable contrast—but this one is rampant.

Above The demonstration bed of ornamental grasses at Wisley shows the huge variety available, but underlines the point that grasses do not mass well. They are best used as individuals or in clumps well separated by plants of contrasting character.

Left The plumy tufts of the annual squirreltail barley, *Hordeum jubatum*, relieve the dazzle of massed flowers in a midsummer border. Grasses can be either annual or perennial. Perennial grasses look neater and more attractive if given a yearly grooming with a wire rake.

Above Johnny Appleseed in a setting of pampas grass. A picture which says much about the value of the human figure for catching your attention. Well-established pampas grass plants can be burnt off in spring to tidy away the old dead leaves and flowers.

THE USE OF BAMBOO

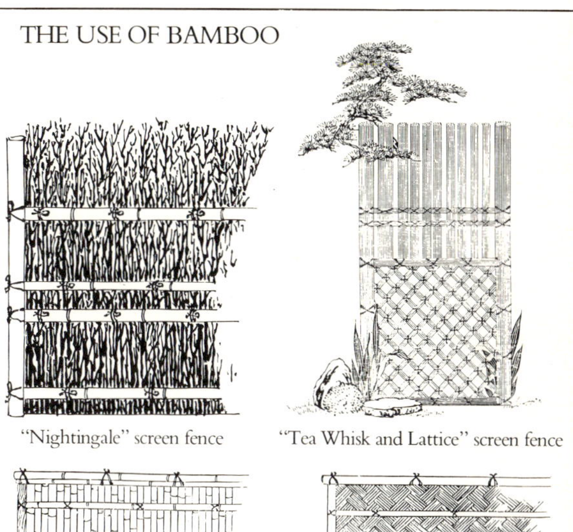

"Nightingale" screen fence

"Tea Whisk and Lattice" screen fence

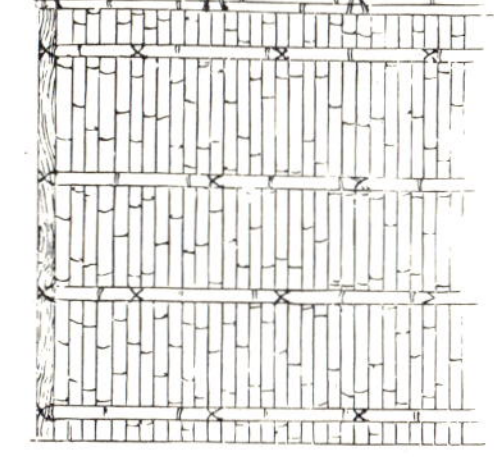

"Kininji" bamboo fence

Plaited bamboo fence

Having such an adaptable material as bamboo easily to hand, in every size, the Japanese use it for every building purpose—as scaffolding, guttering, for pillars, lintels and frames, as cladding and as thatch. Tying it into various forms of fences and gates is a minor art form.

Left A grove of timber bamboos (*Phyllostachys bambusoides*) in the Moss Garden, Kyoto. The 40-foot canes grow to their full height within a few months. The grove is thinned by removing new shoots for food and mature stems for building. Timber bamboo is remarkably winter-hardy, but only grows to its full height in a damp climate with hot summers. Such a universal provider is not surprisingly regarded as sacred.

Above The common hardy bamboo (*Arundinaria japonica*) makes a dense evergreen screen of surprising grace and elegance, nowhere more effectively than beside a pond. Its roots run about with abandon unless checked, but several very similar bamboos stay demurely in clumps. There are even pygmy bamboos for miniature poolside planting. Bamboo roots enjoy moisture, but not actually standing in water.

Ferns and mosses

Below The value of ferns in woodland is at its height in spring with their fresh new shoots, and in autumn, when many of them turn shades of rust and gold. This grove of ferns, contrasting perfectly with the shiny small-scale leaves of camellias, is in the Valley Gardens in Windsor Great Park.

Most gardens get by very happily without an intentional fern, or any moss to speak of. If they are there at all, they come uninvited—and indeed they are not things you can buy in every garden centre.

Yet there are few plants that carry such a cargo of atmosphere. Ferns are the embodiment of green thoughts in a green shade, and if a leafy shadow could take root, moss would surely be the result. There are gardens where any such thing would be irrelevant and ridiculous; where all is sunlight and airy exposure. But there are others, and probably parts of most, where a poor, sour shade could be given a luxurious leafy cloak by planting ferns and encouraging moss.

Moreover, despite their appearance of being the inhabitants of dripping caves, there are ferns, and even mosses, that are tolerant of perpetually dry ground. Since the combination of drought and shade is the ultimate in gardening problems it is odd that we are not greeted by ferns in every dim backyard.

Ferns and mosses are cousins of a sort. They both belong to the flowerless part of the plant kingdom that has an in-between stage in its reproductive process. Ferns produce spores by the million, usually on the undersides of their leaves, where they form rusty patches. The spores drop off, take root, and perform the sexual functions for the fern, as it were by proxy, but never grow into ferns themselves. Instead they produce the "seed" from which the next generation of ferns grows. Mosses have the same habit of alternating sexual and vegetative generations, only with them it is the sexual generation which is the taller, showier (if that's the word) plant.

Most ferns are quite easily propagated by sowing the spores very thinly on moist peat under a pane of glass. The plants that will appear look very like the sexual generation of mosses—almost like small green toadstools. In turn they will produce the tiny fern plants. They need careful weaning in damp conditions before they are hardened off ready for planting out. On the other hand the majority of ferns can quite easily be divided like any herbaceous plant, so long as the pieces are planted in damp soil with peat, leaf-mould or compost.

The easiest way to establish moss is to procure lumps, or even scraps, of whatever kind grows in your neighbourhood. The north-facing slopes of roofs are often a fruitful place to look if you want moss for a dry site. Pin the moss down with hair-grips on bare moist ground where you want it to grow. A light scattering of peat or sawdust among the pieces is a good idea. Happily moss is encouraged rather than killed by contact weedkillers, which will keep down any competition. An occasional watering with a normal dilution of a paraquat-type weedkiller will prevent it being overtaken by more vigorous plants. The fact that the north side of roofs and tree trunks is the place to find it shows that many mosses dislike direct sunlight. Yet nothing can be drier than a roof in summer.

The Japanese are the artists in this genre. For them moss holds the place that grass does in English gardens, but then most of Japan has a steamy summer, which is just what moss likes best. As for ferns, the Japanese manage to pack so much emphasis into one plant, placed just so at the foot of a stone lantern or by a stepping stone in a brook, that you feel the last word has been said on the subject.

Ferns were a passion of Victorian gardeners. North-facing greenhouses were tricked up with a few flints and a trickle of water and designated ferneries. Every idiosyncratic fern (many are given to sporting odd forms) was treasured and given a long Latin name. Hundreds, if not thousands, have been sold in the past. Sadly, comparatively few survive in cultivation.

Of those that have survived the male fern, *Dryopteris filix-mas*, is the toughest and suitable for the driest, most hopeless spots. It has a very pretty golden-green brother, *D. pseudo-mas* (*borreri*), which is scarcely less tough, and looks rather more special. Even tougher, of course, but not to be admitted to your garden, is the ineradicable bracken of sandy heaths.

At the opposite extreme are such delicacies as the maidenhair, its fronds forming perfect arcs on fine black stems (this must have shade); and such intricacies as the cut-and-cut-again-leaved version of the soft shield fern, *Polystichum setiferum* 'Plumoso-divisilobum'. In complete contrast to this laciest of ferns is the one with a totally uncut strap of a leaf—the common hart's tongue.

There are ferns that like bogs, too: the royal fern and the shuttlecock fern only grow to their full dignity in wet ground. But alas only those who garden in subtropical conditions and high rainfall can enjoy the magnificence of the tree-ferns.

Below The entrance gate to a Japanese tea garden (with a lettered fringe to oblige you to bow as you enter) has been colonised by ferns and mosses that thrive in the humid summer of Kyoto. But there are mosses and ferns adapted to dry situations which could create the same effect.

Right A hundred years ago ferns were cultivated in hundreds of varieties. Now few are commercially available. Among those that are, two of the best are (left to right) *Pteris* and *Onoclea*.

Top The palm-like tree ferns of Australasia are the most spectacular of their race, but only hardy in such mild damp climates as the South West of Ireland, where they have become naturalized.

Above There are ferns for all soils from dry to boggy. The royal fern, *Osmunda regalis*, grows well here on the margins of a stream and its bright green foliage invades the water itself.

Left Lichens can be regarded as a sort of mini-moss, although their structure and lifestyle are quite different. They consist of a fungus and an alga growing together in an intimate relationship of mutual dependence. Here they grow in a dry creek in New Zealand with two species of *Raoulia*, a cushion-forming alpine which could also almost pass for a moss.

Heaths and heather

Below Heathers and conifers together can furnish the garden in winter with harmonious colour and form. The mature heather garden of the Royal Horticultural Society at Wisley is one of the best examples of the genre, with tree-heathers and conifers providing solid masses to vary and contain the scene.

There are no half-measures with heathers. Even more than the heavies of their family, the rhododendrons, they impose their personality on any garden where they get a foothold. In theory a little patch of heather sounds a reasonable way to vary the planting. In practice it is all or nothing: you must either embrace the ambience of the heaths and adjust your garden to it, or shun it altogether. Heathers and roses, heathers and delphiniums, heathers and annuals all look equally grotesque together. It is only in the rock-and-peat mode that heathers can sometimes be used as a sub-dominant theme. But you are still playing with fire.

I am speaking of aesthetic, not physical aggression. Heathers are the basic groundcover of rainy, peaty mountains, where their scale matters no more than the length of the grass in a panorama of pasture-land. But bring heathers into the garden and their demure precision of small leaf, small flower, low mound—without the endearing disproportion of alpines, top-heavy with flowers—seems like a rebuke to plants of stature, be they coarse or elegant. One little heather looks absurd, so you plant a group. The group gang together into a mass of even colour and texture, spreading inexorably (but too slowly to be exciting). You are recommended to have a patchwork of different colours and to relieve their monotonous flatness with little conifers. Eventually, after eight or nine years, you have a mature heather garden.

Yet look at the picture above. If you are beginning to suspect that heathers are not my favourite plants, let me freely admit that it is hard to imagine a more inviting mid-winter garden scene. The heathers, in their patterns like crops, play the role of a fertile valley; the conifers are forests and ranges of hills. There could hardly be a more coherent and convincing garden landscape. This is at Wisley, is twenty years old, and is one of the best-planned parts of that great garden.

The test comes when you look at the centre picture above: again a consistent, well-planned and mature piece of garden. But this is summer. Apart from the general warmth of tone and the extra shapes and colours of deciduous trees it is the same as winter. I cannot understand a gardener who would celebrate summer with such a denial of all its qualities.

For what is always advertised as the strong point of the heathers is that they have representatives in flower in almost every month of the twelve. They also have forms with leaves in strikingly different colours which do not need to be in flower to show up distinctly as colour in the patchwork. Some of them also keep their old flowers, withered and tobacco-brown, in such numbers that this colour becomes another element in the heathscape. Although the winter-, summer- and autumn-flowering kinds vary enough close-to to provide considerable interest, the net effect *en masse* is simply of the same plants performing a light-show of colours at a snail's pace.

The vast majority of heathers are natives of South Africa and (I nearly said luckily) tender in northern Europe. All the dwarf or low-growing hardy kinds common in gardens come from Europe's own moorlands. They belong to three genera: *Calluna*, which has only one species, ling or true heather, the springy substance of the Scottish highlands; *Erica*, with a dozen European species; and *Daboecia* with two, one from the Azores and one of the Atlantic coast from Ireland to Portugal.

Yet out of this mere score of species have sprung hundreds of cultivars; enough to provide almost any flower-colour in the range from red to white, against any leaf-colour in the range of green, gold, grey and bronze, at almost any time of year.

A rapid catechism of the heathers from winter to winter begins with the hybrid *Erica* × *darleyensis*, up to two feet or so in height, generally pink in flower, capable of flowering from November to May and tolerant of limy soil. It has a gold-leaved variant and a well-known white form from Germany: 'Silberschmelze'. Hard on its heels comes the shorter, equally hardy and lime-tolerant *Erica carnea* (alias *E. herbacea*) from the Alps and Appenines. Rosy red is its "normal" colour, but as usual there are forms with gold leaves (e.g. 'Foxhollow'), pink forms, "ruby" forms and the popular 'Springwood

Above The bud of the low-growing Irish bell heather, *Daboecia cantabrica*, opens in summer into a hanging bell.

Above Common heather, the "ling" of the Highlands, is summer-to-autumn flowering with densely-packed flower spikes.

Below A heather garden in the height of summer, with its fresh new growth and with the lings about to flower. But it is the fine collection of trees at the top of the picture that give this garden its interest. Cover them up and despite the heathers it could scarcely be described as a summery scene.

Right Heathers provide colour by leaf forms and even in the warm tones of their spent brown flower heads. *Left to right* are the gold-leaved Cornish heath, *Erica vagans* 'Valerie Proudley' in summer, and two lings: *Calluna vulgaris* 'Elsie Purnell' and grey-leaved 'Arthur Davis' in autumn.

Above The autumn lings in Adrian Bloom's famous Bressingham heather gardens. The golden-yellow plants are *Calluna vulgaris* 'Sunset', which has pink flowers. In the foreground is *Calluna vulgaris* 'H.E. Beale', which bears outstandingly long spikes of bright pink flowers. This is a popular plant for cutting for indoor decoration.

Above In the ericas it is the corolla, the inner part of the flower, not the calyx, the outer, which is often rich-coloured and conspicuous.

This is the lime-tolerant *Erica carnea* from the mountains of southern Europe. It flowers in winter, making it one of the most useful of the family.

White'. March signals the end of its flowering season. About this time come two taller but less hardy heaths from the Mediterranean, *E. erigena* and the "tree" heath, *E. arborea*, growing respectively to six and twelve feet. Both smell deliciously of honey; *arborea* with white flowers, *erigena* generally pink or red, but also with a white variant. Zone 8 is about their limit of hardiness: the tree heath is sometimes killed by frost at Kew. Where they can be grown, though, they greatly relieve the insipid mass of the lower heathers.

The first heather of summer is *Daboecia cantabrica*, the Irish bell heather; the rock and peat of Connemara is its home. This is a straggly two-footer, pink or white in flower from June to autumn. The white form and its hybrid 'William Buchanan' are said to be the best. Also in June the common bell heather of many open, peaty moors, *E. cinerea*, comes into flower. At least a hundred clones exist in cultivation, putting up with far warmer and richer soil than they were designed for. Two taller, more straggly heaths, *E. ciliaris* from Dorset and *E. tetralix*, the cross-leaved heath, follow it. These are less tolerant, demanding damp, acid soil. A much better and more reliable plant is the upstanding (to eight feet) lime-tolerant *E. terminalis* from Italy, which is rarely seen in gardens.

Then, well past midsummer, comes the Highland ling, in almost every colour, and sizes from three inches to three feet. At the same time, lasting well into autumn, the Cornish heath, *E. vagans*, flowers in a style of its own, with jostling spires of pink or white reaching up eventually to three feet.

Heather gardens of the sort shown above are not as effortless as they look, for two reasons. First, the ground between the plants must be endlessly weeded until they join up. At the recommended planting distance (eighteen inches for most kinds) this is usually a matter of three or four years. Second, the soil is usually too fat for them: they tend to grow too fast and become gaunt and bare. Neat regularity is only achieved by pruning or shearing: of the spring-flowering kinds after they have flowered; of the autumn-flowering kinds in spring.

Below Of several "tree" or tall shrub species of *Erica* the most beautiful and graceful (but unfortunately tender) is *E. canaliculata* from South Africa. It has reached a height of sixteen feet in Cornwall in a sheltered garden, flowering in soft pink in January and February.

Sub-shrubs

Below Lavender is grown as a crop on the Adriatic islands and elsewhere around the Mediterranean. "English" lavender has narrow flower spikes; "French" (*Lavendula stoechas*) more truncheon-like flower-heads. Cuttings take easily in spring or autumn. All it asks is stony ground and sunshine.

The formal definition of a sub-shrub is a plant that is permanently woody at the base, but whose stems tend to be soft and herbaceous towards their tips. The botanical term is suffruticose. At one point in the seventeenth century frutex threatened to become the English for a shrub; suffrutex for a sub-shrub. We had a lucky escape.

What is or is not suffruticose depends to an extent on the climate. There are many plants that fail to ripen the tips of their new growth in places where the summer is too short or too cool. Hardy fuchsias, for example, are completely fruticose in Ireland; substantially herbaceous in most of England. Pragmatic gardeners therefore use the term sub-shrub for anything that is shrubby by inclination but low, sprawling and soft-wooded, or just simply dwarf in stature.

The biggest single class of plants embraced by this definition must surely be the heathers. Then there are the woody herbs. Then there is an army of popular and useful plants ideal for small gardens and unclassifiable in any other way, particularly the grey-leaved little bushes.

The lower picture opposite gives a good idea of the look of well-furnished stability that little shrubs offer. It has the same advantage, or disadvantage, depending on your tastes, as a garden of heathers: nothing much happens. It looks well-organized and tasteful, but the seasons are marked (in this case) only by the dwarf red berberis coming into leaf, some discreet passages of white flowers on the hebes, and yellow flowers on the Jerusalem sage. The upper right picture is more inert still. Only the pinks are so brash as to disturb its well-bred calm.

This sort of gardening is moving close to the Japanese ideal of once-and-for-all composition. The exquisite miniature of the upper left picture opposite, with not a leaf out of place, is almost Japanese gardening in Western materials. In terms of scale it also overlaps with rock-gardening, though on the whole the plants we are talking about are not alpines but the under-brush of, for example, Mediterranean coastal hills.

Grey-leaved plants are generally adapted to drought and heat: a question mark always hangs over their hardiness in northern gardens. The cotton lavender, *Santolina chamaecyparissus* (*incana*), is one of the hardiest. Clipped occasionally it makes a pale and solid mound of great "design" value. The artemisias, the family of sagebrush and absinthe, have the finest of all feathery grey fronds in *Artemisia arborescens*, but this is not guaranteed against hard frosts. The pale green southernwood is the toughest of them.

The vast genus of the ragworts, *Senecio*, provides some of the most popular grey-leaved plants: the sprawling bush variously known as *S. greyi* and *S. laxifolius*. *S. monroi* is a neater form with smaller crinkly leaves. Far more silvery and outspoken, but also more tender, is *S. cinerarea*, with broad deeply lobed leaves: this is used as tender bedding in cold gardens. Those who do not approve of bright yellow daisies often clip the flower buds off senecios and santolinas in early summer to keep the plants compact.

One of the most varied and intriguing contributors in this field is the New Zealand genus of hebes, which old hands know as shrubby veronicas. At one extreme they offer little bushes like dwarf cypresses (the "whipcords": notably the green-brown *Hebe armstrongii*). At the other they put up tall spikes of lavender-blue flowers (*H. hulkeana*). Then there is *H. rakaiensis*, like box (pages 72–3), *H. pinguifolia* 'Pagei', a frosty little groundcover, and *H. macrantha*, with wide white flowers almost like a campanula.

If you are looking for a dark green dome of great authority, with flowers like scented apple blossom and red berries, *Daphne retusa* would be your answer. If sheets of pink or yellow or orange flowers, the helianthemums. If an indefatigable classic, you could not improve on lavender.

Below All-grey planting with sub-shrubs on and below a low stone wall at Hestercombe, a garden designed by Sir Edwin Lutyens and Gertrude Jekyll in Somerset. The plants are the shrubby *Santolina chamaecyparissus*, pinks and the vigorous little snow-in-summer *Cerastium tomentosum*.

Above Sub-shrubs lend themselves perfectly to miniature compositions. The plants include *Senecio* 'Dunedin', (left), *Chrysanthemum haradjani* (foreground grey), *Acaena* 'Blue Haze' and *Convolvulus cneorum*.

Below Permanent low planting with sub-shrubs at Sissinghurst. From the foreground a dwarf red *Berberis thunbergii*; grey *Hebe pinguifolia* 'Pagei', brown *Hebe armstrongii* and grey Jerusalem sage, *Phlomis fruticosa*.

Above Among the useful sub-shrubby herbs common kitchen sage has several forms with subtly beautiful leaves. This is 'Tricolor'. Others are a deep grey-purple and green suffused with gold.

Above The brown "whipcord" hebe, *Hebe ochracea*, in an unusual combination with a neat little woolly willow from Scotland, *Salix lanata*. Neither has grown more than eighteen inches in five years.

Above There are few sprawling sub-shrubs to compare with the rock-roses or helianthemums for a rapid sheet of bright colour in a dry place in midsummer. This is 'Wisley Primrose'. 'Wisley Pink' is equally good.

Above A bindweed as lovely as a bride: *Convolvulus cneorum* makes an evergreen hummock of silver-silky leaves and flowers all summer with pink buds opening pure white. It loves to sprawl on a sunny terrace.

The herb garden

Herbs are inseparably linked with nostalgia for the seventeenth century; an age when housewives and their maids, in our imaginations at least, spent enchanted mornings together in garden and still-room gathering and disposing of bundles of aromatic plants. Whether we would really enjoy either the process or the results today is immaterial to our instinctive approval of such a natural, wholesome, surely happy and fulfilling business.

We should imagine seventeenth-century tastes as rather more robust than ours, lest we mislead ourselves. I once went to a house in Kent where rosemary and rushes were still strewn on the stone flags in the great hall, Tudor fashion. The combination of crushed rosemary underfoot and smoke from the apple logs piled in the grate gave me a vivid flash-back to the days of our ancestors in doublet and hose. How pallid and genteel our ideas of scent and flavour have become.

How limited in scope, too. The herbals of the seventeenth century were based on the broad faith that everything in the garden had a use, whether for medicine, cookery, preserving, cosmetics, or often quasi-magically to raise or lower the spirits of the depressed or overexcited. The recipes read today as though the symptoms were filled in after the cures were concocted. It may have been so, although most modern drugs are derived from plants. In any case the garden repertoire was uninhibited, as were the recipes. Dozens of plants that we consider "flowers" rather than "herbs" were pressed into service. As a result the herb garden in its original form was a much prettier place than it is today. Today it wears an air of restraint, of containing only rather dowdy plants whose merits are all in their juices. We have either forgotten the uses of the more flamboyant ones, or promoted them into the flower garden regardless.

Yet the same air of restraint gives the herb garden a unity. The prevailing colours are green and grey and brown with a few quiet purple, pink, yellow and soft blue flowers. A separate bed (or better still enclosure) with herbs alone is a restful change from the brighter colours of the rest of the garden. Not all herbs are in scale together—angelica and fennel for example tower like trees over the maquis of the lesser herbs—but all are at least harmonious.

One of the best plans is to grow herbs in a chequerboard pattern, alternating little beds with paving slabs, which provide somewhere to stand while you pick them. The soil in the beds can be varied to suit the plants, and beds for invasive herbs such as mint and balm can be lined with cement down to a depth where even mint roots give up.

Wherever I have seen such a cabinet of herbs it has been almost too much of a conversation piece: so much lore and legend attaches to each plant. But since it does provoke discussion it is a good idea to put a large label in each bed. The names, in the mother tongue, not Latin, have a runic quality which makes you look twice at even the dullest little clump of leaves.

The term herb is by no means restricted to herbaceous plants. Many are annuals. An important minority are the aromatic shrubs and sub-shrubs of Mediterranean hillsides, the plants that grew wild where the first European gardens were made.

The shrubby herbs are all good garden plants whether you use them in the kitchen or not. Bay is one of the handsomest and hardiest of evergreen trees. Thyme in its many varieties is ideal cover for a dry bank or low stone wall. The two culinary thymes are the common and the lemon-scented (which has a pretty golden form). Corsica also has one called *Herba barona*, which reputedly has a caraway flavour. Lavender, though nothing to do with cooking, carries a potent charge of old-garden association. Rosemary is one of the best companions for old roses, and looks good in any border. The form known as 'Miss Jekyll's Upright' makes a superlative marker or point of emphasis, given the shelter of a wall.

Sage, with its zinc-grey leaves, may seem a dull plant, but I

Above The subtle colours of herbs are either delicate or dowdy according to your taste. Here they are grown with complete freedom, wild-garden style, in gravel.

Above and below Medieval gardeners' ingenuity, limited in the scope of the plants they knew, found its outlet in elaborate patterns known as knots, planted with herbs, and filled with coloured earth and stone. These are later, seventeenth-century, plans: a lover's knot and *flowre de luce*.

Above All herbs are best used fresh gathered, but most can be preserved for winter use by drying. Here they hang from the beams of a Spanish kitchen. They are dry within a week, then stored in airtight boxes.

Left The Queen's Garden at the Royal Botanic Gardens, Kew, is planted entirely with plants popular in the early seventeenth century—most of which are "herbs" in the broad sense of having domestic uses.

Below An effective modern "knot" garden planted with box, lavender and petunias. A Tudor gardener would have had his ears boxed for letting the pattern become blurred.

have seen it used to great effect in broad sweeps on a stony hill, and its colour-forms in purple and greeny-gold are excellent. Rue, vile smelling though it is, has exquisitely fretted leaves and is marvellously easy to grow: so much so that the blue-leaved 'Jackman's Blue' has become a cliché with lime-green lady's mantle in old-English gardens. Hard drainage is the rule for all the shrubby herbs. Aim to remind them of their home in Provence.

The annual herbs need more sympathetic soil. They vary from the essential parsley, which needs moisture and appreciates shade, to basil, which insists on the warmest spot. The majority vote with the basil, so it makes more sense to keep your herb bed in the sun and grow your parsley in the shade by the kitchen door. Coriander, dill (the top herb in Scandinavia; scarcely recognized in Britain), sweet marjoram and summer savoury are all annuals that enjoy a warm place with fairly rich, moist soil. The one valuable herb that would prefer to be with the parsley is the rather similar but subtler chervil, the secret of *omelettes fines herbes*.

Alone among the herbaceous herbs mint likes moisture. There is even a lovely mint that lives in water: treading on it wading in a stream is a moment to remember. It seems that only the British and the Arabs cook with mint, but it would be a pity to leave it out of a herb garden. There are two culinary kinds: spearmint (with pointed leaves) and apple mint, whose leaves are round, soft-hairy and have the better flavour. Apple mint also has a white-variegated and a grey form; both attractive enough to plant for decoration alone.

The other herbs will all be happy with a well-drained garden soil, needing little feeding but more or less frequent dividing and replanting. This is particularly true of the two indispensables, chives and tarragon. No doubt alecost, lovage, lemon balm and sweet cicely would appreciate it too. Alas all they tend to get is a leaf torn off, tasted and briefly discussed from time to time.

Above A wide range of herbs can be grown in pots, though this picture is unrealistic in suggesting they can all be grown in the same one. A window box is adequate space to grow enough of all the standard kitchen herbs for household use—except bay, which can be grown in a tub by the front door.

Right It is a pity to segregate all herbs into a separate part of the garden when some of them have so much to offer in handsome leaves and bold, if not bright, flowers. The biennial (or short-lived perennial) angelica is a splendid eye-catcher, here in company with the grey sub-shrub *Santolina chamaecyparissus* (*incana*). Fennel is another stately herb, especially in a bronze-leaved form. Unfortunately its seedlings can easily become deep-rooted weeds.

The lawn

Below Regular stripes emphasize the calm and orderliness of a well-kept lawn. To a lawn fanatic the process of mowing is a pleasure in itself: the noise of the mower, the smell of exhaust and oil and the warm green cuttings. For the richest green and the most pronounced stripes three-quarters of an inch is the best length.

Right The two forms of lawn-mower in use today are the rotary and the cylinder. The rotary mower shown works like a hovercraft, forcing air downwards round the edges to keep the rotating blade "floating". It will cut grass up to six inches long. The cylinder mower produces stripes but balks at two-inch-high grass.

Above Grass has no substitute for combining even greenness with resistance to the traffic of feet. The best alternative for small plots or places awkward to mow (on rockery banks for example) is "Irish moss" or pearlwort, a *Sagina* which forms a fine-textured spongy carpet with tiny white flowers. It needs regular moisture and not too much direct sunlight. In a rock garden it can become a pernicious weed.

Above Subtropical grasses (the commonest are the Bermuda grasses) unfortunately have dormant periods in winter, when they turn a dreary brown. They can be sown with annual cool-climate grasses to hide them in winter or even (according to the Sunset *Western Garden Book*) dyed green. Several non-grass plants are used as substitutes in the tropics. This Indian lawn is planted with *Othiopogon*, or lily-turf.

A consensus in gardening opinion is rare, but few would argue with the proposition that a garden needs a visible floor: that the ground level needs to be firmly established somewhere, preferably centrally, by an open space free, or relatively free, from the jostle of plants.

Paving is ideal for small yards and patios. But on a larger scale something green and soft is more natural and more soothing. Grass is the automatic answer wherever it will grow.

The art of the grassy lawn was developed in England. Some say it was invented by the huge flocks of sheep that cropped, manured and compacted the naturally grassy areas round country houses. It was perfected in Tudor times, when a bowling green scythed to a flawless finish was a status symbol. The word *boulingrin* for a plot of grass passed into French—though never the attitude of mind that went with it.

The air in England is apparently full of grass seed. You have only to leave ground bare to see the process start. The climate favours it—damp summers and moderate winters are ideal. I have made a perfectly acceptable lawn by doing nothing—sowing no seed, laying no turf—simply mowing the naturally occurring plants on a patch of bare ground every other week for a summer. By the end of the first season the grass had the upper hand. By the end of the second year I could use the word lawn. Grass is one of the few plants that survive and thrive with having their heads cut off at frequent intervals.

Not everyone is so lucky. Though grass of some kind will grow almost anywhere in temperate climes, the good lawn

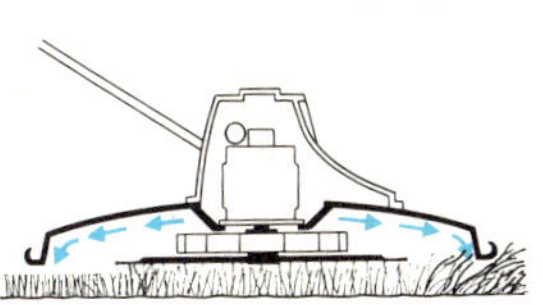

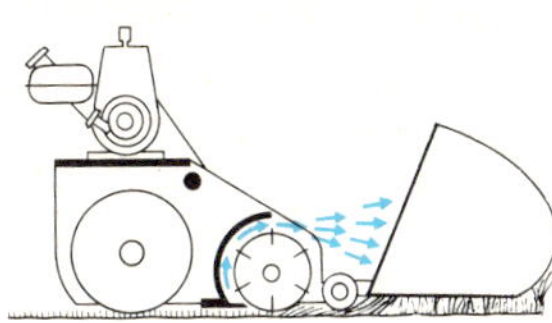

Above The lawn as a meadow at Great Dixter, Sussex. Wild flowers and bulbs, including snakeshead fritillaries, are encouraged to seed themselves. The grass is only cut three times a year, in late July when the flowers have seeded, late August and November to produce short turf as a setting for spring bulbs.

Left Different lengths of grass can be used to great effect to define paths and distinguish spaces. By varying the shape and size of the area of longer grass the whole character of this garden can be altered.

Right The lawn as a restful pool of green is cleverly used in this garden to distract attention from its rectangular boundaries. Instead of emphasizing perspective with parallel stripes the circular lawns focus attention in the heart of the garden.

grasses resent extremes of climate and flourish only where the soil is deep and well drained. When we mow and collect the trimmings we remove nutrients which the roots must replace; if the root-run is shallow, constant feeding becomes necessary. The ideal conditions for a lawn are two inches of sand over a foot of good rich soil and then a fast-draining sub-soil—an unlikely combination in nature. The sand prevents the surface compacting or water-logging; the rich soil invites the roots to run deep; and the drainage makes sure they do not drown.

Given that very few gardeners are likely to prepare such perfect conditions lawn-seed is normally sold in judiciously balanced mixtures of the more or less aristocratic and demanding kinds—the fine-leaved creeping fescues that call for the daintiest treatment; the tougher meadow-grasses (*Poa* species), more tolerant of damp and shade, the vigorous longer-stalked bents and sometimes the not easily discouraged brawny perennial rye-grass. The precise prescription varies by merchant, by region (with allowances made for local climate) and of course by the intended use of the lawn. A football pitch needs very different grasses from a polite suburban sward.

There are lawn fetishists to whom anything but the finer grasses are anathema. Perhaps they should open their eyes to the virtues of clover, which stays green when drought browns the grass, and moreover is self-feeding with its nitrogen-fixing roots, and even—in appropriate sunless places—moss. Moss takes advantage of neglected, starved grass—especially on very acid soil. The broad-leaved weeds such as plantain and dandelion break the even surface of green and spoil the effect. Daisies on the other hand are beautiful in themselves, and are usually sufficiently discouraged by mowing.

A "perfect" lawn is the garden's greatest consumer of energy, in the form of fertilizers and weedkillers and in the Saturday-morning roar of a million mowers getting cracking. And that is only the start of it. A lawn needs regular raking to pull out the "thatch" of dead grass, spiking to aerate the soil and rolling to compact it again.

The energy spent on maintaining lawns in the United States would revolutionize the agriculture of a goodish part of the Third World. The argument for compromise between lawn and meadow is a powerful one. Yet compromise is not easy to put into effect.

In a small garden orderly trimness is likely to be the object of having a lawn at all. Even in a large garden it turns out to be less laborious to mow short regularly than long occasionally—which lets you in for the sweaty business of haymaking. If you mow often enough you need not even collect the cut grass—a saving of both time and fertilizers.

The advantage of delaying mowing until midsummer is that the grasses and other plants have time to flower. Never seeing the flowers of fescue and bent few gardeners realize how pretty they are, especially laced with the wild flowers (weeds with their proper status) that will soon join them—and for that matter the bulbs you can plant to naturalize where the mower will not go till June.

Above The first and still the ultimate cutter—the scythe. Motor-scythes with reciprocating cutter-bars have largely taken its place for very long grass, but traditional bowling-green keepers still occasionally use the scythe after mowing with the cylinder-mower for perfecting the grassy surface down to three-sixteenths of an inch.

Groundcover

In a sense the term groundcover sounds like an admission of defeat. You will not find it in old gardening books that were written with the assumption that labour and leisure were both in plentiful supply. The groundcover concept admits that, restricted though we are in small modern gardens, there is still too much ground for us to pay detailed attention to it all. We want to just cover some of it over to keep it quiet, like putting a blanket over the budgerigar.

As the term is generally used today it means permanent trailing or clump-forming plants, usually evergreens, which quickly join together to form a dense layer of leaves not more than a foot or so high. They block out all light from the soil and thus prevent weeds germinating.

Groundcover is a sort of vegetable paving. Like paving it is a major effort and expense to begin with, but once installed it forms a part of the garden you can relegate to the back of your mind. Sweeping the terrace and tidying the groundcover come into the category of occasional garden housework—mere unskilled chores.

Groundcover has not become a vogue word and a vogue way of gardening simply because we prefer unskilled chores to intricate craftsmanship, however, or because time has mysteriously contracted since the start of this century. There are powerful arguments for it, both ecological and aesthetic.

Ground is not bare in nature. Nor is it ever dug. It has its characteristic permanent coverings of moss, of grass and wildflowers, of bracken or of brambles. Or perhaps there is an overhead canopy of beech trees which at the same time repel invaders with their shade and replenish the soil with their leaves in due season.

Under nature's stable regime the soil is protected from the elements; uncompacted, well-nourished and in perfect condition for the fauna and micro-fauna that give it life.

It is this healthy state of nature that groundcover introduces into the garden. For once a layer of vegetation dense enough to exclude light has covered the surface, a natural routine takes over. The cast-off leaves of trees and other plants fall and filter through to rot on the shady floor and be incorporated in the soil by a thriving population of earthworms. All the weeding and feeding the old-fashioned gardener would do, in other words, is done automatically.

By laying down relatively large carpets of one plant, meanwhile, the gardener has done something it is all too easy to fail at, particularly in a small garden: he has achieved a sense of decision, of a mind made up; the soothing, satisfying, much-to-be-desired quality of aesthetic unity.

Groundcover can maintain order, but it cannot impose it. It is no use hoping that by planting ivy or periwinkle—however densely and lavishly—in ground infested with serious permanent weeds you will eventually smother them into submission. There is nothing labour-saving about groundcover in the early stages. Quite the reverse. Because you are giving your planting a long lease on the ground in question, it needs unencumbered possession. All deep-rooting, persistent weeds must be dug out or poisoned. You cannot be sure that you have seen the last of ground elder or couch or horsetail until you have watched the bare soil for three summer months. And once you have done your planting all new weeds must be methodically suppressed until the cover closes over the ground.

The thicker you plant the sooner your groundcover will become effective. If expense were no object you could achieve total cover in a single season by planting at spaces of only a few inches. But spacing should bear some relation to the natural size of the plant. Dead-nettle can go in at six-inch spacings, but spreading junipers need a yard to take up their natural stance. Overclose planting will force growth upwards into a mound.

With all groundcover, as with almost any plants, it is better to put in many and small than few and big. Most creeping plants can easily be pulled apart into little pieces, each with enough roots to make a start. Plant them well in sympathetic soil and you will not have to wait long. Meanwhile you can either hoe or use weedkiller (with great care) on the remaining bare ground—or you can cover it with a deep mulch to prevent weeds germinating and make those that do easy to pull up. A sheet of black plastic with holes for the new plants is sometimes suggested. It will work (while looking horrible) for plants that do not need to root as they spread. But any persistent weeds under the sheet are liable to find the holes, and once they are entangled with the roots of your groundcover you will have to start again.

Although the main object of groundcover is foliage, there is no need to exclude flowers, and even fruit. The only essential is dense leafage, and for preference a ground-hugging habit.

While we tend to think of groundcover in terms of informal shapes, from the sombre swathes of ivy in public parks to clumps of hostas by a pond or heathers or rock-roses on a sunny bank, the system can work equally well as a substitute for formal "bedding". Intricate parterres can be planted once and for all—not admittedly with such brilliant colours as annuals can give, but with enough tones of green, silver, purple and gold in leaves alone to perpetuate the pattern.

Any permanent planting that fits this bill could be, and sometimes is, included in the definition. Day-lilies, we are told, make excellent groundcover, and so do the cranesbills. The same could be said for most border plants planted thickly and growing well in weed-free ground. Where many of them fail as groundcover in the strict sense is in their tendency to leave a bald centre as they spread outwards. They need lifting, dividing and replanting every now and then. The ideal groundcover plant on the contrary develops a canopy as even as jungle seen from the air.

Bulbs find themselves perfectly at home under low groundcover, so long as it reaches no more than half-way up their leaves. All bulbs need their leaves in the sun while they ripen. Crocuses are happy under creeping bugle; daffodils under ivy. Nerines look spectacular fanning out their bright pink flowers in autumn above foot-high hillocks of grey cotton lavender, sheared over in early summer to keep it close and low.

Below Where a bank is too steep for mowing, groundcover provides a simple way of keeping it tidy. Saint John's Wort does the job so well that it has become a cliché.

Left London Pride makes dense groundcover of beautiful texture and colouring on an intimate scale. Here it encroaches on a miniature pool in a hollowed-out rock, encouraged by the damp and shady conditions. It will tolerate drought but takes its name of *Saxifraga* × *umbrosa* from its liking for shade.

Above The simplest planting is often the most effective. The statue and the pine are allowed their full value by the wave of ivy breaking at their feet. Irish ivy is the best for groundcover.

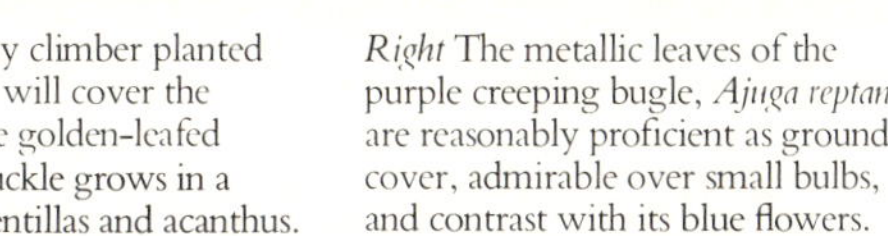

Below Almost any climber planted without support will cover the ground. Here the golden-leafed Japanese honeysuckle grows in a border with potentillas and acanthus.

Right The metallic leaves of the purple creeping bugle, *Ajuga reptans*, are reasonably proficient as groundcover, admirable over small bulbs, and contrast with its blue flowers.

Above The cranesbills (here, *Geranium endressii*) vary in stature from three inches to eighteen, but all cover the ground to exclude weeds.

Below The juniper has produced a score of prostrate, close-textured forms that slowly create admirable groundcover.

The kitchen garden: the principles

Below Orderliness is essential for vegetables, but it need not necessarily mean segregation. The great walled gardens of many Scottish country-houses traditionally grew vegetables and flowers side by side in the best soil available and in the most sheltered place. This is at Ellon Castle, north of Aberdeen.

There is much to be learned from the fact that the kitchen garden, the one part of the garden not planned or planted for beauty's sake alone, is very often the most aesthetically pleasing part of the whole.

The taste for the functional is not new to the post-Bauhaus twentieth century. Addison wrote in *The Spectator*: "I have always thought a kitchen garden a more pleasant sight than the finest orangery. . . . I love to see everything in perfection, and am more pleased to survey my rows of coleworts and cabbages, with a thousand nameless pot-herbs springing up in their full fragrancy and verdure, than to see the tender plants of foreign countries. . . ."

A kitchen garden has the satisfaction of inevitability. There is only one way to set about it. A boat must have a sharp end; vegetables must be grown in rows—or at least regular patches. Their ground must be measured, marked out and made ready. It must be kept fertile and clean. If all this is well done it is more expressive of the harmony of man and nature than anything else a gardener can do. Here we are not just looking for pleasure (which is perhaps why we find it); we are looking for a measurable return for labour. The word efficiency creeps in. Comparison with the price of vegetables in the shops is unavoidable.

The object of growing crops (as opposed to just growing plants) is to produce the maximum quantity of a quality that will satisfy us in as small a space and in as short a time as possible. It is common sense not to grow anything that is being raised commercially at much lower cost. If for example maincrop potatoes are falling off lorries all along your road you will not want to waste ground on them. But good salad potatoes, for example, are hardly grown commercially in Britain at all.

There are other vegetables that flood the market at certain times of year. It is useless to have your own glut at the same time as everyone else. Far better to grow something different for maturity at that time, or (as far as you can) advance or delay your crop so as not to coincide with the glut.

Although the whole principle of growing vegetables is to pump them full of nutrients so that they grow as fast as possible, to be as juicy and tender as possible, it may sometimes be better to reduce the apparent efficiency of your turn-over. For example, you can grow a crop in relatively unfertile conditions, which will make it hardy enough to stay in the ground over the winter. Spring is the leanest time of year for supplies, and leeks, sprouts and cabbages that have survived the winter are marvellously welcome before the first early crops can be forced along.

In general, however, the object is to give vegetables a short life and a pampered one. A perfect kitchen garden needs warmth, sunlight, shelter from the wind, soil in good general "heart" (easily worked and well-drained), additions of fertilizers when they can do most good, an ample supply of water and weeds kept well at bay. In an exposed place shelter from the wind might be the overriding factor. Nothing discourages tender young leaves so much as a howling cold draught. In a hot and sandy place the most important thing will be the amount of moisture-retaining humus you can manage to incorporate into the soil. In a sad bog drainage must come first . . . and so on.

Certain points of layout apply very generally. Shelter from the north and east, by walls if possible, means a quick warm-up in spring. A south-facing slope raises the soil temperature, but there must be an escape route for cold air on frosty nights at the lowest point or a frost-pocket will result. A wind-baffling fence or hedge on the side of the prevailing wind is very desirable, but not if it also shades the ground for a significant part of the day. Plant rows running north-south receive most sunlight. Hard paths are essential when the ground is wet.

Paths also provide a welcome permanent framework and pattern. The custom (at least in substantial kitchen gardens) is to divide the space into three parts for a rotational cycle (to avoid growing the same crops in the same soil twice running; see above right) and keep a fourth part for such permanent fixtures as rhubarb, asparagus or soft fruit, or as an additional step in the rotation of potatoes. If you want both the plan will need five parts.

The rotation system classes almost all vegetables as 1) pea or onion family, 2) cabbage, or *Brassica*, family and 3) a root crop. The three classes like their soil rich and well-mucked in that descending order. Ideally therefore you plan to dig and manure the ground; grow peas, beans, onions and leeks in it first; the next year cabbages and their relations; and in the third year carrots, parsnips and the like. In the latter two years you use fertilizers. Then you start again. Meanwhile, irrespective of rotation, you dart in and out with quick "catch" crops of whatever you think you can get away with: the elementary and instant radish; lettuces; carrots; spinach; endive. . . .

Instruction manuals and seed packets are generally very clear on such matters as spacing: how far apart the plants should eventually be. Closer together they will shelter one another but also compete. As in all garden questions the decision is finally the gardener's own. Would you rather have four small cabbages or two big ones?

Right The principle of the rotation of crops has been practised at least since the Middle Ages, when every third year was a fallow one for the land to recover its fertility. In the eighteenth century the first scientific study of farming developed the idea that different crops took different nutrients from the land and that an ideal system would allow perpetual fertility. The farming journalist and reformer Arthur Young made an international reputation by such indefatigable investigation and record-keeping as that illustrated here. As practised in kitchen gardens rotation has two main objectives, to economize on manure and the labour of digging it in, by only manuring one-third of the garden each year, and planting in it the crops that need it most; and to prevent the build-up of pests and diseases peculiar to one crop or family which would follow if it were grown repeatedly in the same soil. Where no manure but only fertilizers are used it is only the second advantage that applies.

A N N A L S

O F

AGRICULTURE,

COLLECTED AND PUBLISHED BY

ARTHUR YOUNG, Esq. F.R.S.

A FARM OF ABOUT FIVE HUNDRED AND FIFTY ACRES.

Nº.	1779.	1780.	1781.	1782.	1783.	1784.	1785.
1	Turneps	Barley	Oats	Laid	Laid	Wheat	Turneps
2	Barley	Vetches	Turneps	Barley	Laid	Laid	Peaſe
3	Barley	Turneps	Barley	Peaſe	Turneps	Barley	Oats
4	Turneps	Barley	Laid	Laid	Barley	Turneps	Barley
5	Barley	Turneps	Barley	Laid	Laid	Barley	Turneps
6	Laid	Sum. fal.	Wheat	Barley	Turneps	Barley	Laid
7	Oats	Turneps	Barley	Laid	Turneps	Barley	Peaſe
8	Sum. fal.	Wheat	Barley	Turneps	Barley	Laid	Laid
9	Barley	Oats	Turneps	Barley	Laid	Laid	Wheat
10	Barley	Peaſe	Turneps	Barley	Laid	Laid	Barley
11	Laid	Barley	Turneps	Barley	Turneps	Barley	Laid
12	Barley	Laid	Sum. fal.	Wheat	Turneps	Barley	Turneps
13	Turneps	Barley	Laid	Laid	Wheat	Turneps	Barley
14	Turneps	Barley	Turneps	Barley	Laid	Laid	Barley
15	Laid	Laid	Barley	Turneps	Barley	Laid	Barley
16	Turneps	Barley	Peaſe	Turneps	Barley	Laid	Laid
17	Laid	Laid	Barley	Turneps	Barley	Laid	Laid
18	Wheat	Turneps	Peaſe	Turneps	Barley	Laid	Laid
19	Barley	Turneps	Barley	Laid	Laid	Wheat	Turneps

N. B. By *laid*, is meant clover, ray-graſs, &c.

Above France has a strong national style in "*jardins potagers*" often with box hedges and fruit trees as a framework in which vegetables and flowers are grown together.

Left As different a setting as you could well imagine, yet the orderliness of a kitchen garden looks equally in place: this garden is on the beach-front at Santa Barbara, California.

Right The starting point for successful vegetable gardening: thorough manuring in the bottom of a trench. In this case the gardener is preparing a single row for beans in spring beside a row of spring greens planted the previous autumn.

The kitchen garden: the routine

The human race has been eating for a long time but only recording its menus for a short one. The early history of most of our food plants is lost. Many of them are developments of wild plants of the Mediterranean and the Near and Middle East. Plants of these areas tend to have large food storage organs (roots, rhizomes or seeds) evolved to keep through a long dry season and grow like fury when it rains.

The process of selection over thousands of years has obscured the wild origins of some vegetables completely: the onion, for example, has no obvious wild ancestor. But the majority advanced surprisingly little until the dawn of science. The first illustrations we have of vegetables, from the sixteenth century, show how remarkably primitive they were. The seventeenth century brought new introductions: the potato, maize, the tomato, beans and the marrow from the New World, but conservative gardeners did very little with them.

Not until the end of the eighteenth century did methodical selection and breeding begin. Early in the nineteenth century M. de Vilmorin experimented with wild carrots, selecting seedlings with fleshy roots from the majority (which had merely fibrous ones). By sowing their seed, selecting again and repeating the process three times he produced within four generations from the wild plant a vegetable very like that which had taken thousands of years to develop. From that time on, with the principles of selection and breeding increasingly being understood, vegetables constantly improved and diversified almost beyond recognition.

High tide came sometime in the first quarter of this century, when an astonishing range of vegetables for every sort of taste and local conditions was available. Now the tide has turned and is on the ebb. Most modern "improvements" are nothing of the kind as far as gardeners are concerned. The expensive business of breeding new vegetables is undertaken only for commercial growing, where taste is a minor consideration beside uniformity, looks and cropping and storing qualities. Worse still, European Economic Commission regulations have outlawed all the old varieties not on a short list agreed among commercial interests, declaring them to be broadly synonymous with varieties that are on the list, whether

---

Peas and beans are members of the legume family, which includes wisteria, laburnum, the acacia (or locust) . . . all plants that have nitrogen-fixing bacteria in their roots and thus leave the soil better off (as far as nitrogen goes) than they found it.

They come first in the pecking-order of rotation after the big dig, and the manuring that goes with it, partly because the added nitrogen is ideal for the leaves of the brassicas, partly because they have deep roots, but mainly because they appreciate the moisture-holding properties of the manure. Some gardeners have buried soaking newspapers and rags (while their peas were looking the other way) and found that it served the same purpose. Potash is the other thing that is hard to overdo, at least in its harmless form of fresh wood-ash. Like all vegetables except potatoes they prefer the soil alkaline rather than acid. Being big seeds they are easily sown in their permanent places, but since mice enjoy them peas are often dipped in paraffin before sowing.

Broad beans are the ancient European kind, easy, fond of heavy soil, hardy enough to sow in autumn in many places for a spring crop. They need support against wind and should be grown in double rows to to ensure pollination. Their only real problem is blackfly, which concentrate on the growing tip. Pinch this off (it is good to eat) as soon as the first pods have started to form near the bottom of the plant.

Runner beans and French or string beans are both imports from South America; the former, like the tomato, originally as an ornamental climber. Both are too tender for winter planting. The French bean is put in light (but fertile) warm soil in spring; the runner bean not planted out until frosts are over, but then given a veritable underground compost heap of its own; really rich damp ground to delve in. Although every English gardener builds a bamboo tent or wigwam to

---

Brassica may seem a somewhat esoteric way of referring to the cabbage and its relations, but there is a good reason for bracketing them all together: they are all the same plant. Remarkably enough kale, cabbage, red cabbage, savoys, spring greens, cauliflowers, calabrese, Brussels sprouts, broccoli and kohlrabi are simply selections of the wild *Brassica oleracea* of the sea-cliffs of Europe—a crinkly reddish-leaved plant with pale-yellow summer flowers.

In the kitchen garden brassicas share both tastes and pests, being united in thriving only in thoroughly fertile ground with a steady water supply. There are serious pests and diseases that move in on struggling brassicas—the worst by far being club-root. Brassicas of whatever kind should therefore be moved on to a fresh plot every year; the plot that had its three-yearly deep digging and manuring a year ago and has meanwhile grown peas and beans, acquiring extra nitrogen in the process. Keeping the soil decidedly limey discourages club-root. The brassica routine therefore goes: autumn digging and liming with half a pound of ground chalk to each square yard; leave the ground to settle over winter (they like it packed-down and firm); sow seeds thinly in a separate seed-bed with plenty of general fertilizer; transplant the seedlings with a root-ball of soil in good time before they start crowding; plant them firmly so they do not rock in the wind. It is a prudent practice to bury a mothball under each plant to distract pests that home in on the brassica smell.

Kale is the hardiest of the brassicas, essential in the far north as winter greens but in the south generally consigned to the cattle. Brussels sprouts are an old Belgian development of a sprouting kale ("Cottager's kale") which are almost equally hardy, but need constant selection or re-crossing to prevent them becoming kale-like again. F_1 hybrid seeds for sprouts

---

Salads are intended to be eaten uncooked, so they should be grown fast in rich moist ground to give no chance for fibres to form. Of all salad plants lettuce is the most important and versatile; with planning and cloches or a cold frame lettuces can be grown almost all year round.

There are scores of varieties, but four principal and recognizable types: the soft round cabbage-hearted or "butterhead"; the crisp round cabbage-hearted; the loose lettuce with no heart and the Cos—crisp with narrower upright leaves. All grow best in the freshly-manured legume department, but are often sown almost anywhere for a quick catch crop. They like lime.

The secret, as with all salad crops, is to sow little and often, and to thin the rows almost continuously, using even the smallest thinnings for salads as you go. Since some are transplanted, other sown in their rows, and the cloche/frame routine varies from variety to variety and month to month, the seed-packet is the place to learn this information.

Without growing under glass there is a gap in the lettuce season in winter. This can be filled with some of the many versions of chicory. The Italians, with their penchant for bitter flavours (think of Campari) are the champion chicory-growers. In northern Europe the commonest form is the Belgian witloof, commercially forced and blanched and very expensive to buy. But the beautiful red Verona kind or the green 'Pain de Sucre' can easily be grown in the same manner as lettuce, sown in early summer, and stand moderate winters without protection. Any chicory can be made sweeter by forcing. For mid-winter use transplant it into boxes of rich soil in a warm dark place in autumn, or for spring eating cover it with straw and soil in the garden.

Endive is loose- and curly-leaved chicory. The shaggiest and most tangled is a June-sown, late summer crop. The less curly Batavian endive is more like a bitter Cos lettuce, sown in late summer to crop in winter. Again, its bitterness is reduced by blanching.

Other good winter salads include dandelion (sown in spring for late autumn) and corn salad, lamb's lettuce or mache, sown in August in rich soil and harvested leaf by leaf all winter. Cloches keep it in good condition and free of splashing mud.

Of the many possible summer additions to the salad bowl, to be sown as catch crops, the most worthwhile are American cress (for a damp place in shade), the savoury-flavoured rocket (*Eruca*) and the succulent-leaved Golden Purslane (Pourpier doré)—and of course spring onions and radishes. Sow from March onwards.

Compared with these rapid crops of almost weed-like ease celery and bulb (or Florence) fennel are major operations calling for a luxurious moist and peaty bed. Spinach looks for similar conditions. Courgettes and marrows (overgrown courgettes) are like runner beans, asking for a compost heap of their own. The outdoor or "ridge" cucumber, a prickly fruit like a gherkin, asks for the same, while the real cucumber needs the warmth and humidity of a frame. Pollination makes cucumbers bitter, so buy only female varieties.

The cultivation of tomatoes, aubergines and peppers in a greenhouse is not difficult, but they do demand daily attention. If they can be given a warm enough wall outdoors they are less demanding. Moreover the best salad tomatoes of thick flesh and Provencal flavour ('Marmande' is one) are unhappy under glass. In Britain everything depends on the summer—as it does with sweet corn. In a hot season sweet corn can be one of the most exciting, satisfying and beautiful vegetables to grow. Sow it in spring under glass in peat pots—to avoid transplanting damage—and plant it out in a block (not a row) in the sunniest corner of the bean department in June. Rush the cobs to the boiling water as soon as they are plump. In no vegetable is freshness more important.

they taste the same or not. A stiff fine has been imposed on anyone who should transgress these regulations, aimed at a stultifying uniformity—and bound, moreover, to have serious genetic consequences as the breeding potential of the outlawed varieties is lost.

For an amateur the criteria (economy apart) for deciding to grow a vegetable must be either that it is a better variety, or that he can grow it better than commercially available kinds. Growing it better includes having the chance to pick and eat it at exactly the right moment.

On these two pages is a summary of most of the vegetables that concern amateurs: an attempt to elucidate the basic divisions of the kitchen garden and its methodical cropping.

PERENNIAL VEGETABLES

There are four valuable perennial vegetables that are looking for a permanent home—not necessarily in the kitchen garden since all, in their season, are beautiful plants.

Asparagus is the most luxurious, demanding most space and most care, besides taking four or five years to come into full bearing. Yet its commercial price makes it worth growing if the space is there. It requires light or sandy well-drained ground and a copious top-dressing of manure or fertilizer in late winter. Even the odd couple of asparagus plants are worth tucking away somewhere, perhaps in the flower garden. They will provide two or three intimate suppers in summer and glorious golden ferns in autumn.

Globe artichokes, with their jagged grey leaves, are also quite handsome enough for a border and need minimum upkeep. Replanting offsets from the base every four or five years is enough. A straw mulch in winter protects them and gives them a them a good start in spring. Brittany is where they are most at home, so rain is important.

Seakale has some of the best leaves of any perennial, in scallops and volutes of palest grey. Forcing it indoors in winter for its succulent shoots is an epicurean pastime.

Rhubarb sounds more worthy but is scarcely less decorative, and deserves a well-manured corner of any garden. Early summer is the normal cropping time for the sanguine stalks (the leaves are inedible), although they, too, are often forced with a box full of straw to be ready a month or so earlier.

---

let the plant run up as high as possible no harm is done by pinching it out to make it form a bush.

The French eat "their" bean, the haricot, in various states of freshness or dryness: as *haricots verts* in its crisp prime, as *haricots secs* dried and yellow, and as flageolets in between. They are awkward plants to handle and harvest, needing a certain amount of support (even the the dwarf varieties) and being brittle—and also camouflaging their fruit among the stems and leaves. For this reason the purple-podded variety is a boon. It takes half the time of stooping and fumbling to harvest the crop.

Peas were among the first vegetables to be systematically improved, with the object of breeding some of the hardiness of the round-seeded kind into the much sweeter wrinkly, or "marrow-fat", peas. The earliest ones, sown in autumn, are still round and scarcely worth growing in rivalry to commercial frozen peas. It is questionable use of space and effort to grow even the best spring-sown ones today. The (also spring-grown) tender French petits pois and mangetout or sugar peas, which you eat pods and all, are more worth the amateur's time and trouble—especially in small batches sown at intervals to lengthen their season.

Onions grown from seed and leeks are conventionally given a place in the legume plot to take advantage of recent manuring. Most amateurs today however grow their onions from "sets"—small seedling bulbs started in a nursery. All the amateur does is fatten them, which demands nothing more than a general fertilizer. Shallots are the same, except that they multiply offsets instead of growing fat. Nor do leeks need extravagant manuring—they are transferred in summer (in much the same state of maturity as onion sets) from a seed-bed to their final spacing. There is no hardier or more valuable winter vegetable.

---

are therefore common in catalogues. Since Brussels sprouts are tall and top heavy and need to stand all winter, firm soil is essential and staking a good idea.

Cabbages have been developed to mature in each season. Football-like winter cabbages and Savoys (which differ only in their alligator-hide leaves) are sown in spring. Spring "greens" are sown in late summer, transplanted in autumn and remain as little plants all winter. The trick is to give them a sheltered place and feed them with a handful of general fertilizer when the ground starts to warm up so that they grow their loose heads rapidly. Red cabbages are also planted in late summer but take a whole year to mature.

The other versions of *Brassica oleracea* have been developed for their flower-heads rather than their leaves. The glamorous member of the party is the cauliflower, which was originally developed for a Mediterranean climate. None is more greedy for fertilizer or sulks more readily if conditions are not ideal. There are winter cauliflowers now of considerable hardiness as well as the traditional summer ones, and new Australian ones that mature in autumn. Summer cauliflowers are sown under glass in autumn and kept in a frame until spring. Autumn and winter ones are spring-sown in a seed bed like winter cabbages.

In cold areas broccoli is a much surer and easier plant to grow. It is sown in spring for picking over a long period, sprout by sprout, the following late winter and early spring. Calabrese might be called summer broccoli; a short plant like a cauliflower sown in spring to be ready for picking in late summer.

Kohlrabi is the odd one out, linking these brassicas with their first-cousins the turnips and swedes. It is a cabbage with very little leaf and a stem swollen into an ugly ball above ground. It is scarcely epicurean, but a summer standby for dry gardens and meagre soil.

The root vegetables that take third place in the succession of crops, after the brassicas have had the best of the fertility, have no simple organization or allegiance. In general they like a lighter soil than the greenery (not that you can change your soil from one year to another). They do not like fresh manure; it makes their roots divide. Nor for obvious reasons do they like stony ground. They are sown where they are to grow and not transplanted. A general fertilizer is all they need, except of course for ample water. Nothing but tough old roots can come from starved droughty conditions.

Two of the rootcrops, turnips and swedes, are brassicas and need the brassica routine for good health. Turnips in fact break the rules and benefit from rich ground and quick growth. Sow them at intervals in spring for tender summer roots, harvesting them very small. Turnips grown for their palatable cabbage-like tops and coarser roots are sown in autumn. Swedes are like bigger, sweet-flavoured turnips sown in spring to be ready from autumn onwards.

The most generally useful group of roots are the beets—all developments of the same European seaside perennial, *Beta vulgaris*. Sugar beet, mangolds, beetroot, spinach-beet and Swiss chard (or seakale beet) are botanically from the same stable. Of these the first two are purely agricultural; good beetroots can be bought very satisfactorily; but spinach beet and Swiss chard are first-class roots to grow, paradoxically, for their delectable leaves.

While real spinach is a temperamental plant given to running to seed unless the soil is rich enough and the summer damp enough, and in winter needs protection, spinach beet keeps up a perpetual supply of only slightly less tasty leaves with no histrionics. If it is sown in spring it will be bearing well by late summer. Summer sowings crop well in winter. Keep picking the outer leaves to encourage more. Swiss chard is almost as good-tempered though not quite so hardy. Spring sowings are superb in summer, with crisp and juicy white-ribbed leaves. The similar ruby chard has brilliant red leaf-stems. Summer sowings need covering in winter with cloches to be ready for spring cropping.

Carrots are almost a salad crop in summer. A succession of small sowings from spring to midsummer keeps a supply of crisp little roots perfect to eat raw. "Maincrop" carrots are sown in summer and lifted for storage in late autumn: useful for stews but a root without romance. All carrots prefer light sandy soil and need protection from the carrot fly, which is attracted by the smell, particularly during the essential operation of thinning the rows. "Pelleted" seeds, which are big enough to sow singly and thus save thinning, are one way round the difficulty. For heavier soils there are short stumpy carrots which taste just as good.

Parsnips are an old English native, related to parsley and celery (an umbellifer, in fact) and like parsley slow and uncertain of germination, but very hardy and very sweet. Quick-germinating radish seed is usually sown with the parsnips in March to mark the rows. The long deep roots are ready about October.

Salsify is another one-of-a-kind root, a member of the daisy family, which is grown in much the same way as parsnips, but also sometimes left until the following spring when its new shoots and leaves are good to eat in a time of general vegetable dearth.

Celeriac is a godsend for soils too dry or gardeners too lazy to grow the time-consuming celery. It is a sun-loving, surface-dwelling root of evil appearance but excellent celery flavour, either raw or cooked. It needs a long growing season, which means early sowing in a greenhouse or frame, planting out in early June, and moderate feeding and watering until it is as big as a croquet ball in late autumn. Then like all roots it can be lifted and stored in sand out of the reach of frost.

Soft fruit

Below A cage to keep the birds out is a prerequisite for soft fruit growing and is also very useful for early salad crops which are often attacked. If they are not grown in a permanent cage strawberries must be netted before they flower: the flowers are another irresistible temptation to inquisitive birds.

Right Highbush blueberries have been developed this century in the eastern USA, where they are native, as a garden crop for early autumn. They demand distinctly acid soil, plenty of nitrogenous feeding and full sunshine. Ten-foot spacing is not too much for the bushes, which like blackcurrants put up vigorous canes

Among vegetables anything short of apple-pie order is immediately obvious. You cannot just let a kitchen garden drift. Because fruit trees and bushes form a permanent part of the garden picture it is easy to pass lightly over them as scenery, forgetting that they have a purpose and should have a routine as clear-cut as a row of cauliflowers.

There is nothing morally wrong about the relaxed attitude that considers it a bonus if a fruit tree actually produces any edible fruit. In a small garden, though, space must work, and if the black currants are not bending and the gooseberry bushes groaning under the weight of their crops it might be better to yank them out and plant roses instead.

Pruning is the essence of producing a good crop. Unfortunately it is not a thing one can get right by instinct, since the different bushes bear their fruit on wood of different ages. It sounds complicated, and it is.

All soft fruits have one thing in common—the need for well-manured, deep-dug, well-drained but amply watered ground, slightly acid in reaction. Sun is important, but it is not their first need: better the right soil in a degree of shade. They also need conscientious weeding, since their roots are shallow and weeds can give them serious competition. Very light hoeing, herbicides or—perhaps best—a deep mulch are recommended rather than forking over, which damages the roots.

At some stage they all need protection from birds: the bush fruits in winter when their buds have formed and again in summer for their fruit; the cane fruits just in summer. Congregating them all into a fruit cage therefore makes sense. Ideally the cage should have permanent sides but a removable netting top, which can be taken off before snow and also during flowering to allow access for pollinating insects.

With good cultivation and hygiene (not leaving old leaves, rotted fruit, prunings and other rubbish lying about) and plenty of potash (which all fruit needs for ripening its wood), diseases should not be a problem. Chemicals should only be used with reluctance and infinite precaution. When eventually a virus or other bad disease strikes—it will usually catch up with raspberries after eight years or so—burn the plants and replant with new healthy ones in (if possible) a different place.

The formal division of soft fruit into those that grow on bushes and those that grow on canes is a good start for understanding their pruning. The management of cane fruit is discussed in the panel on the right. Bush fruit includes gooseberries and black, red and white currants, each of which have their own idiosyncrasies. Black currants are the easiest to understand: they are sturdy, vigorous, long-lived bushes that fruit on their newly ripened one-year-old stems. The principle is therefore to feed them well and prune them hard, cutting off up to a third of the old wood down to the base each year after it has fruited. Six feet apart is not too far to space them.

Red currants (and white, which are simply a variety of red) bear their fruit, in contrast, mainly on spurs on their old wood, which makes them very suitable for training as cordons. Pruning them consists of shortening all the main shoots by half the length of last year's growth and the lateral (or side) shoots to two buds from their base; in other words keeping a main frame of mature wood with short spurs coming off it at intervals. Only when a main branch grows old and feeble is it cut off at the base and a new one trained to replace it.

The gooseberry routine is more like red currants than black. They also fruit on spurs on old wood, but in addition on one-year-old stems. The object with a gooseberry bush is to build up a permanent framework of strong branches to last several years. The laterals are kept short, ideally in a summer pruning session that encourages new fruit buds. With a well-organized bush (it can also be grown as a cordon) you are less likely to lacerate yourself on the prickles.

CANE FRUITS

Raspberries and blackberries, and loganberries, which are a cross between the two (the work of a Scots exile in California), never make anything worthy of the name of bush. Their nature is to keep pushing up long thin canes from the ground to fruit either in their first or second year.

These cane fruits, to be manageable and productive, must be trained on horizontal wires or against a fence. Each needs slightly different treatment, though the principle for all is the same: constant renewal and tying up.

Raspberries are planted only eighteen inches apart in rows five or six feet apart. They are cut down to near the ground and given a summer to push up new canes, which are tied in to two or three wires, up to about six feet. In their second summer these canes fruit and are then immediately cut off at ground level. A clutch of new replacement canes are meanwhile shooting up in their place. The best six or eight of these are tied up, the rest cut off. Suckers also appear from the roots in the fairway between the rows. These are cut off, or better, pulled out. The exceptions to this routine are autumn-fruiting varieties, which are cut to the ground entirely each February and are up and in fruit by September.

Blackberries and loganberries (and also Boysenberries) have a slightly more complex routine. They need horizontal wires closer together so that their year-old canes can be tied in at oblique angles (see right) to bear fruit while their new canes shoot straight up. The new canes need tying to the top wire while the old ones fruit. The old ones are then cut off and the the new ones tied at the same oblique angles as their predecessors were. Eight or ten feet between plants is a good spacing for them.

Blackberry

from ground level. These fruit on side shoots in their second and subsequent years. No pruning is needed for two years; then one or two of the oldest shoots are removed altogether. Among the best-known cultivars are 'Bluecrop', 'Blueray', 'Ivanhoe', 'Berkeley', 'Earliblue', 'Darrow' and 'Elizabeth'.

Left Redcurrants are less vigorous than black, and demand a different pruning routine: instead of having whole branches cut out they need new shoots shortened, flowering on spurs on old wood. Their juice in jams and jellies helps them to set.

Below The gooseberry is a species of *Ribes*, like the black and red currants. In cultivation it is more like the latter. It thrives on potash and ripens the best and tastiest fruit in fairly cool conditions. Giant gooseberry-growing used to be a minor English competitive sport: the fruit was totally tasteless.

Loganberries are like long (up to 2 inches) rather acid and firm raspberries borne on long whippy canes like those of the blackberry. The canes flower and fruit in their second year. The routine for managing them is described left.

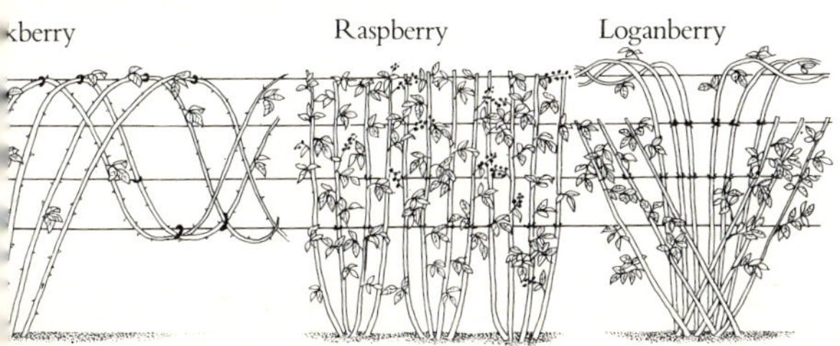

Strawberries, though undeniably soft fruit, are usually grown as part of the vegetable routine and moved every three years or so to newly dug ground. They propagate themselves by sending out runners that root along their length at the tip. If runners which have made good roots are replanted in August in the new bed they will crop the next year, but it is better to pick off the flowers and any new runners and be patient. The following year will be the bumper crop. As soon as the fruit starts to form (but not before) put down a mulch of straw or polythene to keep it off the ground and cover it with bird-netting. When the orgy is over clear up the straw and weeds and cut off all the leaves, and feed the plants with sulphate of potash. "Perpetual" strawberries never have so much fruit at once.

Melons (above 'Dutch Net', below 'Ringleader') need plenty of moisture, but not too much nourishment. A minimum temperature of 60°F (16°C) is needed in the greenhouse or frame. Provided there is enough light they can be grown all year round. The fruit needs support.

Fruit trees

Above The fruit tunnel on an iron frame, a descendant of the medieval arbour, is one of the most charming and practical ways to grow apples or pears as cordons or espaliers. Fairly vigorous rootstocks are needed; growth is controlled by pruning in summer, which also encourages fruit.

Right The traditional orchard of standard apple trees is disappearing in favour of bushes and hedges, which cannot rival it in beauty. These trees are well pruned with open heads to admit light. In gardens such trees are perfect support for climbing roses or clematis, apart from the odd apple.

Above The espalier, with long branches trained horizontally either along wires or against a wall, besides being ornamental is one of the traditional ways of growing apples and pears for intensive production.

Above The fan, trained on wires or against a wall, is slightly easier to achieve than the espalier. It is usually used for peaches, nectarines, plums, cherries and apricots, although apples and pears can also be fan trained.

Above Fig trees are almost impossible to train into tidy symmetry, but some sort of fan against a south-facing wall is the best method. Their roots should be severely restricted to make them crop well.

Above The cordon, a single stem often trained at an angle, is the favourite form of restricted training today as it takes least space. All pruning of cordons is done in summer to avoid stimulating new shoots.

No part of the garden has changed more in this century than what used to be the orchard. The scene pictured above, of spreading standard apple trees, is no longer a domestic one and may soon not be seen in commercial orchards either. The revolution of this century has been the almost universal adoption of dwarfing rootstocks, and with it the chance of squeezing more fruit of more varieties into less space—and also making its management, pruning and picking much easier.

Lovely though the mossy gnarled old apple tree may be, it is a symbol of the past. Where there is room it may well be grown for that very reason. Modern gardeners with little room to spare might do better to be nostalgic about the old standards of craftsmanship that produced such wonders as the illustration above right.

The term "top fruit" applies to apples, pears, plums, cherries, peaches and nectarines: everything that used to be or can be grown on a tree with a trunk. Size-controlling or "dwarfing" rootstocks were classified (at first only for apples) at the fruit research station at East Malling in Kent. Any variety of apple can be grafted on to them and never exceed a predetermined size. They are known by their Malling (or M) numbers: M 27 produces a tree never more than eight feet high; M 9 (the commonest) gives a tree up to ten feet; M 26, M 7 and MM 106 give progressively bigger trees. Quince roots were found to be compatible with pears and made smaller trees than ungrafted pears. Some progress has been made in finding effective dwarfing roots for plums and peaches. Acid (Morello) cherries are always grafted and a manageable size. Sweet ones have long defeated the root experts and remain vigorous trees. But new developments are ready to shrink these too.

In deciding what top fruit to grow the gardener should first look at his local conditions.

The size, form and number of trees will depend on the space,

Above The trade card of a nineteenth-century French fruit nursery demonstrates the skill with which fruit trees were formerly trained. Most here are cordons, either single or multiple (several straight stems from one root) or horizontal (foreground). On the right is an elaborate pyramid. Below the arch is a series of overlapping low fans, another productive form.

Left An autumn exhibit from the Royal Horticultural Society's gardens in 1977 shows that there are still plenty of alternatives to the ubiquitous 'Golden Delicious'. The new techniques of restricted training are making room for more varieties in private gardens and bringing back old names. Britain has a national fruit tree collection which will graft any of 1,880 varieties on demand.

but in small gardens a large variety of very small trees, ideally cordons, is undoubtedly the best policy. Apples in general are least trouble, with no special soil requirements beyond good drainage, generally flowering late enough to escape frost and find enough bees for pollination. But in some districts they are so plagued with bugs that the struggle may not seem worthwhile. Four hundred assorted pests and diseases are said to attack apples in the North Eastern United States.

Pears flower earlier than apples. Late frost is more often a problem. They are generally self-sterile and need another pear tree within a hundred feet. For good crops they also need more nitrogen than do apples. But the chief problem with pears is catching the fruit in its brief moment between greenness and sogginess. 'Comice' and 'Williams' (American 'Bartlett'), though not the easiest to grow, are the most popular because they keep a good texture longest.

Plums, their inferior form damsons and their celestial form gages, also flower early, are often self-sterile, are demanding of space, light, moisture and nitrogen and cannot readily be restricted. Winter pruning brings the risk of disease. Birds, moreover, often entirely strip the buds. The only plum worth growing in a small garden is the best—the gages, which prefer drier soil and more summer warmth than the others. 'Victoria' has the advantage of being self-fertile and also flowering in mid-season, when it can pollinate many others.

Since any trained and restricted fruit takes time and trouble it is logical to choose the most expensive and exotic your conditions will allow. A south-facing wall is an invitation to plant a peach, or better still a nectarine, to train as a fan. Apart from the unavoidable peach leaf curl disease, which means regular spraying with fungicide, a peach is no more difficult to manage than a pear. Success with all fruit lies entirely in appropriate pruning, and where necessary spraying.

Above Modern commercial growers are inclining more and more towards rows of semi-dwarf bushes or cordons grown as a hedge for easy cultivation. Here in France each pear is protected from birds by its individual paper bag.

Above A young apple hedge. Plants on dwarfing rootstocks need permanent staking and generous feeding as the roots themselves are small. Pruning in late summer with electric hedge-shears has proved satisfactory.

Above The "spindle-bush" is an open cone-shaped small tree with its leader permanently staked and branches kept horizontal with string. It is very heavy-cropping in commercial growing but not a pretty form for gardens.

Above The latest idea in fruit-growing is the "meadow-orchard", in which the "trees" are cut right down every second year, then sprayed with a growth retardant as they grow. The second season they crop heavily.

Composing the picture

As every photographer knows, a garden without a strong element of architecture underlying and occasionally emerging from the jumble of plant patterns is a hopeless subject. The eye and the mind both need the reassurance of a firm line somewhere in the picture before they can begin to enjoy the rich diversity of details. In classical gardens the line was provided by vistas, staircases, sculpture, balustrades. In Japan it is natural unsculpted rocks, regarded as the unchanging female principle in contrast to plant growth, the fickle male.

The rock-like element of conscious and finished design is something that is missing from most gardens. Many gardeners will probably say they are happy enough without it; that their pleasure is in growing plants. Yet the best gardens are undoubtedly those with the most coherent and clearly stated theme, or mood, or plan—none of which come by accident.

They were, in fact, designed, either on paper or in someone's head. And in most cases the design was built solidly into the site in the form of walls, paths, hedges and steps, pools and bridges, as the groundwork before the subtler, more transitory furnishing with plants was developed.

Design with plants is the ultimate art of the gardener, but design of the spaces between plants is just as important.

Professional garden designers sometimes shock plant-loving amateurs by specifying with great exactness how high each wall shall be, how wide each bed, and choosing their bricks and paving with extreme care (and at great expense)—then leaving only vague directions about the plants to clothe their engineering. There are, strange to say, effective designers whose plant repertoire is brutally limited and banal. They are effective because they work to a well-thought-out brief. They decide what garden picture they want to achieve, survey what resources are at their disposal, and then apply a series of well-tried principles of design which in the abstract may have an air of unreality, but in practice make all the difference between satisfaction and an uneasy feeling that all is not well.

Humphry Repton, who wrote in the days when abstracts were current coin—and still gives every subsequent writer the feeling that it has all been thought, said and summed up for good—spoke of Unity, Utility and Proportion.

By Unity he meant a consistent theme without jarring incidents. By Utility he intended fitness and likeliness for its purpose: avoidance of the far-fetched. And when he said Proportion he meant keeping the elements in reasonable relative scale—not planting an oak in a rockery.

Unity is the ideal that is very rarely reached—at least by amateur gardeners. There are too many temptations to wander into irrelevant and distracting by-ways. Every magazine article that makes you form a mental picture of another "feature" in your garden is the voice of the devil. Unfortunately it is new features that give most gardeners most fun.

Utility means something much more earthy to us than it did to Repton. Very often it means fitting a quart into a pint pot by concentrating on the utilitarian parts, at the expense of growing all the plants we would like, or indeed of a coherent and pleasing design. The more utilitarian our gardens are, however, the greater the need for fit and suitable materials and a logical, workable plan.

The ideal is a garden that fits the habits of the household and at the same time makes the most of its site; that works as outdoor living space and yet uses the relevant resources of nature to make it beautiful, refreshing and inspiring.

The first part is rarely achieved by amateurs: the second not often by professionals.

A purposeful, deliberate simplicity is immensely effective in garden design. The solid materials used for this path in Westbury Gardens, Long Island, New York are unpretentious brick and rough timber.

The choice of paving

In garden design the cardinal rule is to consider the obvious first. Use the bricks from an unwanted outhouse to pave a path, or timber from an old tree to make a seat. There is a fundamental rightness about using the raw materials of the neighbourhood: stone in places where it lies near the surface and shapes the contours of the land; brick in the clay-bottomed valleys; timber in forest country. Materials cannot be a cliché; only the way they are used.

Since hard surfaces of various kinds are essential, for the drives, the paths to the house doors, the terrace and the main garden paths, and since they loom large in anybody's first impression of the garden, they are worth as much creative thought as the plants round them.

As they will also cost more money than any other essential part of the garden—far more than any plants—they should repay in interest and pleasure, in long life and low upkeep, whatever you spend on them.

Bare, hard, plant-free surfaces have three important functions. The practical one is to provide dry going and prevent summer dust and winter mud from finding its way indoors. The aesthetic ones are to furnish the transition between house and garden, fusing them into one unit; and to stand out in contrast to all the billowing, gesticulating growing things around them, acting as the frame to the picture.

To be functional they must be well-laid, and above all well-drained. Whatever the surface, whether gravel or wood or stone, the paving process should start with the excavation of six inches of soil. If it is good top-soil it is well worth having for other parts of the garden—indeed it would be a crime to bury it under paving.

Into this hole goes four inches or so of rubble, small stones or clinker, or anything hard and permanent that can be made stable by ramming or rolling without packing down solid. For slabs or bricks, a smooth surface of raked sand or fine ashes is needed on top of this.

A path made like this has the added advantage of providing drainage for the garden on either side. If the ground is particularly wet it would be worth excavating a bit deeper and laying land drains in the rubble at the bottom of the hole—thus killing

Above By using the same brick and the same colour of stone as the house this forecourt perfectly fulfils its function of binding house and surroundings together as a unity. The proportions of one material to another are designed to echo the classical rhythm of the English Queen Anne architecture.

Right Marble makes the most formal paving, but only for areas which are free from hard frosts. Having sawn edges the slabs fit together with the finest of joints.

Below The opposite effect is achieved by leaving open joints between irregularly cut slabs.

two birds with one load of stone. The drains would need a slight slope and a ditch or soakaway at the end. The paving needs a camber or gentle tilt too, to prevent puddles.

Given that the choice of surface is influenced by the local geology, there are still opportunities for the imagination in combinations of textures and patterns of laying. The European masters of paving are the Italians, with their marbles of the musical names—Piastraccia, Arabescato, Travertine, Rosso levanto, Carrara, Portoro machia—and their tiles of subtle colours. By using bands and panels of different colours, or perhaps the same material cut to different shapes, they give a terrace or patio the richness of a carpet.

The detail of Japanese garden paving is full of lessons in the vivid handling of simple stone. Stepping-stone paths are used to extraordinary effect, somehow suggesting tentative, even perhaps illicit, traffic. In one famous piece of paving in Kyoto a stepping-stone path accompanies a severe march of rectangular slabs in an interwoven counterpoint, like the flutterings of a geisha round a man of martial calm. In other places a tide of moss seems to be ebbing from a beach of perfect hand-picked pebbles. This may be the poetry of paving, but the prose has no need to be dull. Gravel is the cheapest material both to buy and to lay. Alone and unembellished it has no interest or charm, but give it an edging of two feet of brickwork or stone, or perhaps buried baulks of timber, and the contrast immediately gives it the value it lacked.

There are a dozen different ways of arranging bricks (though they always look better on edge) and they can be banded with stone or concrete or bricks laid a different way. As a general rule two materials or textures are enough—more becomes a muddle.

With rectangular stone or concrete the interest lies in the pattern of joints as well as the colour and texture. They can be regular or all in line, or busily interlocking—and again there can be panels of another material. Concrete with a smooth cement finish is deadly dull, but with the aggregate exposed by brushing before it sets, and with wide joints (perhaps planks on edge) to stop it crazing as it expands, it can have as much personality as stone.

Below Concrete is open to many imaginative uses. This path junction in Arizona uses concrete dressed with irregular cobbles, then with inset logs, then patterned before hardening with an Indian motif. Concrete texture varies according to the aggregate used, and whether the cement is washed off before it sets.

Above Where old naturally worn stones are available one of the most satisfying pavements is a jigsaw of substantial pieces. Stone broken on purpose to make "crazy-paving" is a pathetic parody.

REDWOOD DECKS

The "deck" is one of America's distinctive contributions to garden design, deriving perhaps from the old timber porch but launching out in free shapes into the garden as an easy way of producing levels on sloping ground, at the same time linking indoor and outdoor living areas. Redwood is the perfect timber for the purpose: easily worked, smooth grained and lasting indefinitely. The Californian style of gardening, which has since spread all over the United States, (see pages 234–5) largely depends on the concept of the deck.

Left A chequer pattern of alternating hard and soft materials. This Japanese version is stone and moss. Stone and grass is equally practicable if the stones are set slightly below the level of the turf. Cutting with a rotary mower, rather than a cylinder one, gives the best effect by leaving the grass springy and unrolled.

Above Loose pebbles contrast perfectly with a strip of moss and a patch of gravel. Recently European designers have taken up this Japanese idea and used pebbles extensively as a "labour-saving" groundcover. In reality few things are more laborious than cleaning fallen litter from among the crevices of a pebble beach.

Paths and steps

No single element in the design of a garden is as important as where you put your paths. Once paths are made they dictate, not just to the feet but to the mind, the route to follow, the points from which the planting will be seen, indeed the whole shape of the garden. They are the dynamic element in its structure—the track the eyes move on. Even a path you choose not to follow leads your imagination the way it goes.

Someone once made an analogy between a garden and a golf course. In each case there should be tees from which you survey the scene and drive off, bunkers and rough to waylay you, and greens to arrive at and putt (or potter) on.

Paths are therefore worth thought, observation and experiment. They can emerge naturally from use or they can be imposed according to a plan, but any plan must start by considering who goes where. The first object of a path is a safe dry passage. The groundwork paths of any garden must link the doors of the house to the places people go from them—the front gate, the garage, the greenhouse and the rest.

On the other hand a garden simply criss-crossed with the petrified footsteps of people going about their daily business would be at the same time humdrum and chaotic. The planner's mind must see, if it can, a certain pattern in the necessary routes that can be either regularized or romanticized, according to his intentions for the garden as a whole.

If it is to be based on a rectangular grid with straight lines like the classical gardens of the past, any curving path will look out of place and uncertain. The dictates of geometry make it almost inevitable, too, that a right-angled corner of a lawn or a bed will lie across somebody's urgent path somewhere. A short-cut will soon make itself visible. Better to pave the short-cut, perhaps with stepping stones, and compromise the symmetry of the plan than to have a tell-tale bare patch in the lawn or a hole in the border.

The French view of the English style of curving paths is summed up in what was supposed to be a devastating remark: "On n'a qu'à enivrer son jardinier et à suivre ses pas" (All you need to do is to get your gardener drunk and follow his footsteps).

The curve, now the dominant shape in modern gardens, is far harder to make coherent and convincing; yet it is infinitely more adaptable, and to modern minds more sympathetic. You may still not achieve your bee-line to the garage, but in the spirit of compromise you will not mind turning a gentle corner round a sweet-scented bush.

How many paths should a garden have? In general the answer must be as few as possible—if only to make them look authoritative. Too many look, and make the looker feel, indecisive. Their business is to conduct you to all the best places, and it is just as well if they let you know when you have arrived by bringing you to a landmark; a seat or summer house or a view. Paths should live up to their promises.

It is even more important to be decisive about changing levels. A slight slope is a marvellous opportunity to make the dynamics of the garden work in another dimension. It should be seized and made obvious, at least with a flight of steps, even when the fall is scarcely enough to justify them. From the top you survey the scene below you; from the bottom you are aware of heights above. "Sunk gardens" used to be made to introduce the vertical dynamic in level gardens. They have a value as a psychological incident which is in danger of being forgotten.

With levels as with paths the well-worn division into formal and informal rears its head. Formal, straight-line gardens demand levelling, at least on one axis, with walls supporting the artificial horizontals. Informal gardens are all the better for slopes and undulations—not to mention precipices and ravines—so long as they are properly negotiable by steps.

A formal garden on a steep site demands levelling into terraces to be workable. The actual angle of slope that makes terracing essential is about 30 degrees. Even at a lesser angle you can get the uncomfortable feeling that everything is sliding downhill unless at least a broad level path crosses the slope to "hold" it.

Perhaps the chief reason formality is out of fashion is the cost of the essential groundwork. To "cut and fill"—the technical term for taking earth from one part of the slope and adding it to another—on any scale is a major operation. What complicates it is the fact that top-soil is top-soil and sub-soil is sub-soil in which nothing will grow. If you simply barrow the top-soil from the hump to the hollow you will have double the depth in one place and none in another. To do it properly means taking off all the top-soil first, then cutting and filling the sub-soil, then spreading the top-soil evenly again.

It is also essential, or at least highly desirable, to build a wall to support the upper level. A steep earth bank is one of the hardest spots in the garden to plant and maintain. Grass grows badly and is almost impossible to cut. Shrubs are difficult to establish. A "dry" (or unmortared) stone wall is a wonderful planting opportunity, but a heavy expense unless you live in natural stone country. A brick wall is very formal, as well as expensive (see pages 172–3).

For steps as for paths simplicity and generosity are the secrets of success. Garden steps are not like stairs indoors, trying to climb as fast as possible in as little space as they can manage. The risers should be slight (five inches is ample) and the treads broad—not less than a foot, but more if possible. They should be wide, gradual and substantial in every way. If the height calls for more than a dozen steps it is handsome to have a pause, a landing, perhaps a change of direction. One detail that is always worth while if possible is to give each tread a "nose"—a very slight overhang. The object is to cast a shadow and emphasize the orderly parallels of the treads. The eye looks for such hints of architectural stability in a garden and is strangely satisfied by them.

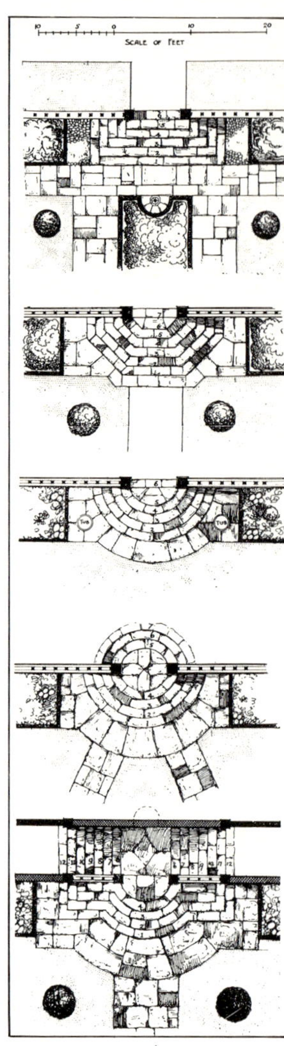

Steps with flair. At the top a flight at Bodnant, N. Wales, with below them a sequence of similar designs from Thomas Mawson's *The Art and Craft of Garden Making*. All follow the principle of fanning the steps out as they descend, an analogy with the eye surveying the prospect below. The bottom two designs, like the picture above, start with recessed steps at the top, giving the flight an ingenious and satisfying symmetry.

Far left The ideal model of a path curving round an artificial obstacle, at the Sento Imperial Palace, Kyoto. The azalea entirely justifies the graceful sweep of gravel.

Left A fine path but an awkward corner apparently needing bamboo rails to stop passengers taking a short cut. A classic example of the Japanese passion for indirectness and asymmetry even when using straight lines. The garden is in the monastery of Daitoku-Ji, Kyoto.

Right How to cut away an awkward slope (in this case the bank of a pond) and substitute an ideal wall for rock plants and a waterside path. A diagram taken from one of Gertrude Jekyll's classic books, *Wall and Water Gardens.*

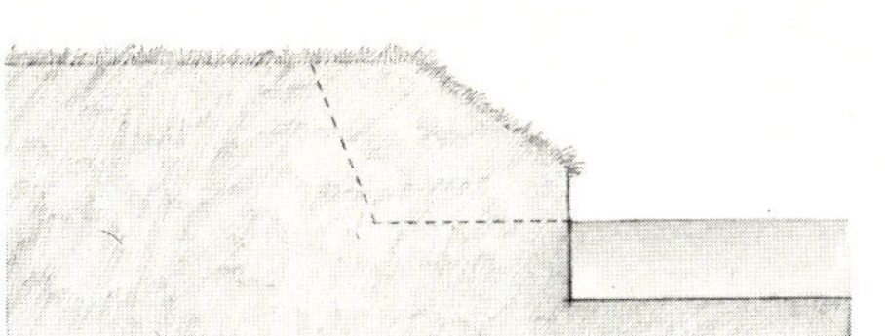

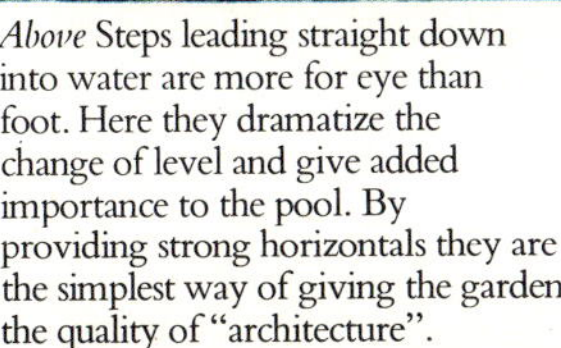

Above Steps leading straight down into water are more for eye than foot. Here they dramatize the change of level and give added importance to the pool. By providing strong horizontals they are the simplest way of giving the garden the quality of "architecture".

Below A mere indication of a path by mowing a swathe of short grass through long is enough to attract the imagination and suggest pleasures beyond. The emergence of the path from under the shade of the trees into sunlight adds to the seductive effect.

Above The virtue of emphasizing slight changes of level. In Emilio Pucci's garden in Italy, designed by Miss Aulenti, an intriguing and entirely satisfying landscape is made by straightening the contours and marking them with ribbons of stone. The eye is led inexorably towards the distant swimming pool, which seems to be coming or going round a corner: a good example of implied movement—the "dynamics" of garden design.

Left The informal equivalent of the steps and pool shown above left, using a curve to help the steps climb unusually steeply. Their dry-stone construction allows self-sown snow-in-summer and *Erigeron* to soften and romanticize the architecture.

Walls and fences

Right A fence that combines being a barrier with some of the quality of sculpture. Telegraph-pole sections of random lengths are concreted into the ground to form a strange stockade. An example of the sort of initiative that is essential with the modern price of traditional garden building materials.

Walls have in the past been so basic to gardens that their sudden transformation into expensive luxuries beyond most gardeners' reach has had a devastating effect on design and techniques. All the books that make casual reference to the protection afforded by south-facing walls have taken on an increasingly poignant tone as the cost of simple bricks and mortar has moved inexorably from the unpleasant to the impossible.

The only walls in most gardens today are the walls of the house and perhaps of the garage. A lucky few still have old garden walls. For the rest the realistic choice is between hedges or barriers of plants, and the range of fences and screens which are the miserable modern substitute for bonded brickwork or morticed stone.

The virtues of walls are not just nostalgic imaginings. They are the appropriate symbol and the actual provider of the shelter and privacy which are proper to a garden. Aesthetically there can be no question that the air of permanence about a wall is a basic garden need. It cannot be met by a fence, which at best looks temporary; at worst rickety and improvised. To provide the look of permanence a hedge is the best substitute. But a hedge takes years to mature. It also deprives the gardener of the great horticultural virtues of a wall: its foot and its surface as the place to nurture plants that need protection, and the warmth that brick or stonework stores long after the sun has gone down.

It is all the more essential then to make the best use of what walls we have, not wasting them on plants that would be equally happy in open ground. Fruit-trees, such climbers as roses that can excel themselves in the extra warmth, shrubs of doubtful hardiness and bulbs that need a summer baking all clamour for a south- or west-facing wall. Even north- and east-facing walls have a degree of protection to offer and suit many woodland climbing plants. The one important proviso to bear in mind is that walls exposed to strong prevailing winds develop powerful up, down and side draughts. Climbers, clingers and wall-trees are good for baffling the wind and protecting soft plants below; but they must themselves have sturdy anchorage in the form of well-fixed wires or trellis.

If high boundary walls are at an absurd premium, at least low edging walls still remain a possibility as scaled-down shelter for smaller plants and bulbs. In country where stone is available, dry-stone walls up to three or four feet are not unduly expensive or difficult to erect. Built with thorough and efficient drainage but packed with good soil they can combine the growing conditions of a rock garden and the lee of a sheltering wall.

There will be places, though, in every modern garden where there is no alternative to a fence. No room (and perhaps no time) for a hedge or a group of shrubs; perhaps a desire to grow climbers or fruit trees. It is worth remembering that solid fences are inevitably more expensive, needing more timber, and almost always uglier than see-through ones. Is it really essential to provide a total barrier? Or will a half-open one have virtually the same effect at a distance? It does not take a fortress wall to define a boundary. The job can be done with a mere visual hint: a row of posts will do it, if a boundary is all you need. If the boundary must be a barrier without a chink then close-boarding may be the unavoidable answer.

With all garden constructions boldness, honesty and simplicity are essential virtues. With most they are also expensive. Fences are no exception. Flimsy matchboard is both ugly and a waste of money: you need the thickest timber you can afford, supported by the strongest uprights.

If you must save somewhere, save on the infilling, but invest in posts that will see you out. By exaggerating the proportions of the posts you will help to give the essential character of permanence and fitness to the whole fence.

Above The sense of enclosure and privacy of a beautiful old garden wall is emphasized by the device of a peep-hole. The local building material in this part of Sussex is flint with brick facings.

In practice no fence stands for ever: however well-cured the timber, the panels or planks will begin to deteriorate and need renewing after five or ten years, depending on the quality of the wood and the dampness of the climate and exposure of the site. One way of preserving and also giving character to a fence which is certainly worth considering—especially in a town garden—is painting it. An imaginative, not a lurid, colour on the fence might be the starting point for colour schemes within the garden.

Nobody has studied fencing with such care and inventiveness as the Japanese. Although permanence is not a quality they particularly respect—even their houses are essentially temporary constructions—they give their fences character and authority by using bold details. They add a deep cap or cornice, or contrasting panels of bamboo and bark, or hold them together with elaborate knots.

This sort of inventiveness and courage is the only answer for gardeners who can no longer afford the first-class materials that were once used as a matter of course in laying out the ground-work of a garden.

Right Up to the end of the seventeenth century walls were practical necessities against deer, cattle and rabbits as well as boundaries of the garden. The invention of the ha-ha or sunk fence made it possible to pretend that the whole landscape was part of the gardener's domain.

Above Original and bizarre materials can be extremely effective in producing a sophisticated and urbane atmosphere. This garden with its walled plant-containers of painted ceramic tiles overlook the sea in Monte Carlo.

Below An unusual dry (a term for any unmortared) wall made of close-fitting granite paving setts with pockets of soil left for plants that will appreciate the warm, dry conditions. Planting in a wall is ideal for rosette plants.

Above Woodland plants appreciate the protection and shade of a north-facing wall, which also has the advantage of back-lighting, particularly effective for such pale plants as Bowles's golden grass, here with *Tiarella cordifolia, Euphorbia epithymoides* and *Mahonia moseri*.

Left A plain close-boarded fence, weathered to a pleasant grey, makes a homely background for roses (left, 'Etude'; right, 'Copenhagen') that deserve something better.

Above Dense cascades of aubrieta completely mask the construction of a dry-stone wall—a point to bear in mind where stone is expensive.

Left The serpentine or crinkle-crankle wall is a tradition in certain parts of England, particularly Suffolk. The curves allegedly give extra protection to the fruit trees, and the wall, though longer, can be built one brick instead of two bricks thick—a slight net saving.

Screens and frames

Above A frame concentrates the eyes on the picture: the disappearing lawn makes exploration irresistible. In Graham Thomas's former garden in Surrey.

Right A filigree summer house without roof or walls makes the lush planting feel like invading jungle.

Below Treillage, the art of building apparently substantial architecture with flimsy trellis, was highly developed in eighteenth-century France. Its revival (*below right*) is overdue.

It is a fundamental of good garden design to provide both a sense of direction and a motive for movement: to lure the visitor from one scene to another, so that however delightful he finds the spot where he is, something compels him to explore farther. The sense of curiosity should always be awake. Leaving a door ajar, either literally or metaphorically, is the simplest way of arousing it.

Thus the gate, the archway, the frame, the transparent screen, the division that does not divide have an important part to play in gardens. These pages show a few of the infinity of variations on this theme.

The garden above demonstrates the principle to perfection. The foreground is the terrace behind a house. The pillars, with their simple cross-beam supporting roses, frame a broad walk between varied plants that call for closer examination and enjoyment. This is the invitation. The fall of light on the walk intensifies the feeling of "out there".

If you could see the other end of the lawn the effect would be weakened, if not lost. The picture would be complete in itself; there would be no further need to investigate. But the lawn curves away out of sight. Thus the frame draws your attention to the view, but the door is only half-way open: there is more to be seen round the corner.

The power of suggestion is strong. It is enough to place two pillars or plant two cypresses athwart a path for the mind to accept that a new space starts. In the same way a barrier needs no strength to stop the mind. No more than a feather-weight hurdle is needed to provide a sense of the limits to an area. Simply by laying in the way a small stone tied up with rope

Left Patterns of fencing can suggest trim domesticity (*left*) or (*right*) public dignity. The painted fence, with such slight extra finish as finials on the posts, can be an economical way of defining spaces with style and authority.

Right A Japanese garden archway conveys a powerful feeling of an even more desirable world beyond. It is conceived entirely as a picture frame: there is no path—the moss is barely trodden. Its massive construction emphasizes the delicacy of leafy sprays while its red doors link it with the turning leaves.

Above Wrought-iron gates have a peculiar way of making the scene beyond inviting: enclosing yet revealing. Although these gates are made of modern light strip iron the strong pattern of curves of thicker metal at the top gives them the necessary sense of solidity.

the Japanese close a path to traffic. It is enough. The eye is adept at picking up pointers provided by anything placed in rows, and the feet can be compelled by the simple repetition of a pleached walk or any regular planting.

Even light alone can be an effective form of invitation. A pool of light, like a clearing in a forest, draws the feet irresistibly. On page 202 is an example where the effect is achieved with beds of low pale flowers among tall dark greenery.

One of the most remarkable examples of the power of suggestion is the art of *treillage*: making bogus architecture with flimsy trelliswork. The power of making light batons suggest massive masonry reached perfection in eighteenth-century France. It is still absurdly easy to trick the eye with false perspectives made of trellis on a flat background. Alcoves and arcades imitated in trellis laid flat on a wall are effective in pushing out the oppressive limits of small town gardens.

This is not to impute virtue to flimsiness or lack of genuine solidity. A look of impermanence is one of the worst faults of most modern garden hardware. Fences, gates, seats, summer-houses all look as though they were only intended to last a season. Economy with materials is not a crime, but it must be honest economy; not the bent strip metal that passes for wrought iron today. Real wrought iron is a totally different thing; richly three-dimensional, involving whole plates and bars of metal. It is better to avoid such materials altogether than to use them meanly. Failing the solid underpinnings a garden really needs to give it its sense of sure foundation it is better to achieve what you can with flights of fancy and imagination—the art of horticultural theatre.

Above A pleached lime walk is a traditional garden barrier by suggestion rather than physical fact. Views between and among its stilt-like trunks are given heightened interest. Pleaching is done by tying together young side branches of neighbouring trees in one flat plane and cutting off or pruning back all the others that point in the wrong direction.

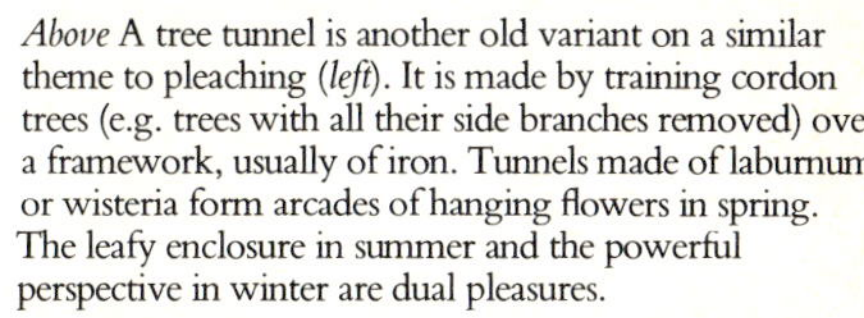

Above A tree tunnel is another old variant on a similar theme to pleaching (*left*). It is made by training cordon trees (e.g. trees with all their side branches removed) over a framework, usually of iron. Tunnels made of laburnum or wisteria form arcades of hanging flowers in spring. The leafy enclosure in summer and the powerful perspective in winter are dual pleasures.

Above An ingenious alternative to the "screen wall", often made of pierced blocks, is made by training ivy along ropes or chains stretched between posts. The ivy is clipped yearly to keep the interstices open, giving a leafy frame to the view beyond.

Above Movable lightweight wickets or hurdles have great possibilities in gardens for blocking a path and suggesting a different route for a different time of year. It gives pleasure by being in contrast, yet in harmony, with the surrounding natural plant forms.

Pots and vases

Above Hanging wire baskets, lined with moss and filled with a not-too-sandy compost, can support a spectacular display. Here the mixture is geraniums with various annuals.

Right An eccentric choice of containers for a mixed collection of house plants, annual marigolds and a hardy chrysanthemum.

Below A cluster of flower pots at the door of Great Dixter, Sussex, bringing together the complementary colours of lilies and cornflowers.

To separate flowers from the ground by growing them in pots, vases or hanging baskets has the effect of singling them out for special attention.

There are many good reasons for doing this. There may be no ground to grow flowers in—the apartment-dweller's perennial problem. The plants may be tender, needing winter protection. They may be plants that have but one brief season of glory and are best kept out of sight at other times. They may be rampant, running-rooted plants that need severe restriction. They may be demanding and difficult, needing special soil conditions you cannot provide in the garden. Or they may simply be exquisite, favourite plants that you want near the eye. Or there may be a place in the garden where it is worth taking the extra trouble for the extra emphasis.

Pots do cost extra trouble. It is almost always easier to grow anything in the ground than in a container, which presents its own cultural difficulties—of which by far the most considerable is the need for regular watering and feeding.

There are four factors which taken together can help to ensure success. The first is that the container should be suitable. Leaving aside the aesthetics—and tastes vary, as these pages show, from second-hand sarcophagi to cast-off paint pots—the essentials are that the container is big enough for a healthy year's growth of roots and shoots, but not so big that soil lies stagnant and unused outside the root zone. Drainage should really come first. Never think that you can give the pot a good topping-up that will last a long weekend. The water must flow through the soil, not lie in it. Ample drainage holes and rubble to help the water on its way are essential for all but a very few, basically aquatic, plants.

The second factor is that the plant is suitable. Although almost any plant can be grown in a pot the sensible kind to choose is one with a well-developed will to live. Legend has it that the aspidistra became the predominant pot plant of Victorian drawing rooms because its jungle training gave it an immunity to the combined fumes of gas-lights and coal-fires. There is good reason for the popularity of pelargoniums, fuchsias, begonias, petunias, ivy, oleanders and the other predictable pot plants you can think of—they can tolerate occasional forgetfulness. But nothing can tolerate total neglect.

A third essential is suitable soil. Rarely, if ever, will it be found in the garden. Considerable research has taken place recently into ideal potting mixes. Some, especially in the USA, now contain no "soil" at all, but a mixture of peat and perlite or cooked clay with slow-release fertilizers. For most purposes a standard potting compost of two parts of sterilized garden soil ("loam"), to one each of peat and coarse sand (or perlite) is right. The soil and peat hold the moisture and nutrients while the peat and sand keep the mixture "open". When plants (trees for example) are to stay in containers for long periods, perlite and its equivalents are more stable than peat or humus, which break down and compact before long. Plants, particularly house plants, tend to be sold in an almost pure peat mixture, which is far from ideal for outdoor containers: it dries out rapidly and is almost impossible to re-wet.

The fourth consideration is where you put the containers. It is easy to imagine that because a plant is in a container it somehow leads an independent existence. But sun, shade and wind matter to it more, not less, than to other plants because its roots as well as its top are subjected to extremes.

Direct southern summer sunshine can be very damaging. At 90°F the roots stop functioning effectively. At least partial shade is essential. At the other extreme roots that are considered winter-hardy in the ground may not be so in a pot, which freezes and thaws more rapidly. Position the pots, in other words, with even more care than you would the plants in open ground.

Left Few things are more welcoming than a front door flanked with pots of flowers. Any of the annuals shown on pages 120–1 or bedding plants on pages 122–3 are suitable, but the aspect of the entrance is important. Choose flowers suitable for the degree of sun and shade it gets. Geraniums are always a safe choice.

Below Permanent planting in a vase can be very effective if the plant and container are chosen to complement one another. A low dense-growing purple-leaved *Sedum spathulifolium purpureum* forms a perfect companion for a shallow white-stone vase. Sedums are easy to establish and need very little maintenance.

Above This watercolour of the turn of the century by the English artist Margaret Waterfield shows one of the favourite pot flowers of the period, *Campanula pyramidalis*, the chimney bell-flower. It is grown as a biennial, sown in spring for the summer of the following year.

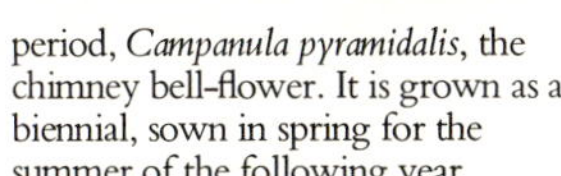

Above A narrow bed of foliage plants, mainly hostas, at the foot of a wall can look two-dimensional. A vase with a similar plant against the wall adds depth as well as variety, making the wall appear further away.

Above The clematis in this glade is detached from the ground as though it were growing in a container. But in reality it is planted under an old mill-stone and grows up from the cool shade it prefers through a hole in the stone.

Left An elaborate Byzantine or Venetian sarcophagus makes a rich centrepiece for a group of grey and white plants in containers. In the foreground a white agapanthus grows in an Italian lemon-pot. Agapanthus gradually expands and may eventually break the pot.

Above Old carved stone sinks and troughs are nowadays in great demand for growing alpine plants. Never again will there be such a collection as Valerie Finnis photographed in a yard in Northamptonshire more than twenty years ago.

Above A cylinder of earthenware with pierced sides sloping in towards its top, sitting in a fitted dish, though technically known as a strawberry pot (they are planted on top and the runners are rooted in the holes) is a good way of growing parsley by the kitchen door.

Statues and seats

Below An eighteenth-century swain who never expected to find himself the focal point of a twentieth-century garden. He stands silhouetted against open fields and sky. Many such figures in modern gardens symbolize trite nostalgia. This jaunty figure and his unusual new context do something quite different.

Of the many ways of directing or compelling attention in a garden the most peremptory is the statue. It is possible to be aware of planting, and proportions, and even architecture without focusing on it. A statue is a command to look. The human figure above all compels us.

In just the opposite way a seat is an invitation; a suggestion. It invites you to pause and turn round; implies that you have come far enough and should review what you have seen; lures you to rest.

Both are signposts which can be used skilfully to define or reinforce the structure of the garden—or heedlessly stuck in at any convenient or conspicuous place.

Sir Francis Bacon was anti-statue. He had clearly had his fill. "They are for state and magnificence; but nothing to the true pleasure . . . of a garden." Anyone submitted to the relentless idolatry of Italian and quasi-Italian gardens of the sixteenth century might have been forgiven for agreeing.

Yet Sir George Sitwell, whose essay on gardens has as much philosophy and true understanding as Bacon's, argues most powerfully that statues "compel attention, stir imagination, strengthen memory, banish the consciousness of self and all trivial and obsessive thoughts".

The danger of statuary is that nowadays it is often a mere half-baked reminiscence of a dead period. An enormous quantity of statuary has passed through the gardens of history. For a long period it encompassed some of the very greatest works of art, and countless copies of them so good as to be precious in themselves. Very few of these survive: weather eventually destroys lead and marble. Those that do remain have the quality of splendid antiques, with enough presence to dominate any garden scene. In such cases the garden should be made round the statue.

Below Garden seats should always look permanent, deliberately placed and rooted to the spot, whether like the solid throne (*left*) with the authority of a judgement seat, or the elegant confection of painted iron beside it, which is too entwined in honeysuckle to move. The third from left, though portable, has a solid simplicity that suggests permanence. Those with overarching bowers, whether of vegetation or carpentry, invite meditation or flirtation. That of cold stone (*far right*) is not so much for use as to draw the visitor's attention to the view.

Below Modern sculpture in the classic context of an eye-catcher in an avenue. The bronze, by the British sculptor Bernard Meadows, is partly polished to add the dimension of reflection. It reflects both parts of itself and its surroundings, linking the two in surprising ways and involving the spectator in the scene.

Unfortunately mass-produced copies of a few favourites (which for some reason are never the best) have become commonplace. In the same sense in which original works of art are alive and add their peculiar vibrations to the scene, familiar copies are dead. As Sylvia Crowe says in *Garden Design*: "It cannot be the genius of the place if it has already been seen in the same role elsewhere."

It is possible to find a new way of using an old statue to make a fresh point. The photograph above left proves it. But luckily the problem is being solved by a new generation of sculptors who have found new ways of creating the essential tension. Where these are abstracts, they have an obvious relationship with the natural rocks which the Chinese and Japanese have admired for so long.

In very small gardens abstract sculpture or *objets trouvés* have particular value. Where a figure would dominate a small yard, and give the feeling of an alien presence, a beautifully shaped stone, or an enigmatic form of metal, perhaps reflecting the light (an idea totally foreign to classical sculpture) has the opposite effect: liberating the imagination and hence enlarging the apparent space.

Detached pieces of architectural detail can have the same effect. Such things as columns or pieces of architrave out of context and out of scale often have great presence. By being surprisingly, almost shockingly, big in a small space they will distract attention from the confining walls and make the area seem larger than it is.

Abstract sculpture also invites you to consider the surrounding plants as abstracts—or rather as sculpture. It tends, however, to ask for plants of bold and distinct draughtsmanship—such things as yuccas, phormiums, grasses or a fig tree. On the whole it is not friendly to flowers.

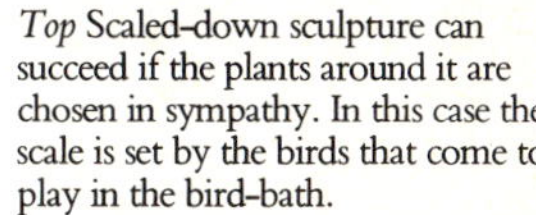

Top Scaled-down sculpture can succeed if the plants around it are chosen in sympathy. In this case the scale is set by the birds that come to play in the bird-bath.

Above left The idea of figures playing in a fantasy world of their own gives the onlooker the role of voyeur. Garden sculpture is rarely as fresh and original as these Victorian figures at Twickenham.

Above A monumental chimney pot treated as sculpture combines the attributes of architecture and abstract. Its placing and the planting round it are both done with exceptional care.

The many moods of water

Below The quintessence of cool shade: the canal at Buscot Park, Berkshire, dropping in slow degrees through a narrowing glade to a lake, is one of the most successful formal water gardens made in this century. The designer was Harold Peto, one of the last garden architects to work in the old formal manner.

The greatest asset a garden can have—greater than four feet of natural potting compost or a view of Mont Blanc—is a permanent stream. Water wakes up a garden. It is the one element which is biddable, to paint pictures and evoke moods at will.

The first gardens were water gardens. In desert countries, indeed, gardens are simply celebrations of places where water is plentiful and it is possible to grow trees to create shade and be cool. But water is scarcely less valuable in climates of perpetual mist for the liveliness and drama a foaming cascade or a mossy weir can bring to the scene.

The range of water's moods is one of the gardener's greatest opportunities. By merely lying in a placid pond it paints a patch of sky on the ground, throwing the light up again and reflecting the clouds, the blue, the colours of the flowers or the green shade of trees. Then the wind stirs and the ripples race, or dance, and another naiad takes charge.

In movement its moods range from the clockwork monotony of a drip to the varied cadences of a cascade or the proud plumes of a fountain. Any manifestation of water, however small, gives a garden life. It need be no more than the little tinkling dribble that runs into a hollow stone at the gate of every Japanese garden—a perfect symbol for the refreshment of the spirit that waits inside.

An unexpected sidelight on the value of fountains and cascades has emerged recently in research into why the hot dry winds of southern Europe, blowing from North Africa, have an irritating and depressing effect—as indeed they do. They are charged, it appears, with positive ions, which seem temporarily to alter the chemistry of the brain. The same research suggests that the air around breaking water, on the seashore, under waterfalls and around fountains, is charged with negative ions, which may have the opposite effect: of soothing and giving a sense of well-being.

The Japanese are the masters of garden water. In most of their classical gardens, tucked under the mountain slopes of Kyoto, running water is plentiful. Where there is none, garden designers feel it is so essential that they pretend it is there, making waterfalls of stone and dry stream-beds of sand.

So sensitive are the Japanese to the behaviour of water and its messages to the senses that not even a shower of rain is wasted. The guttering is arranged so that rain becomes an entertainment. As you sit quietly on the matting watching the drops glistening on the pine needles, or weighing down the tall bamboos in graceful arcs of green, the sound of water, splashing, pattering, gurgling and running, rises to a climax with the shower.

Rather than pushing it hastily away into a hole the gardener is playing games with it. The water from one bamboo gutter glides into the open top of a vertical cane, to splash out below on to a casually placed rock and form a tiny lake, suggested by a dip in the gravel with mossy sides. Another gutter is of bronze hoops down which the water leaps and glistens into a brimming stone basin. Water from a third is made to shoot into a bronze hopper with a ringing sound.

The Japanese live on rainy islands, yet instead of turning their backs on rain as commonplace they revel in it as a sensuous experience. This is the secret of using water, as it is of using plants.

The best example in Europe of the exploitation of every aspect of wateriness is the fourteenth-century Moorish garden of the Generalife, brilliantly sited on a hill above Granada in the route of the snow-water from the Sierra Nevada down to the plain. The limitless water pressure is ingeniously controlled so that while the flow in one place is headlong, in another it ambles along or bubbles with gentle persistence. The famous staircase with liquid handrails is often mentioned: you trail your fingers in a miniature cascade on each side of the stairs. The most postcarded hydraulics of all are the arching jets over the narrow canal in the Patio de la Riadh. But there are scores of other tricks. In one courtyard a natural-looking cave in the hill, curtained with creepers, hides a spring in its mossy roof, constantly dripping water on to ferny rocks. In another a deep stone tank of curious form catches five arcs of crystal water. Before a cloister of creamy stone, honeycomb-roofed, the nipple of a marble font pours out a quiet insistent stream.

Most telling of all, when you have passed through court after court to the brow of the hill, where the ground appears to plunge directly from an alabaster look-out hundreds of feet to the town below, your eye falls, not to the valley floor, but to the little box-hedged garden within speaking distance beneath your feet. From the centre of the garden rises a single sparkling jet to intercept your view of the world of dust.

The spouts and mossy shelves of the Villa d'Este, the preposterous hydraulics of Versailles, the calm lakes of Capability Brown are all great set-pieces of garden waterworks. But the possible moods are endless. It used to be thought very funny to squirt visitors with sudden jets—particularly up ladies' skirts. Water could be droll. It can equally be dignified: nothing adds to the dignity of a building so much as its reflection in a looking-glass of water at its feet.

The only mistake which is often and easily made is to confuse the artfully natural with the frankly artificial. All garden waterworks can be divided into the formal, which includes all pools of regular shape, all fountains and any water in a situation where it clearly could not arrive by itself, and the informal, which can only look right if the mind can accept that it flowed there of its own accord.

Above Many Italian gardens have such flourishes of water, spouting and tumbling in joyful wetness. The Villa d'Este at Tivoli, near Rome, has perhaps the finest collection of waterworks of them all.

Right Water is specially apt for jokes: something usually missing in gardens. The classical Japanese dragon spouting water is comically satirized by this absurd frog.

Below The hand-rinsing basin at the entrance to a silk-merchant's garden in Kyoto. Even such a miniature water garden breathes coolness and refreshment. Visitors to the garden pause to rinse their hands and faces, ritually preparing themselves for the unseen pleasures that await them in the garden.

Above St Petersburg's eighteenth-century fountains were designed to glitter even under a cold northern sky. The figures are gilded, the jets fine and sparkling. All greenery is excluded.

Right The formal cascade is an Italian idea, linking waterfalls and architecture to superb effect. These gardens at the Villa Cicogna in Lombardy have remained unaltered since the sixteenth century.

Ponds and streams

Below A stream need be no more than a foot-wide channel through the turf. This one, lined with concrete, carries the water from one pool to another. The cascade in the background is reproduced in the drawing below. In the foreground is a miniature weir of small stones set in the concrete bed.

"Plant the hills and flood the hollows" is perhaps the best-known maxim ever uttered by a landscape gardener. The likeliest fault with naturalistic gardening is that it will look unnatural. A pond will look unnatural anywhere but at the lowest point in the garden.

It will also look unnatural if there is an abrupt drought by the brink. A formal lily pond can stand in crisp turf and look correctly neat. But if we are to pretend that the water is there of its own accord then the surroundings, or part of them, must look wet as well. This is the principal difficulty in making a naturalistic or informal pond look real without a stream to feed it.

To garden by a constant stream is a happy state few gardeners achieve. I labour on with pumps and pipes (which, incidentally, are the greatest fun) while studying the successes of my riparian friends. It seems to me the finest effects are always made by damming the stream to obstruct its flow and widen it into pools. The pools provide deeper water (with possibilities for fish) and a constant margin, which makes planting much easier, while the abrupt changes in level at the dams, or weirs, or cascades provide movement, drama and soothing sound.

Again the best effects are made by people who do not overdo the planting—either in the water or on the bank. Two-thirds of the water surface at least should be clear of plants to form a simple mirror. And a good proportion of the brink should be clear, too, particularly on the near, or viewing, side. It is too easy to let the rushes, the reeds or the irises get a hold and hide the margin, and a good part of the water. The most brilliant dodge I have seen for avoiding this without constant cutting back of rampant growth (this was in a big natural pool) is steps—flight after flight of them, appearing from every angle among the reeds and mysteriously descending into the deep as if to meet King Arthur.

There are of course natural ponds without streams, but these present the same problem as unnatural ponds. Above all the banks dry out in summer. To garden satisfactorily round any pond, in fact, you must be able to keep it brimming full and, at least now and then, slightly overflowing. If you have no stream and no spring then you must have recourse to a hosepipe.

Happily small pumps give us a means of making a big splash with a meagre supply of water by recirculating it. The natural affinity of rock to water, coupled with modern pumps, has given rise to a new style of gardening, one might say the most positive and creative contribution of this century to small gardens in places without natural advantages. For given rock rising sheer from the water the idiom is immediately rockery or alpine rather than water-meadow or bog. Copious supplies of water are not needed to keep margins wet, except here and there for a patch of primulas. Admitting the unlikeliness of an outcrop of rock and a spring in a small back garden, by borrowing a little of the imagination of the Japanese one can accept a good garden in this style as a miniature landscape with its own laws, naturalistic at one remove from the strictly natural.

Since water is in short supply, the first requirement is to make the pond watertight. The old formula used to be puddled clay; that is heavy clay rammed and trampled down in a foot-thick layer that no water would ever pass. But there is no mechanical method of clay puddling. Today's materials are either concrete or plastic or butyl rubber sheeting. Concrete is the surest and most permanent, the least obtrusive, the most adaptable and subject to the finest adjustments. It is also the most expensive and time-taking to lay. Four inches is the minimum safe thickness. Sheeting of any kind is simple to put down (on a smooth stoneless bed so that no stones can puncture it). But it remains subject to puncture, and it presents you with a problem round the edge: what do you do with the necessary rim just above the water-line? It is not easy to arrange marginal paving and plants so that no sheeting is visible anywhere—and even a glimpse has a sharply disillusioning effect.

Whatever the lining material it is wise to have no right-angled corners. Curves are easier to clean. With concrete it is prudent to have shelving sides so that ice can expand upwards and not force the walls out. With all ponds it is useful to have a sump—a distinct low point in the bottom—to make pumping out easier. Indeed a small pond could usefully have a plug leading to a drain or soak-away. Two feet is plenty deep enough.

The shape of a pond under construction looks decisive and immutable. In practice it is not so important. So long as there is a good water-holding shell the shape of the water surface can be altered at will by building low walls inside it. The little wiggly-edged ready-made plastic pools sold by garden centres are as unnecessary as they are repulsive. A simple rectangle can be turned into a "natural" shape by walls retaining soil inside the pond. On the principle that too many marginal plants spoil the view of the water, however, it is best to start with roughly the final shape, then adapt it with plants either in the water or overhanging it from the banks. The plants for these places are discussed on pages 138 to 143.

More important than the shape is the level. All ponds look best brimming full. To have concrete (or worse plastic) bank showing above the water-line mars all. If the pond is to have an outflow to a stream, a cascade or another pond the height of this weir is your determining factor. The weir should be wide and shallow, not narrow and deep, to hold back as much water as possible. If the levels of the rest of the bank are carefully kept with a spirit level and the final height of the spillway is left till last it should be possible to have the pond filled to the brim and just running over at the weir.

If possible a water garden that strives to look natural, even on its own terms, should be screened or set apart from the rest of the garden. If it has rocks, they can provide a spring show of alpines. Summer will bring on the waterside plants and floating water-lilies. At all seasons there can be fine leaves of every imaginable shape, size and hue and in winter the glowing stems of dogwood and willow. But brilliantly coloured bedding plants, above all bedding roses, should be kept out of sight. Both the pond and the bedding would look banal and absurd in juxtaposition. Even in falsifying—perhaps most of all in falsifying—it is vital to preserve integrity.

STREAM GARDENING

A cross-section to show the principles of a naturalistic stream garden where there is no real stream. The less water there is, the more it needs to be shown off, so this stream starts with a short cascade from a little pool perched among rocks, then drops three feet over an overhang to fall clear and splashing into the main watercourse. The stream is lined with four-inch thick concrete and held back at intervals by concrete weirs, disguised by rocks, to keep a good depth and a steady flow. The deeper ponds are suitable for fish and plantings of water-lilies and other water plants. A small electric pump in the bottom returns the water to the top at the rate of four gallons a minute, though even one gallon a minute makes a respectable splash.

Above A convincing artificial weir in the Royal Horticultural Society's rock garden at Wisley, Surrey. Water-worn limestone rocks convey the impression that the water level is often higher at times of flood. Ferns in the rock crevices add a final touch of realism.

Below Consummate stream-gardening at the Imperial Palace, Kyoto. Clear water over pebbles, with an artificial pebble beach and mock jetty suggesting that a boat might come round the corner at any time. Deep shade is provided by overhanging evergreens.

Above The dark trunks of willows reflected in a still pool epitomize the spirit of natural water-gardening. The planting is lush but casual. The addition of more colour would spoil the effect of tranquil calm. The surface of the pond is free from congestion, leaving a simple mirror.

Below A rockwork cascade built as a showpiece for the Chelsea Flower Show. A lesson in placing natural rocks and blending plants and water together. A powerful pump, however, is required to continuously circulate many gallons of water a minute.

The mouth of the pipe is hidden by rocks to look like a spring.

A precisely level margin is vital, the pond should be full to the brim with none of the lining showing. The height of the weirs is the simple way to adjust the depth.

Stepping stones can be supported on bricks. They should be as close to water level as possible.

The vast variety of suitable stream-side plants is discussed on pages 138 to 141. The banks should be very slightly lower where the ground is to be wet so that a weekly topping up with a hose will reach the plants.

In small ponds strong-growing water-plants are best planted in baskets to restrict their growth.

Pools and fountains

Below and right The formal use of water implies geometry, whether traditional, as at Knightshayes Court, Devon, or innovative, as in this sculptural aqueduct in Denmark. In both cases the water is deliberately framed to stand out and be admired rather than merge into a lush landscape.

A formal pool is quite a different proposition. Here you are not borrowing or recreating the picturesque passage of the hydrological cycle (page 10). You are frankly decorating with water. The emphasis is not on its natural life but on its capacity to reflect, to glitter, splash or cool.

There will be no question of making the pool fit in with the landscape: its purpose is to stand out. An improbable site is all to the good. One of the simplest ways of emphasizing a pool is to raise the water level above the ground: to make it a walled tank. The reflections, being nearer the eye and at an unexpected angle, make more impact than if they are lying tamely at your feet. The famous tank garden at Hidcote carries this principle to an extreme. Almost the whole of a circular yew-hedged enclosure is taken up with a waist-high stone tank, brimming full. Walking round it, running your fingers through the surface, you are intensely aware of the circle of sky framed by the yews, just at your side.

Sir George Sitwell studied the Italian use of water and described some of its effects in his great essay *On the making of Gardens*, "Water-reflections", he wrote, "are actually more delightful than the views they repeat . . . for the gloss of the water-film is like the coat of old varnish that mellows a picture; like the twilight it gives breadth, connection and unity."

Clearly the pool must have something pleasant to reflect. Good architecture makes the best reflections of all. The modern house that is worth reflecting, however, is rare. This is where small figures, statues, pergolas and the tracery of nearby trees are all-important. Half the point of all the balustrades and nymphs and putti round Italian pools is their doubling in the water. Then suddenly "that strange power the eye has of clearing away reflections by the change to a longer focus" shows us the fishes and the submerged plants and their shadows on the bottom.

With formal pools the water is the point; not the plants. There must be plants, and fish, or the water will stagnate (see the panel opposite). Water-lilies have all the qualities of sculptured formality you could want. But they must not be allowed to get out of hand. At least two-thirds of the surface should be open water. It is possible to use only underwater plants and have a clean and healthy pool, but difficult without some degree of shade: constant sunlight promotes the growth of green plankton or algae. Without competition they can make the water too green.

It is better to avoid waterside or water-related plants at the margin: better to emphasize the architecture of the edge and move smartly to grass or plants of contrasting character. Perhaps a single clump of iris or reed, a sudden vertical, will emphasize the strong horizontal of the water. Perhaps, on the contrary, it will just look bitty and indecisive. Certainly one sees many pools where a small concession to marginal planting has grown inexorably until a fringe straggles half-way round the water.

The fountain is to the pool what the stream is to the pond, yet compared with busily trickling cascades fountains are sadly out of fashion. It is quite in keeping with the philosophy of our times that water going uphill is considered wasteful and ostentatious, while water going downhill is environmentally acceptable—or some such cant—even if it first has to be pumped up behind the scenes.

Yet perhaps we overlook the role of fountains as celebrations of light and water: events rather than processes. There is no need for a fountain to be always playing. Even those at Versailles were only turned on for parties.

Even if a fountain is essential to wake up what would otherwise be a dull or sombre pool it can easily be engineered to have several moods: bubbling perpetually, perhaps; surging on Saturdays and rising to a plume only on still, sunny days when there is something to celebrate.

Above Fountains exploit the interaction of water and light. They can reflect many moods from the grandiose to the whimsical, but they are essentially as artificial as vases of flowers.

A SNAIL'S PLACE

The water in a pool or pond is just as full of activity and varied in its population and components as any soil sample. It is not just a simple see-through medium but a living system, composed of water, gases, mineral nutrients (solid and dissolved), plants and animals.

But unlike soil, water rapidly becomes foul if something is missing from the system. A proper economy, a balance of producers and consumers, is essential for any pool or pond to stay clear and smell sweet.

The producers are plants, playing the same role as on land: photosynthesizing and in so doing consuming carbon dioxide and producing oxygen. In most water various kinds of algae, microscopic floating plants, are the most important producers. But in a densely planted or shaded pool bigger plants may have the upper hand.

The consumers are fish, newts, tadpoles, insects, snails and a whole host of greater and lesser fry that eat living plants and each other, and breathe out carbon dioxide.

Below both in the ecosystem come scavengers: animals that eat dead particles, both of plants and animals; and decomposers: microscopic bacteria and fungi, that break down dead and waste matter into simpler substances.

The significance of this to a pond-proprietor is that all these orders of life are essential for a "balanced" system to operate successfully.

Right In a very small urban yard a minute formal pool, scarcely bigger than two paving slabs, is still worth while. The plants in the water have to be grown in pots to prevent them spreading, but goldfish are extremely effective, their quick dashes and slow glides catching your eye from all over the yard. Quiet-coloured "foliage" plants are used round the paving here to concentrate attention.

Left A formal pool is almost inevitably the right choice for a small suburban garden where nothing can make any water look natural; particularly if the gardener's other pleasures lie in bright bedding plants.

SWIMMING POOLS

If any proof were needed that water is not an inert medium it is the amount of chemicals and filtration we need to keep a swimming pool in the state we are pleased to call clean.

Maintaining swimming pools is scarcely gardening, but swimming pools are important components of modern gardens—now certainly the commonest form of "formal" pool. If they were full of black reflecting water they could be a valuable part of any garden plan. Unfortunately the relentless blueness of the majority makes them stand out as sports equipment, almost impossible to harmonize with the proper tranquility of a garden.

Except in the California idiom (see pages 234–5) it is generally best to let a swimming pool dominate a compartment of its own and avoid having to seek uneasy compromise in the rest of the garden. Let it be near the house but screened away; a garden room for bathing—never the centrepiece of the garden. Attempts to disguise them as other than swimming pools by adding fountains, islands and other gimmicks very rarely works.

Taking stock: aspirations and resources

The happy gardener is one who has found a balance between what he would ideally like and what he can afford in time and money. Not perhaps perfect equilibrium: as one of Browning's characters says: "A man's reach should exceed his grasp, or what's a heaven for?"

Victorian gardening books used to begin with a chapter called Choosing a Site, which recommended a gentle south slope on medium loam with a gravel sub-soil, not to mention shelter from the prevailing winds. It is a very rare modern householder who picks and chooses among soils and sub-soils. Today as new gardens become smaller and smaller most gardens of any size are second-hand.

For that reason, a keen gardener is likely to choose an old property that will give him more scope—and hope that its builder read Chapter One. An old garden will also give him some sort of start with mature plants. His approach, therefore, will be quite different from that of somebody moving on to virgin ground.

Both gardeners will in the end impose their will on the place. But a new garden needs building, while an old garden needs watching.

It is as well to credit your predecessor with having had some reasons for arranging the garden as he did. His thinking may not be obvious at first. But the reasons may well emerge as the seasons change. Who knows what bulbs may be lurking? A weed is a weed and must be pulled, but everything else should be left where it is for a year and duly noted while you formulate your plan.

There are two crucial elements in your calculations, both entirely human and both much more important than horticulture. The first is what the garden will be used for, by whom, and when. The second is how much time you, or anyone else, are ready or can afford to devote to it.

From the first question comes a list of the elements you would ideally like. Is the garden to be primarily a playground, an outdoor dining-room, or a picture from the windows of the house? Do you want flowers for arranging? Do you yearn to be cradled in nature's bosom? Is the garden there to fill the freezer, or to let you lie by a swimming pool? Will you be there every day, or only in the evenings, or only at weekends?

A professional designer would ask a client all these things as a matter of course. Amateurs often forget that they are their own clients and press on with plans that have little to do with the way they live, drawing inspiration from their neighbours' gardens or a local garden centre without questioning its relevance to themselves and their lives.

The upkeep question is harder to answer. Perhaps you are keen to start with, but will be side-tracked to fritter away your life playing golf or ten-pin bowls. Perhaps gardening will grow on you and become a passion: when the children leave home you will want acres to devour. Perhaps help will come. Perhaps it won't.

The essential is to be aware of how long gardening operations take. It is not at all easy to generalize—digging, for example, takes much longer on heavier soil; grass-cutting (one of the major time-takers) takes more time in a wet season—but it has to be faced. Weeding can be a perpetual task but it can be organized out of existence with mulches and weedkillers. Given (say) five gardening hours a week, would you rather spend them on repetitive chores such as mowing, or hard physical work such as growing vegetables (which, from digging to cropping, provides the most exercise in the garden) or gentle handicrafts requiring more mental than physical effort, such as raising cuttings or tending alpines?

It is a good idea to look round the garden and list the areas which seem to take care of themselves. There are some parts of my garden where I need only go once a year, if that, to tidy up

One of the most effective ways of developing ideas before starting any practical steps, whether making a new garden or modifying an old one, is to take black and white photographs of it from various angles, have plenty of large prints made, and draw the features you imagine on the photographs. A wax crayon draws on glossy prints—or you can use a tracing-paper overlay. The examples here show two totally different imaginary schemes for an old garden (*above*) which is virtually featureless. On the right it is imagined as a formal garden with a stone-edged pool. On the far right it is an informal garden with a little conservatory overlooking a lawn sloping down to a pond with bog-plants. In both cases a vegetable plot is planned to the left of the house. Obviously any number of schemes can be made and modified.

fallen twigs and perhaps dig up elder or sycamore seedlings. They were not necessarily planned as "labour-saving": they have simple achieved a balance which is more or less self-perpetuating. Areas of heavy shade under trees, for example, may not be thrilling in themselves, but they have a stability that releases your efforts for other parts of the garden—and by contrast they make the sunlit spaces brighter.

The rule is to match your available time to the aspects of gardening you most enjoy, and organize the rest to take care of itself as far as possible. But labour saving can go too far. It is a pity to go out on a fine spring morning with high horticultural anticipation to find that there is nothing whatever to do. I strongly suspect that this is what so often sends householders round to the garden centre looking for kicks. They see some shrub they haven't got, cheerfully in bloom, and hurry home with it. The garden eventually becomes a magpie's nest of ill-assorted plants bought on impulse, with neither unity nor harmony, plan nor purpose.

We return to the idea of a plan. The conventional wisdom of gardening books tells us to make a decision about the lay-out, commit it to paper, and then follow it as circumstances allow.

It is a counsel of perfection that few people follow. In the United States it is common practice to have the place "landscaped" once and for all, but in Europe most gardens emerge over time. Rather than committing themselves on graph paper their owners carry their ideas in their heads, modifying and moulding them as they go along. There is sound sense in this. Creation is much more fun than maintenance. It is a pity to have all your fun at once and have nothing left to look forward to.

Where a plan is probably most helpful is as a survey of the property: its possibilities and drawbacks. A working document like this can record your experience of conditions of wind and weather, sunshine and shade, soil and drainage. By observation of which corners catch most of the sun and least of the wind, where the frost lies longest, where the ground dries out fastest (or lies wettest), you can make an ecological map which will suggest what should go where. There is social ecology too, of course: exposure to the road or the scrutiny of

Right Before even considering the layout, the style or the individual plants a personal stock-taking session will provide a brief to work from. It is helpful to imagine that you are your own client.

On the right is an example of a possible way of assembling the ideas and considerations which will eventually need turning into practical reality. Doodling like this is a good way of trying out different combinations of elements without commitment. Potential inconveniencies soon became apparent.

The outlook in various directions, the state of neighbouring gardens, the prevailing wind and other notes can be added round the edges to see how they impinge on the developing plan. Such questions as changes in levels, soil, drainage and frost pockets can also be marked (see pages 16–17).

South or south-west

Bit of jungle for children, to be converted one day into woodland

Tools, compost bonfire

Vegetables fruit and flowers for cutting

Main view and prettiest part of garden, with green centre for a feeling of space

Herb bed or perhaps conservatory-greenhouse

Eating out area handy for kitchen and living rooms

Main view from windows

Special collection of favourite plants, perhaps miniatures to be enjoyed at close range or place to hide swimming pool behind a screen.

Clothes line, fuel store and other unromantic necessities

Kitchen

Living rooms

Garage, maybe workshops

Approach and parking space

neighbours; nearness to the kitchen for an eating-out place. Views, good and bad, beyond the garden can also be marked.

A ground-plan is also extremely useful for calculating the quantities and details of the garden hardware: its paving, fences and the rest, and precise disposition of plants. It is the method always used by designers (an example is shown at the top of page 104–5). Samples are found in traditional nursery catalogues as a way of packaging the knowledge needed to plant a bed or border. A suggested approach to plant-planning is shown on pages 192–3.

But when it comes to visualizing alterations, a paper plan is not necessarily the best idea. To those not used to dealing with them, designs on paper have a spurious authority. Once you have drawn a possible place for the path or the line of a border, the matter seems settled. It is probably wiser for amateurs to plan on the ground, using canes and string or flower pots or plastic cups with stones in as markers to help them visualize what they propose. Once the concept is agreed, sketches and photographs are invaluable aids. I find that as a non-artist the effort of drawing in itself (especially the perspective) teaches me a great deal about the scene. You cannot draw without observing closely: it is the secret of surveying the garden, as it is of knowing its plants.

Photography has another advantage: it is ruthlessly candid. While your eye can gloss over patches of muddle, a photograph reports them faithfully. It should be in black and white, which brings home the essentials without flattery.

A combination of camera and sketch is best of all. You can draw with a wax crayon on a glossy photograph, or use a tracing-paper overlay and draw on that. Be decided about how far into the future you are projecting; the immediate effect after the alterations or the scene five years hence.

As to priorities, there are two logical starting points (this is for the practical lay-out of the garden, not its planting). They are the working area of tool-shed, compost heap and frames, the centre of horticultural activities, which cannot logically be thrust away into the farthest corner but needs a secluded spot reasonably near the house, and what the French call the *coin de repos*, the place where you will take your ease.

The search for style

Above is an instance of an outward-looking garden where the surroundings suggested very clearly what line to follow. The spirit of the garden harmonizes perfectly with the landscape. Boundaries are defined quietly but effectively by banks, which echo the distant hills.

Below This garden is cut off from the world beyond, but creates a strong identity by using strong features. The purposeful path and gate dispel any feelings of introversion and suggest that the garden's character extends into the world beyond.

Successful gardens, gardens that we remember and return to when we can, have a strong sense of place, a powerful identity that unites their various parts. They may agree with the landscape round about, sharing its views, its land-form and its trees, or they may have to shun it, shutting out a city or a desert behind a high wall and starting afresh to make a fantasy world. To be convincing, though, gardens must be coherent. They must settle on a theme and follow it all the way. They must not be waylaid by irrelevancies or seduced by decorations. They may change key for a passage; certainly they must vary their rhythm. But as music respects the dominant, so they must return to their basic style.

Style can mean many things. In garden design it inevitably has undertones of history. It is impossible to be unaware of the centuries of gardening that lie behind us.

Yet there is no precedent for the way we live; for our affluence curiously coupled with scarcity of space and time; for our reliance on society in general without being able to rely on other individuals; for our access to boundless knowledge without the time or the mental training to make use of it. Nothing like us has happened before in history. We cannot garden like our ancestors, and if we could it would be a mere pastiche. We have to find a true style for ourselves in our present condition. And this is where we run into trouble. There are too many prepacked ideas on offer in books, magazines and catalogues. The resulting muddle is all too obvious where-ever we look—including, I hasten to add, in my own garden.

It seems perhaps easier, certainly safer, to take our ideas from books and magazines than directly from our own observations, our experience of nature, or even from other people's gardens. But observation is where style starts. The finest essay on style today is in Russell Page's *The Education of a Gardener*. He describes how as a designer he has learnt to look for a starting point. He walks not just round the garden but round its neighbourhood, again and again, noting consciously (and subconsciously) elements that make up its character: the native plants, plants that flourish in other gardens, building materials, building details, the lie and rhythm of the land. The very breadth of the sky and the way the clouds pass may be hints.

Then he selects. From a notebook cluttered with details he distils what seems the essence of the place. This of course is where his artistry lies: it would be foolish to pretend that everyone can diagnose what is essential with such deft economy. But there is a plodding method.

Inevitably the scale is the first consideration. It is useless to think in terms of wide skies in a hemmed-in yard. By the same token fussy planting in an open landscape will be wrong. One tall tree can dominate the sense of scale in a garden, making other trees look puny. But add a seat, some steps—something on a human scale, and the small trees are given their dignity, the tall one its grandeur.

Climate comes next. The garden should be appropriate for the prevailing weather. In England this is easy: there are relatively few days in any season when it is not reasonably pleasant to be outdoors. Shade is rarely considered necessary. Shelter from the wind is the characteristic need which has given England its tradition of high walls and splendid hedges. In Scandinavia a sun-trap is the most important thing: the garden should look south and have no trees overhead more solid than birches. In Spain, shade is all that matters. California today is full of people reproaching themselves for having attempted eastern-type gardening in a rainless land. Two years of drought suddenly made western plants fashionable.

Then the underlying geology makes itself felt in the shapes of the landscape; fluid or flat or craggy. Traditional building materials—stone of a certain colour, brick or timber—agree with the geology; there was neither means nor reason to build

Above Soil and situation should set their stamp on a garden. This is a sunny bank on dry chalky soil at Upton House, Banbury: a property of the National Trust.

Left It is much harder to find a theme in the aridity of a new suburban plot. This American example creates a fantasy world with its own consistency.

Above Where the geology shows on the surface, in building stone, a sense of unity and sure style is easier to achieve. The single flower colour balances the mass of the stonework.

Below Woodland soil and shade have here dictated a totally different style. There is just enough of a hint of gardening in this almost-natural wood designed by James Russell.

Above A truly simple cottage garden, even with an outside privy, can also be dignified by consistency in planting. The unity of scale and limited range of colours give this garden memorable quality.

Left Gadgetry and gimmickry, gnomes and windmills, can still add up to a native sense of style if they are followed through with conviction

Below Everything goes wrong when planting is haphazard, without consistency or scale. Here the angular hedge, the round pond and the scattered bushes have no common theme or purpose.

with anything else. Today concrete is common currency, yet even concrete can be handled and finished in a way sympathetic to local traditions. For not only colours and textures but scale and proportions were dictated by the local resources.

The soil expresses itself in the dominant local plants. The trees give the country its characteristic outline and texture. This is the broadest hint of all. In cities and suburbs, however, where all the trees are deliberately planted, there is more likely to be confusion. To add to the medley with yet another nurseryman's job lot of one green tree, one gold and one purple is certainly in keeping. But to impose a style worth the name is a tall order.

In many modern gardens the social environment is a more important factor than the underlying ecology. The sort of street, the size of plot, the styles of buildings around are overwhelmingly relevant.

Whatever the eye and the mind perceive as the indicators of the sense of place can form the basis of a style—so long as it genuinely arises from the place itself and what people have done to it in the past; not out of generalized reminiscence.

This is where courage is needed. For having selected, you must stress. You must carry the theme to its logical conclusion, eschewing rival ideas which can only detract from the effect. Self-discipline is essential to produce a recognizable style.

A limitation of any kind makes the decision easier. A very acid or chalky soil planted simply with the plants that like it best already begins to have a coherent style. The best-conceived small gardens are often those of specialists, having the unity of single-mindedness—boring though a whole garden of irises or saxifrages may be to more frivolous minds.

A well-kept kitchen garden or orchard is always enjoyable, because a forthright workmanlike honesty is forced on it. The utilitarian style need not be tedious at all—even if it is hard to make it original. Far better to have a row of nut-trees and a row of artichokes than a blue spruce and a sickly palm in a patch of unloved lawn.

The language of design

The terminology of design is by no means essential to amateurs planning improvements. A garden has scale and structure, or does not have them, whether they are so described or not. But designers' jargon has the virtue of giving access to designers' concepts. Some of the terms you will find in textbooks and magazines are themselves useful tools in deciding why one arrangement looks right and another wrong. This little glossary may help to clarify them.

Accent Used to denote any feature that draws attention to itself, usually by being in a minority: a blue flower in a white border, or (very commonly) an upright conifer in a heather bed. The eighteenth-century word, working on rather a different scale, would have been "eye-catcher". Accents are essential to provide punctuation for the eye as it reads its way over the terrain. They lend seasoning to blandness and resolve all sorts of difficulties—so long as they are few, firm and apposite. Too many simply cancel each other out and make a restless undecided scene.

Anchor plant Something bold and solid used as the starting point for a composition. Also used of planting near a building to break the line of its foundation and as it were anchor it to the ground.

Association Perhaps sufficiently defined on pages 194–5, where various felicitous ones are discussed. Association of plants from wildly different habits (alpine with bog plant, cactus with birch) is seldom a good idea—although it works in many flower borders.

Asymmetry The opposite of symmetry; the cardinal rule in all naturalistic gardening. Symmetry and asymmetry are in reality not so mutually exclusive as they sound: asymmetry can with skill be so balanced that it can form part of an otherwise symmetrical composition. On the other hand a house with a classically symmetrical front suggests a symmetrical garden and usually looks better for it.

Axis The central joining line, or point where the mirror seems to be, in a symmetrical composition. Or any decisive line on the ground, which might be a path, a canal, or just a marked gap in the planting round which the design of the whole seems to pivot. The axis of any space suggests the direction to follow. Classical European gardens all have a strong central axis, sometimes expressed in avenues many miles long. Other radial avenues would be the axes of other points of view.

Balance One of the hardest qualities to define, since it can be either as obvious as the two sides of an avenue, or so subtle that it is not apparent at all. It is arrived at by answering a weight or mass in one part of the composition by another which seems to have the same value, and so keeps an equilibrium. A vertical could balance a horizontal, or a small dense mass (see *Density*) a big diffuse one if they had the same importance to the eye of the viewer.

Boldness A term only used approvingly when a good idea has come off. Boldness is necessary to striking design, but it should be remembered that really bad design is very often the result of rash boldness.

Borrowed scenery A fashionable import from the Japanese which would be better translated as "the view". Prospects beyond the garden are just as much part of the scenery as objects within it. They can often be hidden by planting close to the viewer, but should be welcomed if they have anything

Accent

Anchor plant

Asymmetry

Axis

Density

agreeable or even tolerable to add, since the small world of the garden usually gains by comparison with the world beyond. Hills, trees and other considerable objects are part of the garden's skyline, and hence its composition, whether within it or without. A distant hill can be made an element in a balanced garden picture. Any distinct character given by plants outside the garden should be recognized and allowed for inside it. Harmony is almost always better than contrast.

Colour An important resource for design, but in many cases ephemeral and thus less important than shape or "form". See pages 196–203.

Composition The arrangement of elements that go to make up the garden, including the plants and the paths, the solids and the spaces between them. Although few gardens are consciously "composed" as an overall design, any garden can (and probably should) be analysed as a composition, and can usually be improved by judicious addition and omission.

Density The apparent weight of an object, suggested by its appearance of solidity or otherwise. Dense objects have far more impact than diffuse ones. Tracery of branches has no density: a clipped ball of box has a great deal. Density is all-important in achieving balance.

Development (over time) By far the hardest aspect of design to visualize and allow for, since it will completely change the picture remarkably soon. It is essential to know how fast plants grow before installing them, and be aware of discrepancies that will soon need correcting if the plan is to be saved. All design is done with some future time in mind: it is best to be positive about when that time is supposed to be. If it is this summer, plant annuals. Most well-designed gardens look best at the point when they begin to need surgery for over-growth.

Exotic Strictly speaking, any plant not native to the region, but to a designer something which not only is but looks foreign and out of context. Often used of plants with big leaves (or other parts) that suggest the tropics. Occasional exotic plants in this sense can be effective *accents*. A sustained passage of them can be really exciting. But freely mixed with less demonstrative plants they are usually inappropriate and disturbing.

Focal point An accent in an axis: an obvious eye-catcher. Or just the point where perspective lines converge. One view can (or at any rate should) only have one focal point.

Formal Now usually means on the classic European mould, using straight (or geometrically curved) lines and usually symmetry. "Informal" is any other style, from eighteenth-century landskip to twentieth-century "wild" gardening or "island beds".

Foundation planting Plants put round the base of a building to soften its emergence from the earth and make it look as though it "belongs"—often an impossible task. See above under *Anchor plant*.

Framing One of the easiest and most effective tricks of design. It can be achieved with an arch, a pergola, an overhanging branch . . . photographers often cheat and do it with a broken-off spray of leaves. A view seen out from under something, or in between two somethings, is almost always immeasurably improved. See pages 174–5.

Harmony As difficult as framing is easy. Harmony is not contrast, nor is it uniformity. It is finding relationships in unalike things and emphasizing what they have in common by the way and in the proportions in which they are brought together. Neighbouring colours in the spectrum can be harmonious; a selection of various shapes of small leaf may be harmonious; a goldfish and a water-lily will be harmonious. There is usually a sort of harmony in distinct one-ecology gardening: a rock garden, for example. But boredom, not harmony, is achieved by simply playing safe.

Line A pictorial quality at its most obvious in, for example, bare branches in winter, but everywhere present in the "drawing" of plants and other objects. Line is one of the factors in which contrasts can be made or harmonies found. Weeping willows or bamboos, for example, have obvious, very expressive, lines; but so does a beech tree, which forms tiers of leaves, or a fern, which makes a grid-like pattern. The illustrations at the foot of pages 194–5 show thoughtful uses of the "lines" of border plants.

Mass is complementary to line, and means the whole bulk of an object. The "masses" of deciduous plants change totally from summer to winter. Masses divide and define the spaces or "voids" round them. A garden without evergreens or at least densely twiggy deciduous plants therefore largely loses its definition and plan in winter. Masses have *density* (which see) which can be used to achieve *balance* (which also see). Dark masses are more "massive" than light ones.

Natural A word often distorted in meaning to apply to curves as opposed to straight lines. Nature is well-provided with both. A curve can easily look "forced" and unnatural.

Nucleus The central feature round which the garden plan is conceived or arranged—often the garden door of the house and the sitting-place outside it. Convention suggests that the garden be most elaborate, contrived and highly coloured at its nucleus, becoming less so as you move away from it. Large gardens however usually have several nuclei linked by sustained passages of interesting planting, or at least deliberate and obvious routes.

Ornamental Previously a term of approval in gardening, but beginning to be regarded as dangerously frivolous.

Proportion Such relation of the size of one part to another as makes the whole pleasing and harmonious, with nothing out of scale. The proportions of garden enclosures, for example, can convey definite impressions of repose or otherwise. A long narrow space tends to be unrestful, like a corridor. Unless that is the intention, it would be improved by dividing it into a series of rooms with a more static feeling. As used in classical garden literature proportion meant due deference to the well-defined rules of architecture.

Repose One of the traditional benisons of the garden, achieved through a sense of security from disturbance and by harmonious surroundings. Well-defined boundaries therefore contribute, and loud contrasts of colours or shapes detract.

Richness In gardens as in food, a desirable quality up to a certain point. Richness in gardens is given by the variety of ingredients and their effective display. Certain colours (purples and oranges for example) contribute towards a rich effect. Richness and simplicity are rare bed-fellows, but together they constitute the ideal.

Framing

Line

Spatial (definition)

Surprise

Scale An alpine plant is out of scale and ridiculous in a border of tall plants; so is a delphinium in a rockery. In general all the components of a garden should agree in the sense they convey of the size of the whole. A very big garden, for example, should have wide paths. On the other hand a deliberately odd scale can be striking and enjoyable. Tiny yards in Japan are sometimes almost filled by huge stone lanterns. The Chinese rely largely on contrasts of scale (small leads to large; high to low) in their warren-like gardens.

Simplicity An effect for which designers strive. It demands conviction and single-mindedness, which are rare qualities among amateurs planning their own gardens. It is much easier for a professional to take a sweeping decision to plant (say) only ivy. He will not be there to be bored by it. Ideally an impression of simplicity can be gained without sacrificing *variety* by the careful study of the *harmony* of the parts. Simplicity is very much in vogue as the corollary to labour-saving. Keen gardeners will probably not pay much attention to either of them.

Spatial definition The function of *masses* (which see). Clear and deliberate boundaries between one part of a garden and another give it a sense of decision and purpose which is highly desirable. In small gardens vague thickets of shrubs are not so effective as hedges or other definitive dividers: in large parks on the other hand spaces may be defined by loose groups of trees. A marked change of level can also define a space. Even different lengths of grass can do it.

Structure The bones of the garden: the paths, fences and hedges; the house itself; permanent plantings of trees and shrubs; everything you would put down as the framework if you were drawing a map of the garden. A firm, well-considered structure is the great virtue of the Italian/French tradition, continued in England in such gardens as Hidcote and Sissinghurst, which are plotted as a series of rooms. Functional modern gardens are structured differently. It is the relationship of house to pool to eating area to parking space that dictates the structure.

Surprise (or unexpectedness) The happy effect produced by concealing, then revealing, a feature—as for example by a bend in a pathway. Devastatingly dismissed by the remark (in Peacock's *Headlong Hall*) "Pray sir, by what name do you distinguish this character, when a person walks round the grounds for the second time?" In practice an interrupted view leads to anticipation of something worth seeing beyond, and therefore draws the viewer on . . . and funnily enough it does work a second time.

Symmetry see *Asymmetry*.

Tension The result of contrasting objects of different character but similar value (for example, density or mass) to the eye. Tension implies an interesting and unexpected balance. A matching pair of urns has no tension: a single urn balanced by a cypress might well express it.

Unity The general agreement of all the parts with a common theme, however vaguely defined. The lack of any jarring or out of place elements. See pages 188–9.

Variety Variety is the life (and unity the soul) of a garden. Without variety there can be no harmony, contrast or tension. But of all garden virtues it is the most often overdone. The result: a muddle.

An approach to planting

The border below is shown with the plants that will give it shape and interest in winter boldly outlined. Assuming that (as in the photograph below) it is seen principally from the left-hand end—perhaps a living-room window—the winter plants are positioned to enclose the border and give it the feeling of being furnished without taking up too much of the space needed for later plants. Little winter- or very early spring-flowering bulbs could be added in the front of the border, particularly at the left-hand end to tempt you into the garden on bright days.

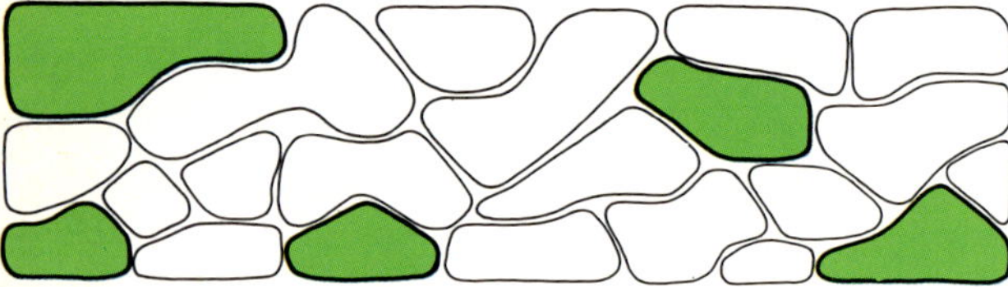

The emphasis in spring is on groups in the front of the border to present the maximum effect when seen from the left-hand end. Spring-flowering plants tend to be smaller than those that flower later and would be hidden at the back of the border, although long-lived bulbs can be used in combination with the more permanent border plants and shrubs throughout the planting. If bulbs are planted under perennials that need frequent lifting and dividing they will inevitably be damaged in the process. The evergreens are still giving full value at this time of year.

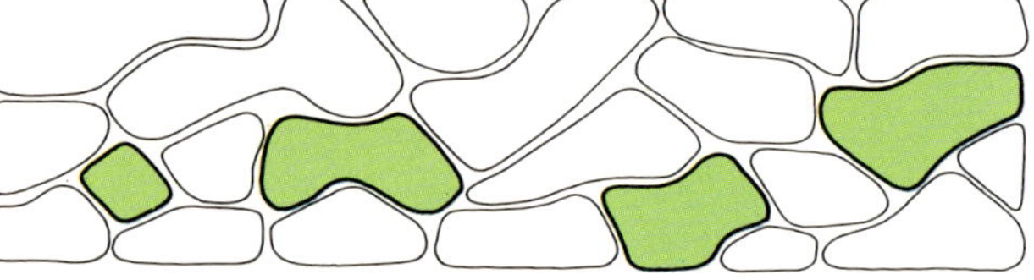

In early to midsummer the main stress of flowers is in the centre of the border, with outposts at either end. This spacing is the best way of giving the impression of a flowery climax while keeping space for later-flowering plants.

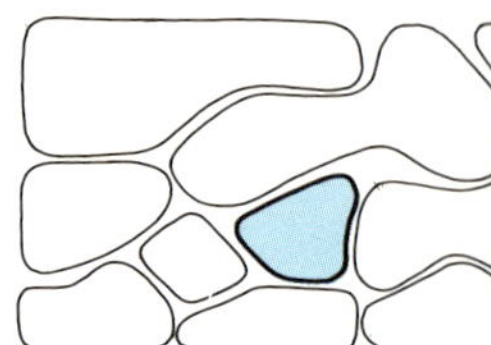

Below Stage six of the approach described below is to decide on the range of colours you want for each season and to write them in, either on the separate seasonal plans or as here on one master-plan of the whole border. Where it is helpful the planting for any particular season can be shaded in or outlined in bold. The colours chosen are yellow and orange nearest the viewpoint (on the left), then the hot colours giving way to cool white and blue in the centre, with blue and purple reiterated further away to enhance the sense of distance. At this stage you will have begun to assemble ideas for particular plants and combinations of plants which can be pencilled in where their colours, seasons and sizes are appropriate.

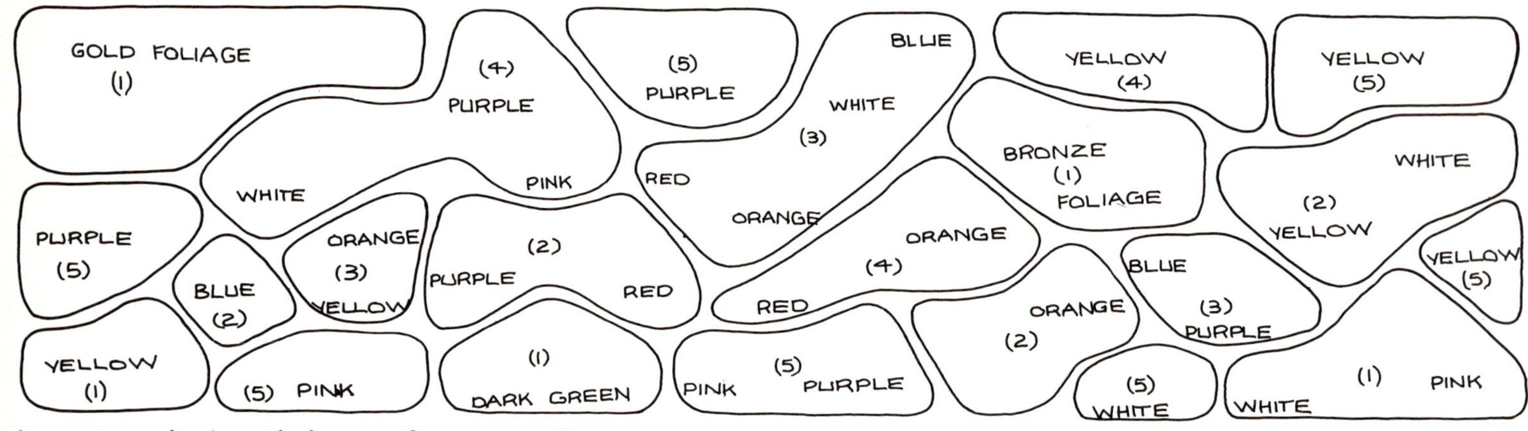

Approaches to planning with plants vary from the meticulous to the hit-and-miss. There are gardeners who will not stir until the whole garden is mapped out like a military campaign, and others (the majority, I strongly suspect) who wander round vaguely with their latest plant acquisition in their hands. They try vainly to visualize it in flower, out of flower; next year, five years hence, and finish by planting it in the only available space—or so they think until they find their fork crunching deep into a lurking bulb.

The latter are not lost souls. They include excellent gardeners who simply have poor memories and unmethodical minds. Some of the most experienced gardeners never make deliberate plans but go by "feel", often shifting plants from place to place as they outgrow their positions, or simply to enjoy the effect of a new combination of shapes and colours. Experience brings confidence in moving plants about—some plants even seem to enjoy it.

There is no absolute or right way of planning for planting. There are conventional ways, which can be found at the end of many nursery catalogues. I have tried to improve on these in the light of my own experience, adding in particular what I find one of the most difficult garden disciplines—imagining all the seasons and remembering the flow of events in any given corner of the garden. The way of planning suggested here was designed to help with this problem and produce a scene on any scale (be it a whole small garden, a border or a view from a window) which is satisfying and interesting at all times of the year.

It begins by dividing the growing year into five changes of scene. As the earlier pages exploring the resources of plant materials show this is an exaggeration for some classes of plants and an under-estimate for others.

Right In drawing up a planting scheme it is helpful to begin with rough sketches like these to plan the general effect. These show two alternative treatments of a border, the first formal with an obvious structural pattern, the second informal but still deliberate and balanced.

Later summer flowers are concentrated nearer the principal viewpoint where they will arrest the eye and allow the general impression of pleasant green, with perhaps the beginning of autumn colour in leaves or fruit, to fade away into the distance. The tactic of using brighter and warmer colours in the foreground and cooler greys and blues in the background to emphasize perspective could be used here. By this time of year space which was used for spring flowers can be re-used with perennial plants that make their growth late.

As most plants are fading and beginning to look bedraggled by the last flowering season the late-flowering plants are scattered through the border to hide or distract attention from their predecessors. Seed heads that hold up well can add greatly to the interest. There is as much colour now from leaves and fruit as from flowers, and evergreens begin to stand out again as the scene turns to yellows and browns. The interest of the border can be maintained well into winter by resisting the urge to tidy away perennials as they die down.

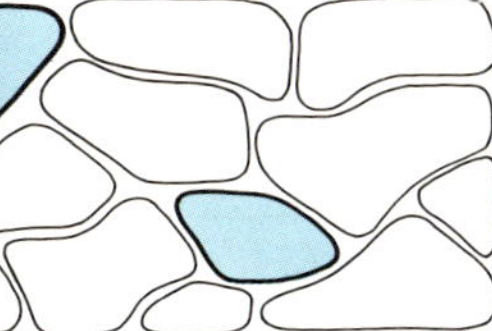

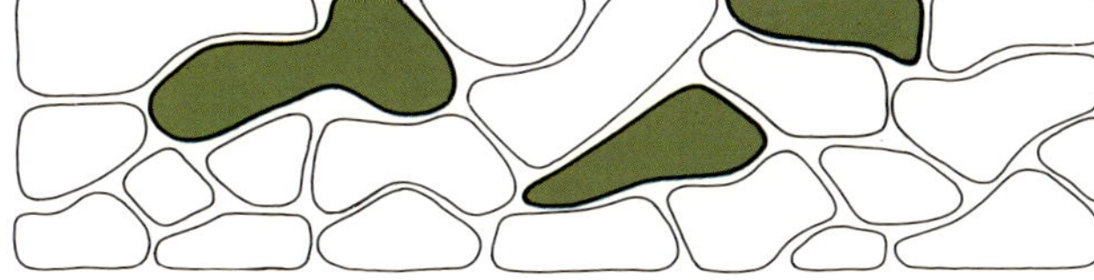

Below A final possible stage before ordering the plants for a border (or any planting scheme) is to impose a grid over the plan. The square of this grid represents nine inches on the ground. By using it in conjunction with reference books that tell you the eventual spread of each plant you can establish exactly how many plants will be needed to fill their allotted space in due season. In this example the grid is coded both for season and flower-colour.

B- BLUE
P- PURPLE
K- PINK
W- WHITE
R- RED
O- ORANGE
Y- YELLOW
G- GREEN
1- WINTER
2- SPRING
3- EARLY SUMMER
4- HIGH SUMMER
5- AUTUMN

1G	1G	1G	1G	1G	1G	1G	1G	1G	1G	1G	4P	4P	4P	4P	5P	5P	5P	5P	5P	5P	5P	5P	3B	3B	3B	4Y	4Y	4Y	4Y	4Y	4Y	4Y	4Y	5Y	5Y	5Y	5Y	5Y	5Y	5Y
1G	1G	1G	1G	1G	1G	1G	1G	1G	1G	1G	4P	4K	4K	4K	5P	5P	5P	5P	5P	5P	5P	5P	3B	3B	3B	4Y	4Y	4Y	4Y	4Y	4Y	4Y	4Y	5Y	5Y	5Y	5Y	5Y	5Y	5Y
1G	1G	1G	1G	1G	1G	4P	4P	4P	4P	4P	4P	4K	4K	4K	4K	5P	5P	5P	5P	5P	5P	3W	3W	3B	1G	1G	1G	1G	1G	4Y	4Y	4Y	4Y	5Y	5Y	5Y	2W	2W	2W	2W
1G	1G	1G	1G	1G	4W	4P	4P	4P	4P	4P	4K	4K	4K	4K	4K	4K	3R	3R	5P	5P	3O	3O	3W	4O	1G	1G	1G	1G	1G	1G	1G	1G	2Y	2Y	2Y	2W	2W	2W	2W	2W
1G	1G	1G	1G	4W	4W	4W	4P	4P	4P	3O	3O	3O	4K	4K	4K	3R	3R	3R	3R	3R	3O	3O	4O	4O	4O	1G	1G	1G	1G	1G	1G	1G	2Y	2Y	2Y	2W	2W	2W	2W	2W
5P	5P	5P	5P	5P	4W	4W	4W	4W	3O	3O	3O	3O	4K	4K	2R	2R	2R	3R	3R	3R	3R	4O	4O	4O	4O	4O	1G	1G	1G	1G	1G	2Y	2Y	2Y	2Y	2W	2Y	2Y	5Y	5Y
5P	5P	5P	5P	5P	2B	2B	3Y	3Y	3Y	3O	2P	2P	2P	2R	2R	2R	2R	2R	3R	3R	4R	4O	4O	4O	4O	4O	4O	2O	2O	3B	3B	3B	3P	2Y	2Y	2Y	2Y	5Y	5Y	5Y
5P	5P	5P	5P	2B	2B	2B	3Y	3Y	3Y	3Y	2P	2P	2P	2P	2R	2R	2R	2R	4R	4R	4R	4R	4R	4O	4O	4O	2O	2O	2O	2O	3B	3P	3P	3P	3P	1K	1K	1K	5Y	5Y
5P	5P	1Y	1Y	2B	2B	2B	2B	5K	3Y	3Y	2P	2P	1G	1G	1G	2R	2R	4R	4R	4R	4R	5P	5P	2O	2O	2O	2O	2O	2O	2O	3P	3P	3P	3P	1W	1W	1K	1K	1K	5Y
1Y	1Y	1Y	1Y	1Y	5K	5K	5K	5K	5K	3Y	3Y	1G	1G	1G	1G	1G	5K	5K	5K	5P	5P	5P	5P	5P	2O	2O	2O	2O	5W	5W	5W	5W	3P	1W	1W	1W	1K	1K	1K	1W
1Y	1Y	1Y	1Y	1Y	5K	5K	5K	5K	5K	5K	1G	1G	1G	1G	1G	1G	5K	5K	5K	5K	5K	5K	5P	5P	2O	2O	2O	5W	5W	5W	5W	5W	1W	1W	1W	1W	1W	1W	1W	1W

Left The method of planning suggested here is described in terms of this kind of traditional border. It can equally be applied to any piece of planting from a little yard to a considerable garden landscape. The intention is to create a firm framework to which each season will bring new beauty and interest. In a landscape the units might be trees rather than plants and bulbs but the same principles will apply: the preliminary disposition of shapes, including particularly evergreens, to form a strong and balanced outline; then a succession of seasonal events from early-flowering trees to late-autumn colour.

For planning purposes the principle phases of the garden picture are:

1 Winter-early spring (say January-March, depending on your climate zone)
2 Full spring (April-May)
3 Late spring-early summer (May-June)
4 Full summer (July-August)
5 Late summer-autumn (September-December)

The suggested procedure is as follows:

1 Decide on the limits of the scene you are concerned with (which may be self-contained like a border, or include everything you can see from your terrace or window).

2 Decide what season or seasons you want to concentrate on remembering that if you try for flowers all year round there will be relatively few at any one time. A big garden can afford to have compartments planned to create a sensation once a year and fade into the background or not be visited at all afterwards. It is a matter of opinion in a small garden whether it is better to aim for continuous but rather subdued interest or one or two seasons of memorable floweriness.

3 Do a rough drawing of the scene, possibly using a photograph as a basis as on pages 190–1. Take as your viewpoint the place you will most often see it from. Take into account the position of the sun in relation to the viewer: a north-facing border, for example, is lit from behind for much of the time.

4 Sketch in evergreens or firmly shaped and dense, deciduous trees or shrubs for structure and solidity in winter. These will give you a structure of basic heights and masses in which to integrate all the plants. At this stage you might arrive at a sketch like one of those at the top of the page.

5 Make a plan (from above) of the part of the garden in question and divide it into areas corresponding to plants or groups of plants of appropriate sizes and interesting shapes. If you are dealing with a landscape these may be trees or clumps of trees; in a border single shrubs or groups of anything from three to perhaps two dozen plants. It can be helpful to impose a grid pattern over the whole plan to help you with the scale.

6 Repeat this plan for each of the five seasons, as in the examples across the top of these pages. Allocate an appropriate amount of the planting to each of the seasons in which you intend the scene to be interesting or colourful and flowery. This is done in the example above by outlining the plant groups which will constitute the "event" of each season.

7 Decide on the range of colours you want for each season. As an example, this could easily flow from blue, yellow and white in spring with a gradual dropping of the blue and white and introduction of red and orange to an autumnal blaze of all the warmest colours. There is no reason why a border should stick to one colour scheme, but every reason to make sure that colours you are planning to complement one another will in reality appear at the same time. Harmonies and clashes are just as much a matter of timing as of juxtaposition. Making a separate plan for each season is helpful here, too.

8 Introduce interesting shapes and textures. Remind yourself, that is, that flowers are not everything.

9 Look up what plants can provide the colour or other interest you want at the relevant season. There is no one reference book to do this in, but many help. Notes taken in other people's gardens are very often the best way to discover the size, shape, colour and character of plants you want, and to collect ideas for combinations.

10 Distribute the plants you have chosen in their appropriate seasonal sectors, bearing in mind their needs for sun or shade, or particular soils.

Apposite associations

The gardens to left and right are both good examples of shapes and textures coming before colour. On the left, the round shape of the border matches the bulk of the weeping willow; the little upright conifers framing the path balance the main vertical feature: the pair of Lawson cypresses. The balance of the whole is helped by the pale dome of the weeping silver pear. Light tones alternate with dark and dense masses with diffuse ones. The interplay of height and depth in the planting disguises the limitations of the site and creates the illusion of a much greater space. The garden belongs to Mrs H. A. Anderson, Surrey.

On the right is a much more deliberate composition in receding planes of different textures leading to the focal point. Most of the textures are fine: closely-clipped small-leaved plants. But the three tall "wings" of the stage on the right are progressively finer-textured as if to emphasise the distance. In bold contrast, the huge leaves of an ornamental vine give the foreground life. The yellow of a giant mullein catching the light on the left finally balances the picture with another "accent". Some successful design comes about by design and some by happy accident. The chief lesson here is the deliberate simplicity and restraint of the basic planting, allowing deviations to make memorable, rather than muddled, effects. This is Hidcote, a National Trust property.

Above The herbaceous *Phlomis russelliana*, *Lychnis* and the shrubby *Ozothamnus rosmarinifolius* all have a strong vertical character but contrast strikingly in both tone and texture.

Above Abundant interest is provided not by colour but by three bold forms of flower, *Veronica virginica* 'Alba' (front), with *Macleaya cordata* and (right) *Echinops ritro*, the globe thistle.

It is an excellent idea to plan your basic planting in black and white before you even consider colour. It may eventually be the colour that will beguile you and create the mood of the garden, but just because colour *is* so beguiling it can blind you to weaknesses in composition, and leave boring patches where no one shape or texture stands out to give point to the rest.

Everyone can think of associations of two or more plants that have made him pause and look twice; perhaps appreciate some shape or texture for the first time; or perhaps just given him the pleasure that harmonious composition of any kind can give. A good garden is full of these incidents, from its general plan down to touches of minutest detail.

Such associations can take place on one or several planes. They can be contrasts or complements, involving shapes, sizes, tones, textures, modelling or form, bulk and apparent weight. They can take place entirely on an intellectual level: because we know that a group of plants grow together in a certain mountain range, or are all indigenous to the region of the garden, or were collected or bred by one man. They could all be roses Josephine grew. E. A. Bowles had a corner of his garden where he planted all the deformed and contorted plants he could find. There are countless reasons for planting this next to that before considering what is now often the overriding one: colour.

On the previous page I touched on the relationships between different forms: the way in which importance in the garden picture is related to density as well as to size. Tones as well as masses have their apparent importance—a fact that black and white pictures show much better than pictures in colour. Dark tones recede; light ones advance towards you. There can be a fundamental contrast between two otherwise very similar plants—and hence an apposite association—just because one reflects more light than the other.

Left A miniature but successful example of the association of evergreen leaves: the fingery *Helleborus foetidus* under an ivy-clad wall with the dwarf form of box used for low hedges. Here all the greens are similar: the contrast is only between the shapes and sizes of the leaves.

Above A Japanese temple-garden where plant textures play the dominant role with colours and even shapes subordinated to them. The effect is heightened by looking towards the light. Pine (left foreground), heavenly bamboo (right foreground), hard shiny camellias and soft light-absorbing maple-leaves form a jigsaw of subtly different textures.

Left Association by ecological fitness nearly always works. The cool damp climate of the Scottish Highlands suits Himalayan primulas and the blue poppy to perfection. Everything that revels in the same conditions looks right together.

Contrast for its own sake can easily be (and often is) overdone. A garden that sets out to alternate big with little, light with dark, matt with shiny, relentlessly all around you is fidgety and unrestful. It is essential to establish a dominant theme or scale first; then to look for the right variation on it. A single fern growing by a rock in a wide area of moss is far more effective than a scattering of the same fern here and there throughout the moss. On the other hand scattering different ferns at random would be a greater mistake.

Perhaps the most telling associations of all take the form of a visual pun, when in one sense two plants are the same; in another quite different. An example might be plants of precisely the same shade of green but on a totally different scale. Sylvia Crowe gives as an example box and banana leaves used in the gardens of the Alcazar, Seville. Another example might be bergenias and winter heliotrope in early spring. The leaves of both are big, bold, roundish in outline and low on the ground, but the bergenias are richly glossy, the heliotrope's completely matt. Another is bridal wreath, *Francoa ramosa*, with the wand flower, *Dierama pulcherrima*; two tall, slender waverers to interweave their white clusters and purple bells.

In a wider garden scene, a mixed border for example, there are bound to be contrasts and complements to be picked up and enjoyed if you can detect them in the general jumble (though many border plants, particularly the daisies, are depressingly similar in structure). Here the secret is to choose a particular motif and make it sufficiently obvious. Gertrude Jekyll's famous border was interrupted by a doorway flanked by terrifying great clumps of the prickly *Yucca gloriosa*. Next to it came a great tumble of the big spurge of lighter grey-green colour (*Euphorbia characias wulfenii*), but in long knobs instead of spikes. Then farther along the border the sword-leaves of irises reminded one of the opening chord of yucca.

Above One virtue of limiting planting to a narrowly-defined range of colours is that it throws the emphasis on the shapes of the plants. Broad jumbled leaves of variegated hostas (foreground), contrast with lilies with narrow, orderly, comb-like ones against a bright but neutral background of gold-variegated dogwood. The plants to take over and flower later are phlox (among the lilies) and the round-leaved *Ligularia* 'Desdemona'.

The nature of colour

Some of the world's greatest gardens have limited themselves so radically in the use of colour that one can almost say it was omitted from their philosophy entirely. The great Italian Renaissance gardens were compositions in form and mass, light and shade—but not in colour. At Versailles the flower colour in the parterres was entirely coincidental to the great architectural and spatial concept. The English landscape garden was thought of in terms of spaces, planes, modelling—and, of course, historical and literary associations. The colours were green, stone and water. Organized plant colour in fact came late into the consciousness of garden designers. Sir William Chambers is said to have been the first to suggest the substantial grouping of flowers of one colour to form a patch.

Today we tend to put more emphasis on colour, both in flowers and leaves, than on any other single aspect of gardening; yet with remarkably little knowledge or understanding. Most gardeners are entirely undiscriminating. Many nurseries sell seeds of popular flowers in "mixed shades". Their criterion is brightness, regardless of quality, or of what the colours may do to one another. Similarly among trees and shrubs any colour is conceived to be an improvement on "mere" green: purple- and gold-leaved trees proliferate not because those colours are good in themselves or do anything more than muddle the picture, but because they are, simply, "colours".

There are a few gardeners who have a painter's—and it needs to be a painter's—understanding of the relationships between colours and the harmonies that are possible with their careful use. The musical image is apt, for what happens when colours interact can be almost as powerful, and yet remains as mysterious, as the mingling of musical sounds.

What, for a start, is colour? It is reflected light, edited by the pigment of the surface that is reflecting it. Unreflected daylight is more or less white. White light is a combination of all the colours of the spectrum (or rainbow). The function of a pigment is to absorb some parts of the mixture and reflect back the others—which we see as its colour. The more pigments there are the more light is absorbed, and the colour is said to be "saturated". Not only the pigments but also the texture of the surface affects the reflection. A piece of satin and a piece of velvet may be dyed precisely the same colour yet the satin will appear lighter, since its texture reflects more light.

Pigments are coloured molecules, which like all molecules contain electrons that determine which colours are absorbed and which reflected. If the electrons have short, rapid wave movements they absorb the short light waves, which are blue, and by consequence reflect its opposite, which is yellow.

Not only do we find a wide range of pigments in plants, but their ability to absorb or reflect depends on the chemistry of other substances present in the plant. Proteins, tannins, sugars and acids are all able to affect their colour.

Of the two main classes of pigments one is insoluble, existing in the sap as minute solid particles. These are the carotenoid (yellow to orange) pigments, including xanthophyll, which provides the yellow of roses, and carotene, which makes carrots (and shellfish) red. The question "why did the lobster blush?" is sternly answered by the rejoinder that a combination of carotene and proteins kept it blue while it was on the seabed. But when the water boiled the proteins took their leave.

The second great class of pigments are the anthocyanins, which are soluble in water and hence liable to even more volatile behaviour, readily reacting, for example, to the acidity of cell-sap. Among the anthocyanins are pelargonidin ("geranium red"), delphinidin ("delphinium blue") and cyanidin, the red of roses until a recent genetic mutation brought pelargonidin into the sap of the startling 'Super Star'.

Between them these three cover the spectrum, with the exception of yellow. Not just acidity but combinations with sugars and tannins make delphinidin, for example, vary between greenish-blue and magenta, and pelargonidin between scarlet and violet-blue. As far as simple acidity is concerned they react like litmus paper, turning red in the presence of acid and blue in an alkaline solution.

It is the anthocyanins that give a reddish tinge to new shoots and leaves; many roses are examples. Again in autumn they form in the sap in reaction to high light intensity and low temperatures—turning the leaves, as their chlorophyll ebbs, to the vivid reds, oranges and purples of autumn.

So these are the "true" colours of plants; their pigments. But if colour is reflected light, the other important element is the light being reflected. For the intensity and "temperature" of daylight vary all the time, from dawn to noon to dusk, with the angle of the sun and with the passing of clouds. They vary even more with the latitude and the humidity. In Britain the light is always slightly soft and blue. Mediterranean and subtropical light give harsh contrasts and violent shadows.

The more intense the light, the stronger, more absorptive, more "saturated" the colour it needs to give a truly "coloured" impression; the dimmer the light, the more the reflective power of pale colours makes them glow. Pastel colours look feeble at noon in summer even in Britain; far more so in Mediterranean light—but towards dusk they show up more and more. By nightfall red flowers have disappeared altogether, while white ones shine like lamps.

Above "Shadows are in reality, when the sun is shining, the most conspicuous things in the landscape next to the highest lights"—John Ruskin's remark explains the rich variety of colours provided by only two kinds of flower, a peony and a pansy, both red, with rain bending their petals so that the light is reflected quite differently from either side, giving the effect of completely different tones.

Below Brilliant noon-day sun can kill even colours as bright as the scarlet geranium in the vase. Colour-schemes to be effective in southern areas of very bright light must include colours of great intensity to absorb a high proportion of the sun's rays, or the result will appear washed-out.

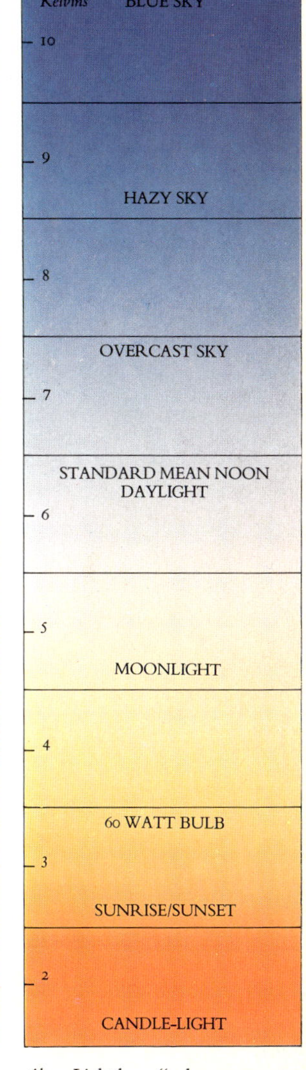

Above Light has a "colour temperature", conventionally measured in "degrees Kelvin"—a measure of the temperature to which a notional black object would have to be heated to emit light of a given colour. The chart above shows the colour temperature of light from various sources, ranging from the low-temperature light of a candle to the very high-temperature light of a bright blue sky. Despite appearances, and the conventional feeling that blue is a "cool" colour and red a "warm" one, the photograph *above left*, taken at noon, has a much higher colour temperature than the photograph on the *left*, taken in the glow of dusk.

Left In an English garden at dusk in summer all dark, non-reflecting colours rapidly disappear, leaving only the pastel colours and whites, which take on the brilliance of lamps in contrast to the gathering gloom.

Colour: contrast and harmony

Below The borders below were planted to illustrate and exploit the two sides of the spectrum which are normally ill-at-ease together in gardens; colours containing blue on the one hand and yellow on the other. Either side looks better on its own. At Barrington Court, Somerset: a National Trust property.

The sort of colour co-ordination taken for granted in decorating and furnishing a room is rare in garden planning. Partly I suspect it is because most of us are very vague about the precise colours of flowers. They come and go leaving an imprecise memory. Hardly anyone goes to the trouble of finding their exact match on a colour chart, or even picking a flower and carrying it over to another plant to see whether the two "go" together or not. Timing is not so simple—we may think two plants will complement one another only to find that one has finished flowering before the other has really started.

Time is the enemy in another way as well. We only find that our two rhododendrons look perfectly horrible in flower together after we have spent several years nurturing them. So we live with the swearing colours and comfort ourselves with the untruism that natural colours cannot clash.

In a garden colours are never seen singly as they are on a colour card. There is always a context of surrounding colours—with green, of course, normally dominant. Which means there is always an interaction: the colours are always affecting each other for better or for worse, for louder or quieter, for lighter or darker.

The language of colour is concerned with defining and naming particular points on the spectrum or colour wheel and describing the relationship between them. Colours which are neighbours in the spectrum normally harmonize with each other, while those on opposite sides of the wheel contrast. Red and green, for example, are "complementary": that is, in maximum contrast.

Red, yellow and blue are described as "primary" colours because all other colours can be produced by mixing them. Side by side they produce violent contrasts, having nothing at all in common. The three mid-points between the primary colours are green, orange and violet. Although they also contrast the effect is less violent; they have certain pigments in common. Various "triads" of colours produced by turning an imaginary triangle in the colour wheel are classic examples of successful and satisfying colour-planning. Sage/plum/buff and citrus/slate/russet bear the same relationship to each other as red/yellow/blue, yet in fact harmonize rather than contrast.

In technical terms each colour is given three "attributes" or "dimensions": its hue (that is where it occurs on the spectrum; if you like the "pure" colour); its tone or brightness (which means how much of the pigment is present; therefore how much light it absorbs; therefore how intensely "coloured" it appears); and its saturation, or purity. In the spectrum the colours are fully saturated—as pure as possible. Any mixture with grey or white lessens their purity and hence their degree of saturation.

Contrast and harmony depend not just on the relative positions of the hues in the spectrum but also on their other "dimensions". There can well be a contrast between neighbouring colours if one is very dark in tone and the other very light, or one is intensely saturated and the other washed out. Conversely colours that, judging by their place on the spectrum alone should contrast strongly, can appear harmonious if they share a common dimension in, let us say, a very light tone or a very dark one.

It is easy to exaggerate the difficulties with this barrage of jargon. In practical gardening experience there is an unexpectedly simple rule of thumb at hand, which is that the spectrum divides more or less evenly along a line drawn between green and red, into those flowers and leaves containing blue in their make-up and those containing yellow. Many very effective colour schemes are made by the free use of one or the other of these two ranges, with only very limited and careful (if any) interpolation from the other.

THE STUDY OF COLOUR

Colour has been analyzed and described many times in many ways, but no analysis or description can substitute for the sight of a sample. Colour-cards and the colour wheel are not to be scorned as aids by anyone who hopes to achieve harmonious effects with flowers. Practice in matching colour samples greatly increases awareness of colour. To a gardener who has only thought of colour in vague terms such training opens new windows.

Certain areas of the spectrum are straightforward and easy to handle. Yellows are an example. Others are more sensitive. One particular area is notorious for our imprecision in referring to its colours, and for the dowdy, muddy effects that are easily created by lack of care in handling them. This is the passage between red and blue shown in the colour samples on the right.

There seems to be little general agreement as to the precise relative places of such flower-colours as lavender, lilac and violet in this range.

The captions to the colour samples show a suggested order for the commoner colour-names between red and blue.

Colour samples, however, are misleading in suggesting that colours can be viewed in isolation. In practice they never are, but are always affected by their surroundings.

The colour-patches below are examples of the ways in which colours appear to change in the presence of other colours, depending not just on their hues (or relative places in the spectrum) or their other dimensions of tone and intensity but on their relative masses and even positions.

The phenomenon of the "after-image" is important here. When the eye has been resting on a strong colour for a while its opposite or complementary colour (for example red complements green) appears as an after-image overprinted, as it were, on the next colour to be seen. In the examples below this accounts for the apparent redness of the blue flash on the green background.

Above Colours alter in relationship to other colours. The dark green as background to a light flash looks darker still, but has less "colour" when it is seen as a flash on a paler ground. The pale green appears much paler when surrounded by dark green. Such effects are constant and, with practice, predictable.

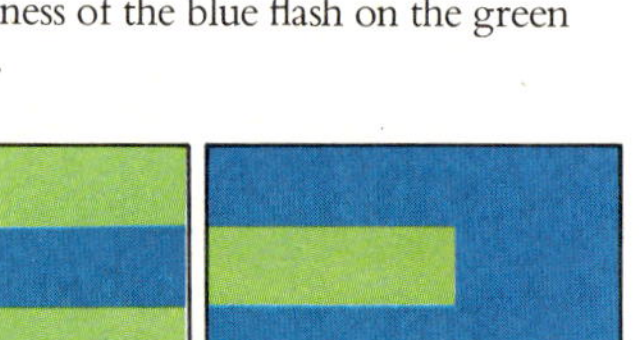

The large area of green seems greener in relationship to the blue flash, but when it appears as a flash on a blue ground the effect is more yellow. At the same time the eye detects redness in the blue flash on green but not in the same blue as background; the result of the "after-image" of the green on the blue.

The pure hue at the left is re at half-strength **rose**: as a ve light tint it becomes **pale pi**

Red moving towards blue is **magenta** at its most intense; fading to **mallow** and at its lightest to **orchid pink**.

The half-way hue between r and blue is **purple**, fading fi to **violet**, then **mauve**, then **lavender**. **Lilac** is another n for a pale purple tint.

Blue with red added is **genti** at its most intense, **delphiniu** at about half-strength, becoming **periwinkle** as it grows paler.

Pure or **spectrum blue** is extremely rare in flowers. A slightly paler form is **hydrangea** blue. **Forget-m not** is a washed-out pure blu

Above A range of colour samples from red to blue printed to show the pure hue on the left fading to a pale tint. The pure, or intense, colour is "saturated". The lighter tones are progressively less saturated. But the hue remains characteristic of the parent (intense) colour even in a very pale version.

Right When colours are closely related in tone, as these pinks and love-in-a-mist are by lightness, their hue—or actual place in the spectrum—may be unimportant. Another sort of relationship takes over to make a sympathetic picture.

Right A fierce fight between complementary colours of strong value can be acceptable when they are well-matched—and in fairly small doses. Here the golden new leaves of *Mahonia aquifolium* 'Moseri' clash with the fierce magenta flowers of *Geranium macrorrhizum*.

Above The colour wheel is a conventional way of demonstrating the relationships between the colours of the spectrum by dividing them into segments of equal width. It ignores the fact that the wave-bands of different colours as seen, for example, in a rainbow are wider or narrower in order to show the complementary colours directly opposite one another.

This very early colour wheel was painted in 1839 by the French chromatographer Chevreul, who designed the Gobelin tapestries of the period. Since his time the range of colours available in paint pigments and dyes has been enormously enlarged. Turquoise, for example, was very subdued until the 1930s when I.C.I. produced the brilliant pigment known as monastral blue.

Above An example of mismanagement with colour. The blue-pink of the dianthus (left) and the yellow-pink rose (top) show that yellow- and blue-pinks should be kept apart.

Left A subdued range of woodland greens and browns in an unusual approach to formal bedding. It is effective here because all the colours are "muddied" to the same degree.

Below A "riot" of colour sometimes works because almost all the possible clashes are used at once: extreme contrast is the theme. There is no denying it presents a lively picture.

A single colour

The short cut to making a big impact with colour, as with everything else in the garden, is to be ruthlessly single-minded. If you can bring yourself to devote a part of your garden to one colour only, with variety limited to heights, shapes and tones, you will have a picture people will take away with them. It need only be for one season that you impose the rigid discipline. It is possible to have a garden that is yellow in spring and red in the autumn: but for total conviction the whole setting, including the leaves of the background shrubs, or hedge, or trees, must join in the scheme.

The monochrome garden seems to have been yet another invention of the astonishing Gertrude Jekyll in the last quarter of the nineteenth century. As a painter she studied and understood colour better than any gardener before her. In devoting whole self-contained sections of gardens to single colours her idea was to set moods in motion. Like all designers she wanted to manipulate the reactions of her audience. By making them pass through an archway from a cool enclosure of blues and greys to a glowing gold and yellow garden she could be sure of exclamations: "It's like sunshine after rain!"

Strong doses of one colour undeniably affect the mood of the viewer. If yellow is warming and cheering, soft blues and mauves are soothing, red and orange are exciting, white is at once peaceful and lively, fresh and yet somehow formal.

White is much the easiest single colour to handle. The choice of white flowers is almost infinite. A remarkable number of flowers that we think of as being other colours have a white form as well. There are white agapanthus as well as blue, white campanulas, white phlox, white roses, white (or at least cream) red hot pokers, white Michaelmas daisies, white daffodils, white lilies, white clematis, white veronicas, white cyclamen, white honesty. . . . With a white garden, in fact, the skill comes in relating the plants to each other and creating a setting that makes their whiteness tell. In the famous white garden at Sissinghurst, shown opposite, Vita Sackville-West used quantities of grey-leaved plants as a transition between the enclosing dark green of yew and box and the stark whiteness of the flowers. White directly against dark green would have been too obvious and startling. Gently creamy-white flowers also help to keep the mood calm, where laundry whiteness all around might prove dazzling and irritating.

In any colour scheme the leaves have a part to play at least as great as the flowers. In silver-grey schemes—perhaps the most fashionable today—the leaves do the whole job, with a few innocuous flowers allowed in as contrast, but most (since many useful grey-leaved plants have unremarkable daisy flowers of brassy yellow) actually sheared off while they are still in bud.

There is no reason why carefully chosen leaves of different shades of green, and the few green flowers of any worth, should not be used to make an all-green garden. In practice, however, all the emphasis would inevitably fall on the contrasting shapes and textures of the plants. Green is a colour; indeed, the most important in the garden. But since it is all round us, to try to single it out for attention is like painting with white ink on white paper.

Of all colours red is the hardest to handle on its own. There are not so many truly red flowers (or leaves) to choose from. Early in the year, in fact, there are practically none except tulips. The red borders at Hidcote, illustrated above right, make use of such bulky and permanent furnishing as the purple-leaved cobnut and a dark red form of the Norway maple (which is cut back to a stump each winter to make it produce over-size leaves) to give a dark background to such flowers as dahlias and crocosmias, scarlet bergamot and orange day lilies. Although reds come out to meet you in good light in a green setting, in poor light and *en masse* they tend to retreat and become dark holes in the picture. A dusky copper background helps to throw the lighter reds forward. Certainly the total effect is rich and strange.

Yellow has the advantage that there are so many gold-leaved and variegated plants, including plenty of evergreens, to stabilize the picture. Gertrude Jekyll used anything that captured the right shade, not scorning, for example, golden privet, though privet is scarcely a conventional border plant. Yellow flowers are never in short supply, but do look relentless without the relief of some white and cream here and there. A yellow border can either be cooled (to great effect) by a leavening of blue, or warmed with touches of orange among such flowers as day lilies, nasturtiums, California poppies or chrysanthemums that lie naturally on the red side of yellow. Either course will seem consistent and correct—both together will start a seed-packet riot.

A blue corner is scarcely possible—there are so few flowers that can truly be called blue in the pure sense of a gentian or a meconopsis. But in the lilac-violet-lavender segment of the spectrum, where the Michaelmas daisies lie, there are possibilities for the tenderest and most romantic garden picture. Gertrude Jekyll's Michaelmas daisy border, illustrated below, is the triumphant expression of an artist's self-discipline.

Silver foliage, in its full range from filigree to plate (in this case from *Artemisia arborescens* to *Salvia argentea*, with softly furry leaves) proves one of the most popular single-colour themes.

Left The Michaelmas daisy border in Gertrude Jekyll's own garden, at Munstead Wood, Surrey, here painted by her friend George Elgood, was to start a fashion for gardens limited to one colour, or at least a narrow part of the spectrum. In this case it was limited to one season as well.

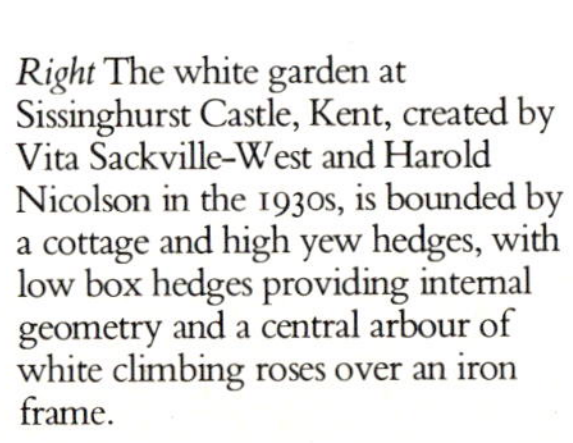

Right The white garden at Sissinghurst Castle, Kent, created by Vita Sackville-West and Harold Nicolson in the 1930s, is bounded by a cottage and high yew hedges, with low box hedges providing internal geometry and a central arbour of white climbing roses over an iron frame.

Below The red border at Hidcote, Gloucestershire now, like Sissinghurst below, a National Trust property, is possibly the only one of its kind. Dahlias, crocosmias, scarlet bergamot and orange day lilies provide the reds. Purple-leaved cobnut and a Norway maple provide the darker background.

Below The famous gold borders at Pyrford Court, Surrey, also designed by Gertrude Jekyll, look rather less dazzling today than when they were planted, as the background evergreens have taken over space once allotted to yellow flowers.

More tactics with colour

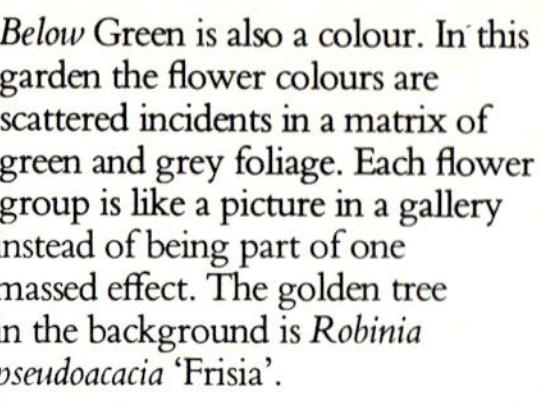

Below Green is also a colour. In this garden the flower colours are scattered incidents in a matrix of green and grey foliage. Each flower group is like a picture in a gallery instead of being part of one massed effect. The golden tree in the background is *Robinia pseudoacacia* 'Frisia'.

Between planning a garden in a single colour and conceiving and managing a complex and coherent colour scheme is a difference as great as between decorating a room and painting a picture. True garden picture-makers are rare indeed. Most of us have to be content with the inherent pleasure in cheerful colours pleasantly organized—avoiding, as far as we can, the "riot" threatened on so many seed packets.

Up to a point the seasons dictate the rules. Winter reduces the palette but finds a lovely equilibrium in its muted range of browns, greys and purples. Spring juggles with contrasts of the most daring kind. Summer provokes us with its heavy green mantle to set out our most flaunting colours. Autumn strikes great chords of harmony with its turning leaves, dominating whatever we do.

The gardener's thoughts on colour are bound to be seasonal (as we have seen in *An approach to planting* pages 192–3). They will grow in coherence and authority if they follow certain rules experience has shown to be widely applicable.

The first is that colour-contrasts in themselves quickly become wearisome: especially if the colours are in anything like equal quantities. It is no new discovery that red stands out in sharp relief against green, or that grey and purple foliage are powerful foils for each other. There may well be a place for both these contrasts somewhere in your garden, but only as an isolated and climactic moment. It is almost always a mistake to make contrast a theme.

For reasons that reach too far into the science of optics for me to follow it takes more effort for the eye to focus on red than on other colours. If red and colours near it are to be prominent it is best to group them in a gradual and harmonious progression so that the eye can take them in. Blue on the other hand is one of the colours most easily focused. A graduated set of blues has little stimulus in it, but calls for contrast from yellow or white to make it come alive.

Any contrast should be heavily weighted on one side or the other, with one colour unmistakably dominant. Where the contrast involves a strong colour and a weaker one it is the weaker one that should predominate in area. Small areas of light colours among large ones of stronger tones seem feeble and indecisive, whereas one strong colour dotted here and there on a quiet ground can be very effective.

In general it is best not to play any strong contrast straight, but to lead up to it with an intermediate colour that prepares the eye. Gertrude Jekyll recommended leading up to any particularly brilliant flower colour with a related but quieter one. When she wanted to change gear in her borders from one part of the spectrum to another she would reduce speed, as it were, with low-toned colours, make the shift in this range where almost anything goes, then gradually build up to higher speeds and faster cornering in the new range.

The most useful all-rounders for such bridge passages are white and grey. Grey-leaved plants are invaluable as intermediaries in any colour scheme. The popularity of little grey shrubs must be partly due at least to the fact that it is hard to misplace them. Not only are light tones always more amenable and adaptable than strong and dark ones, but of all light tones silver-grey has most friends and fewest enemies.

Moreover, to the picture-maker there is a great advantage in having certain more or less permanent pivotal points, which foliage, with its long season, provides much better than flowers. My main borders pivot round what I conceive to be the perfect harmony of box and common juniper; a regular association in the Pyrenees and Cevennes of south-west France. Both are evergreen. Both change colour subtly with the seasons. Box is everywhere accepted as an ideal foil for almost anything. The juniper is not exactly a grey plant, but neither is it green. It is a thing of moods and shadows like old lichened stone. With these two quiet plants dominant—the juniper as a line of pillars down the centre of the borders; the box as low hedges and a pyramid in each corner—I find that even a magpie collection of flowers that have caught my fancy begins to have a certain coherence. This coherence, however, is more noticeable in the relatively low-angled light of morning and evening than at noon.

Humphry Repton remarked that all natural objects look best with the light behind them; all man-made objects with the sun on them. It is certainly true that back-lighting has a striking power of flattery. Plant your flower borders to the south and west of where you will sit of an afternoon to enjoy them and all (or most) of your chromatic crimes will be forgiven you.

As to the tricks you can play with colour: it is a well-established fact that certain colours in certain lights advance towards you while others recede. I have already mentioned the power of red to detach itself from the background. Blue gives the opposite impression: it seems to slink away.

Right and below right Red has the quality of approaching the viewer: blue the reverse. The red azalea and the blue bank of gentians (right) are only a few feet apart though the distance appears much greater. *Below* A sudden patch of red distorts the perspective of a well-composed view by bringing the distance closer.

By painting a misty background in blues and greys and related quiet colours it is possible, even in a small garden, to produce the illusion of greater depth; especially with the help of red and other vibrant colours in the foreground. Conversely putting red at the far end of a vista has the effect of apparently shortening the distance, which can upset the perspective.

Another trick, which is perfectly exemplified by the picture at the bottom of the opposite page, is to create an artificial pool of light—in this case with creamy tulips in a clearing among dark evergreens. Variegated-leaved plants can be similarly effective in sunless places when given a background of very dark leaves.

Nor should we forget that paint can play tricks as well as plants. Gates and doors in gardens tend to be painted away into the background as far as possible in tones of green, brown and grey. The Japanese have no such inhibitions. One of their most telling strokes is a sudden orange-painted temple gateway in a setting of tree-green and rock-grey.

Above Flowers and leaf-colours in the walled garden at Crathes Castle, Scotland are controlled with great sublety to give an overall tapestry effect. Purple-leaved smokebush makes a richly sombre centrepiece strong enough to dominate a wide range of bright reds, yellows, oranges and pinks.

Far left The mauve of a distant bank of aubrietia is picked up with scattered anemones of the same colour among a drift of white ones in the foreground.

Left Pale yellow tulips among forget-me-nots in a clearing among dark rhododendrons creates the effect of a patch of sunlight.

Above Scarlet tulips in long grass jump out of the picture to create an effect quite disproportionate to their numbers. The pointilliste scattering of red is extremely effective in holding together an idyllic spring scene. Had the flowering cherries been pink instead of white the tulips might well look wrong.

Left A palette limited to variegated leaf-colours only can be very effective. Here the shapes and textures of the leaves provide ample liveliness and variety.

Right Gardeners often forget the possibilities of paint on doors, gates, fences or summer-houses as an integral part of their colour-scheme.

The development of the modern garden

Our present set of ideas of what constitutes a garden has long roots back into history; not just of our own countries but of all civilized lands.

As far as we know gardening first started, quite independently, in two places—Egypt and China. Egyptian gardens were based on irrigated smallholdings in the desert, Chinese on Imperial hunting parks in what was then the richest country in plant life the world has known since the Ice Ages.

These two sources started traditions that were diametrically opposed in every way, and which can be summarized as the formal and the informal; the straight-edged and the flowing; the architectural and the naturalistic.

Until the beginning of the eighteenth century the Egyptian tradition, transmitted through the Greeks and Romans, the Persians, the Moors, the Italians and the French, reigned supreme in the West, but had no influence at all in the East—east of India, that is. Then suddenly the English started to garden in what was to all intents and purposes the Chinese way. There is no direct evidence of influence. Yet it is hard to believe there is no link waiting to be discovered.

The English style was taken up wholesale in the century that followed and has been, with the exception of occasional classical revivals, the dominant mode of thinking about gardens since. In turn, however, it has borrowed from the vocabulary of the classical style, so that today in most deliberately planned gardens the two idioms are inextricably mixed.

None the less there remains the basic dichotomy of what we now call the "formal" and the "informal"—which goes straight back to the diverse roots of our gardening ideas.

The principal development that has overlain this chopping and changing of styles has been the stress laid on plants for their own sakes. The story of modern gardening, from the late eighteenth century on, has been the story of greater and greater interest in plants and more and more variety, with correspondingly less emphasis on the design of the garden.

The limit of the undesigned garden was reached with the concept of the woodland garden, which started in the middle of the nineteenth century and reached its climax in the middle of this. Woodland gardening is closely linked to the cult of the rhododendron. (The finest Himalayan kinds need sheltered forest-like conditions.) Some woodland gardens began as collections of specimen trees and surprised their owners by turning into woods as the trees grew. Some of the best have a plan of glades and vistas derived in part from the classical, in part from the naturalistic schools. Many, however, are simply highly coloured woodland with all the thought given to the cultivation and juxtaposition of plants.

Where layout is concerned, if there is a significant modern departure from the twin traditions it is towards abstract shapes echoing ideas in painting and sculpture. Modern patios and small gardens frequently have no straight lines or traditional formality, yet their flowing forms are definitely not of nature's making. Their spiritual ancestors are the works of Mondrian, Picasso or Moore.

This section is not a history of gardening. It is a series of flashbacks to the moments of fulfilment in garden design, when styles we still refer to were crystallized by a combination of terrain, climate, social history and fashion.

It represents these originals and some of the cross-fertilizations of ideas between them—a subject which is still in some cases little understood. And it details the components of each style: components which have now become part of our gardening vocabulary.

Plus ça change. . . . A modern garden in Holland, at Walenburg near The Hague, combines the axial formality of the seventeenth century with modern freedom in planting. A plan which satisfies both the desire for order and the sense of poetry.

In a Persian garden

Mediterranean, and hence all Western, gardening had its origins in Egypt between three and four thousand years ago. Since Egypt is a natural desert, depending entirely on irrigation from the Nile for its fertility, its gardens were planted round reservoirs and along canals of the kind used for irrigation. The canals were straight for practical reasons; trees planted for shade naturally followed them in straight rows. It was logical to have the main water tank for supply, for fish, for the sacred lotus and for general *agrément* in the centre.

Hence, the theory goes, the axial designs, the straight lines, the "formality" of all classical Mediterranean-inspired gardens to our own day—via the Persians, whose style swept eastwards to India and westwards to Spain with the spread of Islam, and the Romans, whose adaptation of Egyptian style was repeated by the Renaissance.

The Persians have a special place in the story of gardening. No race has been so captivated by the pleasure of gardens. In the words of the historian Arthur Upham Pope "the need for a garden is more deeply rooted, more articulate, and more universal in Persia than the Japanese passion for flowers or the English love of country". The vast aridity of Persia and its pitiless sky made the high-walled garden, with the shade of its trees and its air cooled by streams and fountains, the simple recipe for paradise. Mohammed's promise of paradise, in fact, is precisely that—a steady supply of black-eyed houris "of resplendent beauty, blooming youth, virgin purity and exquisite sensibility", in a garden pavilion shaded with palms and pomegranates, beside streams not only of water but of wine and honey. The word "paradise" originally meant a hunting park, and it is still a Persian word for garden.

The Persian garden plan remained resolutely formal; an elaboration of the Egyptian plan, commonly based on the form of a cross. Two main waterways divided the garden in four—representing, it is said, the four quarters of the universe. Often the centre of the cross was a brimming tank, lined with blue tiles to accentuate the freshness of the water. In bigger gardens subsidiary canals divided and subdivided the space again and again. Little tinkling water jets made sure that you heard the water as well as saw it. Tall chenar trees (oriental planes) shaded the centre, while round the edges cypresses, pines, poplars, date palms, almond, orange and other fruit trees cooled and scented the air.

The season for flowers is brutally short in Persia, which must have intensified their pleasure in them for the brief duration of spring. The canals were sometimes lined with borders of flowers (as they are in the Generalife gardens in Granada, a direct descendant) and flowers were encouraged to grow promiscuously in long grass (or clover, which stayed green for longer) under the trees. Tulips, irises, primulas, narcissi, jonquils, hyacinths, hollyhocks, evening primroses, violets, anemones, pinks and carnations, lilies, lilac and jasmine are all mentioned. Many bulbs are natives of Persia, but the Persians were also the first people to go plant hunting abroad. Their most treasured flower of all was the rose—partly, it may be, because it went on flowering when other flowers were past. Almost certainly trade or conquest had introduced the Chinese perpetual-flowering rose.

By the thirteenth century, following the almost incredible campaigns of the Mongol emperor Genghis Khan, the routes to China were well established and the Chinese influence can be seen distinctly in Persian painting. All the surviving paintings of gardens date from this period or later, and many of them show strangely Chinese-looking features; not only details of architecture but naturalistic meandering streams with rocky margins. In fact Chinese gardening. Whether such gardens were ever actually made or not, it is the first meeting of East and West in garden art.

The key to the gardens of the Islamic world is the idea of an oasis. All round stretch bare hills in the burning sun. Within the garden walls the essentials are cool shade and the sight and sound of water.
This conjectural reconstruction of a fourteenth-century Persian garden in spring shows the features common to all Islamic gardens—a high surrounding wall, straight tile-lined channels of water, bubbling and sparkling fountains, trees for shade and fruit, a pavilion or "kiosk", and a strong emphasis on flowers, in beds and pots.

There are no statues, as Islamic law forbids idols in human form. Kiosks often took more elaborate forms than this, sometimes rising to several stories, and often completely surrounded by water.

Spring is a fleeting season in Persia. Early in the year the fruit trees and the native bulbs bloom. Shortly afterwards, before the chenar trees are fully in leaf, comes the high season for flowers; then all is over for the year save the roses. Persia's native roses include the brilliant yellow and red *Rosa foetida*. Lacking flowers in summer the Persians used faience tiles on every surface to provide colour. Some early paintings show wide pavements of green tiles as a substitute for grass which would inevitably be brown for most of the year.

Miniatures of the fourteenth century onwards show that Persia was strongly influenced by Chinese ideas. Many of them show kiosks in scenes of naturalistic Chinese landscape.

Low hedges of clipped myrtle surround beds of mixed flowers and bulbs by the steps to the kiosk. Beside the pool a spring wells up in the paving and flows into the main channel. Ornamental fowl were another way of bringing colour into the garden. Peacocks are native forest birds of India, from Assam south to Ceylon.

The garden is divided in four by its main canals. The name Chahar-Bagh, meaning fourfold garden, is still common in Persia and India. The biggest gardens repeated the grid system of canals, since ground beyond the sight and sound of water could hardly be considered as garden. The grandest of all gardens in this style were made in the sixteenth and seventeenth centuries by the Moghuls in India and Kashmir.

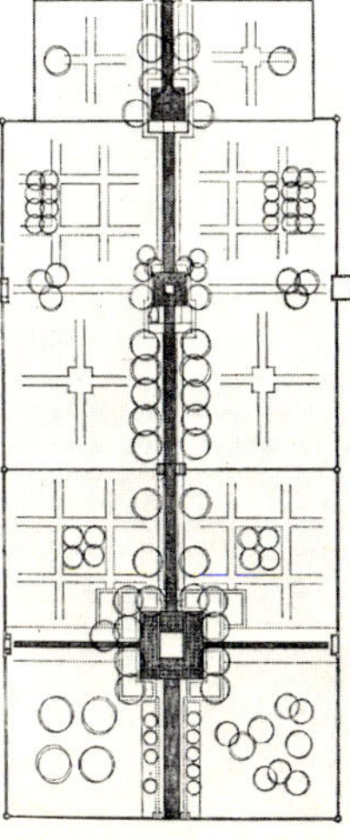

Left The plan of the Moghul Shalamar Bagh, the great Kashmir garden of Shah Jahan built in 1642 shows the grid system of canals extended.

Right A fourteenth-century Persian miniature of the lovers Humay and Humayan in a garden shows a completely informal park-like scene more like a Chinese garden.

Far right Lovers in a sixteenth-century Moghul garden of the period of the great Emperor Akbar have a formalized and artificial setting far removed from the hunting-park.

Italian gardens: origins and influence

Below The Roman Renaissance of the sixteenth-century filled gardens with architecture again. The Villa Aldobrandini at Frascati was built in about 1600 on a typically Roman hillside site with a monumental water cascade as its centre-piece. In front of the villa was a complicated formal parterre of flowers.

Top The strongly architectural basis of Italian gardens stems directly from Ancient Rome. The Emperor Hadrian's villa at Tivoli rambled over 700 acres, with endless courtyards, pools, gardens and grottoes, all encompassed with columns and enlivened with fountains and statuary.

Above A reconstruction of the younger Pliny's more modest villa on the coast south of Rome shows the way the gardens penetrated into the heart of the house. Loggias and porticoes were carefully arranged to take advantage of winter sun and summer breezes.

Left The traditional Tuscan garden aims to combine the homely intimacy of medieval secret gardens —box-edged plots within high walls—with airy sites and long views. The sixteenth-century Villa Capponi, overlooking Florence, is one of the most perfect examples.

It is easy to gain the impression that the history of Italian gardens is written in the margins of the history of Italian architecture. All the characteristic features seem to be builders' work: staircases, balustrades, cascades, pavilions and pavements—even the cypress avenues are imitations of colonnades. Certainly when we speak of a garden in the Italian style we mean one with more than a modicum of masonry—and thus, alas, one of a kind that will probably never be built again.

The origins of the style are obviously found in Ancient Rome. The rich Romans were as adept as anyone has ever been in the theory and practice of making themselves comfortable. They took the greatest pains to site their villas on hillsides with exceptional views, where cooling breezes would reach them, above the malarial valleys. Within the villas there were courts and colonnades designed for every phase of wind and weather: a cloister for exercise, for example, would face south-east to catch the low winter sun but escape the summer heat. With outdoor dining-rooms and enclosed swimming pools (heated and unheated) the interpenetration of house and garden was total. Spanish patios give us some idea of the principle—but perhaps California furnishes the best modern examples of such indoor-outdoor living.

When the Renaissance picked up the threads of Roman design the evidence of ancient practice was best preserved in the ruined buildings. Other gardens, beyond the immediate precincts of the villa, had disappeared. We now know that there was scarcely a mode of gardening that the Romans did not practise; from the purely formal, to the woodland, to the "landscape", to the fantastic cave-and-grotto. One of their weaknesses was topiary, which they practised to excess. But when Pliny remarks "on a sudden in the midst of the elegant

Right and *below* By 1600 the Baroque taste was allowing grottoes and wild woodland to invade the fringes of the formal garden. The source for the cascade at the Villa Aldobrandini (*right*) is a "natural" piece of rockwork in the woods, although its destination (*below*) is strictly architectural and formal.

Left At the height of the Renaissance, with classical order and symmetry triumphant, there was still room for garden follies. The sixteenth-century Villa d'Este at Tivoli, famous for its virtuoso waterworks, also possessed a scale model of Ancient Rome, seen crumbling on the right-hand side of the picture.

Above The Villa Pietra at Florence is an idealized conception of a timeless Italian garden made by an English scholar in the twentieth century. As a series of intimate green rooms on a hillside it is in keeping with Tuscan tradition. The green "theatre" is an idea with classical roots often repeated in Italian gardens.

Right In contrast to the above the Italian extravaganza at San Simeon, W. Randolph Hearst's "castle" in California, is the nearest the modern world provides to the feel of Ancient Rome. The grandiose swimming pool harks back to Hadrian's villa opposite even if the scale is puny in comparison with the original.

Above The beauty of the northern Italian lakes has tempted gardeners since the days of "sweet Catullus' all-but-island, olive-silvery Sirmio". The Sirmio of the Roman poet was on the south shore of Lake Garda near Verona. It may have looked something like the eighteenth-century Villa Balbianello, *above*, on Lake Como. The most famous of all the lake gardens is Isola Bella in Lake Maggiore, an entire island coverted into garden architecture, started in the seventeenth century and still not entirely finished.

regularity you are surprised with an imitation of the negligent beauties of rural nature", it is hard to know what picture we should conjure up.

The little garden-making that went on in the Dark Ages was probably confined to the monasteries and the courts of emperors and kings. The royal pleasure-grounds in Palermo and Naples were some sort of hybrid of Islamic hunting-park (inherited from the conquering Saracens) and Roman villa. The great thirteenth-century treatise on agriculture, Crescentius' *Liber Ruralium Commodorum*, describes flowery parks and menageries that seem more Moorish than medieval. But he also describes what was clearly the standard domestic garden of the Middle Ages—the *hortus conclusus*, or walled enclosure, with a fountain, turfed seats, vine-shaded arbours and beds of flowers and herbs.

This was certainly the sort of Tuscan garden Boccaccio described in the *Decameron* in the middle of the fourteenth century. It was Boccaccio's friend Petrarch who first accomplished what William Kent was to repeat, with so much more publicity, three hundred and fifty years later: he "leaped the fence and saw that all Nature was a garden". Petrarch, who lived at one time in Provence, climbed Mont Ventoux to admire the view—an excursion his contemporaries considered dangerously eccentric. He also delved back into Virgil for instructions on how to proceed with his gardening.

As the Renaissance gathered force in the Florence of the Medicis precepts for gardening were eagerly gleaned from the classics, notably by the architect Alberti. The most revolutionary garden was that of the Villa Medici, of about 1460, at Fiesole. The Tuscans, however, were fond of their old enclosed gardens and inclined rather to adapt them with a grotto here, a statue there, possibly to align them along a central axis in the classical fashion, rather than uproot them and start great building works. There are still gardens round Florence that are more medieval than Renaissance.

It was in Rome that the fully fledged Renaissance garden first emerged, as a prelude to the rebuilding of St Peter's. In 1503 Pope Julius II commissioned Bramante, who was later to draw up the plans for the basilica, to build the Vatican gardens—and build was the word. The Cortile del Belvedere at the Vatican became the prototype for dozens of works of imaginative roofless architecture. The elements are stairs, colonnades, statues in niches, and fountains. Nature was scarcely allowed to breathe.

Bramante's successors, Ligorio and Vignola, brought the Italian garden to its climax with their masterpieces of the middle years of the sixteenth century: the Villa d'Este at Tivoli, the Villa Farnese at Caprarola, and the Villa Lante near Viterbo, which is described on the next pages.

It is hard for us to imagine them as they looked when they were built, "white from the mason's hand". Gertrude Jekyll wrote, "precious qualities come by age, both of masonry and vegetation. The abrasion of hard edges and the falling out of mortar are a gain, for the lichen laps over the bruised moulding and the mortar is replaced by a cushion of moss."

But as time went by the fashion did begin to shift away from a sense of total control. It may just have been that the trees were growing up and adopting picturesque attitudes in the once strict gardens, but by 1600 Baroque taste was actively encouraging them to do so. By the time the Italian style was eclipsed by the French in the seventeenth century, areas of wild wood and naturalistic grottoes were the height of fashion.

Italian gardens: components of a style

The garden-architects of the Renaissance coined an idiom so powerful that its freshness is now hard to comprehend. We have all seen so many grand flights of stone stairs, monumental fountains, niches, cascades, double ramps, terraces and balustrades, along so many axes leading to so many porticoes in front of the grand villas, hotels and casinos of the world that it takes a slight mental effort to look at the picture opposite with fresh eyes.

The Villa Lante has been chosen so often by critics as the most perfect garden in Italy, and one of the most beautiful spots on earth, that it is worth looking for its special qualities. What makes this particular formalized hillside so enchanting and satisfying?

First, it is clearly a garden for the garden's own sake. It was begun in 1566 as a country retreat for Cardinal Gambara. He is said to have commissioned Vignola, who had established his reputation in the long-drawn-out construction of Cardinal Farnese's palatial villa and gardens at Caprarola nearby. Gambara wanted something simpler, with more emphasis on garden beauty and little on the house—so little in fact that it is chopped in half and becomes two dignified but modest pavilions that introduce the garden rather than the usual reverse arrangement.

The axial plan—everything along a central straight line—is thus made to refer solely to the garden itself. The stress falls principally on the elaborate water-parterre in the foreground; as polished and humanized an outdoor space as it is possible to imagine. Then the eyes and feet are drawn upwards to find the source of all this sparkling water, and are led inexorably, in a series of detours (enough to make you face in every direction as you go, and glance back repeatedly at the scintillating fountain and the spacious view beyond) into closer and closer acquaintance with the water and, almost imperceptibly, deeper and deeper into the heart of green nature.

On the way the water takes many forms: spouts, jets and runnels; a rippling rectangle in the middle of a dining-table where wine was cooled and perhaps dishes floated from guest to guest; a formal cascade between recumbent river-gods; and then a long foaming channel in imitation of the Cardinal's arms—the claws of the crayfish—repeated to keep the water white and writhing between the encroaching walls of green.

All this leads to an upper terrace where small pavilions flank a shady spring and paths radiate away into deep groves of ilex: a classical reference as fundamental as could be.

What the garden is saying, although to simplify it so is to miss half the point and all the nuances, is that there is an essential link between the utterly humanistic and artificial brilliance of the water parterre and the mysterious primeval source of its life: the woodland spring. Later Baroque gardens were to dally with the wild woods, bringing them by degrees into the picture. Here they are clearly defined as the all-important context for a human *tour de force*.

You are free to choose either end of the garden as the climax or, as the Cardinal probably intended, to regard the tension between the two, played out in garden terms, as the point and purpose of the villa.

The Villa Lante is a relatively small garden, but none of the garden masterpieces of Italy are very big—certainly nothing on a scale approaching the French extravaganzas of the next century. It is partly because of this modest human scale that their message is so clear and convincing. Perhaps, of all the gardens ever made, they have the strongest sense of comprehensive unity. When their style has been revived, as it was with a vengeance in the nineteenth century in countless expensive and usually meretricious examples, it has generally been amid distractions that have robbed it of its single-minded clarity. Italian is a term of honour; Italianate a term of reproach.

The Villa Lante is at Bagnaia, near Viterbo, 37 miles north of Rome. Work on the villa occupied some 40 years and only one of the two pavilions was built in the lifetime of its begetter, Cardinal Gambara. The work was completed by his nephew, Cardinal Montalto. Since about 1600 little has changed save the mellowing of the masonry and the spreading of the trees. Evergreen oaks with their dense crowns and planes with their dappled shade are the two principal trees. They were originally planted to form dense *boschi*, considerably more architectural in effect than the present tall woodland. Today the superb view from the top terrace down over the garden and across the rooftops of the village into the distance is framed by old planes.

Above It is right to be reminded, amid the serenity and even solemnity of such gardens in their old age, that they were built for fun as well as philosophy. Even the most sophisticated churchmen were amused by practical jokes. Guests at the Villa Lante were led into an enclosed garden where they were soaked to the skin by concealed water jets.

Left Giacomo Barrozzi (1507–1573), called Vignola after his birthplace, is traditionally credited with the design of Villa Lante, though no direct evidence exists that he designed it.

The formal parterre in front of the twin pavilions, forming the frontispiece of the garden and its main feature on entering, is about eighty yards square. Half of the box-edged beds, and the wall and gate separating the garden from the village of Bagnaia, are omitted from this painting. The box beds, some in scrollwork and some in simpler geometry, have been filled at various times with different flowers particularly chosen for their scent. Lemon trees are stood out in the square box-edged enclosures at the corners of the beds and along the walks. The crayfish coat of arms of Cardinal Gambara is cut in box on the ramp between the two pavilions.

The water-parterre surrounds what has been called the most beautiful fountain in Italy. Four figures hold aloft the arms of Cardinal Montalto, crowned with a star streaming water at every point. In the ponds "float" little stone boats. The stonework is kept deliciously moist by a central jet and various spouts, which gives it the gleam of polished bronze.

Flowers had a secondary role in Italian gardens of the Renaissance, but they were still much loved. The common red "geraniums" of today give no idea of the range of roses, irises, violets and pansies, hyacinths, carnations, hollyhocks, jasmine, lilies, lavender, poppies, primroses, narcissi and other old flowers that were cultivated in the parterres of the sixteenth century. Orange and lemon trees, originally imported from Sicily where the Saracens took them, have always played an important part. In most parts of Italy they have to be grown in pots so they can be moved indoors during the winter.

France: the grand manner

Below This imaginary garden based on the concept of Versailles necessarily reduces the scale of Le Nôtre's operations to show some of the detail. The Palace of Versailles alone with its forecourts would have filled the whole space. Even with this compromise only the immediate gardens are shown.

To epitomize French gardening with the work of Le Nôtre is not to belittle what went before him. French medieval gardens were as fine as any in Europe.

During the sixteenth century a fury of building and garden-making swept through France. Every great château was endowed with a girdle of glorious gardens in what might be called a high-flying medieval manner. Although Renaissance ideas were in full flood it proved impossible to apply logic and symmetry to craggy old castles. Du Cerceau's great volume of surveys of *Les Plus Excellents Bastiments de France* shows every detail of dozens of these gardens. Their flavour can still be tasted at Villandry (see pages 214–15).

By the beginning of the seventeenth century, with a Medici as Queen of France, the royal palace gardens in Paris (the Tuileries and the Luxembourg) were largely Italian in plan. Those of St Germain-en-Laye downstream on the steep banks of the Seine, begun for Henri IV in 1594, were directly inspired by the Villa d'Este.

At the same time French gardeners were working out their own versions of Italian models in a style more suitable to France. Most influential among them was Claude Mollet, royal gardener at the Tuileries, who is credited with the creation of *parterres de broderie* of an elegance never seen in Italy, and also with insisting on the importance of the avenue. When Le Nôtre was born in 1613, son of one of Mollet's staff, the milieu for his genius was set, and he was in the midst of it.

Nicolas Fouquet, Chancellor to the young Louis XIV, met Le Nôtre through his fellow-student, the painter Le Brun, and commissioned him to design the gardens of his palace at Vaux le Vicomte. Fouquet, however, over-reached himself with his great *fête champêtre* of 17 August 1661 and the jealous and malicious young king ruined and imprisoned him. Louis XIV then stole Le Nôtre (and most of Fouquet's garden).

Suddenly the scale of gardening was astonishingly enlarged. Already the French, generally gardening on flat land as opposed to the Italians' hillsides, disposed their parterres more generously under their castle walls. But now the decimal point was moved. The unit of measure was no longer one human being but a curtsey of courtiers. Le Nôtre declared: "I cannot abide a limit to a view." He drove his canals by kilometres, and his avenues and allées were not suffered to stop before the horizon.

Sheer scale alone immediately made his work revolutionary. But his success in handling such sweeps of landscape came from the application of strict principles. He always deliberately pushed back the planting from the building, making it stand proud from flat parterres or, sometimes, water. He took the Italian principle of an axial plan and used it to the limit, with a vast clearing as the main axis, walled with trees in perfect symmetry. The main cross-axes were always at right angles; between and within them diagonals and clearings and *jeux d'esprits* of every sort might multiply. He was recreating the criss-crossing rides of the great hunting forest of Chambord and Cheverny on the Loire, but filling them with elegant and spectacular incidents in infinite variety. He used long reflecting waters: the moats of older châteaux, or reminders of them. Above all he used fountains. Louis XIV was a hydromaniac, if there is such a thing. Never were fountains so many, so massive, or so marvellous. There was never enough water for the King's desires. Thousands of troops were added to the builders labouring on endless aqueducts to bring more.

Le Nôtre designed gardens for many of the French nobility, but Versailles is the epitome of them all. It manages to be a great work of art, built with overweening pride and callous brutality, yet with extraordinary imagination and love. Needless to say Versailles was envied and imitated by every ruler in Europe. But none ever approached it in artistry or majesty. None had Le Nôtre.

Right A series of vividly detailed engravings by Du Cerceau records the gardens of the greatest châteaux of France in the sixteenth century. There was little chance to apply Renaissance ideas of relating garden to house along a central axis when the house was a fortress. This engraving of the Château de Montargis shows the sort of lavish development of medieval ideas spiced with Italian details which was typical of the time. At Montargis the gardens girdled the castle, beyond the moat, with an inner ring of parterres (including mazes) traversed with great galleries of carpentry; then a high wall with a decorative frieze; then a larger area of orchards and kitchen gardens.

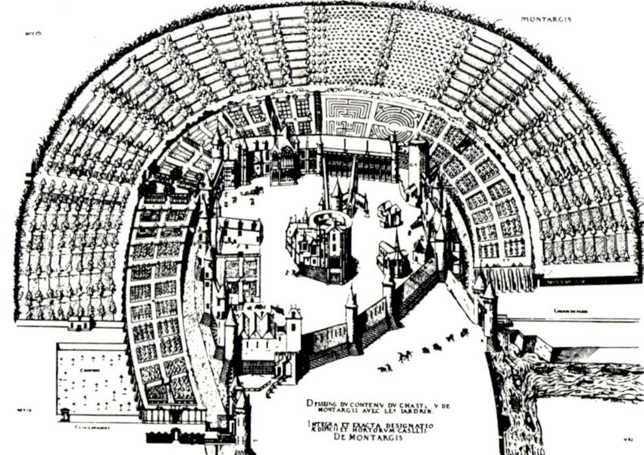

Right André Le Nôtre (1613–1700) painted in his middle years. Son of a gardener, an artist by training, Le Nôtre was as warm and unpretentious as his designs were logical and grand. When Louis XIV suggested he take a coat of arms he replied he already had one: "Three slugs surrounding a spade and crowned with cabbage leaves."

Left Of all the imitations of Versailles by foreign potentates the gardens of the Charlottenburg Palace at Berlin, recently fully restored, probably give the clearest idea of the original appearance of the parterres. Only aerial photography can do justice to their immaculate "embroidery".

It was Le Nôtre's principle to make the approach to the building plain, austere and imposing and also, in the last resort, defendable with high walls and railings. The building itself was always the culminating point of the garden, standing clear of the trees and implying the dominance of the proprietor over all he surveyed. The garden front, in the greatest possible contrast, was as rich with decoration as the entrance was stark and austere.

The first principle of a Le Nôtre garden is the dominating central axis, from the centre of the garden front, across the open parterres, along the broadest of the many rides, as far as the eye can see. At Versailles the axis is largely occupied by the wide Grand Canal that runs for more than a mile.

The trees along the rides, or allées, were planted in dense blocks of mixed kinds clipped into hedge-fronts as high as the gardeners could reach. Their free-growing branches above the clipping eventually provided a form of cornice, strengthening the architectural impression of these defined spaces.

Statues and vases of flowers in their hundreds lined the allées. At Versailles 95 sculptors were kept at work under Charles le Brun. Models of new work were made in plaster, painted to look like marble or bronze, put in place and left for the King's decision on which material should be used.

In the bosquets, or blocks of woodland, countless architectural incidents were hidden, ranging from fountains to theatres. An extraordinarily rich diversity of ornament was tucked away among the trees, never detracting from the main vistas, but always adding tempting diversions to a walk.

Dutch improvements in floriculture encouraged the growing of more flowers, though always in pots so they could be changed as they faded. The Trianon, a secondary palace in the park at Versailles, had flower beds in which the scent of tuberoses was so strong that ladies were overcome.

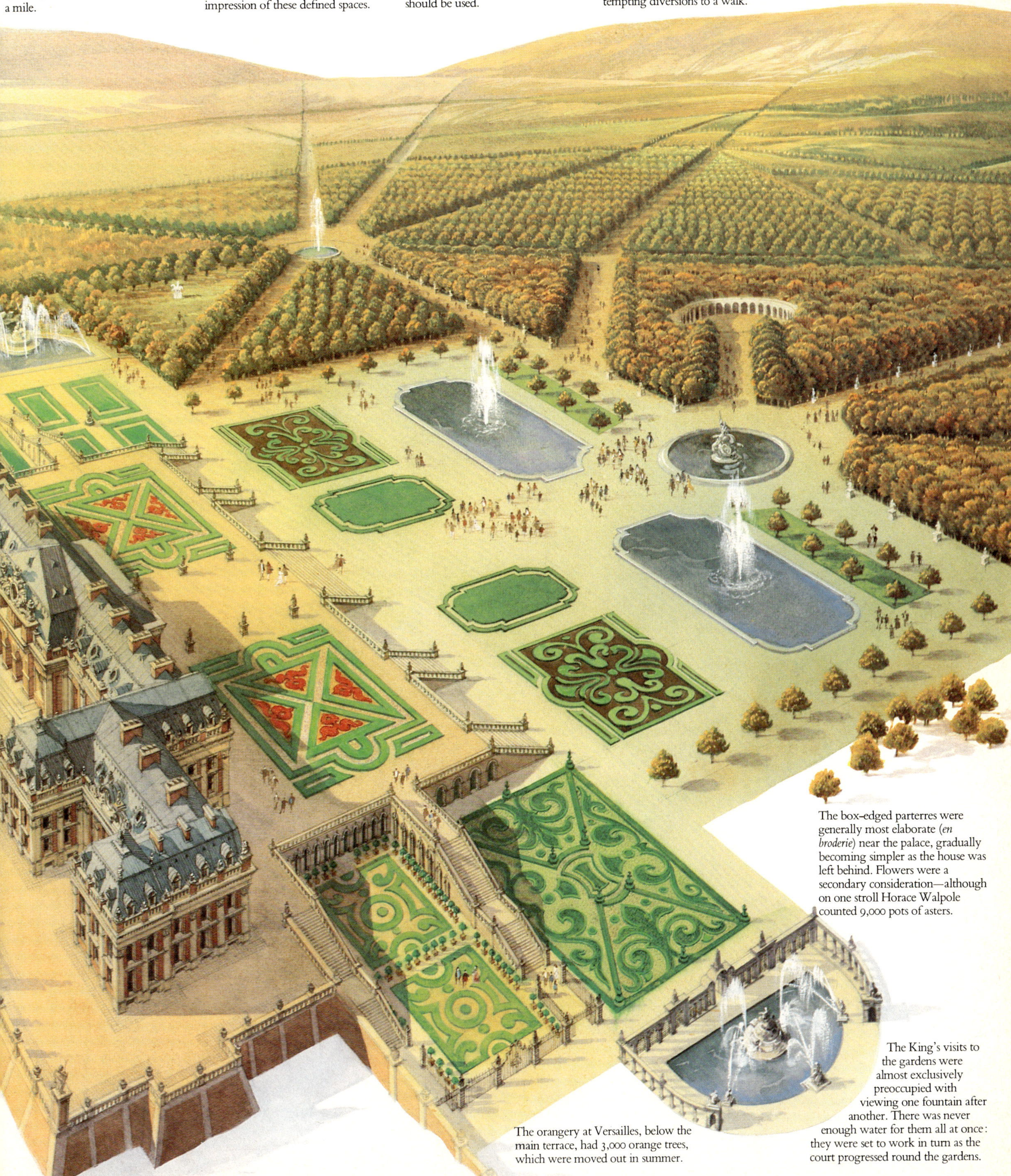

The box-edged parterres were generally most elaborate (*en broderie*) near the palace, gradually becoming simpler as the house was left behind. Flowers were a secondary consideration—although on one stroll Horace Walpole counted 9,000 pots of asters.

The King's visits to the gardens were almost exclusively preoccupied with viewing one fountain after another. There was never enough water for them all at once: they were set to work in turn as the court progressed round the gardens.

The orangery at Versailles, below the main terrace, had 3,000 orange trees, which were moved out in summer.

France since le Nôtre

By the end of the seventeenth century more than half the country within fifteen miles of Paris was covered with the gardens of the courts of Louis XIV and Louis XV. Far from being the exception, Versailles was simply the biggest and best of scores of such gardens, one abutting on another.

The pupils of Le Nôtre continued to pour out such performances until they became the basic garden style of almost every château in France, not to mention all the courts of northern Europe. They continued to draw inspiration from Italy and refine Italian ideas with French sophistication. Their innumerable cascades, for example, were built of finest coursed ashlar in contrast to Italy's relatively crude masonry. They carried the art of *treillage* to new heights of elaboration and finesse and made grottoes with all the hydraulic automatons and singing birds they could devise.

Yet inevitably the mood changed. Versailles without the personality of the Sun King became oppressive, sad and boring. Even in his lifetime he demanded constant change, for any garden that relies so heavily on architecture and inanimate objects, without the mystery of developing plants to keep adding interest, can become stale. The court moved on; it fell into disrepair.

About 1750 a number of events fired the move to a new direction. At court Madame de Pompadour rebuilt the Trianon, made a working dairy, and started cultivating flowers. News came back from England (the two countries were briefly at peace) that gardens were being remodelled on new and natural lines. And letters from missionaries in Peking gave enthusiastic if imprecise accounts of Chinese gardens, in which nothing was symmetrical, but different parts of the garden, marked by buildings in different styles, signified different moods: "*Scènes enchantés, horribles, riantes.*"

Within another ten years the signs of the times were clear. In 1760 a very good English poem celebrating nature, James Thomson's *The Seasons*, was translated into French and became a craze. In 1763 Jean-Jacques Rousseau's *La Nouvelle Héloïse* became a best-seller. Rousseau, according to the critic Taine, "made the dawn visible to people who had never risen till noon, the landscape to eyes that had only rested hitherto on drawing-rooms, the natural garden to men who had only walked between tonsured yews and rectilinear borders".

In the same year the Marquis de Girardin began France's first "landscape" garden at Ermenonville, where, fifteen years later, Rousseau was to die and be buried, by moonlight, on the Ile des Peupliers. The year Rousseau died Queen Marie-Antoinette set to work with an English gardener to create the Petit Trianon. Le Nôtre's world was dead and the world of romantic fantasy had begun.

By the time the Queen had finished with the Petit Trianon it boasted (or had boasted, for buildings were pulled down almost as soon as they were put up) a pagoda, a Chinese aviary, a theatre, a temple of Diana, Turkish fountains, a dairy and a farm, a hermitage, a *salon hydraulique*, an ancient temple on a large rock, a thatched cottage and a stone bridge. Finally it acquired the little hamlet that still exists, complete with operating peasantry, and furnished by the English gardener with masses of flowers. At this point the Revolution interrupted operations.

But as soon as the Revolution was over the fury of the *style anglo-chinois* really hit France. Thomas Blaikie, a Scots former undergardener at the Petit Trianon, was employed on all sides to design gardens. The Revolution and the anglo-chinois between them destroyed many of the truly French gardens of the old houses and put in their place "*le jardin anglais*"; at its best a total funfair of kiosks, ruins and assorted follies; at its worst a boring travesty of the English model.

The enlightening feature of this age was the new passion for flowers. The Empress Joséphine at La Malmaison collected not only every rose there was but every new plant she could find. Redouté and others made matchless paintings of them. The passion for new plants extended to trees, and *bouquets des arbres étrangers* appeared alongside every château.

The English style has co-existed with the French ever since. There have been various classical revivals, but without much hope, for the distinctive French style is the Grand Manner which, without a genuine megalomaniac at the helm, is apt to end in pompous pastiche.

Where French gardening is at its best today is in suitably scaled-down versions of the classic style, with all its cool and *hauteur* and, above all, in the national style that goes straight back to the crowded cultivation of the sixteenth century. *Jardin de curé*—"parson's garden"—is the expression for the sort of straightforward plot where flowers, vegetables and well-trained fruit-trees grow side by side. The onion lies down with the rose. The soul of France is here; beauty arises from the logic and the discipline.

Where French gardening is at its worst is in the Garden-centre style, which today obliterates everything native and necessary and replaces it with blue and yellow conifers, and red roses and geraniums.

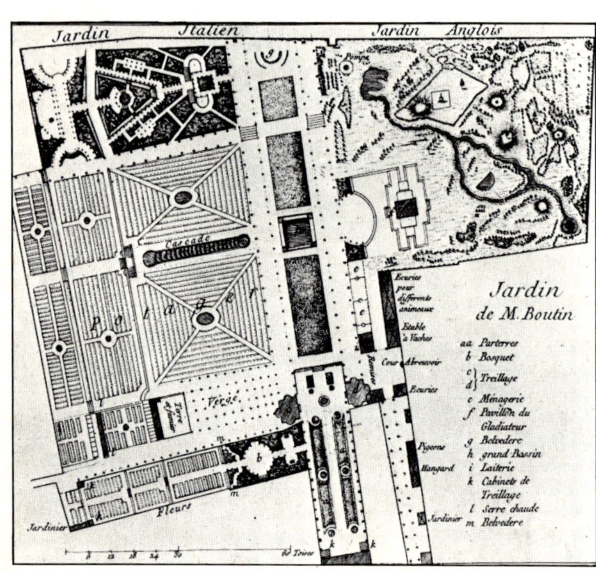

Left A plan of a Parisian garden modified about 1770 catches the French garden in a mood of indecision, with perfect examples of the traditional French style, the formal "Italian" style and the informal "English" style. The English style was to gain the ascendancy for large gardens, while the French style has been simplified but never really abandoned

Right The glory of French gardening in the early nineteenth century was the cultivation of flowers, particularly roses, encouraged by the passionate collecting of the Empress Joséphine and her patronage of the painter Pierre-Joseph Redouté. He painted this portrait of *Rosa indica vulgaris*, known in England as 'Parsons's Pink China', in 1817.

Below This ultimate kitchen garden, the apotheosis of the potager, was made early in the twentieth century at the Château de Villandry near Tours as a free reconstruction of the sixteenth-century gardens portrayed in du Cerceau's engravings. The vegetables are chosen for their colours and changed twice a year.

Right In the same Gallic spirit of combining usefulness with pleasure and orderliness this more modest bourgeois potager carries on the great tradition. Espalier fruit trees divide the walks: dwarf box hedges surround the beds. The juxtaposition of vegetables and flowers is taken as a matter of course.

Left The spirit of museumism invaded France and her gardens in the second half of the eighteenth century and prevailed for over a century. No mingling of architectural styles was too bizarre. This "Chinese" rockery surrounded by Greek or Egyptian monuments is part of a large sample sheet of possible follies.

Above centre The demand for formal gardens, created this twentieth- the old school is still alive in France. Russell Page, who has designed many of the best modern French gardens, created this twentieth-century version of the traditional canal-and-parterres scheme for a private client in the 1950s.

Above The relaxation of the Riviera has produced a more intimate style of garden which somehow blends English and Italian elements; informality in planning with fine features in stone on hillside sites. The Vicomte de Noailles' garden at Grasse contains one of the best private plant collections in France.

Dutch gardens

Examples of the classical styles of Islamic, Italian, French and English gardening have survived in such numbers that they seem familiar and unsurprising. Not so the Dutch style of the seventeenth and eighteenth centuries. Fashion and fortune have swept away the whole tradition.

What is a Dutch garden? The few old gardens that go by the name have little in common besides formality. Was there ever a characteristic Dutch style? To confuse the issue the Dutch, referring to what the world knows as a Dutch garden, call it English (rather as the French and English credit each other with the pox and other unedifying things).

The truth is that the Dutch, dedicated florists since time immemorial, became aware of garden design in the same northern Renaissance as the French, inherited much the same ideas of symmetry and stateliness as the French, and in due course imitated designs coming out of France.

But the needs of prosperous burghers growing flowers in a flat landscape under a grey sky were so different from the aristocratic showmanship of France that a distinctly Dutch way of gardening rapidly emerged, characterized above all by its scale. The Dutch gardened small. Even a big garden was divided into cosy little enclosures. As far as the towpath of the canal was all the view they were interested in.

The Japanese, who also garden small, keep it simple. They try to express limitless Nature with a distillation of her attractions: a rock, a tree, a fern. The Dutch took the opposite view, filling their little yards with the most elaborate furnishings they could devise. As florists they loved marbled, frilled, striped, doubled flowers. Apart from tulips, hyacinths, ranunculus, crown imperials, carnations, roses and auriculas were their favourites. Some say their taste for the highly coloured and artificial came from their trading contacts with the Orient and the Indies; some from their often cheerless weather. They made fitting beds for their fancy flowers in intricately flowing designs, trimmed with box hedges and punctuated with obelisks, statues and conceits of topiary. Topiary was carried to such lengths that it became identified in foreign minds with Holland, though in fact it goes back to the Romans. Avenues were a Dutch passion. Where the scale ruled out tall trees, clipped hedges (usually of hornbeam) were a common feature—and may well be a Dutch invention.

A watery approach was considered essential. In much of Holland it was also inevitable, as the land reclaimed by drainage from the sea is divided by regular canals. Where canals were absent prosperous houses were provided with moats to create the same effect. The swans that paddled these waters were another important feature. Fountains presented a problem. Tall jets were impossible. The low water pressure of a country without hills would allow no more than a falling arc. Where water would not glitter, therefore, gilt was employed. Fountains, statues and gates were painted and gilded with none of the modern reticence that decrees that lead should be grey and wrought iron black.

The garden on the right is a reconstruction of one of many similar villas that lined the banks of the Vecht, a 20-mile stretch of river between Utrecht and Muiden on the Zuider Zee near Amsterdam. The Vecht was to Amsterdam what the Brenta was to Venice 200 years earlier. Scores of trim houses and their gardens faced the waterway in what seems from engravings of the time to have been an atmosphere of perpetual regatta, with drinking parties and little orchestras and merchants' wives sitting in their gazebos gossiping about the waterborne passers-by.

All this is gone. Modern Holland gardens in an international style, still on a comfortable domestic scale, perhaps with special emphasis on bulbs, but without the charming formalities and conceits of the days of her merchant splendour.

The imaginary late-seventeenth-century Dutch garden above is divided into many little enclosures, either by hornbeam hedges or by shady tunnels consisting of a wooden framework wreathed in climbers. In the central parterre flowers are massed in intricate designs in box-lined beds. Near the house a gilded fountain dribbles into a square basin surrounded by a low railing and obelisks of tightly trimmed bay trees. Yews in wedding-cake or chessman shapes are set about at regular intervals. Statues are painted or gilded. So are the posts of the pergolas—in some gardens even tree-trunks were smartly painted blue and white. Orange trees in tubs are set out in serried ranks for summer after spending winter in a heated orangery. At the waterside iron gates provide a "clairvoyée" through which the good burgher can clearly see who is passing, while his wife plays cards in the brick gazebo with its painted shutters.

Above Abel Grimmer in the sixteenth century painted the forerunner of such a garden in his *Spring*. The design was simpler; the beds simply edged with spade-smoothed soil, but the tunnel-like arbour, the low railings, the trees in tubs and the general sense of order are already in evidence. Tulips began to arrive in Holland from Constantinople, via Vienna, towards the end of the sixteenth century.

Above The villa-lined Vecht River near Amsterdam in an eighteenth-century engraving, with the villa of Theodorus Boendermaker at Brenkelm in the foreground, showing its hedges, its clairvoyées and summerhouses. The whole district between Utrecht and Amsterdam had become one vast garden. Engravings exist of scores of similar gardens, yet not a single example survives.

Above The influence of Dutch design on later gardens has been surprisingly small. Such "Dutch" gardens as the above, at Hampton Court, are so called because they are enclosed and intimate with formal parterres. This garden dates back to England's Dutch king, William III. Hampton Court gardens were largely designed by Daniel Marot, a pupil of Le Nôtre at Versailles before he left to become court gardener to William.

Above Training living trees, usually elms, into tree houses was a long-lived Dutch conceit. In the large illustration above (upper right) a ring of elms has been made to form a leafy room on stilts.

China: the mother of gardens

Left The mountains of central China with their fantastic peaks have been a major influence in shaping the Chinese idea of natural beauty. This T'ang dynasty painting is of the Emperor Ming Huang's flight to Shu.

Above Rocks reminiscent of the mountains are dominant features in almost every Chinese garden. The more weirdly eroded and contorted they are the prouder the gardener. This is the Yu Yuan Garden.

If European gardening tradition begins with the systematic reclamation of a desert, Chinese gardening starts with the enjoyment of a landscape of unimaginable beauty, fertility and variety—an oriental Garden of Eden.

Where the flora of Europe had been decimated by the ice ages, and even North America's seriously depleted, eastern Asia had kept its primeval diversity of plants intact. The north China plain, at the time when Chinese gardening began, perhaps about 2000 BC, had a flora of unique richness: trees, shrubs and flowers of almost every family.

The gardener's contribution in such circumstances was simply to order and emphasize what was already there. Buildings and bridges, terraces, steps and gateways turned wooded lakes into gardens without a tree planted or a seed sown. The hunting parks of the early emperors were simply the landscaped enclosed.

Of course the Garden of Eden did not last. The population grew; the forests were cut down; a more sophisticated nobility found a mere house in a wood insipid and looked for more extravagant ideas.

The Han dynasty, contemporary with the ascendancy and greatness of Rome, was the first to unify China. The emperor Wu, like Caesar Augustus not so long after him, was tempted by the notion of immortality. It was Wu who hankered after the legendary Mystic Isles, the home of the Immortals, supposed to lie somewhere in the mists of the North China Sea. The story goes that, failing to find them in reality, he decided to recreate them in fantasy; and so created the lake-and-island garden that has been reproduced, with variations, again and again both in China and Japan.

The myth was an elaborate one. Some of the isles were supported on the backs of giant tortoises. They could be reached only if the traveller was carried by a bird—the giant crane. In Wu's garden these beasts were symbolically represented by suitable rocks. Rocks were also collected to form the islands and give the lake shore something of the feeling of a sea coast. Wu laid the foundations of the garden art of China.

The Han dynasty cracked in about AD 200 and its prosperity gave place to wars and uncertainty. Its bulwark to the north, the Great Wall, was overrun by barbarians and its nobles and scholars, artists and writers took refuge beyond the Yangtze river in the south in an unfamiliar landscape of mountains, forests, crags and cataracts. Buddhism came north from India to meet them. Monasteries were built in inaccessible eyries. Painters and poets turned from the lively human commentary which had been the pride of Han civilization and contemplated the wilderness.

China had already arrived at its Rousseau and Wordsworth. A description of a fourth-century monastery could almost be from *The Prelude*. "Within the grounds Hui Yuan laid out a grove for meditation. The mist condensed on the trees and dripped on the mossy paths. Every spot seen by the eye and trodden by the foot was full of spiritual purity and majesty."

In due course the cult of the wilderness descended to the plain. China's experience of her own mountains, not ancient and rounded by millenia of erosion like the Lake District but geologically young, sharp-cragged and spectacular, became part of her notion of the beautiful. Garden-making on the old lake-and-island pattern returned, but with its soft contours changed. Rocks themselves, as reminders of the mountains, became objects of extreme admiration. The bigger and craggier the better.

By the end of the sixth century a new emperor was displaying his power and security by lake-and-island garden-making on a scale worthy of Louis XIV. The Western Park was seventy miles in circuit, employed a million men to build it, and contained four huge lakes—one of them thirteen miles round. The architecture that set off this preposterous park was gaudy and grandiose. Endless red palaces and pavilions with roofs of glittering coloured tiles and upswept eaves lay among the lotus-covered lakes, the weeping willows, the acres of grotesque rocks.

This was the picture that greeted the first Japanese envoy to China in AD 607. Japan had already learned something of China's splendour via Korea, which lies between the two, and had long been a colony of its great neighbour. It seems that the Japanese genius for assimilation is nothing new: within a few years of the envoy's return Japan had the first Chinese-style lake-and-island garden of her own.

Giant strides are inevitable in the long history of China, but so conservative are the Chinese that centuries have gone by without perceptible change. Six hundred years of high

Above Japan came under Chinese influence in the seventh century and immediately adopted the flamboyant style of the Chinese court in contrast to her own rustic simplicity. This is the Chinese gateway of a Kyoto monastery.

Above The geology and land-form of Japan is entirely different from China's. But in the same way natural scenery, above all the pine-clad rocks of the Inland Sea, has been the inspiration of her garden style.

Above Most enigmatic of all Japan's garden styles is the dry landscape. The first and still the most famous was built at the monastery of Ryoan-Ji in 1490, and consists of fifteen stones on a bed of gravel.

Left The oldest surviving garden in Kyoto is the twelfth-century Moss Garden, Saiho-Ji. The Zen creed was already calling for perfect naturalism. This dry cascade is entirely man-made, yet appears completely natural.

Above The garden of the Silver Pavilion, Ginkaku-Ji, was the last work of the Muromachi era—contemporary with the Medicis in Florence. Its romantic naturalism is interrupted by outcrops of white sand.

civilization lay ahead, at least for parts of the empire: the period of the T'ang and Sung dynasties. Landscape-painting and gardening advanced hand in hand to reach what is generally considered their highest point of achievement in the twelfth century under the Sung emperor Hui Tsung.

The flowering of Japanese culture took place at the same time, in the three hundred and fifty peaceful years of the Heian period. Fashions and manners we think of as distinctly Japanese were developed from the Chinese by this astonishing court. We know from its literature, including the famous *Tale of Genji*, that it reached as high a point of wordly refinement and sensibility as any civilization before or since.

The Japanese contribution to the Chinese original was an intense love of nature. Japan is one of the loveliest countries on earth. Where China has the stark contrast of mountain and plain and the extremes of a continental climate, Japan is all a chaos of volcanic hills, swathed in forests almost as rich in plants as China and with the gentler weather of islands. It turns its back on Siberia and looks towards the Pacific. The seasons are pronounced but not extreme: summer is hot; winter snowy but not intensely cold; spring and autumn are long, slow and glorious. Rain comes and goes all year round, giving the earth a patina of moss, enabling trees to grow on the rocks of the rugged coast, feeding an infinity of springs and rills.

The Heian capital was Kyoto. The site seems to have been chosen for its beauty, more as a resort than a seat of government. Wooded hills cradle it and a thousand streams from the hills murmur and splash in its hundreds of gardens. Boating on the garden lakes, writing poems to the flowers, choosing stones and designing cascades, even sitting all morning to watch the fluttering smoke of a bonfire were the pastimes of the Heian court.

No original Heian garden exists today, but a reconstruction was made in 1894 to celebrate Kyoto's 1,100 years as the capital. The Heian shrine, as it is called, is one of the gayest, most delightfully contrived gardens on earth, with whole orchards of cherries, thickets of azaleas, islands of water lilies and acres of irises. There are plenty of rocks, but they are submerged in flowers. How near to the original it is we shall never know, but to view smoke uncurling in such a place would seem completely right. Genji is believable there.

Gradually, though, the Japanese love for the simple and rustic reasserted itself. The highly coloured Chinese style was transformed into something more in tune with the Japanese mind; a way of gardening in which nature was given all the credit; in which the art was to conceal art and make the garden appear simply a part of a perfectly harmonious natural world. Zen Buddhism, which arrived in Japan about this time, preached canons of art which exactly coincided with the mood: avoidance of the trite, the obvious, the emphatic.

By the year 1200 the art of naturalistic landscape was mature. The famous Moss Garden in the western hills of Kyoto dates from this period. Its dry cascade, composed of flat-topped boulders, is totally convincing as a natural rocky outcrop. Unlike earlier and later gardens the stones in no way suggest mountains on a different scale.

In due course fine rocks became objects of enormous value and prestige, to be given as favours; even plundered as booty. A successful warrior, in the centuries of upheavals that followed the Heian peace, would carry off his enemy's garden, rocks, trees and all, as the greatest treasure he possessed.

Chinese influence was not dead. The masterpieces of Sung art were prized and imitated in Japan even though it was hard to reconcile their romantic fantasy with Japanese naturalism. The Sung style with rocks was to set them boldly on their ends: horizontal strata pointing skywards in imitation of China's rugged, unweathered hills.

Examples of both styles exist in Kyoto. Out of the conflict of ideas came the finest landscape gardens ever built: the estate gardens of the Muromachi period, contemporary with Renaissance Florence, and itself something of a Renaissance. The Gold and Silver Pavilions are the two masterpieces of the period, built in 1394 and 1482, at the beginning and end of this great artistic climax.

Above The sandpile at the Silver Pavilion is reputed to have become a famous feature by chance. It was probably a store of spare sand for the paths. A larger area is also covered with white sand in an abstract shape.

Above A little waterfall in the woods at the Silver Pavilion is typical of the skilful rockwork of the fifteenth century. Until the 1930s this perfect piece of naturalism had been buried under fallen earth.

Developments in Japan

The great Muromachi period of the fourteenth and fifteenth centuries that created the Gold and Silver Pavilions was followed by a century of bloodshed, during which castles were the order of the day. The seventeenth century, however, saw another wave of garden-making—the last of great landscape gardens—in which most of the existing lake-and-island gardens were made or remade. All the Imperial villa gardens belong to this time.

It is almost impossible to believe, seeing these perfect landscapes, that they had no influence on what was to happen in England less than a century later. Enlarge the scale, substitute classical architecture, and Stourhead lies before you. The curving lakeshore, the soft sweeps of grass, the advancing woods and scattered temples are all familiar. Even the rocks and islands could almost be English. What really gives the game away is the pines: each tree pruned with infinite art into an exaggeration of a pine's proper posture. The maintenance of a Japanese garden is mostly pruning the trees. To the Japanese it is the only way that they can be in proportion and harmony with their surroundings. If there is a parallel in Europe it is in the French style of trimming trees into walls of green. As for the English, they let their gardens run wild, by these standards, from the moment they plant them.

It was not just lordly landscapes that grew to perfection in the Muromachi renaissance. Little temple courtyards were arranged as contemplative gardens with transcendent artistry. The most famous of these strange abstractions in sand and stones, Ryoan-Ji (see page 219), dates from the same generation as the Silver Pavilion, the climax of Japanese landscape art. It consists simply of fifteen apparently random boulders scattered in groups about a walled yard, emerging from a surface of gravel raked to resemble, one supposes, the waves of the sea. The garden is viewed from the wooden platform that runs along the open side of the house; only the duty-monk with his rake is allowed in. Twenty generations have mused on its meaning . . . if it has one.

The same period invented the tea ceremony, which

The tea ceremony was invented by a Zen monk at the end of the fifteenth century, reputedly in a small house in the Silver Pavilion garden. The object of the ritual was to impress the participants with the virtues of urbanity, courtesy, purity and imperturbability—in a world where their opposites were very much more common.

The tea-garden above is based on an early nineteenth-century drawing and represents the full development of the convention. Guests entered through the gate in the foreground and went to the covered bench to wait.

THE IMPERIAL VILLAS OF KYOTO

The three villas were all built, and their gardens made, within fifty years in the seventeenth century. They are as varied as they are consummately skilful.

The Katsura villa is the quintessence of urbanity: of startlingly simple architecture and remarkably elaborate gardening. Fitting four tea-houses and innumerable bridges, rocks, lanterns and pines into the walk round one small lake the garden does seem, perhaps, over-busy, but each separate picture on the stroll round is a cameo beyond criticism.

Shugaku-In, in the hills the other side of Kyoto, has a totally different effect. The message here is escape into the country. The centre of the seventy-acre garden is as remarkable as the little hamlet at Versailles with its milkmaids: suddenly you are walking through rice-fields with peasants in their straw hats toiling around you. And its climax is dramatic beyond words. The path leads steadily uphill between tall hedges which block out any view. Just as you begin to wonder where you are climbing to, and why, the hedges disappear to leave you high on the hillside in possession of a prospect of mountain and lake stretching to infinity. The view is unique in Japanese gardens, which are normally in valleys looking upwards to the hills.

Best of all the Imperial gardens, perhaps, is the Sento villa in the heart of Kyoto. All the sensibility of centuries of cunning gardeners seems distilled into this perfect lakeside walk. Nothing is overstated. A single gentle cascade feeds the lake. A single white azalea blooms on a promontory. The long stone bridge is buried in a vast wisteria. By the jetty a skiff lies motionless, sunk to the gunwales, suggesting the futility of moving from this perfect place.

Above The gardens of the Sento Imperial palace in the heart of Kyoto have a timeless tranquillity that is perfectly expressed by the purposely sunken boat at the jetty.

Above right The Katsura Imperial villa has a much busier garden, full of incident and whimsy, although the villa itself has an austerity that has inspired many modern architects.

Right The view from the high terrace of the Shugaku-In villa stretches far over the man-made lake, remarkably perched on a hillside, to the wooded mountains surrounding Kyoto.

(Beyond is a privy, with a kettle of hot water for washing). The host sounded a gong and the guests, not more than five, filed, on the stepping stones, past the well, first to the stone basin with its laver for a ritual cleansing, then to the tea-house. Its low door meant entering in a humble posture. Lanterns lit the path at night. The essence of the garden is a mood of rustic calm with a patina of mossy age, impeccably swept and sprinkled for dewy freshness. Its plants are the traditional pine, plum, and nanten, or heavenly bamboo.

crystallized the culture of Japan into a ritualistic form. The path to the tea-house became loaded with symbolism as the place of preparation. So another style of gardening on a small scale came into being, again employing simple means to reach a definite spiritual, or perhaps moral, end.

Both styles were developed throughout the seventeenth century in countless examples (though very few were as high-brow as Ryoan-Ji). Courtyard gardens tended to become gently suggestive of scenery, using water where it was available, imitating it where it was not with dry cascades of stone and swirling rivers of sand round mossy promontories. In most gardens some particular tree is singled out for attention and shorn and propped into a singular shape. Clipped evergreens are used to suggest more rocks, or perhaps distant hills. Where the real hills can be seen they are "borrowed" into the garden to form part of the composition.

In complete contrast with Western gardens, which use the widest possible palette of plants, far wider than the natural flora round them, the Japanese sternly exclude all but a narrow conventional range. The woods around Kyoto hold a far greater variety than its gardens. Flowers are not neglected. They are cultivated in great variety and remarkable perfection. But rarely as part of the garden picture, rather as clusters of pots round the kitchen door.

Today there are so many of the smaller kinds of garden and their derivatives in Japan that it is almost impossible to follow their historical development. Nor perhaps does it matter very much. No doubt it is difficult for Japanese visitors to Europe to distinguish between Decorated and Perpendicular.

It seems, though, as if the inspiration waned in the eighteenth century. In place of monks and warriors a new middle class took to gardening, and inevitably looked for "rules" to follow among the works of pure imagination they inherited. Professional gardeners were happy to supply them, inventing a great deal of mumbo-jumbo, which for a long while stood between their successors and a straightforward appreciation of a great treasury of garden art.

Above The 1890s saw the revival of original gardening by a great designer, Jihei Ogawa, who made this apparent woodland glade for Prince Yamagata on a two-acre site, Murin-An, in the heart of Kyoto. So skilful is the planting, the use of the stream and the glimpse of distant hills, that it is impossible to believe you are surrounded by traffic. The only planting in the grassy centre is low-clipped evergreen azaleas.

The West learns from Japan

Below left A walk by the lake in the garden of the Sento Imperial villa, Kyoto, which might have been made in eighteenth-century England. It is scenes like this that prove there is no real gulf between Japanese and Western ideas of garden beauty whether or not there were early points of contact.

Below These two pictures relate Japanese and European forms even closer together. The upper one is the little courtyard of a traditional Kyoto inn. The lower is a scene from the New Forest in England. Because there is no overt stylistic mannerism the nationalities of the two could be transposed.

When Japanese gardening first began to influence the West and whether there is any relationship at all before the end of the nineteenth century remains an unresolved question. Looking at the picture above, of a piece of gardening that might have been done in England in the eighteenth century (but which was done in Japan a hundred years earlier), it is hard to believe that no plans, or rumours of plans, passed between the two.

Apparently they did not, and the West had its first coherent account of Japanese garden-making in 1893 from Josiah Conder's book *Landscape Gardening in Japan*. The West was curious, but not very impressed. Conder, unfortunately, was guided by Japanese professional gardeners of an era of mannerism and decadence—in fact, of Japanese Victorianism. There is little sign of the brilliant clarity and decisiveness, or the exquisite sense of scale and texture that we have since learned the Japanese are masters of.

Early Western imitations of Japanese gardens have been given a bad press. But clearly a great deal of the fault lay in the state of what they were imitating.

The true quality of earlier Japanese gardens was not revealed until the 1930s, when the scholar and artist Mirei Shigemori published his twenty-six-volume study of the classical masterpieces. The Second World War intervened, both in the restoration of the old gardens and in their appreciation by the West. It is only recently, in fact, that we have had a chance to see the perfection of the real thing.

Fifteenth-century Japan sounds a very remote period and place to modern Western gardeners. But hardly any era of any country's history has produced so much of artistic relevance to today. The very simple modular architectural style of houses that developed in that period still continues and has deeply influenced the West. The philosophy and method of their gardens have even more to offer.

The Japanese art is one of concentrating the attention on essentials: be they strong shapes or subtle nuances. It is the art of editing—the most necessary part of gardening. In a Japanese garden you become intensely aware of the characters of the plants and objects around you. Some, such as the tonsured trees, because they are so strange; others, such as the pebbles and moss, because they are so appropriate, so well ordered, and so well kept.

Above all Japanese ideas are relevant to small gardens. Many gardens in Japan are mere door-yards. If it is too much to ask the Western eye to see a microcosm of a wild sea coast in two or three rocks, a bamboo and a diminutive reflecting circle of water, there is another sense in which concentrating on a few well-chosen, well-proportioned, natural objects achieves that link with nature which we seek in gardens.

Japanese gardeners garden for the permanent picture. They will go to any lengths to perfect a view and then any lengths to keep it precisely so, unaltered year after year, season after season. The bones of the garden are evergreens and, of course, the all-important rocks.

On the stage of this static garden seasonal changes become dramatic happenings. It begins with the great festival of cherry blossom, when the whole country is an operetta orchard, with people in their best clothes picnicking under the pink-frothy trees; then the massed ranks of azaleas, clipped into rigid forms which seem incongruous as they burst into flower. Later irises by the water with tame carp in their brilliant motley cruising between them combine to make a startling picture. And so eventually to the year's climax, when the maples smoulder and blaze in gardens and woods.

The Japanese style is much more readily acceptable in America than in Europe—certainly more than in England. American gardeners already agree with the idea of setting a permanent scene, relying heavily on evergreens, in which the seasons pass as actors. Climate has a great deal to do with it. So has laziness. No so the English, who, if they love gardening at all, must always be pottering about watching the daily development of their plants. The owner's involvement is a very English thing. Japanese and American gardens have this in common: they are largely maintained by contractors.

Conversely, just as each dish in a Japanese meal is served separately, often exquisitely, in a tiny bowl, so I suspect a Japanese would find England's riotous mixed borders like our meat and two vegetables with plenty of gravy—a gross and inexplicable waste of good things by mixing them together.

Right The dry landscape of the Zen temples has been revived in modern Japan by Mirei Shigemori. He made this abstraction in the traditional materials of rocks, gravel and moss in 1961, proving that five hundred-year-old ideas are still current and valuable.

Below and *below right* Meanwhile the West begins to find its feet in the Japanese idiom. These examples, from the USA (left) and Germany, have adopted the materials of Japan but not yet reached the sureness of touch. On the left the stone lantern is a declaration of Japanese intention; on the right it is the rocks used for their own sake. It is the choice and, above all, the control of the plants that lacks authority.

Left Some Japanese forms transplant perfectly to Europe. This tea-house and bridge were built over the river Avon near Salisbury in the 1930s. The willows and watercress have taken them to their bosoms.

Above A city garden that tries to synthesize Eastern and Western ideas has difficulty in making the transition. Tidy walled beds lack the naturalism, however mannered, that gives coherence to Japanese door-yards.

Below Abstractions in concrete in a California garden have unmistakable Japanese undertones. The interaction of rectangles and curves is American, but the eaves of the house, the gravel, the stepping stones are Japanese.

Early English gardening

In a simplified, but not absurd, version of history, Europe's three great national gardening styles that emerged after the Middle Ages have followed each other like a series of timed detonations, with England's coming last.

The Medieval style was nationless, and also curiously timeless. One can argue that it still persists in a million back gardens all over Europe and beyond.

The first explosion was in Italy in about 1500, followed by a century of inspired gardening, with its influence spreading far and wide. France's followed in about 1650 and had a briefer conflagration—chiefly because it centred on one man of genius. England's followed rather less than a century later and had a longer flowering, a greater development, and finally the greatest influence of all.

To complete this pocket sketch we must include the Dutch, not as creators of a revolutionary style but as the industrious nurserymen who, from about 1550 to the present day, have been important improvers and innovators and the main suppliers of many kinds of plants, from bulbs to trees.

The main point about the medieval garden was that it was enclosed, separated from the various other outdoor areas where people kept pigs or practised fighting, and intended as a place of beauty and tranquillity. All early representations of gardens show the same sort of arrangement: a high wall surrounding a grassy plot with a fountain, a few trees (or sometimes no trees but tall flowers in the grass), usually a seat or seats covered with turf and frequently an arbour—a wooden gallery with plants trained over it. The arbour appears less in the earlier pictures but has a long career, reaching its climax in the sixteenth century, and still battling on today in the form of the pergola. A bathing, or at least a paddling, pool was an occasional, more luxurious, feature. Tents, imported by the Crusaders, were set up for parties.

One can imagine such gardens remaining largely undesigned. If there were flower beds, they were in simple shapes, sparsely planted. Except in the gardens of monasteries and the parks of palaces, prestige and display were not involved.

The rigid medieval structure of society began slowly to alter in the fifteenth century. The invention of printing, the capture of Constantinople by the Turks, the voyages of the Portuguese and the rediscovery of the classics in Italy brought a fundamental change in men's attitudes. If they fought no less they thought more. In England when the Tudors won the Wars of the Roses and fifty years later closed the monasteries, men who would have been otherwise engaged were free to write, draw, observe and plan in secular affairs. In no time, I suspect, they were finding out about plants and dreaming up improvements to the garden.

The Tudor king Henry VIII had famous, if somewhat childish, gardens full of painted wooden beasts, topiary and labyrinths, and "knots"—the crude English forerunners of the later parterres. By the middle of his reign came the first sure sign that people were curious about plants and wanted to know more: the first English translation of a herbal. By the year after his death in 1548 there appeared the first original English book on plants, William Turner's *The Names of Herbes*. Shortly after the first practical gardening book in English, Thomas Hill's *The proffitable arte of gardening* (1568) was published, written for the gentlefolk in their modest country manors. Unlike the castles of the French these were straightforward houses whose gardens could start at their windows.

These two books started a flood of English garden and plant literature that has never paused since, and which has no equivalent elsewhere. The Elizabethans and Jacobeans were writing at the moment of crystallization of the English language with a freshness, enthusiasm and accuracy that still makes us humble and grateful. Sir Francis Bacon's famous

Left Medieval gardens were usually portrayed as small, round and invariably surrounded with a wall, a wattle fence or a palisade. Sometimes an inner garden, or *hortus conclusus*, was railed off.

Below An illustration from Thomas Hill's *The Gardeners Labyrinth*, 1571, shows the Elizabethan garden developing from the simplicity of the middle ages to a more elaborate design, surrounded by a hedge, with fountains, beehives, an arbour, railed beds and a rain-making device.

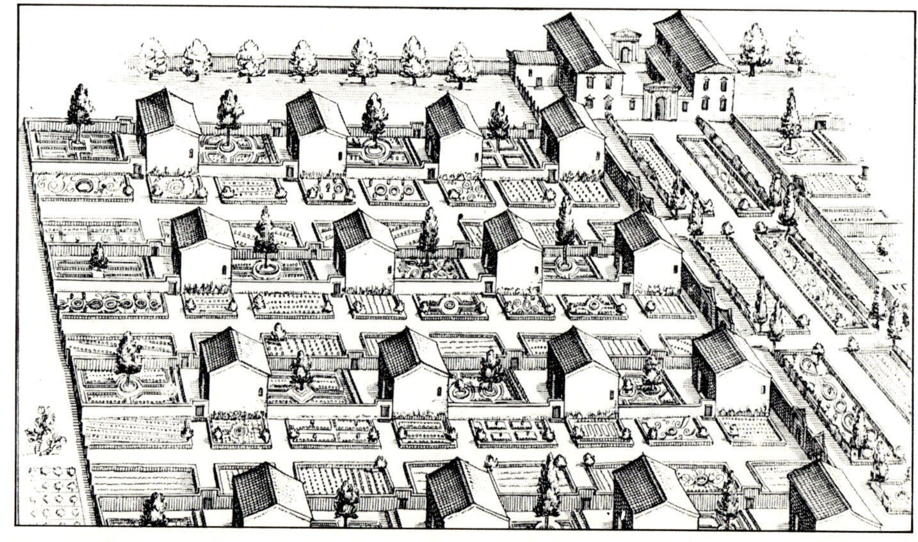

Bottom Though far from England, this 1607 monastery near Turin, where each hermit had his own garden, shows the typical treatment of small plots derived from the middle ages and handed down as a living tradition to the modest back-gardens of our own century.

Below Scotland, with a wilder landscape and climate than England, was not so apt to be tempted to pull down its ancient garden walls. Scots gardeners have tended to be craftsmen in a conservative spirit. The parterre at Pitmedden, based on the seventeenth-century design, has no surviving equivalent in England.

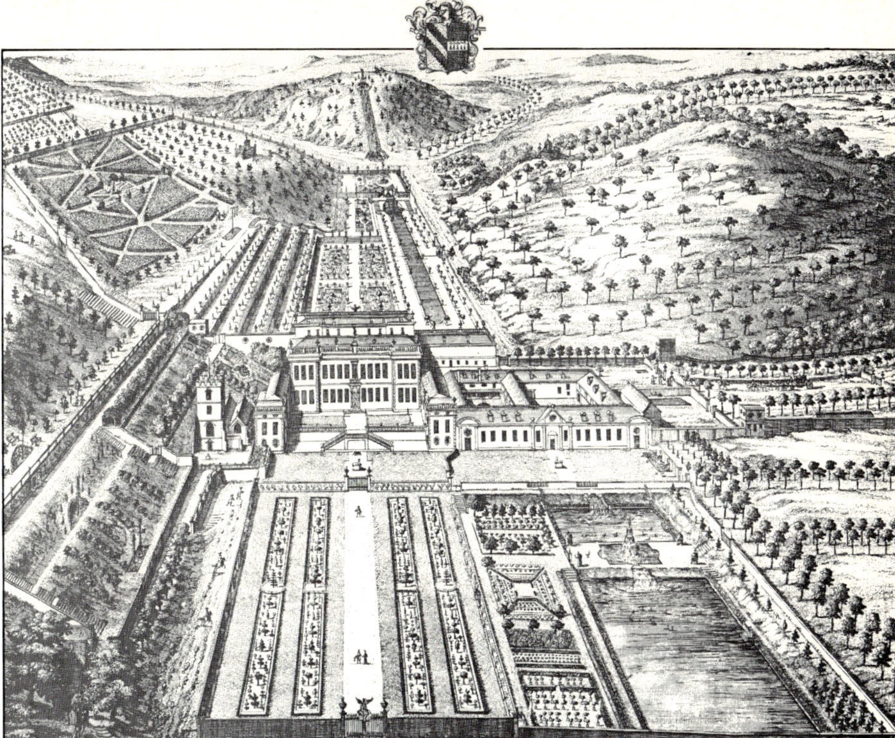

essay is the best surviving description of an Elizabethan garden: in spirit magical—in design and detail remarkably naive.

There was money to build ambitious gardens in Elizabeth's reign, and vast formal layouts were undertaken, just as they were in contemporary France—though the English would have been out of date by French standards.

England caught up in the reign of James I. In 1607 the Huguenot Salomon de Caus arrived, followed in 1620 by his brother Isaac. The de Caus brothers were masters of the Renaissance garden arts of perspective, groundworks and hydraulics. They had studied the new gardens of Italy at first hand and found an eager clientele in England. At Ham House, Moor Park, Richmond and many of the royal houses (above all at the Earl of Pembroke's Wilton) England's great Renaissance gardens took shape. We shall never know how successfully they attempted the Italian form of garden beauty without the climate or the hillside sites of Italy. The Civil War and the Commonwealth destroyed the royal gardens. The rest were swept away by the landscape movement. At any rate their vogue was brief. When Charles II was restored to the throne in 1660 the Le Nôtre style of gardening was the model every English gentleman was eager to follow.

Just as important as the succession of foreign fashions invading England was the increasing number and knowledge of plants. First Gerard in Elizabeth's reign, then the Tradescants developed private botanical gardens and eagerly collected every new plant they could lay their hands on. The story of the feverish hunt for new plants in the old world and the new is told on pages 58–65. With the growing mania for gardening arose a nursery industry to supply it. In the 1680s the first professional firm of nurserymen, designers and contractors appeared: the great Brompton Park nursery to be known as London and Wise.

The accession of the Dutch king William in 1688 provided yet another twist and new direction to what was becoming the principal passion of the English gentry. For two generations, before and especially after 1700, it is possible that in synthesizing all the influences of the previous century the English were making some of the finest gardens the country has ever known. But the wits did not think so. The essayist Addison and the poet Pope were bored by symmetry and regularity. At the same time, newly rich and confident young Englishmen were making a firsthand acquaintance with Italy. They found it much more romantic and interesting than they expected. They came home in a mood to bulldoze out of existence what they saw as the many derivative formalities descended, however indirectly, from the medieval garden. They wanted the real classical Italy, ruins and all.

Above One of the famous series of engravings by Knyff and Kip of English country houses towards 1700 shows a typical synthesis of Italian, French and Dutch ideas at Dyrham Park near Bath, probably designed by George London of London and Wise. The site could hardly be handled in the French way, with radiating allées, so Italian-style terraces and ramps were built on a cross-axis to the Franco-Dutch parterres and canals. Without encircling woods the young avenues stalk rather dejectedly away.

Left The same house today, looking the other way. The landscape movement swept all away and left what seems virgin parkland; only the statue of Neptune from the top of the cascade is left.

Right Surviving examples of England's late seventeenth-century "French period" are rare. At St Paul's Walden Bury, in Hertfordshire, there remains a typical *patte d'oie*, or goose-foot, of radiating allées flanked with statuary; a common sight in England before the landscape movement.

Below The poet Pope's famous Twickenham garden in 1744. Walpole said, "It was a singular effort of art and taste to impress so much variety and scenery on a spot of five acres." Its influence in de-formalizing the English garden was undoubtedly immense.

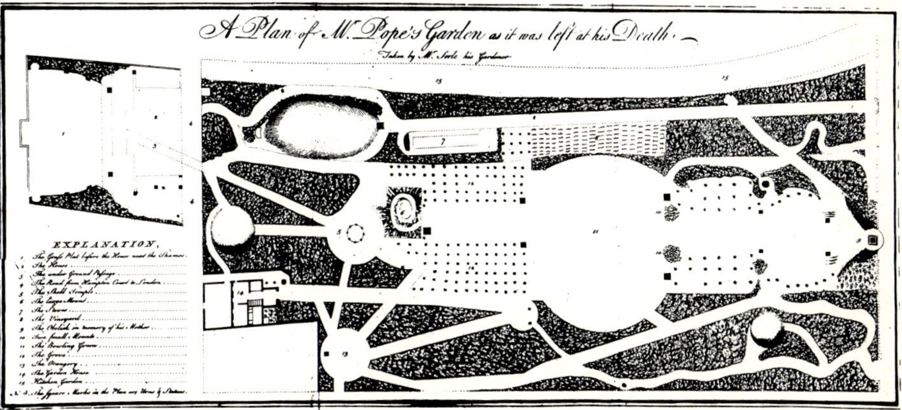

English landskip

There is still much learned debate about the exact origins of the English landscape movement. As early as 1685 Sir William Temple returned from the Hague with a second-hand account of "irregular" Chinese gardening or Sharawadgi. Addison, in *The Spectator* in 1712, attacking the excesses of topiary, gives favourable mention to Chinese gardens.

The notion of an alternative to symmetry was there, yet the rage was still all for the French and/or Dutch style. It seems that the strength of tradition was too strong to be easily shaken off. It had to be prised, little by little, by a variety of critics, painters, gardeners, pattern-makers and poets.

It was in the 1720s that the mood began to change, with published plans by Stephen Switzer and Batty Langley at first merely easing the stiffness of regularity. Charles Bridgeman at Stowe was perhaps the first practising gardener to deliberately adapt the French model to the English landscape, using ha-ha's to bring parkland flowing into the picture. Sir John Vanbrugh was the eccentric architectural genius who would have ignored rule-books anyway to create the scenes of his fancy. His courage was infectious. Pope, in his small garden (page 225), undoubtedly had a wide influence. Claude's and Poussin's paintings are given credit for offering an ideal of classical landscape to follow. From the French themselves the English had learned not to be afraid of size. Perhaps in the English character there is a Celtic longing for the undefined, unregulated, mysterious and suggestive.

Whatever the cause, in about 1730 William Kent, working at Stowe for Lord Cobham, "leaped the fence". Suddenly there was no beginning and no end to the garden; it was all "landskip" (in the spelling of the day) to be idealized as an earthly paradise with strong classical overtones.

Kent was an architect and painter who succeeded in composing pictures with sweeping lawns, water, trees and architecture. The architecture was as important to the landscape garden as terraces and stairs had been to the earlier formal gardens; but in a different sense. Each building not only functioned as an accent to beckon the eye but also as some sort of moral, philosophical, or poetical allegory.

It was Palladio's Venetian neo-Roman style that particularly appealed to the aristocratic English taste. In it they clearly saw much more than mere pleasing proportions: it was a reminder of Roman virtues, suggesting "innumerable Subjects for Meditation" and "giving a great Insight into the Contrivance and Wisdom of Providence". One might imagine a Chinese mandarin or a Japanese monk referring to his garden in this way, but surely not a courtier at Versailles.

To make the plain rolling English countryside a fit setting for such Insights, streams were dammed to form lakes, and trees planted in "belts" and "clumps": a belt round the periphery as a screen and windbreak, and clumps on knolls to flank buildings and advance in wings to give lateral interest.

Once the formula was devised it became very easy to repeat —as Kent's successor, Brown, who had also worked at Stowe, found to his infinite profit. He set up in business as a landscape gardener in 1751, found that every potential client's property had distinct "capabilities"—which gave him his famous nickname—and proceeded to remove as blots on the landscape all those gardens in the old style that stood in his way.

That Brown had talent, amounting almost to genius, there is no doubt. But the English have had fits of hating him ever since for obliterating their garden heritage. For within little more than a generation Brown and his imitators had swept away almost all the great formal gardens and replaced them with grass—grass right up to the doors of the mansion. Not even a terrace was suffered to stand in the way. All was to be, as his contemporaries began to complain, "one uniform, eternal green".

The most famous and to many the most beautiful garden of the English landscape movement is Stourhead in Wiltshire, designed not by a professional but by its owner, the banker Henry Hoare, between about 1740 and 1770. He dammed a stream to form a series of lakes, planted trees in shelter belts and clumps to frame views, and set classical buildings as eye-catchers in a composed sequence to be revealed in following a particular walk. The house was left out of account entirely.

The illustration reconstructs Stourhead as it was towards the end of the eighteenth century, when the plantations had grown but before they were diversified with a great collection of new species, and most of the spaces round the lake filled with rhododendrons and other shrubs.

The house *top right* was built in the 1720s to command a long view many miles eastward to Salisbury Plain. The builder's son flooded the valley behind and started the landscape garden. The margins of the lake are lined with stone to prevent the invasion of rushes or reeds. Few shrubs were planted. The intention was contrast between open water, smooth turf, tall trees and stately buildings.

The intended circuit of the garden started from the lawn south of the house, led to a viewpoint as a prelude, then down to the arching wooden bridge (which was demolished in 1798). Over the bridge it turned left and followed the lakeside among trees, then passed through the Grotto with a statue of Neptune where a rivulet enters the lake, then turned the corner to the Pantheon, which commands a view back to the buildings on the far shore. This and the other masterly Palladian buildings were designed by the architect Henry Flitcroft.

The path led over the dam in the foreground up to the temple of Apollo on a knoll, looking over to a distant obelisk above the woods. Then back to the village with its stone bridge, an ancient gothic market cross, a Gothick greenhouse (which no longer stands), the pedimented Temple of Flora and the boathouse. At various times such features as a turkish tent of painted canvas were added, and later a Gothick gardener's cottage.

Visitors today start their tour at the village, looking first across the lake from the bridge towards the Pantheon.

Museumism

With Brown the Landskip style of gardening reached its logical zenith, just as the French had with Le Nôtre. Neither style had anywhere to go next, except to compromise and complicate, which the successors of both inevitably did.

It must be said that Brown, like Le Nôtre, was dealing with the rich and great. We may be sure the smaller manors and rectory gardens proceeded with their flower beds exactly as before. But garden fashion has never been debated by modest lovers of flowers.

The element missing in Brown's landscapes, according to a vociferous contemporary school of thought, was the picturesque. They were looking for more than clumps of trees, temples and serpentine lakes. They objected to "this flat, insipid, waving plain" and demanded either a return to ancient ways, or higher drama in the landscape—in some cases both.

While Brown was clearing away all but the bare essentials the expansion of empire was giving the English a taste for the exotic—in architecture, in scenery and in plants. Kew Gardens was born. Chambers gave it its Pagoda. Horace Walpole built Strawberry Hill in the Gothick style. No doubt curry and chutney came onto the national menu. It was all very well having a fashionable park in shades of green, but where were you to put the new trees, shrubs and flowers (let alone the old ones) or build follies in the latest style?

The follies presented little problem. A steady stream of fantastic architecture, from tinselly little Chinese tea-houses to sombre mock ruins complete with owls and ivy, joined the noble neo-Romans in the park.

But the cry for flower beds and shrubberies and somewhere to plant "specimen" trees was bound to mean a muddying of the pure landskip spring; and it did. Brown's successor was Humphry Repton, the ideal man to introduce the necessary variety without losing the thread. His writings on garden design still read as perfect good sense. He reintroduced terraces and flowers near the house as a foreground to the landscape, allowed walled gardens for privacy and shelter for flowers, planted "shrubbery walks" and set aside areas for collecting rare trees. He painted his proposals for individual clients in his famous Red Books, with before-and-after views. By the time of his death, in 1818, his idea of variety within a garden bound together by "proportion" and "unity" was accepted as the norm—or rather the ideal.

Within a decade of his death there was scarcely a department of what we now consider to be modern gardening that had not been launched. Variety, however, proved very much easier to find than Unity. Nineteenth-century gardeners fell into the same trap as designers in every other medium: they did not know when to stop.

There was a new class of gardener who had made his fortune in the Industrial Revolution and had no liberal or classical education to guide him. There was a new class of garden: the villa garden—no broad acres but enough money to pay for any freak of fancy. The (later Royal) Horticultural Society had been founded in 1804 and gave new impetus and prestige to the cultivation of new plants. Suddenly glass became cheap enough for the middle class to afford greenhouses.

Calm in the midst of this frenzied scene sat the extraordinary John Claudius Loudon, founder and editor of *The Gardener's Magazine*. No writer has worked so hard to absorb and make sense of such a mass of material. His *Encyclopaedia of Gardening*, first published in 1822, makes the previous standard work, Philip Miller's *Gardener's Dictionary* (of 1731, and many later editions) seem medieval. Loudon and his wife produced edition after edition of painstaking, detailed history, description, instruction and advice.

"Gardenesque" was the unfortunate title he coined for the style he promulgated, which was intended "to display the art of the gardener—the individual beauty of trees, shrubs and plants in a state of cultivation".

It is hard to overestimate the influence of Loudon. He made an honest attempt to synthesize the best of gardening of all times and places. His plans are a development of Repton's, but lay more stress on collecting new plants and on the business end of things; the kitchen garden, nursery, greenhouse and frames. He laid the ground rules for all the new gardens of the nineteenth century save the grandest. The grandest went to excesses, reviving, in its most florid form, whatever past style took their fancy, with "Italian" as the favourite, and decorating them with a profusion of exotic plants.

Books appeared to urge the collecting of every conceivable class of natural object both indoors and out. Shirley Hibberd's *Rustic Adornments* is the archetype of this eclectic mood. Undoubtedly there was good sense and taste and tradition, and there were certainly lovely flowers, in countless gardens unflapped by fashion. But a Cleansing of the Temple was due.

Above The landscape style, applied to a modest country house near Glasgow, left it apparently in the middle of a field. The only concession to gardening was a walk round the perimeter (foreground) with a seat and a few flowers. Alexander Nasmyth, the painter, was also a garden designer.

Above By 1770 the craze for forming outdoor museums of architectural styles had already resulted in such preposterous juxtapositions as this at Shugborough. Designed by James Stuart for Lord Anson, it combined (left to right) a Chinese pavilion, a Greek peristyle and a copy of the "arch of Hadrian" at Athens all in a setting of more or less open country.

Right As the middle class grew and its gardens got smaller writers like Shirley Hibberd compressed Loudon's "gardenesque" style, with its landscape roots, into little urban rectangles. Similar designs, without the geometrical beds, are still being published in popular books today.

Left The Horticultural Society was founded in 1804. Cruikshank's cartoon of a meeting in 1825 describes the members as "A Pink of Fashion", "A Bulb from Holland with offset" (foreground), "A monstrous Medler", "A sprig of Nobility running to seed", and so on. The Society actively promoted plant exploration in its early years, having correspondents in China and sending, among others, David Douglas to North America. At a conference in 1899 it effectively founded the science of genetics. From its foundation it has been the world's premier horticultural organization, promoting experiments and setting standards.

Above Humphry Repton's "Red Book" for the Duchess of Devonshire's garden at Endsleigh, Devon, shows (left) the existing garden, with Repton in the chair directing his assistants with their surveyors' poles. Right is the scene as he intended to improve it, adding a conservatory and a terrace, reshaping the ground towards the river and clearing some of the trees. The biggest change is the cultivation of flowers in the foreground, relegating the landscape to a backdrop. Thus Capability Brown's disciple reinstated the gardening Brown had banished. Repton made scores of such plans for country houses all over England.

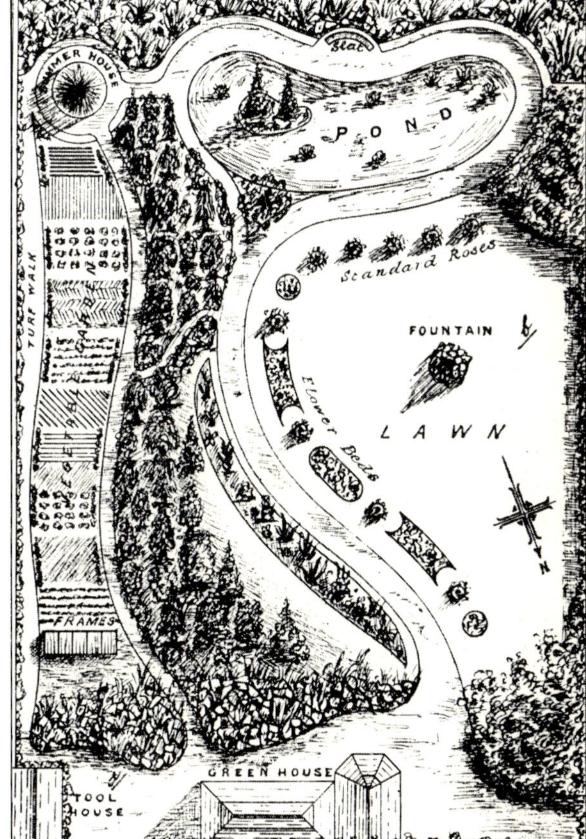

Right A suburban villa garden of three acres from J. C. Loudon's *Suburban Gardener and Villa Companion*. Loudon's enormous output of gardening information in the 1820s and 1830s bridged the gap between the last great landscaper Repton, and a million Victorian gardeners.

Left The mania for collecting new trees created a totally new kind of scenery: the arboretum. Sheffield Park in Sussex was a Capability Brown landscape until specimens of every sort of tree were planted, with the great North American conifers towering above all.

Below right The nursery industry rose on the horticultural tide. This ship carried plants from Holland to the International Exhibition in Paris.

The culmination: the Victorian country house

A great English country-house garden in the last quarter of the nineteenth century epitomized the feeling that plants were made for man. Never was so much technology or manpower devoted to horticultural display. The craft of gardening, as distinct from the art, had reached its zenith. The Industrial Revolution, coinciding with the ceaseless import of novelties, made the mastery of their cultivation one of the great status symbols of the time. To employ coal, glass and iron to bring unheard-of exotics into bloom, thousands of miles from their native jungles, gave Victorians every sort of satisfaction.

The gardener-engineer who made the greenhouse a symbol for the Victorian age was Joseph Paxton. A farmer's son from Bedfordshire, he had trained at the Horticultural Society's gardens at Chiswick, and at the age of twenty-three was appointed head gardener at Chatsworth, the Duke of Devonshire's palace in Derbyshire.

Within a few years he had revolutionized this great garden, formed an arboretum with 1,670 species and varieties of trees, given it the tallest fountain in Britain—a jet 267 feet high—and built the most extensive greenhouses in the country. Paxton became nationally famous in 1850 when he persuaded the giant Amazon water-lily, *Victoria regia*, to flower for the first time in cultivation. It had been named for the Queen as the most magnificent tribute the plant kingdom could pay her. The water-lily has flowers a foot wide and leaves six feet across. Paxton built a warm-water tank, with a paddle wheel to simulate the flow of the Amazon, and erected over it an iron glasshouse of entirely novel design.

At the same time, Paxton heard that the Commission considering designs for the building to house the Great Exhibition the following year had turned down all the 250 plans submitted. His inspiration came at a board meeting of the Midland Railway at Derby. On his blotter he drew a plan for a modular glass and iron building, like the *Victoria regia* house, but 2,100 feet long and 400 feet wide. Its apparently fragile engineering, he said, was based on the leaves of the great water-lily itself. Within a year of its drawing, the great glasshouse was built in Hyde Park, opened by the Queen, and popularly christened the Crystal Palace.

This then was the mood, and this the confidence, that created gardens, not only close to the scale of Le Nôtre but with an elaboration of planting that would have made the master blench. A typical great house garden would be divided into as many as ten departments, with up to ten men in each, in charge of the innumerable greenhouses, the rose-gardens, the herbaceous borders, the fruit and vegetable gardens, the rock and water gardens, the lawns and shrubberies, the trees, and above all, the bedding. As John Sales of the National Trust has written, "No opportunity for display was lost, especially near the house, and the geraniums were relentless." Rich people, it was said, used to show their wealth by the size of their bedding plant list: 10,000 for a squire, 20,000 for a baronet; 30,000 for an earl; and 50,000 for a duke. On the morning after a storm, the gardeners would be out at dawn, replacing battered plants with spares from the greenhouses. One banker is said to have insisted on different climbing roses against the walls of his house each weekend of the summer.

This whole style might best be described as gargantuan gardenesque—following to the letter Loudon's definition of showing off the work of the gardener. Flourishing plants and impeccable maintenance had become their own justification. A pleasing garden picture was a well-kept one, full of masses of brilliant colours and, preferably, strange shapes. The notion of a picture in the painter's sense, as a composition of unity and harmony, dominated the eighteenth century and returned with the twentieth. For almost the whole of the nineteenth it was lost in the excitement of a bottomless hamper of new toys.

Horticulture as a craft reached its climax in the later years of the nineteenth century. It was the cultivation of new plants with new technology that fascinated the Victorians. The great nursery firms led the way, with such clients as the banker owners of the mansion illustrated here to egg them on. All the emphasis was on novelty. It was not enough that plant-hunters were shipping home unheard-of species every day: the nurseries vied with each other in the new-born art of plant-breeding. Rivalry and jealousy were sometimes intense. The head gardener of one great English mansion was sent out every year on a tour of the nurseries of Germany, France, Holland and Belgium to scour for new varieties to bring home. If he liked them and his employer was pleased with them he would buy every plant to secure a monopoly. It was considered a virtue in plants to be tender and need the shelter of a greenhouse.

The mansion was surrounded by elaborate formal parterres bedded out twice or often three times a year with the most brilliant display the gardeners could contrive. The summer bedding was often of "stove" or hot-house plants, the more bizarre and tropical-looking the better. Scarlet geraniums were massed by the thousand.

The design of the garden was often entirely eclectic, with everything from Tudor knots to Japanese stepping-stones. Within the vast walled enclosures (*below*) were orchards, nursery beds, vegetable grounds and a magnificent central vista of herbaceous borders related not to the house but to the greenhouses and the operational parts of the garden.

Rank upon rank of working greenhouses and frames were needed for the production of bedding plants and the perfecting of vegetables and fruit, particularly out of season. A gardener who could conjure up strawberries at Christmas was a man to reckon with. Many such country house gardens had a skilled staff of fifty or more, besides innumerable "boys".

The display greenhouses (as distinct from the working ones) were often richly ornate and constituted complete indoor gardens of tender plants. Under the dome here, for example, was a tall rocky cascade imitating a tropical jungle in a profusion of such enormous-leaved plants as tree ferns and bananas.

An ornamental lake in an uncertain blend of classical and romantic styles forms the focus for a collection of exotic trees. We owe the magnificent mature arboreta of today to the Victorian passion for acquisition.

The not-so-grand manner

Above An engraving from William Robinson's *The English Flower Garden*, 1883, shows the sort of Italianate excess that was anathema to him. But formality had its supporters up to World War I.

Right Gertrude Jekyll drew her inspiration from the gardens of Surrey cottages—the favourite subject of her friend the painter Helen Allingham. The makings of many modern gardens are visible.

Above Miss Jekyll's architect partner, Edwin Lutyens, laid massive foundations in brick and stone for her subtle and sensitive planting. Hestercombe in Somerset is one of the best-conserved examples. A central strip of water with stone edges was a favourite device.

Right Jekyll and Lutyens used the Surrey farmhouse style on a manor-house scale at Vann, another of their Surrey gardens. This idealization of the rustic undercurrent of English gardening, stretching back to Elizabethan times, ignored all the garden styles that had come and gone between.

"The first purpose of a garden is to give happiness and repose of mind, which is more often enjoyed in the contemplation of the homely border . . . than in any of those great gardens where the flowers lose their identity, and with it their hold of the human heart, and have to take a lower rank as mere masses of colour filling so many square yards of space." So in 1896 Gertrude Jekyll summed up the argument that changed the direction of gardening yet again.

With the bewildering increase in kinds of plants, technical resources and possible styles throughout the nineteenth century the greatest challenge was that of choice. Writers tended to recommend everything indiscriminately. It was time for a clear-eyed look at what was, and was not, beautiful in the garden and in nature.

Miss Jekyll was a spinster of the cultivated gentry; a painter and a very gifted writer. In the country lanes and cottage gardens round her home in Surrey she found more that was truly worth looking at than in the great centres of horticulture.

At almost the same moment a very different character, a vehement young gardening journalist from Ireland called William Robinson, wrote a book called *The Wild Garden* and, in 1871, started a magazine he called *The Garden*. Miss Jekyll became a contributor in 1875. *The Garden* became the vehicle for revolutionary views, castigating carpet-bedding and all that it stood for, fulminating against formalism, and declaring, (at its most moderate) that "we should not have any definite pattern to weary the eye, but we should have quiet grace, and verdure, and little pictures month by month".

Love of plants was at the core of it. In *The Garden*, and the many books by its contributors, writing about plants developed a new sensitivity. Robinson's *The English Flower Garden* of 1883 was the bible of the movement. Miss Jekyll's *Wood and Garden*, 1896, was probably its masterpiece. Nobody had written with such clarity and authority before on, for example, the precise use of colour, or why one plant set off another to perfection.

By great good fortune Miss Jekyll met and formed a partnership with a young architect, Edwin Lutyens. He designed houses and gardens; she planted them. Lutyens was the original genius needed to settle the still-open question of the design of the garden. While others were still reviving Jacobean or Restoration gardens Lutyens coined a new style of his own: a development of farmhouse vernacular into something monumental and full of power.

Left The grand woodland style started with the mid-Victorian introduction of Himalayan rhododendrons. Many splendid examples, such as Wakehurst Place, here, are now in their prime.

Above The true cottage style means infinite devotion to individual plants that together form pictures of great charm. The author Margery Fish practised and preached it in her Somerset garden at East Lambrook.

While the argument raged on about whether gardens should be formal or informal Lutyens designed immensely formal, or at least architectural, gardens and Miss Jekyll planted them. Between them they produced the equation of a maximum of architectural definition—whether symmetrical or not was beside the point—in the planning, and a maximum of informality in the planting.

By dividing up the garden space into definite separate rooms Lutyens gave his partner the chance to paint a multitude of distinct pictures with plants. There was space in quite a small area for a woodland glade, cottagey effects, a formal pool, borders of different colours or for different times of year, a bog garden and a rock garden, if they were screened from each other in a carefully articulated plan.

Both Robinson and Jekyll professed to have learned a great deal from cottage gardens. It was certainly not artistic arrangement they learned from the higgledy-piggledy of little plots at the cottage door. It was a sort of humility; the beauty lay in the plants and often their haphazard association. Mostly they were either old garden plants or native flowers.

This attitude has been the key to almost all the English gardens that have been recognized as great in this century. The exceptions are the great woodland gardens, which stride off in a mood of their own into a never-never land somewhere in the foothills of the Himalayas.

Among the most celebrated gardens in the new manner, with enclosures of exuberant but carefully considered planting as their theme, are Hidcote Manor in the Cotswolds, started about 1907; Sissinghurst Castle in Kent, started about 1930; and Crathes Castle near Aberdeen, started about 1929. Of original Lutyens-Jekyll gardens unfortunately very few have survived in a recognizable state. But thousands of others have adopted the principle consciously or unconsciously. Inevitably though it is Miss Jekyll's part, rather than Lutyens's, that modern gardeners play. The planting has to try to make up for lack of architecture or even, often, of a plan.

It is not a revulsion from the bricks and mortar themselves but their cost that has shaped more recent styles. One of the most influential of these has been the "island" beds advocated by Adrian Bloom, using free-flowing "landscape" beds filled with border flowers, or sometimes heathers and conifers. On a big scale the effect can be very fine, as at Bloom's own garden at Bressingham. Reduced to an urban rectangle it can be much less effective than a wall-to-wall cottage muddle.

Above Some of the best current examples of the herbaceous border, a major feature of the Robinson/Jekyll garden, are at Crathes Castle near Aberdeen, now a property of the National Trust for Scotland.

Left "Island" beds, of indeterminate flowing shapes, were introduced in the 1940s by Adrian Bloom as a new and more "natural" way of growing border flowers. His Dell garden at Bressingham in Norfolk is the best example of the style.

Gardens for people

Americans have made almost every kind of garden. Starting with the English seventeenth-century model (the best example existing anywhere today being the reconstruction of colonial Williamsburg), they have progressed through homely backyards, opulent imitations of the French and Italian styles and serious and successful versions of the English landscape, to arrive at a style which is uniquely their own: a fusion of influences from almost everywhere, which is now returning what it has borrowed with interest.

The specifically American style was developed in California in the 1930s and 1940s, largely through the vision of one architect, Thomas Church. His philosophy is summed up in the title of his most influential book, *Gardens are for People*.

Church compared the first Californian gardens, made by Spanish settlers on a model going back to Moorish patios, with the English landscape style, which had crossed the Rockies from the East. The rich of post-Goldrush California did not stint themselves for lawns, flower beds and exotic trees—all promiscuously watered as the only way of keeping them alive.

But Church saw that the natural way of life in a Mediterranean climate does not divide the house and garden into habitat and setting. The dichotomy of indoor/outdoor, inherited from England, was irrelevant. In this century, the principal style of house built in California has been the bungalow, combining the feeling of confinement with the opportunity to step out of the house, at any point, into the garden. Where William Kent leaped the fence, Thomas Church jumped through the window.

The logic is inescapable: fuse house and garden into one. It was the old way of the Spaniards, and across the Pacific, Japan provided strong support.

The answer was to conceive the garden as an extension of the house and, literally, build it at the same time. A great deal of wood and stone or brick might be expensive at the outset, but it cut down drastically on maintenance. The main components of the garden were no longer the lawns, borders and shrubberies but the features of a private resort: swimming pool, sundeck, barbecue, sand-pit, games area, car-park and perhaps a vegetable plot. Among these functional spaces were interwoven elements of planting, also for practical purposes—trees for shade, bushes for screening, and occasionally, as a purely horticultural treat, a big container of bright flowers or a soft carpet of moss.

Church's genius lay where the genius of great designers always has: in identifying the essential character of the site and interpreting it in his clients' terms. The opportunities in the seaside hills of California are magnificent. The views, the rocks, the shape of the land, the forms of the old live oaks, even the pale layers of the sea-fog were there to be exploited.

Abstract art, Cubism in particular, provided themes in flowing and interlocking shapes which Church used, where the site allowed, to free the garden from any feeling of boundaries. The hills themselves flowed and interlocked in sympathy. Often the sites were so steep that a third dimension of steps and "decks" (usually of native redwood planking) gave the garden an even greater feeling of being a house without roof or walls.

Once the style was established the State boundary did not stop it. In other parts of the United States there were other reasons for not wanting a traditional garden. The harsh climate makes Americans reluctant gardeners, just as England's teasing mildness is constantly bringing us to the garden door to see what bud is bursting. The California garden as Church and his associates conceived it adapts well to un-Californian conditions. It shuts down well in winter and is quickly ready for action in summer. Hence the rapid spread of the same sort of hard-edge design to Scandinavia.

In all the gardens of the past there have been the active participants, usually paid gardeners, and the passive ones whose role was to stroll about gossiping, admiring the flowers and the fountains and wondering how much it had all cost. America introduced a new concept, the garden as a play-space, decorated with plants but almost independent of them, where the main activity is not gardening but relaxing, swimming, playing with the children or entertaining friends.

It began in California in the 1930s. The garden portrayed here is an imaginary one in the style of Thomas Church, the most influential designer of the time. It draws its character from its typical California hillside site with long views of golden grassland dotted with evergreen oaks. It was Church's principle to retain as much as possible of the natural terrain; to emphasize boulders, bridge natural gullies, and particularly to single out the best trees on the site and prune them carefully into interesting open sculptural shapes, providing both shade and a frame for the view between their trunks or branches.

As the garden base, in place of conventional lawns, he laid down solid floors, sometimes on several levels, of stone or planking, often (as here) with rectangular shapes in counterpoint with the free forms of contemporary art.

The climate allows many ideas which would be impractical or inappropriate in northern Europe. The swimming pool is often the focal point, with an attendant building of its own as changing-room and perhaps outdoor cookhouse. Garden furniture is scarcely different from indoor furniture. Church devised gardens that needed little gardening for people who had the money and the space but not the inclination to spend their time stooping, nor gardeners to do it for them.

Above A famous Thomas Church garden of the 1950s at Woodside, California, takes advantage of densely wooded surroundings to create a tropical atmosphere, emphasized by the South Sea island style of the building.

Left Very steep hillside sites have produced some of America's most memorable garden designs. Here a wooden "deck" hangs onto the side of the house with a tree from the slope below growing up through it.

Right In contrast to country gardens where the scenery can dominate, Church often designed town gardens with abundantly "horticultural" planting in practical container-beds. The ambience here is sophisticated street-cafe.

What next?

Below An example of original modern gardening of the very highest quality, by Russell Page in Italy. It brings together ideas from many sources, the English landscape school and Japan certainly among them, to compose a timeless Elysian scene—yet on quite a small scale, and needing little skilled upkeep.

Above left A unique early eighteenth-century garden at Studley Royal, Yorkshire, using formal geometrical shapes but the simple grass, water and trees of the landscape era could have been built tomorrow. It has every quality we can look for in big-scale modern gardening.

On the last thirty pages we have examined the legacy of the gardens of the past and the climactic moments when distinct new styles emerged as works of art for their time. Our times, however, are different. Every factor likely to affect garden-making: resources of plants, resources of knowledge, resources of labour, way of life and artistic inspiration have changed completely in this century.

We have far more species of plant available than our ancestors did; which makes choice harder than ever. We have far more knowledge of the workings of plant life. We have a fraction of the time and practically none of the task force. As for artistic inspiration, not many gardeners yet find themselves inspired by the works of the twentieth century.

In these circumstances our legacy is partly a help, partly a hindrance. The helpful part is the vast body of information on how to grow things which has taken centuries to accumulate. What is less helpful is that while the grandees and leaders of fashion have been spending their fortunes on new versions of Elysium, more and more stylistic conventions have accrued to the simple idea of a garden. It is not easy to shake them off or ignore them. They are written and rewritten into every gardening textbook as part of the received wisdom of the subject. Yet we must shake them off, or at least be extremely selective among them, if we want to plan gardens that are a pleasure and not a worry.

The central tension of late-twentieth-century gardening is between the knowledge and love of plants and the lack of time to care for them. It does not matter that the lack of time is largely illusory: that labour-saving is a false god. In due course, when there is more leisure than we know what to do with, no doubt labour-intensive crafts will come back, gardening among them. For the moment most of us would rather use all the mechanical and chemical aids we are offered and have more time for "ourselves". At the same time we are just beginning to grow wary of lavishing fuel and herbicides on gardens as substitutes for unobtainable man-power. At heart we know it is a short-term expedient.

It seems as though the only way to resolve the tension is to discover or invent what sounds like a contradiction of the first principle of gardening: a garden that needs the minimum of control. Under ideal circumstances it would be simply a reversion to a natural ecosystem with the lightest of editing. The woodland or "wild" garden, at least in theory, is the nearest we have come to this.

It is more likely, though, especially in a town, to mean creating a new and unnatural one, which is what is usually meant in America by "landscaping". The American trend is to have the garden professionally "fixed" in such a way that it will stay fixed—or at least only require a weekly call from a contractor to hose it down. It is not so far, after all, from the Japanese concept of gardening. Unfortunately the results are all too often either inert and characterless or bizarre and unnatural; the very opposite of what a satisfying self-perpetuating garden could and should be.

The rules for future gardening start with the very fundamentals; start in fact at the beginning of this book. They insist that you take your lead from the climate and the soil: to fight either is to make co-operation with nature impossible.

There will always be plant collectors who will have none of this. For them the peat bed and the alpine house were invented For a keen gardener in a restricted space there is no better way of widening the horizons than to miniaturize: like Blake to see infinity in a grain of sand.

Just to collaborate with nature, though, is not gardening. The future ecological gardener's contribution will be to identify the essence of the site and to dream up an ideal version

Above The precarious place of gardening in a great modern city: a roof-garden in New York. Conditions are appalling for plants and not much better for people.

Right Another Russell Page garden; this one on a Mediterranean island, using plants that convey the feeling of fertility yet remain in character.
Far right An urban German garden using stacked concrete containers, some with water, some with plants, to increase planting space and give a strong architectural character.

of it. If it is a wood or the remains of a wood, to emphasize the trees for all they are worth. If it is a marsh, to bring the rustling reeds to the very door. If it is a desert, to gaze out over sand-dunes and succulents. If it is an urban yard, to polish it into quintessential urbanity. If it is a lifeless suburban house-lot, to mould it round the house and its occupants, which are the reason for its existence.

On these pages are some outstanding examples of what has been done in this spirit, or with this effect, in widely different settings. At present they are very much exceptions. Most gardeners are hesitant about breaking with horticultural convention. Convention, in Europe at least, is still in favour of what you might call decorative gardening.

In Loudon's time the "gardenesque" rejoiced in all the artificial things gardeners could do with plants. The "decorative" style is not so much concerned with showing off the gardener's skill as in displaying the plants in beautiful associations with each other.

Perhaps we need not go to the extremes of ecological, no-hands gardening. Somewhere between emphasis on cultivating plants and composing idealized landscapes there is a perfect middle course. The great gardeners, certainly those of the last hundred years, have performed the balancing act perfectly. What is admirable about the gardens that have set the pace and influenced the style of modern gardening is that they give as much weight to plants and their cultivation as to pictures and their composition. It is a tall order. It calls for understanding of the natures of plants, and observation of their design and behaviour, at the same time as an artist's eye.

It means mastering the underlying principles of plant life, taking in its variety, and making a well-considered choice. The choice, and the resolution to stick to it, is the crux of the matter. Nobody can do everything—least of all in gardening.

Above A Scandinavian garden that needs nothing but the enfolding woods. The garden is simply a wooden platform under the existing trees; any more would distract from the spirit of the place. An admirable example of restraint.

Above A garden in Arizona that makes a virtue of desert conditions, using dramatic drought-tolerant plants as sculpture in dunes of stone. Again the designer has let the site dictate, with remarkably powerful results.

Below The Brazilian painter and garden designer Roberto Burle Marx has abandoned all old world conventions and adapts the techniques of abstract painting. He uses great sweeps of one plant to form abstract shapes.

Looking it up

Books play such a large part in an interested gardener's life that a grasp of garden literature is an essential tool. Instinct, rule of thumb, even a deep grounding in the relevant sciences, are all very well. But all good gardeners are constantly looking things up. The further they delve into any aspect of gardening the more eager they are to read everything that has been written on it. There is always something to learn—even if it is only another person's point of view.

The technical literature of all subjects is constantly being rewritten. So vast is the body of gardening literature that it is not easy to tell when it is merely being rewritten and when it is being newly researched and freshly thought. The only way to find out is to go back to previous eras to see what was being said.

From the scientific point of view it is only of antiquarian interest to go back more than a hundred years. On the botanical side two hundred years takes you back to Linnaeus. From the purely horticultural point of view of tools and techniques it is fascinating to see how much and how little has changed over a similar period—particularly to see how far ahead of us our grandfathers were in pure craftsmanship.

The history of garden design is still almost a virgin subject. Remarkably little has been written until very recently about the way our ancestors planned their gardens. Antique books are still the prime source of information.

As for the love of plants and their literature, there is something to be learned at every stage of history, with perhaps the most perfect expression of the wonder and joy they bring in the pioneer English writers of the seventeenth century.

Having written a book intended to introduce readers to as many aspects of the vast subject as possible it seems fit to say where my own information comes from, and to indicate where you can most fruitfully pursue all the hares I have tried to start.

This, then, is a necessarily abbreviated list of the books I find most helpful and delightful. Although they are listed under headings indicating their main value or interest, many of them could have been listed several times under different headings.

General reference

The Gardeners and Florists Dictionary Philip Miller 1724, 2 vols. Last ed 1807.
An Encyclopaedia of Gardening John Claudius Loudon 1822. Latest ed 1871 (by Mrs Loudon).
The Illustrated Dictionary of Gardening Editor G. Nicholson 1884, 4 vols. Latest ed 1901.
The Royal Horticultural Society's Dictionary of Gardening Editor F. J. Chittenden 1951, 4 vols. 2nd ed 1956 (with supplement).
Sunset Western Garden Book Edited by Sunset Books: David E. Clark 1967.
The Modern Flower Garden C. E. Lucas Phillips 1968.
The Readers' Digest Encyclopaedia of Garden Plants and Flowers 1971.
The Collingridge Encyclopaedia of Gardening Arthur Hellyer 1976.
Hortus Third Revised by staff of Liberty Hyde Bailey Hortorium, Cornell University, 3rd ed 1976.

General inspiration

The Wild Garden William Robinson 1870. 7th ed 1929.
Wood and Garden Gertrude Jekyll 1899. 13th ed 1926.
Home and Garden Gertrude Jekyll 1900. Last ed 1926.
Colour Schemes for the Flower Garden Gertrude Jekyll 1908. 6th ed 1925.
On the Making of Gardens Sir George Sitwell 1909. Last ed 1949.
Some English Gardens Gertrude Jekyll and George J. Elgood 1910. Last ed 1935.
My Garden in Spring Edward Augustus Bowles 1914. Last ed 1972.
My Garden in Summer Edward Augustus Bowles 1914.
My Garden in Autumn and Winter Edward Augustus Bowles 1915. Last ed 1972.
In Your Garden Victoria Sackville-West 1951. 4th ed 1953.
A Chalk Garden Sir Frederick E. Stern 1960. Last ed 1974.
The Well Tempered Garden Christopher Lloyd 1970. Last ed 1978.
Mediterranean Plants and Gardens Viscomte de Noailles and R. Lancaster 1977.

Scientific background

The Living Garden Sir Edward Salisbury 1935. Last ed 1946.
Plant Physiology in Relation to Horticulture J. K. A. Bleasdale 1973.
Plant and Planet Anthony J. Huxley 1974.
Water, Soil and the Plant E. J. Winter 1974.

History of gardens and gardeners

The Garden of Pleasure André Mollet 1670.
The Suburban Gardener and Villa Companion John Claudius Loudon 1838.
Rustic Adornments for Homes of Taste Shirley Hibberd 1870. Revised ed 1895.
Garden Craft in Europe H. Inigo Triggs 1913.
Men and Gardens Nan Fairbrother 1956 (N.Y.), 1957 (London).
Italian Gardens Georgina Masson 1961.
The Shell Gardens Book Editor Peter Hunt 1964.
British Botanical and Horticultural Literature before 1800 Blanche Henry 1975, 3 vols.
Dictionary of British and Irish Botanists and Horticulturalists Ray Desmond 1977.
The Shell Gardens Book Arthur Hellyer 1977.
The Chinese Garden—History, Art and Architecture Maggie Keswick 1978.
The Garden as Fine Art F. R. Cowell 1978.

History of plants

Herball John Gerard 1597. Enlarged ed 1663.
Paradisi in Sole John Parkinson 1629. Last ed 1976.
Sylva, or a Discourse of Forest Trees, and the Propagation of Timber in His Majesties Dominions 1664, 2 vols. 4th ed 1812.
The Old English Herbals Eleanour Sinclair Rohde 1922. Last ed 1972.
Plant Hunting in China E. H. M. Cox 1945.
The Quest for Plants Alice M. Coats 1969.
The Development of Garden Flowers Richard Gorer 1970.
Book of Flowers Alice M. Coats 1973.
Evolution of Crop Plants Editor N. W. Simmonds 1976.
"Leaves from Gerard's Herball—arranged for Garden Lovers by Marcus Woodward" 1978.

Trees and shrubs

Trees and Shrubs Hardy in the British Isles W. J. Bean 1914, 4 vols. 8th ed 1970–79.
Modern Rhododendrons E. H. M. and P. A. Cox 1956.
Effective Flowering Shrubs Michael Haworth-Booth 1962.
Clematis Christopher Lloyd 1965. Last ed 1978.
Dwarf Conifers H. J. Welch 1966.
Hillier and Sons' Manual of Trees and Shrubs 1972.

Roses

The Old Shrub Roses Graham Stuart Thomas 1955. Revised ed 1961.
Shrub Roses of Today Graham Stuart Thomas 1962. Revised ed 1974.
Climbing Roses Old and New Graham Stuart Thomas 1965. Revised ed 1978.
The Complete Rosarian Norman Young 1971.

Border plants

The English Flower Garden William Robinson 1883. 16th ed 1956.
Collins' Guide to Border Plants Frances Perry 1957.
Perennial Garden Plants, or the Modern Florilegium Graham Stuart Thomas 1976.

Alpines

The Alpine Flora Henry Correvon and P. Robert 1914.
The English Rock Garden Reginald Farrer 1919, 2 vols. 5th ed 1938.
Alpines in Colour and Cultivation Thomas Cyril Mansfield 1942. Last ed 1945.
The Peat Garden and its Plants Alfred Evans 1974.
Manual of Alpine Plants Will Ingwersen 1978.

Bulbs

Collins' Guide to Bulbs Patrick Synge 1961. Last ed 1971.
Dwarf Bulbs Brian Mathew 1973.
The Larger Bulbs Brian Mathew 1978.

Greenhouses

The Greenhouse Frederick George Preston 1951.
The Small Greenhouse Deenagh Gould-Adams.

Water gardening

Water, Bog and Moisture Loving Plants Amos Perry 1930. 3rd ed 1936.
Water Gardening Frances Perry 1938. Revised ed 1961.

Groundcover

Plants for Ground Cover Graham Stuart Thomas 1970. Revised ed 1978.

Garden design

Observations on the Theory and Practice of Landscape Gardening Humphry Repton 1803. Last ed 1806.
The Art and Craft of Garden Making Thomas Mawson 2nd ed 1909. 5th ed 1926 (with Edward Prentice Mawson).
Gardens are for People Thomas D. Church 1955.
Garden Design Sylvia Crowe 1958.
The Education of a Gardener Russell Page 1962. Last ed 1971.
Room Outside John Brookes 1969.
The Small Garden John Brookes 1977.

A gardener's directory

An inventory of garden terms, tasks and tools; of gardens and gardeners, garden designers, plant collectors and writers. Words in capital letters indicate that further information is given under those headings.

A

Abbotsbury, Dorset. Well-known seaside garden with subtropical plants, palms and famous camellias.

Abbotswood, Gloucestershire. A grand Cotswold garden of the early twentieth century, with spacious formal lawns, wood, stream and rock gardens.

Aberconway, The Lord (1913–). Third Baron of BODNANT in North Wales, where his father created a terrace and woodland garden with a spectacular view of Snowdonia, famous for rhododendrons. He looks after the garden for the NATIONAL TRUST. President of the RHS (Royal Horticultural Society) since 1961. Awarded VMH 1961. His father was President 1931–53.

Abercrombie, John (1726–1806). One of the many great Scottish gardeners who have worked in England, in his case for the royal family at the Royal Botanic Gardens at KEW. He wrote *Every Man His Own Gardener* (1767), which ran to 24 or more editions.

Achene. A one-seeded FRUIT which does not split open to release its seed, for example the "seeds" on the surface of a strawberry.

Acid soil. Soil without LIME, formed in areas without chalk or limestone. Acid soils tend to breed BACTERIA more slowly than limy (ALKALINE) soils and thus contain more undecayed vegetable matter, which makes them spongy and "open" but with limited fertility. Acid soil is necessary for most of the huge and important *Erica* family, which includes rhododendrons, azaleas, the heathers and many other highly decorative plants. Acidity is measured on the pH scale, which counts the number of hydrogen ions. A pH of 7 is neutral. More than 7 is alkaline; less, acid.

Acuminate. Botanist's term for a common shape of leaf tip with concave curves up to the last minute, then a convex point. See LEAF SHAPES.

Acute. Botanists' term for a leaf tip coming to a sharp point. See LEAF SHAPES.

Adams, Ansel (1902–). An outstanding twentieth-century landscape photographer, recognized for his commanding photographs of mountainous terrain.

Adventitious. Used to describe buds, roots and shoots, arising in an abnormal place—for example, shoots from the CALLUS formed over a wound, or SUCKERS arising from roots.

Aerial roots. Roots formed above ground. Ivies and climbing hydrangeas, for example, cling to walls or trees with aerial roots. EPIPHYTES have only aerial roots.

AGM (Award of Garden Merit). The RHS has several levels of plant commendation, given on the advice of specialist committees. Award of Garden Merit is the highest, awarded to plants which have been well tried in gardens and proved "of good constitution and excellent for ordinary garden decoration". The first AGM was given in 1922. The year of award is always cited after the initials. See also AM and FCC.

Air-layering. A method of propagating woody plants that are difficult to STRIKE from CUTTINGS and have no stems that can be bent down to the ground for LAYERING in the conventional way. The bark is wounded and the wound wrapped in damp moss and covered with a layer of polythene sheet tightly tied above and below. Roots will form from the wound into the moss. The stem is then cut just below the layer and treated as a rooted cutting. The new plant should be hardened off gradually. It can take weeks or even months for the roots to develop.

Aislabie, John (1670–1742). Former Chancellor of England and a most talented and original garden designer, whose huge moon-shaped ponds at STUDLEY ROYAL, Yorkshire, are formal gardening on the scale and in the mood of the landscape movement which was to follow.

Aiton, William (1731–93), and **William Townsend** (1766–1849). Father and son, the first and second superintendents of KEW. The elder compiled the great *Hortus Kewensis* (1789), the catalogue of plants at Kew, and the younger revised it (1810).

Alcàzar gardens, Seville. A unique living museum of Spanish gardening history, including gardens in the Moorish, Renaissance and modern styles.

Alkaline. The opposite of ACID. The soils of deserts and other rainless places tend to be alkaline. Extreme alkalinity is dangerous to all plants, and any alkalinity to some families (see ACID). On the other hand, the natural FLORA of alkaline soils (for example the English Downs) is normally richer and more varied, and general fertility higher.

Allée (French) or **alley.** A ride or walk cutting through massed trees, originally in French seventeenth-century gardens, having its sides formally clipped, often up to a considerable height.

Ally. Word used by botanists to mean plant falling into the same general grouping as another. "Bulbs and their allies" meaning BULBS, CORMS, TUBERS and RHIZOMES.

Alpine. Used by gardeners to mean any plant suitable (small enough) for growing on a rock garden. More strictly, a native of the mountains. Most real alpines flower in spring, soon after the snow melts.

Alpine house. Extremely airy, well-ventilated and unheated greenhouse to protect alpines from winter wet and keep their blooms in perfect condition.

Alstroemer, Claes. Pupil of LINNAEUS. He sent seeds of the Peruvian lily from Spain. Linnaeus rewarded him with immortality by calling the plant *Alstroemeria.*

Alternate. Used to describe leaves or buds that occur at intervals on alternate sides of a stem, as distinct from those that occur OPPOSITE one another.

Alton Towers, Staffordshire. One of the most preposterous of early nineteenth-century folly gardens, made for the Earls of Shrewsbury. It includes a ruined neo-Gothic mansion, a Roman colonnade and bath, a Chinese pagoda-fountain and a druidical stone circle. Now an amusement park.

AM (Award of Merit). The Award of Merit, confusingly enough, is the lowest rank of commendation given by the RHS (since 1888). It signifies that a committee likes the look of a plant, but that it has not been tested in gardens. See AGM and FCC.

American Association of Botanic Gardens and Arboreta. Publishes *Bulletin of the Association of Botanical Gardens and Arboreta*, a 48-page quarterly geared for professionals in public horticulture. Los Angeles, California 90024.

American Horticultural Society. Issues *American Horticulturist*, a 46-page colour journal for the knowledgeable amateur gardener. Mount Vernon, Virginia 22121.

American plants. An archaic term for the members of the *Erica* family, especially rhododendrons and azaleas; possibly because early rhododendrons came largely from America, or because so many were sold there by British nurseries.

American Society for Horticultural Science. Publishes on alternate months *Journal of the American Society for Horticultural Science*, a scientific journal for professional horticulturists. Alexandria, Virginia 22314.

American Society of Landscape Architects. Publishes six times a year *Landscape Architecture*, a journal established in 1910 for professional landscape and building architects and city and regional planners. Contains 96 pages in colour. McLean, Virginia 22101.

Amherst, Countess Sarah (1762–1838). Wife of an English Governor-General of India (1823–28) and one of the first botanists to explore the Himalayas. She sent home (in the 1830s) seeds of *Clematis montana* and *Anemone vitifolia* and introduced the spectacular "Amherst" pheasants to Europe.

Anglesey Abbey, Cambridge. A 100-acre landscape garden with fine avenues and an important collection of sculpture, started in 1926 by Lord Fairhaven with the help of designer Vernon Daniel. Perhaps the last private garden to be made on such a scale. A property of the NATIONAL TRUST.

Annual. A plant with a whole life-span, from seed to flowering and death, of a year—or usually considerably less.

Anther. The active part of the STAMEN, the male organ of a flower. See FLOWERS.

Aphids. Insect pests also known as greenfly, blackfly, plant louse or blight. They attack leaves and shoots by sucking their sap, which reduces vigour, causes leaf curling, flower malformation and premature leaf fall. Aphid wounds are entry points for disease-causing organisms; mainly FUNGI. Control aphids by spraying with an appropriate INSECTICIDE.

John Abercrombie

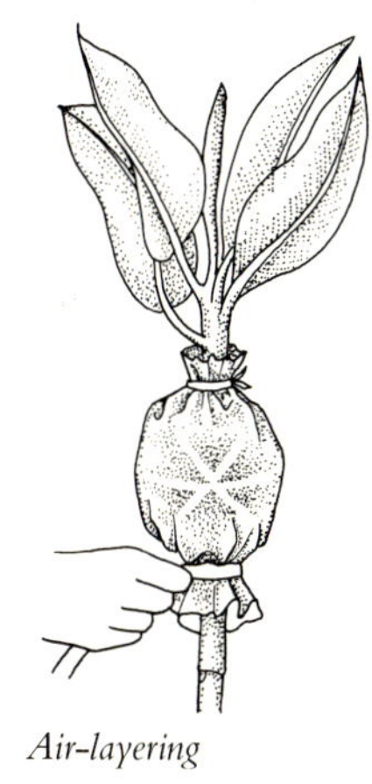

Air-layering

Alternate

Alton Towers: the pagoda fountain

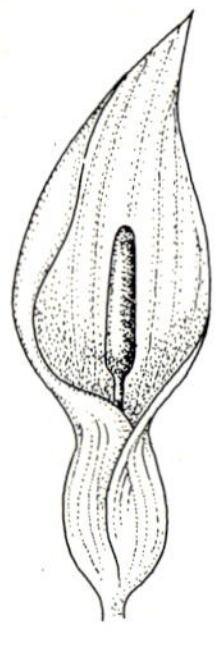

A member of the Arum family: see Aroid

Liberty Hyde Bailey

Sir Isaac Bayley Balfour

Sir Joseph Banks

Aquatics. Plants that naturally grow either completely or partially submerged in water. They oxygenate the water and are food for the fish as well as decorating a pond—but beware vigorous species.

Aranjuez. Royal palace near Madrid with great eighteenth-century formal gardens in the French manner.

Arbor Day. Observed in many states on the last Friday in April, the day is set aside to plant trees.

Arborescent. Tree-like or tending to become a tree. Some plants so called, for example, *Artemisia arborescens*, are bushes.

Arboretum. A tree collection (see, for example, ARNOLD ARBORETUM and WESTONBIRT).

Arbour. Any kind of small-scale garden shelter, but particularly one built of trellis with climbing plants.

Armillary sphere. A skeleton sphere made up of hoops to show the motions of the heavenly bodies. A highly decorative sculptural object in gardens.

Arnold Arboretum, Jamaica Plain, Boston, Massachusetts. The 265-acre arboretum of Harvard University created in the 1880s by C. S. SARGENT and now containing America's most important collection of woody plants, was responsible for many plant-collecting expeditions, to China in particular. Important for scientific studies and the introduction of ornamental plants.

Aroid. Any member of the Arum family, whose flowers are formed into a phallic central protuberance (the SPADIX) wrapped in a single cloak-like BRACT (the SPATHE). Arum, anthurium, philodendron, lysichitum are examples.

Ascott, Wing, Buckinghamshire. One of the best surviving examples of a grand Victorian garden. Now a NATIONAL TRUST property.

Attiret, Père Jean Denis (1702–68). French Jesuit missionary in China. His enthusiastic *Description of the Emperor's Garden* (1762) precipitated the craze for garden CHINOISERIE.

Augusta, Princess (1719–72). The German wife of Frederick, Prince of Wales, who was responsible for the first significant botanic garden at KEW.

Auxin. A plant hormone. See also HORMONES.

Avenue. An approach. Now always meaning one lined with two or more rows of trees, a method of dignifying a path since time immemorial and unfashionable only during the excesses of the English LANDSCAPE MOVEMENT. The first writer to enjoin the extensive planting of avenues was ANDRE MOLLET in his *Jardins de Plaisir* published in 1651.

Awl-shaped. Adjective describing narrow leaves with sharp, curving points. See LEAF SHAPES.

Awn. A whisker-like extension on the end of a seed, fruit, leaf or petal but particularly the extensions on the seeds (lemmas) of many GRASSES.

Axil. The angle or junction between a stem and a leaf growing from it. The bud within the angle is described as axillary.

B

Back-cross. A hybrid crossed with one of its own parents.

Backhouse. A famous English gardening name borne by two unrelated families. James Backhouse & Sons of York were ALPINE specialists in the nineteenth century. William Ormston Backhouse (1885–1962) and his father and grandfather were plant breeders; the first two generations were best known for daffodils, the third for wheat in Argentina.

Bacon, Francis (1561–1626). Elizabethan statesman, philosopher and essayist, whose essay *Of Gardens* (1625) begins "God almighty first planted a garden, and indeed it is the purest of human pleasures. . . ." His description of his ideal garden, of 30 acres, is the best account of Jacobean ideas of garden design.

Bacteria. A group of single-celled microorganisms important to the life of plants. Bacteria help break down plant and animal tissues in the soil, making nutrients available for absorption by plant roots. They may also cause plant diseases such as soft rot or abnormalities such as crown gall.

Bagatelle, France. Villa and garden in the Bois de Boulogne, Paris, built in 1777 by the architect Bélanger for the Comte d'Artois, youngest brother of Louis XVI, in two months for a wager. The 60-acre garden is in the English style and famous for its roses and spring bulbs.

Bailey, Liberty Hyde (1858–1954). America's first great scientific gardener, dean of New York State College of Agriculture from 1903 to 1913 and author of the *Standard Cyclopedia of Horticulture* (1914–17), *Hortus* (1930), *Hortus Second* (1941) and many other books. The Liberty Hyde Bailey Hortorium at New York State College commemorates him and produced *Hortus Third* (1976), a third edition of his great work.

Balfour, John Hutton (1808–84). Scottish scientist and botanist. Regius Keeper of the Royal Botanic Garden, EDINBURGH, for many years.

Balfour, Sir Isaac Bayley (1853–1922). Regius Keeper of the Royal Botanic Garden, EDINBURGH, after his father (above). He built the magnificent rock gardens, directed the comprehensive study of rhododendrons, enlarged the gardens and made them of the greatest horticultural use and beauty.

Ballard, Ernest (1870–1952). Nurseryman of Colwall, Herefordshire, famous for his development of the Michaelmas daisy. Awarded VMH 1949.

Balustrade. A fence (usually of stone) consisting of a rail or coping on a row of balusters, bulging pillars originally modelled on "the blossom of the wild pomegranate". The word is corrupted in English into "banister".

Bamboo. Woody stemmed members of the grass family, the Gramineae, mainly natives of the Tropics, with a few hardy kinds. Some are clump-forming; others spread by RHIZOMES. The stems, known as canes, are hollow between the JOINTS in most species but extremely strong. Thus bamboo canes are ideal for supporting top-heavy plants. See also pages 144–5.

Banks, Sir Joseph (1743–1820). Scientist and naturalist of great wealth and energy, leader of the British scientific world for 40 years. He sailed with the *Endeavour* on Cook's first voyage (1768–71) to Australia, succeeded LORD BUTE as Superintendent of KEW and became President of the Royal Society at the age of 35. He commissioned, organized or encouraged innumerable expeditions to collect plants and natural history specimens. In 1804 he was among the seven founders of the HORTICULTURAL SOCIETY.

Banister, John (1650–1692). A botanist who catalogued the plants of Virginia, which resulted in the first printed account of American flora (1688).

Barrington Court, near Ilminster, Somerset. One of the few remaining examples of GERTRUDE JEKYLL's garden design on a large scale, with a famous iris garden. Now a property of the NATIONAL TRUST.

Barry, Sir Charles (1795–1860). Architect of the Houses of Parliament, also designed the Italianate gardens of Shrubland Park, Suffolk with NESFIELD, Harewood House, West Yorkshire, and many others in England.

Bartram, John (1699–1777). Appointed the King's Botanist in America by George III. Planted America's first BOTANIC GARDEN, which included plants sent to him from Europe. Introduced 200 species of plants to cultivation; sent plants and seeds from the United States to PETER COLLINSON in England for distribution.

Basal leaves. The lowest leaves of a plant, arising at or near soil level, often of different shapes from those on the stem.

Base dressing. The application of manure, COMPOST, LIME or FERTILIZER to the soil by digging it in. Opposite of TOP-DRESSING, where the dressing is spread over the soil.

Bean, William Jackson (1863–1947). Former curator of KEW, where he worked for 46 years, and author of *Trees and Shrubs Hardy in the British Isles* (first edition 1914). His work, generally referred to simply as "Bean", is a landmark in garden literature, combining botany and personal experience, observation and judgement. The eighth edition is published between 1970–79 under the general editorship of SIR GEORGE TAYLOR, largely assisted by Desmond Clarke. It remains the standard reference book on woody plants in the temperate zones. Awarded VMH 1917.

Beard. The name of the growth of hairs along the upper surface of the lower petals of some irises.

Bed. A plot for flowers in the centre of a garden, as opposed to a BORDER, which is round the edge.

Bedding plants. Plants which are put in place for one season only—as opposed to "border" plants, which are permanent. They may be ANNUALS or BIENNIALS, or tender plants borrowed from the GREENHOUSE. Since bedding plants use the nutrients in the soil and are then dug up and taken away, "beds" have to be constantly fed and renewed.

Bedgebury Pinetum, near Goudhurst, Kent. The British national conifer collection, begun in 1924 and now run by the Forestry Commission. The mature trees in a series of steep valleys make it one of England's most memorable landscapes.

Bell glass. A large bell-shaped glass jar developed in France for protection of early crops and called a CLOCHE (a bell). Now little used. But the word cloche is used for protective structures of other designs.

Bellingrath Gardens, Theodore, Alabama. A 75-acre landscaped woodland and water garden famous for its oaks, azaleas, camellias and rose garden. Also within its grounds is the Boehm Gallery, housing an extensive collection of Boehm porcelain.

Beloeil, Château de. The home of the Princes de Ligne since the fourteenth century, near Brussels. The magnificent LE NÔTRE-style garden has six miles of hornbeam hedges 20 ft high.

Belon, Pierre (1518–63). A physician from Brittany, one of the first botanical travellers who journeyed to Crete, Constantinople, Egypt and Palestine. His account of the journey, *Les Observations*, was published in 1554.

Belvedere. A pavilion or raised turret or lantern on the top of a house, open for the view or to admit the breeze; a summer house on an eminence. Also the name of the Papal villa in the Vatican gardens.

Benmore, Strathclyde, Scotland. A 100-acre woodland garden. An outstation of the Royal Botanic Garden, EDINBURGH, on the rainy west coast of Scotland. Important collections of conifers, giant and dwarf rhododendrons and other rain-loving plants.

"Bentham and Hooker". The familiar name of the *Handbook of the British Flora* (1858) by George Bentham, revised by SIR JOSEPH HOOKER in 1886. Bentham's basic approach became the ancestor to all known plant classification systems.

Berceau (French). Trelliswork forming a covered walk which provides a support for greenery: an almost universal feature of early French and Dutch gardens.

Berso (Italian). Same as BERCEAU (above).

Bicton Garden, Colaton Raleigh, Devon. One of the finest examples left in Britain of formal French garden design; said to be by LE NÔTRE but unlikely as he died 35 years before its inception. Has one of Britain's best conifer collections.

Biennial. A plant which completes its life-cycle in two growing seasons, forming a leafy plant in the first year, then flowering and seeding in the second before dying.

Bigeneric. A HYBRID derived from crossing two different GENERA. For example × *Fatshedera lizei*, a hybrid between *Fatsia japonica* and *Hedera helix*.

Bipinnate. A doubly divided PINNATE leaf. See LEAF SHAPES.

Birr Castle, County Offaly, Ireland. Medieval castle in an eighteenth-century park; altered, in the nineteenth century, by the addition of an ARBORETUM and of new gardens designed by the present Earl and Countess of Rosse (the daughter of the late Leonard Messel of NYMANS).

Biternate. A leaf divided into three, each leaflet again divided into three. See LEAF SHAPES.

Blanching. Excluding light from a plant to prevent the formation of green pigments, a process normally used to make it more tender and attractive at table.

Bleeding. The release of sap from a pruning cut, especially common in grape vines. It can be avoided by pruning in late summer to autumn.

Blenheim Palace, Woodstock, Oxfordshire. The palace of the Dukes of Marlborough, built 1705–24. The palace and gardens were designed by VANBRUGH and the gardens laid out by LONDON AND WISE, nurserymen of Kensington. "CAPABILITY" BROWN transformed it into a natural landscape in 1760s. Magnificent formal PARTERRES, designed by Achille Duchêne, were reintroduced near the palace early in the twentieth century.

Blickling Hall, Norfolk. One of the most influential English gardens of this century in its use of border flowers on the grandest scale to complement a Jacobean mansion in an eighteenth-century park. Designed in the 1930s by NORAH LINDSAY. Now a property of the NATIONAL TRUST.

Blind. A term for young plants that have lost their growing point through damage by pests or other injury. Once blind they do not, or only very belatedly, make a new growing point or further growth.

Blomfield, Sir Reginald (1856–1942). Architect, garden-designer and author of *The Formal Garden in England* (1892). His views on design were diametrically opposed to those of his contemporary WILLIAM ROBINSON.

Bloom, Alan (1906–). Nurseryman, steam-engine collector and author. Founded his nursery, specializing in HERBACEOUS PERENNIALS and ALPINES in 1930. Moved in 1946 to BRESSINGHAM, Diss, Norfolk, where his enormous plant collection is displayed in the ISLAND BEDS he has strongly promoted. Many excellent new cultivars have been raised at Bressingham. Awarded VMH 1972. Bloom's son Adrian continues the tradition, specializing in heathers and dwarf conifers.

Boboli Gardens, Florence, Italy. The hillside gardens behind the Pitti palace. Designed by Tribolo for the Medicis family early in the sixteenth century. Its conservative Tuscan style, with architecture subordinate to site and plants, was altered to a more architectural Roman scheme in the succeeding century. The amphitheatre was a famous setting for pageants and parties. The baroque *isolotto*, an elaborately statued oval pool, is the most original feature.

Bodnant, Gwynedd, Wales. A superb Italianate and woodland garden with a famous view of Snowdonia, designed by LORD ABERCONWAY *c.* 1900; now famous for its rhododendrons, camellias, magnolias, embothriums and euchryphias. A property of the NATIONAL TRUST.

Bog plants and gardens. Plants accustomed to living in permanently wet ground. Their roots can exist on the oxygen in water where others would drown. In some cases, there are special air-conducting channels running down into the roots from the aerial parts. Bog gardens are made without drainage for bog plants, but with drainage for many others that also like damp ground.

Bolting. The premature production of FLOWERS in a vegetable caused by a check to growth; often hot, dry weather or inadequate watering following transplanting, or starvation. Some plants or strains inherit this tendency. Lettuce, spinach and beetroot are prone to this trouble.

Bonemeal. Organic FERTILIZER made from ground-up animal bones. A good source of phosphate (20–30%) and a slight source of nitrogen (1–4%). Valuable for releasing its constituents very slowly and particularly effective in sandy and gravelly soil.

Bonpland, Aimée (1773–1853). French surgeon and botanist, companion of ALEXANDER VON HUMBOLDT on his South American travels.

Bonsai. The Japanese art of training trees to look mature, gnarled and natural while restricting their roots, by pruning, to grow in a small pot. Bonsai trees of great age are highly valued in Japan. The practice is spreading alarmingly in the West.

Bordeaux mixture. A general-purpose protective FUNGICIDE, originally devised to combat FUNGUS diseases in vineyards. It contains copper sulphate and hydrated lime and is usually supplied ready-made in powder or paste form to be mixed with water and sprayed on foliage.

Borde Hill, Sussex. One of a dozen important ACID SOIL gardens made in Sussex at the end of the last century. Still owned by the family of Colonel Stevenson Clarke, its creator.

Border. First used for part of a garden about 1400, and generally distinguished from BEDS in the centre of a garden. The term "border plants" is now taken as synonymous with HERBACEOUS PERENNIALS (or hardy perennials).

Bosco (Italian) or **Bosquet** (French). A grove of trees, particularly a thickly planted block forming part of the "architecture" of the garden. French *bosquets*, as used, for example, by LE NÔTRE, were dense and regular and had their sides clipped with military precision. The English "boskage" is something altogether more relaxed and romantic.

Bell glass

Belvedere

Bonsai tree

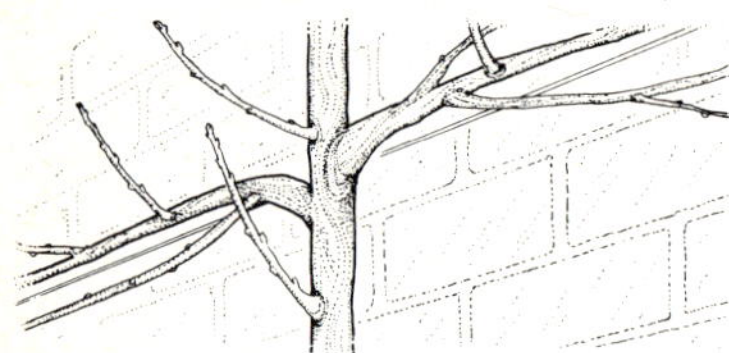

Breastwood

Christopher Brickell

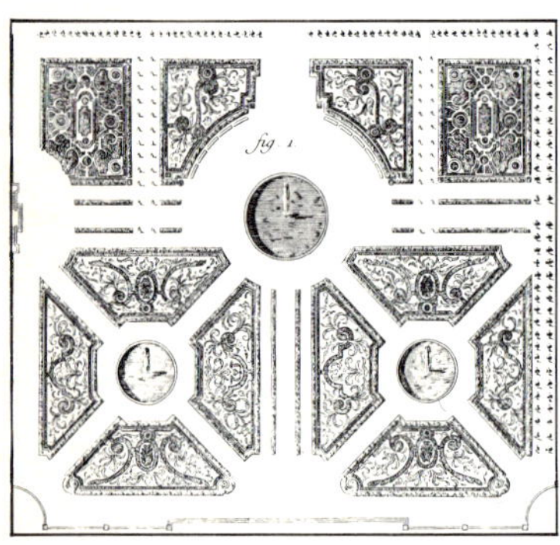

Parterre de broderie

"Capability" Brown

Boskoop. Nursery town in Holland on peaty polder land with a high water table causing remarkable growth of plants. Nearly half the world's production of trees and shrubs for gardens comes from Holland and most are from the 1,000 nurseries of Boskoop.

Botanical Magazine, Curtis's. The first periodical devoted to scientific horticulture. Launched by William Curtis in 1787, with three hand-coloured plates, it has continued up to the present time, though since 1947 the plates have been mechanically coloured. Between 1922 and 1970 it was published by the RHS, though more botanical than horticultural in content. Since 1970 it has been published by the Bentham-Moxon Trust at KEW. See also CURTIS FAMILY.

Botanic garden. A garden that grows plants primarily for their botanical, as opposed to horticultural, interest. Traditionally, plants are grouped in beds according to their families regardless of appearance. Many botanic gardens, such as KEW, are centres of crop plant research and development.

Botanical Society of America. Publishes *American Journal of Botany* monthly, a professional botanical journal of more than 1,000 pages, and *Plant Science Bulletin*, an 8-page quarterly for the professional and semi-professional botanist. Bronx, New York 10458.

Botrytis. A FUNGUS usually seen as a greyish mould which causes such plant diseases as paeony blight and lily disease.

Bottom heat. Heat applied to plants from below. Employed usually in a frame or greenhouse for propagating plants from cuttings or seed or for growing tender plants. Heat is provided by decomposing manure (the old method), electric cables under the soil, hot water pipes or small oil heaters.

Bowles, Edward Augustus (1865–1954). The greatest amateur gardener of his day, revered as a plantsman, author, counsellor and friend by a huge circle of gardeners. He was a central figure at the RHS for half a century and his garden at Myddelton House, Enfield, just north of London, was a place of pilgrimage—now sadly neglected. Bulbs were his speciality, but his knowledge was encyclopaedic, his learning profound, and his judgement of plants, plant literature and men remarkable. He wrote three books, all classics, for intelligent gardeners, published *c.*1914: *My Garden in Autumn and Winter, My Garden in Spring* and *My Garden in Summer*. Awarded VMH 1916.

Boyce Thompson Southwestern Arboretum, Superior, Arizona. Famed for its collection of drought-resistant plants and other flora of the southwest.

Bract. A leaf or leaf-like structure often to protect the forming flower, occurring at the base of a flower stalk or the stem of a flower cluster or, as in COMPOSITE plants, forming part of the flower head itself.

Bradley, Richard (*d.*1732). The first Professor of Botany at Cambridge (1674); author of *New Improvements of Planting Both Philosophical and Practical* (1717). He wrote on systematic hybridization, published the first description of successful fruiting of the pineapple in England and made a study of glasshouses which was well before its time in recognizing the need for regulated heat rather than architectural perfection.

Bramante, Donato (1444–1514). Italian Renaissance architect, a rival of Michelangelo. His design for the Vatican gardens for Pope Julius II firmly established the architectural basis of Italian garden design.

Bramham Park, Yorkshire. The best example of a seventeenth-century French-style garden in Britain until 1962 when a gale blew down many of the beech trees forming the boskage along the ALLEES. Fascinating now (after replanting) as an immature example of its style, reminding us of the way Louis XIV saw VERSAILLES.

Branklyn, Perth, Scotland. Perhaps the most famous small private garden in Britain. Comprising two acres around a bungalow, it was begun in 1922 by John and Dorothy Renton and planted with enormous variety, richness and skill as woodland glades. A property of the NATIONAL TRUST for Scotland.

Break. To grow out from an AXILLARY BUD, naturally or artificially. In chrysanthemums, pinching out the growing tips induces the BREAK BUDS to appear, and encourages branching. It also means a departure from the normal form of a plant, a "SPORT"; much appreciated by commercial breeders.

Break bud. In chrysanthemum growing, the flower bud which naturally terminates the stem of a young plant. Usually it is pinched out or it aborts, the growth of the plant continued by side shoots (BREAKS).

Breastwood. Shoots growing forwards from a tree which is intended to be trained flat against a wall.

Brickell, Christopher D. (1932–). Director of WISLEY GARDEN since 1969. One of today's leading gardener-botanists.

Bridgeman, Charles (*d.*1738). English landscaper now credited with the transition from formal to naturalistic style in the early years of the eighteenth century. Bridgeman is credited with the introduction of the HA-HA, the device which opened up the garden to the surrounding landscape. His work at STOWE, ROUSHAM and others is much overlaid with that of his successors WILLIAM KENT and "CAPABILITY" BROWN and new research is only now discovering the extent of his innovation.

Brier (or Briar). Strictly any wild rose bush, but to gardeners it means the rootstock usually of dog rose (*Rosa canina*) or Japanese brier (*R. rugosa*) on to which a ROSE VARIETY IS BUDDED OR GRAFTED.

Britton, Nathanial Lord (1859–1934). The first director of the New York Botanical Garden, responsible for the development of the herbarium. He also worked to codify botanical nomenclature.

Broadcast sowing. The wide scattering of seed as opposed to careful sowing in straight rows or drills. Grass seed and fertilizers are both sown and spread in this way.

Broadleaf. A plant, especially a tree, with broad rather than needle leaves. In fact any tree which is not a conifer.

Broderie, parterre de (French). Elaborate curvilinear design in dwarf box hedges. Similar in effect to embroidery. Said to be an invention of Catherine de Medici's gardener in Paris, CLAUDE MOLLET.

Bromeliads. Members of the family Bromeliaceae. ROSETTE-forming plants, they are often EPIPHYTIC, although some are soil-dwelling and inhabit semi-deserts.

Brooklyn Botanic Garden. New York's most attractive and interesting garden, with a fine plant collection, excellent Japanese gardens and popular courses of instruction. Its quarterly publication *Plants and Gardens* is one of America's leading gardening journals.

Brown, Lancelot ("Capability") (1716–83). A gardener from Northumberland who learned landscaping from WILLIAM KENT at STOWE. In 1751 he began a career which altered the face of England, ruthlessly sweeping away the old formal gardens to replace them with naturalistic "landskip". The list of his work includes half the great country houses of England—BLENHEIM, CHATSWORTH, KEW, Longleat and SHEFFIELD PARK. He has been much reviled as a destroyer, both at the time and since, but his vision of English parkland is now accepted as natural and right.

Bud. An embryo shoot, flower or flower cluster, usually protected by closely overlapping scales. In fruit trees there are two kinds—the growth bud and the fruit (flower) bud. A terminal bud occurs at the tip of a shoot; an axillary bud is found in the AXIL of a leaf. In herbaceous plants, particularly chrysanthemums, a crown bud is a flower bud at the tip of a shoot and surrounded by smaller flower buds.

Budding. A method of grafting used in particular for fruit trees and roses. A single bud of the desired plant is removed with a small piece of bark and inserted into a slit in the plant which is to furnish the roots. See pages 52–3.

Bulb, bulbil. A bulb is a modified BUD usually formed underground with fleshy scales or swollen leaf bases which store food during a rest period. The term is commonly used for all flowers with this or similar modes of growth. A bulbil is a small bulb which in some plants, such as the tiger lily, forms on their stems. See CORM, TUBER, RHIZOME. See pages 124–31.

Bunyard, Edward Ashdown (1878–1939). Gardener, gourmet and author of the *Handbook of Hardy Fruits* (1920–25), *The Anatomy of Dessert* (1933) and *The Epicure's Companion* (1937). Among his interests, rare at the time, was the cultivation of "old" roses. His *Old Garden Roses* was published in 1936.

Burbank, Luther (1849–1926). American gardener and plant-breeder of plums, berries and lilies.

Burpee, Washington Atlee (1858–1915). Built the firm of W. Atlee Burpee and Co into one of the world's best-known seed houses and was the first to establish a successful mail-order seed business. He developed and introduced many new plant varieties.

Burroughs, John (1837–1921). American naturalist and writer.

Buscot Park, Berkshire. The formal walk to a large lake is one of the few examples of HAROLD PETO's work open to the public. A property of the NATIONAL TRUST. See the photograph on pages 182–3.

Bute, John Stuart, 3rd Earl of (1713–92). Courtier, botanist, politician and first (though unofficial) director of KEW. Bute was an intimate friend and advisor of the Prince of Wales and of PRINCESS AUGUSTA, and tutor to their son the future King George III. His passionate interest in gardening led him to encourage the Princess to start their botanic garden.

C

Cactus. Any of 2,000 species of fleshy, SUCCULENT plants in the family Cactaceae designed to withstand long periods of drought. All bear spines, and often hairs, wool or felt, on special organs called areoles. In most cacti the main body of the plant is a swollen stem which may be a flattened pad (*Opuntia*), spherical (*Mammillaria*), column-shaped (*Cerus*) or leaf-like (*Zygocactus*). Leaves are usually absent or reduced in size to spines.

Caerhays Castle, Cornwall. Home of the WILLIAMS family with a remarkable plant collection including seedlings from many Himalayan expeditions, particularly rhododendrons and camellias.

Calcicole, calcifuge. Plants sensitive to LIME. A calcicole plant thrives in a limy soil but can usually survive if lime is absent. A calcifuge plant cannot grow in the presence of lime. Heathers and rhododendrons are calcifuges.

Callaway Gardens, Pine Mountain, Georgia. Features 2,500 acres of trails to observe Appalachian plants and wild flowers, notably native azaleas and hollies, in addition to lakes and other recreational facilities.

Callus. New corky tissue formed by a plant to heal a wound on a stem, root or leaf stalk. Cuttings usually form a callus and then put out new roots from (or near) it. Callus helps to seal the joint where a plant is GRAFTED.

Calyx. The SEPALS or outermost ring of modified leaves that form a FLOWER. Usually green and inconspicuous but may look just like PETALS (as in clematis) or replace them (as in the winter aconite *Eranthis hyemalis*).

Cambium. The very thin layer of growing cells in stem and root sandwiched between the wood (XYLEM) tissues and conducting (PHLOEM) tissues. Dividing cells of the cambium add to these tissues, which cannot themselves reproduce.

Cambridge University Botanic Garden, Cambridge. A 40-acre teaching garden run by Cambridge University with unique twin rock gardens; one of sandstone, one of limestone. Its flower beds are arranged systematically: plants of the same family grown together, each family shown in relation to the others. Good collections of roses and tulips, glasshouses and a garden for winter effects.

Canal. In gardens, a formalized stretch of water, usually a long rectangle and often occupying the middle of the central vista.

Capsule. A dry FRUIT which splits open on ripening. In some cases, e.g. violet, the seeds are forcibly ejected. The fruit is formed of two or more joined female parts of the flower (CARPELS).

Carpel. A single female unit of a FLOWER, usually composed of a STIGMA, on which POLLEN lands, a STYLE down which a pollen-tube grows and an ovary in which FERTILIZATION takes place.

Carpet bedding. Bedding with small plants tightly packed together to form a carpet-like patterned surface. A popular Victorian style, now rarely seen except in public parks where the necessary greenhouses and gardeners are available.

Carson, Rachel (1907–1964). Author of *The Sea Around Us* (1951) and *Silent Spring* (1962), the latter an eye-opening account of the hazards of insecticides and chemicals on the environment.

Cascade. A waterfall in which the water runs rapidly down a stepped slope, rather than dropping straight. Or a series of small waterfalls. A favourite device in Italian gardens, adopted and formalized by the French. The word was first used in English by JOHN EVELYN in 1641.

Caserta, near Naples, Italy. Palace of King Carlos III of Naples with enormous gardens in the French style; modelled on VERSAILLES, designed by Vanvitelli in 1751. The last great palace garden to be made in Italy.

Castle Howard, North Yorkshire. One of the most influential gardens of the English LANDSCAPE MOVEMENT, designed with VANBRUGH and LONDON AND WISE by the 3rd Earl of Carlisle between 1705 and 1738 in the style later to be associated with "CAPABILITY" BROWN. Still magnificent and still owned by the Earl's descendants.

Catch crop. Fast-maturing plants such as lettuces and radishes which are grown in the soil prepared for another, slower-growing crop.

Catkin. A dense spike of petalless, usually unisexual, flowers often, but not invariably, pendent and wind-pollinated. Male and female catkins often look very different, as in many willows (*Salix*), where the males, covered with yellow pollen, are much the prettier.

Chambers, Sir William (1723–96). Architect who made a brief visit to China and published *Designs for Chinese Buildings* (1757), which had more influence in France than in England. In the same year he was made architect at KEW, where he built the PAGODA and other follies. He was a rival and critic of "CAPABILITY" BROWN and possibly the first designer to suggest massing flowers according to their colours.

Sir William Chambers

Champney, John (*fl* 1800s). Rice planter and gardener of Charleston, South Carolina, USA. Made the first cross (in 1802) between China and "old" roses. The resulting rose became known as 'Champney's Pink Cluster', the parent of the Noisettes and hence all modern bedding roses.

Chantilly, Château de, France. Royal palace north of Paris, rebuilt since the Revolution, with one of LE NÔTRE's finest gardens.

Chatsworth, Derbyshire. The palace of the Dukes of Devonshire, famous in gardening history since the seventeenth century when LONDON AND WISE made the spectacular cascade. "CAPABILITY" BROWN redesigned the park, one of the most beautiful in England with wild moorland as a backdrop. SIR JOSEPH PAXTON started his career here and built a famous conservatory, now replaced with another of *avant-garde* design.

Chelsea Physick Garden

Chelated iron. A form of iron readily available to plant roots and used to treat plants suffering from CHLOROSIS (lack of green pigment) often caused by iron deficiency. The chelated iron is watered on the soil in such products as Sequestrene.

Chelsea Flower Show. The world's greatest annual gardening event, held by the RHS in the grounds of the Royal Hospital, Chelsea, in late May every year (except in wartime) since 1913. The show lasts for four days, with a 3½-acre marquee for the main flower exhibits. Model gardens and every conceivable "sundry" from greenhouses to antiquarian books fill the rest of the grounds.

Chelsea Physick Garden. London's oldest botanical garden, founded in 1673 by the Society of Apothecaries for the study of medicinal plants. It occupies four acres on the north bank of the Thames in Chelsea and now grows some 5,000 species of plants, still for the purpose of study by colleges and hospitals. The London climate allows such tender plants as the olive to flourish. Great gardeners at Chelsea have included PHILIP MILLER (for nearly 50 years), WILLIAM FORSYTH of the forsythia, WILLIAM CURTIS of the BOTANICAL MAGAZINE and JOHN LINDLEY, later of the RHS. The garden contains the first rockery to be built in England.

Chimaera. Plant containing two distinct kinds of tissue with different inherited characteristics. Chimaeras result from spontaneous genetic changes (MUTATIONS). GRAFTING can produce artificial chimaeras. *Laburnocytisus adami* is an example, produced by grafting purple-flowered broom on laburnum.

Chinoiserie. The Chinese style, particularly as it manifested itself in eighteenth-century gardens as brightly coloured fretwork pavilions and bridges. In Britain it was treated as just another form of decoration, but in France it was confused with the English style to become "anglo-chinois"; a force that revolutionized French gardens in the latter part of the century. See also ATTIRET, CHAMBERS. See pages 228–9.

Peter Collinson

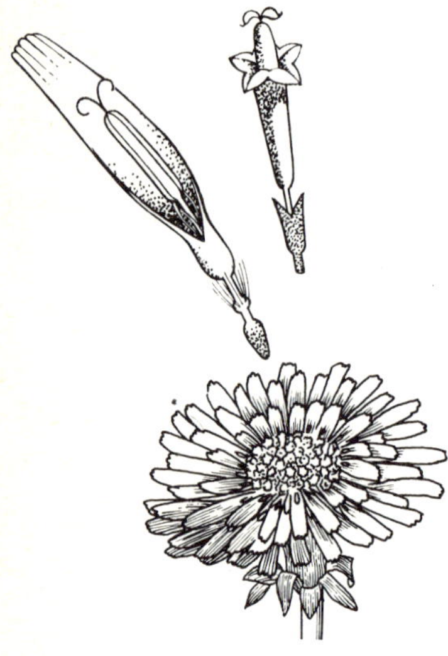
A composite flower

Conservatory

Corona

Chlorophyll. The pigment in green plants which is essential to their survival. It absorbs sunlight and uses the energy in the process of PHOTOSYNTHESIS to build sugars from water and carbon dioxide. See pages 28–9.

Chloroplast. Minute body in the plant cell containing CHLOROPHYLL in which PHOTOSYNTHESIS takes place. See pages 40–1.

Chlorosis. The fading of the bright green colour in leaves to pale green or yellow. Caused by a variety of diseases and by deficiencies of minerals such as potassium or iron. See pages 24–5.

Chromosome. A chromosome is found in the nucleus of all living cells at the time of cell division. It is a carrier of the genes, units of inheritance, which control the plant's appearance and development. See page 49.

Church, Thomas (*d.*1978). The leading garden architect of California since the 1940s. His book *Gardens are for People* (1955) set out his way of working, making outdoor rooms for relaxation more than horticulture. His use of abstract shapes, careful pruning of trees, "decks" to adjust levels and ground cover are now the California vernacular. His many well-known students include Mai Abergast and Lawrence Halprin.

Clairvoyée. Screen, usually of iron railings, through which one can "clearly see" the view. An idea used before the invention of the HA-HA, and indeed after it, particularly in both French and Dutch gardens.

Clamp. A pile of root vegetables such as potatoes completely covered with straw and earth for storage during the winter.

Cleveland, Horace Wm. Shaler (1814–1900). Landscape architect in western states who introduced landscape architecture to the planning of new towns.

Climber. Any plant with a natural ability to climb or used for "climbing" in gardens. See also RAMBLER. See pages 100–103.

Cloche. A glass or clear plastic structure like a small open-ended tent (if with side walls, it is a "barn cloche") designed to act as a miniature greenhouse and bring on vegetables or fruit ahead of season. They are usually put end to end to cover a row. Cloches are also used to raise plants from SEEDS or CUTTINGS. See also BELL GLASS.

Clone. A group of plants produced by vegetative means from the same parent, therefore having identical inherited characteristics. All the runners from one strawberry plant, for example, form a clone.

Clusius (Charles de l'Ecluse) (1526–1609). Pioneer Flemish botanist and creator of the first BOTANIC GARDEN in northern Europe at LEYDEN (from 1594). He translated early works on the plants of the New World into Latin, worked at Vienna for Maximilian II and was instrumental in introducing the tulip to Holland.

Coats, Alice M. (1905–78). Trained as a painter, she later became a garden historian. Author of *Flowers and their Histories* (1956), *The Quest for Plants* (1969), *The Book of Flowers* (1973). The last is a magnificent illustrated history of four centuries of botanical painting and drawing.

Coats, Peter (1910–). Garden designer, photographer and writer. Gardening editor of *House & Garden*, author of beautifully illustrated books, including *Guide to Great Gardens of Britain* (1977), *Flowers in History* (1970) and an autobiography, *Of Generals and Gardens* (1977).

Cocker & Sons. Specialist rose nursery established in 1841 at Aberdeen, Scotland, and still in the Cocker family. Close links with the rose-breeding HARKNESS family have given rise to many successful roses bred jointly including 'Alec's Red' (1970) and 'Silver Jubilee' (1978).

Collinson, Peter (1694–1768). A London linen-draper whose correspondence with the plant collector JOHN BARTRAM of Philadelphia over 33 years led to the introduction of large numbers of American plants to Europe.

Comber, Harold Frederick (1897–1969). Plant collector and nurseryman, son of the head gardener at NYMANS. Travelled in the southern Andes and Tasmania collecting seed. Author of *A New Classification of the Genus Lilium* (1949). In 1952 joined JAN DE GRAAFF at the Oregon Bulb Farms in Oregon, USA. Awarded VMH 1936.

Composite. Any of the 13,000 species in the daisy family Compositae. Includes chrysanthemums, cinerarias and zinnias. Composites are found worldwide. Their flowers are made up of tightly grouped small flowers (FLORETS) either tubular or strap-shaped. The SEPALS of each floret are often modified to hairs or bristles, which assist seed dispersal.

Compost, garden. Plant remains collected in a heap or pit to decay together, with the help of BACTERIA and other micro-organisms, into a valuable form of organic enrichment for the soil. See pages 24–5.

Compost, John Innes. See JOHN INNES COMPOST.

Composts, seed and potting. Mixtures of organic and inorganic materials, such as peat and sand, formulated for such specific garden purposes as growing seed, potting plants, striking cuttings or top-dressing the soil. Such composts have various recipes, but most contain all or most of the following: PEAT or sterilized loam (or both), sand, superphosphate, powdered chalk, hoof and horn meal or a general FERTILIZER. The JOHN INNES series of composts is among the best known, although today Levington composts, using all peat instead of loam, are more popular. See pages 26–7.

Compound. Describes parts of a plant composed of several units. A compound leaf comprises several leaflets, a compound FLOWER several florets, a compound FRUIT more than one ripened flower OVARY.

Compton, the Hon and Rev Henry (1632–1713). A botanically minded Bishop of London, whose diocese included the American colonies and who shrewdly chose botanists as missionaries. His garden at Fulham Palace became an important centre for new plants from America.

Cone. Flowering or fruiting spike of a CONIFER. Cones are always of separate sexes. Male cones are usually small and inconspicuous. Female cones develop hard scales, which open to release the winged seeds they protect.

Conifer. Any CONE-bearing tree, but also includes the yews and junipers that have fleshy fruits. Most conifers are EVERGREENS with scale, needle or strap-shaped leaves and have resinous wood.

Conservatory. Strictly distinguished from a greenhouse as having central beds in which permanent plants are placed, as well as side shelves for pots of flowers. More loosely, it is any greenhouse used as much by people as plants, especially one attached to a house where plants can be enjoyed in winter or bad weather.

Container, container-grown. A container is any kind of pot, plastic wrap or can in which a plant is sold. "Container-grown" means that a plant has spent its life from seedling or cutting in a container. Plants lifted from "open ground" and put in containers just before sale will be missing half their roots.

Contractile. Describes the roots of certain plants such as crocus CORMS and dandelions that have the power of shrinking longitudinally in order to pull the plant deeper into the soil.

Coppice. Trees or bushes regularly cut back to low stumps (STOOLS) to promote the growth of many straight stems useful in the garden as PEA STICKS and supports. Chestnut and hazel are traditional trees for coppicing.

Cordate. Heart-shaped. Used to describe a leaf with paired, rounded lobes at its base. See LEAF SHAPES.

Cordon. A tree (or plant) that is trained by removing all LATERAL branches (or side shoots) to form one main stem. Fruit trees, such as apples and pears with fruit-bearing SPURS, are most commonly trained in this way. Sweet peas and tomatoes can also be cordon-trained.

Corm, cormlet, cormel. A corm is a swollen stem base found below ground which stores food reserves. Unlike a BULB, it is not layered but the whole is covered with papery scales. Cormlets or cormels are small corms formed at the base of the parent and sometimes on stems above ground. All can give rise to new plants. Gladiolus and crocus are two common examples.

Corolla. The modified leaves forming the PETALS of a FLOWER. Usually a different colour from the SEPALS (CALYX). Petals may be separate or joined together.

Corona. Any outgrowth between the PETALS and STAMENS of a flower, for example the "trumpet" or crown of a narcissus or the protrusions from the stamens of the milkweed *Asclepias*, which make nectar.

Correvon, Henri. Swiss botanist and ALPINE specialist. His book *La Flore Alpine*, with admirable plates by Philippe Robert in a subdued art-nouveau style, was translated into English in 1911 and gave great impetus to the craze for alpines and rock gardens.

Corymb. A flower cluster with flower stalks of variable length arising from different levels of the stem to produce a flat head. Candytuft is a good example. See FLOWERS, FORMS OF.

Cotyledon. Seed leaf. Embryo leaf or leaves contained within the seed. These usually emerge and expand into green leaves on germination, but in some cases are retained below ground as food stores, the first leaves above ground being true ones. Flowering plants are divided into those with two seed leaves (DICOTYLEDONS) and those with one seed leaf (MONOCOTYLEDONS).

Coulter, Thomas (1793–1843). Irish doctor, plant hunter and adventurer in Mexico and California, where he met DAVID DOUGLAS, who named the big-cone pine (*Pinus coulteri*) after him. Coulter also discovered the California tree poppy (*Romneya coulteri*).

Country Life. British weekly magazine since 1897, which has always had admirable gardening articles and given a lead in the study of garden history. Among the many *Country Life* books is the three-volume *Gardens Old and New* (1900–8).

Cox, Euan H. M. (1893–1977). Botanist, gardener and author. Travelled with REGINALD FARRER in the eastern Himalayas in 1919. From 1929–40 he was founder and editor of *New Flora and Silva*, reviving WILLIAM ROBINSON's idea of a highbrow gardening magazine. Author of *Plant Hunting in China* (1945) and, with his son Peter (1934–), co-author of books on rhododendrons.

Cranborne Manor, Dorset. A sixteenth-century stone manor house with very beautiful gardens in the SISSINGHURST style. The property of the Cecil family, who are also active gardeners at Hatfield House.

Crarae Lodge, Strathclyde, Scotland. One of the world's most remarkable man-made landscapes, a rocky gorge by Loch Fyne densely clothed in exotic plants revelling in the almost-perpetual rain.

Crathes Castle, Banchory, Scotland. A gaunt baronial castle enriched with a masterpiece of modern gardening, planted by Lady Burnett in the 1930s in a framework of eighteenth-century yew hedges. A very rich variety of plants arranged in colour schemes of great subtlety. A property of the NATIONAL TRUST for Scotland.

Crenate. Term for a leaf with rounded teeth around its edge. See LEAF SHAPES.

Cross. See HYBRID.

Crowe, Dame Sylvia (1901–). Author and landscape architect whose work has included landscapes of new towns and power stations and advising the Forestry Commission on suiting its planting to the landscape. Her books include *Tomorrow's Landscape* (1956) and *Garden Design* (1958), which is still a standard work.

Crown, crown bud. A crown is the upper part of an underground stem (ROOTSTOCK) from which shoots grow. It is also the "trumpet" of a flower. In chrysanthemums a crown bud is one terminating a side shoot that forms on the main stem after STOPPING, or naturally after the abortion of a BREAK BUD.

Crucifer. Any of the 3,200 species of plants in the cabbage family Cruciferae. Flowers have four petals arranged in a cross shape. Most crucifers are found in cold, temperate regions and most are herbaceous. Important garden crucifers include the cabbage, wallflower (*Cheiranthus*), mustard (*Sinapis alba*) and the bedding plant alyssum.

Culm. The stem of a plant, particularly the hollow jointed stems of GRASSES and BAMBOOS.

Culpeper, Nicholas (1616–54). London herbalist and author of the *Complete Herbal* (1653), one of the most popular of all guides to herbs and their medicinal uses.

Cultivar. Short for "cultivated variety". The correct term for what most gardeners know as a "variety", that is a horticulturally selected plant. Also known as a CLONE.

Cultivator. A cultivator is a person or tool which improves or breaks up the surface of the ground. The tool is shaped like a deep, narrow, heavy rake. A rotary cultivator is motor-driven and has a revolving head with TINES all round.

Cunningham, Allan (1791–1839) and **Richard** (1793–1835). Two brothers who worked as plant collectors for KEW in Australia. Allan had a long career: for fifteen years he scoured the Australian bush. His brother died on his first excursion.

Cup. The crown, "trumpet" or CORONA of a narcissus that is shorter than the petals. A daffodil is a narcissus with its cup or corona equal to or longer than the petals.

Curd. Gardeners' name for the head of a broccoli or cauliflower.

Curtis, Charles H. (1870–1958). A great botanist and gardener, editor of the "GARDENERS' CHRONICLE" from 1919–50. No relation to the Curtis family below. Awarded VMH 1930.

Curtis family: William Curtis (1746–99). Quaker apothecary who founded CURTIS'S BOTANICAL MAGAZINE in 1787. Author of *Flora Londinensis* (1770). His cousin and son-in-law Samuel Curtis (1779–1860) was a nurseryman and author of *A Monograph on the Genus Camellia* (1819). He inherited the *Botanical Magazine* but did not edit it.

Cutting. Any part of a plant removed from its parent and treated so that it produces roots and, in time, a complete new plant. Cuttings may be composed of stems, roots or leaves. See STRIKE, PROPAGATION, RIPE, HALF-RIPE.

cv. Abbreviation of CULTIVAR.

Cyme. Dome-shaped or flat-topped flower-head or INFLORESCENCE in which the central flower opens first. See FLOWERS, FORMS OF.

Cypress Gardens. The name of several gardens in the south-eastern United States which incorporate parts of cypress swamps. Huge bald (or swamp) cypresses (the deciduous *Taxodium distichum*) with buttressed trunks rise from dark pools. Azaleas and camellias grow admirably in the peaty soil. The most famous are at Cypress Gardens, Florida, and Charleston, South Carolina.

D

Damping down. The wetting of benches and floors in greenhouses and frames to increase air humidity.

Damping off. The action of disease-causing FUNGI on seedlings which makes them collapse and die. Usually caused by the fungus *Pythium debaryanum*, which flourishes when seedlings are too crowded or too wet. Treat with an appropriate FUNGICIDE.

Dartington Hall, Totnes, Devon. A famous modern garden surrounding an old stone manor, now a college. The principal designers were Beatrix Farrand in the 1930s and Percy Cane in the 1950s. The best-known feature is a series of giant grass terraces, the Tiltyard.

Darwin, Dr Erasmus (1731–1802). Scholar, poet and gardener. Author of *The Botanic Garden*, an extraordinary, immensely popular verse essay on gardening and botany. Grandfather of Charles, author of *The Origin of Species*.

David, Jean-Pierre Armand (1826–1900). French missionary-naturalist who taught and botanized in remote western China. He discovered (but did not introduce) the handkerchief tree (*Davidia involucrata*).

Dawyck, Stobo, Scotland. A great collection of trees on the banks of the Tweed; the origin of the FASTIGIATE Dawyck beech. Developed since the late nineteenth century into a woodland garden by the planting of shrubs and bulbs under the trees.

Dead-heading. Removing faded flowers from a plant, partly for its appearance but also to prevent it from spending its energy on producing seeds. Dead-heading often produces, as in rhododendrons, a better crop of flowers the following year, or, as in perpetual-flowering roses and many herbaceous plants, and especially annuals, it encourages more flowers to follow.

de Busbecq, Ghiselin. Sixteenth-century ambassador of the Holy Roman Empire to Suleiman the Magnificent at Constantinople, who probably introduced *c.*1550 many Turkish and Middle Eastern plants, including tulips and crown imperials, to Europe.

de Caux, Isaac (*fl.*1625–45). Garden architect, responsible in part for the great gardens of Hatfield House and Wilton. Possibly son of Solomon de Caux, designer of the famous Castle Gardens of Heidelberg.

Euan H. M. Cox

A crucifer flower

Nicholas Culpeper

William Curtis

Olivier de Serres

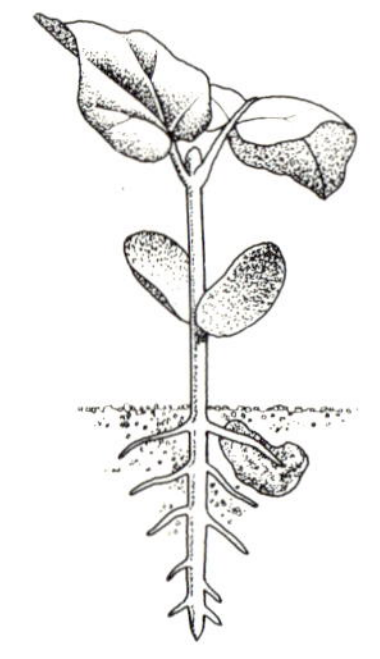

Dicotyledon

Andrew Jackson Downing

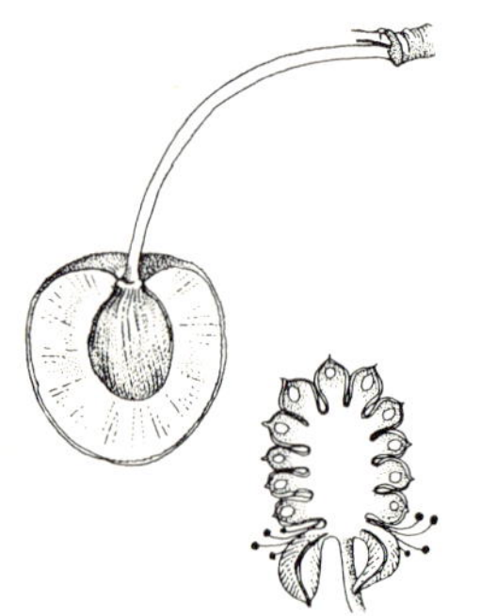

Drupes: cherry and raspberry

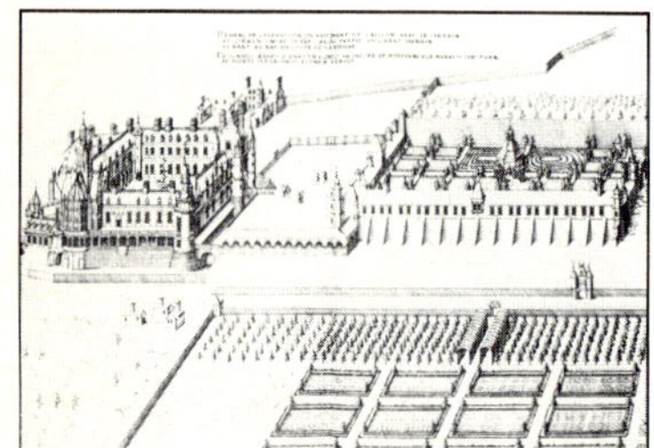

Engraving of Château de Gaillon by Jacques Androuet du Cerceau.

Deciduous. A plant that loses all its leaves at one time of the year, usually late autumn. The opposite of EVERGREEN.

de Graaff, Jan. The most important breeder of lilies, on his Oregon Bulb Farms at Sandy, Oregon, USA, founded in the 1920s. He has developed such important strains as the Mid-Century, the Bellingham and the Olympic hybrids and supplies a large proportion of the lily bulbs sold in Europe as well as in the USA.

Dehiscent. A FRUIT or CAPSULE that bursts open to release its contents. The poppy is an example.

de Jussieu family. A family of famous botanists: three brothers from Lyon, France, Antoine, Bernard and Joseph; their nephew Antoine-Laurent and his son Adrien. Joseph (1704–79) travelled and collected plants in Central and South America, discovering the heliotrope (*Heliotropium peruvianum*).

Delavay, Jean-Marie (1838–95). French missionary-botanist in China who sent home seeds of innumerable important plants, including paeonies, primulas, rhododendrons, irises, incarvilleas. Many of them bear his name.

Dendrology. The study of trees.

Dentate. Of a leaf with a regularly toothed edge and with the ends of the teeth pointing outwards. See CRENATE and SERRATE. See LEAF SHAPES.

de Passe, Crispin (*fl.*1615). Dutch engraver, author of *Hortus Floridus* (1614) translated as *A Garden of Flowers* (1615).

de Ruiter, Gesbert (1926–). Leading Dutch rose breeder. His creations include 'Europeana' (1963), 'Diorama' (1965) and 'Michelle' (1970).

de Serres, Olivier (1539–1619). Early French agricultural and horticultural writer from the Ardèche. His *Théatre d'Agriculture* contains exact views of gardens of the period.

des Barres, Arboretum. Nogent-sur-Vernisson, France. The French national tree collection, at the former home of the VILMORIN family. Now a forestry school with some fine specimens of rare trees.

Descanso, La Canada, California. Picturesque gardens with giant oaks shading extensive plantings of rhododendrons and camellias.

Dibber, dibble. A bluntly pointed wooden tool for making holes in the soil. Seeds or seedlings are "dibbled", or planted, in the holes. Dibbers can often be made from a broken spade handle by sharpening it to a blunt point.

Dickson & Sons Ltd, A. Northern Ireland. Old family firm of rose breeders whose varieties include 'Shot Silk' (1924), and 'Grandpa Dickson' (1966).

Dickson, James (1738–1822). Scottish-born botanist, nurseryman and herbalist of London; a founder of the RHS and of the LINNEAN SOCIETY. The New Zealand tree fern is named *Dicksonia* for him.

Dicotyledon. Plant with two seed leaves or COTYLEDONS in each seed, often appearing at germination. Dicotyledons are one of the two divisions of flowering plants (angiosperms). The parts of the dicotyledon flower are usually arranged in fours or fives and the leaves are net-veined. See also MONOCOTYLEDON.

Digitate. Of a leaf with finger-like divisions composed of separate small leaves (leaflets) all arising at the summit of a single stalk. Horse-chestnut is an example. See LEAF SHAPES.

d'Incarville, Pierre N. le C. (1706–57). The first of many French missionary-botanists in China, in correspondence from Peking with JOSEPH DE JUSSIEU in Paris and PHILIP MILLER and PETER COLLINSON in London. He sent many specimens to Europe and some seeds, including the Chinese Tree of Heaven (*Ailanthus altissima*), *Albizzia julibrissin, Sophora japonica, Cedrela sinensis* and *Koelreuteria paniculata.*

Dioecious. A plant in which male and female FLOWERS are borne on different individuals. To ensure fruit production among dioecious plants males and females must be planted near one another or POLLEN transferred manually. See MONOECIOUS.

Diploid. Refers to the usual number of CHROMOSOMES present in the nucleus of any cell. Half of these chromosomes are derived from the male parent and the other half are derived from the female parent. See page 49.

Disbudding. Removing side shoots and/or FLOWER BUDS from a stem. Disbudding encourages the growth of the remaining buds.

Disk floret. One of the little tubular flowers in the middle of a RAYED composite (daisy) flower.

Division. The deliberate separation of a clump-forming plant into two or more different parts as a means of vegetative PROPAGATION.

Dombey, Joseph (*d.*1796). French botanist, pupil of DE JUSSIEU, who braved nature and the Indians, and (far worse) the Spanish authorities, to collect plants in Peru and Chile from 1778–84. The magnificent evergreen southern beech (*Nothofagus dombeyi*) salutes him.

Dormancy. A period of inactivity, necessary to most plants, at least in the temperate zones. It can take many forms, from dropping leaves and forming new buds to withdrawal underground. Some seeds need to undergo several months of dormancy before they will germinate.

Dot plant. Taller plants "dotted" among shorter, especially in old-fashioned formal bedding schemes.

Double, semi-double. Flowers with more than the usual complement of PETALS. In a double flower some of the sexual organs (STAMENS or CARPELS) are transformed into petals. A semi-double has fewer petals than a double. Also used of a daisy-type COMPOSITE with some or all of the DISK FLORETS changed to RAYS.

Double digging. A thorough method of digging, also known as bastard trenching.

Douglas, David (1799–1834). The best known of all dauntless plant hunters, a Scotsman from Scone. He was sent to the West Coast of North America by the HORTICULTURAL SOCIETY in 1825 and spent most of the rest of his life discovering and shipping home plants from the almost unknown western flora. They include the Douglas fir (*Pseudotsuga taxifolia*), seven or eight pines, the flowering currant (*Ribes sanguineum*), Oregon grape (*Mahonia aquifolium*), dogwood (*Cornus alba*), California poppy (*Eschscholzia californica*), lupins, such annuals as limnanthes, nemophila, godetia, clarkia. Douglas was killed by a bull after falling into a bull pit in Hawaii.

Downing, Andrew Jackson (1815–52). American garden architect and author of *A Treatise on the Theory and Practice of Landscape Gardening Applied to North America* (1841), many times reprinted and widely influential in the mid-nineteenth century. Popularized gardens for public use: many public parks, including Central Park in New York, were the result of his crusade.

Drainage. The run-off of water from below the SOIL which is essential to prevent waterlogging and poor soil aeration. Where necessary drainage can be provided by a system of pipes below the soil laid at a gradient. See pages 22–3.

Drawn. Describes a weak, spindly stem. Caused by lack of light, overcrowding, overwatering or overheating. It can be a help in procuring propagating material from plants which are difficult to root from cuttings.

Drift. Word much used by gardeners, designers and writers to mean a substantial, but casual- and natural-looking patch of one plant. Daffodils or snowdrops, for example, are planted in "drifts".

Drill. A narrow, straight, shallow furrow in the soil in which seeds are sown. The drill may be flat-bottomed or V-shaped.

Drummond, Thomas (*d.*1835) and **James** (1784–1863). Scottish brothers who were naturalists and plant hunters. Thomas worked in western USA, was a friend of DAVID DOUGLAS and introduced the Texan *Phlox drummondii*. James was a pioneer in Western Australia in an area rich in strange flowers, which he roamed for 30 years, sending his finds to SIR WILLIAM HOOKER at KEW.

Drummond Castle, Crieff, Scotland. A craggy castle overlooking an elaborate 13-acre PARTERRE of Victorian design.

Drupe. A FRUIT such as a cherry with a fleshy covering (pericarp) enclosing one or more seeds or "stones". Small drupes (drupelets) may be grouped, as in a raspberry.

du Cerceau, Androuet. A famous French family of architects of the sixteenth and seventeenth centuries. Jacques (?1510–85) is best known for his engravings of *Les Plus Excellents Bastiments de France*, which include detailed plans of the great gardens of the time.

Duke Memorial Gardens, Durham, North Carolina. These gardens, on the grounds of Duke University, feature a formal terrace garden in continuous bloom, colourful annuals and perennials, and a rock garden.

Dumbarton Oaks, Washington, D.C. Federal style mansion built in 1801 and privately endowed gardens belonging to Harvard University. The scene of regular scholarly conferences on questions of garden history. Of particular interest are the elegant terrace gardens and the glass-enclosed orangery.

E

Earthing up. Piling soil around plants either to keep parts of them white (BLANCHING) or to protect them from wind damage or excessive cold.

Edinburgh Royal Botanic Garden, The. One of the world's most important botanic gardens and the great centre for rhododendron studies, with what is usually called the best rock garden anywhere, made in 1908–14 under PROFESSOR BAYLEY BALFOUR. It has spectacular glasshouses, both Victorian and ultra modern.

Edzell Castle, Tayside, Scotland. A small enclosed garden restored in the 1930s in a medieval style, overlooked by the ruined Edzell Castle and three remarkably ornate walls of red sandstone.

Ehret, Georg Dionysius (1708–70). Son of a Heidelberg market-gardener who became one of the greatest of all botanical artists. From 1736 to his death he worked in London, often painting the first flowering of new plants in cultivation.

Eliot, Charles (1859–1897). Took an active part in designing the park system of Boston, and was a sometime partner of FREDERICK LAW OLMSTED.

Ellacombe, Rev Henry Nicholson (1822–1916). One of the brotherhood of Victorian gardening parsons. His garden at Bitton, Gloucestershire, was famous for its plants. In his book *In a Gloucestershire Garden* he wrote "I was long ago taught... that it is impossible to get or keep a large collection [of plants] except by constant liberality in giving." Awarded VMH 1897.

Elliptic. Of leaves, PETALS and BRACTS with the outline of an ellipse. See LEAF SHAPES.

Elwes, Henry J. (1846–1922). Gardener and dendrologist. Author of *The Genus Lilium* (1880) and, with AUGUSTINE HENRY, of *The Trees of Great Britain and Ireland* (1906–13), a seven-volume work of impressive scholarship which gives the impression that the authors inspected every worthwhile tree not only in Britain but all over the world. Awarded VMH 1897.

Endosperm. The food store in a SEED. Found surrounding the embryo plant and used by it during GERMINATION. See pages 50–1.

English Flower Garden, The. WILLIAM ROBINSON's most famous work, published in 1883 with contributions from all the great amateur and professional gardeners of the day. Most of the book is a detailed plant catalogue. The latest revised edition (16th) was published in 1956.

Entire. Term for a leaf edge completely without indentations.

Epiphyte. A plant that grows on another, using it for support but not as a source of nourishment; that is not parasitically. Many epiphytes have AERIAL ROOTS adapted to obtain moisture from the air and are also called air plants. Examples include lichens, BROMELIADS and ORCHIDS.

Ericaceous. Any of the 1,350 species of plants in the heather family Ericaceae, which includes azaleas and rhododendrons. Mostly shrubs and trees native to cold and temperate regions and high mountains in the Tropics. FLOWERS may be saucer, bell, urn or tubular in shape, the six PETALS partially or completely fused. Most are CALCIFUGES that will not grow on limy soil.

Espalier. A lattice-work of wood or wires to train trees on. Also a method of training fruit trees, such as apples and pears that fruit on SPURS by selecting LATERAL branches to grow in a particular shape, usually horizontally in opposite pairs on each side of the main stem.

Etiolated. A weak, spindly stem. See DRAWN.

Evelyn, John (1620–1706). "A man of means, of unblemished character, and a dilettante, who helped to advance English civilization." Evelyn designed several gardens, wrote the enormously influential *Sylva: a Discourse on Forest Trees* (1664), translated the work of DE LA QUINTINIE into English, and started to write a great gardening book, *Elysium Britannicum*. His diary records the making of his garden at Sayes Court, Deptford, Kent.

Evergreen. A plant that keeps its foliage for at least a year. The opposite of DECIDUOUS. A wintergreen retains its leaves for one year only.

Exbury Gardens. The great rhododendron gardens of the ROTHSCHILD family in Hampshire where many famous CROSSES have been made, particularly of azaleas.

Exotic. A plant introduced from another country. Not native or endemic.

Eye. An undeveloped BUD on a potato or dahlia TUBER or a rose bush. Also a stem CUTTING of a grape vine with one bud on its side or tip. In flowers it is a bloom with a centre of a different colour.

F

F_1 hybrid. Plant produced in the first generation of breeding from a cross between parents of two different true-breeding CULTIVARS within a SPECIES. Such HYBRIDS are more vigorous and usually heavier cropping than their parents. Seed from F_1 hybrids does not breed true.

F_2 hybrid. Plant produced by the interbreeding of first generation or F_1 hybrids. Usually less vigorous than F_1s, but like them not true breeding.

Fairchild Tropical Garden, Miami, USA. One of America's finest tropical gardens and a major botanic collection with 500 different species of palms, also cycads, aroids, BROMELIADS, orchids and FERNS.

Falls. The lower PETALS of irises which hang downwards. In some species they bear a growth of hair that is known as a BEARD.

Family. Group of plant GENERA sharing a set of basic characteristics such as flower composition. Most family names end in -aceae, but there are exceptions, such as Compositae (daisies), Graminae (grasses) and Labiatae (dead nettles and their ALLIES). Several families are grouped together to form a plant "order". See also GENUS, SPECIES.

Fan. The shape of a trained tree such as a peach or an apricot. The branches are trained to grow straight and to radiate from the top of a central trunk.

Farrer, Reginald (1880–1920). Plant collector and author, pioneer and popularizer of rock gardening. His first book, *My Rock Garden* (1907), coined a number of pithy phrases still current among rock-gardeners such as "a dog's grave". His great work was *The English Rock Garden* (1919). Few writers have been so nimble with epithets and imagery to describe plants, or conveyed such infectious enthusiasm. In 1914–15 with WILLIAM PURDOM and in 1919 with EUAN COX he visited western China and Tibet. He died on this last expedition.

Fasciation. A condition in which the tip of a stem proliferates many growing points in parallel, fused together, usually on one plane giving a feathered effect, often curling or spiralling. The condition can be continued by CUTTINGS or grafts, but is sometimes inherited. It is prized in CACTI and FERNS. Affected plants are known as cristate. The cause may be FUNGI, mites or BACTERIA, and possibly radiation.

Fastigiate. A variety of tree or shrub with erect instead of the normal spreading branches. The Lombardy poplar is a common example.

FCC (First Class Certificate). FCC is an intermediate award to plants considered "of great excellence" by the appropriate committee of the RHS, without detailed knowledge of their garden performance. See also AGM and AM.

Feathered, flaked, flamed. Terms for the markings on PETALS. In feathering, fine markings of a different colour spread round the petal edges. In a flamed flower the petals are feathered with an extra central band of colour. In a flaked flower the petals are streaked and banded in one or more colours over a ground colour.

Fern. A non-flowering plant that reproduces by means of SPORES borne on the underside of the leaf-like fronds. They abound in the Tropics but occur worldwide. Many of the at least 10,000 known species are shade and moisture lovers. See also pages 146–7.

Fern-leaved. Describes a deeply and daintily divided leaf of any plant. An example is the fern-leaf beech (*Fagus sylvatica* 'Heterophylla').

The enclosed garden of Edzell Castle

An espalier

John Evelyn

Eye on a potato; eye in a flower

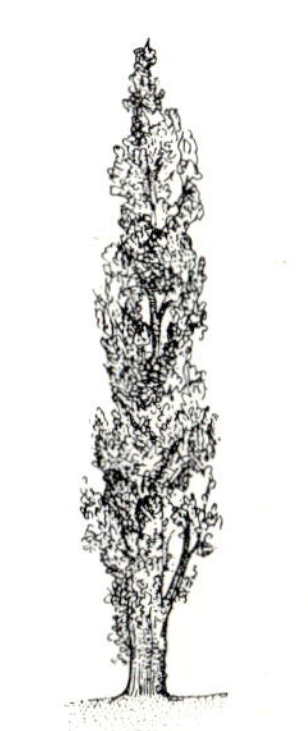

A fastigiate tree

Valerie Finnis

A flore pleno flower

Fertilization. The fusion of male and female sex cells. If POLLEN and female cell are on the same plant then self-fertilization can occur; if on different plants it is cross-fertilization. See page 47. See also FLOWER.

Fertilizer. Material rich in elements vital to plant growth added to the SOIL to increase its fertility. Fertilizers may be organic materials such as dried blood, bonemeal or powdered hoof and horn or be made up of inorganic substances (chemical fertilizers). The main elements supplied by fertilizers are nitrogen, phosphorus, potassium, magnesium, sulphur and the TRACE ELEMENTS (those needed in minute quantities). Sodium and chlorine may also be added. Liming fertilizers usually supply only calcium and magnesium. Fertilizers may be in liquid soil (TOP-DRESSING) or dug in (BASE DRESSING). See LIME, NITROGEN PHOSPHATE, SUPERPHOSPHATE. See pages 24–5.

Filament. The slender extension on which POLLEN-producing parts of the FLOWER (ANTHERS) are borne. Anther and filament together form a STAMEN.

Fimbriate. Fringed. Describes the border of a leaf or PETAL.

Finial. An ornament on a gate-post or pier, the apex of a roof or the top of a dome. Often a ball, a pineapple or an urn.

Finnis, Valerie (Lady Scott). Contemporary plantswoman and garden photographer. Created alpine section of old Waterperry Horticultural School. Has gardens at Boughton House, Kettering, Northamptonshire with a wide variety of shrubs and plants. Awarded VMH 1975.

Flaked. See FEATHERED.

Flamed. See FEATHERED.

Fletcher, Dr Harold R. (1907–78). Botanist and historian. Director of WISLEY (1951–54), Regius Keeper of the ROYAL BOTANIC GARDEN, EDINBURGH (1956–70), a great authority on rhododendrons and primulas and author of the exhaustive and enthralling *The Story of the Royal Horticultural Society 1804–1968* (1969). Awarded VMH 1956.

Flocculate. To improve the texture of clay SOIL by adding LIME, which makes the fine particles aggregate in small crumbs. From the Latin word for wool.

Flora. The whole of the plant world, as opposed to the fauna or animal life. Also the plants of a particular area or a book describing them.

Flora and Sylva. A luxurious but short-lived gardening magazine published by WILLIAM ROBINSON 1903–5. Now a collector's piece.

Flore pleno. Botanical term describing a flower with extra petals (a DOUBLE). Often denoted by the words plena or pleniflora or abbreviated to fl. pl.

Floret. Any of the small individual flowers making up a COMPOSITE flower such as a daisy. May be tubular or strap-shaped. Tubular florets in the flower centre are usually known as DISK FLORETS, strap-shaped ones around the edge as RAY FLORETS. Composite flowers may be entirely composed of tubular or strap-shaped florets.

Floribunda. Simply means having lots of flowers. Floribunda roses are modern cluster-flowering bushes closely related to HYBRID TEAS. See pages 86–93.

Flower. The special organ of sexual reproduction in higher plants. The parts are borne on a specialized, sometimes swollen, stem-tip, the receptacle. A flower consists of two sets of modified leaves, the outer SEPALS or CALYX and the inner PETALS forming the COROLLA. Inside these are the male and female parts. The male organs (androecium) comprise POLLEN-producing ANTHERS on extensions or FILAMENTS. The female parts (gynoecium or PISTIL) comprise one or more CARPELS each made up of STIGMA, STYLE and OVARY. See pages 46–7. See also FLOWERS, FORMS OF.

Foliage plant. A plant grown for the sake of its leaves rather than for its flowers or fruit. The leaves may be colourful, or large or a striking shape.

Folly. Any fanciful construction in a garden which is there for appearance rather than use. The word reputedly derives from the French *feuillée*, meaning leafy—and therefore presumably originally meant a green arbour. Another view is that it simply means the builder is a fool.

Fontainebleau, Château de, France. Royal palace south of Paris, first beautified in the sixteenth century by François I, later by Catherine de Médicis, Henry IV and Louis XIV. Napoleon called it the "house of the centuries"; it had been altered so many times. The gardens retain traces of the layout drawn by DU CERCEAU.

Forcing. The act of hurrying plants into maturity by artificial means, usually by raising the temperature. Sometimes combined with the exclusion of light as in forcing rhubarb. A forced plant of this sort grows by using its reserve stores of food. Forcing is also used to describe the out-of-season (in winter) culture of fruits and vegetables under glass.

Fork, "forking over". A more useful and sympathetic tool than a SPADE for many purposes. Good for digging heavy ground that sticks together in clods. Essential for forking out deep-rooting weeds. "Forking over" is a general loosening of the soil surface, particularly in spring after winter rains have compacted it. It can take the form of shallow digging or just pronging the ground with a twisting motion of the fork. It should not be done near shallow-rooting plants or roses: for these a MULCH is better treatment.

Form. A term used loosely by botanists and gardeners alike for any plant deviating in minor ways from the norm of a SPECIES, whether a botanical or a cultivated VARIETY. It is lower in rank than a variety.

Forma. A botanical TAXON lower in rank than a VARIETY.

Forrest, George (1873–1932). Scottish plant collector whose introductions from western China were to have even more of an impact on European gardens than those of E. H. WILSON. Forrest visited the area seven times between 1904 and 1932, financed by various syndicates of amateurs, in particular J. C. WILLIAMS. His bag included 300 new rhododendron species, 150 new primulas, *Gentiana sino-ornata*, *Camellia saluenensis* (parent of *C.* × *williamsii*), *Pieris forrestii*, magnolias and numerous lilies. Awarded VMH 1921.

Forsyth, William (1737–1804). Gardener to King George III, he was successor to PHILIP MILLER at the CHELSEA PHYSICK GARDEN, where he built the first rock garden in Britain, using stone from the Tower of London and lava brought by SIR JOSEPH BANKS from Iceland. He concocted a famous "plaster", which he

FLOWERS, FORMS OF

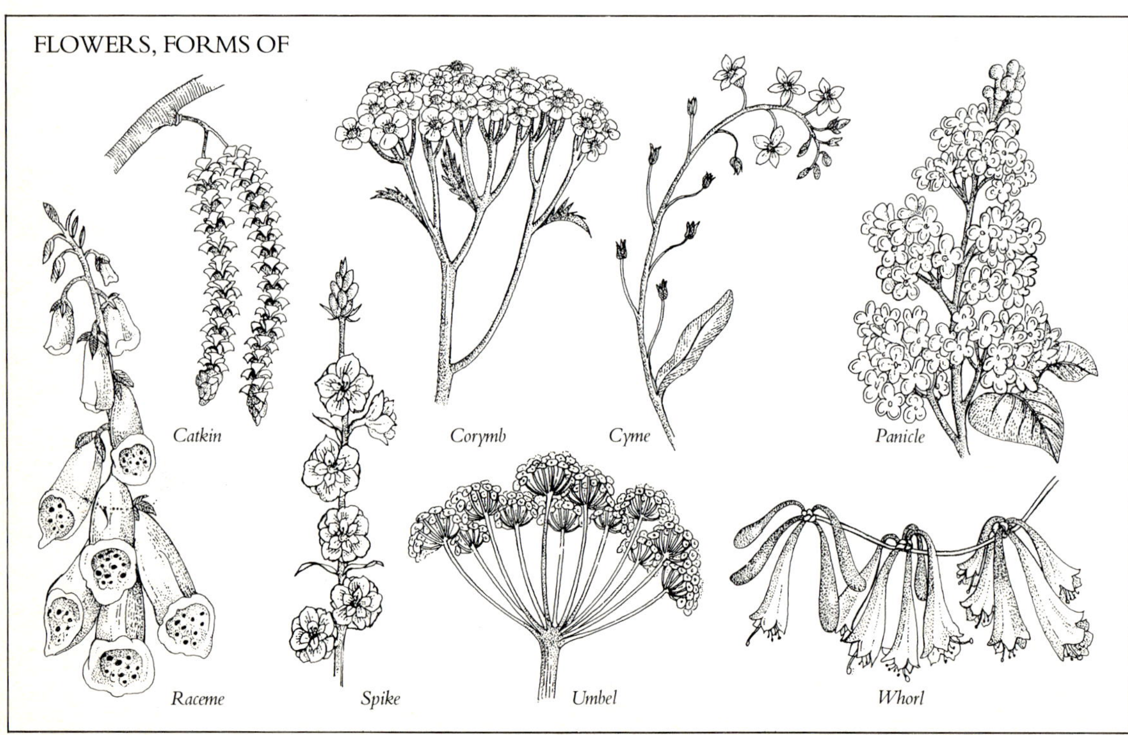

claimed could cure diseased trees, and was the oldest of the founder-members of the HORTICULTURAL SOCIETY. The forsythia is named after him.

Fortune, Robert (1812–80). Scottish plant collector who had the remarkable luck to be the first into China after the opening of that country in 1842 after the Opium War. He was sent by the HORTICULTURAL SOCIETY, returning after many adventures in 1846 with a hoard of treasures including "Japanese" anemones (*Anemone hupehensis*), chrysanthemums, *Dicentra spectabilis*, winter jasmine (*Jasminum nudiflorum*), forsythia (*Forsythia viridissima*), weigela (*Diervilla florida*) and winter honeysuckle (*Lonicera fragrantissima*). He made several more Chinese journeys for the East India Company and others to procure tea-plants, which he successfully introduced to India. In 1860 he went to Japan for Standish and Noble and returned with another rich haul, including *Saxifraga fortunei*.

Foucquet, Nicolas (1615–80). Chancellor of France and early patron of LE NÔTRE, he ruined himself in building the palace and park of VAUX-LE-VICOMTE. Many of his statues were later used at VERSAILLES.

Fountains. See pages 180–1, 184–5.

Frame. A most useful device for providing sheltered conditions for small plants. Often called a cold frame, it consists of a low-walled box with a sloping LIGHT for cover. It is ventilated by raising the lower edge of the light with a wedge. Heating can be provided by an electric cable buried in the soil or (the old method) by putting the frame on top of a heap of fermenting manure. Frames are used for germinating seeds of half-hardy plants, providing close conditions for cuttings, HARDENING OFF plants before planting them out, raising early salad crops, sheltering slightly tender plants in winter, keeping alpines in pots dry, and giving extra warmth to summer crops such as melons and cucumbers.

Fraser, John (1750–1811), Scottish plant hunter, protégé of WILLIAM FORSYTH, he made several voyages to North America, collecting for (among others) the Russian royal family. His important discoveries include *Rhododendron catawbiense* and *R. calendulaceum*, *Aesculus parviflora*, *Hydrangea quercifolia*, a rudbeckia and an evening primrose. His son (also John) accompanied him on his later travels.

Frémont, General J. C. (1813–90). Legendary adventurer, soldier and explorer of western USA, known to botany chiefly for his travels in the Mojave desert and remembered by *Fremontodendron californicum*, a splendid yellow-flowered bush.

Friable. Used to describe SOIL which is easily crumbled into small pieces or powder.

Frost damage. The destruction of plant parts that occurs when cells are ruptured by temperatures below freezing point. Plants susceptible to frost damage are described as tender or half-hardy. Plant parts most susceptible are those in an active state of growth that contain much water. See page 13.

Fruit. The ripened female parts of the flower developing after FERTILIZATION and containing SEED. True fruits are those in which only the walls of the CARPELS (true female units) are affected. In false fruits or pseudocarps other parts of the flower such as the SEPALS are involved. When ripe, the fruit may be dry or succulent. Dry fruits that open to release their seeds are called DEHISCENT, those that do not are indehiscent. Indehiscent fruits include ACHENES and NUTS, dehiscent fruits include CAPSULES, LEGUMES and siliquas. Succulent fruits include berries and DRUPES. Among the many kinds of false fruit are the strawberry, apple (pome) and pineapple.

Fruticose. Describes a shrubby plant, that is one with stems that are mainly or entirely woody.

Fumigation. The killing of pests, especially INSECTS, mites and FUNGI, with poisonous vapour. Sulphur is most commonly used to kill fungi; hydrocyanic gas, nicotine and tetrachlorethane to kill insects.

Fungicide. Chemical used to kill FUNGI or check their growth. Fungicides are most effective against fungi such as powdery mildews which grow on the plant surface, less so against those that penetrate plant tissues, for which prevention is better than cure, though SYSTEMIC fungicides have been developed which circulate in the sap of the plant. Copper salts and sulphur are among the most effective fungicides available.

Fungus, fungi. Any member of a huge group of non-flowering plants that have no green pigment (CHLOROPHYLL). Fungi either live as PARASITES, obtaining food from other living organisms, or as SAPROPHYTES, which gain nourishment from decaying organic matter. Most fungi consist of small threads (hyphae) forming a spawn or mycelium on which are borne fruiting bodies containing reproductive SPORES. Some fungi cause plant diseases, including black spot, scab and mildew; others are useful as natural decomposers in the soil. See MYCORRHIZA.

G

Gall. Outgrowth on a plant. Most commonly caused by an INSECT but can arise from bacterial, fungal or eelworm activity. In insect galls the plant reacts to the prescence of insect eggs by producing an abnormal growth which protects the eggs during development. Many galls are harmless but some distort buds, leaves or fruit. An "oak-apple" is an example.

Garden Club of America. Publishes biannually *Garden Club of America Bulletin*, a 60-page bulletin primarily for civic-minded women interested in gardening. New York, New York 10022.

Garden, The. The monthly journal of the RHS. WILLIAM ROBINSON founded and edited a magazine with the same title from 1871–1927.

Gardeners' Chronicle. First published on 2 January 1841. Among its four founders (who also founded *Athenaeum* and *Punch* in the same year) were DR JOHN LINDLEY and SIR JOSEPH PAXTON. The greatest gardening magazine for many years. Now a horticultural trade journal.

Garden History Society, The. Scholarly society, founded by Peter Hunt in 1965, which publishes a quarterly journal, *Garden History*, organizes conferences and tours and keeps a register of current research.

Garfield Park Conservatory, Chicago, Illinois. An outstanding American CONSERVATORY, featuring exotic and desert plants.

Garinish Island, Ireland. A strange marriage of Italianesque formality and modern woodland gardening on what was almost a bare rock in Bantry Bay. Designed by HAROLD PETO to take advantage of the mild (but blustery) Atlantic climate. Many rare and tender plants.

Gazebo. The same as a BELVEDERE. The word first appeared in 1752 in reference to a "Chinese turret", so it may be a corruption of an oriental word—or it may be mock Latin, from "gaze" and "bo", as in "lavabo".

Generalife, Granada. The greatest monument to the garden art of Moorish Spain. A sequence of courts linked by a theme of playing water, with sudden views of Granada, the Alhambra and the distant Sierra Nevada.

Genetics. The science of heredity. See pages 48–9.

Genus. A group of plants with common characteristics agreed by botanists probably to have evolved from a common ancestor. A genus is comprised of one or more SPECIES. Thus the genus *Iris* contains over 800 species, including *Iris germanica* and *Iris reticulata*. The first part of the Latin name, or binomial, denotes the genus. Where several genera are thought to have a common ancestor they are grouped together to form a plant FAMILY.

Gerard, John (1545–1612). Herbalist and gardener, author of the celebrated *Herball, or generall Historie of Plantes* (1597), which he largely borrowed without acknowledgement from the work of the Dutchman Dodoens. The *Herball* was revised and corrected by Thomas Johnson (1633) in another famous edition.

Germination. The emergence of a plant from a seed. Occurs only in the correct conditions of light and temperature sometimes only after a period of DORMANCY. In germination the seed first absorbs water which mobilizes food stores for the embryo plant. In flowering plants the appearance of the RADICLE (first root) is the sign of germination. This is normally followed by the emergence of the seed leaves.

Gessner, Conrad von (1516–65). Swiss scholar and naturalist. He is credited with having popularized the tulip, after seeing one in an Augsburg garden in 1559. All garden tulips are known botanically as *Tulipa gesneriana*.

Gilpin, William Sawrey (1724–1804). Vicar of Boldre, Hampshire, and author of books on natural scenery, including *Forest Scenery* (1791), which influenced the romantic/picturesque gardening movement. His observation of trees was acute and is still worth reading.

John C. Frémont

John Gerard

Asa Gray

The great grape vine at Hampton Court

Glabrous. Not hairy.

Gland, glandular. Glands are secretory organs in any part of the plant which make substances such as oils, sugar or water. NECTARIES are among the most complex glands. Glands borne on thin stalks, such as the stinging glands of nettles, are called glandular hairs.

Glasnevin Botanic Garden, Dublin, Ireland. The national botanic garden of Ireland, started in 1795. A great collection with remarkable glasshouses, and peat, rock and water gardens.

Glaucous. Describes a blue or grey-green leaf or FRUIT covered with a waxy bloom. A grape is a glaucous fruit; a Scots pine needle a glaucous leaf.

Grafting. The process by which parts of two different plants are bound together so that they unite to become a single plant. The top part of the graft which produces flowers and fruit is the SCION, the lower rooting section is the STOCK. The scion may also be placed in a slit made in the bark of the stock. Where the stock and the scion join is known as the union. See also BUDDING. See pages 52–3.

Grass. Any of the 10,000 plant species in the (monocot) family Graminae. Found worldwide, grasses can be creeping or tufted and nearly all are herbs. The leaves are usually long and narrow and several flowers are carried together in spikelets. Grasses are important food sources and much used for lawns. The BAMBOOS are woody grasses.

Gray, Professor Asa (1810–88). Distinguished American botanist, Professor of Natural History at Harvard 1842–88, author with JOHN TORREY of a *Flora of North America* (1838–43). One of the founding fathers of the ARNOLD ARBORETUM.

Grease band. A ring of grease put round the trunk of a fruit tree or the stem of a rose to trap disease-causing organisms (particularly INSECTS) or to prevent them from climbing up to the leaves, flowers or fruit. The "grease" is made from plant extracts, the band is made some 4 in wide and set below the lowest branch.

Great Dixter, East Sussex. House and garden designed in the 1900s by EDWIN LUTYENS for Nathaniel Lloyd, the father of the present owners. The garden is now famous as the subject-matter of CHRISTOPHER LLOYD's books and articles. He also keeps a small commercial nursery of excellent plants, especially clematis, in the gardens.

Greenhouse. Glass building for protecting plants from the weather. The two basic models are "lean-to", with a single roof slope up to a supporting wall, and "full-span", with slopes both ways, which admits more light but is more costly to heat. There are also "three-quarter span", "Dutch" and combined shed and greenhouse types. Since the entire ecosystem in a greenhouse is under the gardener's control, great care is needed in watering, shading, ventilation, pest-control and general hygiene. See pages 32–3. See STOVE.

Green manure. A quick-growing crop cultivated expressly to be dug into the ground to improve the texture of the SOIL. On light soil it has the advantage of holding nutrients in the soil that would otherwise be LEACHED away by rain, and releasing them slowly as the dug-in crop decays. On heavy soil, it opens up the texture and improves the drainage. Mustard, rape, Italian rye grass and vetches are typical green-manure crops.

Grey-leaved. Describes a plant with leaves bearing a grey or blue-grey bloom or a coating of hairs. Grey-leaved plants have particular garden value for offsetting bright colours. See also GLAUCOUS.

Gronovius, Johan Fredrik (1690–1762). Scholar and naturalist of Leyden, Holland; friend of Linnaeus; author of *A Flora Virginica.*

Grotto. A cave, natural or (especially) artificial, considered picturesque in a garden and agreeable as a cool retreat from the sun. The idea was Italian, but has been imitated almost everywhere. Buildings obviously not caves but adorned with shells or craggy stone are sometimes called grottoes.

Groundcover. Plants, especially low-growing EVERGREENS such as ivy, periwinkle or pachysandra, grown to provide an agreeable, even, relatively trouble-free blanket over the soil. Lawns are the commonest groundcover, but are seldom called such. See pages 156–7.

Guillot, Jean-Baptiste. Famous nineteenth-century French rose breeder of Lyon who created 'La France' (1867), the first HYBRID TEA rose.

H

Habitat. The locality or environment in which a plant grows, such as marshland, woodland or open country.

Ha-ha. A sunk fence, that is a ditch with one sloping side and one vertical, the latter usually supported by a wall. Originally (1712) spelt Ah! Ah! (exclamation of surprise on discovering, or falling into, one). Supposedly introduced by BRIDGEMAN, the ha-ha allowed garden designers to dispense with walls for keeping cattle or deer from the garden, and encouraged them to consider the whole landscape as part of their design.

Hairy. Any part of a plant bearing hairs. These hairs may be feather-like, star-shaped or scale-like. A hairy plant is called hirsute if the hairs are stiff and densely packed, setose if hairs are very stiff and straight, pilose if the hairs are long and sparse. Tomentose describes woolly, felty or downy hairiness. Pubescent also means downy and villous applies to long hairs.

Half-hardy. Any plant between TENDER and HARDY.

Half-ripe. Describes a CUTTING taken from the tip of a young shoot of a tree or shrub just as it stops growing and starts to become woody at the base. See also RIPE.

Half-standard. A plant with an upright stem clear of head-forming side branches for 3–4 ft. Describes trained fruit trees and plants, such as chrysanthemums in particular, but not roses, in which a full STANDARD has a clear stem of about 4 ft.

Hall, Dr George R. (1820–99). American physician who lived and collected plants in Japan 1855–61. He introduced *Wisteria floribunda, Hydrangea paniculata* 'Grandiflora', *Magnolia kobus* and *M. stellata*, and the evergreen honeysuckle (*Lonicera halliana*) named after him.

Hampton Court Palace, Surrey. The most important remaining example in Britain of the formal French garden style of the seventeenth century. It was designed by LONDON AND WISE for William and Mary. The basic plan and the radiating lime avenues still stand, but no attempt is made to maintain seventeenth-century formality in PARTERRES and TOPIARY. The famous maze was added by Queen Anne and the great vine (under glass) was planted in 1769.

Hanbury, Sir Thomas (1832–1907). Enthusiastic amateur and benefactor of the RHS. Hanbury presented the original 60 acres of WISLEY GARDEN to the Society in 1903. His own garden, created with his brother Daniel, still exists at LA MORTOLA on the Mediterranean.

Haploid. Refers to the number of CHROMOSOMES present in the nucleus of the sex cells after division by meiosis. During meiosis two cell divisions occur which result in the cell nucleus containing half the usual number of chromosomes. See page 49.

Hardening off. The process by which a plant is gradually acclimatized to an environment of lower, more fluctuating temperature and sometimes lower humidity. A cold FRAME may serve as an intermediate environment.

Hardiness. Used in temperate and cold climates to mean the degree to which a plant is susceptible to FROST DAMAGE. A HARDY plant can live year-round without protection, a HALF-HARDY or TENDER one needs protection during the coldest months of the year. In hot countries "hardiness" may refer to a plant's resistance to drought.

Hardy. Describes a plant capable of surviving for the whole of its lifespan without any form of protection. Half-hardy plants may need some protection, depending on the severity of the winter. See pages 12–15.

Harkness & Co Ltd, R. Famous nursery established *c.*1879 at Bedale, Yorkshire by John (1857–1933) and Robert (1855–1920). In 1892 Robert opened a branch at Hitchin, Hertfordshire, which specialized in roses. The Harkness's long friendship with COCKER & SONS has led to joint informal rose-breeding ventures. Introduced 'Ena Harkness' (1946). 'Southampton' (1972) and 'Compassion' (1974) are two of their popular roses.

Harlow Car, West Yorkshire. The "WISLEY" of the north of England. The display garden of the NORTHERN HORTICULTURAL SOCIETY at Harrogate, started in the 1950s in a fine valley site with stream and rock gardens. The climate is cold so plants are effectively tested there for northern gardeners.

Hartweg, Theodore (1812–71). German collector employed by the HORTICULTURAL SOCIETY in Mexico (1836–40), where he found important fuchsias, many orchids, and the great Montezuma pine (*Pinus montezumae*). In California (1846–8) his discoveries included Monterey cypress (*Cupressus macrocarpa*) and two valuable ceanothus (*Ceanothus rigidus* and *C. dentatus*). He also collected seed of the coast redwood (*Sequoia sempervirens*) and introduced it to England.

Heathcoat-Amory, Sir John and Lady. Creators of KNIGHTSHAYES, one of the best twentieth-century English gardens. Since Sir John's death, the garden has been run in partnership with the NATIONAL TRUST. Sir John was awarded VMH 1966.

Hedge. An ancient way of dividing land and controlling stock, usually in conjunction with a ditch, formalized for garden use in remote times. Also a feature of Japanese and Moorish gardens.

Heel. When a side-shoot is pulled and not cut from a parent plant, a small piece of older tissue with wood and bark at its base comes with it. This is called a heel. Such CUTTINGS often root more easily than those without.

Heeling in. The temporary planting of shoots or roots in the soil to keep them moist until they can be planted in permanent positions. Used to retard the growth of severed shoots intended for GRAFTING.

Henderson, Peter (1822–90). Scottish-born American nurseryman in Jersey City. Author of *Gardening for Profit* (1865), *Gardening for Pleasure* (1875) and other books.

Henry, Dr Augustine (1857–1930). Doctor employed as a Customs officer by the Chinese at Ichang on the upper Yangtze river. In this remote place he botanized intensively, corresponding with KEW and discovering many plants, including *Lilium henryi* and *Rhododendron augustinii*. Later in Yunnan he realized that the Chinese were destroying whole forests and urged that a young collector be sent. Messrs VEITCH sent E.H. WILSON, who was greatly helped by Henry. Back home Henry collaborated with H. J. ELWES on the great *Trees of Great Britain and Ireland* (1906–13).

Herb. Any non-woody, non-shrubby plant. Can be ANNUAL, BIENNIAL or PERENNIAL. Often a plant with stems that die back to ground level at the end of the growing season. In common usage it has become applied to aromatic plants used for culinary flavouring or in medicines. A herbal is a book describing such plants. See pages 152–3.

Herbaceous. Describes any PERENNIAL herb that dies back to ground level each autumn or winter, though many non-woody EVERGREENS are customarily included in the term. Also applied to borders filled largely or entirely with such plants.

Herbicide. Despite the name, used of any chemical for killing plants. A herbicide (weed killer) may be selective, killing particular plants or groups only. Non-selective herbicides include paraquat, simazine and sodium chlorate. Dalapon is a selective herbicide used for killing grasses such as couch. See page 45.

Hergest Croft, Hereford and Worcester. One of England's remarkable private arboreta, with mature exotic trees and shrubs in garden, field and woodland making a series of beautiful, apparently semi-wild, pictures.

Herrenhausen, Hanover, Germany. The Hanoverian VERSAILLES, contemporary with its original and not much less grandiose. There is no longer a palace, but the gardens are splendidly maintained, with a famous "green theatre", a knot garden, a rose garden, spectacular waterworks and a great lime ALLÉE.

Hessayon, Dr David (1928–). The world's best-selling gardening author. His series of *Be Your Own Gardening Expert* books has sold over 20 million copies. With his American wife Joan Parker Hessayon he wrote *The Garden Book of Europe* (1973).

Hestercombe, Somerset. One of the most complete examples remaining of the partnership of EDWIN LUTYENS and GERTRUDE JEKYLL, made in 1910. Restoration from neglect was begun in the early 1970s.

Hever Castle, Kent. An original and bizarre but very effective Italianate garden made by Viscount Astor (started 1903) to display his collection of classical antiquities. The long, cloistered CASCADE is one of the most brilliant creations of twentieth-century garden design.

Hibberd, Shirley (1825–90). Popular Victorian gardening author whose books including *Rustic Adornment for Homes of Taste* (1856) epitomize the florid eclectic taste of the time.

Hidcote Manor, Gloucestershire. One of the most influential English gardens of the twentieth century, made from 1907 by Major LAWRENCE JOHNSTONE. It is designed as a series of outdoor rooms, each with its own sense of scale and range of colours. See pages 200–201.

Highland and Durand Eastman Park Arboretum, Rochester, New York. One of the largest and finest ARBORETA in the United States, noted especially for its lilac collection.

Hill (Hyll), Thomas (*fl*1540s–70s). Author of the first gardening book printed in England: *A Most Briefe and Pleasante Treatyse Teachyng how to Dresse, Sowe and Set a Garden* (*c.*1558) and of the later *Gardener's Labyrinth* (1577) (under the pen-name Didymus Mountain), which gives us clear illustrations of an Elizabethan garden.

Hillier Nurseries (Winchester) Ltd, Hampshire. One of the world's most important tree and shrub nurseries. Founded in 1864 by Edwin Hillier. His grandson Harold Hillier (VMH 1957) developed the most comprehensive list of hardy woody plants ever offered by a nursery, with some 7,000 kinds. *Hilliers' Manual of Trees and Plants* is one of the gardener's most valuable publications. In 1977 Hillier gave his JERMYNS ARBORETUM to the Hampshire County Council.

Hobbie, Dietrich. German nurseryman and rhododendron breeder, at Oldenburg near Bremen, who has bred fine and prolific hybrids suitable for gardens in cold climates.

Hooker, Sir Joseph Dalton (1817–1911). Son of SIR WILLIAM HOOKER, and in due course (1865) his successor as Director of KEW. Traveller to the Antarctic (1839–43) with Captain Ross and also on a famous expedition to Sikkim in the Himalayas (1848–1851), which revealed for the first time the riches of rhododendrons. He introduced 43 new species. At the age of 53 he made a perilous journey in Morocco. With George Bentham he published a standard British flora (BENTHAM AND HOOKER) and *Genera Plantarum* (1862).

Hooker, Sir William Jackson (1785–1865). The first official Director of KEW. A Norfolk man, for 20 years Professor of Botany at Glasgow. In 1841 he was appointed to Kew with AITON as Curator. He made Kew a public park, encouraging visitors, planned much of its present appearance, was responsible for the Palm House, and initiated research into the flora of all the British dominions. His own great love was ferns. His son Joseph was his assistant for ten years.

Hormone. Substance produced by a plant which regulates its growth and development. AUXINS are one kind of hormone. Hormones control all aspects of plant growth and operate in minute quantities. Preparations containing large amounts of hormones may be used as selective weed-killers and to help rooting of cuttings. See pages 40–1.

Horticultural Club, The. A social club for keen amateur gardeners founded in 1876, which meets regularly at the RHS for dinners, lectures, garden visits.

Horticultural Society (of London). The original name of the RHS. Queen Victoria made it "Royal" in 1861.

Hortus Third. A concise dictionary of plants cultivated in the USA and Canada (1976). A standard work updating previous volumes of 1930 and 1941. See LIBERTY HYDE BAILEY.

Hose-in-hose. Abnormality of a flower in which one perfect flower is found inside another. Particularly affects primulas, where the CALYX is PETALOID. Also known as a duplex. See DOUBLE.

Hotbed. Formerly a bed of manure, which gives off heat as it decays. Young and tender plants were raised on top of it to benefit from the heat. For modern use see BOTTOM HEAT.

Hovey, Charles Mason. Founder in 1835 of *The American Gardener's Magazine*. A nurseryman and breeder of strawberries and camellias.

Humboldt, Alexander von (1769–1859). Prussian scientist, naturalist and explorer of South America. Commemorated by the Humboldt Current but not, strangely, by any familiar plants. Charles Darwin described him as "the greatest scientific traveller who ever lived". See pages 60–61.

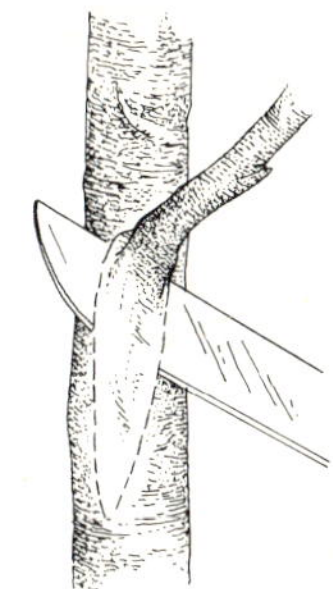

Heel

Augustine Henry

Thomas Hill

A hotbed

Involucre

Isola Bella

Gertrude Jekyll

Humus. The black or dark brown substances that result from the decay of organic matter in the SOIL. Humus improves the texture of soil by increasing its sponginess and water retention. The micro-organisms in humus help break down chemicals in the soil into forms that can be absorbed by plants. See also COMPOST.

Hunnewell Pinetum, Wellesley, Massachusetts. Important tree collection started in 1852 by H. H. Hunnewell.

Huntingdon Botanical Garden. The formal European garden plan includes vistas, views of the San Gabriel Mountains and Valley, and Italian renaissance details. Also features twelve-acre desert garden with three thousand kinds of cacti.

Hurst, Dr Charles Chamberlain (1870–1947). Pioneer geneticist at Cambridge, whose work on roses, in partnership with his wife Rosa, established the most probable heredity of garden roses. See pages 86–7.

Hussey, Christopher (1899–1970). An English gentleman-scholar whose writings on country houses, largely in COUNTRY LIFE, "helped to turn preservation from a minority cult into a major national concern". His family home, SCOTNEY CASTLE in Kent, is now a property of the NATIONAL TRUST.

Hybrid, hybrid vigour. A plant resulting from cross breeding between two different SPECIES, true-breeding VARIETIES or GENERA. Hybrids are sometimes sterile and never true-breeding. They are denoted with the sign × as in *Erica* × *veitchii*, a cross between *E. arborea* and *E. lusitanica*. Hybrids may be larger and more fruitful than their parents, whence the term "hybrid vigour". See F_1 and F_2 HYBRIDS.

Hybrid Teas. The typical modern bedding rose, with one flower to a stem, derived by elaborate breeding from the Tea roses of China. See pages 86–7 and 92–3.

Hydroponics, hydroculture. The culture of plants in a soilless base such as water or aggregates (sand, vermiculite, perlite or gravel). The latter involves sub-irrigation and is usually a commercial technique. Plants are supplied with a balanced solution of all the essential nutrients for life. The technique is used to grow many plants, particularly bulbs, tomatoes, carnations and house plants.

Hyll, Thomas. See HILL, THOMAS.

Hypocotyl. The stem linking the seed leaves (COTYLEDONS) and roots of a germinating seed. In some plants, such as radishes, the hypocotyl swells to form an organ for storing food. See PLUMULE, RADICLE.

I

Inarching. A form of GRAFTING in which the rooting part of the graft (the stock) and the graft (the scion) are bound together with the scion rooted in a pot or sitting in a jar of water. Usually a piece of bark is removed from each and the stems bound together with the barkless areas touching. When the graft has "taken" the binding is removed and the unwanted parts of stock and scion cut away.

Incinerator. An invaluable help in a small garden where a bonfire would take up too much room. Diseased plants *must* be burnt. An old oil-drum pierced with holes and stood on bricks makes a good incinerator.

Incised. An edge that is deeply and sharply cut. Used to describe a leaf, BRACT, SEPAL or a PETAL.

Indumentum. A covering of short hairs.

Inflorescence. The arrangement of flowers on the stem. Branching flower-heads include the CYME, PANICLE and UMBEL. An inflorescence may be made up of many small flowering units (FLORETS) as in the COMPOSITES. See FLOWERS, FORMS OF.

Ingram, Capt Collingwood (1880–). Plant collector, universally known as "Cherry" Ingram from the standard book he wrote on flowering cherries. His garden at Benenden, Kent (since 1919) is an historic collection of plants he has raised, usually from collected wild seedlings. Awarded VMH 1952.

Innes, John (1829–1904). London property developer who bequeathed the money that founded the John Innes Horticultural Institution, originally at his home at Merton, Surrey. It was the world's first institution for the scientific study of gardening problems and introduced JOHN INNES COMPOST. In 1967 the Institute moved to Norwich, Norfolk.

Insecticide. Any chemical used to kill insects and related pests without harming affected plants. Leaf-eating types (e.g. sawflies and many caterpillars) are killed with stomach poisons such as lead arsenate dusted or sprayed on. Sucking insects, such as APHIDS, are killed by fumigation dusts, or contact washes such as nicotine or malathion. Insecticides can also be applied to the SOIL, where they are taken up by the plant and permeate the entire sap stream of the plant (SYSTEMIC).

Insects. Important to gardeners for both their beneficial and harmful effects. Helpful insects include bees and other pollinators and those ladybirds that devour insect pests. A great variety of adult and larval insects (caterpillars) harm plants by eating them, sucking their sap and transmitting diseases. See APHID, INSECTICIDE, POLLINATION.

Intercrop. A short-term crop planted and grown between the rows of another crop with a longer maturation period, for example, lettuces between cabbages.

Internode. The part of a plant stem between the JOINTS (NODES), where leaf buds or leaves arise. Cuttings taken between joints are known as internodal cuttings.

Inverewe Gardens, Poolewe, Scotland. A seaside garden in north-west Scotland taking advantage of the mild Gulf Stream climate to grow a great collection of "tender" plants from New Zealand, Australia, South America, South Asia. Started by Osgood Mackenzie in 1864. Now owned by the NATIONAL TRUST for Scotland.

Involucre. One or more rings of SEPAL-like BRACTS surrounding a flower-head. Involucres are very common in COMPOSITE flowers. In the globe artichoke (*Cynara scolymus*) they are large and fleshy.

Involute. When leaves or petals roll inwards at the edges.

Irregular. Describes an asymmetrical FLOWER.

Island beds. A popular style of planting in beds of irregular curving outlines that can be isolated or grouped in a lawn. Light and air-circulation are better than in a border with its back to a hedge or wall. When well planned they can be very effective, but the random curve is a difficult shape to get right. See BLOOM.

Isola Bella, Italy. An island in Lake Maggiore converted into a great stone "ship" covered with terraced gardens. The work of Count Carlo Borromeo between 1630 and 1670; though only finished in the twentieth century.

J

Jackman family. Nurserymen at Woking, Surrey, for four generations, up to 1967; raisers of *Clematis* × *jackmanii*, the most popular of all clematis, in 1863.

Jacquemont, Victor (1801–32). French naturalist, a pioneer in Kashmir, commemorated by the whitest-stemmed and most beautiful of birches, *Betula jacquemontii*.

Jardin des Plantes, Paris. The KEW gardens of France, on the left bank of the Seine in Paris. Famous since the seventeenth century.

Jeffrey, John (1826–54). Scottish collector employed by the Oregon Association, a syndicate of Scottish landowners, to prospect for new conifers in Oregon, USA. His finds included the grand fir (*Abies grandis*) and the western hemlock (*Tsuga heterophylla*), both of outstanding importance.

Jekyll, Gertrude (1843–1932). A gifted artist who turned to garden design and authorship because of failing sight and became, through her gardens and her books, the most potent influence on twentieth-century English gardening. She contributed to WILLIAM ROBINSON's publications and worked in partnership with the architect EDWIN LUTYENS on many gardens, very few of which survive in recognizable form. She drew her ideas largely from the Surrey countryside, and closely studied the cottage gardens of the area round her home, MUNSTEAD WOOD, near Godalming. Her sense of form and colour was acute and her pen, at its best, accurate and eloquent enough to convey her perception. Her *Wood and Garden* (1899) and *Colour Schemes for the Flower Garden* are masterpieces. Such later gardeners as VITA SACKVILLE-WEST and GRAHAM THOMAS have been her apostles.

Jellicoe, Geoffrey A. (1900–). Architect and landscape designer, known for landscapes that range from the classical Ditchley Park, Oxford which is almost on LE NÔTRE's scale, and the John F. Kennedy Memorial at Runnymede. Author with J. C. Shepherd, of *Italian Gardens of the Renaissance* (1925), and with his wife

Susan (who is also a photographer) of several books including *Modern Private Gardens* (1968) and *The Landscape of Man* (1975).

Jensen, Jens (1860–1951). Midwestern landscape designer who operated in the English nineteenth-century idiom but was one of the first landscape designers to think in terms of ecology. Collaborated briefly with Frank Lloyd Wright.

Jermyns Arboretum, Hampshire. One of the most important tree collections in Europe, and one of the youngest. Begun in the 1950s by HAROLD HILLIER to supply the family nursery firm with propagating material. He gave it in 1977 to the Hampshire County Council, who have formed a trust with plans to enlarge it.

John Innes Compost. A formula for making the ideal compost for seeds and cuttings, developed in the 1930s by the JOHN INNES HORTICULTURAL INSTITUTE. The formulae are given on page 27.

Johnston, Lawrence (1871–1958). The creator of HIDCOTE. A rich American amateur gardener, born in Paris, who loved plants and had a genius for placing them. He collected with "CHERRY" INGRAM in South Africa and GEORGE FORREST in China and also gardened near Menton on the French Riviera. In 1948 he gave Hidcote to the NATIONAL TRUST.

Joint. The point (node) at which a leaf or leaf bud develops on a stem. Joints are often prominent in plants with hollow or pithy stems such as BAMBOOS. Depending on the distance between joints, stems are described as long- or short-jointed. Because the joint contains growth tissue (CAMBIUM) most cuttings root best if severed just below a joint.

Josephine de Beauharnais (1763–1814). Consort of Napoleon I and Empress of France. A great gardener whose collection of roses at MALMAISON, near Paris, was the most famous in history. She encouraged plant hunting and commissioned P. J. REDOUTÉ to paint his famous plant portraits.

Juvenile. A distinct form of leaves present only on young plants and/or young shoots. In many junipers, for example, the juvenile leaves are pointed and the mature ones scale-like.

K

Kalm, Pedro (1715–79). Pupil of LINNAEUS, he travelled to America where he was greatly helped by BARTRAM. Linnaeus commemorated him with the lovely calico bush (*Kalmia latifolia*).

Keel. The two lower petals of a leguminous flower, such as a pea, which are joined to form a boat-shaped structure.

Kent, William (1685–1748). Architect and garden designer who developed the new landscape style, following BRIDGEMAN. Lord Burlington employed him at his Palladian villa at Chiswick. The greatest memorials to his work are at STOWE, Buckinghamshire and ROUSHAM HOUSE, Oxfordshire.

Kerr, William (*d.*1814). The first professional plant collector to live in China (1803–11), jointly sponsored by KEW and the East India Company. His range was limited to Canton and Macao, but he sent back many good plants including *Rosa banksiae*, *Nandina domestica*, *Pieris japonica*, *Pittosporum tobira* and *Lilium tigrinum*. The kerria commemorates him.

Keukenhof Gardens, Lisse, Holland. The showcase for the Dutch bulb industry. A 65-acre garden near The Hague, where millions of bulbs make a remarkable spring display, in formal beds, in woodland and in every possible setting.

Kew, Royal Botanic Gardens, Surrey. The world's greatest botanical institution, founded in the eighteenth century by the Royal family, given to the nation in 1840. An enormous collection of supreme historical and horticultural interest, now supplemented by the gardens of WAKEHURST PLACE, Sussex, as an outstation with more favourable growing conditions. See also BUTE, BANKS, AITON, HOOKER, CHAMBERS, NESFIELD, PALM HOUSE, TAYLOR, BOTANICAL MAGAZINE.

Kiftsgate Court, Gloucestershire. A twentieth-century garden, neighbour to HIDCOTE, best known for its old shrub and species roses. The great rambler *Rosa filipes* 'Kiftsgate' originated here.

Killerton Garden, Devon. Outstanding tree and shrub collection on a favoured hillside within sight of Dartmoor. A NATIONAL TRUST property.

Kingdon-Ward, Frank (1885–1958). Explorer, plant collector and author of 23 books. First employed by Bees of Chester in 1911 to hunt the eastern Himalayas for alpines. His territory during nearly 50 years of collecting included Assam, Burma, Tibet and western China and his specialities were rhododendrons, primulas, lilies, gentians—and the wonderful Himalayan blue poppy (*Meconopsis betonicifolia*), which he introduced from Tibet in 1925.

Kitchen garden. The most business-like part of most gardens and therefore often the best planned. The French custom of growing flowers among vegetables, combined with the necessary straight lines and small plots, gives their *jardins potagers* immense charm. See pages 158–165.

Knap Hill Nurseries Co Ltd, Woking, Surrey. Knap Hill azaleas took their name from the nursery, which is now owned by SLOCOCK's. See WATERER FAMILY. See pages 98–9.

Knight, Richard Payne (1750–1824). Man of taste and, with his Shropshire neighbour SIR UVEDALE PRICE, chief opponent of the landscape theories of "CAPABILITY" BROWN. Knight's poem *The Landscape* sets out his taste for the picturesque and romantic, foreshadowing the excesses of Victorian gardening.

Knightshayes Court, Devon. One of the most ambitious and successful modern English gardens made since WWII. Designed around a Victorian mansion by SIR JOHN AND LADY HEATHCOAT-AMORY it includes a famous formal pool (illustrated page 184) and intensely gardened woodlands with a huge collection of plants. Now jointly run with the NATIONAL TRUST.

Knot. A formal ornamental flowerbed originating in Tudor times, named for its twisted designs formed with dwarf evergreens. See PARTERRE.

Kordes, Wilhelm. One of the outstanding rose breeders, of Holstein, Germany, and, with TANTAU, one of the two largest rose firms in the world. Kordes succeeded in making a fertile hybrid between two Japanese roses: the hardy and healthy *R. rugosa* and the sprawling *R. wichuriana*. The resulting *R.* × *kordesii* has been used to produce such first-rate climbers as 'Dortmund' (1955) and 'Parkdirektor Riggers' (1957). His other successes include 'Iceberg' (1958), 'Peer Gynt' (1968) and 'Ernest H. Morse' (1964). His son Reimer is now in the business.

Kurume. Town on the island of Kyushu, Japan. Famous for its many varieties of EVERGREEN azalea. See pages 98–9.

L

Labiate. Lipped. Describes a flower with one or more petals forming a lip. Also any of the 3,500 species in the dead nettle family Labiatae. Many are valued as herbs because they secrete oils. Lavender, thyme, sage and rosemary are examples.

Laciniate. Jagged or cut into narrow segments of unequal size. Used to describe leaves or petals. See LEAF SHAPES.

La Mortola, Ventimiglia, Italy. One of the most important botanical gardens of the Mediterranean. Seventy acres near the Italian-French border at Ventimiglia, created by SIR THOMAS HANBURY after 1866. Now owned by the Italian Government.

Lanceolate. Shaped like a lance or spear. Usually applied to narrow leaves three to six times as long as they are broad, and broadest below the middle. See LEAF SHAPES.

Landscape (or Landskip) movement. The revolutionary development in English garden design begun in the first half of the eighteenth century and culminating with the work of "CAPABILITY" BROWN. The movement spread to the Continent by the mid-eighteenth century, causing the destruction of many of the finest old gardens. See pages 226–7.

Langley, Batty (1696–1751). An industrious and talented designer, writer and artist who did much to popularize the "new irregular style" of gardening by publishing designs and pattern books that were widely followed. Gothick follies were his speciality.

La Quintinie, Jean de (1628–88). Head gardener to Louis XIV at VERSAILLES. JOHN EVELYN translated into English his *The Compleat Gard'ner* (1693).

Lateral. A side shoot or stem which grows out from a BUD. In fruit trees, laterals, if pruned correctly, are the basis of fruiting SPURS.

Layering. Method of VEGETATIVE PROPAGATION in which shoots are induced to form roots while still attached to the parent plant. Used for increasing plants difficult or slow to root as CUTTINGS. See also AIR-LAYERING. See pages 52–3.

Josephine de Beauharnais

Frank Kingdon-Ward

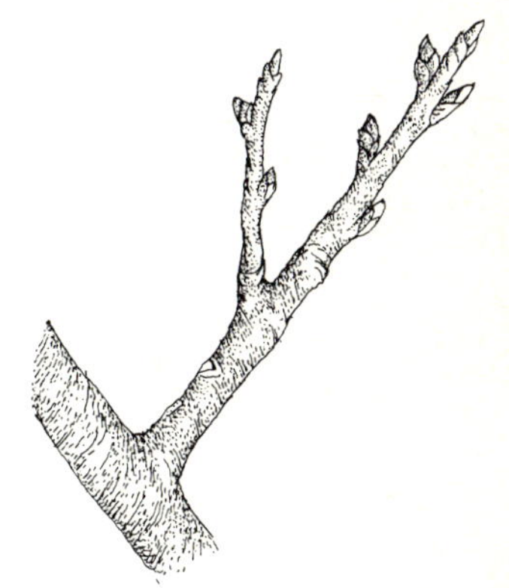

A lateral

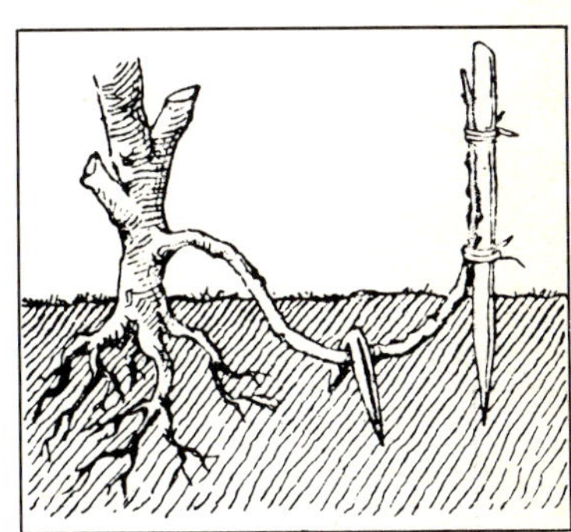

Layering

Legume

Levens Hall

John Lindley

Leaching. The loss of nutrients in the soil when rain dissolves them and carries them down beyond the reach of roots. It is a cause of infertility of light soil in high-rainfall areas, and a reason why fertilizers should be applied little and often rather than in one big dose.

Leader. The uppermost, usually central shoot of a woody plant and its main branches. Also called the terminal shoot. See also LATERAL.

Leaf. A modified outgrowth of the stem with all the tissues spread out flat to take full advantage of air and light. Leaves are vital to plant life for they usually contain the green pigment CHLOROPHYLL which absorbs light for PHOTOSYNTHESIS. They are enormously varied in shape and form. A simple leaf has a single blade, a COMPOUND leaf has several blades or leaflets. Leaves may be modified to TENDRILS, SPINES, scales or BRACTS. See also STOMATA.

Leaf mould. An invaluable source of HUMUS made by piling autumn leaves in deep mounds until they decay and become crumbly. Excellent as an alternative to PEAT in some POTTING COMPOSTS, for putting round the roots of trees and shrubs being planted, as a MULCH on the surface round woodland plants or to feed lawns. The best leaf mould is made of oak or beech or other small leaves. Large leaves, such as horse chestnut and plane, are less suitable as they decay slowly and their leaf ribs remain. Leaf mould from trees on limy soils will be ALKALINE and could damage CALCIFUGE plants.

Lee, James (1715–95) **and Kennedy, Lewis** (*b.* 1709). Famous London nurserymen who set up the Vineyard Nursery *c.* 1745 in Hammersmith. James Lee was also an author and was the first translator of LINNAEUS's work into English (1760).

Legume, leguminous. A member of the legume or pea family (the third largest family of flowering plants) which includes herbs, shrubs and trees. The FLOWERS have two side PETALS (alae or wings) and two lower petals combined to form a keel enclosing male and female parts. Legume roots have NODULES containing BACTERIA that can fix NITROGEN from the air.

Leichtlin, Max (1831–1910). Nurseryman of Baden-Baden, West Germany, who introduced many rare plants into cultivation, notably from the Near East.

Le Nôtre, André (1613–1700). The greatest French garden designer, who worked on a scale never seen before in Europe, at VAUX-LE-VICOMTE, CHANTILLY, Dijon and, above all, VERSAILLES for Louis XIV. Despite the grandiosity of his style, with mile-long avenues, canals and innumerable fountains, he was known as a kind, humorous and approachable man. The many gardens "by Le Nôtre" outside France are by his pupils and imitators.

Lenticel. A pore in the bark of a tree trunk or woody stem which allows air to reach the tissues behind the bark. The pore contains very loosely connected cork cells. They are seen on most cherry trees.

Leonardslee, Sussex. Great woodland garden made famous in the 1890s by SIR EDMUND LODER. He raised the famous Loderi rhododendrons there.

Levens Hall, Cumbria. One of England's few remaining formal gardens, with TOPIARY, now grotesquely but impressively oversize, in the style of 1700 and earlier. The parkland, on the other hand, foreshadows the naturalist LANDSCAPE school to come 50 years later.

Levington compost. See COMPOST.

Leyden, Holland. The first town in northern Europe to make a BOTANIC GARDEN, in 1577. CHARLES DE L'ECLUSE (Clusius) was appointed to direct and expand it in 1592. For two centuries it remained an important distribution point for new plants and still exists with part of its original design intact.

Light. The glazed roof of a cold FRAME which can be removed or lifted to let in air for toughening or HARDENING OFF plants.

Lime. An inorganic substance containing calcium oxide, a chemical that reacts with water in the SOIL and carbon dioxide from the air to produce carbonate of lime, which in turn neutralizes acids in the soil. Lime may also contain magnesium compounds, which have a similar effect. The calcium in lime prevents "topple"—the wilting of flower stalks at their growing points. Lime is added to some FERTILIZERS and is applied as a TOP-DRESSING. The addition of lime to heavy clay soils binds (FLOCCULATES) its minute particles together into small crumbs which "opens" the texture of the soil.

Lindley, John (1799–1865). Secretary and the dynamo behind the HORTICULTURAL SOCIETY (later the RHS). Author of *The Theory and Practice of Horticulture* (1840) and *The Vegetable Kingdom* (1846). The RHS Library at VINCENT SQUARE is named after him.

Linear. Long and narrow. Describes the shape of leaves, PETALS and BRACTS with parallel sides which are at least 12 times as long as wide. See LEAF SHAPES.

Linnaeus (Carl von Linné) (1707–78). Swedish naturalist. The father of modern taxonomy (the science of classifying natural objects). His greatest single contribution was to establish the binominal

LEAF SHAPES

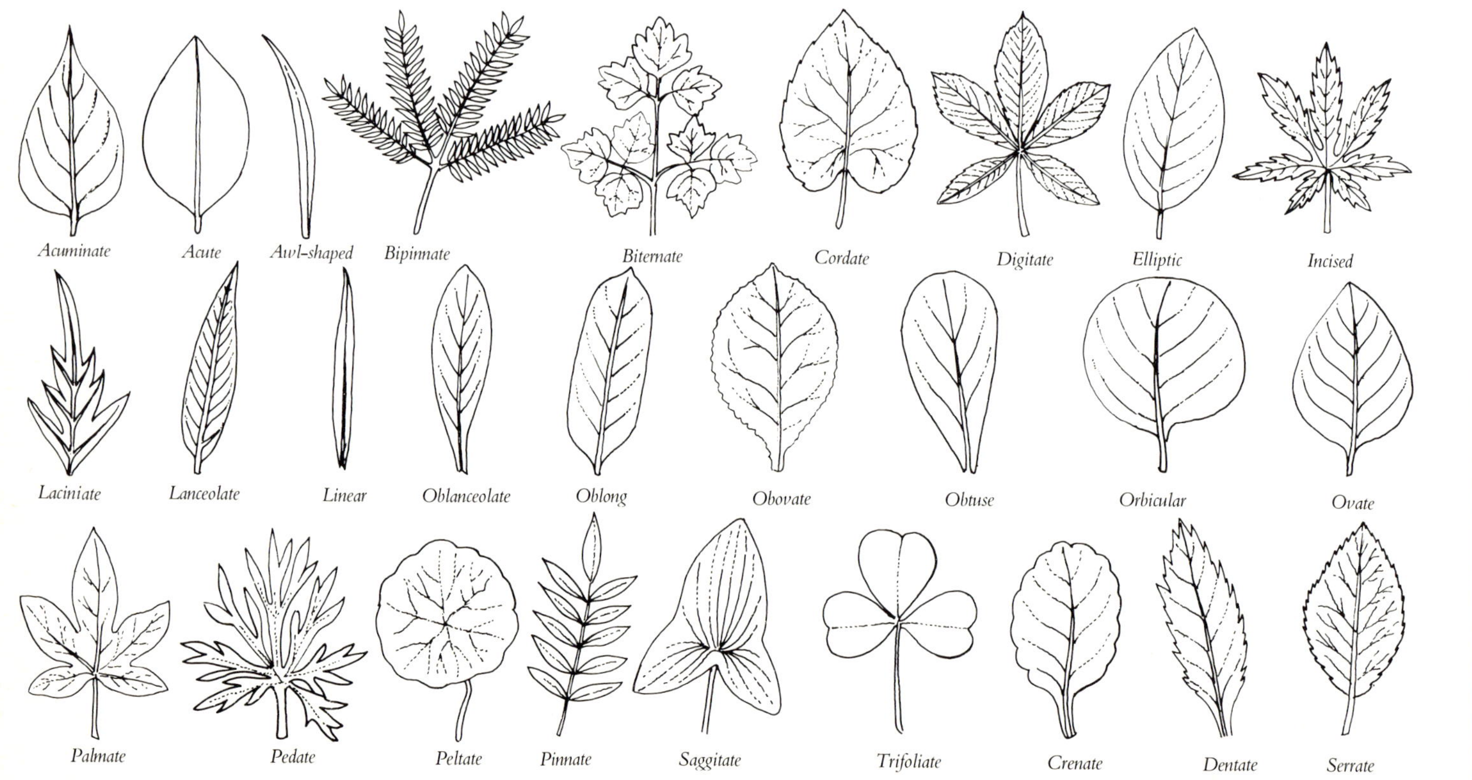

Acuminate · *Acute* · *Awl-shaped* · *Bipinnate* · *Biternate* · *Cordate* · *Digitate* · *Elliptic* · *Incised*

Laciniate · *Lanceolate* · *Linear* · *Oblanceolate* · *Oblong* · *Obovate* · *Obtuse* · *Orbicular* · *Ovate*

Palmate · *Pedate* · *Peltate* · *Pinnate* · *Saggitate* · *Trifoliate* · *Crenate* · *Dentate* · *Serrate*

system (a specific and a generic name) by describing and naming 12,000 species of plants and animals in his own collection of specimens, now at the LINNEAN SOCIETY. His initial "L" appears after their full names in all scientific works. By concentrating on the number and arrangement of the sexual parts of plants he laid the foundation of a natural system of classification.

Linnean Society. A learned London society, founded in 1788, 10 years after the death of LINNAEUS, to "cultivate the study of natural history in all its branches". One of its founders, Sir James Smith, bought Linnaeus's library and collection of plants and animals. They remain at the Society's London premises in Burlington House, Piccadilly, to this day. It was at a meeting of the Society in 1858 that the theory of evolution by natural selection was first promulgated.

Lip. A flat lobe formed from one or more flower petals. Also called a labellum. A single-lipped flower is described as LABIATE; one with upper and lower lips as bilabiate. Orchids have very elaborate lips.

Lloyd, Christopher (1921–). The most articulate and one of the most scholarly of contemporary gardener-writers, author of several books including *The Well-Tempered Garden* (1970), *Clematis* (revised 1978) and a weekly contributor to COUNTRY LIFE. See GREAT DIXTER.

Lobb, William (1809–63) and **Thomas** (1817–94). Cornish brothers who worked as plant collectors for VEITCH & CO, nurserymen of Exeter and London. William went to southern USA, introducing to Britain the monkey puzzle tree (*Araucaria araucana*), and later travelled to western USA, introducing the wellingtonia (*Wellingtonia gigantea*) and *Thuja plicata. Berberis darwinii* and *Embothrium coccineum* were among his plants from South America. Thomas collected in the Far East. His introductions were principally orchids and tender rhododendrons.

Lobe. Any part of a PETAL, leaf or other plant organ divided from the remainder of the structure by a deep indentation. Oak leaves are examples.

Loddiges, Conrad (*c.*1739–1826). Dutch-born nurseryman of Hackney, London, from the 1770s. He introduced many American plants from William, son of JOHN BARTRAM, and specialized in greenhouse and hothouse plants, being the first to grow orchids on a commercial scale. His commercial catalogue contained some 4,000 trees and shrubs, including 1,500 roses, 300 heathers, 150 palms and 30 eucalyptus.

Loder family. Landowners in Sussex who have given a rhododendron flavour to a considerable tract of country. Sir Robert Loder's estate LEONARDSLEE was inherited by his elder son Sir Edmund (1849–1920), who raised the famous Loderi hybrid rhododendrons there. His younger son Gerald (1861–1936), later Lord Wakehurst, bought the neighbouring property of WAKEHURST PLACE and developed its already fine collections. Leonardslee is still in the family; Sir Giles Loder continues the tradition.

Logan, Dumfries and Galloway, Scotland. An old garden enjoying one of the mildest climates in Britain. Now an outstation of the ROYAL BOTANIC GARDEN, EDINBURGH, growing a collection of "tender" plants.

Loggia. A gallery or arcade open to the air on one or both sides—originally designed as a shady walk in Italian gardens.

London, George (*d.*1714) **and Wise, Henry** (1653–1738). The greatest English nurserymen and garden contractors of the late seventeenth and early eighteenth centuries. They had 100 acres of nurseries at Brompton Park, London, and laid out LE NÔTRE-style gardens at HAMPTON COURT and CHATSWORTH, where their great CASCADE still runs. Most of their work was obliterated by the LANDSCAPE MOVEMENT.

Longwood Gardens, Kennett Square, Pennsylvania, USA. One of America's greatest gardens. The former du Pont estate, on a site first planted as an ARBORETUM *c.*1800, it has magnificent old trees. Almost every department of gardening is represented on a grand scale, including splendid greenhouses with winter interest.

Loudon, John Claudius (1783–1843). Prolific editor and encyclopaedist, his *Encyclopaedia of Gardening* (1822) was the most comprehensive ever published. In 1826 he founded THE GARDENER'S MAGAZINE, the first popular gardening paper. His *Suburban Gardens* (1838) and *Suburban Horticulturist* (1842) set the standards and much of the style of the new middle-class Victorian garden—a style he christened "gardenesque"—designed specifically for displaying the vast range of new plants. His wife Jane Wells Loudon (1807–58) worked just as hard and survived him to continue producing books.

Lutyens, Sir Edwin (1869–1944). Architect and designer who early in his career met the much older GERTRUDE JEKYLL and collaborated with her on many garden projects. He is best remembered as the last great country-house architect, brilliantly infusing vernacular materials and styles with originality and vigour of his own. His garden designs are full of bold and interesting stonework.

Luxembourg Gardens, Paris. Palace and gardens built in 1615–20 for Queen Marie de Medicis. The gardens were designed by ANDRÉ MOLLET, with most elaborate PARTERRES and a fountain by Rubens. The Queen had asked for something like the BOBOLI Gardens in Florence, where she was brought up. They are one of Paris's prettier parks.

M

Maiden. A fruit or other tree derived by BUDDING or GRAFTING in its first year of growth. A maiden is untrained and unpruned. Also applied to roses and other shrubs. A "well-feathered" maiden has many side shoots.

Mainau, Lake Constance, West Germany. Island-garden between Germany and Switzerland with a remarkably mild temperate climate. Count Bernadotte of Sweden grows tropical and sub-tropical plants and a vast collection of roses, bulbs and dahlias there.

Malmaison, la, France. The country house of the Empress JOSEPHINE near Paris, where she collected many rare plants, particularly roses.

Marly, France. A small château and gardens near Versailles designed for Louis XIV in 1679 by Jules Mansart. Underground water was pumped from Marly by a famous device which used the power of the Seine to supply the fountains of Versailles. Only the park remains.

Marx, Roberto Burle (1909–). The leading landscape architect of Brazil, the creator of the modern garden movement in that country and a potent influence on designers abroad.

Masson, Francis (1741–1806). The first plant-collector employed by KEW. On an outstandingly successful trip to South Africa in 1772–75 he collected a vast number of plants, including pelargoniums and heaths. After further extended journeys to the West Indies and the Cape, he spent the last years of his life plant hunting in North America.

Mawson, Thomas (1861–1933). Garden designer and author of *Art and Craft of Garden Making* (1901). His nurseries were in Lancashire, and some of his best gardens were built in the Lake District—although by LUTYENS's standards they seem dull and derivative.

Maximowicz, Carl (1827–91). Russian botanist, the greatest expert of his day on the plants of northern China and Japan. He explored Japan from 1861 to 1864 for PETERHOF, the great BOTANIC GARDEN at St Petersburg, introducing countless important plants to the West.

Meilland family. An old family of rose breeders in France, now among the world's biggest growers at Tassin, near Lyon, and at Antibes. Francis Meilland (*c.*1911–58) bred the best-selling 'Peace' at Antibes in 1939, established an international network for testing roses, the Universal Rose Selection group, and was a champion of plant breeders' patent rights. His son Alain succeeded him. Other famous Meilland roses include 'Grandmère Jenny' (1950), 'Moulin Rouge', 'Baccara' (1956) and 'Charleston' (1963).

Melbourne Hall, Derbyshire. A garden of great interest to historians, unchanged since it was made in the early 1700s by LONDON AND WISE in the French formal style.

Mendel, Gregor (1822–84). The father of genetics. Mendel was Abbot of Brunn in Austria, and his work on peas uncovered the basic "Mendelian" laws of heredity (1866). It was not until 1899 that the importance of his work became known, at the RHS Conference on Hybridization.

Michaux family. French botanists. André (1746–1803) travelled to the Near East and Persia (where he found *Rosa persica*) and with his son François (1770–1855) to North America, where they settled at Charleston, South Carolina, and explored from Florida to Hudson's Bay. He introduced the ginkgo to America, and wrote the first study of American oaks.

J. C. Loudon

Sir Edwin Lutyens

A maiden

Roberto Burle Marx

Philip Miller

Alan Mitchell

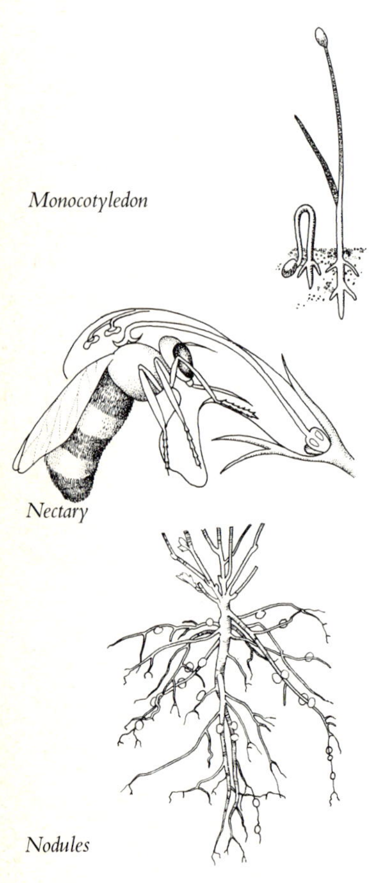

Monocotyledon

Nectary

Nodules

Miff. One that displays peevish ill-humour. First used of difficult, sulky plants by REGINALD FARRER and still often found in gardening contexts.

Miller, Philip (1691–1771). Gardener of the CHELSEA PHYSICK GARDEN for nearly 50 years, and author of *The Gardener's and Florist's Dictionary* (1731), which remained the standard horticultural reference book for the rest of the century.

Missouri Botanical Gardens, St Louis, Missouri. Features a fourteen-acre Japanese garden, a climatron (a giant greenhouse built as a geodesic dome that maintains two climatic zones with tropical and sub-tropical plants in a natural setting) and a collection of orchids.

Mitchell, Alan F. (1922–). Dendrologist to the Forestry Commission, in charge of WESTONBIRT ARBORETUM and the National Pinetum at BEDGEBURY, author of *A Field Guide to the Trees of Britain and Northern Europe* (1974). A great enthusiast with a unique knowledge of tree habits on both sides of the Atlantic. Awarded VMH 1970.

Mlokosewitsch, Ludwig F. (1831–1909). A Polish nobleman and naturalist who became the greatest living expert on the natural history of the Caucasus. An exquisite single yellow paeony bears his unforgettable name.

Mollet family. Three generations of royal gardeners under Kings Henri IV and Louis XIII of France and James I of England. The first Mollet laid out the Château d'Anet. His son Claude (*b.*1563) laid out part of FONTAINEBLEAU and much of the Tuileries. His other son André wrote *Le Jardin de Plaisir* (1651). In their time they devised the PARTERRES and ALLÉES which were to become familiar in the work of LE NÔTRE.

Monocarpic. Describes a plant that fruits only once and then dies. Not usually applied to ANNUALS or BIENNIALS but to plants that grow for several years before flowering and fruiting. The century plant, *Agave americana*, may grow for 50 years or more before fruiting and dying.

Monocotyledon. "Monocot" for short. One of the two divisions of flowering plants. Monocots produce one seed leaf (COTYLEDON) during GERMINATION. Grasses, palms and most bulbs are examples. All others are DICOTYLEDONS and produce two seed leaves.

Monoecious. A plant with male and female flowers separate but borne on the same plant. See DIOECIOUS.

Monotypic. A GENUS of plants made up of a single SPECIES. An example is the Japanese "heavenly bamboo" (*Nandina domestica*).

Moraine. In nature the bed of scree, small stones and rubble around and below a glacier. In gardening, it is a specially constructed bed for the cultivation of ALPINES, made from rubble and coated with fine chippings. See also SCREE.

Morton Arboretum, Lisle, Illinois. The grounds contain an outdoor collection of 4,000 different kinds of woody plants.

Morris Arboretum, Chestnut Hill, Pennsylvania. Victorian-style English landscape garden with mature specimens of trees and shrubs from Asia, a fine collection of holly and magnolia, a formal rose garden, and a garden of tropical medicine plants.

Mosaic. The light green or yellow mottling on leaves symptomatic of certain VIRUS diseases, such as tobacco mosaic virus which affects tomatoes.

Mosses. Non-flowering plants with leaves of one cell thickness and stems bearing root hairs but with no internal conducting vessels. Most form cushions or mats that thrive in damp and shady situations. Opinions are divided about whether mosses are a good thing in lawns, but they will upholster the ground as nothing else can under the right conditions. Their water-retaining properties make them useful for packing live plants. See PEAT.

Mottisfont Abbey, Hampshire. A NATIONAL TRUST property with a great collection of old roses, the work of GRAHAM THOMAS.

Mount. A standard feature in medieval and Tudor gardens, providing a vantage point for overlooking the gardens and the outside world.

Mount Usher, County Wicklow, Ireland. Established in the 1860s and remarkable proof of the value of family tradition: this outstandingly beautiful 20-acre garden full of fine plants is now in the fourth generation of the WALPOLE family.

Mount Vernon, Mount Vernon, Virginia. Estate of George Washington, first president of the United States. The gardens, one of the earliest and best examples of American gardens, have an unusually wide range of plant material.

Muir, John (1838–1914). American naturalist, explorer and writer who helped found Sequoia and Yosemite National Parks.

Mulch. A bulky organic material such as grass cuttings, PEAT, COMPOST, straw or strawy manure spread on top of the SOIL to help water retention (by preventing evaporation); to provide some nutrients; to furnish HUMUS and keep the soil "open". It also prevents weeds from becoming established and encourages the growth of useful BACTERIA. Black plastic is also used to mulch against weeds. It is not very attractive but it is at least effective.

Munstead Wood. The home of GERTRUDE JEKYLL, at Godalming, Surrey, designed for her by EDWIN LUTYENS, and the subject of much of her writing and exemplar of her ideas.

Mutant. The botanist's term for what a gardener calls a SPORT. See also MUTATION below.

Mutation. The change in the constitution of hereditary material (the gene) that gives rise to a new form, a MUTANT or SPORT. May occur spontaneously or be induced by agents such as chemicals or X-rays and may affect the whole plant or only part of it. See also SPORT.

Mycorrhiza. Threads of FUNGUS found in association with the root cells of some plants. The relationship is mutually beneficial (symbiotic), the fungus gaining nourishment and the roots gaining chemicals made available by the fungus. ORCHIDS, heaths and most forest trees are examples of plants for which they are essential.

N

National Arboretum, Washington, D.C. An ARBORETUM with its emphasis on botanical, horticultural and forestry research and public education as well as plant breeding and propagation studies. It also features seasonal displays of flowering shrubs and trees.

National Trust, The. A charitable trust founded in 1895 to acquire and maintain places of historical interest or natural beauty. Now the third largest landowner in Britain (after the State and the Crown), its properties include 68 notable gardens representing virtually every facet of the nation's gardening history and comprising probably the greatest plant collection on earth. Standards of upkeep, plantsmanship and historical accuracy are impeccable. The gardens are administered by a gardens advisor, John Sales, and his assistants with GRAHAM THOMAS as consultant. For gardens owned by the Trust see their separate entries.

National Park Service. The US government agency, established in 1916, is responsible for the national parks that protect land and wildlife, national monuments, and historical parks and sites of the nation.

Naturalize. To establish a plant in a garden in conditions where it reproduces itself freely, as though in the wild. Such bulbs as snowdrops and daffodils are often naturalized.

Naumkeag Gardens, Stockbridge, Massachusetts. The estate, built in 1885 for Joseph Choate, Ambassador to England, is now a museum. The formal gardens feature rocks and sculptures from Japan.

Nectary. A GLAND producing a sugar solution known as nectar. Usually situated in the base of a flower but may be found on the leaves. The nectar attracts pollinating insects.

Nematodes. Microscopic soil-dwelling plant pests known as roundworms or eelworms but no relation to earthworms. The free-living forms inflict physical injury, while parasitic forms live at the expense of the plants they inhabit, sometimes causing GALLS on stems and invading buds, leaves and roots. In roots the symptoms are known as root knot. Nematodes are best eradicated by soil sterilization.

Nesfield, William A. (1793–1881). Garden designer and painter, he laid out a large part of KEW for SIR JOSEPH HOOKER and designed the HORTICULTURAL SOCIETY's gardens in Kensington. Most of his work was in the grandiose Italianate manner.

Neutra, Richard (1892–1970). California architect who developed outdoor living space as an extension of interior functions: a concept that requires a mild climate. See pages 234–5.

New York Botanical Garden, Bronx, New York. The 239-acre park includes some untouched old woodland of eastern hemlock and tulip trees and features 12,000 plant species and the greatest collection of cacti in the United States. It specializes in plant breeding and research and plant physiology. Extensive greenhouses and an annual flower show make the garden a great attraction. Published bi-monthly is *The Garden*, a 40-page colour journal for amateur gardeners and botanists.

Nitrogen (N). An element vital to plant growth. Without it plants are stunted, have few, pale leaves and delayed flower, fruit and TUBER formation. Nitrogen is present in most soils but not in sufficient quantity for heavy regular crops. It is supplied in FERTILIZERS as sodium nitrate or ammonium sulphate. See pages 24–5.

Node. The site on a stem at which leaves or leaf buds arise. See JOINT, INTERNODE.

Nodule. A small swelling, particularly in the root of a LEGUMINOUS plant such as clover, containing BACTERIA able to "fix" NITROGEN in the air and make it available to the plant. In return the bacteria obtain sugars from the plant. Nodules help to increase SOIL nitrogen content.

Noisette, Louis and Philippe. Eighteenth-century French brothers, nurserymen respectively in Paris and Charleston, South Carolina, USA. In 1814 Philippe sent Louis a seedling from 'CHAMPNEY's Pink Cluster', the first Sino-European rose hybrid, which became known as *Rosa noisettiana*.

Nursery. Where young plants are reared and prepared for sale, or for planting out in their permanent stations.

Nut. A hard FRUIT that does not split to release the single seed within, which is protected with a covering skin. Most nuts are housed in a cup or cupola. Nut is also used to describe fruits that are not true nuts such as walnut and horse-chestnut.

Nuttall, Thomas (1786–1859). English plant hunter, explorer of western USA, author of *Genera of American Plants* (1818) and curator of Harvard University Botanic Garden (1822–34). After many expeditions Nuttall finally crossed the Rockies in 1834. The western dogwood (*Cornus nuttallii*) bears his name.

Nymans, Sussex. One of the supreme examples of turn-of-the-century gardens, the work of the Messel family, now a property of the NATIONAL TRUST. Many first-rate garden plants originated here and superb specimens still dominate RHS shows.

Nymphenburg Gardens, Munich, West Germany. The palace of the Elector with gardens originally laid out in the Dutch style in 1701, then elaborated with VERSAILLES-type fountains in 1715; later partly reworked in English LANDSCAPE style.

O

Oblanceolate. Describes a plant structure, particularly a leaf, that is spear shaped (LANCEOLATE) but is wider above the middle. See LEAF SHAPES.

Oblong. A plant structure that is elliptical but has blunted rather than rounded ends and parallel sides. See LEAF SHAPES.

Obovate. Describes an OVATE LEAF that is wider above the middle. See LEAF SHAPES.

Obtuse. Describes any plant part that is blunt or rounded at its end. See LEAF SHAPES.

Old Westbury Gardens, Old Westbury, Long Island. A walled garden in the Italian grand manner which has extensive lawns and boxwood plantings and seasonal displays of annuals and biennials.

Olmsted, Frederick Law (1822–1903). America's first landscape architect and city planner, the designer (with Calvert Vaux) of New York's Central Park, instigator of America's first National Parks, consultant and designer of many parks, including those of Boston, Berkeley, Chicago and Cincinnati.

Opposite. The term for leaves arising in pairs on exactly opposite sides of a stem and in the same plane. ALTERNATE pairs may lie in different planes.

Orchid. Any of the 15,000 species of plants in the family Orchidaceae found worldwide but particularly abundant in the Tropics. Many are EPIPHYTES, living on other plants and using them as support but not as a food source. Some orchids live as SAPROPHYTES—they have no green pigment (CHLOROPHYLL) and obtain nourishment from the HUMUS in which they live by means of a fleshy underground stem (RHIZOME). Most orchids depend on fungi called MYCORRHIZA with which their roots have a mutually beneficial (symbiotic) relationship. The majority are tender plants needing a warm GREENHOUSE with high humidity but constant changes of air —an expensive hobby, in fact.

Organic Gardening. A monthly magazine that caters to amateur and professional home gardeners.

Oval. Used to describe leaves and BRACTS that are broadest in the middle and taper equally to rounded ends. See LEAF SHAPES.

Ovary, ovule. In the female part of the FLOWER (PISTIL) the ovary is the structure containing the female sex cells or ovules, which develop into seeds after FERTILIZATION. The egg cell within each ovule contains half the normal amount of genetic material (CHROMOSOMES). An ovary placed above the flower-bearing structure (receptacle) is known as "superior". The receptacle extends above an "inferior" ovary.

Ovate. Egg shaped; used of leaves that are twice as long as wide and broadest below the middle. See LEAF SHAPES.

P

Page, Russell (1906–). The most distinguished European garden designer of the second half of this century. Since World War II a large part of his work has been in France, Italy, Belgium, Switzerland and the USA. His book *The Education of a Gardener* (1962) is a masterly exposition of his methods and theories. His current work shows an increasing subtlety to meet the necessity of low maintenance.

Pagoda. A manifestation of CHINOISERIE popular in the late eighteenth and early nineteenth centuries. The biggest and most famous in the West was built by SIR WILLIAM CHAMBERS at KEW in 1759.

Palladio, Andrea (1518–80). Italian architect, imitator of the Roman style on principles of his own devising. His buildings in Venice, Padua and particularly his villas on the Brenta, north of Venice, were the inspiration of the Palladian School of Lord Burlington, WILLIAM KENT and others in England in the early eighteenth century.

Palmate. Adjective describing a leaf shaped like an open hand. See LEAF SHAPES.

Palm house. A greenhouse tall enough and warm enough to grow palm trees in, especially the magnificent one at KEW, otherwise known as the Great Stove, designed and built by SIR JOSEPH PAXTON from 1836 to 1840 on similar lines to his CHATSWORTH prototype for the Crystal Palace.

Pan. A shallow flowerpot, used for sowing SEEDS and for the cultivation of certain ORCHIDS and ALPINES. Hard-pan is a hard, impermeable layer of SUB-SOIL that impedes drainage.

Panicle. Form of flower-head technically defined as a branched CORYMB or RACEME. See FLOWERS, FORMS OF.

Parasite. Any plant or animal that lives at the expense of another (the host) from which it obtains shelter and nourishment. Complete plant parasites such as dodder (*Cuscuta*) have no leaves or roots. Incomplete parasites such as mistletoe (*Viscum*) have leaves but lack roots and cannot live without a host. See EPIPHYTE.

Parkinson, John (1567–1650). Apothecary to James I and King's botanist to Charles I, with a garden in Long Acre, London. Author of *Theatrum Botanicum* (1640) and the much-loved *Paradisi in sole Paradisus terristris: or A Garden of all sorts of pleasant flowers which our English ayre will permitt to be noursed up* (1629). The Latin title is a pun meaning "the earthly paradise of park-in-sun". Of all early flower books this is the most delightful.

Parterre (French). Literally "on the ground". A level space ornamented with flower beds of often elaborate shapes, intended to be viewed from above. Parterres were highly developed in France in the late sixteenth and early seventeenth centuries.

Patte d'oie (French). Literally a goose's foot, the bone pattern of which resembles the radiating AVENUES or ALLÉES of a formal French garden. Hence a meeting of five or more radiating avenues.

Paxton, Sir Joseph (1803–65). A horticultural and engineering giant of Victorian England, head gardener, then agent at CHATSWORTH to the Duke of Devonshire, where he built the Emperor Fountain. Between 1836 and 1840 he built the Great Stove at KEW. Designer of the Crystal Palace for the Great Exhibition of 1851. One of the founders of the GARDENER's CHRONICLE.

Russell Page

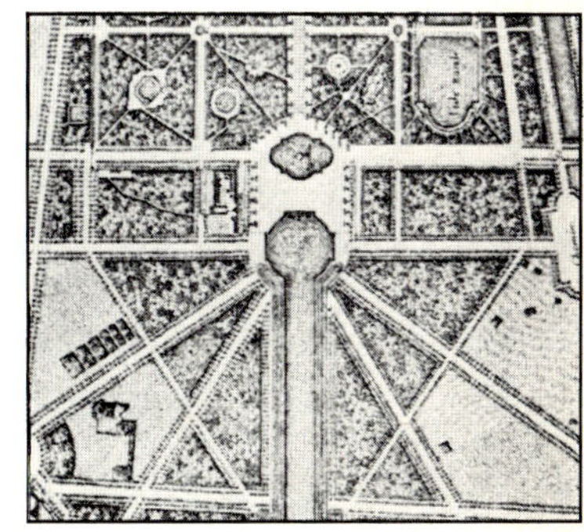

Patte d'oie

Joseph Paxton

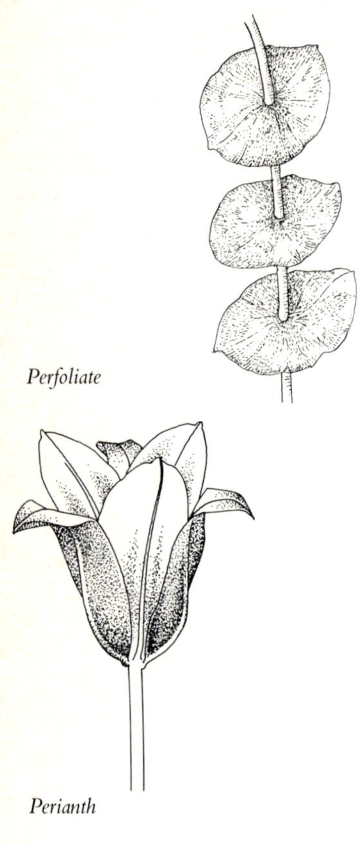

Perfoliate

Perianth

Piping

Pollarding

Peat. The SOIL from a bog, made up of partially decayed vegetation, particularly the moss SPHAGNUM and various sorts of sedges. An invaluable ingredient in gardening composts, providing water-holding capacity and improving the physical structure of soils, whether light or heavy. Horticultural peats are classified as either sedge peat or moss peat, in coarse, medium or fine grades. Peat has little or no food value for plants, but provides an ideal unresisting foraging-ground for roots. It must always be wet or damp when used.

Peat garden. A bed built up with peat blocks supporting very peaty soil. A twentieth-century invention for growing woodland and certain ALPINE plants that relish an easy, damp and ACID root-run. High atmospheric humidity or frequent watering and a certain amount of shade are essential. See pages 138–9.

Pedate. Shaped like a bird's foot. A deeply lobed PALMATE leaf, the side lobes again cleft. See LEAF SHAPES.

Pedicel, petiole. Types of plant stalk. A pedicel is the stalk on which a single FLOWER is borne and is applied particularly to flower clusters. A petiole is a stalk on which a leaf blade is borne.

Pelleted seeds. Seeds covered individually with a soil-clay mixture. Pelleting prevents wastage of seeds, makes them easier to handle and saves THINNING.

Peltate. Shield shaped. Describes a leaf this shape with a stalk attached to the lower surface rather than to the edge (margin). See LEAF SHAPES.

Perennial. A plant that lives for more than two years. Often applied exclusively to herbaceous perennials, plants producing stems that die down every year. See MONOCARPIC, ANNUAL, BIENNIAL.

Perfect. A perfect flower has a complete set of sexual organs, male and female—as opposed to one that is unisexual or altogether sterile.

Perfoliate. Describes a plant with leaves totally united or joined at their bases around a stem so that the stem seems to pass through a single leaf. The JUVENILE leaves of some *Eucalyptus* species are examples.

Pergola. A walk of pillars and cross-members with plants trained to grow up and cover it. A feature of Italian gardens since Roman times, often covered with vines. Medieval and later gardens had elaborately carpentered galleries on the same principle.

Perianth. The two sets of modified leaves that form the COROLLA and CALYX of a flower made up, respectively, of PETALS and SEPALS. Sepals and petals may not be clearly distinguished and modified leaves or BRACTS may take on the functions of the perianth partially or completely.

Pernet-Ducher, Antoine (1859–1928). The famous Lyon (France) rose breeder who succeeded, in 1883–93, in introducing the "blood" of the 'Persian yellow' rose into HYBRID TEAS. The first Pernet rose was called 'Soleil d'Or' (1898). Other Pernet roses included 'Mme Caroline Testout' (1890). Jean Gaujard (1903–), breeder of 'Opera' (1947) and 'Femina' (1960) who joined the Pernet-Ducher firm in 1925, is now running the business.

Perpetual. Used of roses that flower more than once. It rarely means in constant bloom but when used of vegetables such as spinach, it means that it can be cut and will regrow all season long.

Perry, Francis. A contemporary leading horticultural author, journalist and lecturer. The first woman member of the RHS Council and the first woman vice-president of the RHS. Awarded VMH 1971.

Pesticide. Chemical used to kill pests, mostly insects.

Petal, petaloid. A petal is one of the modified leaves forming the COROLLA of a FLOWER. Petals are usually showy and often brightly coloured. Any other part of the flower that looks like a petal, for example a SEPAL OR BRACT, is described as petaloid.

Peterhof (Petrodvorets), Leningrad, USSR. The eighteenth-century Russian VERSAILLES, at Peter the Great's new capital, then called St Petersburg. Peterhof has been restored now to its formal grandeur, including its famous gold-plated fountains. Illustrated page 181.

Petiole. See PEDICEL.

Peto, Harold Ainsworth (1854–1933). Architect and garden designer who was deeply influenced by Italian gardens, but sought to interpret rather than imitate. His work at BUSCOT PARK, Berkshire and GARINISH ISLAND, County Cork, is imaginative and admirable. See page 180.

pH. A measure of acidity and alkalinity used in gardening in reference to SOIL. pH values range from 0–14. A pH less than 7 indicates acidity, one more than 7 alkalinity. pH 7 is neutral. CALCIFUGE plants, however, insist on a pH of 6.5 or less.

Phillips, Brigadier Cecil E. Lucas (1898–). Author of *The Small Garden* (1952), *The Modern Flower Garden* (1968) and other excellent and amusing gardening books; also many war books.

Phloem. The tissues within a plant that transport food materials. See XYLEM.

Phosphate. The chemical form in which phosphorus (P) is usually applied to the SOIL. Phosphorus deficiency causes poor lateral growth, spindly stem formation and poor development of flowers and fruit. See FERTILIZER, SUPERPHOSPHATE.

Photosynthesis. The chain of chemical reactions vital to the life of green plants. With the aid of the green pigment CHLOROPHYLL, the energy in sunlight is trapped by the leaves and used in photosynthesis to convert carbon dioxide from the air and water transported from the roots into sugars. Oxygen is released as a by-product. See pages 28–9.

Pinetum. A conifer ARBORETUM, or collection of conifers.

Pinna, pinnate. A pinna is a sub-unit or leaflet of a COMPOUND leaf and may have its own leaf stalk or PETIOLE. Such a leaf, with leaflets on either side of the leaf stalk or axis, is described as pinnate. See LEAF SHAPES.

Piping. A CUTTING taken by pulling a young shoot from the main stem at a JOINT. Used exclusively for PROPAGATING pinks and carnations.

Pistil. The combined female organs of a FLOWER. It consists of an OVARY containing female sex cells or ovules, a STIGMA, on to which POLLEN is deposited, and usually a STYLE separating stigma and ovary.

Pitmedden House, Grampian, Scotland. A recent reconstruction of a seventeenth-century PARTERRE garden, made by the NATIONAL TRUST for Scotland.

Plants and Gardens. The quarterly publication of the BROOKLYN BOTANIC GARDEN.

Pleaching. Technique for forming a dense hedge by interweaving the branches of well-spaced plants, usually such trees as lime or hornbeam, and often leaving bare trunks as stilts. A pleached alley is a garden walk lined with pleached trees.

Plumule. The stem of an embryo plant contained within a SEED. Enlarges during GERMINATION to form the first stem of the plant. See RADICLE, HYPOCOTYL.

Plunge. To sink pots containing plants into SOIL, or beds of sand, PEAT or weathered boiler ash, either up to their rims or, for BULBS, to a depth of several inches. Plunging keeps the roots cool and prevents evaporation.

Pollard. A tree regularly cut back to the main trunk at a height of five to six feet—just above the browsing height of cattle and deer. Like a COPPICE stool a pollard puts out vigorous straight boughs. After being pollarded many times it forms a thick trunk with a knot-like top.

Pollen. The dust-like grains produced by the male organs (ANTHERS) of a FLOWER. Each grain is composed of two coats of tissue and contains two sperm cells. The pollen grain germinates and produces the pollen tube down which the sperm cells travel before FERTILIZATION. See also POLLINATION.

Pollination. What happens when pollen lands on the STIGMA of a FLOWER. Pollen may come from the same plant (self-pollination) or from a different one (cross-pollination), being brought by the wind or by an agent such as an insect. Wind-pollinated (anemophilous) flowers produce much dry pollen. Insect-pollinated (entomophilous) flowers produce less pollen, which is often sticky, and have insect attractants such as NECTARIES.

Pompon. A dahlia, chrysanthemum or other flower with small, densely petalled or floreted globe-like blooms. From the French for a tuft.

Pope, Alexander (1688–1744). Poet and passionate gardener, whose small garden at Twickenham, Middlesex, was almost a workshop for the young LANDSCAPE MOVE-

MENT. In his poems he satirized the old formal school of design.

Pot. Traditional baked clay flower pots are now largely superseded by plastic for permanent use, or polythene, "whalehide" (tarred paper) or compressed PEAT for a brief period of "growing-on". The last two have the advantage that the plant can be planted pot and all without disturbing its roots. Clay pots range in size from 18 in to $1\frac{3}{4}$in diameter and are sometimes named from the number made in a single cast of clay; the higher the number the smaller the pot, for example, a "48" has a 5 in diameter; a "16" has a $8\frac{1}{2}$in. Clay pots being porous need watering more often than plastic and should be soaked well before use.

Potanin, Grigori Nicholaevich (1835–1920). Russian botanist. Explored western China with his wife Alexandra, who died on the journey and is commemorated by the ornamental rhubarb *Rheum alexandrae*; and made a large botanical collection.

Potash. Name for the inorganic compound potassium oxide added to the SOIL in FERTILIZER or on its own to provide plants with the essential mineral potassium (K). Potassium deficiency leads to stunted growth, browning of leaf margins and tips and poor colour in flowers and fruits. Potassium also gives plants some resistance to disease and cold.

"Potting-up", "Potting-on". "Potting-up" is the first time a plant is moved from seed tray or propagation unit to a pot of its own. "Potting-on" is when it is promoted to a bigger pot.

Poulsen, Svend. The Danish rose breeder who, *c.* 1910, crossed Polyantha POMPON with HYBRID TEA roses producing Poulsen roses; these, crossed with Hybrid Teas, produced the first FLORIBUNDAS. His son Niels has bred many excellent roses, including 'Copenhagen' (1964) and 'Chinatown' (1963).

Prick out. To transfer seedlings from the SOIL where they germinated into POTS, PANS or BEDS so that they are more widely spaced. Usually performed when seed leaves (COTYLEDONS) are fully formed and with true leaves just visible.

Propagation. The increase of plants sexually by SEED or vegetatively by such means as LAYERING, DIVISION, GRAFTING, CUTTINGS, BUDDING, TUBERS, CORMS, RHIZOMES or SUCKERS. Vegetative propagation ensures that new plants are exact replicas of their parents, propagation by seeds does not.

Pruning. The removal of stems, branches or roots of a tree or shrub. Pruning is performed to alter plant shape, to increase vigour, to remove dead or damaged parts or to help improve the quantity and quality of FLOWERS and FRUITS. The extent and time of pruning varies from species to species.

Pubescent. A plant part covered with down or soft hairs. See also HAIRY.

Puddling in. A way of making sure all the fine roots of a bare-rooted plant are in contact with the SOIL, by dunking them in liquid mud just before planting.

Purdom, William (1880–1921). Plant collector in China for KEW and best known as guide and companion to the author REGINALD FARRER. Introduced several first-rate plants to Britain, including *Viburnum fragrans* and *Clematis macropetala*.

Pyramid. A fruit tree trained to the shape of a pyramid with an upright central trunk and horizontal side branches. A dwarf pyramid grows to about 7 ft, a full pyramid to as much as 25 ft.

Pyrethrum. An INSECTICIDE made from the powdered flower heads of *Chrysanthemum cinerariafolium* and *C. coccineum*. It is not poisonous to man and can be applied as a dust or as a spray.

Q

Queen Mary's Rose Garden, Regent's Park, London. The greatest rose garden in Britain, started in 1932, based on a grand circle of beds each tight-packed with one VARIETY, surrounded by pillars and ropes for ramblers. It continues to grow, with new varieties being planted.

Quintinye, Jean de la. See LA QUINTINIE, JEAN DE.

R

Raceme. An elongated, unbranched FLOWER-head or INFLORESCENCE bearing short-stalked flowers. The top of the inflorescence continues to grow and produce new buds as the lower flowers open. See SPIKE. See FLOWERS, FORMS OF.

Radicle. The root of an embryo plant, the first root to appear as the SEED germinates. See PLUMULE, HYPOCOTYL.

Rambler. A plant, especially a rose, with long but lax stems, tall if supported but essentially droopy in habit. See also CLIMBER.

Ray. A strap-shaped flower-part (FLORET) of a composite plant such as a daisy, that is its apparent PETALS. Also the spoke-like flower-bearing stem of an UMBELLIFER such as a carrot.

Ray, Rev. John (1627–1705). Essex clergyman, author of the first authoritative *British Flora* (1670) and of *Historia Plantarum Generalis* (1686–1704), an important survey of botanical knowledge.

Recurved, reflex. Bent backwards or curved downwards. Adjectives used to describe leaves and PETALS. A recurved part is gently curved, a reflex one sharply bent. A part that bends upwards and inwards is described as incurved.

Redouté, Pierre-Joseph (1759–1840). Belgian plant-painter, perhaps the most popular of all time. He worked in Paris, largely for the Empress JOSEPHINE at LA MALMAISON. His major books include *Histoire des Plantes Grasses* (1799–*c.* 1832) (Succulents), *Les Liliacées* (1802–16) (Lilies) and *Les Roses* (1817–24), by which he is best known.

Reeves, John (1774–1856). A tea inspector for the East India Company in China who acted as agent for the HORTICULTURAL SOCIETY (from 1817 for some 20 years) in procuring many plants, including azaleas, camellias, paeonies, chrysanthemums and roses, probably the first double-flowered "Japanese" cherry and possibly the wonderful *Wisteria sinensis*. Also obtained paintings of plants by native artists, now in the RHS Library.

Reflex. See RECURVED.

Rehder, Dr Alfred (1863–1949). Botanist at the ARNOLD ARBORETUM, USA, author of the standard *Bibliography of Cultivated Trees and Shrubs* (1949).

Remontant. Repeat-flowering, used of roses and strawberries in much the same sense as PERPETUAL.

Repton, Humphry (1752–1818). The natural successor of "CAPABILITY" BROWN as England's leading landscape architect, but a less dogmatic, more adaptable artist. He allowed terraces and flowers to creep back to the foreground whence Brown had banished them. In the "Red Books", which he made with before-and-after paintings for prospective clients, we see the beginnings of the Victorian romantic style. His writings on the theory of design, in *The Art of Landscape Gardening* (1807), are still among the best today.

Respiration. Respiration takes place in all living cells. It is a cellular process that involves the oxidation of organic substances which results in a release of energy.

Reversion. The change of a plant back to its original form, whether affecting the whole or part of the plant. Most often occurs among SPORTS. In grafted plants reversion means the "take over" of the graft by the stock (root) plant. VARIEGATED plants often revert in part to their normal green form. Unless this part is cut off it will eventually dominate the plant, having more vigour.

Rhizome. A swollen, creeping, underground stem bearing roots, leafy shoots and flowering stems. A rhizome is an organ of storage and, for the gardener, of vegetative PROPAGATION. Bearded irises are an everyday example.

Ridging. A method of digging in which the dug SOIL is piled up in long, ridge-shaped mounds to expose it to frost, which helps to break it down. The soil is dug to one spade's depth and each ridge made up to 3 ft wide.

Ringing or **bark-ringing.** The removal of a complete or incomplete ring of bark from a tree branch or trunk. Ringing stops or slows the downward flow of sap, preventing the formation of too much vegetative growth and encouraging FLOWER and FRUIT formation.

Ripe. Used of the shoot of a woody plant when it has matured and taken on its woody character. Generally leafless but may have some leaves at the tip. See CUTTING, HALF-RIPE.

Rivers, Thomas & Son Ltd. Britain's oldest nursery firm, specialists in fruit trees and roses, established at Sawbridgeworth, Hertfordshire, in 1725 and still in the same family. Their breeding produced the famous 'Conference' pear in the 1890s. Varieties of plum, peach, nectarine and gage bear their name.

Svend Poulsen

John Ray

Humphry Repton

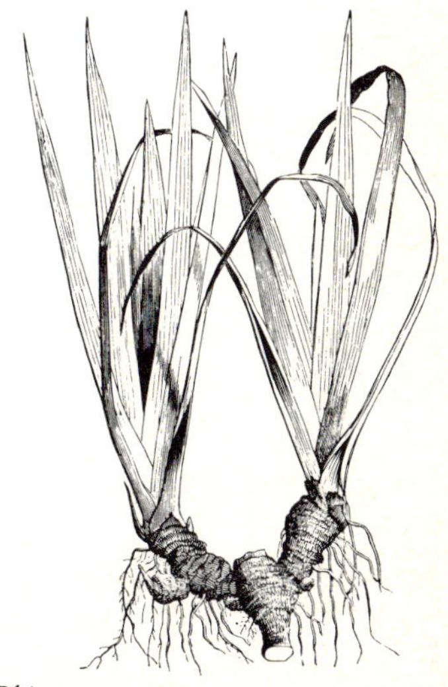

Rhizome

William Robinson

Thomas Rochford I

Rosette

Leopold de Rothschild

Robin, Jean. Seventeenth-century director of the JARDIN DES PLANTES in Paris and friend of JOHN TRADESCANT I. The false acacia or locust, *Robinia pseudoacacia*, is named after him.

Robinson, William (1838–1935). The most famous and controversial gardening journalist of the nineteenth century. He became a foreman at the Royal Botanic Society's Gardens in Regent's Park. He then worked for *The Times*, travelling in France at the time of the 1867 Paris Exhibition. His first book was *Gleanings from French Gardens* (1868). In 1870 he visited the USA and back in London published *The Wild Garden* the same year. In 1871 he started *The Garden* magazine and it was at its offices in Covent Garden that in 1875 he met GERTRUDE JEKYLL, with whom he developed a strong friendship. His best-known book, *The English Flower Garden* (1883), contained contributions from all the eminent gardening writers of the day. He spent the considerable fortune he made with his pen on developing the garden and estate round his house, the Elizabethan Gravetye Manor, East Grinstead, Sussex, which is now a hotel. Robinson's theme was that plants should be made to look natural in the garden. He therefore abhorred bedding-out and (theoretically) all formal gardening. His ideas were timely and his style persuasive.

Rochford, Thomas, & Sons. The world's biggest house plant nursery, founded by Thomas Rochford I in 1877 in the Lea Valley near London. The fourth Thomas Rochford is now in the business.

Rock garden, rockery, rock plants. A rocky bank, natural or, more usually, artificial, planted with low-growing plants in imitation of a mountain slope. The vogue for rockeries started in the mid-nineteenth century and reached a peak in the 1920s. See pages 132–37.

Rock, Joseph (1884–1962). Austrian-born American naturalist who, from 1922, spent some 27 years in western China, working for the ARNOLD ARBORETUM, USA, the National Geographic Society and others. One of the last Western botanists to work in China.

Rogue. Any plant whose characters are not as the gardener intended, as for example a CULTIVAR in which one, or more, individuals fails to come true to type. The appearance of rogues may be due to the unexpected expression of hereditary characters or genetic changes or to accidents in sorting BULBS or packeting SEEDS.

Rohde, Eleanour Sinclair (1880–1948). Gardening historian, author of *The Old English Gardening Books* (1924), *The Old English Herbals* (1922), *The Scented Garden* (many editions), and other scholarly and elegant works.

Roller. An implement little seen in modern gardens, but formerly much used for compacting lawns and gravel or sand paths. Modern theory considers it more important to aerate a lawn by spiking.

Root. The part of the plant that develops from the RADICLE of the germinating SEED. Roots are designed to absorb water and mineral salts and to provide a firm anchorage. The absorbing is done by small root hairs situated near the growing root tip. The two main root systems are branched or fibrous roots and TAP ROOTS. Some plants have roots above ground. AERIAL ROOTS of some ORCHIDS absorb moisture from the air, and roots of ivy act as climbing organs.

Rooting hormones. Preparations of HORMONES (growth-regulating substances) usually in powder form, into which CUTTINGS are dipped to encourage root formation. Different preparations are available to treat soft, semi-woody and woody cuttings.

Rootstock. An underground stem such as a RHIZOME or TUBER from which leaf- and flower-bearing shoots and roots arise. In many cases the rootstock may be used for VEGETATIVE PROPAGATION. Also the stock on to which a shoot of another plant is GRAFTED. See GRAFTING, SCION.

Roper, Lanning (1912–). American-born horticulturist and garden designer who has worked for most of his life in Britain. Garden correspondent of the *Sunday Times* (1951–75).

Rose, James. Contemporary American landscape designer who conceives of gardens as a result of interplay between the organism (owner) and the environment.

Roseraie de l'Hay, le, Paris, France. The masterpiece of formal gardening with roses. They are trained over arches, along vistas, on pillars and into umbrellas. A comprehensive collection tracing the development of the rose.

Rosette. The arrangement of plant parts, particularly leaves, into a rose-like form.

Rotation, crop. The changing of the position of crops each year so that each is replaced by one as different as possible. Crop rotation ensures that fertilized, manured soil is used to best effect and helps reduce the build-up of pests and diseases.

Rothschild family, de. Many English de Rothschilds have been keen gardeners, including Baron Ferdinand (1839–98), who built Waddesdon Manor, Buckinghamshire; Leopold (1845–1917), who gardened at Gunnersbury House, Acton, and ASCOTT, Wing, Buckinghamshire; and his son Lionel Nathan (1882–1942), who made the famous EXBURY GARDENS on the Beaulieu River in Hampshire. Here he raised some of the finest rhododendron and azalea hybrids now in existence. His son Edmund (1916–) continues the family tradition of hybridization and has opened the gardens to the public.

Rousham House, Oxfordshire. One of the key documents of the English LANDSCAPE school: a complete *c.* 1730 garden by CHARLES BRIDGEMAN and WILLIAM KENT, altered only by time.

Rowallane, County Down, Northern Ireland. A woodland garden of 50 acres with an immense variety of woody and herbaceous plants. Started in 1903 by H. Armytage Moore, now a property of the NATIONAL TRUST. Several good garden plants have been selected here and bear the name.

Royal Botanic Garden, Edinburgh. See EDINBURGH ROYAL BOTANIC GARDEN.

Royal Botanic Gardens, Kew. See KEW, ROYAL BOTANIC GARDENS.

Royal Horticultural Society, The. Founded 1804 at Hatchard's Bookshop, London, as the HORTICULTURAL SOCIETY. Since 1904 its headquarters have been at VINCENT SQUARE, Westminster, and since 1903 its gardens at WISLEY, Surrey. From its foundation it has been the world headquarters of horticulture. The Society has some 70,000 members, organizes the CHELSEA FLOWER SHOW and regular shows and competitions at Vincent Square, holds trials and demonstrations and gives individual advice at Wisley. It also maintains the world's greatest gardening library, publishes a monthly journal, THE GARDEN, and many other books and booklets. It gives many awards to both plants and gardeners; for these see AGM, AM, FCC and VMH.

Royal National Rose Society, The. Formed as the National Rose Society in 1876, dubbed Royal in 1965. An enthusiasts' Society with some 45,000 members, with trial and display grounds at Chiswell Green, St Albans, Hertfordshire. Publishes *The Rose Annual*.

Rugose. Wrinkled. Usually applied to leaves with a wrinkled surface (as in *Rosa rugosa*).

Runner. A long, slender shoot growing along the ground and rooting where it touches the soil, usually at its tip, to form a new plant. Runners are used for vegetative PROPAGATION. The strawberry is the classic example.

Russell, James P. C. (1920–). Plantsman and garden designer, who revived the SUNNINGDALE NURSERIES, Windlesham, Surrey (from 1944), where he was joined in 1956 by GRAHAM THOMAS. They were sold to the WATERER group in 1968. He now lives at The Dairies, Castle Howard, North Yorkshire, and is making a large collection of plants for the CASTLE HOWARD Estate.

Rustic work. Fences, seats, arbours and other garden impedimenta made of untrimmed branches and twigs, or even iron or concrete in imitation of them. A Victorian fashion mercifully long past, but still surviving in some places.

S

Sabine, Joseph (1770–1837). Secretary of the HORTICULTURAL SOCIETY (later the RHS) from 1810 to 1830. A man of vision and energy, responsible for the Society's first garden, its successful publications and its fruitful expeditions.

Sackville-West, Victoria (Vita) (1892–1962). Poet, novelist, journalist (for 14 years garden correspondent of the *Observer*) and creator of the most famous twentieth-century English garden at SISSINGHURST CASTLE, Kent. In 1913 she married Harold (later Sir Harold) Nicolson. They bought Sissinghurst in 1930 and planned it together. Her growing knowledge and love of plants is still fresh in the seven books she made of her *Observer* articles, including *In Your Garden* (1951) and *In Your Garden Again* (1953) edited as *V. Sackville-West's Garden Book* (1968).

Sagittate. Shaped like an arrow-head. See LEAF SHAPES.

Sanders' Encyclopaedia of Gardening. A remarkably concise dictionary of garden plants first published in 1895 by the late T. W. Sanders (*d.*1926), at that time editor of *Amateur Gardening*, and revised and reprinted many times.

Santa Barbara Botanic Garden, Santa Barbara, California. Features native California perennials, woody trees and shrubs in landscape settings.

Saprophyte. Any plant that lives exclusively on the dead bodies of plants or animals. Saprophytes have no CHLOROPHYLL and cannot use sunlight to make food. They help decay organic matter in the soil and make essential chemicals available to plant roots. See PARASITE.

Sargent, Professor Charles Sprague (1841–1927). Patrician Bostonian who created the ARNOLD ARBORETUM and directed it for 54 years. Author of *The Silva of North America* (14 volumes, 1891–1902). He travelled to Japan in 1902, bringing home the superlative cherry *Prunus sargentii*, and employed many plant hunters, including E. H. WILSON, who became his Curator.

Savill, Sir Eric (1895–). Gardener and land agent of the family firm of Alfred Savill & Sons, who created some 400 acres of new gardens in Windsor Great Park for Kings George V and VI, including the VALLEY and SAVILL GARDENS, which many consider the finest twentieth-century gardens in Britain.

Savill Garden, The, Windsor Great Park, Buckinghamshire. The first (started 1932) of a series of gardens made for the Royal Family by SIR ERIC SAVILL in this park. The rest are known as the VALLEY GARDENS. All are informal, basically woodland and stream gardens, not linked to any house. One of the greatest pieces of modern gardening.

Scape. A long flower stem that grows directly from the base of a plant, such as a daffodil. It is usually leafless.

Scion. A bud or shoot taken from one plant and grafted on to another (the ROOTSTOCK). See pages 52–3.

Scotney Castle, Lamberhurst, Kent. Another of the magic circle of great gardens on the Kent–Sussex borders. A dramatically picturesque garden with a ruined moated castle as its eye-catcher. The home of the HUSSEY family. Now a property of the NATIONAL TRUST.

Scree. In nature a scree is a collection of rock debris at the base of a cliff. In the garden it is a bed made of small stones used for growing ALPINES. See also MORAINE.

Secateurs. Pruning shears with crossed blades, scissor fashion, invented in the 1890s. Up to then the only shears were like sheep-shears: two blades joined by a curved spring. Most pruning was done with a knife. In an alternative form known as "anvil" secateurs, a single blade cuts the stem against a flat bar. Both kinds have the advantage over the traditional pruning knife of supporting the stem while they cut it, so needing only one hand.

Seed. The structure resulting from FERTILIZATION of the ovule of the female part of the FLOWER and usually contained within a FRUIT before being dispersed. The seed consists of a single embryo plant covered with a protective coat. Outgrowths such as plumes or wings on the covering often aid dispersal. See pages 50–1.

Selective. Term for a WEEDKILLER that kills some plants but not others.

Semi-double. A flower with more than the usual complement of petals but not a full DOUBLE.

Sepal. One of the outer ring of modified leaves forming the CALYX of a FLOWER. Often green and inconspicuous but may be showy like PETALS (petaloid) as in clematis. Sepals may be carried singly or be united. They help protect the flower bud before it opens and may remain attached to the FRUIT to aid dispersal.

Serrate, serrulate. With toothed edges. A serrate leaf has sharp teeth that point forwards, a serrulate one has small rounded or pointed teeth. See LEAF SHAPES.

Sessile. Without a stalk. Used to describe leaves or FLOWERS attached directly to a stem.

Set. Organ of vegetative PROPAGATION, particularly dahlia and potato TUBERS or onion and shallot BULBS, but also used of willow cuttings. To "set" is to plant them. Also describes FRUIT or SEED that has started to develop from fertilized flowers.

Sharawadgi. A term first used by SIR WILLIAM TEMPLE in his essay *Upon the Gardens of Epicurus* (1685) to express the "beauty of irregularity" as perceived by the Chinese in their gardens. Temple served as Ambassador in Holland, where he may have heard reports of Chinese or Japanese gardens. He was the first European writer to question the domination of the straight line in gardening.

Sheffield Park, Sussex. A "CAPABILITY" BROWN landscape modified in the nineteenth century by the addition of two more lakes and a CASCADE. From 1909 to 1948 A. G. Soames planted the woods and lakesides with a great collection of trees and shrubs, making it the most famous garden in Britain for autumn colour. A property of the NATIONAL TRUST.

Shenstone, William (1714–63). Minor poet and an innovator in garden design. On his estate at The Leasowes, near Birmingham, he made a *ferme ornée*, a romantically pretty and perfect farm.

Sherwood Gardens, Baltimore, Maryland. These gardens are designed primarily for spring bloom, and are beautiful in season: azaleas, dogwood, flowering crab and tulips predominate.

Shrub. Any plant with many woody stems, the main ones usually arising from near the base. See SUB-SHRUB.

Siebold, Dr Philipp Franz von (1791–1866). Physician with the Dutch East India Company in Japan 1826–30. The first collector to introduce Japanese plants to the West in numbers, via LEYDEN, Holland.

Simple. Describes any leaf with a single blade. Also a HERB from which a medicine with one constituent chemical can be extracted.

Singling. The removal of seedlings or larger plants to leave more space for those remaining. See also THINNING.

Sissinghurst Castle, Kent. One of the most popular and influential gardens in Britain, created by VITA SACKVILLE-WEST and her husband Sir Harold Nicolson from 1930. Its relatively small area is divided into "rooms" with different themes or colour schemes, all dominated by a Tudor Tower. The standard of gardening (now maintained by the NATIONAL TRUST) is extraordinarily high.

Sitwell, Sir George (1860–1943). Eccentric and brilliant gardener on his estates at Renishaw in Derbyshire, and Montegufoni, near Florence, Italy. His book *On The Making of Gardens* (1909) is among the most original and vivid contributions to garden literature.

Sloane, Sir Hans (1660–1753). Physician, author of *The Natural History of Jamaica* (1699) and philanthropic landowner of the CHELSEA PHYSICK GARDEN. The British Museum was founded partly on Sir Hans Sloane's collections.

Smith, Geoffrey (1928–). Gardening writer and broadcaster, author of many books including the *Mr Smith* series on fruit, flowers and vegetables. Superintendent of the NORTHERN HORTICULTURAL SOCIETY's garden at HARLOW CAR (1954–74) and an expert on northern gardening.

Smith, Sir James Edward (1759–1828). Naturalist. Bought Linnaeus' collections in 1784 and founded the Linnean Society in 1788 of which he was president 1788–1828. Author of many books including *Exotic Botany* (1804–5).

Snag. A stump mistakenly left on a stem after pruning. It may develop unwanted shoots in the next growing season or be an entry point for disease-causing organisms.

Société Nationale d'Horticulture de France. The French national gardening society, founded 1827, with headquarters in the Rue de Grenelle, Paris. It fulfils many of the functions of the RHS, having a library, trial grounds and shows, but it has only 7,000 full members; many more are members of affiliated societies.

Soil. The soil is made up of mineral particles surrounded by living and dead organic substances loosely known as HUMUS, with air spaces between. Water clings to the surface of the particles. Soils vary in texture according to the minerals they contain. The main divisions are sand, loam and clay. Of these sandy soils naturally hold least water, clay soils the most. The TOPSOIL is the upper layer of soil, suitable for the growing of plants, which can be broken up to form a TILTH. Below this is the SUB-SOIL. See pages 20–7.

Vita Sackville-West

Scape

Sir George Sitwell

Sir Hans Sloane

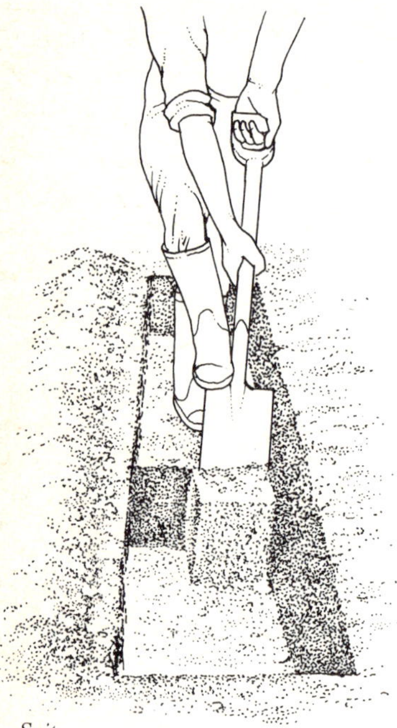
Spit

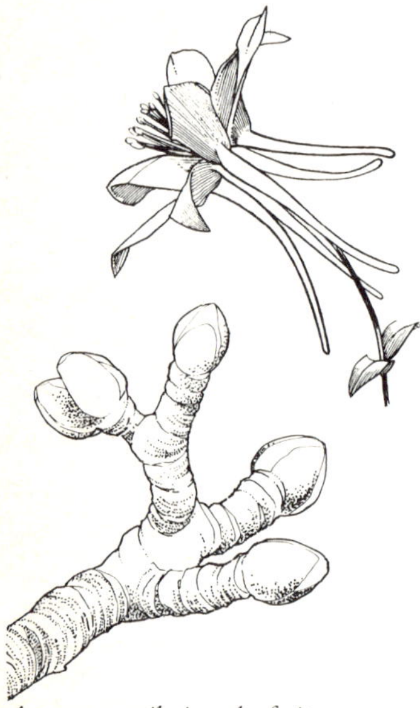
A spur on aquilegia and a fruit spur

Stipule on a rose

A chrysanthemum stool

Soil block. A compressed block of SOIL or PEAT with a hollow in which SEEDS or small plants can be planted.

Spade. An essential digging tool once made in many patterns for different types of soil and gardener. The choice available now is chiefly of size, of straight or pointed blade and of handle grip. It is worth investing in a good steel spade which, if kept clean, will make digging much easier.

Spadix. A fleshy, elongated FLOWER-head (INFLORESCENCE) in which small, insignificant flowers are embedded in pits. The spadix is normally sheathed in a SPATHE.

Spathe. A modified leaf often found wrapped like a cloak around a SPADIX, as in the ARUM family.

Species. A group of mutually fertile plants (or animals) sharing essential characteristics that are distinctive and breed true from generation to generation. Details such as petal colour and leaf shape may vary between individuals. Each species is given a two-word Latin name or binomial, in *Viola biflora*, for example, *Viola* is the GENUS name, *biflora* the species. Plants with persistently different detailed structures may be grouped into sub-species or varieties. See HYBRID, VARIETY. See also pages 38–9.

Sphagnum. A GENUS of MOSS particularly useful to gardeners as a sterile, porous rooting medium. The walls of the moss cells are penetrated by pores which enable the plants to absorb a great deal of water. Dry sphagnum is light, firm and elastic, making an ideal material for packing plants for transportation.

Spike. An elongated FLOWER-head (INFLORESCENCE) in which stalkless (SESSILE) flowers occur. The flower-head is unbranched and the lower flowers open first. See FLOWERS, FORMS OF.

Spit. In reference to digging it describes SOIL taken out to one spade or fork's depth.

Spore. Reproductive body of a non-flowering plant such as a FERN, MOSS or FUNGUS, the equivalent to the seed of higher plants. Fungal spores are important to the gardener as they transmit many plant diseases.

Sport. A plant differing from its parent stock as the result of a spontaneous change (MUTATION) in the material composing one or more of its hereditary units, or genes. In the wild, such changes are the result of cosmic radiation, but plant breeders use X-rays and the drug colchicine to produce the same effects. See pages 48–9.

Sprays. Chemicals in solution sprayed on to plants to combat pests or diseases. To achieve the maximum wetting effect the spray should be fine, should be applied to the undersides as well as the tops of leaves, and should contain a "wetting agent" such as soap to lower the surface tension.

Spry, Constance (1886–1960). Gardener, flower-arranger and author of *Flower Decoration* (1934), *Autumn Flowers* (1951) and *Favourite Flowers* (1959). Also founder of the well-known School of Cookery.

Spur. In flowers (such as columbine and delphinium) a hollow extension, usually containing nectar. Also a short side-branch on an older branch of a fruit tree, bearing several closely placed BUDS.

Staking. Support for newly planted trees of any size is best provided by a stout stake placed on the side of the prevailing wind and driven into the hole before the roots are spread in it. The tree must be tied firmly to the stake and the tie regularly checked to see that it is not damaging the bark. The stake should be needed only for two or three years.

Stamen. The male organ of a FLOWER, consisting of a POLLEN-producing ANTHER borne on a stalk, the FILAMENT. The filament may be very short and the anther united to a petal. Within the anther pollen is made in pollen sacs, which split to release their contents.

Staminate. Term for a unisexual flower that has male organs (STAMENS) but no female organs.

Standard. A tree or shrub with an upright stem that bears no branches for an appreciable distance, usually about 6 ft. In peas and other LEGUMINOUS flowers the standard is the upright rear petal, in irises it is the three upright petals. See also HALF-STANDARD.

Stanley Smith Horticultural Trust. A charitable trust endowed by the late Stanley Smith for the benefit of horticulture. Its considerable income has helped research, travel, publications and buildings. The chairman is SIR GEORGE TAYLOR.

Station sowing. The sowing of SEEDS individually or in small groups in the sites where plants are to grow to maturity. It saves seeds and the effort of transplanting.

Stearn, Professor William T. (1911–). One of Britain's senior botanical scholars, former librarian of the RHS and chief scientific officer of the British Museum (Natural History), retired 1976. Author of *Botanical Latin* and many other books and papers. Awarded VMH 1965.

Stellate. Star-like, usually of leaf-hairs with several horizontally radiating arms.

Sterile. Describes any plant that bears no viable sex cells, seeds or fruits. HYBRIDS and MUTANTS (SPORTS) are often sterile and must be propagated vegetatively, as must DOUBLE flowers. A self-sterile plant is one whose POLLEN will not fertilize the ovules of the same plant.

Stern, Sir Frederick (1884–1967). Creator of the famous chalk garden at HIGHDOWN, Sussex. Chairman of the John Innes Horticultural Institution 1947–61, author of *A Chalk Garden* (1960). Awarded VMH 1940.

Stigma, style. The stigma is the part of the female organs of a FLOWER (PISTIL) which receives the POLLEN. It is usually sticky. Only if the stigma is properly receptive will the pollen germinate and grow down the style to the ovary. The stigma is often elaborately branched or hairy in wind-pollinated flowers. See POLLINATION, pages 46–7.

Stipule. A leaf- or scale-like growth from the base of the leaf stalk (PETIOLE). Stipules are usually borne in pairs, one on each side of the leaf stalk. They protect leaf buds and sometimes young leaves.

Stock. The root-bearing part of a plant to which a graft is attached. Also known as a ROOTSTOCK.

Stolon. A shoot that gives rise to a new plant at its tip. The stolon may hang downwards, as in the blackberry, or grow horizontally, either above or below the ground. A stolon can be used for vegetative PROPAGATION.

Stomata. The openings in a leaf through which oxygen, carbon dioxide and water vapour pass during the processes of RESPIRATION and PHOTOSYNTHESIS. The loss of water vapour is known as transpiration. Each stoma is bordered by a pair of "guard cells", which can expand and contract by absorbing or releasing water. In land plants stomata are usually most numerous on the undersides of the leaves.

Stool. An underground stem (much the same as ROOTSTOCK) but generally used of HERBACEOUS PERENNIALS in the winter or resting stage, and particularly for chrysanthemums. A chrysanthemum stool produces shoots that can be removed and rooted as cuttings. It also means the stump remaining after a tree has been cut down, from which COPPICE-shoots arise.

Stopping. A kind of PRUNING in which the growing tip of a shoot, often the central or terminal shoot, is removed. Stopping encourages the production of side shoots.

Stourhead, Stourton, Wiltshire. The *locus classicus* of the English LANDSCAPE MOVEMENT. Made by the Hoare family from *c.* 1744 and later enriched with more diverse plantings. A property of the NATIONAL TRUST. See pages 226–27.

Stove. Old-fashioned term for a hothouse.

Stowe, Buckinghamshire. Great landscape garden developed throughout the eighteenth century by designers CHARLES BRIDGEMAN, WILLIAM KENT and "CAPABILITY" BROWN for Lords Cobham and Temple. Complex and magnificent, but leans heavily on its architectural features. Now a school and a property of the NATIONAL TRUST.

Strain. Term used by gardeners, not botanists, for a disease-resistant or extra-fine selection of an existing CULTIVAR.

Stratification. A technique for provoking the GERMINATION of a large number of seeds with hard or thick, fleshy outer cases by mixing them with sand, soil or peat, or between layers of sand, in containers, and exposing them to the weather for one or two winters.

Strike. To take a cutting, that is, to prepare it and plant it. Once it has formed roots, it is described as struck or taken.

Strybing Arboretum at Golden Gate Park, San Francisco, California. The ARBORETUM displays conifers, rhododendrons, native perennials, shrubs, woody trees and a magnolia collection, and has demonstration gardens of ground-cover, vines, annuals and perennials, and ornamental plants. The library is a West Coast centre for plant information.

Studley Royal and Fountains Abbey, Yorkshire. A unique formal landscape garden, using geometrical shapes but the simple materials (water, grass and trees) of the LANDSCAPE era. The work of JOHN AISLABIE between 1720 and 1742. The neighbouring Fountains Abbey ruins were later given a romantic landscape setting.

Stuyvesant, Peter. An early citizen of New York whose farm, the Bouwerie, served as a nursery for seventeenth-century settlements on Long Island and up the Hudson River.

Style. See STIGMA.

Sub-shrub. A small PERENNIAL plant with woody stem bases having soft tips. These tips die back each year. Also called an under-shrub. Sometimes also used by gardeners for any small shrub.

Sub-soil. The distinct layer of SOIL below the TOP-SOIL containing less organic matter and therefore less nutrients for plants. When large plants are planted, the sub-soil should be broken up and enriched with COMPOST or manure, but not brought to the surface.

Succulent. Any plant with fleshy leaves and/or stems containing juice or sap, adapted to life in arid environments. In some succulents leaves are absent or much reduced. See CACTUS, XEROPHYTE.

Sucker. A shoot arising from the roots or underground stem of a plant in addition to the main shoot or shoots. Suckers may be used as rooted CUTTINGS. In grafted plants suckers have the characters of the rooting part of the GRAFT (stock) and are usually vigorous and undesirable.

Suffruticose. Alternative name for a SUB-SHRUBBY plant, that is, a woody PERENNIAL with soft shoot tips that die back annually.

Sunningdale Nurseries, Windlesham, Surrey. Historic nurseries started in 1847 by Charles Noble whose premises were also at Sunningdale, and John Standish. Famous for its beautiful gardens and for rhododendrons in particular until the 1930s. Revived by JAMES RUSSELL in the 1940s. Since 1968 it has been the mail-order section of the WATERER group.

Sunset Magazine. Published in Menlo Park, California, USA. The leading authority on gardening on the West Coast and desert of the USA. The Sunset *Western Garden Book* is a detailed directory of very high quality, frequently revised.

Superphosphate. An inorganic FERTILIZER which is a mixture of monocalcium phosphate and calcium sulphate. When dissolved in the soil superphosphate provides plants with large amounts of the vital element phosphorus (P). Commercial superphosphates are graded by the amount of phosphoric acid they will release. See PHOSPHATE. See pages 24–5.

Sutton's Seeds Ltd. Important mail-order seed merchants, founded in Reading in 1806 and run by the Sutton family for four generations. In 1976 the business moved from Reading to Torquay in Devon. There is a retail shop in Covent Garden, London.

Symbiosis. Relationship between two different kinds of organisms from which both partners benefit, as when a FUNGUS (MYCORRHIZA) inhabits plant roots and both gain chemicals essential to survival. Lichens are composed of an alga and a fungus mutually dependent for growth and the reproduction of the whole plant. See NODULE.

Synge, Patrick M. (1910–). Author, gardener and botanist. Editor of the RHS Journal (1945–69) and publications and of the second edition and Supplement (1969) of the *RHS Dictionary of Gardening*. His many books include *Plants with Personality* (1939), the *Collins Guide to Bulbs* (1971), which are his special interest, and *Devon and Cornwall Gardens* (1977). Awarded VMH 1969.

Synonym. A different name for the same plant—unfortunately a common occurrence since the application of the International Rules of Nomenclature keeps changing Latin plant names faster than nurseries, let alone gardeners, can keep up with them.

Syon House, Middlesex. The Thames-side palace of the Dukes of Northumberland, notable for magnificent trees, a permanent gardening exhibition and a popular garden centre.

Systemic. Term for a chemical applied by gardeners (for example an INSECTICIDE or FUNGICIDE) that circulates in the sap of a plant and so kills the insect or fungus that feeds on it.

T

Tantau, Mathias. Contemporary German rose breeder (one of the two largest breeders in the world) who produced the almost fluorescent vermilion 'Super Star' (1960). Other famous roses include 'Fragrant Cloud' (1964), 'Blue Moon' (1964), 'Duke of Windsor' (1967), and 'Whisky Mac' (1968).

Tap root. Large ROOT growing vertically downwards into the soil and designed to draw water from deep levels. The root is often swollen with stores of carbohydrate and is useful as food crops such as beets, carrots and turnips.

Tar-oil wash. Spray applied to fruit trees during the DORMANT season to kill the eggs of such insects as APHIDS, apple suckers and capsid bugs. It is messy stuff which can damage grass and any green plants. Apply carefully, on a calm day.

Taxon (pl. taxa). The unit of classification, for example, FAMILY, GENUS, SPECIES or VARIETY.

Taylor, Sir George (1904–). A much travelled, influential and genial botanist from Edinburgh. Former Director of KEW, Director of the STANLEY SMITH HORTICULTURAL TRUST and Professor of Botany to the RHS. Awarded VMH 1955.

Temple. A garden temple is a summer-house with more than a nod in the direction of classical mythology. The idea took hold with the eighteenth-century English LANDSCAPE MOVEMENT when the garden was seen as an aid to reflection, introspection and a sort of pantheistic worship—for which a temple was perfectly appropriate.

Temple of Flora, The. A series of dramatic paintings of exotic flowers illustrating LINNAEUS's sexual system, commissioned and published by Dr Robert Thornton between 1799 and 1807. The project cost the doctor his fortune and the plates have been dismissed as vulgar and pretentious, but they continue to attract lovers of the beautiful and bizarre.

Temple, Sir William (1628–99). Scholar and diplomat who gardened at Sheen and Moor Park, Surrey. See SHARAWADGI.

Tender. Describes any plant likely to be damaged by low temperatures. The most vulnerable parts are soft newly sprouted and non-woody shoots. See pages 12–15.

Tendril. Any thread-like, twisting growth that helps a plant climb, by coiling or looping round any available support. Tendrils may be modified stems, leaves, leaflets or leaf stalks. Some tendrils have suckers (holdfasts) at their ends.

Terminal. At the end. Describes the uppermost, usually central, FLOWER or stem of a plant.

Tetraploid. Term for any plant which has four sets of CHROMOSOMES present in the nucleus of its cells as opposed to the usual two sets. Tetraploids may result from accidental or artificial MUTATION. They may also be more vigorous than the normal, DIPLOID, forms. See also TRIPLOID.

Thinning. Reducing the number of plants growing in a plot, box, pot or elsewhere to make more space available to those remaining. Used especially for seedlings and immature plants. Also the removal of alternate trees or "fillers" in an orchard and the pruning of shoots from a fruit tree to prevent overcropping.

Thomas, Graham Stuart (1909–). Gardener, author, artist and lecturer. His books, many illustrated by his own paintings and drawings, which have become classics in their field, are written with scholarship and charm: *The Old Shrub Roses* (1955), *Shrub Roses of Today* (1962), *Climbing Roses Old and New* (1965), *Colour in the Winter Garden* (1957), *Plants for Ground Cover* (1970), *Perennial Garden Plants* (1976). *Gardens of the National Trust* (1979) records much of his work since 1950 as Gardens Consultant to the Trust. Awarded VMH 1968.

Threave School of Practical Gardening, Dumfries and Galloway, Scotland. Garden school run by the NATIONAL TRUST for Scotland. A very good collection of plants, largely laid out in ISLAND BEDS.

Thrower, Percy (1913–). Britain's most popular television gardener, trained in the royal gardens at Windsor. Author of many books. Now a partner in the nursery firm of Murrell's of Shrewsbury, rose specialists. Awarded VMH 1974.

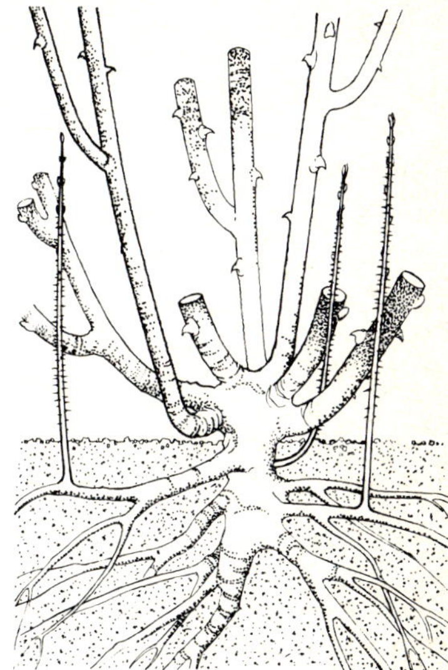

Sucker

Tap root

G. S. Thomas

Topiary

A truss

Kasteel Twickel

Thunberg, Carl Peter (1743–1828). Pupil of LINNAEUS and plant collector. Physician to the Dutch East India Company in Japan, introducer of many Japanese plants and, with MASSON, a pioneer of South African botany.

Tilth. SOIL that will crumble when broken down with a fork and rake, forming an easily worked surface layer essential for seed sowing. The quality of the tilth depends on the stickiness, plasticity and friability (crumbliness) of the soil.

Tine. The prong of a FORK or CULTIVATOR.

Tomentose. Woolly. See HAIRY.

Toothed. Describes any plant part, but particularly a LEAF, with indentations like teeth around its edge. See CRENATE, SERRATE.

Top-dressing. Spreading FERTILIZERS or other substances on the SOIL surface without digging them in. Also removing the top 1 to 2 in of soil in a pot or tub and replacing it with COMPOST.

Top-soil. See SOIL.

Topiary. The practice of cutting trees and bushes into ornamental shapes. It was popular with the Romans and probably before them. Topiary was revived in the Middle Ages, was a craze in the seventeenth century, became popular again in the nineteenth century and is now once again coming into fashion. The two best materials, for large and small shapes respectively, are yew and box.

Torrey, Dr John (1796–1873). Great American botanist and co-author with ASA GRAY of a *Flora of North America* (1838).

Tournefort, Joseph Pitton de (1656–1708). Professor of Botany to Louis XIV. He made, and wrote a lively account of, a great botanical progress through the Levant: through Greece, Turkey (where he found *Rhododendron ponticum* and the common yellow azalea, *Rhododendron luteum*, on the shores of the Black Sea), Syria and Persia.

Trace elements. A group of six elements —iron, manganese, copper, zinc, boron and molybdenum—needed by plants in minute quantities. Many FERTILIZERS contain some or all of these elements without which a variety of abnormalities in plant development occurs. See pages 24–5.

Tradescant family. John Tradescant I (*c.* 1580–1638), naturalist and collector, considered by many to be the father of English gardening. Head gardener at Hatfield House and later to King Charles I. One of the first English plant hunters (in Russia, Spain and the gardens of Holland and France). His son John Tradescant II (1608–62) inherited his father's passion, travelling several times to Virginia, USA, for plants. He was also the royal gardener. The Tradescant collection of "curiosities" at Lambeth, London, came into the possession of the antiquary Elias Ashmole, who bequeathed it to Oxford University as the original Ashmolean Museum.

Treillage. Trelliswork, or a pattern of wooden laths, normally 1 in wide and $\frac{1}{4}$ in thick, used as a screen, to add height to a wall, to create TROMPE L'OEIL effects, to support CLIMBERS and, in certain French examples, to form elaborate architectural features. See page 174.

Trenching. An old-fashioned method of deep digging.

Trengwainton, Cornwall. One of the most important plant collections in a county where many TENDER things thrive; it includes rhododendrons from KINGDON-WARD's seed. A NATIONAL TRUST property.

Tresco Abbey, Isles of Scilly. A subtropical garden on a 750-acre island in the Gulf Stream. Still in the Dorrien-Smith family, who started it in 1834. Windbreaks of Monterey pine and cypress make it possible to grow plants that are TENDER everywhere else in Britain on what was once a bare rock.

Trifoliate. With three leaves or leaflets.

Triggs, H. Inigo. Architectural and garden historian. Author of *Garden Craft in Europe* (1913).

Triploid. Describes any plant whose cells contain $1\frac{1}{2}$ times the normal number of CHROMOSOMES. Triploids may arise from breeding between different DIPLOID and TETRAPLOID forms or SPECIES (hybridization) or from accidental or intended changes (MUTATIONS). Triploids may be more vigorous than the normal diploid forms but are usually sterile or have low fertility.

Trompe l'oeil. A device, picture or pattern to deceive the eye. In gardens false perspective is the commonest trick, achieved, for example, by TREILLAGE imitating a receding arcade, or by having apparent parallels approach each other to make a vista look longer than it is.

Trumpet. Any FLOWER shaped like a trumpet or cone. Also the crown or CORONA of a narcissus when it is as long or longer than the surrounding PERIANTH.

Truss. A cluster of flowers or fruits.

Tuber. Swollen plant stem or root, usually found underground. Tubers contain stored food. Root tubers such as potatoes bear EYES, BUDS from which new tubers or complete plants are generated. In stem tubers, such as dahlias, new growth arises from the attached stem or crown. See also PROPAGATION.

Tusser, Thomas (1524–80). Author of *Five Hundred Pointes of Good Husbandrie* (1573), a rhyming guide to, among many other things, gardening, for example, "In Marche and in Aprill, from morning to night; In saving and setting, good housewives delight." An immensely popular book in Elizabethan England.

Twickel, Kasteel, Delden, Holland. Possibly the finest private garden in Holland and one of very few remaining from the eighteenth century with the characteristic PARTERRES, TOPIARY and orange trees. Also well known in modern horticulture for good new plants, for example, lavender 'Twickel Purple'; and for its rose garden and rock garden.

Type. A SPECIES or GENUS which embodies the essential characteristics of its FAMILY or group, and from which that family is usually named.

U

Umbel, umbellifer. An umbel is a FLOWER-head (INFLORESCENCE) in which flowers are borne on stalks arising from a single point on the stem like the spokes of an umbrella. In a compound umbel each "spoke" bears smaller rays, each with an umbel at its tip. An umbellifer is any of the 1,800 species of plants in the family. Umbelliferae found worldwide and characterized by having flowers arranged in umbels. Garden umbellifers include fennel and caraway. See FLOWERS, FORMS OF.

University of California Botanical Garden, Berkeley, California. The research collections feature plants from various geographical areas, including Tibet, western China, Africa, Australia, New Zealand and South America.

Unwins, Ltd, W. J. family firm of seedsmen established 1903 at Histon, Cambridgeshire, originally famous for sweet peas.

V

Valley Gardens, The, Windsor Great Park, Berkshire. A continuati on of the gardening in the Park begun by SIR ERIC SAVILL in the SAVILL GARDENS. Since World War II Savill planted its various hills and valleys to create "natural" woodland garden. The "Punch Bowl" is a natural amphitheatre full of evergreen azaleas.

Vanbrugh, Sir John (1664–1726). Dramatist and architect of BLENHEIM PALACE, Oxfordshire, and CASTLE HOWARD, North Yorkshire. Exactly how much he contributed to the gardens' designs is unclear, but his enormously vigorous and impressive designs made a great impact on the taste of the time.

Van Tubergen Ltd. Important Dutch BULB firm, founded *c.* 1852, with the well-known Zwanenburg Nursery in Holland, and a London office. Many new bulbs have been introduced to gardens through their services and the names tubergeniana and Zwanenburg recur in bulb catalogues.

Variegated. Describes plants with yellow, cream or white markings on their leaves due to an absence of the green pigment CHLOROPHYLL. Seed from most variegated plants will produce normal green ones. Many are unstable and tend to revert to the normal all-green condition, unless all-green shoots are pruned. Variegation may also be caused by malnutrition or disease, in which case it is usually called CHLOROSIS.

Variety. Term used loosely by gardeners for any distinct form of a SPECIES or HYBRID. Strictly speaking, all varieties in cultivation should be known as CULTIVARS. Variety really means a true-breeding variant of a species in the wild.

Vatican Gardens, Rome, Italy. The Papal gardens were BRAMANTE's masterpiece in the early sixteenth century. Today, almost everything has been altered. Their most famous feature is the VILLA PIA, designed by Pirro Ligorio in 1560.

Vaux-le-Vicomte, Seine-et-Marne, France. The château and garden of Nicolas Foucquet, one-time Chancellor of seventeenth-century France, situated between Paris and FONTAINEBLEAU. The château and his entertainments there were so lavish that he was ruined. Vaux-le-Vicomte was the first major work of LE NÔTRE, which with CHANTILLY brought him to the attention of King Louis XIV.

Vegetative. Term for reproduction that does not involve the processes of FERTILIZATION and seed production. Vegetative parts of a plant include TUBERS, BULBS, CORMS, RHIZOMES and STOLONS, and CUTTINGS from roots or shoots.

Veitch family. The most famous British nurserymen of the nineteenth century, introducing over 1,100 new plants into gardens. The firm was started in 1808 in Exeter by John Veitch (1752–1839). In 1863 the founder's grandsons separated, the Exeter firm becoming Robert Veitch & Son and its London branch, in Chelsea, James Veitch & Sons. The latter became the greatest nursery of its time. Veitch's many plant collectors included the LOBB brothers, Charles Maries and E. H. WILSON as well as three Veitches. Sir Harry Veitch, (1840–1924) great-grandson of the founder, had no successor and wound up the London business in 1914. The Exeter firm continued until the death of Anna Veitch in 1969.

Vernalization. The production of growth from a seed or vegetative organ, such as a BULB, outside its normal growing season. In vernalization seeds or vegetative organs are first subjected to low temperatures and then provided with the light, warmth and water needed for growth. The process is used for FORCING bulbs and for growing ALPINES.

Versailles, Palace of. The gardens were the great creation of LE NÔTRE for King Louis XIV, begun *c.*1662 when 1,200 trees and scores of statues were transported from the unfortunate Foucquet's VAUX-LE-VICOMTE. It is clear from the King's instructions for touring the gardens that his greatest pride was in the fantastic fountains. Additions and improvements continued until about 1688. By that time imitations of Versailles were springing up in every capital in Europe. The gardens were neglected and overgrown by the mid-eighteenth century, when Madame de Pompadour installed a model dairy in the Petit Trianon. Today the gardens are wholly restored save for the most ambitious fountains. See pages 214–15.

Villa Aldobrandini, Frascati, Lazio, Italy. Archetypal baroque garden with a CASCADE issuing from a rocky GROTTO in wild woods to rush down an elaborate stairway ending in a great formal semi-circular "nymphaeum". Designed by Giacomo della Porta in 1598; it is still owned by the Aldobrandini family. See pages 210–11.

Villa Barbaro, Maser, Veneto, Italy. The villa is a masterpiece by PALLADIO of 1560. Palladio also designed the gardens, in conservative Venetian style but for the *giardino segreto* (secret garden), which is powerfully architectural and Roman, having a semi-circular pool and fountain lined with statues.

Villa Balbianello, Lake Como, Italy. One of the most romantic gardens of Lake Como. Situated on a peaceful promontory, it was laid out in 1790 with terraces, fountains and a LOGGIA among the flowers looking up the lake.

Villa Borghese, Rome, Italy. The great seventeenth-century layout of alleys and avenues, almost in the French style, was replaced with an "English" park in 1773. Now Rome's major public gardens.

Villa Capponi, Arcetri, near Florence, Italy. A perfect small Tuscan garden of the late sixteenth century which commands magnificent views of Florence and is preserved in its original simple plan of three "rooms": an open grassy terrace, a lemon garden with box PARTERRES, and a *giardino segreto* (secret garden).

Villa Carlotta, Cadenabbia, Lake Como, Italy. A simple eighteenth-century terraced garden overlooking Lake Como, elaborated in the nineteenth century with a romantic, "English" woodland garden and stream.

Villa Cicogna, Bisuschio, Lombardy, Italy. A well-preserved sixteenth-century garden, with a famous stepped CASCADE and a GROTTO-gallery below the terrace as a shady retreat. Still owned by the original family. See page 183.

Villa d'Este, Tivoli, near Rome, Italy. The most theatrical of Rome's Renaissance gardens, designed *c.*1570 by Pirro Ligorio (1500–83) for Cardinal Ippolito d'Este. The theme is a long climb up a strange hydraulic hill, where water appears in a different guise at every turn, spraying or splashing or hurrying past. The famous terrace of 100 fountains is one of the pauses on the way. Diversions include a scale model of ancient Rome and various GROTTOES. Despite later alterations, the total effect and the view from the top are uniquely splendid.

Villa Farnese, Caprarola, near Rome, Italy. A palatial villa built for Cardinal Alessandro Farnese by Giacomo Barozzi da Vignola (1507–73) on a typical hillside site. Two separate walled PARTERRE-gardens are divided from the villa and each other by moats and belts of trees. A path leads uphill through woods to a hidden PARTERRE of fountains and sculpture. As Georgina Masson in *The Gardens of Italy* says, "No other garden in Italy contains a surprise as ravishing as this."

Villa Gamberaia, Settignano, Tuscany, Italy. A Tuscan garden of the early eighteenth century, recently meticulously restored, with a long grassy terrace commanding a view of Florence, PARTERRES now filled with water, and the usual *giardino segreto* (secret garden).

Villa Garzoni, Collodi, Tuscany, Italy. A mid-seventeenth-century garden after the Roman fashion, particularly the monumental staircase leading up a steep hillside. With baroque details in the naturalistic CASCADE among rough rocks and the planting which merges into the Tuscan landscape.

Villa Lante, Bagnaia, Lazio, Italy. Giacomo Barozzi da Vignola's masterpiece for Cardinal Gambara, widely considered Italy's finest garden. Two pavilions at the foot of a wooded hill are separated by a characteristic Roman series of stairs climbing against the flow of a CASCADE. Before them lies a water-PARTERRE centred on a great star-fountain. The whole is intact, scarcely changed from about 1570. See pages 210–11.

Villa la Pietra, Florence, Italy. A scholarly Englishman's idealization of an Italian garden, created by the Acton family early in the twentieth century on the site of an older garden.

Villa Medici, Rome, Italy. An intact example of sixteenth-century Roman design. PARTERRES of flowers stand well back from the house. Beyond them lies the BOSCO. The arbours that once provided height and shade in an otherwise flat landscape are now missing.

Villa Orsini, Bomarzo, Lazio, Italy. A strange sixteenth-century garden of obscure origins, haunted by grotesque monsters carved out of rocky outcrops. There is no symmetry or pattern and the woodlands that lent it mystery have largely gone, but the giant primeval tortoise lurking by the stream is still disturbing.

Villa Pia, Vatican Gardens, Rome, Italy. A retreat built for Pope Pius IV in 1560 by Pirro Ligorio in the seclusion of a wooded grove. Essentially a summer-house, all prettiness and symmetry, reflected in gently stirring water.

Villa Rizardi, Pojega di Negrar, Veneto, Italy. A perfect late eighteenth-century garden in the Valpolicella, one of the last to be made in the old Italian style with cypress AVENUES, secret gardens, a BELVEDERE and a fine "green theatre".

Villa Taranto, Pallanza, Piemonte, Italy. An English garden on the shores of Lake Maggiore, begun in 1930 by Captain Neil McEacharn. Now a public park of 100 acres with masses of flowers.

Villandry, Château de, near Tours, France. A twentieth-century reconstruction of a sixteenth-century castle garden, the work of the Spanish Dr Joachim Carvallo from 1906. The principal feature is a $2\frac{1}{2}$-acre square PARTERRE of ornamental vegetables: a unique *tour de force* calling for two complete plantings a year, in March and June, each of some 30,000 plants. The flower parterres are on the same scale, with 19 miles of box hedges.

Vilmorin-Andrieux Ltd. French family seed nursery founded in 1745 by Philippe Victoire de Vilmorin. Nineteenth century de Vilmorins included Louis (1816–60) whose contributions to agriculture included the development of sugar beet. His sons, Henri (1843–99) and Maurice (1849–1918) were also dedicated horticulturists. Maurice is remembered for sponsoring plant hunters, particularly the French missionary-botanists including JEAN-MARIE DELAVAY. Maurice de Vilmorin's garden was at DES BARRES where he established a vast collection of trees and shrubs, now the property of the French government. The Vilmorin firm, now in La Ménitré and La Costière, is one of the two biggest seed producers in France.

Sir Harry Veitch

Villa Garzoni

The garden at Villandry

A wardian case

Anthony Waterer

Ellen Willmott

Vincent Square. The Westminster headquarters of the RHS. The Old Hall, in the square itself, contains the LINDLEY Library, the council room and offices. The New Hall, in Greycoat Street, opened in 1928, contains the lecture and committee rooms. Most flower shows are held in the larger New Hall.

Virus. Disease-causing micro-organism. Viruses cannot survive outside living cells. Inside the cell they "take over" the hereditary material in order to effect their rapid multiplication. They have no independent mobility and most plant viruses are transmitted by sap-sucking insects. In plants the symptoms of virus disease include chlorotic patterning such as MOSAICS on leaves and petals, a reduction in fruit or flower formation, severe crippling or stunting and death. A virus may be "carried" in a plant showing no disease symptoms.

Vista. A view—particularly a long narrow view, as opposed to a panorama, which is a wide sweep.

VMH. Victoria Medal of Honour. The highest honour bestowed on gardeners by the RHS, instituted to celebrate the diamond jubilee of Queen Victoria in 1897. The number of holders at any one time was increased from 60 to 63 in 1900 to mark the total number of years of Queen Victoria's reign.

W

Wakehurst Place, Sussex. One of the LODER family's Sussex gardens made *c.*1900 around an Elizabethan mansion. Now an out-station of KEW, with ideal conditions for many TENDER plants. Developing still, but already one of the great ARBORETA.

Wallich, Nathaniel (1786–1854). Danish surgeon and naturalist, director of the Calcutta Botanic Garden 1817–47. He introduced many fine plants from Nepal, including *Lilium giganteum*, *Cotoneaster frigida* and the Bhutan pine, *Pinus wallichiana.*

Walter Hunnewell Arboretum, Wellesley, Massachusetts. Has one of the oldest collections of conifers in the eastern United States, and unique TOPIARY specimens.

Wardian case. A glass case resembling a miniature greenhouse invented by Dr Nathaniel Bagshaw Ward (1791–1868) for protecting plants in such unhealthy environments as the salt-sprayed decks of East India ships. Its invention was of extreme importance to plant collecting as the lengthy transportation of newly discovered plants had been, until that time, the chief cause of failure.

Waterer family. The two branches of this family of nurserymen were founded by Michael Waterer (1745–1827), who established the famous KNAP HILL NURSERIES of Woking, Surrey, *c.*1796, which he left to his brother Hosea. He also established a nursery at Bagshot (Waterers' of Bagshot) in 1829, which he left to his brother John (*d.*1868). Hosea left Knap Hill to two nephews, Robert Godfrey and Anthony Waterer, who was the breeder of the Knap Hill azaleas. Bagshot passed to three brothers, Frederick, John and Michael, who concentrated on rhododendrons, including the renowned 'Pink Pearl' (1890). In 1914, the Bagshot Waterers amalgamated with Crisp's of Twyford, Berkshire to become John Waterer Sons & Crisp. In 1967 they were bought out and became known as the Waterer group, which includes Dobbie & Co Ltd of Edinburgh and SUNNINGDALE NURSERIES as their mail-order department. The Knap Hill Nurseries were sold to SLOCOCK'S NURSERIES in 1976.

Water shoot. A long, unfruitful shoot arising on a tree or shrub from a DORMANT bud that would not normally develop. Caused by hard pruning and most common on vigorous plants grown in good, fertile soil.

Weedkiller. See HERBICIDE.

Westonbirt Arboretum, Gloucestershire. Britain's greatest ARBORETUM, made by the Holford family from 1829 and now run by the Forestry Commission, who are enlarging it by adding the neighbouring Silk Wood. Many enormous conifers dominate glades full of flowering trees and especially Japanese maples, brilliant in autumn. See also ALAN MITCHELL.

Whip. A very young tree, still pliable.

Whorl. A group of three or more flowers or leaves arising at a single place on a stem and radiating from it. Such an arrangement is described as verticillate. The branches of most conifers also arise in whorls.

Williamsburg Restoration, Williamsburg, Virginia. Scrupulously rebuilt and maintained reconstruction of English town gardens in the eighteenth century. Emphasis is on formal patterns rather than on plants themselves.

Williams family. Distinguished gardeners at CAERHAYS CASTLE, Cornwall. John Charles Williams (*c.*1860–1939) was a principal sponsor of GEORGE FORREST and bred the superb *Camellia* × *williamsii*. He also contributed to the breeding of outstanding daffodils by his first cousin Percival Dacres Williams (*d.*1935) of Lanarth. Julian Williams, grandson of J. C. Williams, took over Caerhays in 1955 on the death of his uncle, the Rt Hon Charles Williams.

Willmott, Ellen (1860–1934). An extravagant and influential gardener at Warley, Essex, where she had a garden staff of 100, and in Savoie, France. Friend of GERTRUDE JEKYLL; a sponsor of E. H. WILSON in China; raiser of many good plants (named either Willmott or Warley) and author of *The Genus Rosa* (1910–14). Awarded VMH 1897.

Wilson, Ernest Henry (1876–1930). Most famous and horticulturally important of all plant hunters in China. His first voyage there in 1899 was to collect *Davidia involucrata* for VEITCH's nursery. From 1907 to 1910 he hunted chiefly for the ARNOLD ARBORETUM, of which he became Curator. As many as 600 out of his 1,000 or so introductions are still in cultivation. At least 100 have won awards as first-rate garden plants, including the regal lily (*Lilium regale*), *Clematis montana*, *Rosa moyesii*, *Anemone hupehensis*, and innumerable maples, berberis, cotoneasters, honeysuckles, magnolias, rhododendrons, cherries, sorbus and viburnums.

Winterthur, Winterthur, Delaware. The gardens contain extensive naturalized plantings, especially of azaleas and wild flowers, and one of the largest collections of rare and native conifers in eastern United States. The museum in the grounds is noted for its collection of American decorative arts from 1640 to 1840.

Wisley Garden, near Ripley, Surrey. The display, experimental and teaching gardens of the RHS since 1903, now covering some 200 acres. The best known of the many features are the great rock garden and ALPINE meadow; Battleston Hill, with its rhododendrons, azaleas and lilies; the massive HERBACEOUS borders; the rose gardens; the greenhouses, model vegetable garden and the comprehensive PINETUM. Trials are held continuously in the Portsmouth Field. Suburban-size model gardens are a recent addition and a new ARBORETUM was opened by Queen Elizabeth II in 1978. Although there is no overall plan, and the architectural features are weak or worse, this is the most important garden for gardeners in the world.

Witch's broom. An abnormal cluster of shoots on a tree branch, usually caused by a FUNGUS but sometimes the result of an hereditary change (MUTATION). Witch's brooms are the source of many varieties of dwarf conifer.

Woolly. Describes any plant part covered with hairs that give it a wool-like appearance. Also known as TOMENTOSE.

Wrest Park, Silsoe, Bedfordshire. A little-known but historically important great garden, where "CAPABILITY" BROWN for once spared the formal "French" plan and added to it in his own manner.

Wye College. The University of London college of agriculture and horticulture, near Ashford in Kent.

Wyman, Donald. Horticulturist of the ARNOLD ARBORETUM since 1935. Author of *Trees for American Gardens* (1951).

X

Xerophyte. A plant adapted to survive long periods of drought. Xerophytes may have no leaves, or small and/or rolled leaves modified into spines. Other characters include hairiness, hard or SUCCULENT stems or leaves, and waxy coatings.

Xylem. The woody tissue within a plant composed of tubes which carry water. See also PHLOEM.

Y

Young, William (*d.*1785). Queen's botanist in America: credited with the first introductions of twenty-five plants from America to Britain, including the Venus fly-trap.

Z

Zonal. A plant part with a region, often ring-like, of a different colour from the remainder. Zonal pelargoniums, for example, have rings of darker or lighter colour on their leaves.

Index

Numerals in roman type denote text entries
Numerals in *italic* type denote illustrations
Numerals in **bold** type denote a major entry

Acknowledgements

The publishers would like to extend their thanks to the following individuals and organizations who have helped in the production of this book: Professor P. R. Bell, Professor of Botany, University College London; Dr H. G. Dickenson, Lecturer in Botany, University of Reading; Forestry Commission; Mr J. Harkness; Dr D. Idle, Lecturer in Botany, University of Birmingham; Mr R. Legge; Dr D. Wilkie, Reader in Botany, University College London; Ruth Binney; John Innes Horticultural Institute; Rothampstead Experimental Station; Hugh Synge; Brent Elliot; Mr P. F. Stageman; Mr Charles Notcutt; Mr Adrian Bloom; The National Trust Waddesdon Manor; Martyn Rix.

Indexer Michael Kendall

ARTWORK CREDITS

Page 10 Chris Forsey; **11** Chris Forsey, Mick Saunders, Venner Artists; **13** Chris Forsey, Alan Suttie; **14–15** Clare Roberts, Arka Graphics; **16–17** Brian Delf, Alan Suttie; **20–21** Harry Clow, Alan Suttie; **22–23** Chris Forsey; **24–25** Chris Forsey; **26–27** Cynthia Swaby; **28–29** Mick Saunders; **32–33** Chris Forsey; **38–39** Mick Saunders, Chris Forsey; **40–41** Chris Forsey; **46** Alan Suttie; **47** Chris Forsey; **48–49** Chris Forsey; **50** Harry Clow; **51** Chris Forsey; **54–55** Chris Forsey; **58–59** Arka Graphics; **60–61** Arka Graphics; **62–63** Arka Graphics; **64–65** Arka Graphics; **77** Chris Forsey; **79** Peter Morter; **86–87** John Davis; **94–95** Barbara Everard; **98–99** Mick Saunders; **100–101** Basil Smith; **102–103** Chris Forsey; **105** Chris Forsey; **106** Mary Grierson; **107** Kevin Dean; **108–109** John Davis; **110–111** Basil Smith; **112–113** John Davis; **114–115** Chris Forsey; **116–117** John Davis; **118–119** Chris Forsey; **120–121** Basil Smith; **123** Tony Graham; **124–125** Basil Smith; **127** Mary Grierson; **128–129** John Davis; **137** William Giles; **145** Peter Morter; **147** Peter Morter; **155** Trevor Hill; **162–163** Chris Forsey; **171** Chris Forsey; **173** Chris Forsey; **182–183** Peter Morter; **188–189** Peter Morter, Chris Forsey; **192–193** Chris Forsey; **197** Alan Suttie; **198** Chris Forsey; **206–207** Peter Morter; **210–211** Peter Morter; **212–213** Peter Morter; **216–217** Peter Morter; **220–221** Peter Morter; **226–227** Peter Morter; **230–231** Peter Morter; **234–235** Peter Morter; **239** Chris Forsey; **240** Mick Saunders; **242** Tony Spalding; **224** John Davis, Vana Haggerty; **245** Vana Haggerty; **246** Vana Haggerty; **247** Vana Haggerty; **248** John Davis, Vana Haggerty; **251** Vana Haggerty; **252** John Davis; **253** Vana Haggerty; **254** Mick Saunders; **255** Vana Haggerty; **256** John Davis, Vana Haggerty; **258** Vana Haggerty, John Davis; **260** Chris Forsey; **261** John Davis; **262** John Davis, Chris Forsey; **263** Chris Forsey; **264** Vana Haggerty

PICTURE CREDITS

The publishers acknowledge the co-operation of photographers, photographic agencies and organizations as listed below. Abbreviations used are:
t top; *c* centre; *b* bottom; *l* left; *r* right; *u* upper; *f* far; *n* near; EC Eric Crichton; HS Harry Smith Horticultural Photographic Collection; MEPL Mary Evans Picture Library; NHPA Natural History Photographic Agency; RHS Royal Horticultural Society; RHS/LL/CB Lindley Library of the Royal Horticultural Society, photo by Chris Barker; SHP Saling Hall Press; TM Tania Midgley; VF Valerie Finnis.

Cover and page 4: *Papaver orientale* from Edwards, *New Botanical Garden*, 1812, volume 2, plate 42. Courtesy of Lindley Library of the Royal Horticultural Society/Photo: Chris Barker.
1 John Hedgecoe. **3** John Hedgecoe. **7** VF. **8–9** Kenneth Scowen. **10** John Hedgecoe. **11** *t* TM; second from top Meteorological Office Library, by permission of the Controller of Her Majesty's Stationery Office. **12** *t* VF; *b* Susan Griggs/Photo: Anthony Howarth. **12–13** Bruce Coleman/Photo: John Shaw. **13** *t* TM; *cr* Pierre Mackiewicz; *b* John Garrett. **17** Robin Fletcher. **18** *tl* Photo Researchers, Inc./Photo: A. de Menil; *cr* Donald Smith. **18–19** William MacQuitty. **19** *t* TM; second from top Pamela Schwerdt; *bl+cl* Bernard Alfieri; *cr* TM; *br* A. H. M. Synge. **20** *tl* Ardea/Photo: Christopher K. Mylne; *bl* R. & C. Foord; *r* K. A. & G. Beckett. **21** *tl* Ardea/Photo: Adrian Warren; *bl* Paul Brierley; *fr* Naru Inui. **22** *tl* Barnaby's Picture Library/Photo: A. Christie; *tr* Paul Brierley; *c* VF. **23** Fotogram/Photo: DeLuc. **24** *t* Ardea/Photo: Su Gooders; *b* Mansell Collection. **25** *l+b* TM; *tr* Biofotos/Heather Angel. **26** John Garrett. **27** *tr+tl* John Garrett; *bl+c+br* Michael Busselle. **28** A. D. Schilling. **29** *tl* Ardea/Photo: A. P. Paterson; Row *l* to *r*: William MacQuitty; K. A. & G. Beckett; Oxford Scientific Films; Biofotos/Heather Angel; *bl* Donald Smith; *br* Biofotos/Heather Angel; second from bottom Timothy Beddow. **30–1** Robin Fletcher. **31** *bl* S. & O. Mathews; *br* Brian Furner. **32** *t* TM; *b* Jessica Strang. **33** from top to bottom: TM, Don Wildridge; Pat Brindley; John Topham Picture Library/Photo: Mayo. **34–5** Susan Griggs/Photo: Farrell Grehan. **36** RHS/LL/CB *Anemone pavonia* by P. J. F. Turpin, before 1840. **37** *t* VF; *b* Reproduced from *Field Guide to the Trees of Britain and Northern Europe* by Alan Mitchell by permission of Collins Publishers. **38** Mansell Collection. **39** *l* Robert Harding Associates, courtesy the Linnean Society; portrait of Linnaeus from "The Temple of Flora" by R. J. Thornton, engraved by Meyer after Hofmann and Bartolozzi; *r* Robert Harding Associates, courtesy Linnean Society. **40** *tr+tl* Biophoto Associates/Dr G. F. Leedale. **41** Row *l* to *r*: Paul Brierley; John Topham Picture Library/Photo: Windridge; John Topham Picture Library/Photo: Windridge; *bl* R. & C. Foord; *br* Bruce Coleman/Photo: John Shaw. **42** *bl* Tony Stone Associates; *br* Mansell Collection. **42–3** Donald Smith. **43** *ul+bl* TM; *ur* EC; *cb+br* R. J. Corbin. **44** John Hedgecoe. **45** *tl* John Hedgecoe; *bl+bc* TM; *tr* Ardea/Photo: Su Gooders; lower *r* Biofotos/Heather Angel. **46** Paul Brierley. **47** *tl* Ardea/Photo: Ake Lindau; *fr* Oxford Scientific Films; Row *l* to *r*: Naturfotograferna/Photo: Arne Schmitz; Biofotos/Heather Angel; Ardea/Photo: John Mason; Paul Brierley; *b* Bruce Coleman/Photo: Jessica Ehlers. **48** *t+c* Susan Griggs/Photo: Farrell Grehan. **49** *bl+br* Paul Brierley; lower *l* J. K. Burras; *t* Oxford Scientific Films. **50** Paul Brierley. **51** *ul* Bernard Alfieri; *c* HS; *tr* Oxford Scientific Films; *cl* Bruce Coleman/Photo: Pekka Helo; lower *r* R. J. Corbin; *b* R. & C. Foord. **52** *l* TM; *tr* SHP; *br* R. J. Corbin. **53** *t* Reproduced from *Famous Trees* by Richard St. Barbe Baker and S. R. Badmin by permission of Times Newspapers, Ltd.; *lc* R. J. Corbin; *lb* HS; Centre column, *t* to *b*: R. J. Corbin; EC, courtesy Twyford Laboratories; *cr* Ann Ronan Picture Library; *br* HS. **56** *tl+tr* VF; *b* The Picture Library. **57** *tl+b* VF; *tr* SHP; *c* S. & O. Mathews. **58** All RHS/LL/CB: *fl* Regnault, *La Botanique*, 1774, ii, pl. 12; lower *l* *Botanical Magazine*, 1816, xl, iii, pl. 1808; *ur* *Botanical Magazine*, 1788, ii, pl. 44; *br* Edwards, *New Botanical Garden*, 1812, ii, pl. 42. **59** *bl* RHS/LL/CB Jacquin, *Icones Plantarum Rariorum*, 1781–86, i, pl. 78; *nl* Jan van Huijsum, "Flowers in a Terracotta Vase", reproduced by permission of National Gallery; *bnr* Robert Harding Associates, courtesy Musée National d'Histoire Naturelle; *bfr* T. F. Hewer; *tl* MEPL; *tc* RTHPL; *tr* RHS/LL/CB John Renton the Younger, "George Loddiges". **60** *tl* Ashmolean Museum; *cl* Photo of painting by John Wollaston from Hunt Institute for Botanical Documentation, courtesy National Portrait Gallery, Smithsonian Institution; *bl* courtesy Library, Royal Botanical Gardens, Kew; all others RHS/LL/CB: *cr* L'Heritier, *Cornus*, 1788, pl. 50; *tr* Hill, *Vegetable System*, 1761, ii, pl. 51; *br* Cavinilles, *Icones et Descriptiones Plantarum*, 1791, i, pl. 80. **61** *tl* Mansell Collection; *bl* Cartoon by John Nash courtesy Joe Elliott; *tr* Photo of painting by George Gastard from Hunt Institute for Botanical Documentation, courtesy Linnean Society; all others RHS/LL/CB; *cl* *The Gardener's Chronicle*, Oct. 3, 1931, p. 226, by permission of Haymarket Publishers Ltd.; Centre column, *t* to *b*: Duhamel, *Arbres et Arbustes*, ed. 2, 1801–9, i, pl. 13; Cavinilles, *Icones et Descriptiones Plantarum*, 1791, i, pl. 65; Hooker, *Icones Plantarum*, 1884, vii, pl. 672; *Botanical Register*, 1884, xxx, pl. 57; *cr*, three drawings *l* to *r*: *Botanical Magazine*, 1789, iii, pl. 103; Andrews engr., *Heaths*, 1805, ii, pl. 96; *Botanical Register*, 1815, i, pl. 35. **62** *bl* courtesy Library, Royal Botanical Gardens, Kew; *br* MEPL; all others RHS/LL/CB, as follows: *tl* *Botanical Register*, 1828, xiv, pl. 1168; *tc* *Botanical Magazine*, 1813, xxxix, pl. 1592; *tr* Plenck, *Icones Plantarum Medicinalium*, 1789, ii, pl. 143; *bc* *Hooker's Botanical Miscellany*, 1830, i, pl. 70. **63** Top row, *l* to *r*: RHS/LL/CB Bonpland, *Description des Plantes Rares*, 1813, pl. 55; RHS/LL/CB J. W. Loudon, *Ladies' Flower Garden of Ornamental Greenhouse Plants*, 1848, page 149 in ic, pl. 30; photo of lithograph from Hunt Institute for Botanical Documentation, courtesy Royal Botanic Gardens and Herbarium, Sydney; Second row, *l* to *r*: RHS/LL/CB *Andrews' Botanical Repository*, 1800, vol. 1, no. 135; RHS/LL/CB Bonpland, *Description des Plantes Rares*, 1813, pl. 13; photo from Hunt Institute for Botanical Documentation, courtesy Mrs. Rica Erickson, Nedlands, Australia; Bottom row, *l* to *r*: RHS/LL/CB *Cockayne's New Zealand Plants and Their Story*, 1967, reproduced by permission of Alexander Turnbull Library, Wellington, New Zealand; courtesy R. A. Dorrien-Smith; RHS/LL/CB Schneevoogt, *Icones Plantarum Rariorum*, 1793–95, pl. 43; RHS/LL/CB Delile in Redouté, *Liliac*, 1815, viii, pl. 448; all others RHS/LL/CB; *lc* *Botanical Magazine*, 1889, cxv, pl. 7065; *uc* *Botanical Magazine*, 1893, pl. 7296. **64** All RHS/LL/CB: *bl* Stapf in *Botanical Magazine*, 1930, cliii, pl. 9185; Centre column, *l* to *b*: J. E. Smith, *Exotic Botany*, 1804–5, i, pl. 6; *Botanical Magazine*, 1912, cxxxviii, pl. 8647; Sweet, *British Flower Garden*, 1834, vi, pl. 253; *tr* *Revue Horticole*, 1835, p. 548; *br* Siebold & Zuccarini, *Flora Japonica*, 1835, pl. 98. **65** *cl* RHS/LL/CB Boynton in *Addisonia*, 1931, xvi, pl. 529; RHS/LL/CB Jacquin, *Icones Plantarum Rariorum*, 1786–93, iii, pl. 553; Second column from left, *t* to *b*: *RHS Journal*, 1943; RTHPL; collection of the author; Third column from left, *t* to *b*: all RHS/LL/CB: *Iconotheae Botanicae*, 1903; *Illustration Horticole*, 1858, v, pl. 157; Trattnick, *Thesaurus Botanicus*, 1819, pl. 52; *Botanical Magazine*, 1911, cxxxvii, pl. 8411; Fourth column from left, *t* to *b*: Mansell Collection; RHS/LL/CB *Botanical Magazine*, 1796, x, pl. 327; RHS/LL/CB Thunberg, *Icones Plantarum Japonicarum*, 1805, v, pl. 4; reproduced from *History of Japan* by Engelbert Kaempfer, 1906 edition, vol. 2, figure 105, by permission of Robert MacLehose Ltd. **66–7** Paul Miles. **68** *t* NHPA/Photo: M. Savonius; *b* G. S. Thomas. **69** both SHP. **70** A. D. Schilling. **70–1** K. A. & G. Beckett. **71** *tl* EC; *tr* K. A. & G. Beckett; *cr* Neil Holmes; *bl* TM. **72** *tl* NHPA/Photo: Paul Miles; *tr* TM; *cr+bl* SHP; *br* Paul Miles. **73** *bl+cr+t* TM; *br* John Sims; *tr* SHP. **74** *t* Biofotos/Heather Angel; *b* SHP. **75** *tr* Biofotos/Heather Angel; *c* A. D. Schilling; *fr* VF; *b* A-Z Botanical Collection. **76** *tl* Photo Researchers, Inc.; *b* SHP. **76–7** Paul Miles. **77** *t+b* SHP; *c* TM. **78** *tr+br* TM; all others SHP. **79** *t* SHP; *b* Pat Brindley. **80** *t* TM; *c* Georges Leveque; *b* Don Wildridge. **81** Top row, *l* to *r*: K. A. & G. Beckett; TM; Second row: both VF; Bottom row, *l* to *r*: Biofotos/Heather Angel; Pat Brindley; Roche Photography; *c* TM. **82** *t* John Hedgecoe; *b* EC. **82–3** SHP. **83** *tfl+tfr+b* TM; Left column, *t* to *b*: TM; TM; EC; Right column, *t* to *b*: TM; EC; EC. **84** *t+bl* TM; *c* R. & C. Foord; *br* HS. **85** Top row, *l* to *r*: VF; Bavaria-Verlag; TM; Neil Holmes; Second row, *l* to *r*: EC; TM; Bottom row, *l* to *r*: SHP; John Sims; *b* TM; second from *b* Marilynn Zipes. **88** *t* G. S. Thomas; *cl+bc* TM; *cr+bl+br* Biofotos/Photo: Hazel Le Rougetel. **89** *tr* Ardea/Photo: A. P. Paterson; Centre column, *t* to *b*: R. & C. Foord; Robert Harding Associates; VF; *br* VF; *cl+bl* Michael Warren; *cr* TM. **90** *t* Jeremy Whitaker; *tr* Wolfram Stehling; *br* SHP. **91** *tl* Natural Science Photos/Photo: P. H. Ward; *tr+br* William MacQuitty; *bl* Biofotos/Photo: Hazel Le Rougetel. **92** *tl* SHP; *tr+cr* HS; *cl* Robert Harding Associates; *c+b* VF. **93** *fr* corner SHP; Top row, *l* to *r*: SHP; HS; TM; Second row: both TM; *b* TM; second from *b* HS. **94** Roy Lancaster. **96** RHS/*The Garden*. **96–7** Jessica Strang. **97** Top row, *l* to *r*: TM; John Sims; TM; HS; Centre column, *t* to *b*: Robert Harding Associates; TM; HS; Right column, *t* to *b*: TM; John Sims; TM. **98** *t* William MacQuitty; *cl* TM; Column, *t* to *b*: Roy Lancaster; TM; TM; *bl* VF. **99** Picturepoint. **100** HS. **100–1** Patrick Matthews. **101** *tl* TM; *tr* William MacQuitty; *bl* VF; *cr* Paul Miles; *br* Patrick Matthews. **103** *tl* EC; *bl* A. D. Schilling; *cb* Susan Griggs/Photo: Michael Boys; *tr* Madelaine Anderson; *br* S. & O. Mathews. **104** Reproduced from *Some English Gardens* by George S. Elgood and Gertrude Jekyll, Longman's 1905 by permission of the Estate of Gertrude Jekyll. **105** *l* VF; *ur* TM; *br* SHP. **106** *t+br* VF; *bl+bc* courtesy Mary Grierson. **107** *tl+cl* R. & C. Foord; *tr* HS; *cr* Neil Holmes; *bl* SHP. **110** *lc* TM; *c* Bernard Alfieri; *tr* EC; *bl* HS; *bc* SHP. **111** *tl* VF; *tr* HS; *cr* Ardea/Photo: A. P. Paterson; *cl* EC; *bl* TM. **114** *tc+bl* SHP; Column, *t* to *b*: VF; Robert Harding Associates; Michael Warren; Michael Warren; VF. **115** *tl* John Sims; *cl* Michael Warren; *b* TM; Box, top row, *l* to *r*: Pat Brindley; NHPA/Photo: M. Savonius; Ardea/Photo: Su Gooders; Box, bottom row, *l* to *r*: Pat Brindley; Ardea/Photo: Su Gooders; Don Wildridge. **118** Bruce Coleman/Photo: EC. **118–19** SHP. **119** *cl* Georges Leveque; *tr* G. S. Thomas; *br* Pat Brindley. **122** *t* EC; *b* J. K. Burras. **123** *lc* Ardea/Photo: A. P. Paterson; *tr* Bernard Alfieri; Top row: all Pat Brindley; Bottom row, *l* to *r*: A-Z Botanical Collection; Pat Brindley; A-Z Botanical Collection. **124** Neil Holmes. **124–5** Paul Miles. **125** *tr* Robert Harding Associates/Photo: Sassoon; *cl* VF; *cr* Susan Griggs/Photo: Farrell Grehan; *br* Biofotos/Heather Angel. **126** *l* Neil Holmes; lower *r* R. & C. Foord; *t* EC. **126–7** SHP. **127** *bc* John Sims; *br+tr* EC; *tl* R. & C. Foord; *cl* SHP; *cr* S. & O. Mathews. **130** *t* SHP; *c* R. & C. Foord; *bl* John Sims; *br* EC. **131** *t* S. & O. Mathews; lower *l* John Sims; *tr* Bernard Alfieri; *c* R. & C. Foord; *rc* SHP; *bl* NHPA/Photo: N. Savonius; *bc* TM; *br* Biofotos/Heather Angel. **132** *tl* VF; *tr* R. & C. Foord; *bl* F. & N. Schwitter. **133** *t+uc* F. & N. Schwitter; *lc+bl+bc* VF; *br* Douglas Dickins. **134** *l* Wilhelm Schacht; *tc+tr* EC; *cr* TM; *b* R. & C. Foord. **135** Top row, *l* to *r*: R. & C. Foord; NHPA/Photo: N. A. Callow; Second row, *l* to *r*: EC; R. & C. Foord; EC; Bottom row, *l* to *r*: K. A. & G. Beckett; Alfred Evans; *b* NHPA/Photo: Brian Hawkes. **136** *tr* Reproduced from *Alpine Flora* by H. Correvon and P. Robert, printed by Atar, Geneva, 1911. **136–7** all other photos: Roy Elliott. **138** *t* K. A. & G. Beckett; *bl* VF; *br* Ken Akers. **139** *bl+cr* SHP; *br* Ken Akers; *t* TM;. **140** *b* A; *t* EC. **140–1** SHP. **141** *t+br* SHP; lower *cl* Paul Miles; upper *c* HS; *bl* Biofotos/Heather Angel; *tl* TM. **142** *tr* TM; *c* John Sims; *br* Bruce Coleman/Photo: David Hughes. **143** *tr+tl* Biofotos/Heather Angel; *tc* A-Z Botanical Collection/Photo: E. Lloyd Jones; second from top, right Biofotos/Heather Angel; Centre row, *l* to *r*: R. J. Corbin; Biofotos/Heather Angel; Michael Warren; Bottom row, *l* to *r*: VF; EC; TM. **144** *bl* Pat Brindley; *br* TM. **144–5** TM. **145** *bl* SHP; *br* EC. **146** SHP. **146–7** SHP. **147** *t+c* Pat Brindley; *b* Biofotos/Heather Angel. **148** *t* Michael Warren; *cr+b* R. & C. Foord. **149** Top row, *l* to *r*: all S. & O. Mathews; Second row: both Michael Warren; *bl* Bruce Coleman/Photo: EC; *br* R. A. G. Beckett. **150** André Martin. **151** *tl* VF; *bl+cr* SHP; *tr* Paul Miles; *c* Robert Harding Associates; *cb* Pat Brindley; *br* HS. **152** *t* TM; *c+b* Reproduced from *The Old English Gardening Books* by Eleanour Sinclair Rohde by permission of Minerva Press. **153** *tl* Bruce Coleman/Photo: EC; *tr* Anthony Denney; *c* A-Z Botanical Collection; *cr* TM; *b* HS. **154** *t* John Hedgecoe; *bl* J. K. Burras; *br* Patrick Matthews. **155** *l* Jessica Strang; *tr* Christopher Lloyd; *cr* Don Wildridge; *br* VF. **156** TM. **156–7** John Sims. **157** *tl+bl* SHP; *tr+fr+cr* TM; *br* John Sims. **158–9** *t* G. S. Thomas; *b* Paul Miles. **159** *t* Museum of English Rural Life, University of Reading from *Annals of Agriculture*; *c* VLOO/Photo: J. C. Mayer; *b* Bernard Alfieri. **162–3** *t* John Topham Picture Library/Photo: Windridge; *b* HS. **163** *tl* Derek Fell; *tr* Ardea/Photo: John Mason; second from *t* Bruce Coleman/Photo: EC; *bl+bc* HS; *br+r*, second from *b* Brian Furner. **164** *tl* HS; *cl+cr* EC; *bl* Ardea; *br* Iris Hardwick Library. **164–5** Ardea/Photo: Su Gooders. **165** *tr* MEPL; *c* RHS/*The Garden*; lower *c* SHP; *br+rc* Long Ashton Research Station; *bl* East Malling Research Station. **166–7** Franklin Photo Agency. **168** *t* Jeremy Whitaker; *bl* Robin Fletcher; *br* Paul Miles. **169** *tl* Patrick Matthews; *cl* TM; *bl+br* Reproduced from *The World of the Japanese Garden*/Photo: Takeji Iwamiya by permission of John Weatherhill Publishers; *tr* Robert Perron. **170** All photos SHP. **171** *tl* TM; *cr* Carla de Benedetti; *bl* SHP; *br* VF. **172** *c* S. & O. Mathews; *t* F. & N. Schwitter. **173** *tl* Georges Leveque; *bl* A-Z Botanical Collection; *c* Patrick Matthews; *tr* SHP; *br* VF; *bc* Michael Busselle. **174** *uc* G. S. Thomas; *lc* SHP; *bl* Reproduced from *Garden Craft in Europe* by H. Inigo Triggs by permission of B. T. Batsford, Ltd.; *br* Elizabeth Whiting & Associates/Photo: Michael Nicholson; *tl* Paul Miles; *tr* Bruce Coleman/Photo: J. Ehlers. **175** *l* Jeremy Whitaker; *tr* Reproduced from *The World of the Japanese Garden*/Photo: Takeji Iwamiya by permission of John Weatherhill Publishers; *cl* VF; *cr* Peter Hayden; *bl* Paul Miles; *br* S. & O. Mathews. **176** *t* HS; *bl* SHP; *br* Jessica Strang. **177** *tc+c* TM; *tr* John Sims; *tl* Reproduced from *Flower Grouping in English, Scotch and Irish Gardens* by Margaret Waterfield by permission of J. M. Dent & Co. Ltd.; *cr* SHP; *bc+bl* VF; *br* Biofotos/Heather Angel. **178** *t+br* TM; *bl+bc* SHP. **179** *tl* John Hedgecoe; *c* Jessica Strang; *cr* John Sims; all others TM. **180** Tony Mott. **180–1** TM. **181** *bl+tl* William MacQuitty; *tr* HS; *c* SHP; *br* Rose Porter. **182** SHP. **182–3** SHP. **183** *tl* SHP; *tr+cr* TM. **184** *t* John Bethell; *cr* William MacQuitty; *br* S. & O. Mathews. **184–5** *tl* Brigitte Baert/Photo: Michel Nahmias; *tr* Biofotos/Heather Angel; *bl* George Hyde; *cr* Benjamin Smith; *b* TM. **186–7** SHP. **188** *t+b* Wolfram Stehling. **189** *tl+cl* G. S. Thomas; *tc* Muriel & Arthur Orans; *tr* Muriel Hodgman; *cr* VF; *b* A-Z Botanical Collection; *ub* Paul Miles. **192** TM. **194** *t* G. S. Thomas; *bl+bc* SHP. **195** *l* G. S. Thomas; *br* Paul Miles; all others SHP. **196–7** SHP. **197** *r+b* SHP. **198–9** G. S. Thomas. **199** *bl* RHS/LL/CB Cercle chromatique from *Expose d'un Moyen de Definir et de Nommer les Couleurs* by M. E. Chevreul, 1861; *b* F. & N. Schwitter; *ub* Iris Hardwick Library; all others SHP. **200** *l* Reproduced from *Some English Gardens* by George S. Elgood and Gertrude Jekyll, Longman's, 1905 by permission of the Estate of Gertrude Jekyll; *tr* VF. **201** *tl* TM; *tr* Peter Coats; *b* Peter Hayden. **202** *bl* TM; *br* SHP. **202–3** SHP; *c* G. S. Thomas. **203** *t* SHP; lower *t* G. S. Thomas; *c* Cressida Pemberton-Pigott; *bl* HS; *br* Jessica Strang. **204–5** Elias Canneman. **207** *bl* Reproduced from *The Gardens of Mughal India* by permission of Gordon Patterson; *bc* Ms. Add. 18113, f. 40b, "Humay and Humayun", 1396A.D., reproduced by permission of the British Library; *br* Illustration from the "Romance of Amir Hamza", Mughal, *c.* 1565, Victoria & Albert Museum/Photo: Cooper-Bridgeman Library. **208** *tl+r* Tony Mott; *b* Peter Hayden; *cl* Reproduced from *Garden Craft in Europe* by H. Inigo Triggs by permission of B. T. Batsford, Ltd. **209** *br* John Hillelson/Photo: Rene Burri; all others Tony Mott. **210** *t* Tony Mott; *c* MEPL. **212** *c* Reproduced from *Garden Craft in Europe* by H. Inigo Triggs by permission of B. T. Batsford, Ltd.; *br* Mansell Collection; *bl* Verwaltung der Staatlichen Schlösser und Gärten, Schloss Charlottenburg. **214** *bl* Service Photographique, Caisse Nationale des Monuments Historiques et des Sites © Arch. Photo. Paris, by Jacques Musy, S.P.A.D.E.M.; *br* Mansell. **214–15** *t* SHP; *b* Ecole Nationale Supérieure des Beaux-Arts. **215** *t* VLOO/Photo: J. C. Mayer; *c+b* Paul Miles. **216** *b* Museum of Fine Arts, Antwerp/Photo: Scala. **217** *bc* © British Tourist Authority/Photo: Brian Boyd. **218** *tl* National Palace Museum, Taipei, Taiwan, Republic of China; *tr* © Paolo Koch; lower *r* SHP. **219** *tl* John Hillelson/Photo: Dennis Stock, Magnum; *tc* Orion Press; all others SHP. **220** SHP. **221** *bl+br* SHP; *ul* Vautier/Decool. **222** *l+tr* SHP; lower *r* S. Relph. **222–3** Paul Miles. **223** *tl+cl* SHP; *tr* George Taloumis; *bc* Wolfram Stehling; *br* Roche Photography. **224** RHS/LL/CB All reproduced from *Medieval Gardens* by Sir Frank Crisp, Vol. II by permission of the Bodley Head. **225** *tl* Peter Hayden; *tr* courtesy of the National Trust, Dyrham Park; *c* National Trust/Photo: John Bethell; *ub* SHP; *b* Reproduced by permission of the British Library, print courtesy of M. R. Brownell, Garden History Society. **228** *t* Richard Green Galleries; *b* National Trust/Photo: Geoffrey Shakerley. **229** *tr+tl* RHS/LL/CB Humphrey Repton's *Fragments*; second from top, left Cruikshank cartoon, "Exhibition Extraordinary in the Horticultural Room", reproduced by permission of the RHS/Photo: Chris Barker; third from top, left SHP; *bl* RHS/LL/CB J. C. Loudon, *The Suburban Gardener*; *br* MEPL; *rc* RHS/LL/CB Shirley Hibberd, *Rustic Adornments*, 1895 edition. **232** *tl* Reproduced from *The English Flower Garden* by William Robinson, 1883 by permission of John Murray Publishers Ltd.; MEPL; *cl* Paul Miles; *b* TM. **233** *l* SHP; *tr* VF; *rc* G. S. Thomas; *b* Michael Warren. **235** *bl+br* Paul Miles; *bc* Photo © Morley Baer, garden designed by Kipp Stewart. **236** *l* Peter Hayden; *br* Brian Shuel. **236–7** Paul Miles. **237** *tl* Derry Moore; *tr* Wolfram Stehling; *cl* Camera Press; *cr* George Taloumis; *b* Luiz Claudio Marigo. **239–266** All read from top to bottom, as follows: **239** MEPL; Arthur Hellyer. **240** From *Liberty Hyde Bailey* by Philip Dorf, Cornell University Press, 1956; Royal Botanic Garden, Edinburgh, reproduced by permission of the Regius Keeper; Ann Ronan Picture Library. **241** Ann Ronan Picture Library; Mansell Collection; Camera Press/Photo: Swedowsky & Weiss/Curtis. **242** Courtesy RHS/Wisley Garden; MEPL; MEPL. **243** RTHPL; MEPL. **244** Mansell Collection; MEPL. **245** Courtesy Peter Cox; RTHPL; MEPL. **246** MEPL; RHS/LL/CB Reproduced from *Landscape Gardening*, 10th edition, 1921, revised by Frank A. Waugh by permission of Chapman & Hall, London, and John Wiley, N.Y.; Jean-Loup Charmet. **247** Arthur Hellyer; Mansell Collection. **248** VF; Mansell Collection; Mansell Collection. **250** Mansell Collection; Popperfoto/Photo: Donald MacLeish. **251** RHS/*The Garden*; MEPL; Ann Ronan Picture Library. **252** RTHPL; National Portrait Gallery. **253** Mansell Collection; Popperfoto; Ann Ronan Picture Library. **254** Reproduced from *The Gardener's Assistant* by Robert Thompson, Gresham Publishing Co., 1905; MEPL; RTHPL. **255** RTHPL; RTHPL; Abril Press/Photo: Chico Nelson. **256** Photo courtesy Hazel Le Rougetel from French edition of *Gardener's Dictionary*, 1785; courtesy Alan Mitchell. **257** Oxford Botanic Garden/Photo: J. W. Thomas; courtesy Russell Page; RHS/LL/CB from *Les Jardins de France*, vol. 2; RTHPL. **258** Ann Ronan Picture Library. **259** Royal National Rose Society; Mansell Collection; Mansell Collection, reproduced from *The Gardener's Assistant* by Robert Thompson, Gresham Publishing Co., 1905. **260** Photo: Donald Merrett, courtesy Paul Miles; reproduced by courtesy of the House of Rochford; RTHPL. **261** RTHPL; RTHPL; Mansell Collection. **263** Courtesy G. S. Thomas. **264** Mansell Collection; Paul Miles. **265** RHS/*The Garden*; Italian State Tourist Department; French Government Tourist Office. **266** Mansell Collection; MEPL; RHS/LL/CB *The Gardener's Chronicle*, 1897, vol. I, p. 307, by permission of Haymarket Publishers, Ltd.; RHS/*The Garden*.